Edward Louis Colen Ward

The Scrap-Book

Being a Thousand Gems of Prose and Poetry

Edward Louis Colen Ward

The Scrap-Book
Being a Thousand Gems of Prose and Poetry

ISBN/EAN: 9783744693028

Printed in Europe, USA, Canada, Australia, Japan

Cover: Foto ©Thomas Meinert / pixelio.de

More available books at **www.hansebooks.com**

THE SCRAP-BOOK

BY

E. L. C. WARD, LL.B.

IT BEING

A Thousand Gems of Prose and Poetry

BY
A THOUSAND AUTHORS

NEW YORK
WM. L. ALLISON COMPANY
1899

COPYRIGHT, 1899, BY E. L. C. WARD.

GIFT OF

A. J. Morrison

THE SCRAP-BOOK.

DEAR SIR:—This is a work which suggested itself twenty years ago, and to which I have since labored. It was suggested because the scrap-book I then had was the most popular book in my library. I judged other people by my friends, and went to work to supply what experience taught me was wanted.

WHY I CALL IT THE SCRAP-BOOK:

1st. Because it is an old-fashioned, popular name, dear to all.

The following poems of James Whitcomb Riley are copyrighted by, and published with the consent of, Bowen Merrill Co., Indianapolis, Ind. :—

PAGE		
23	Old Trundle-bed, . . .	"ARMAZINDY."
58	Long afore he knowed, .	"PIPES O' PAN."
65	Days gone by, ...	"PIPES O' PAN."
69	The Song I never Sung,	"ARMAZINDY."
169	Man in the Moon, . . .	"RHYMES OF CHILDHOOD."
240	Runaway Boy, ...	"RHYMES OF CHILDHOOD."

4th. Because being old, it is yet a novelty.

GENERAL REASONS FOR IT.

1st. A scrap-book is universally popular. Here is a maturely made one, full of cream; and without the reader's trouble of making.

2d. It contains much very choice and chaste original matter that can be found nowhere else.

3d. It contains much old matter, that is ever dear, and wanted by all, that can be found in no other book.

4th. As a book of recitations and quotations it is new, and fits all classes.

5th. It preserves in a handy book form, a portion of the best current American literature—not heretofore in books.

THE SCRAP-BOOK.

DEAR SIR:—This is a work which suggested itself twenty years ago, and to which I have since labored. It was suggested because the scrap-book I then had was the most popular book in my library. I judged other people by my friends, and went to work to supply what experience taught me was wanted.

WHY I CALL IT THE SCRAP-BOOK:

1st. Because it is an old-fashioned, popular name, dear to all.

2d. Because it is generic, and if any scrap-book, or blank book for that purpose is called for at the book-stores, this, ready made, will be shown, and perhaps sold.

3d. Because the books nearest it (viz.: Field's Scrap-Book, books of Essays, Irving's Sketch-Book, and others) have all been popular and large sellers.

4th. If Volume I. took, and went, the same copyright offers a large field for succeeding volumes of it, that also would help sell more of Volume I., and *vice versa*.

WHY IN THIS SHAPE?

1st. Because it carries with it the old, familiar scrap-book idea.

2d. Because it avoids the stereotyped idea of the usual books of quotations and selections, which are alone from the Standard Authors, and already in existence in another book form.

3d. Because it gives variation and restfulness to the rainy-day leisure-hour reader.

4th. Because being old, it is yet a novelty.

GENERAL REASONS FOR IT.

1st. A scrap-book is universally popular. Here is a maturely made one, full of cream; and without the reader's trouble of making.

2d. It contains much very choice and chaste original matter that can be found nowhere else.

3d. It contains much old matter, that is ever dear, and wanted by all, that can be found in no other book.

4th. As a book of recitations and quotations it is new, and fits all classes.

5th. It preserves in a handy book form, a portion of the best current American literature—not heretofore in books.

6th. It has a thousand good things from as many authors who, with their friends, will wish copies, and be instrumental in helping to push it on the market.

7th. It fills the bill as an occasional helper, and comes to the rescue of the newspaper and miscellany, the speaker and reciter.

8th. It is not like the average book, inviting only a temporary run, with only a class of readers; but is suited to all classes, and never goes out of style, or date.

9th. Foreigners wish American folk-lore and The Scrap-Book contains it.

These are my reasons for offering The Scrap-Book, as the product of twenty years' labor of love.

Yours very truly,
E. L. C. WARD.

INTRODUCTION.

It is just as true that the world loves a scrap-book, as it is that it loves the lover. Why it has not heretofore been given this want in handy popular form has long been a mystery to the writer. Long since have the fields of literature been well covered, yet the old-fashioned scrap-book has been left to the individual, and the ground between the book and the current literature of the day has remained comparatively untouched, in the face of the fact that in the newspaper and periodicals of the day is a class of the finest literature of the age. Writers now address themselves more to current literature than formerly; hence, many of the finest gems in prose and verse appear from week to week and are lost with the short life of the paper or magazine in which they are published. It will be admitted, therefore, that many of them deserve better fate, and that the language would be enriched by their preservation. It is to this class of literature The Scrap-Book addresses itself; and it would be incomplete were not in it also found many old gems which are familiar to the public, and copies of which are wanted by all. Many of their writers have long since passed over the river, and are unknown to the writer, if not to the world. Hence an apology is due, perhaps, to many of those helping to make up The Scrap-Book, insomuch as, in some instances, they were not consulted as to the selections used, or that imperfect and incomplete credits may, in some instances, be given. The scope of our labors, and the means at hand, would suggest it as an impossibility that it should be otherwise. In a few instances it may also be possible that selections have been made from others whose writings are not released. In many instances permission and aid have been cordially granted by those, without extracts from whose writings, no scrap-book would be complete. And in all cases, we trust that no individual damage has been done by the making of selections which was intended as the highest compliment of the writer to their merit and authors.

It is called The Scrap-Book, because that is really what it is. Simply a scrap-book. To this end, we have endeavored to preserve its identity as such, and trust the public will thus generously accept it; and that those who have contributed to its make-up, will accept its dedication as the highest regard of its

AUTHOR.

THE SCRAP-BOOK.

ME AN' MARY.

There's a lot o' joy in livin', an' a lot o' fun in life
When a fellow has a sweetheart an' is thinkin' of a wife,
An' that kinder now reminds me that I lived on honey-comb
When Mary did the milkin' an' I drove the cattle home.

I was kinder shy an' bashful, an' what folks would say was "green";
An' the writin' in the Bible put down Mary "seventeen";
I'd been thinkin' of the city—bein' much inclined to roam,
But I wondered, if I left her, who would drive the cattle home?

But there warn't so much in farmin', or in drivin' cows to milk;
It kept me down to cotton jeans an' Mary fur from silk;
An' so, though I was up to go—for leavin' of the loam,
As I said before, I wondered who would drive the cattle home?

You see, they kinder knowed me—been a-drivin' of 'em so!
An' Mary had to milk 'em at a certain time—you know!
Would they come up in the twilight, would they know the time o' stars?
An' who, like me, could coax 'em, an, let down for 'em the bars?

I remember it was springtime—'bout the settin' of the sun;
An' I'd drove the cows to Mary, an' the milkin' had begun;
An' I said: " I'm sorry, Mary, that the two of us must part;"
An' I kept a-whistlin', careless, like 'twould break nobody's heart.

But she looked acrost the meadows with her blue an' beamin' eyes,
Which was like a dream o' heaven, an' jest took in all the skies!
An' then—an' then—I can't tell how—I couldn't think or see—
"Do you like the city livin', or the cattle, more than me?"

Warn't no milk in that ere farmhouse that evenin'—not a drop!
The cows got in the cornfield an' jest eat up half the crop!
But the dish that I was feedin' from was sweet with honey-comb
From the red, sweet lips o' Mary as I kissed her goin' home!
I lost sight o' the city life, whatever it might be;
One acre in the country was enough, an' more, for me!
An' I've made my mind up certain, an' I ain't inclined to roam
While Mary does the milkin' an' I drive the cattle home!

A MOTHER'S PICTURE.

Only a mother's picture,
   Stained by my falling tears;
Only a mother's picture,
   Snatched from the wreck of years,
But it carries me back to my childhood;
   Back to my boyhood days,
Thoughts of the old home come o'er me,
   Thoughts of the good old ways.

I think of my father and mother;
  Their voices I seem to hear,
But only this picture is left me
  Of all that I once held dear.
The old home; the home of my childhood,
  Had fallen to deep decay;
The brothers, the sisters and parents
  In the churchyard are laid away.

But oft at the hour of midnight,
  When silence is over all,
Voices from out of the darkness
  Sadly seem to call,
Thoughts of the old home come o'er me,
  While I ponder here alone,
And my heart cries out in sadness
  As the breezes sigh and moan.

But only a mother's picture,
  Stained by my falling tears,
Brings back these old home visions
  From out of the mist of years.
Only a mother's picture,
  Stained by my falling tears;
Only a mother's picture,
  Yet the comfort of my years.
    —Louis E. Thayer.

THE EMPTY CRADLE.

There's a little empty cradle,
  Standing in a darkened room,
And a loving mother's prayers
  Echo through the silent room;
For to-day the snow-white pillow
  Brings no little head sweet rest,
And the dainty bed's sad smoothness
  By no little form is pressed.

By its side the lonely mother,
  Choked with grief and unshed tears,
Kneels and prays for strength and comfort
To sustain her through the years
She must spend in yearning sorrow,
  Thinking of that happy time
When her home was filled with laughter,
  Making sweet and merry chime.

All the longings and the heartaches,
  Of the mother in her woe,
All the bitter pain unceasing,
  Only childless mothers know;
For howe'er well-meant the effort,
  None can any comfort give,
And her heart seems full to bursting,
  Such a burden 'tis to live.

But there comes a time when sunbeams,
  Shining in the sombre room,
Change her prayers to praises,
  And vanishes the saddening gloom;
Now her heart hath found sweet comfort;
  And her weariness sweet rest,
In the thought, "whate'er betides us
  Jesus doeth all things best."
    —Minnie Martin Fuller.

WHEN THE CIRCUS WAS IN TOWN.

Dar ain't no day lack show-day, when
  de circus comes to town,
Wid all its spotted hosses, its varmints
  an' its clown;
Hit's long ways 'head of Christmas an'
  ef here de whole year roun',
I'd be a happy nigger while dat circus
  wuz in town.

Hit jes' puts a kind o' feelin' all in a feller's bones
Dat makes him feel lack spendin' jes'
  ev'ry cent he owns
To git inside dat circus—an' it's inside
  I'll be boun',
You'll alluz fin' dis pusson when the circus is in town.

How well I's rickolectin'—long sens niggers wuz sot free,
Ole Moster come aroun' one day an'
  say—says he to me:
"I want you all to promise that the
  fact'ry shan't shet down,
But you'll all keep on a-workin' when
  that circus comes to town."

An' he 'low'd pore-bucks an' niggers
  wuz all de sort what went
An' spent der time an' money inside a
  circus tent;
An' he 'low'd ef ev'rybody wuz lack him
  de circus groun'
Would look lonesome as a grave-yard
  when de circus come to town.

Well, mos' de niggers promist dat dey
    sho'ly wouldn't go
An' fool away der money a-messin' wid
    dat show;
But I jes' sorter mumbled an' it mought
    a sorter soun'
Mos' lack some sich a promise 'fore the
    circus come to town.

But 'twarn't a plum-shore promise, kaze
    I know'd I couldn't stick—
Hain't never mist a circus but wunst
    when I wuz sick;
An' shore enough nex' mornin' when
    dey come purradin roun'
I klean forgot Ole Moster, kaze de circus wuz in town.

I know'd he wouldn't miss me kaze I'd
    seed him go away—
An' hearn him tell Ole Mistes he'd be
    gone all of dat day—
So I made lack he done tole me to go
    chop wood fer Parson Brown,
And sneaked off to dat circus dat wuz
    showin' down in town.

My conscience sorter bit me, yit sumpin
    seemed to say:
"I'd never miss dis circus—dey ain't
    one ever' day,"
An' while I felt uneasy an' as sneakin'
    as a houn',
I marched into dat circus big as any
    man in town.

But 'fore I'd got good sot down I mos
    nearly had a chill,
Fer right dar sot Ole Moster a laffin' fit
    to kill;
I 'pear'd I didn't see him, but when
    he begin to frown
Den I know'd he know'd I seed him
    when de circus was in town.
            —SAM BEAN.

SOME OTHER DAY.

THERE are wonderful things we are
    going to do,
        Some other day;
And harbors we hope to drift into
        Some other day.

With folded hands and oars that trail,
We watch and wait for a favoring gale
To fill the folds of an idle sail
        Some other day.

We know we must toil if ever we win,
        Some other day.
And we say to ourselves there's a
    time to begin
        Some other day;
And so, deferring, we loiter on,
Until at length we find withdrawn
The strength of the hope we leaned
    upon
        Some other day.

And when we are old and our race is
    run
        Some other day,
We fret for the things that might have
    been done
        Some other day.
We trace the path that leads us where
The beckoning hand of a grim despair
Leads us yonder, out of here,
        Some other day.
    —ALFRED ELLISON *in the
        Chicago Record.*

DON'T USE BIG WORDS.

IN promulgating your esoteric cogitations and in articulating your superficial sentimentalities and amicable philosophical or psychological observations beware of platitudinous ponderosity. Let your conversational communications possess a clarified conciseness, a compacted comprehensibleness, coalescent consistency, and a concatenated cogency. Eschew all conglomerations of flatulent garrulity, jejune babblement, asinine affectations. Let your extemporaneous descantings and unpremeditated expatiations have intelligibility and veracious vivacity without rhodomontade or thrasonical bombast. Sedulously avoid all polysyllabic profundity, pompous prolixity, psittaceous vacuity, ventriloquial verbosity, and vaniloquent vapidity. Shun double ententes, prurient jocosity, and pestiferous profanity, obscurant or apparent. In other words, talk plainly, briefly, natu-

rally sensibly, purely, and truthfully.
Keep from slang, do not put on airs,
say what you mean, mean what you say,
and DON'T USE BIG WORDS!

THE LORD'S PRAYER.

A SCHOLAR was asked to suggest an improvement in the translation of the Lord's prayer. He suggested the following:

Our Father, in heaven,
Hallowed be Thy name;
May Thy Kingdom come,
And Thy will on earth be done;
Daily our necessities meet,
And, forgiving us our trespasses,
Incline us to so forgive others;
Deliver us from temptations and evil,
And by Thy mercy judge and save us.
      Amen.

FARE THEE WELL.

FARE thee well! and if forever,
 Still forever, fare thee well;
Even though unforgiving, never
 'Gainst thee shall my heart rebel.

Would that breast were bared before thee
 Where thy head so oft hath lain,
While that placid sleep came o'er thee
 Which thou ne'er canst know again.

Would that breast, by thee glanced over,
 Every inmost thought could show,
Then thou wouldst at last discover
 'Twas not well to spurn it so.

Though the world for this commend thee—
 Though it smile upon the blow,
Even its praises must offend thee,
 Founded on another's woe;

Though so many faults defaced me,
 Could no other arm be found,
Than the one which once embraced thee,
 To inflict a cureless wound?

Yet, oh yet, thyself deceive not;
 Love may sink by slow decay,
But by sudden wrench, believe not
 Hearts can thus be torn away:

Still thine own its life retaineth—
 Still must mine, though bleeding, beat;
And the undying thought which paineth
 Is—that we no more may meet.

These are words of deeper sorrow
 Than the wail above the dead;
Both shall live, but every morrow
 Wake us from a widow'd bed.

And when thou would solace gather,
 When our child's first accents flow,
Wilt thou teach her to say "Father!"
 Though his care she must forego?

When her little hands shall press thee,
 When her lip to thine is press'd,
Think of him whose prayer shall bless thee,
 Think of him thy love had bless'd!

Should her lineaments resemble
 Those thou never more may'st see,
Then thy heart will softly tremble
 With a pulse yet true to me.

All my faults perchance thou knowest,
 All my madness none can know,
All my hopes, where'er thou goest,
 Whither, yet with *thee* they go.

Every feeling hath been shaken;
 Pride, which not a world could bow,
Bows to thee—by thee forsaken,
 Even my soul forsakes me now.

But 'tis done,—all words are idle—
 Words from me are vainer still;
But the thoughts we cannot bridle
 Force their way without the will.

Fare thee well!—thus disunited,
 Torn from every nearer tie,
Sear'd in heart, and lone, and blighted,
 More than this I scarce can die.
      —LORD BYRON.

HELP THE HOMELESS.

Cheer them in thy sweet compassion;
  Point them to the mercy seat;
Help the homeless on life's journey;
  Gently lead the stumbling feet;
Save from wrong and sin and blame;
Help before their lives are blighted
  With the scorching brand of shame.

Ye, who fondly treasure riches,
  And whose stately mansions fair
Shield thy daughters pure and lovely,
  As thy dearest earthly care;
Wake thy sleeping hearts to pity,
  For the poor whose daughters toil;
Build a home and from thy bounty
  Rescue now, ere sin despoil!

Give a mite or donate millions;
  Bless, as you with homes are blest;
One above will keep the record
  Of the money you invest.
Homes are reared to shield the fallen,
  And their builders builded well,
But the better part were chosen,
  Had they helped them ere they fell.
—Margaret Scott Hall.

MOTHER AT PRAYER.

Once, says a writer, I suddenly opened the door of my mother's room and saw her on her knees beside her chair, and heard her speak my name in prayer. I quickly and quietly withdrew with a feeling of awe and reverence in my heart. Soon I went away from home to school, then to college, then into life's sterner duties. But I never forgot that one glimpse of my mother at prayer, nor the one word—my own name—which I heard her utter. Well did I know that what I had seen that day was but a glimpse of what was going on every day in that sacred closet of prayer, and the consciousness strengthened me a thousand times in duty, in danger, and in struggle. When death came at last and sealed those lips, the sorest sense of loss I felt was the knowledge that no more would my mother be praying for me!

UNANSWERED.

Why is it the tenderest feet must tread
  the roughest road?
Why is it the weakest back must carry
  the heaviest load?
While the feet that are surest and firmest have the smoothest path to go,
And the back that is straightest and strongest has never a burden to know?

Why is it the brightest eyes are the
  ones soon dim with tears?
Why is it the lightest heart must ache
  and ache for years?
While the eyes that are hardest and
  coldest shed never a bitter tear,
And the heart that is smallest and meanest has never an ache to fear?

Why is it those who are saddest have
  always the gayest laugh?
Why is it those who need not have
  always the "biggest half?"
While those who have never a sorrow
  have seldom a smile to give,
And those who want just a little must
  strive and struggle to live?

Why is it the noblest thoughts are the
  ones that are never expressed?
Why is it the grandest deeds are the
  ones that are never confessed?
While the thoughts that are like all
  others are the ones we always tell,
And the deeds worth little praise are
  the ones that are published well?

Why is it the sweetest smile has for its
  sister a sigh?
Why is it the strongest love is the love
  we always pass by?
While the smile that is cold and indifferent is the smile for which we pay,
And the love we kneel to and worship
  is only common clay?

Why is it the things we can have are
  the things we always refuse?
Why is it none of us live the lives, if we
  could, we'd choose?
The things we all can have are the
  things we always hate,
And life seems never complete, no
  matter how long we wait?
—Elizabeth Stewart Martin.

THE OLD MILL.

THE more modern civilization has rooted out many things that are still dear to the human heart, and among them is the old-fashioned "water mill." For nowadays, as some one has said, "There are more dams by a mill-site, but fewer mills, by a dam-site!"

Yes, the ages of steam and electricity have made many revolutions, and among them the relegation of the old water mill to a thing of the past. Yet, who does not have almost sacred recollections of the old mill, the stream, the "deep tangled wildwood," and all about it? Who does not remember its whirl and splash, the big wheels—and the great Pacific ocean of your first view of waters! And the old miller and his white hat and dust-covered clothes; his boats and his long fishing poles. Yes, down the vistas of the past, these scenes all come back to you, and you almost want to go back and live life over again, as you remember them and how you used to go a-fishing at the old mill. And then the swimming! You never will forget that it was there you first learned to swim; and the times you had! How you ducked Johnny Jones, and saw Bill Smith fall off the old log, "over his head," and was fished out by the miller's son!

There were great events in the average boy's life, and at the old mill were many of them, for it was there that took place the great contests in swimming, marbles, cock-fights, and horse swaps. They didn't have baseball and bicycles then, but they had many other things there. It was there the gossip of the neighborhood was discussed. It was there the important notices of sales, elections, etc., were posted; and it was there the local politician got in his best work, just before the election. The miller, too, was an important individual, for he heard everything, knew "everybody" and was umpire at the games, and referee at the cock-fights and "horse disputes."

As a detective, information bureau, and weather prophet, he was the recognized leader; and what he didn't know about the "changes in the moon," and how they affected the "craps," and the fishes "biting," was not worth knowing!

And then after the crops were laid by, what barbecues, picnics and fish-frys they had at the old mill! It was just the place for it, and the cool shade, crystal spring and long table, on the grounds, were always ready for it. The moon, and the "apple-jack" stills were always in order for a picnic and barbecue, but the fish-fry had to wait for the change in the moon, and for the miller to set his nets! And on such occasions, how the politicians would just "happen by" and what a "run of custom" the mill would have from those not invited to the picnic or fish-fry! One or two fiddlers, perched upon the improvised stand, furnished the music—and such dancing! How rosy would be the cheeks of the girls as they fanned with their sun-bonnets! How the musicians would call out: "First couple to the right," "Ladies chain," "Grand right and left," "Promenade all," etc.

After a while dinner would be announced (which meant a welcome for all), and amid such scenes, exercises and enjoyments, even a poor dinner would appear fit for the gods. But think of such dinners as they had, and with what mirth and zest were they enjoyed. It is needless to say they were all happy and still have pleasant recollections of the old mill.

By and by, after all had become literally tired out by enjoyments, that is to say, "About an hour by sun," (five or six o'clock), they would "break up," and return to their several homes, the last one of them—even the miller's dog—being ready and willing to make an affidavit that he had "had a good time!"

And, then again, the old mill was another important place when the people had still another turn. It was there most of the revivals and protracted meetings had their terminations. Different scenes and surroundings, to be sure; yet it was the common baptismal font of the section. It was there they "gathered by the river," whether it flowed by the throne of God, or not.

Here many were baptized in a very different spirit from the way the boys baptized Jonny Jones, and each other. Yes, it was the "baptizing grounds" for all churches, races and colors, and right big times did the boys have when the colored preachers came with their long lists of candidates for baptism, and we never shall forget what a fool, that cheerful idiot, June Vann, made of himself, as an old colored woman arose from the water, shouting as she arose, "Glory! I see Glory!" by saying, "It was a terapin, fer I seed him myself!"

Yes, the dear old mill,—whose mind does not turn back to it, with almost sainted memories!

WIFE AND I.

SHE who sleeps upon my heart
  Was the first to win it;
She who dreams upon my breast
  Ever reigns within it;
She who kisses oft my lips
  Wakes their warmest blessing;
She who rests within my arms
  Feels their closest pressing.

Other days than these shall come,
  Days that shall be dreary;
Other hours may greet us yet,
  Hours that shall be weary.
Still this heart shall be thy home,
  Still this breast thy pillow;
Still these lips meet thine as soft
  As billow meeteth billow.

Sleep, then, on my happy heart,
  Since thy love hath won it;
Dream then on my loyal breast,
  None but thou hast done it.
And whene'er our bloom shall change
  With its weary weather,
May we in the selfsame grave
  Sleep and dream together.

LIFE'S ONWARD CURRENT.

FOREVER onward is the march—
  From beastly hoof to hand—
From savage to the seer and sage—
  From Saurian types to man;
From man to angel—limitless
  As are the starry spheres,
Progression hath not halt nor bound
  In God's eternal years!

From darkest cloud the lightning flash,
  From nothing—life divine,
From gloom to glory is the law,
  The unvarying design.
A world of good invites our eyes,
  And charms the willing mind—
But he who only misery finds
  Blasphemes the life Divine.

No treacherous gift was life to man,
  With deadly hate concealed,
For Love Divine the method planned
  And all will be revealed
When o'er the clouds that hover here
  The risen soul surveys
The mansions of the eternal spheres,
  The land of endless days.
              —THE ARENA.

HER SECRET.

'TWAS twilight. In the shadow of the porch
  We sat and watched the coming of the moon,
And when at last we saw night's silvery torch
  We both regretted it had come so soon.

Then suddenly she jumped up from her seat,
  And with a cry into my arms she fell;
I clasped unto my breast the burden sweet,
  And gently urged her secret she would tell.

She was a summer maiden, and I knew
  Full well she suffered not from love's attack
And I was right, for when her breath she drew
  She gasped,. "That horrid bug's crawled down my back."
              —NEW YORK EVENING SUN.

CARE FOR FATHER.

DOES any one care aught for father?
  Does any one think of the one
Upon whose tired, bent shoulders
  The cares of the family come?

The father who strives for your comfort,
  And toils on from day to day,
Although his steps ever grow slower,
  And his dark locks are turning gray?

Does any one think of the due bills
  He is called upon to pay—
Millinery bills, college bills, book bills?
  There are some kind of bills every day.
Like a patient horse in a treadmill,
  He works on from morn till night.
Does any one think he is tired?
  Does any one make his home bright?

Is it right, because he looks troubled,
  To say he's cross as a bear?
Kind words, little actions and kindness
  Might vanish his burden of care.
'Tis for you he is ever so anxious;
  He'll toil for you while he may live;
In return he only asks kindness,
  And such pay is easy to give.

EVENING.

DIM falls the light o'er all the dreaming
  woods;
  Athwart the distant western sky are
    gleams
Of gold and amber; pearly, rose-edged
  clouds,
  Looking so passing fair, one almost
    dreams
The opening gate to Paradise hath lent
  Some tinge of glory to the dying day;
And earth-bound souls, with longing,
  ling'ring gaze,
  Would fain rise up and move along
    that way.

A stillness sweet and solemn all around;
  The song of birds is hushed; there
    falls no quiver
Of rustling leaf, or shaking, trembling
  reed,
  Upon the fair faint brightness of the
    river.

The crescent moon gleams coldly, dimly
  forth;
  And in the deepening blue of heaven
    afar,
A tender watcher o'er the troubled
  world,
  Shineth one solitary glitt'ring star.

The shadows deepen on the distant hills;
  The highest peak but touched with
    ling'ring light;
And down their purpling sides soft,
  misty clouds
Wrap all the valleys in a dusky night.

And far away the murmur of the sea,
  And moonlit waves, breaking in foamy
    line.
So Night—God's Angel, Night—with
  silvery wings,
Fills all the earth with loveliness divine.
    —CHAMBERS'S JOURNAL.

DON'T FORGET THE RAINY DAY.

BOYS, our youth too fast is fleeting,
  Life's glad morning cannot last,
And the moments swift retreating
  Warn us that 'will soon be past.
There will come a sure declining,
  And I would this to you say:
While the sun is brightly shining,
  Don't forget the rainy day.

Sunshine cannot last forever,
  Storms will come and winds wage
    strife,
And as sure will dark clouds gather
  On the horizon of life.
Let us, then, in youth remember
  Life is not one long, bright May,
Sure will come the dread December,
  Sure will come the rainy day.

As the busy bee doth gather
  In bright days her winter store,
So should we for life's bleak weather
  Garner ere the summer's o'er.
Yes, ere life's bright spring doth leave us,
  Let us strive aside to lay
Something that may shelter give us
  When shall come the rainy day.

FALLEN.

The iron voice from yonder spire has
  hush'd its hollow tone,
And midnight finds me lying here in
  silence and alone;
The still moon thro' my window sheds
  its soft light on the floor

With a melancholy paleness I have
   never seen before.
And the summer wind comes to me with
   its sad Æolian lay,
As if burthened with the sorrows of a
   weary, weary day ;
Yet the moonlight cannot soothe me of
   the sickness here within,
And the sad wind takes no portion from
   my bosom's weight of sin.

Yet my heart and all its pulses seem so
   quietly to rest,
That I scarcely feel them beating in my
   arms or in my breast ;
And these rounded limbs are resting
   now so still upon the bed,
That one would think to see me here
   that I was lying dead.
What if 'twere so ? What if I died—
   died as I am lying now,
With something like to virtue's calm
   upon this marble brow ?
What if I died to-night ? Ah ! now
   this slothful heart begins to beat ;
A fallen wretch like me, to pass from
   earth so sadly sweet !

Yet am I calm—as calm as clouds that
   slowly float and form,
To give their tearful strength to some
   unpitying summer storm ;
As calm as great Sahara, ere the simoon
   sweeps its waste,
Or as the wide sea, ere the white waves
   all its shores have laced.
Still, still I have no tears to shed ; these
   eyelids have no store—
The fountain once within me is a fountain now no more.
The moon alone weeps for me now—the
   pale and thoughtful moon ;
She weeps for dying Mary, through all
   the night's sweet noon.

What if I died to-night, within these
   gilded, wretched walls,
Upon whose crimson trappings no eye
   of virtue ever falls ?
What would its soulless inmates do when
   they had found me here,
With cheek too white for passion's
   smile, too cold for passion's tear ?
Oh ! one would come and from these
   arms unclasp the bauble bands,
Another wrench the jewels off my fairer,
   whiter hands ;
This splendid robe another's form would
   grace, oh ! long before
The moonlight came again to sleep upon
   the floor.

And when they'd laid me down in earth
   where pauper graves are made,
Beneath no bending willow's angel-
   haunted shade,
Who'd come and plant a flower o'er
   poor Mary's friendless grave,
Or trim the tangled wild grass that no
   Summer wind could wave ?
Who'd raise a stone to mark it from the
   ruder graves around,
That the passing stranger's footsteps
   might respect the spot of ground ?
No stone would stand above me, no
   little waving tree,
No hand would plant a flower o'er a
   fallen wretch like me.

     *   *   *   *   *

What if I died to-night ? And when
   to-morrow's sun had crept
Where late the softer moon in virgin
   beauty slept,
They'd come and find me here, oh !
   who would weep to see me dead ?
Who'd bend the knee of sorrow by the
   pulseless wanton's bed ?
There's one would come—my mother !
   God bless the angel band
That bore her, ere her daughter fell, to
   yonder quiet land !
Thank God for all the anthems that the
   gladden'd angels sung
When my mother went to Heaven, and
   I was pure and young.

And there's another, too, would come—
   A man upon whose brow
My shame has wrought the winter snow
   to rest so heavy now ;
Yes, he would come, with manhood's
   tears all burning down his cheek,
Had reason's kingdom stronger been
   where virtue grew so weak.
My sisters and my brothers all, thank
   God ! are far away ;
They'll never know how died the one
   who mingled in their play—

They'll never know how wretchedly
    their darling sister died—
The one who smiled whene'er they
    smiled, who cried whene'er they
    cried.

I'm all alone to-night ! How strange it
    is that I should be alone !
This splendid chamber seems to want
    some Roue's wonted tone !
Yon soulless mirror, with its smooth
    and all unvarnished face,
Sees not these jeweled arms to-night in
    their unchaste embrace.
Oh ! I have fled the fever of that heated,
    crowded hall,
Where I might claim the richest and
    the gayest of them all—
Where I could smile upon them, with
    that easy, wanton grace,
Which subdues the blood of virtue that
    would struggle in my face !

But I hate them all. I scorn them, as
    they scorn me on the street ;
I could spurn away the pressure that
    my lips so often meet ;
I could trample on the lucre that their
    passion never spares,
For they've robbed me of a heritage of
    greater price than theirs.
They can never give me back again
    what I have thrown away—
The brightest jewel woman wears
    throughout her little day ;
The brightest and the only one, that
    from the cluster riven,
Shuts out forever woman's heart from
    all the hopes of Heaven.

What if I died to-night ? What if I died
    as I am lying here ?
There's many a green leaf withers ere
    the Autumn comes to sear !
There's many a dewdrop shaken down
    ere yet the sunshine came,
And many a spark hath died before it
    wakened into flame !
What if I died to-night, and left these
    wretched bonds of clay,
To seek beyond the hollow sphere a
    brighter, better day ?
What if my soul passed out and sought
    that haven of the blest,
"Where the wicked cease from troubling, and the weary are at rest ? "

Would angels call me from above, and
    beckon me to come
And join them in their holy songs in
    that eternal home ?
Would they clasp their hands in gladness when they saw my soul set
    free ?
And point beside my mother to a place
    reserved for me ?
Would they meet me as a sister, as one
    of precious worth,
Who had won a place in Heaven by her
    holiness on earth ?
Oh ! God, I would not have my soul to
    go out upon the air,
With all its weight of wretchedness, to
    wander where ? Oh ! where ?
        —H. T. S.

THE BABY—WHAT IS IT?

A LONDON newspaper recently offered a prize for " The best definition of a baby."

The following is a selection from some of the best definitions submitted :

The bachelor's horror, the mother's treasure, and despotic tyrant of the most republican household.

A human flower untouched by the finger of care.

A tiny feather from the wing of love, dropped into the sacred lap of motherhood.

The morning caller, noonday crawler, midnight brawler.

The magic spell by which the gods transform a house into a home.

A stranger with unspeakable cheek, that enters a house without a stitch to his back, and is received with open arms by every one.

A bursting bud on the tree of life.

The only precious possession that never excites envy.

The latest edition of humanity, of which every couple think they possess the finest copy.

A native of all countries who speaks the language of none.

The unconscious mediator between father and mother, and the focus of their hearts.

About twenty-two inches of coo and

The Baby.
An Inhabitant of Lapland.

UNIV. OF
CALIFORNIA

wriggle, writhe and scream, filled with suction and testing apparatus for milk, and automatic alarm to regulate supply.

A quaint little craft called Innocence, laden with simplicity and love.

A curious bud of uncertain blossom.

A thing we are expected to kiss, and look as if we enjoyed it.

The smartest little craft afloat in home's delightful bay.

A mite of humanity that will cry no harder if a pin is stuck into him than he will if the cat won't let him pull her tail.

A little stranger, with a free pass to the heart's best affections.

The most extensive employer of female labor.

The pulp from which the leaves of life's book are made.

A padlock on the chain of love.

A soft bundle of love and trouble which we cannot do without.

The sweetest thing God ever made and forgot to give wings to.

A pleasure to two, a nuisance to every other body and a necessity to the world.

An inhabitant of Lapland.

That which makes home happier, love stronger, patience greater, hands busier, nights longer, days shorter, purses lighter, clothes shabbier, the past forgotten, the future brighter.

THE MYSTICAL SEA.

O LOVE, I'm wandering back to-day
  Through the valleys of memory ;
They lie betwixt mountains far away.
The mountains of Hope and of Youth
  are they,
And I'm dreaming again of that night,
  to-day,
    By the mystic southern sea.

O love, I loved you that far-off night
  By the mystical southern sea.
The breeze was light and the stars were
  bright,
And the sea-gulls flashed in their circling flight,
As we sat alone, on that far-off night,
  When you whispered your love for
    me.

Oh, I kissed your lips, and I clasped
  your hands,
By that mystical southern sea,
While softly the waves were kissing the
  sands,
And ships went a-sailing to distant
  lands,
And I kissed your lips, and I clasped
  your hands,
    When you whispered your love to
    me.

O love, a storm has swept the shore
  Of that mystical southern sea ;
The waves still kiss as they kissed before ;
But the ships that sailed will return no
  more,
And the youth, and the love, and the
  hopes of yore
    Will never come back to me.
      —ALBERT B. PAINE.

WHEN THE SKIES CLEAR OFF.

THE prospects will be brighter,
The burdens will be lighter,
An' the souls of us be whiter
  When the skies clear off !
With sweeter roses springin',
An' sweeter birds a-singin',
An' all the bells a-ringin'
  When the skies clear off !

The silver—it'll jingle,
Till your fingers tingle, tingle ;
Old friends'll meet and mingle
  When the skies clear off !
An' trouble, like a feather,
Will go sailin' out the weather,
We'll sing and dance together
  When the skies clear off !

There's a sign o' light a-comin' ;
An' you hear the wagon hummin';
You'll be marchin' to the drummin'
  When the skies clear off !
No matter what's the trouble—
It'll break just like a bubble,
An' you'll drive in harness double
  When the skies clear off !

LOVE'S FIRST KISS.

Sweetheart, 'twas but a while ago—it
    scarce seems yesterday,
Though now my locks are white as snow
    and all your curls are gray—
When, walking in the twilight haze, ere
    stars had smiled above,
I whispered soft: "I love you," and you
    kissed me for that love!

The first kiss, dear! and then your
    hand—your little hand so sweet,
And whiter than the white, white sand
    that twinkled 'neath your feet—
Laid tenderly within my own! Have
    queens such lovely hands?
No wonder that the whip-poor-wills
    made sweet the autumn lands!

It seemed to me that my poor heart
    would beat to death and break,
While all the world, sweetheart! sweet-
    heart! seemed singing for your
    sake;
And every rose that barred the way in
    glad and dying grace,
Forgot its faded summer day and, lean-
    ing, kissed your face!

I envied all the roses then, and all the
    rosy ways
That blossomed for your sake are still
    my life's bright yesterdays;
But thinking of that first sweet kiss and
    that first clasp of hands,
Life's whip-poor-wills sing sweeter now
    through all the winter lands!
        —Frank L. Stanton.

THE NEW BABY.

There came to port last Sunday night
  The queerest little craft,
Without an inch of rigging on;
  I looked and looked and laughed.

It seemed so curious that she
  Should cross the unknown water,
And moor herself right in my room—
  My daughter, O my daughter!

She had no manifest but this,
  No flag floats o'er her water;
She's too new for the British Lloyd—
  My daughter, O my daughter!

Ring out wild bells, and tamed ones
  too;
Ring out the lover's moon!
Ring in the little worsted socks!
Ring in the bib and spoon.

Ring out the muse, ring in the nurse!
Ring in the milk and water!
Away with paper, pen, and ink—
  My daughter, O my daughter!
        —Chas. G. Peeler.

GROWING OLD.

The tallest lilies droop at eventide,
  The sweetest roses fall from off the
    stem;
The rarest thing on earth cannot abide,
  And we are passing, too, away like
    them;
    We're growing old.

We had our dreams, those rosy dreams
    of youth;
  They faded, and 'twas well. This
    afterprime
Hath brought us fuller hopes; and yet,
    forsooth,
  We drop a tear now in this later
    time
    To think we're old.

We smile at those poor fancies of the
    past—
  A saddened smile, almost akin to
    pain;
Those high desires, those purposes so
    vast,
  Ah, our poor hearts! they cannot
    come again!
    We're growing old.

Old? Well, the heavens are old; this
    earth is, too;
  Old wine is best, maturest fruit most
    sweet;
Much have we lost, more gained, al-
    though 'tis true,
  We tread life's way with most uncer-
    tain feet.
    We're growing old.

We move along, and scatter, as we pace,
Soft graces, tender hopes on every hand :
At last, with gray-streaked hair and hollow face,
We step across the boundary of the land
    Where none are old.
    —ATLANTA CONSTITUTION.

THE RAINY DAY.

THE day is cold, and dark, and dreary ;
It rains, and the wind is never weary ;
The vine still clings to the mouldering wall,
But at every gust the dead leaves fall,
And the day is dark and dreary.

My life is cold, and dark, and dreary ;
It rains, and the wind is never weary ;
My thoughts still cling to the mouldering Past,
But the hopes of youth fall thick in the blast,
And the days are dark and dreary.

Be still, sad heart ! and cease repining ;
Behind the clouds is the sun still shining ;
Thy fate is the common fate of all,
Into each life some rain must fall,
    Some days must be dark and dreary.
        —LONGFELLOW.

THE HOUSE OF NEVER.

THE house of Never is built, they say,
Just over the hills of the By-and-By,
Its gates are reached by a devious way
Hidden from all but an angel's eye.
It winds about and in and out
The hills and dales to sever.
Once over the hills of the By-and-By
And you're lost in the house of Never.

The house of Never is filled with waits,
With just-a-minutes, and pretty-soons,
The noise of their wings, as they beat the gates,
Comes back to the earth in the afternoons.

When the shadows fly across the sky,
And rushes, rude endeavor,
To question the hills of the By-and-By
As they ask for the house of Never.

The house of Never was built with tears;
And lost in the hills of the By-and-By
Are a million hopes and a million fears,
A baby's smiles, and a woman's cry.
The winding way seems bright to-day,
Then darkness falls forever,
For over the hills of the By-and-By
    Sorrow waits in the house of Never.
        —CHICAGO DISPATCH.

CARDS AS A BIBLE.

A PRIVATE soldier by the name of Richard Lee was taken before a magistrate for playing cards during divine service. It appears that a sergeant commanded the soldiers at the church, and when the parson had read the prayers, he took the text. Those who had a Bible took it out, but this soldier had neither Bible nor Common Prayer Book, but pulling out a pack of cards, he spread them out before him. He just looked at one card and then at another. The sergeant of the company saw him and said, " Richard, put up the cards ; this is no place for them."

" Never mind that," said Richard.

When the service was over the constable took Richard before the justice.

" Well," said the mayor, " what have you brought the soldier here for ? "

" For playing cards in church."

" Well, soldier, what have you to say for yourself ? "

" Much, sir, I hope."

" Very good. If not, I will punish you more than man was ever punished."

" I have been," said the soldier, " about six weeks on the march. I have neither Bible nor Common Prayer Book. I have nothing but a pack of cards, and I'll satisfy your worship of the purity of my intentions." And spreading the cards before the mayor he began with the ace : " When I see the ace it reminds me there is but one God. When I see the deuce it reminds me of Father and Son. When I see the tray it reminds me of Father, Son and Holy Ghost. When I see the four spot it reminds me of the four evangelists that preached, Matthew, Mark, Luke and John. When I meet the five it reminds me of the five wise virgins that trimmed their lamps—there were ten, but five were foolish and were shut out. When I see the six it reminds me that in six days the Lord made the heaven and earth. When I see the seven it reminds me that on the seventh day he rested from the great work he had created, and hallowed it. When I see the eight, it reminds me of the eight righteous persons that were saved when God destroyed the world, viz.: Noah and his wife with three sons and their wives. When I see the nine it reminds me of the nine lepers that were cleansed by our Saviour; there were nine out of ten who never returned thanks. When I see the ten it reminds me of the ten commandments which God handed down to Moses on tablets of stone. When I see the king it reminds me of the King of heaven, which is God Almighty. When I see the queen it reminds me of the queen of Sheba, who visited Solomon, for she was as wise a woman as he was a man. She brought with her fifty boys and fifty girls, all dressed in boy's apparel, for King Solomon to tell which were boys and which were girls. King Solomon sent for water, for them to wash; the girls washed to the elbows and the boys to the wrists, so King Solomon told by that."

"Well," said the mayor, "you have given a good description of all the cards but one."

"What is that?"

"The knave," said the mayor.

"I will give your honor a description of that, too, if you will not be angry."

"I will not," said the mayor, "if you do not term me to be the knave."

"Well," said the soldier, "the greatest knave that I know is the constable that brought me here."

"I do not know," said the mayor, "if he is the greatest knave, but I do know that he is the greatest fool."

"When I count how many spots there are in a pack of cards, I find 365, as many days as there are in a year. When I count the number of cards in a pack, I find there are fifty-two, the number of weeks in a year, and I also find there are four suits, the number of weeks in a month. I find there are twelve picture cards in a pack, representing the number of months in a year, and on counting the tricks, I find thirteen, the number of weeks in a quarter. So you see, a pack of cards serves for a Bible, almanac and Common Prayer Book."

IF SHE HAD LIVED.

IF she had lived—how sweetly sad the thought
Of all she might have been; what different ways [days
Her steps had led me, what more happy
Her gentle presence to my life had brought, If she had lived.

If she had lived, perhaps the golden prize
We call success had sooner neared my hand,
And, won at last, the favor of the land
Might seem more worthy to my happier eyes, If she had lived.

If she had lived, the earth and air and sky
Might seem to hold a deeper right to be,
The leaves more sadly fall from shrub and tree,
The flowers she loved might sorrow more to die, If she had lived.

If she had lived, perhaps each day were given
A fuller promise, as the east unbars
Morn, noon and sunset, twilight, and the stars
Might seem more radiant—earth more like to heaven, If she had lived.

If she had lived, perhaps the tide of years
Had borne me on more calmly to the sea,
Whose shore is Life—and Nature's harmony [If she had lived.
Might sound a sweeter echo in my ears,
—ARTHUR CLEVELAND PALMER.

THE OLD RAIL FENCE.

WHERE skies are blue and birds sing sweet,
Where sparkling waters in ripples flow,
Mirroring in deep places fleecy cloudlets,
Where winds in soft murmurs blow,

Where the lark merrily sings as he upward flies,
Where the fruit of the soil is the toiler's recompense,
There bordering the lanes and meadows,
Wrapped in the wild running apricot is the old rail fence.

It stands there where the gray dawn melts,
Flushing with rose a broad expanse of blue,
Where the sun's rays shut up the morning-glories
That hold in their hearts drops of dew.
It is kissed by the cold, silent moonbeams
That flitter through the shifting leaves,
And back and forth between its rails
The spider its silvery webbing weaves.

Zigzag it winds over the hill and runs
Like a line of sentinels the fields between,
A foil to the yellow in the tasselling corn,
To the clover's darker green.
It is the resting-place of the farmer
While he listens to the politician's debate,
And in the corner on the matted grass
The lover pleads to know his fate.

It is there the plowboy dreams
As he leans on his plow at the end of his row,
While the sun as it sinks down in the west
Floods the fields with a golden glow.
His thoughts wander over the hill far away,
He longs the world beyond to see ;
Dreams on unmindful of night's gathering gloom
Until a distant call rouses him from his reverie.

Ah, little he knows of the world with its busy marts,
Where truth and honesty are discounted with gold ;
Where the poor are as in chains fettered,
Where virtue is bought and sold.
Where fame is but a bauble when won,

Where love, if not blasted with gold, flies ;
Where friendship is like the gathered rose—
Ere you taste its fragrance it withers, then dies.

Oh, give me the country with its woodlands deep,
With its orchards in bloom by south winds blown ;
Where 'neath tangled grasses our loved ones sleep,
In the shadow of the old church with ivy o'ergrown.
Where the owls' "too-whoo" breaks the hush of night,
Where the wild rose fills the air with its sweet incense ;
Where the catbird calls and the mocking-bird sings,
Where entwined in vines lives the old rail fence.

Where in springtime between half-blown clover leaves dandelions peep,
Where the crab-apple and primrose scent the dell,
Where the cowslips yellow nod to the tender young grass,
And the anthers gold show in wind-tossed lily bells.
Oh, I love to think of my childhood days, of the days that are gone,
When I roamed the field, plucked the flower—
It is an oasis in the weary march of time,
It is like the bloom of the ivy that clings to the crumbling tower.

—ALMA RITTENBERRY.

HOME TOGETHER.

THE road is rough before our feet,
  The hills are steep and high,
And clouds are gathering overhead
  To shut away the sky.
Perhaps our paths may run apart,
  In dark and stormy weather,
But at the nearing evening-time,
  We'll be at home together.

Oh, friend of mine, I grieve to lose
   The grasp of loving hands;
How much we need each other here,
   Each fully understands.
But if our pathways meet no more
   In meadow-land or heather,
Believe that when the night is come
   We'll be at home together.

So here's a hand that's true, my friend,
   And steadfast, come what may;
God grant our paths run side by side
   And part not all the way;
But if it be that part we must—
   God only knoweth whether—
There's comfort in the thought that night
   Will bring us home together.
            —EBEN E. REXFORD.

SOME TIME.

SOMETIME, when all life's lessons have been learned,
   And suns and stars forevermore have set,
The things which our weak judgments here have spurned,
   And things o'er which we grieved with lashes wet,
Will flash before us, out of life's dark night,
   As stars shine most in deeper tints of blue,
And we shall see how all God's plans were right,
   And how what seemed reproof was love most true.

And we shall see how, while we frown and sigh,
   God's plan goes on as best for you and me;
How, when we called, He heeded not our cry
   Because His wisdom to the end could see.
And e'en as prudent parents disallow
   Too much of sweet to craving babyhood,
So God, perhaps, is keeping from us now
   Life's sweetest things, because it seemeth good.

And if, sometimes, commingled with life's wine,
   We find the wormwood, and rebel and shrink,
Be sure a wiser hand than yours or mine
   Pours out this potion for your lips to drink.
And if some friend we love is lying low
   Where human kisses cannot reach his face,
Oh, do not blame the heavenly Father so,
   But wear your sorrow with obedient grace!

And you shall shortly know that lengthened breath
   Is not the sweetest gift God sends his friend,
And that, sometimes, the sable pall of death
   Conceals the fairest boon his love can send.
If we would push ajar the gates of life,
   And stand within, and all God's workings see,
We could interpret all this doubt and strife,
   And for each mystery could find a key.

But not to-day. Then be content, poor heart!
   God's plans, like lilies, pure and white unfold,
We must not tear the close-shut leaves apart;
   Time will reveal the calyxes of gold.
And if, through patient toil, we reach the land
   Where tired feet with sandals loose, may rest,
When we shall clearly know and understand,
   I think that we would say, "God knew the best!"
            —MRS. MAY RILEY SMITH.

MORAL COURAGE.

THERE are two kinds of courage, and perhaps one of the greatest defects in the average man is not to know the difference between courage, and moral courage. The question of right and wrong, ought,—(or owe it)—enters into the one, while the other often has no foundation to stand upon. The one has the indorsement of God and man, while the other is often the product of a low or diseased nature. The serpent has courage; the cock has courage; the lion has courage to kill his best friend as well as his foe; the bull has courage to attack a red flannel, though there be no enemy behind it, and often loses his own life because of an imagined enemy; the bully has courage; and is always looking for some one to knock the imaginary chip from his shoulder. The effect of a diseased mind or body, uncurbed temper and feverish impetuosity are often called courage, while discretion and the sense of right and wrong, often make the bravest men appear to be cowards. The brave man, however, cares but little for appearances; while to the coward, appearances are everything. The one asks, Is it right? is it duty? do I owe it? The other says, I will make the world think I have courage, although it knows I have nothing else to boast of.

This was recently illustrated by one of nature's noblemen, who, for some imaginary offence, was bantered for a fight by one of those little fellows having more the nature of a wasp than a man.

"No," said the moral-couraged hero, "I will not strike you, though you may deserve it, for it would be neither brave nor right. I only strike in defence, and from you there is no need of defence!

"My teaching is to better my fellow-men, rather than to strike or punish them for their weakness and misfortunes. My duty is to help them rather than to harm them. I am by nature endowed with a strong arm, a broad hand, a good head and eye, with swift feet and gentle voice: These, I think, God gave me for better purposes than to be used against my fellow-men. I think He rather intended that I should use my eyes to see, and my feet to run to the assistance of an unfortunate, my head to counsel him, my hand to reach down and help him up, my arm to help to sustain him after he is up, while my voice admonishes him of his errors and strives to reform him to higher aims, and to better ends.

"No sir," said he, "If you want to fight, you must go elsewhere to find your man, but if you will be cool and permit your better nature to assert itself, I don't think you will wish to fight, as it is self-evident you really couldn't do much of it."

Here were the two kinds of courage. As is always the case, the moral kind triumphed.

THE OLD TRUNDLE-BED.

OH, the old trundle-bed where I slept
    when a boy,
What canopied king might not covet the
    joy?
The glory and peace of that slumber of
    mine,
Like a long, gracious rest in the bosom
    divine;
The quaint, homely couch, hidden close
    from the light,
But daintily drawn from its hiding
    place at night,
Oh, a nest of delight, from the foot to
    the head,
Was the queer little, dear little, old
    trundle-bed!
Oh, the old trundle-bed, where I wondering saw
The stars through the window, and
    listened with awe
To the sight of the winds as they tremblingly crept
Through the trees where the robins so
    restlessly slept;
Where I heard the low, murmurous
    chirp of the wren,
And the katydid listlessly chirrup again,
Till my fancies grew faint and were
    drowsily led
Through the maze of the dreams of the
    old trundle-bed,
Oh, the old trundle-bed! Oh, the old
    trundle-bed!
With its plump little pillow and old-
    fashioned spread;
Its snowy-white sheets and the blankets
    above,
Smoothed down and tucked round with
    the touches of love;

The voice of my mother to lull me to
    sleep
With the old fairy stories my memories
    keep
Still fresh as the lilies that bloom 'ore
    the head
Once bowed o'er my own in the old
    trundle-bed !
        —JAMES WHITCOMB RILEY.

MEASURE FOR MEASURE.

HE pleaded full oft, but she never would
    say
If she meant in the future to wed
    him ;
And thus, in capriciousness, day after
    day
A most woful existence she led him!
She seemed from his looks, that were
    downcast and sad,
To derive a particular pleasure,
But clearly forgot that a love-slighted
    lad
Is quite apt to give measure for meas-
    ure !
She loved him, of that there was never
    a doubt,
And forgot she his feelings was hurt-
    ing,
As often with others she'd saunter about,
All the while most decidedly flirting!
He fretted at this, yet he told her again
    She was still his heart's dearly-
    prized treasure,
But said if his pleadings were all to be
    vain,
He would surely take measure for
    measure !
She laughed and turn'd off, but was
    sorry ere long,
For she heard he was wooing another!
She sought him, and owned she was
    much in the wrong
And declared she lov'd him, and none
    other !
"Too late!" he replied, "I'm engaged
    to be wed ;
So you now may repent at your lei-
    sure !
I've done in despair what I formerly
    said,
, And have given you measure for
    measure !"
        —YOUNG LADIES JOURNAL.

THE BEAUTIFUL SNOW.

Many have claimed it, but J. W. WATSON is perhaps the author.

OH ! the snow, the beautiful snow !
Filling the sky and the earth below ;
Over the house-tops, over the street,
Over the heads of the people you meet,
    Dancing,
        Flirting,
            Skimming along ;
Beautiful snow ! it can do nothing
    wrong,
Flying to kiss a fair lady's cheek,
Clinging to lips in a frolicsome freak.
Beautiful snow, from the heaven above,
Pure as an angel, and fickle as love !

Oh ! the snow, the beautiful snow !
How the flakes gather and laugh as
    they go !
Whirling about in its maddening fun,
It plays in its glee with every one,
    Chasing,
        Laughing,
            Hurrying by !
It lights on the face and it sparkles the
    eye,
And the merry dogs, with a bark and a
    bound,
Snap at the crystals that eddy around—
The town is alive and its heart in a
    glow,
To welcome the coming of beautiful
    snow !

How the wild crowd goes swaying
    along,
Hailing each other with humor and
    song !
How the gay sledges, like meteors, pass
    by,
Bright for the moment, then lost to the
    eye—
    Ringing,
        Swinging,
            Dashing they go,
Over the crust of the beautiful snow ;
Snow so pure that it falls from the sky,
To be trampled in mud by the crowd
    rushing by,
To be trampled and tracked by thou-
    sands of feet,
Till it blends with the filth in the hor-
    rible street.

Once I was pure as the snow—but I fell!
Fell like the snowflakes, from heaven to hell;
Fell, to be trampled as filth in the street;
Fell, to be scoffed, to be spit on and beat;
    Pleading,
      Cursing,
        Dreading to die,
Selling my soul to whoever would buy,
Dealing in shame for a morsel of bread,
Hating the living, and fearing the dead!
Merciful God! have I fallen so low!
And yet I was once like the beautiful snow!

Once I was fair as the beautiful snow,
With an eye like the crystal, a heart like its glow;
Once I was loved for my innocent grace—
Flattered and sought for the charms of my face!
    Father,
      Mother,
        Sisters, all,
God and myself, I've lost by my fall;
The veriest wretch that goes shivering by,
Will make a wide swoop, lest I wander too nigh,
For all that is on or about me I know,
There is nothing as pure as the beautiful snow!

How strange it would be that this beautiful snow
Should fall on a sinner with nowhere to go!
How strange it should be when the night comes again,
If the snow and the ice struck my desperate brain,
    Fainting,
      Freezing,
        Dying alone,
Too wicked for prayer, too weak for my moan
To be heard in the crash of the crazy town
Gone mad in their joy at the snow's coming down,
To be, and to die, in my terrible woe,
With a bed and a shroud of the beautiful snow!

THE SCENES OF CHILDHOOD.

"How dear to my heart are the scenes of my childhood,
When fond recollection presents them to view."

EVERY one has doubtless had these thrilling lines to flash through his memory as he gazed upon the "scenes of his childhood." And what a sweet, solemn thought it brings over us, to look upon the fields of our past enjoyment—the *scenes of our childhood!* True, Time the tomb-builder, may have brought changes; but these only serve to make the spot more endearing. You gaze upon the old buildings—the roof that you used to know so well, is now all covered with moss. The steps that your infant feet trod have gone to decay. The entire building has undergone so many changes that you say, "It don't look like it used to." The old well, too, has changed its look. Yet, it is there. The old "moss-covered bucket" still hangs in the well! What an enchanting scene! There have been changes, but no change short of death, can blot from memory's page the impressions of youth. You think of the days that you have spent there in glee —then you were young, a boy. But now you are a man, drawing nearer and nearer every day to the brink of the grave. You sit down, and go over (to yourself), the old family register. There's little Nell, that played with you here in former days, that has long since been consigned to the tomb. Little Willie too, lies there by her side. Grandpa, who used to call us around his knee and tell us stories to make the winter's night seem shorter, has left us long ago. I recollect his death well; I see the room now in which I took my last gaze at his aged face. My aunt too is gone. She died the year after grandpa did. All the things, bitter mingled with sweets, come, link by link, to form memory's chain. Everything that you see, that was of old, has eonnected with it a history. A history, too, of fond remembrance. Each scene has a silent enchantment—not for it as at present—but for the sake of by-gone days. You visit the old family burial-ground. It is hallowed by rustic silence and beauty. There rest aunt, grandpa, little Willie, and by his side sleeps little Nell. You meditate and ask, oh, how long ere I rest there with them?—and almost wish the time had come!

THE RIVER TIME.

Oh! a wonderful stream is the river Time
   As it runs through the realm of tears,
With a faultless rhythm and a musical rhyme,
   And a broader sweep, and a surge sublime,
As it blends with the ocean of years.

How the winters are drifting like flakes of snow,
   And the summer like buds between,
And the years in the sheaf so they come and go
   On the river's breast, with ebb and flow,
As it glides in the shadow and sheen.

There's a magical Isle up the river Time,
   Where the softest airs are playing;
There's a cloudless sky, and a tropical clime,
And a song as sweet as a vesper chime,
   And the Junes with the roses are staying.

The name of this Isle is the Long Ago,
   And we bury our treasure there,
There are brows of beauty, and bosoms of snow,
They are now heaps of dust, but we loved them so—
   There are trinkets and tresses of hair.

There are fragments of song that nobody sings,
   And a part of an infant prayer,
There's a lute unswept, and a harp without strings,
There are broken vows and pieces of rings,
   And the garments she used to wear.

There are hands that are waved when the fairy shore
   By the mirage is lifted to air,
And we sometimes hear through the turbulent roar
Sweet voices we heard in the days gone before,
   When the wind down the river is fair.

Oh! remembered for aye be that blessed Isle,
   All the days of our life till night,
When the evening comes with its beautiful smile,
And our eyes are closing to slumber awhile,
   May that Greenwood of soul be in sight.
              —L. G. CLARK.

TO A KISS.

Humid seal of soft affections,
   Tend'rest pledge of future bliss,
Dearest tie of young connections,
   Love's first snow-drop, virgin kiss!

Speaking silence, dumb confession,
   Passion's birth and infant's play,
Dove-like fondness, chaste concession,
   Glowing dawn of brighter day.

Sorrowing joy, adieu's last action,
   When ling'ring lips no more must join,
What words can ever speak affection
   So thrilling and sincere as thine.

YOU KNOW YOU DO.

When "some one's" step comes up the walk,
   Your cheeks take on a rosier hue,
And though no other hears his knock,
   You hear it well—you know you do!

When "some one" talks about the grain,
   And bows to pa, yet looks at you,
You see his glances—ah! tis plain—
   And give them back—you know you do!

And though it may be very wrong,
    When pa is quite ignored for you,
You sing to him your prettiest song,
    You cunning thing—you know you do!

And when he talks of other girls,
    Of hateful Kate, and Jennie, too,
You fling at him your auburn curls,
    You jealous thing—you know you do!

You keep your eyes upon the clock,
    And wish 'twould jump an hour or two,
So that your pa would cease his talk
    And go to bed—you know you do!

And when the folks to bed have gone,
    And left "some one" alone with you!
You wish the clock would stop its tongue,
    Or you stop it—you know you do!

He blushes deep, and looks afraid
    To be thus left alone with you!
But your eyes tell there ne'er was maid
    But could be wooed—you know you do!

You peep at "some one" 'neath your curls,
    Until with love you burn him through,
And make him hate all other girls
    In love for you—you know you do!

And when his arm steals around your chair,
    You give a smothered scream or two,
As if you didn't want it there,
    But oh, you do—you know you do!

You nestle closer up to him,
    Your head droops on his shoulder, too;
You think it nice to have a "Jim,"
    You naughty thing—you know you do!

You let him kiss your blushing cheek!
    Somehow your lips meet his lips, too!
You tempt him silly things to speak,
    You shameless flirt—you know you do!

And when he timidly doth press
    His wish to make a wife of you,
With happy heart you answer "Yes."
    You darling girl—you know you do!
        —MOLLIE MILLER.

UNTIL DEATH.

MAKE me no vows of constancy, dear friend,
    To love me, though I die, thy whole life long;
And love no other till thy days shall end—
    Nay, it were rash and wrong.

If thou can'st love another, be it so;
    I would not reach out of my quiet grave
To bind thy heart if it should choose to go—
    Love should not be a slave.

My placid ghost, I trust, will walk serene
    In clearer light than gilds these earthly morns,
Above the jealousies and envies keen,
    Which sow this life with thorns.

Thou would'st not feel my shadowy caress,
    If, after death, my soul should linger here;
Men's hearts crave tangible, close tenderness,
    Love's presence, warm and near.

It would not make me sleep more peacefully
    That thou wert wasting all thy life in woe
For my poor sake;
    What love thou hast for me bestow it ere I go!

Carve not upon a stone when I am dead
    The praises which remorseful mourners give
To women's graves—a tardy recompense—
    But speak them while I live.

Heap not the heavy marble on my head,
  To shut away the sunshine and the
    dew;
Let small blooms grow there, and let
    grasses wave,
  And raindrops filter through.

Thou wilt meet many fairer and more
    gay
  Than I; but, trust me, thou can'st
    never find
One who will love and serve thee night
    and day
  With a more single mind.

Forget me when I die! The violets
  Above my rest will blossom just as
    blue;
Nor miss my tears; even nature's self
    forgets,
  But while I live be true.
      —FRED HARRINGTON.

THE NEW WOMAN.

SHE talked with great intensity of each
    man's base propensity, and spoke
    with volubility of woman's higher
    plane;
She dwelt on domesticity with mental
    elasticity, and said that such felicity
    was really quite in vain.

With gestures oratorical and phrases
    metaphorical, she voiced the pow-
    ers numerical that woman had un-
    told.
And spoke with zeal dramatical of vot-
    ing systematical, and ballot-boxes
    spherical, and votes not bought with
    gold.

She said in each vicinity the doctors of
    divinity would come from feminin-
    ity; in bloomers they would be;
And matrons with rapidity would lose
    all their timidity, and no more as-
    ininity in congress would we see.

And while with such audacity she
    showed her great capacity, and
    talked with great didacity, her hus-
    band learned to sweep;
And while with such agility she dwelt
    on her utility with such intense pug-
    nacity, he puts the twins to sleep.
      —NEW YORK SUN.

OLD JINGLES.

THE following time-honored jingles
regarding marriages and births, quoted
from an interesting collection, entitled
"Old Superstitions," are always of interest:

Marry Monday for wealth,
Marry Tuesday for health,
  Marry Wednesday the best day of all.
Marry Thursday for crosses,
Marry Friday for losses,
  Marry Saturday no luck at all.

Born on a Monday,
  Fair of face;
Born on a Tuesday,
  Full of God's grace;
Born on Wednesday,
  Merry and glad;
Born on a Thursday,
  Sour and sad;
Born on a Friday,
  Godly given;
Born of a Saturday,
  Work for a living;
Born of a Sunday,
  Never shall want;
So there's the week
  And the end on't.

Monday's child is fair of face;
Tuesday's child is full of grace;
Wednesday's child is merry and glad;
Thursday's child is sour and sad;
Friday's child is loving and giving;
Saturday's child must work for a living;
But the child that is born on a Sabbath
    day
Has a shining journey down life's way.
      —NEW YORK LEDGER.

A BUSINESS LETTER.

"MARRIAGE is daily becoming a
more commercial affair."—A Society
paper.

DEAR FRED:—Your favor of the 3d,
  Has had my very best attention,
But yet I cannot, in a word,
  Accept you on the terms you men-
    tion;

Indeed, wherever you may try,
  According to the last advices,
You'll meet, I fear, the same reply—
  "It can't be done, at current prices!"

In vain an ancient name you show,
  In vain for intellect are noted,
Blue blood and brains, you surely know,
  At nominal amounts are quoted,
And then, I see you're weak enough,
  To offer "love sincere, unstudied"—
Why, sir, with such Quixotic stuff
  The market's absolutely flooded!

But—every day this fact confirms—
  The time is over for romances,
And whether we can come to terms
  Depends alone on your finances.
So, would you think me overbold
  If I, with deference, requested
A statement of what funds you hold?
  In what securities invested?

For, candidly, in such affairs
  A speedy bid your only chance is,
A boom in Yankee millionaires
  May soon result in marked advances;
With you I'd willingly be wed,
  To like you well enough I'm able,
But first submit your bank book, Fred,
  To your (perhaps) devoted Mabel.
         —PUNCH.

THE PENITENT'S PRAYER.

GO SIN NO MORE.

O, GRACIOUS Lord! stretch forth Thy hand,
  And lead me from the path of sin,
I pray Thee, give my poor heart strength,
  And let Thy glory shine within.
O, cleanse my weak, polluted soul,
  And from its sins, Lord, set it free;
Thou knowest how I need Thy help—
  I am not what I ought to be.

O, give me power to love Thee more,
  And bid my worldly sins depart;
Speak words of promise to my soul,
  And give religion to my heart.
I know, dear Lord, Thy blessed Son
  Died on the cross for such as me—
O, help me, give me strength to pray—
  I am not what I ought to be.

Tear from my heart the bolts that lock
  Its fastened doors, inclosing sin,
And let Thy sweet redeeming love
  Like beams of glory shine therein,
I look to thee with pitying eye,
  And plead for grace on bended knee;
Have mercy on my sinful soul—
  I am not what I ought to be.

Dear Lord, wipe from my soul my shame,
  My every thought and act control;
Grant me forgiveness for my sin.
Have mercy Lord, upon my soul,
  I am unworthy of Thy love—
I am unfit Thy child to be;
O, take me, sinner as I am,
  And make me what I ought to be.
         —WILL S. HAYS.

THE BUSY MAN.

IF you would get a favor done
  By some obliging friend,
And want a promise, safe and sure,
  On which you can depend,
Don't go to him who always has
  Much leisure time to plan,
But if you want your favor *done*,
  Just ask the busy man.

The man with leisure never has
  A moment he can spare.
He's always "putting off," until
  His friends are in despair.
But he whose every waking hour
  Is crowded full of work
Forgets the art of wasting time;
  He cannot stop to shirk.

So, when you want a favor done,
  And want it right away,
Go to the man who constantly
  Works thirty hours a day.
He'll find a moment, sure, somewhere
  That has no other use,
And fix you, while the idle man
  Is framing an excuse.
         —WILLIAM H. HILLS.

WHO knows? God knows: and what
  he knows is well and best.
The darkness hideth not from him, but
  glows   [rose of east or west,
Clear as the morning or the evening
         —CHRISTINA ROSETTI.

THE ETERNITY OF GOD.

WITHOUT BEGINNING, THE SAME YESTERDAY, TO-DAY AND FOREVER.

ALL animated things grow old and die. The rocks crumble, the trees fall, the leaves fade, the grass withers. The clouds are flying and the waters are flowing away from us. The firmest works of man, too, are gradually giving way. The ivy clings to the mouldering tower, the brier hangs out from the shattered windows, and the wall-flower springs from the disjointed stones. The founders of these perishable works have shared the same fate long ago. If we look back to the days of our ancestors, to the men as well as the dwellings of former times, they become immediately associated in our imagination, and only make the feeling of instability stronger and deeper than before. In the spacious domes which once held our fathers the serpent hisses and the wild bird screams. The halls which once were crowded with all that taste and science and labor could procure, which resounded with melody and were lighted up with beauty, are buried by their own ruins, mocked by their own destruction. The voice of merriment and of wailing, the steps of the busy and the idle, have ceased in the deserted courts, and the weeds choke the entrance, and the long grass waves upon the hearthstone. The works of art, the forming hand, the tombs, the very ashes they contained, are all gone.

While we thus walk among the ruins of the past a sad feeling of insecurity comes over us, and that feeling is by no means diminished when we arrive at home. If we turn to our friends we can hardly speak to them before they bid us farewell. We see them for a few moments, and in a few moments more their countenances are changed and they are sent away. It matters not how near and dear they are, the ties which bind us together are never too close to be parted, or too strong to be broken. Tears were never known to move the King of Terrors. Neither is it enough that we are compelled to surrender one or two or many of those we love; for though the price is so great, we buy no favor with it, and our hold on those who remain is slight as ever. The shadows of all elude our grasp and follow one another down the valley. We gain no confidence, then, no feeling of security, by turning to our contemporaries and kindred. We know that the forms which are breathing around us are as short-lived and fleeting as those were which have been dust for centuries. The sensation of vanity, uncertainty and ruin is equally strong, whether we muse on what has long been prostrated, or gaze on what is falling now or will soon. If everything which comes under our notice has endured for so short a time, and in so short a time will be no more, we cannot say that we receive the least assurance by thinking on ourselves. When they on whose fate we have been meditating were engaged in the active scenes of life, as full of health and hope as we are now, what were we? We had no knowledge, no consciousness, no being; there was not a single thing in the wide universe which knew us. And after the same interval shall have elapsed which now divides their days from ours, what shall we be? When a few more friends have left, a few more hopes deceived and a few more changes mocked us, we shall be brought to the grave, and shall remain in the tomb; the clods of the valley shall be sweet unto us, and every man follow us, as they are innumerable before us. All power will have forsaken the strongest; and the loftiest will be laid low, and every eye will be closed and every voice hushed, and every heart will have ceased its beating. And when we have gone ourselves, even our memories will not stay behind us long. A few of the near and dear will bear our likeness in their bosoms till they, too, have arrived at the end of their journey and entered the dark dwelling of unconsciousness. In the thoughts of others we shall live only till the last sound of the bell which informs them of our departure has ceased to vibrate in their ears. A stone, perhaps, may tell some wanderer where we lie, when we came here and when we went away; but that will soon refuse to bear us record. Time's effacing fingers will be busy on its surface and at length will wear it smooth, and then the stone itself will sink or crumble, and the wanderer of another age will pass, without a single call upon his sympathy, over our unheeded grave.

The Eternity of God is a subject of contemplation which, at the same time it overwhelms us with astonishment and awe at things which surround us, affords us an immovable ground of confidence in the midst of a changing world. All these dying, moulding inhabitants of time must have had a creator, for the plain reason that they could not have created themselves. And their creator must have existed from all eternity, for the plain reason that the first cause must necessarily be uncaused. As we cannot suppose a beginning without a cause of existence, that which is the cause of all existing things must be self-existent and could have had no beginning. And as it had no beginning, so also is it beyond the reach of all influence and control; as it is independent and almighty, it will have no end. Here, then, is a support that will never fail, here is a foundation which can never be moved—the everlasting Creator of countless worlds, the high and lofty One that inhabiteth eternity. What a sublime contemplation! He inhabits eternity, occupies this inconceivable duration, pervades and fills throughout this boundless dwelling. Ages on ages before even the dust of which we are formed was created, He had existed in infinite majesty, and ages on ages will roll away after we have returned to the dust from which we were taken and still He will exist in infinite majesty, living in the eternity of His own nature, reigning in the plenitude of his own omnipotence, forever sending forth the word which forms, supports and governs all things, commanding new-created lights to shine on new-created worlds, and raising up new-created generations to inhabit them. The contemplation of this glorious attribute of God is fitted to excite in our minds the most animating and consoling reflection. Standing, as we are, amid the ruins of time and the wreck of mortality, where everything about us is created and dependent, proceeding from nothing and hastening to destruction, we rejoice that something is presented to our view which has stood from everlasting and will remain forever. When we have looked on the pleasures of life and they have vanished away; when we have looked on the works of nature and perceived that they were changing, on the monuments of art and seen that they would not stand, on our friends and they have fled while we were gazing, on ourselves and felt that we are as fleeting as they; when we have looked on every object to which we could turn our eyes, and they have all told us that they could give us no hope nor support, because they were so feeble themselves, we can look to the throne of God. Change and decay have never reached that; the revolution of ages has never moved it; the waves of an eternity have been rushing past it, but it has remained unshaken; the waves of another eternity are rushing toward it, but it is fixed and can never be disturbed. And blessed be God, who has assured us by a revelation from himself that the throne of eternity is likewise a throne of mercy and love; who has permitted and invited us to repose ourselves and our hopes on that alone, which is everlasting and unchangeable. We shall shortly fill our allotted time on earth, even if it should be unusually prolonged. We shall leave behind us, all which is now familiar and beloved, and a world of other days and other men will be entirely ignorant that we once lived. But the same unalterable Being will still preside over the universe through all its changes, and from His remembrance we shall never be blotted. We can never be where he is not. He is our Father and our God forever. He takes us from earth that He may lead us to heaven, that He may refine our nature from its corruption, admits us to His everlasting habitation and crowns us with His eternity. Beyond the clouds the sun is shining, and we are only travellers from earth to eternity. Remember the lonely epitaph in the city of the dead :

"Remember, friend, as you pass by,
As you are now so once was I.
As I am now soon you will be;
Prepare for God and eternity."

DRIFTWEED.

EVERMORE we are drifting out with the
   restless tide,
Out to the ultimate ocean, whose waters
   are wild and wide ;
But somewhere there is a Gilead sweet
   with the healing balm,
And the storm may rage, but the rainbow is arched in the skies of calm.

Windeth the river weary through forests
   no foot hath trod,
Where the darkness is shut from the
   shining of the lamps in the windows
   of God ;
But out from the gloom it flashes in the
   light of the day to be,
And mingles its lonely waters with the
   tide of the splendid sea !

We are not hopeless—homeless ! wherever our feet may roam,
We are still on the King's own highway—still near the King's own home !
And soon with the journey ended—the storm and the darkness past,
We shall enter in at the portals, and reign with the King at last !
           —F. L. S.

NEVER TROUBLE TROUBLE.

MY good man is a clever man,
   Which no one will gainsay ;
He lies awake to plot and plan
   'Gainst lions in the way,
While I, without a thought of ill,
   Sleep sound enough for three ;
For I never trouble trouble till
   Trouble troubles me.

A holiday we never fix
   But he is sure 'twill rain,
And when the sky is clear at six
   He knows it won't remain.

He 's always prophesying ill,
   To which I won't agree,
For I never trouble trouble till
   Trouble troubles me.

The wheat will never show atop—
   But soon how green the field !
We will not harvest half a crop—
   Yet have a famous yield !
It will not sell, it never will !
   But I will wait and see,
For I never trouble trouble till
   Trouble troubles me.

He has a sort of second sight,
   And when the fit is strong
He sees beyond the good and right
   The evil and the wrong,
Heaven's cup of joy he'll surely spill
   Unless I with him be,
For I never trouble trouble till
   Trouble troubles me.
         —NORRISTON HERALD.

SO WE GROW OLD.

A BROKEN toy ; a task that held away
A yearning child heart from an hour of play,
A Christmas that no Christmas idols brought,
A tangled lesson, full of tangled thought,
A homesick boy ; a senior gowned and wise ;
A glimpse of life, when lo ! the curtains rise
   Fold over fold,
And hangs the future, like a boundless sea—
The world all action and reality—
   So we grow old.

A wedding and a tender wife's caress ;
A prattling babe, the parent's heart to bless :
A home of joys and cares in equal part ;
A dreary watching with a heavy heart ;
And death's dread angel knocking at the gate.
And hope and courage bidding sorrow wait

Or lose her hold;
A new-made grave, and then a brave return
To where the fires of life triumphant burn—
　　So we grow old.

A fortune and a general meed of fame,
Or direful ruin and a tarnished name,
A slipping off of week and month and year,
Faster and faster as the close draws near;
A grief to-day, and with to-morrow's light
A treasure that transforms the sullen night
　　From lead to gold;
A chilling winter of unchanging storm;
A spring replete with dawns and sunset warm—
　　So we grow old.

Old to ourselves, but children yet to be
In the strange cities of eternity.

WHATEVER COMES.

LIFE is a struggle for the most—
　Bare rooms, and common fare,
And helpless friends—a weary host—
　And toil and stifling air.
But great men came from such as these,
　The country's life to save;
And manhood is not nursed in ease—
　Whatever comes, be brave.

Some will speak ill, some envy you,
　Some criticise, or blame;
Some whom you trusted prove untrue,
　Friends only in the name;
Some will ignore you if your dress
　Be poor, some scorn your sphere;
But keep a heart that loves to bless—
　Whatever comes, have cheer.

You will be tempted in the race;
　Debt is an easy snare;
And pride has oft a Janus face,
　And vice a winsome air;
And love of wealth and power may lead
　To dally with the wrong;
But to your better self give heed—
　Whatever comes, be strong.
　　　　　—SARAH K. BOLTON.

SEPTEMBER.

SUMMER lingers in her realm fair,
　A soft sweet glow pervades the air,
　She smiles at winter, bids him wait,
　And tribute pay at her royal gate,
With kingly robes she decks the trees,
　Distills rare fragrance through the breeze,
Gathers all that's sweet and most dear,
From all seasons and blends it here.

The insects hum upon the hill,
　And wooded vales are hushed and still,
The songsters have flown, the mellow air
Seems yet to thrill with bird-notes rare,
The cool sweet breeze as it wanders by
　Bears the roses' last fragrant sigh,
The sound of dropping nuts we hear,
And children's voices ringing clear.

The fields are now all bedight,
　With king cotton's blossoms white,
Gathering its snowy wealth we hear,
　The workers song sound sweet and clear.
And lo! the sun-kissed apples now,
　Blush red upon the fruitful bough,
The garnered sheaves like sentinels stand,
O'er th' harvest treasures of our land.
　　　　　—MRS. W. A. FULLER

AS AGE COMES ON.

As age comes on the pulses beat
A slower measure, and the feet,
　More cautious tread, with duller sense,
Born of our much experience,
The changing year and day we greet.

The zest in life, the eager, sweet
Enthusiasms—ah, how fleet
　They seem to fade, to vanish hence,
　　As age comes on!

But though we fail in youthful heat,
Life fuller grows—grows more complete,
　Till it involves the world's immense
Within our helpless impotence—
For hearts where faith and love keep seat,
　　As age comes on.

THREE WAYS TO MARRY.

There are three kinds of matrimony. If a man marries for love, then he gets a wife; if he marries for convenience and comfort, he gets a mistress, and if he marries for a dower he gets a madam. He is loved by his wife, honored by his mistress and suffered by his madam. A wife he has for himself, a mistress for his house and friends and a madam for society. A wife will agree with him, a mistress will oblige him and a madam will dictate to him. If he is ill his wife will nurse him, his mistress will visit him and his madam will inquire after his health, and if he dies his wife will shed tears, his mistress will sigh and his madam will wear mourning.

—Jacob Cohen.

THE OLD-TIME BRINNEL CUR.

Talk about yer blooded dogs, with great long pedigrees,
An' prizes took at bench-shows an' records broke with ease,
But the pup that's struck my fancy more than any dog with fur,
Is that choicest chum of childhood—the ole-time brinnel cur.

He wa'n't much on appearances, his shaggy looks wa'n't fair,
With tail chopped off an' years slit up an' eyes all hid with hair,
But he got there on the home-stretch, though he smacked o' cuckleburr;
An' he never failed to show down—that ole-time brinnel cur.

He wa'n't as likely lookin', p'r'aps, as other dogs you've seed,
But he was the gamest article of all the canine breed;
When he started on the warpath they wa'n't nothin' could deter
The nerve that took possession of that ole-time brinnel cur.

He wus a model of true grit, that nothin' couldn't down,
An' could lick regermints o' purty dogs Like they have in town;
He made the tramps steer clear o' him, wus dreaded near an' fur,
Fur he never knowed no danger—that ole-time brinnel cur.

He was true to every trust in life an' faithful to the end,
An' I'll never cease to love him as my boyhood's warmest friend;
He would sacrifice his own self to do me a service, sir,
An' my lovin' heart will not fergit that ole-time brinnel cur.

He wa'n't nothing but a dog, an' yit he seemed like folks to me,
An' his love wus jest as true as any human love could be,
An' when I had a scrap them days— which I did, you may infer—
I could allers count fur certain on that ole-time brinnel cur.

An' when mother died o' fever an' they buried her that spring,
That pore ole dog seemed strickener than almost anything;
He whined aroun' so pitiful an' wouldn't hardly stir,
Though he wa'n't nothin' only just a ole-time brinnel cur.

You can ridicule the notion, but I know it's gospel true,
That ole dog's heart wus broken by the blow that struck us two,
An' I won't let him be slandered now, by any low-flung slur,
Fur a noble nature dwelt within that ole-time brinnel cur.

One mornin' when I missed him—the dear, old faithful slave—
I foun' him in the orchard there, stretched out on mother's grave;
He had died there while a-mournin'— plague take this pesky blur—
Fur the best of all, good mother, my ole-time brinnel cur.

I never think o' her, somehow, but what I think o' him,
An' I know now how it was, I lost my two best friends in them;

So here's a sigh an here's a tear, sir, to
 the memory of her
An' that choicest chum of childhood—
 the ole-time brinnel cur.
      —RUFUS M'CLAIN FIELDS.

DREAMIN' OF HOME.

I CAN'T jest tell what's come to her, an'
 yet, I think it's clear
That somethin's goin' wrong o' late—
 to see her sittin' there,
A-dreamin' in the doorway, with that
 look into her eyes,
As if they still was restin' on the old-
 time fields and skies.

She's always dreamin', dreamin' of the
 life we left behind—
The cozy little cottage where the mornin'-glories twined ;
The roses in the garden—the yellow
 sunflowers tall ;
The violets—but she herself the sweetest flower of all !

You see, she use to sit there in the mornin's—so content ;
The sunflowers follerin' the sun, no
 matter where he went ;
The brown bees sippin' honey an' a-buz-
 zin' round the place ;
The roses climbin' up to her an' smilin'
 in her face !

An' now, she can't forget it ; when I
 tell her, "Little wife,
There ain't no use in grievin' for that
 simple country life,"
She twines her arms aroun' my neck,
 an' smilin' sweet to see,
She whispers : "We're so fur away from
 where we use to be !"

There ain't no use in chidin', or in sayin' words o' cheer ;
There's nothin' in this city life like she
 was use to there,
Where preachin' come but once a
 month, an' street cars didn't run,
An' folk they told the time o' day by
 lookin' at the sun.

An' larks got up at peep o' day an'
 made the medders ring !
I tell you, folks, when one's brought up
 to jes' that kind o' thing,
It's hard to git away from it—old feelin's
 bound to rise
An' make a-runnin' over in a woman's
 tender eyes !

So there she sits a-dreamin', till I git to
 dreamin', too ;
An' when her head droops on my breast
 and sleep falls like the dew,
An' closes them bright eyes o' hers, once
 more we seem to be
In the old home, where we'll rest some
 day together—her an' me !
      —FRANK L. STANTON.

FORESHADOWINGS.

TO-NIGHT, to-night, dear, as we said
 good-bye,
 I heard a something that was new
 and strange
In the old words, in every short reply :
 And you were not unconscious of the
 change,
You did not seem to feel my hand grow
 cold
 Within your clasp, nor press it as of
 old.

And I can feel a shadowy something
 there
 Where only fondest trust was wont
 to be ;
A something, yes, intangible as air,
 Yet deeper than the globe-encircling
 sea.
I might have asked you, but it is too
 late
To change the workings of unerring
 fate.

And yet sometime, so surely as the day
 Gives place to night, so surely must
 I know
The truth and hear those things that
 you will say ;
 Yet, womanlike, I but postpone the
 blow,
Yet was not brave to-night to let it fall,
Yet was not brave enough to risk my
 all.

I know you will be gentle as you speak
  The words that will efface my every
    claim ;
Your lips will falter, and I think your
    cheek
  Will pale at this last speaking of my
    name.
I know that you must feel some vague
    regret,
For all the past cannot be buried yet.

And O, so often in the coming years
  Old memories of the silent past will
    rise ;
Some perfume will recall its joys and
    tears ;
  Old dreams will be reflected from the
    skies ;
A careless word, a chord of some lost
    strain,
A smile, a glance, will call it back again.

Ay, when you look back through the
    golden mist ·
  That always glorifies the long ago,
And see those summer days when sun-
    beams kissed
  All earth and life to one respondent
    glow,
This love will stand from all the rest
    apart,
Waking some long stilled chord within
    your heart.
    —Eva MacDonagh Smith.

THE YOUNG WIDOW.

She is modest, but not bashful,
  Free and easy, but not bold ;
Like an apple, ripe and mellow,
  Not too young, not too old ;
Half inviting, half repulsing,
  Now advancing and now shy ;
There is mischief in her dimple,
  There is danger in her eye.

She has studied human nature,
  She is schooled in all her arts ;
She has taken her diploma
  As a mistress of all hearts ;
She can tell the very moment
  When to sigh and when to smile ;
Oh, a maid is sometimes charming,
  But a widow all the while.

Are you sad ? How very serious
  Will her handsome face become !
Are you angry ? She is wretched,
  Lonely, friendless, fearful, dumb !
Are you mirthful ? How her laughter
  Silver-sounding, will ring out !
She can lure and catch and play you
  As the angler does the trout.

Ye old bachelors of forty,
  Who have grown so bold and wise,
Young Americans of twenty,
  With the love-look in your eyes ;
You may practice all the lessons
  Taught by Cupid since the fall,
But I know a little widow
  Who can win and fool you all.
    —Sir Edwin Arnold.

THE BLUE-BACK SPELLER.

I'd been mighty busy plowin',
  When there came a half a peck
Of letters sent from Raleigh,
  And askin' me, direct,
To come and take a hand with them
  At spellin' in a Bee
For helping on a set of folks
  They called the Y. M. C.

I'd been a famous speller
  In the days of old Lang Syne,
But that was thirty years ago
  And I hardly thought to shine.
But Charlie Cook said, " Risk it,"
  And I wasn't loath to show
That the good, old blue-back speller
  Is one thing that I know.

The house was well nigh crowded,
  When the time came for the *Bee*,
And after some persuadin',
  There came up along with me,
M. D. and D. D. doctors
  And M. A's., full a score
And editors and teachers,
  And of lawyers several more.

T'was funny, then to see 'em,
  As the hard words came like hail,
A-pausin' and a-stammerin',
  And a-turnin' almost pale,
But, law ! it all came to me
  Like it use to long ago,
And I saw the blue-back speller,
  With each long and even row.

And I gave 'em with the column,
　The place, the side, the page,
For I saw those words like faces
　Of old friends that do not age,
But those learned folks kept droppin',
　Like the leaves off any tree,
And at last there wasn't standin',
　But a D. D. up with me.

And then there came a poser,
　And the Doctor he went down,
And a shout went up that startled,
　Half the sleepy folks in town.
But I didn't care for prizes,
　The thing that made me glad,
Was to down 'em with the blue-back
　I studied when a lad.
　　　　　　　　—F. E. H.

SAXBY TO INGERSOLL.

"If in this life only we have hope
. . . . we are of all men most miserable."—I. Corinthians xv. 19.

I heard you last night, Colonel Robert,
You handled your subject with care,
The words from your mouth flowed like honey,
　As you "jollied" poor dead old Voltaire.
I have never disputed your talent,
And although you have fallen from grace,
And do not believe in the Bible,
What
　Book
　　Do
　　　You
　　　　Give
　　　　　In its place?

Some say that you lecture for money—
Well, parsons all preach for the same—
And neither yourself nor the parson
Can satisfy hunger with fame.
But what I am anxious to get at—
As a lawyer, please take up my case—
If God is a myth and misnomer,
What
　God
　　Do
　　　You
　　　　Give
　　　　　In His place?

I'm doubtful about my religion—
'Tis true I'm not burdened with much—
For I'm "mixed" on the creeds of the Churches
And "fogged" by the free-thinking Dutch.
Voltaire I admire as a student,
But in none of his works can I trace
Where he helps us along with our future—
He
　Takes—
　　But
　　　Leaves
　　　　Nought
　　　　　In its place!

I've just read your oration on Conkling—
It is masterly, scholarly, grand—
As a tear-tearer, Bob, you're a daisy,
And can beat any man in the land.
But I'm anxious to wind up in Heaven
When on earth I have finished my race,
If you take my Elysium from me—
What
　Abode
　　Do
　　　You
　　　　Give
　　　　　In its place!

You remind me of men who are bathing
(We all of us want to be clean)
We undress ere we plunge in the water
And strongly object to be seen.
If some one had stolen our clothing,
We'd never again show our face
If the thief had departed and left us
No
　Pants
　　And
　　　No
　　　　Hat
　　　　　In its place!

What use are your doubts and dissensions?
They bother a man all his life,
When peace by the Bible is offered
Why lie on a pallet of strife?
Don't imagine I'm mad when I tell you
I think, Bob, you're off of your base.

When you take from the patriot his
    country
And
  Give
    Him
      No
        Land
          In its place!

I'm no hog—and perhaps I'd refuse it
If offered the whole of the earth,
For our dollars we cannot take with us,
No matter how much we are worth.
I have been at the bedside of Christians,
And seen the sweet smile on their face
As they thought of the home that
    awaits them—
Can
  You
    Give
      Such
        a
          Home
            In its place!

But, pshaw! You're as good as they
    make 'em!
We must all, in this life, play a part;
And, I've only to look in your face, Bob,
To see you've a great, noble heart.
To scoop in the ducats by talking
Is not an eternal disgrace;
But—our mothers are dead—and we'll
    meet them
There, Bob!—You
      Know
        The
          Place.
        —HOWARD SAXBY.

OUR WEDDING ANNIVERSARY.

A DOZEN moons have come and gone,
Since you and I became as one;
With heavenly light they seemed to fly
Across our star-bespangled sky;
And though with waning light they
    pass'd,
Each left us happier than the last.
In number twelve, in love but one,
Still shines our constant honey-moon.

Fierce winter's cold and pelting storm
Has left our hearts untouch'd and
    warm;
Inconstant spring has tried in vain,
To quench our love with showers of
    rain;
Nor summer's sun with scorching eye
Could drink affection's fountain dry;
Still less shall autumn's yellow leaf,
An emblem prove that love is brief.

The changing seasons but portray,
This earthly body's swift decay;
Our souls ascending, then shall fly
To glorious immortality.
There freed from earth, still clinging
    fast,
Till Time shall end; and when, at last,
The Resurrection morn shall rise,
And spread its glories through the skies,
We'll stand before the great white
    throne,
In faith, in hope, in love still one.
        —CHAS. A. READ.

TWO MYSTERIES.

THE mystery of sleep!
Who knoweth all the secret of the deep
Unbroken silence that doth still prolong
The life it keepeth, making it more
    strong?
No one can know
Where the tired soul doth go, [waking;
Nor understand the slumbering or the
And yet, while life endureth
How many ills sleep cureth!
    What hope that springeth up with
        morning's breaking
New pleasure maketh.
The soul forsaketh
The griefs of yesterday when it awaketh.

The mystery of death,
The stopping of the palpitating breath,
The deep, strange silence that doth more
    prolong   [throng!
The slumber! ah! what questions
"Where? Where?" we say,
"Doth the fled spirit stay?"
    Nor understand the living or the dying.
And yet, while time endureth
'Tis death alone that cureth, [sighing—
    And bringeth to its end life's day of
The soul a little longer slumbereth
And, when its rest is taken,
To stronger life immortal shall awaken!
        —JULIA H. MAY.

Suppose. —Page 38.

UNIV. OF
CALIFORNIA

MAMMY GETS THE BOY TO SLEEP.

Come er long, you blessed baby;
Mammy'll tell you story, maybe;
Dat's right, clamb up in my lap
Lak er man, an tek er nap,
Wuk so hard he almos' dead;
Mammy's arm will res' his head,
Pore chile oughter bin in bed
    An hour ago.

Tell you 'bout de possum, honey?
De mammy possum got er funny
Leetle pouch, er bag o' skin
Lak' you totes yore marbles in—
All long her underside,
Whar de baby possums hide
When dey's skeered, er wants ter ride—
    Quit wigglin' so!

Some time dat mammy—pore old critter—
Has sixteen babies at one litter;
Wide-mouf, long-nose, squirmin' things,
Wid tails dat twist lak fiddle-strings.
Sixteen lak you to mek er fuss,
Ter tote, an feed, rock, an' nuss—
Keep still! Hit's no 'sprise ter us
    Possum's hair's gray!

Honey, when de houn' dawgs ketch 'im
Tell drop dat possum he done dead;
No sign er life from foot ter head;
Wid eyes shut tight, he lay and smile,
An' fool dem houn' dawgs all de while.
Play lak you's er possum, chile—
    Yes, dat's de way.

Possum in de oven roastin',
Slice sweet taters roun' 'im toastin',
Taste so good when he git done!
Mammy'll give her baby some.
Eyes—shet—tight—yes dat's de way—
Houn' dawgs goin' er way—
Bless de boy, no possum play
    In dat sleep!

RECESSIONAL.

God of our Fathers, known of old—
  Lord of our far-flung battle line—
Beneath whose awful hand we hold
  Dominion over palm and pine—
Lord God of Hosts, be with us yet,
Lest we forget—lest we forget.

The tumult and the shouting dies—
  The Captains and the Kings depart—
Still stands thine ancient sacrifice,
  An humble and a contrite heart,
Lord God of Hosts, be with us yet,
Lest we forget—lest we forget.

Far-called our navies melt away—
  On dune and headland sinks the fire,
Lo, all our pomp of yesterday
  Is one with Nineveh and Tyre!
Judge of the Nations, spare us yet,
Lest we forget—lest we forget.

If, drunk with power, we loose
  Wild tongues that have not Thee in awe—
Such boasting as the Gentiles use,
  Or lesser breeds without the Law—
Lord God of Hosts, be with us yet,
Lest we forget—lest we forget.

For heathen heart that puts her trust
  In reeking tube and iron shard—
All valiant dust that builds on dust,
  And guarding calls not thee to guard,
For frantic boast and foolish word,
Thy mercy on Thy People, Lord!
    Amen.
    —Rudyard Kipling.

SOMETIME.

When "sometime" comes then we shall taste the joys for which we long;
The shadows will be sunbeams then, and every sigh a song.
The sweet, deep hopes we cherish and within our breasts entomb
Will all come back to life again and fill our hearts with bloom.
The dreary waste of desert sand will blossom as the rose,
And every brook will bubble sweetest music as it flows;
Our hungry souls that now exist on just the meagre crumbs
Will then sit down to princely feasts of love, when "sometime" comes.
When "sometime" comes then all the year will be a glad, sweet June,
And all the music of our lives will be in perfect tune.

The paths we tread will lead us on
   through blossom-scented dells
Where we shall ever listen to the chime
   of fairy bells.
The thornless roses all the day with
   dewdrops will be wet,
And joy will come untangled in the
   meshes of regret,
And time will flit as gladly as the wild
   bee when it hums
Its drowsy song from honeyed flower to
   flower when "sometime" comes.
When "sometime" comes then all of
   life will be a dream of truth,
And we shall feel again the charms and
   innocence of youth,
And sing the glad sweet songs we sang
   in those bright summers when
We played in careless joy nor knew
   the weary thoughts of men,
And all the friends we held so dear, the
   ones who loved us so,
Will all come back to greet us from the
   happy long ago;
The girls with dolls and dishes and the
   boys with flags and drums,
We'll see them all together once again
   when "sometime" comes.
—CHICAGO JOURNAL.

DEFINITIONS OF A KISS.

THE Tid-Bits offered a two-guinea prize for the best definition of a kiss. Seven thousand answers were received. The prize was awarded to Benjamin J. Greenwood, of Tulse Hill, London, whose definition is herewith framed:

> An insipid and tasteless morsel, which becomes delicious and delectable in proportion as it is flavored with love.

The following is a selection from some of the best definitions submitted:

What the chimney-sweeper imprinted on the rosy lips of the scullery maid when she told him she favored his soot.

The sweetest fruit on the tree of love. The oftener plucked the more abundant it grows.

A thing of use to no one, but much prized by two.

The baby's right, the lover's privilege, the parent's benison and the hypocrite's mask.

That which you cannot give without taking and cannot take without giving.

The food by which the flame of love is fed.

The flag of truce in the petty wars of courtship and marriage.

The acme of agony to a bashful man.

The only known "smack" that will calm a storm.

A telegram to the heart in which the operator uses the "sounding" system.

Nothing, divided between two.

Not enough for one, just enough for two, too much for three.

The only really agreeable two-faced action under the sun, or the moon either.

The sweetest labial of the world's language.

A woman's most effective argument, whether to cajole the heart of a father, control the humors of a husband or console the griefs of childhood.

Something rather dangerous,
   Something rather nice,
Something rather wicked,
   Though it can't be called a vice,
Some think it naughty,
   Others think it wrong,
All agree it's jolly,
   Though it doesn't last long.

A kiss from a pretty girl is like having hot treacle poured down your back by angels.

The thunder-clap of the lips, which inevitably follows the lightning glance of the eyes.

A report at headquarters.

Everybody's acting edition of "Romeo and Juliet."

What the child receives free, what the young man steals, and what the old man buys.

The drop that runneth over when the cup of love is full.

That in which two heads are better than one.

A kiss is three parts of speech—a

transitive verb, an invisible noun, and a visible conjunction.

Printing without ink, leaving no visible impression.

Woman's passport to her husband's purse, and a man's passport to a woman's heart.

When lips of lovers meet in bliss,
The pleasing act is termed a "kiss,"
But when the pair have wed each other
The vapid thing is called a "bother."

Love's artillery, that is brought into action immediately on the call "to arms."

Contraction of the mouth due to enlargement of the heart.

The sounding-line used by a woman to fathom the depths of man's weakness.

An old-fashioned telegraphic arrangement for transmitting from one person to another various sensations that cannot be transmitted correctly by any other medium known.

Nature's Volapuk—the universal language of love.

A woman's trump card in a game of love.

An article that is always accepted and (im) printed, but not always published.

The action of the lips by which the real sentiments of the heart are either affectionately expressed or falsely disguised.

I am just two and two, I am warm, I am cold,
And the parent of numbers that cannot be told.
I am lawful—unlawful—a duty, a fault,
I am often sold dear—good for nothing when bought.
An extraordinary boon and a matter of course,
And yielded with pleasure when taken by force.

A gift which is sometimes expected, seldom rejected, though often returned.

A speech without words.

A lip salve often tried as a specific in affections of the heart.

The missing link between body and soul.

The only delight of the gods that mortals have been permitted to enjoy.

The safety-valve to an exuberance of tender feelings.

The lovers' privilege and the pug dog's right.

What the child gives, the lover steals, the foolish waste and the old value.

The most popular lip salve on the present day.

A tonic which in childhood may be administered with safety, but with great caution when childhood is past.

The lover's flag of truce after a quarrel.

Love's happiest expression and sorrow's tenderest balm.

A cannon off the red.

The anatomical juxtaposition of two orbicularis oris muscles in a state on contraction.

A good impression made by the seal of love.

It is like the wind that blows—it is felt but not seen.

The "pons asinorum" of courtship.

A demonstration of love which will dry the baby's tears, thrill the maiden's heart and soothe the ruffled feelings of a tired wife.

A smack for catching the matrimonial fish.

The sovereign tincture in our household dispensary.

What man struggles for before marriage, what woman struggles for after marriage.

Draughts of nectar from the lips of innocence.

Cupid's crushing smack, the crews of which are generally love-sick.

The striking of a love-match.

A simple thing in which a whole world of meaning is sometimes hidden.

The stars in the firmament of love.

The best plaster for the wounds given in domestic tilts.

The poorest mother's richest gift.

A cheeky application.

A kiss resembles a short sermon, consisting of two heads and an application.

Cupid's sealing wax.

The essence of tu-lips (two lips).

The only gift a generous lover likes to get back again.

Temporary facial friction generating instantaneous rapture and bliss.

The soul's ambassador.

The dew gathered from the lips of earth's fairest flowers.

A game for two, always in fashion.

A rock in the sea of life, on which the good ship Bachelor was wrecked.

The cream of courtship.

That which is exchanged between two persons, is something while in the act of exchanging, nothing after the exchange is made, and for which neither can show value received.

Matrimonial bird-lime.

A kiss is love's press telegram.

The heart's thirst appeased at the fountain of a loved one's lips.

Woman's food, man's luxury, boy's physic.

A lubricant, without which the machinery of love gets rusty.

An unspeakable communication.

MY HOME.

"OH, is there no home for the wounded and weary,
The heart that is broken and eye that is teary,
The mind that is sad and soul that is dreary,
Oh, is there no home in some planet on high,
'Mid the numberless stars of the beautiful sky?

Yea, God hath provided a mansion above,
Whose timbers were grown in the garden of love,
Whose walls are as bright as the sheen of the snow,
As the sheen of the shield of the sun in his glow;
He has built me a home in some planet on high,
Mid the numberless stars of the beautiful sky.

He gave to my fathers a home on this earth,
But sin has dissevered the ties of my birth,
And life is a shadow, a mist of the morning,
That fades from the hills with the light of the dawning;
But still there's a home in some planet on high
'Mid the numberless stars of the beautiful sky.

I know not the orb that will be my abode,
But I know it was formed by the finger of God,
That my mansion is empty and I must await
Till He shall command me to enter the gate,
Till the angel of death in mercy shall come
To bear me to dwell in my beautiful home;
My home that is built in some planet on high,
'Mid the numberless stars of the beautiful sky."

TRYING TO FORGET.

I HAVE said that I would forget the past
And the sweet, sweet days gone by,
Forget the love that I fondly dreamed
Would be mine through eternity.
I have tried to forget it all, I say,
But sweet visions will rise
Of a boyish face, so dear to me,
With its loving, laughing eyes.

The tender words I have heard so oft,
Still ring through heart and brain,
They ring and sting, till my pulses throb
With a bitter, maddening pain.
Yet why should I think of those broken vows
With such passionate regret,
I must rise above and beyond it all,
But I cannot quite forget.

I cannot keep those sweet memories back,
They are far too strong for me,
They come and go, they rise and fall,
Like the waves of a troubled sea,

They dash against my broken heart
  Those memories — they are so strong—
They leave me like a stranded ship
  Whose helm and anchor are gone.

But yet I know in some future time,
  Though scattered and wrecked by the blast,
Though tossed about by the waters wild,
  I shall reach a haven at last.
I shall reach the haven "where still waters lie,"
  Where no memories the world can fret,
And only then when my life is o'er
  Can ever my friend forget.

AN OLD-FASHIONED CALENDAR.

THIRTY days has September,
April, June, and November,
All the rest have thirty-one,
Save February alone,
Which has but twenty-eight, in fine,
Till leap year gives it twenty-nine.

Sixty seconds make a minute,
  Sixty minutes make an hour,
If I were a little linnet
  Hopping in her lofty bower,
Then I should not have to sing it,
Sixty seconds make a minute.

Twenty-four hours make a day,
  Seven days will make a week,
And while we all at marbles play,
  Or run at cunning "hide and seek,"
Or in the garden gather flowers,
We'll tell the time that makes the hours.

In every month the weeks are four,
  And twelve whole months will make a year,
Now I must say it o'er and o'er,
  Or else it never will be clear,
So once again I will begin it,
" Sixty seconds make a minute."

THE AFTERGLOW.

OH, wait for the afterglow
When the sun in the sky sinks low,
And the long light dies
In the Summer skies,
Then wait for the afterglow.
Oh, wait for the afterglow
When the crimson clouds fade and go,
And the wind, full west,
Brings a vague unrest,
Then wait for the afterglow.

Oh, wait for the afterglow
When the heart of the earth beats slow !
One pause—it must tell
All its hidden spell
In the light of the afterglow.

Oh, wait for the afterglow
When the light of this life sinks low,
And the long day dies
In the half-drawn sighs,
Then wait for the afterglow.

Oh, wait for the afterglow
When with hand clasped in hand we'll go
Toward the tender west
And in perfect rest,
Then wait for the afterglow.

Oh, wait for the afterglow
When the pulse of this life beats low,
And we know so well
What it meant to tell,
In the light of the afterglow.
    —GEORGIA E. BENNETT IN KEOKUK (*Iowa*)
    Unitarian Calendar.

THOUGHTS OF OTHER DAYS.

THERE'S a good old sacred mem'ry that
  is hangin' round the past,
And it kinder sweetens livin' anywhere
  your lot is cast ;
The burden that you carry may be
  growin' mighty great,
But that good old by-gone feelin' sorter
  lightens up the weight.

No matter about your raisin'—whether
  poor or whether good,
Somehow a feller likes it when he looks
  back, and he should ;
Because you then were livin' as you'll
  never live again—
And that good old by-gone feelin' is of
  pleasure and of pain.

So many of us wander from our boyhood's happy home,
And we never find another, though for
  years and years we roam ;
Our hearts grow cold and stony from
  the storms of all these years,
But that good old by-gone feelin' often
  fills our hearts with tears.

For it brings back dear old mother, and
    the home we loved so well—
The children's even circle, and the tales
    they used to tell—
The school-day fun and frolic and the
    old familiar plays;
Yes, that good old by-gone feelin' is of
    bright and happy days.

But those days have gone forever with
    their joys and with their cares,
And with them gone the mother with
    her tender love and prayers;
And the friends we loved and cherished
    have gone for evermore,
But that good old by-gone feelin', it
    comes to us o'er and o'er.

Well a feller's friends may leave him,
    and his money take its flight;
The health that once stood by him turn
    to sickness in a night—
He may lose his position, and all else
    beneath the skies,
But that good old by-gone feelin'—it is
    his'n till he dies.
        —SAM BEAN.

WHAT DREAMS MAY COME.

HAUNTING me, ever there comes and
    goes
A line from an old song's tender close,
    Its burden the sweetest—the saddest,
    too,
For the altered lives it has echoed
    through—
"Love, had you loved me," the words
    are few,
But through them an infinite passion
    flows.

"Love, had you loved me;" perhaps
    the key
To many a grief this thought may be;
To a sorrow that stares at the magic
    strain
And steps from its prison, barred in
    vain,
To crush with the old, relentless pain
The heart that has guarded it faithfully.

Ah, fondest and truest, whose brown
    eyes shine
With the tenderest love-light, I am thine
Forever, thou heart of my heart—and
    yet
The breath of an April violet
Wakens a longing, a deep regret
For eyes as blue, that were never mine.

"Love, had you loved me," what life
    would be
Attuned to that passionate melody!
Sad hearts unblest, that must still repine
For the draught untasted of Love's
    rich wine,
Better the memories that haunt this
    line
Of "Love had you loved me," so
    mournfully,
        —ELLA M. SEXTON.

THE DRUMMER'S GRIP.

THOUGH the rain and sleet are falling,
    And the roads are "awful muddy,"
Though all men "hard times" are
    bawling,
    Though a fellow's nose gets ruddy,
Though the rivers may be frozen,
    And the frosts may bite and nip,
They can never stop the advent
    Of the drummer and his grip.

Though the trains may all be smashing,
    Though the horses all go lame,
The drummer, like the bed-bug,
    Will get there just the same,
And when his time is over
    Will come smiling from his trip,
For he always "makes connections,"
    Does the drummer with his grip.

Ah, he teaches us a lesson,
    With his energy and grit,
Things that "paralyze" most people
    Don't astonish him a bit.
And he's ever bright and cheerful
    And a smile is on his lip,
He's a daisy from away back,
    Is the drummer with his grip.

Give him a kind word always,
    He'll give you back the same,
For the doings of some "black sheep"
    Don't give the whole tribe blame,
For down, clear down to Hades
    Some so-called "GOOD MEN" slip,
While along the road to Heaven
    Goes the drummer with his grip.

WHY EVE HAD NO HELP.

A LADY furnishes some of the reasons why Eve did not keep a hired girl. "There has been much said about the faults of women and why they need so much waiting on. Some one (a man, of course,) has the presumption to ask: "Why, when Eve was manufactured of a spare rib, a servant was not made at the same time to wait on her?" She didn't need any. Adam never came whining at Eve with a ragged sock to be darned, buttons to be sewed on, gloves to be mended right away—quick now! because he never read the papers until the sun went down behind trees, and stretching himself yawned out, 'Isn't supper ready, my dear?' Not he. He made the fire and hung the kettle over it himself, we'll venture, and pulled the radishes, peeled the potatoes and did everything else he ought to do. He milked the cow, and fed the chickens, and looked after the pigs himself, and never brought half a dozen friends to dinner when Eve hadn't any fresh pomegranates. He never stayed out until eleven o'clock at night, and then scolded poor Eve who was sitting up and crying inside the gate. He never loafed around corner groceries while poor Eve was rocking little Cain's cradle at home. He did not call Eve up from the cellar to get his slippers and find them in a corner where he left them. Not he. When he took them off he put them under a fig-tree beside his Sunday boots. In short, he did not think she was especially created for the purpose of waiting on him, and he wasn't under the impression that it disgraced a man to lighten his wife's cares a little. That's the reason Eve didn't need a hired girl, and without it her descendants did."

MY TEMPLE OF FANCY.

IN my garden is a temple of fancy,
  Not built of airy castles high,
But a temple of trust—where 'tis sweet
    to be just—
  Erected under God's own eye.

It is a beautiful garden of fancy,
  Not fashioned after life's narrow ways,
But a garden of light—where lillies white—
  Were planted to brighten the days.

And around the walls of my temple,
  The fresh, green ivy creeps,
That day by day—if we will we may—
  Ascend and leave the deeps.

And thus in my garden and temple,
  Away from the world's wild fray,
In a measure slow—my fancies come and go—
And I glean life's best thoughts that way.
    —MARY AGNES JACOB.

GOOD MOTTO.

A GENTLEMAN, whose life had been stormy in its yesterday, and threatened to be tumultuous in its to-morrow, visited a friend. On being shown to the guest chamber his eyes fell upon the following "Good Night," a beautiful motto for such an apartment:

Sleep sweetly in this quiet room,
  O thou, whoe'er thou art,
And let no mournful yesterdays
  Disturb thy peaceful heart;
Nor let to-morrow scare thy rest
  With dreams of coming ill;
Thy Saviour is thy changeless friend,
  His love surrounds thee still.
Forget thyself with all the world,
  Put out each glaring light;
God's stars are shining overhead
  And He can give Good Night.
He cares for every weary one,
  In peace the soul can keep,
And when we miss the earthly sun,
  Give His beloved sleep,
    Good Night!

SOME OF THESE DAYS.

SOME of these days all the skies will be brighter;
Some of these days all the burdens be lighter;

Hearts will be happier, souls will be whiter
    Some of these days,
    Some of these days!

Some of these days in the desert up-springing.
Fountains shall flash while the joy-bells are ringing,
And the world with its sweetest of birds shall go singing
    Some of these days,
    Some of these days!

Some of these days! let us bear with our sorrow;
Faith in the future, its light we may borrow;
There will be joy in the golden to-morrow
    Some of these days,
    Some of these days!
        —FRANK L. STANTON.

GOD.

O! THOU Eternal One! whose presence bright
  All space doth occupy, all motion guide;
Unchanged through Time's all-devastating flight—
  Thou only God! there is no God beside!
Being above all beings! Mighty One!
  Whom none can comprehend and none explore;
Who fill'st existence with Thyself alone;
  Embracing all—supporting—ruling all—
  Being whom we call God—and know no more!

In its sublime research, Philosophy
  May measure out the ocean deep—may count
The sands or the sun's rays—but, God! for Thee
  There is no weight nor measure; none can mount
Up to Thy mysteries. Reason's brightest spark,
  Though kindled by Thy light, in vain would try
To trace Thy counsels, infinite and dark;
  And thought is lost ere thought can soar so high,
Even like past moments in eternity.

Thou from primeval nothingness didst call
  First chaos, then existence. Lord! on Thee
Eternity had its foundation; all
  Sprang forth from Thee; of light, joy, harmony,
Sole origin; all life—all beauty Thine.
  Thy word created all, and doth create;
Thy splendor fills all space with rays divine,
  Thou art, and wert, and shalt be glorious! great!
Light-giving, life-sustaining Potentate!

Thy chains the unmeasured universe surround;
  Upheld by Thee, by Thee inspired with breath!
Thou the beginning with the end hast bound,
  And beautifully mingled life and death!
As sparks mount upward from the fiery blaze
  So suns are born; so worlds spring forth from Thee;
And as the spangles in the sunny rays
  Shine round the silver snow, the pageantry
Of Heaven's bright army glitters in Thy praise.

A million torches lighted by Thy hand
  Wander unwearied through the blue abyss;
They own Thy power, accomplish Thy command,
  All gay with life, all eloquent with bliss,
What shall we call them? Piles of crystal light,
  A glorious company of golden streams—
Lamps of celestial ether, burning bright—
  Suns lighting systems with their joyous beams?
But Thou to these art as the noon to night!

Yes! as a drop of water in the sea,
All this magnificence in Thee is lost.
What are ten thousand worlds compared
   to Thee?
   And what am I, then? Heaven's
     unnumbered host,
Though multiplied by myriads, and
   arrayed
In all the glory of sublimest thought,
Is but an atom in the balance, weighed
   Against Thy greatness—is a cipher
     brought
   Against infinity! What am I, then?
     Naught!

Naught! But the effluence of Thy light
   divine,
Pervading worlds, hath reached my
   bosom, too;
Yes! in my spirit doth Thy spirit shine,
   As shines the sunbeam in a drop of
     dew.
Naught! But I live, and on Hope's
   pinions fly
Eager toward Thy presence; for in
   Thee
I live, and breathe, and dwell—aspiring
   high,
   Even to the throne of Thy divinity.
   I am, oh, God! and surely THOU
     must be!

Thou art! directing, guiding all, Thou
   art!
   Direct my understanding, then, to
     Thee!
Control my spirit, guide my wandering
   heart.
Though but an atom 'mid immensity,
Still I am something fashioned by Thy
   hand!
I hold a middle rank 'twixt Heaven
   and earth,
On the last verge of mortal being stand,
   Close to the realms where angels
     have their birth,
   Just on the boundaries of the spirit-
     land!

The chain of being is complete in me;
   In me is matter's last gradation lost,
And the next step is spirit—Deity!
   I can command the lightning, and
     am dust!

A monarch and a slave! a worm!
   a god!
Whence came I here, and how? So
   marvellously
Constructed and conceived! Unknown?
   This clod
Lives surely through some higher
   energy—
For from itself alone it could not be!

Creator? Yes! Thy wisdom and Thy
   word
Created me—Thou source of life and
   good!
Thou spirit of my spirit, and my Lord!
   Thy light, Thy love, in their bright
     plenitude,
Filled me with an immortal soul, to
   spring
Over the abyss of death, and bade it
   wear
The garments of eternal day, and wing
   Its heavenly flight beyond this little
     sphere
   Even to its source—to Thee—its
     Author there.

Oh, thought ineffable! Oh, vision blest!
   Though worthless our conception all
     of Thee,
Yet shall Thy shadowed image fill our
   breast,
And waft its homage to the Deity!
God thus alone my lowly thoughts can
   soar—
   Thus seek Thy presence. Being wise
     and good!
'Midst Thy vast works, admire, obey,
   adore!
And when the tongue is eloquent no
   more
   The soul shall speak in tears of
     gratitude.
   —FROM THE RUSSIAN OF DERZHAVINE.

LEARN A TRADE.

ONE of the greatest drawbacks to the young men of the day is, they do not learn trades. They may be nice and clever, but unless they have trades and can earn livings, they are not wanted, except for positions they do not care to fill. There is no end to the supply of clerks,—everybody wishes a clerkship, just as they wish an umbrella on a hot day, to keep them out of the sun; and yet to be a clerk, even, requires training and experience. Ask the young man if he has that experience, and he will say "No, but I can soon pick it up."

The trouble is, the average business man don't wish to pay for the schooling in "picking up" a trade or business. He wishes one who has already picked up the business at his own expense and effort. It is the man that has a specialty, and has learned it well, that is wanted. Even fewer of them are wanted in the commercial world than in the industrial and mechanical. A good artisan or mechanic always commands wages. If not in one place, he does in another. But in order to do so, he must first learn his trade, or business; he does not before so doing. He must learn it well, and fully, and some one must be paid the tuition. If it is not the teacher, as in the professions, it must be by hard toil and labor in the workshop, or in the school of experience. No use in accepting a job, thinking the boss may be deceived, and you will get in by stealing either your trade or unearned money of your employer. The deception will not work long, and yours will be the first services dispensed with, while the skilled expert will be retained, even at higher wages.

Young man, go to work. Learn a trade. Don't fool yourself by imagining you are too good, or too rich to do so. Perhaps you may be to-day, and to-morrow "there may be none so poor as to do you reverence." How will you then earn your living? What will you do? What service can you render humanity in exchange for your expense upon it? Who will pay your bills, when mother and father are gone? These are questions sure to come up, put them off as you will, and it is wisdom to provide for their early answer. If you don't earn, you can't pay, long. If you can't pay, the world cares nothing for you, however, different may be your opinion, nor will it care whether you get bread or go hungry. Don't fool yourself on those points, but throw away that switch cane, lay aside your cigarettes, hang up your dude clothes and realize that it is a race for a living, and that he gets the best, who deserves the most. Go to work, if at small wages. Learn a trade, if you have to work for nothing for five years. After that you can be independent and earn back your five years' labor; and if you don't need your trade, it will not be in your way, and if you do, it will be a God-send in time of need. Learn a trade; be a man, and not a pap-sucking, job-hunting dude, all your life!

THE RIGHT WILL RIGHT ITSELF.

WHEN overcome with anxious fears,
   And moved with passion strong,
Because the right seems losing ground,
   And everything goes wrong,
How oft does admonition say:
   "Put trouble on the shelf;
Truth will outlive the liars' day,
   And right will right itself."

By all the triumphs of the past,
   By all the victories won,
The good achieved, the progress made
   Each day, from sun to sun;
In spite of artful ways employed
   By perfidy or pelf,
One thing we can rest assured,
   The right will right itself.

Unshaken in our faith and zeal,
   'Tis ours to do and dare,
To find the place we best can fill,
   And serve our Maker there;
For he is only brave who thus
   Puts trouble on the shelf,
And trusts in God, for by His aid
   The right will right itself.
        —NEW YORK LEDGER.

THE OLD TIME RELIGION.

IT would appear that religion is at least one thing that would never change in style, or go out of date, for it is universally admitted that the creature owes reverence and devotion to the Creator. We believe that all men, everywhere, acknowledge this, though their ideas of the Creator may differ, but it is the creeds and forms they are required to subscribe to, that brings on the rebellions and causes so much trouble. Most churches admit these are man-made, and after all, are simply non-essential opinions; yet upon a test their members are passed upon and judged by those "Non-essentials," in spite of the modern pretensions of liberality and charity. Somehow this did not seem to be so much the case when Jesus was on earth, nor even a short time back when the Old Time Religion was abroad in the land. Come to think of it, Christ did not say very much about denominations and creeds anyway; and he was surely very indifferent to church-rolls, fashionable congregations and paid choirs. Indeed it has only been a short time since these cut very much figure in religion anyway. And while they are very good in their way, have they not been permitted to creep in and really divide the worship that should be exclusively the Creator's? Are there not plenty of people who are educated to the idea that there is really but little chance of reaping God's blessings except through their peculiar creed and church? The different branches of the common church may disclaim it, yet it looks very much that way. We cannot think this was so much the case only a short time back when it was more a question of "Hang together," or being hung separately! For well do many remember, who are still living, the good old days of the camp meetings! How the people came from far and near to some sequestered spot, that seemed to be hallowed by nature, and blessed by God, to enjoy their season of worship. In ox-carts, in wagons, in buggies, on horseback, on foot, they came. At the campground there were no four-dollar-a-day hotels, Saratoga trunks, or fine churches. Their fare was what they found, or provided, their houses tents, or covered wagons, their churches brush arbors, and their canopy the blue sky that arched above them. There was nothing said here about creeds and isms, but each recognized the other as a brother of the same brotherhood and son of the same Godhead, although he had no Bible, and could not read a creed.

These people had a God and church big enough for all, and united in a worship that must have been pleasing to Him, and that almost made the angels weep for joy!

And then the good Old Time Religion at the protracted meetings!—Who does not remember them? How, when the crops were "laid by" and themselves and their neighbors were all helped, they packed well-filled baskets with good things and repaired to the neighboring church to remember God, and give thanks for His blessings! Sometimes it was with the church of one denomination, and sometimes with another,—but that didn't matter as it was God, and not the church, they were worshipping. And how they sung and prayed! There weren't books enough to go 'round, so two or three sung "out of the same book." When books were very scarce, the hymns were "lined out" by the minister, and as the melody rolled upward the curtain of heaven almost appeared to rise!

Then after the singing, how some good brother would lead in prayer!

He wasn't very learned, perhaps, yet his prayer was eloquent, and said just like he knew what he was praying for, and meant for the Lord to hear. "Amen" would come from this corner and that, and, after he had finished praying, the good old minister would turn the pages of the old, big red-bound, Bible that lay on the pulpit, and read the Scriptures, and how he would accent and try to impress every word,—and how still were all as he read! Then, he would announce his text, and such preaching! Such amens that would be echoed from different parts of the congregation! Occasionally some brother or sister would "get happy" and arise and "shout" about the church, and tell the bad boys and girls to flee the wrath to come.

Then how the preacher would "call for mourners" to come out from "the world, the flesh and the devil," by kneeling at the altar, to be the subjects of prayer and mercy. And how they came, weeping and asking the forgiveness of God and man!

After the morning services were over, the "meeting" would be adjourned for the dinner hour. And such dinners! Some would be spread upon the grass, some upon improvised benches, removed from the church, and others upon long pre-arranged tables. Guests were invited to eat at different tables, and right warm was the rivalry of the sisters to get one or more of the ministers to break bread with them; and even as good as were these people, the ministers were accused of being sufficiently human to show partiality, and to manifest a disposition to linger longest around the weighty and well-loaded tables! Be this as it may, there was a plenty and a welcome for all, and no tramp or stranger was permitted to depart without a well-filled stomach, and a "God-bless-you."

Then after the dinner and a bounteous supply of fruits, melons, etc., how the men would bring out their long-stemmed pipes and "home-spun tobacco" and enjoy their smokes!—And the ladies,—yes, some of them—would hurdle out of view of the ministers with their "tooth-brushes." (Don't laugh for the snuff factories are still running on full time!)

And oh, how Deacon Bowen would look at the boys as they got out their "taws" and dug a hole for "knucks" or struck a ring for marbles! "Boys," he would say, "this is the Lord's ground.—Remember." This would be quite enough for the disappearance of the last marble, and each boy would look at the good deacon, and at each other, as if he wished to apologize for something. After dinner-hour, all would again gather in the church, or brush arbor, as the case might be, and begin services again, which were often continued from three days to three weeks, and during which many a man and woman made new resolutions, turned over a new leaf, and started on better lives. Besides this, these meetings were a kind of court, with both civil and criminal jurisdiction, and right there were many a balance struck, and judgment rendered, but few of which, I believe, will ever be reversed by the Supreme Court of all. Yes, they had no paid choirs, "no brand-new organ, Sue," no cushioned pews, no stained-glass windows, no fine church buildings, no creeds, no isms, yet somehow God and the Holy Spirit seemed to be with them, and to pervade the very atmosphere around them. The people were plain, clad mostly in homespun, yet were honest for honesty's sake and good for pleasure and for duty's sake. The ministers, too, were plain, everyday men. They knew what it was to work and to sympathize; and although they had no D.D.'s to their names, and knew but little of the various theories, creeds and isms, yet they always had full houses when they preached. They did not have then what is now known as the "Parsonitis" rarely got "debilitated" as soon as the rich wanted to go off to the springs, and were never given long vacations on full pay; nor, indeed, were they given very full pay at any time. They required no announcements in the papers, needed no big "revivalist to warm over the flock" and required no Salvation Army to reach the less fashionable.

The saying that "you have no use for a minister, except in case of a marriage, or a funeral" was then unknown; and the "Preacher," as he was then called, was, indeed, something more than a "church, or society pet."

Yes, he was a truly beloved, and useful citizen. A "power in the land" for all that was good and ennobling. And though he was plain and unassuming as he went about, living as well as doing his Old Time Religion, he everywhere found a welcome and the most profound respect. And, somehow, when you were sick and worried with the perplexing cares of life; somehow, next to the old family physician, with his saddle-bags, you would prefer to see that plain old minister, and feel the touch of his magic hand.

Yes, somehow, you felt if he was only on your side all was right; or would be made right, with God.

MOTHER'S OLD STEEL THIMBLE.

I'VE been rummaging a casket, filled
  with relics of the past,
And I turned them idly, one by one,
  until I found at last,
Wrapped in a piece of homespun and
  laid away with care,
The dingy old steel thimble that my
  mother used to wear.

O, what a flood of memories sweeps in
  upon my soul,
As the coarse and faded covering I
  carefully unroll,
And dim with dust of useless years, I
  see before me there,
The battered old steel thimble that my
  mother used to wear.

Rough with the toil of mother-love in
  cheerless days of yore,
It was the only ornament those dear
  hands ever wore,
And I tenderly caress it as a treasure
  rich and rare,
This precious old steel thimble that my
  mother used to wear.

Companion of her widowhood, her
  faithful friend for years,
Made sacred by her patient toil and
  sanctified by tears,
No costly gem that sparkles on the
  hand of lady fair,
Could buy the old steel thimble that my
  mother used to wear.

In a quiet little churchyard she has
  slumbered many a year,
Yet in this holy hour I seem to feel her
  presence near,
And hear her tender benediction as I
  bow in grateful prayer,
And kiss the old steel thimble that my
  mother used to wear.

The memory of that mother's love shall
  be a beacon light,
To guide my wayward footsteps in the
  path of truth and right,
And the key that opens heaven's door,
  if e'er I enter there,
Will be the old steel thimble that my
  mother used to wear.

FADING.

THE Past is fading, fading,
  Never to come back again
The cypress tree is shading
  Half the sunny plain.
Unchanged, I wot, is each well-known
  scene,
Not a branch shows new in the hedge-
  rows green.
Just so the lark from the meadow
  sprung,
When life and I alike were young;
Just so the primrose heed'd to light.
  Yet, Nature's self pervading,
    Is the sense of something gone;
  The Past is fading, fading,
    And the wheel of Time rolls on.

The Past is fading, fading,
  And gathered in its hold,
Its mighty pinions laden,
  Is much we prized of old.
The grass grows rank o'er many a
  grave
Of the young and joyous and gay and
  brave;
Many a well-loved voice is hushed,
Many a golden hope is crushed,
Many a happy dream is over,
With a smile of kindred, friend and
  lover.
  The Past is fading, fading,
    The blood runs cold and slow;
  Harsh wisdom is degrading
    The creeds of long ago.

The Past is fading, fading,
  We cling and pray in vain,
Where the cypress tree is shading
  The tombs of all the slain,
Slain by the years and put aside,
The darlings of love, the idols of
  pride.
One by one the frail links part,
Hand drops from hand and heart from
  heart;
One by one the sweet things given
To brighten earth go back to Heaven,
  Till love and life pervading,
    Sighs the sense of something
      gone;
  And the Past is fading, fading
    And the wheel of Time rolls on.

HAPPY EVERY DAY.

Sidney Smith cut the following from a newspaper and preserved it for himself:

When you rise in the morning, form a resolution to make the day a happy one to a fellow creature. It is easily done; a left-off garment to the man who needs it, a kind word to the sorrowful, an encouraging expression to the striving, trifles in themselves light as air, will do it at least for twenty-four hours.

And if you are young, depend upon it, it will tell when you are old; and if you are old, rest assured it will send you gently and happily down the stream of time to eternity. By the most simple arithmetical sum, look at the result. If you send one person, only one, happily through each day, there are three hundred and sixty-five in the year. And supposing you live forty years only after you commence that course of medicine, you have made 14,600 beings happy; at all events for a time.

THEY ARE DEAD.

There was a man who never told a lie—
    But he's dead.
Never said it was wet when the weather was dry;
Never said he'd caught fish when he hadn't caught one;
Never said he'd done something that he hadn't done;
Never scolded his wife, and never got mad,
And wouldn't believe that the world was so bad;
A respecter of men, defender of woman,
Who believed the divine, and in that which was human;
Meek as Moses—he never understood.
And the poor man died of being too good.
    And he's dead.

There was a woman who never had gossiped a bit—
    She's dead too;
Who hated all scandal, nor listened to it;
She believed in mankind, took care of her cat,
Always turned a deaf ear to this story or that;
Never scolded her husband—she never had one:
No sluggard was she, but rose with the sun.
Never whispered in meeting, didn't care for a bonnet
Or all of the feathers that one could put on it;
Never sat with the choir nor sang the wrong note;
Expressed no desire to lecture or vote;
For the poor soul was deaf as a post—also dumb;
You might have called forever, and she wouldn't have come.
    And she's dead.
    —Jeannette La Flamboy, in the Outlook.

"AND YOU'LL REMEMBER ME."

One evening as the sun went down
    Among the golden hills,
And silent shadows, soft and brown
    Crept over vales and rills,
I watched the dusky bats a-wing
    Dip down the dusky lea;
Hearkening heard a maiden sing,
    "And you'll remember me."

"When other lips and other hearts,"
    Came drifting through the trees;
"In language whose excess imparts,"
    Was born upon the breeze,
Ah! love is sweet and hope is strong,
    And life's a sunny sea,
A woman's soul is in her song;
    "And you'll remember me."

Still rippling from her throbbing throat,
    With joy akin to pain,
There seemed a tear in every note,
    A sob in every strain;
Soft as the twilight shadows creep
    Across the listless lea,
The singer sang her love to sleep,
    With, "You'll remember me."
    —Cy. Warman.

Love's Season.
Has buried Autumn in walls of snow;
And bound and fettered where bold
Frost cast her,
Lies outraged Nature in helpless woe.

Page 53.

LIVING ON THE FARM.

How brightly through the mist of years
My quiet country home appears!
My father, busy, busy, all the day,
In ploughing corn or making hay;
My mother, moving with the light,
Among her milk pans, ever bright;
We children, just from school set free
Filling the garden with our glee—
The blood of life was flowing warm
When I was living on a farm.

I hear the sweet church-going bell,
As o'er the fields its music fell;
I see the country neighbors round,
Gathering 'neath the pleasant sound;
They stop awhile beside the door,
To talk their homely matters o'er—
The springing corn, the ripening grain,
And "how we need a little rain;"
"A little sun would do no harm;"
"We want good weather for the farm."

When Autumn comes, what joy to see
The gathering of the husking bee,
To hear the voices keeping tune,
Of girls and boys beneath the moon!
To mark the golden ears so bright,
More golden in the yellow light!
Since I have learned the ways of men,
I often turn to these again,
And feel life wore its highest charm,
When I was living on a farm.

DREAMING.

Let me dream of days gone by;
 Happy days of sun and song,
 Never sad and never long—
Peaceful as the star-kissed sky.

In my heart there lurked no care,
 Not a cloud of anxious thought;
 Life with joy alone was fraught,
Earth and sky were always fair.

Brightly blending each with each,
 Days of pleasure came and went;
 Each on wing of rapture sent—
Each my heart fresh joy to teach.

As they dawned and flitted past,
 By the golden sunlight tipped,
 Carelessly their sweets I sipped—
Nothing doubting they would last.

Ah, I knew not while asleep
 In my youthful innocence,
 There could be no sure defence
'Gainst the tears I soon should weep.

Swiftly as the lightning stroke
 Cleaves the startled clouds in twain
 Love, with all its joy and pain,
From its sleep, my soul awoke.

Love—ah me, how sweet the word—
 Lingered with me for awhile,
 Kissed me with its sunny smile—
Left me like a wounded bird.

With it, from my stricken heart,
 Went the light of life and earth;
 In their bloom and song and mirth
I no longer had a part.

From the present comes no gleam
 Round my life its cheer to cast—
 Let me live, then, in the past,
Dreaming of a broken dream.

THE INQUIRY.

Tell me, ye winged winds, that round
  my pathway roar,
Do ye not know some spot where mortals weep no more?
Some lone and pleasant dell, some valleys in the west,
Where, free from toil and pain, the weary soul may rest?
 The loud wind dwindled to a whisper low,
 And sighed for pity as it answered—"No."

Tell me, thou mighty deep, whose billows round me play,
Know'st thou some favored spot, some island far away,
Where weary man may find the bliss for which he sighs—
Where sorrow never lives, and friendship never dies?
 The loud waves, rolling in perpetual flow,
 Stopped for a while and sighed to answer—"No."

And thou, serenest moon, that, with
  such lovely face,
Dost look upon the earth asleep in
  night's embrace,
Tell me, in all thy round, hast thou
  not seen some spot
Where miserable man might find a happier lot?
  Behind a cloud the moon withdrew
    in woe,
    A voice, sweet, but sad, responded—
      "No."

Tell me, my secret soul, O tell me,
  Hope and Faith,
Is there no resting-place from sorrow,
  sin and death?
Is there no happy spot where mortals
  may be blest,
Where grief may find a balm, and
  weariness a rest?
  Faith, Hope, and Love, best boons to
    mortals given,
    Waved their bright wings and whis-
      pered—" Yes, in Heaven."

—CHARLES MACKAY.

FATHERHOOD OF GOD, AND BROTHERHOOD OF MAN.

I WILL not ask my neighbor of his creed,
  Nor what he deems of doctrine old or
    new,
Nor what rites his honest soul may
  need
  To worship God—the only wise and
    true—
Nor what he thinks of the anointed
  Christ,
Nor with what baptism he has been
  baptized.

I ask not what temptations have beset
  His human heart, now self-debased
    and sore,
Nor by what wayside well the Lord he
  met,
  Nor where was uttered, "Go and sin
    no more."
Between his soul and God, that busi-
  ness lies;
Not mine to cavil, question, or despise.

I ask not by which name among the
  rest
That Christians go by he is named or
  known
Whether his faith has ever been "pro-
  fessed,"
Or whether proven by his deeds
  alone,
So there be Christhood in him, all is
  well;
He is my brother, and in peace we
  dwell.

If grace and patience in his actions
  speak
  Or fall in words of kindness from his
    tongue.
Which raise the fallen, fortify the weak,
  And heal the heart by sorrow rent
    and wrung;
If he give good for ill and love for hate—
Friend of the friendless, poor and deso-
  late—

I find in him discipleship so true,
  So full, that nothing further I de-
    mand.
He may be bondman, freeman, Gentile,
  Jew,
  But we are brothers—walk we hand
    in hand.
In his white life let me the Christhood see,
It is enough for him, enough for me.
—EXCHANGE.

THE BEAUTIFUL GATE.

AT the beautiful gate I kneel in my
  longing,
  Where the strong river sobs out its
    restless moan;
With eyes that are blinded in hot tears'
  swift thronging,
Kneel pleading, consoling, burdened,
  alone,
    At the Beautiful Gate.

O river, be silent thy ebb and thy flow-
  ing!
  Still the rush of thy waters, their
    waiting forbear,
Till I hear in the lull 'twixt the coming
  and going,
  A voice that I love floating out on the
    air
    Thro' the Beautiful Gate.

Lo, I kneel praying, pleading ; unheeding death's arrow,
My soul catching rapture, forgetting its fear,
As the wide shores bend nearer, the river grows narrow,
And a face shines within of heaven's faces most dear
By the Beautiful Gate.

O my love ! O beloved ! stand fast by the portal.
O earth-love unchanging in infinite life !
Stand close ; till my soul made eternal, immortal,
Find place beside thine, beyond grieving and strife
At the Beautiful Gate.
—Louise Dunham Goldberry.

TO KNOW AND HEAR.

Could we but know the sun would shine to-morrow,
We would not mind the storm-clouds of to-day ;
And half the trouble that our sad souls borrow,
Would spread its raven wings and flee away.

Could we but know the kind words we have spoken
Fell like the dew upon some thirsty sod,
Far oftener would some cheerful, loving token
Point from earth's dreary wastes the way to God.

Could we but know the load of shame and sorrow
That presses heavily on the sin-stained breast,
We should not idly dream away to-morrow,
But rise and lead the erring one towards rest.

Could we but know that those who cross the river
Wait for our coming on the other shore,
We would not weep when earthly love-ties sever,
But wait with patience till life's voyage is o'er.

Could we but hear our loving Father calling
His burdened children up to rest in peace,
Like a low benediction on our spirits falling,
Would be his summons, bringing sweet release.
—Mrs. L. J. H. Frost, *in The Watchman.*

GAMBLING.

Humanity has a great inclination to gamble, and gamblers are usually of two classes. One of them is a class which desires excitement and stimulation, and craves it just as an opium-eater craves opium, or a drunkard craves whisky. The other is a class that desires something for nothing, and like the vulture does not care upon what, or whom, it preys. Either of these tastes, or natures, is brought on largely by inheritance, or by laziness and vicious culture ; and it is the latter class that is specially dangerous. For but few people set out to be gamblers, and it is not the good-natured gambler that requires mental stimulance, that is especially to be dreaded. There is a kind of honor among these, and many of them are big-hearted and noble fellows. They must have their stimulants, and must set a bad example ; yet when the example is set, and the mental excitement had, they are sticklish for the observance of the gambler's code, and defy the world to beat them in generosity and downright charity. Their contests are usually with their class, and it is really a game of chance with them ; and in which the world knows or cares but little as to which is the victim or victor. In either case it is " blackjack against thunder," and but little matters it to which pocket the stakes are transferred. It is usually done in secret, the stakes jointly held for that purpose, and outside of their wives and children (who are usually well provided for by some " hook or crook ")— it matters but little to the world which holds the aces, or the bob-tailed flush.

All professional gamblers,—like Masons or Odd Fellows—seem to know each other, and if one "goes broke," they help him up, and he rarely stays broke. Their example and occasionally "roping in a sucker," are really the worst features of it with them, and they are entirely unworthy of many of the otherwise noble men engaged in it. But, if even these quasi-palliations may be said of the gamblers who prey upon each other, what can be said of the hungry, lanky friend who engages in it to dodge work and to get something for nothing? He hasn't even the show of generosity, nor the nobility of a thought of charity. This vampire really offers no game of chance. His victims are the unarmed, and his weapons loaded dice, or stacked cards. He has nothing save a shrivelled soul to lose, and only plays to win. He has no class, except confederates. He has no friends, except by license to rob. He has no wife or babes whose honor and well-being he cares, or respects. There is, in fact, no law, human or divine, that he recognizes, and no brotherhood except for plunder. The real difference between him and the burglar and robber is, the courage required; and the burglar and robber have the further advantage of withholding their influence for bad from others. The burglar and robber may rob, steal and even kill; yet they do not go about duping others into their nefarious work, nor persuade them, that, after all, it is popular and not so bad. The burglar and robber keep in the dark and conceal their work and examples. The burglar and robber respect their friends and stay with their class. This "slick duck" wears good clothes and passes in disguise for what he is not. He often goes in good company, and is found among real ladies and gentlemen; and with his pleasant address and oily tongue, it is then perhaps that he finds families to despoil, hearts to crush, and young men and boys to entice, like flies into the net of a spider. His apparent gentility throws off suspicion and makes his dupes but easier prey; and it is not at the much abused cards and gambling table he alone gets in his work. It is in stocks, schemes, boards of trade, counting rooms and directors' meetings that his influence outcrops, and his same loaded dice appears in another form. The girl who entertains him but little suspects his true nature, the money-loving parents perhaps are carried away with his Napoleonic "financiering"—which really means to play with loaded dice in some form.

While the young men delight in the teaching to "make money" without working for it, later on, perhaps, the girl weeps over a crushed heart and ruined life, the parents realize their stocks, bonds and money lie at the bottom side of the loaded dice, and the young men look through different bars than those of the spider web, or take hasty leave for a change of climate. Alas, alas, "Man's inhumanity to man," and the evil influence of gambling!

It is surprising how little the press and pulpit have said against this class of gambling, and how common it is becoming. "Chance," "Chance," "Chance," from the centre-table to the monopolies and trusts, which play only with loaded dice! At baseball, in futures, at poker, in the lottery, on the exchanges—everywhere they are gambling! Even at the church fairs they are "raffling" and "selling chances" —trying to get something for nothing; or at least, much for little: If it is wrong in the gambler, why not doubly so in the church? Loaded dice, loaded dice, and the world seems to have declared war against them, and to be trying to whip them out of their own game!

Isn't it about time to give up the fight; or at least, get a new game? Will not thievery, shrewdness and loaded dice always win?

What show has the sucker, and how long will the crop hold out?

THE LITTLE DOG UNDER THE WAGON.

"COME, wife," said good old farmer Gray,
"Put on your things, 'tis market day—
And we'll be off to the nearest town,
There and back ere the sun goes down,

Spot? No, we'll leave old Spot behind.
But Spot he barked and Spot he whined,
And soon made up his doggish mind
    To follow under the wagon.

Away they went at a good round pace,
And joy came into the farmer's face;
"Poor Spot," said he, "did want to come,
But I'm awful glad he's left at home;
He'll guard the barn, and guard the cot,
And keep the cattle out of the lot."
"I'm not sure of that," thought Spot,
    The little dog under the wagon.

The farmer all his produce sold,
And got his pay in yellow gold,
They started homeward after dark,
Home through the lonely forest. Hark!
A robber springs from behind a tree—
"Your money or else your life," said he;
The moon was up, but he didn't see
    The little dog under the wagon.

Spot ne'er barked, and Spot ne'er whined,
But quickly caught the thief behind;
He dragged him down in the mire and dirt,
And tore his coat and tore his shirt,
Then held him fast on the miry ground;
The robber uttered not a sound—
While his hands and feet the farmer bound,
And tumbled him into the wagon.

So Spot he saved the farmer's life,
The farmer's money; the farmer's wife;
And now a hero grand and gay,
A silver collar he wears to-day;
Among his friends, among his foes,
And everywhere his master goes,
He follows on his horny toes,
    The little dog under the wagon.
      —NEW ORLEANS PICAYUNE.

A VOICE OF THE NIGHT.

ONCE upon a front stoop, beery,
I with eyes quite red and bleary,
    Tried to punch a keyhole in the door,
While my better half lay napping,
And my muddled brain was mapping—
    Mapping how to save my gore.

"Let me in, dear," gently said I,
Trying to conceal the red eye—
    "Let me enter, I implore!"
But the silence was unbroken,
And of life the only token
    Was a weird, sonorous snore;
Simply that and nothing more.

"I say, my dear, the keyhole's growed up,
And I—why I am almost snowed up!"
    I cried out in a perfect roar;
But the time did slowly drag on,
For she knew I had a jag on,
    And the hour was nearly four,
So she just kept up that snore,
With me pounding on the door;
    Simply that and nothing more.
      —B. M. M.

NO TELEPHONE IN HEAVEN.

"Now I can wait on baby," the smiling merchant said,
    As he stooped and softly toyed with the golden, curly head.
"I want oo' to tall up mamma," came the answer full and free,
"Wif yo' telephone an' ast her when she's coming back to me.

"Tell her 'at I's so lonesome 'at I don't know what to do.
An' papa cries so much I dess he must be lonesome, too;
Tell her to tum to baby, 'tause at night I dit so 'fraid,
Wif nobody there to tiss me, when de light bedins to fade.

"All froo de day I wants her, for my dolly's dot so tored,
Fum de awful punching buddy dive it wif his 'ittle sword;
An' ain't nobody to fix it, since mamma went away,
An' pore 'ittle, lonesome dolly's dittin' thinner every day."

"My child," the merchant murmured, as he stroked the anxious brow,
"There's no telephone connection where your mother lives at now."

"Ain't no telephone in heaven?" and
   tears sprang to her eyes,
"I fought dat God had everyfine wif
   Him up in the skies."
             —EDWARD N. WOOD.

MY SWEETHEART.

Her height? Perhaps you'd deem her
   tall—
To be exact, just five feet seven;
Her arching feet are not too small,
Her gleaming eyes are bits of heaven.
Slim are her hands, yet not too wee—
I could not fancy useless fingers;
Her hands are all that hands should be,
And own a touch whose memory lingers.

The hue that lights her oval cheeks
   Recalls the pink that tints a cherry,
Upon her chin a dimple speaks
   A disposition blithe and merry.
Her laughter ripples like a brook;
   Its sound a heart of stone would soften;
Though sweetness shines in every look,
   Her laugh is never loud nor often.

Though golden locks have won renown
   With bards, I never heed their raving;
The girl I love hath locks of brown,
   Not tightly curled, but gently waving.
Her mouth? Perhaps you'd term it
   large—
Is firmly moulded, full and curving;
Her quiet lips are Cupid's charge,
   But in the cause of truth unswerving.

Though little of her neck is seen,
   That little is both smooth and sightly;
And fair as marble is its sheen,
   Above her bodice gleaming whitely.
Her nose is just the proper size,
   Without a trace of upward turning,
Her shell-like ears are wee and wise,
   The tongue of scandal ever spurning.

In mirth and woe her voice is low,
   Her calm demeanor never fluttered;
Her every accent seems to go
   Straight to one's heart as soon as uttered.

She ne'er coquets as others do;
   Her tender heart would never let her.
Where does she dwell? I would I knew!
   As yet, alas! I've never met her.
             —SAMUEL MINTURN PECK.

LONG AFORE HE KNOWED.

JES' little bit o' feller—I remember
   still—
Ust to almost cry for Christmas, like a
   youngster will.
Fourth of July's nothin' to it—New
   Year's ain't a smell;
Easter Sunday—circus day—jes' all
   dead in the shell.
Lord, though at night, you know, to set
   around and hear
The old folks work the story off about
   the sledge and deer,
And "Santy" shootin' 'round the roof,
   all wrapped in fur and fuzz—
Long afore
      I knowed who
           "Santy Claus" wuz!

Use to wait, and set up late, a week or
   two ahead;
Couldn't hardly keep awake, nor
   wouldn't go to bed;
Kittle stewin' on the fire and mother
   sittin' here
Darnin' socks and rockin' in the skreeky
   rockin' cheer;
Pap gap', and wunder where it was the
   money went.
And quar'l with his frosted heels, and
   spill his liniment;
And me a-dreamin' sleighbells when
   the clock 'ud whirr and buzz,
Long afore
      I knowed who
           "Santy Claus" wuz!

Size the fireplace up, and figger how
   "Old Santy" could
Manage to come down the chimbly,
   like they said he would;
Wisht that I could hide and see him—
   wundered what he'd say
Ef he ketched a feller lyin' fer him that
   away?

But I bet on him and liked him, same
  as if he had
Turned to pat me on the back and say ;
  " Look here, my lad,
Here's my pack—jes' he'p yourself, like
  all good boys does ! "
Long afore
        I knowed who
              " Santy Claus " wuz !

Wisht that yarn was true about him, as
  it 'peared to be—
Truth made out o' lies like that un's
  good enough fer me !
Wisht I still was so confidin' I could
  jes' go wild
Over hangin' up my stockins like the
  little child
Climbin' in my lap to-night, and beggin'
  me to tell
'Bout them reindeer, and " Old Santy
  that she loves so well.
I'm half sorry for this little girl sweetheart of his—
Long afore
        She knows who
              " Santa Claus " is !
              —JAMES WHITCOMB RILEY.

HOPE.

IT is not hope to sit and dream
  And fancy happy days to be ;
It is not hope to idly dream
  The future will be glad and free.
He hopes in truth who gives to toil
  The earnest of a faithful heart,
Who plants the future in the soil
  Of noble deeds of life or art.
He hopes who knows the future's hours
  Will be all clear and sweet and
    bright—
Because he feels that precious flowers
  Of joy must bloom from seeds of right.

A BOOK OF DREAMS.

IN the gathering evening's purple shade
  We sat alone, and the shadows came
Like loving spirits, and touched and
    played
  O'er her fair hair's gleaming and
    golden flame.

And she read to me from a book of
    dreams
  Where a poet's heart had been poured
    away,
And a great life's starshine lent its
    beams
  To a glory grand as the soul of day.

And the lofty words and the thoughts
    sublime
  Seemed then to quiver and to re-
    joice,
As their meaning melted to fitting
    rhyme
  In the tender music of her sweet
    voice ;
And the spirit secrets of life and love
  That the dreamer told in her mystic
    wise,
Were with me and speaking, around
    and above,
  And deep in the blue of my dear
    love's eyes.

But she, ah, never, perhaps, she'll
    know
  What dreams gave answer to those
    she read,
How a heart's deep passion and bitter
    woe
  Gave echo in sobs to the words she
    said.
How a soul's deep love and a heart's
    wild want
  Went dreaming away, where the
    angels sing,
Where Fancy finds in the secret haunt
  Of Longing a Hope that is like a
    wing.

She'll never know how the azure beams
  Of her dear eyes sent me to foolish
    sleep,
How her words awakened the legion
    dreams
  That dwell in the heart and its inner-
    most deep ;
How passions and splendors and kisses
    rained
  From the clouds of the sleeping in
    tendrous wise,
Till my soul no longer was bruised and
    pained
  As in waking hours of life it lies.

Till heaven and stars and the morning's gate
And wild, sweet pinions of joy were mine,
And I looked in the soul of the world and Fate
And talked with the glories that are divine.
Till Love and Life and the sacred thrill
Of Fate and Genius were all my own,
And the wings of my brave enfranchised Will
Drooped only before the eternal throne.

She little knows how the years of love.
The years of the love that was all in vain
Were lost in a glory that came to prove
That beauty must follow the hell of pain.
How, rising and rising along the sound
Of her voice's glory, my heart was given
To look in the eyes of the joys around,
In the groves and the gardens of God in heaven.

Aye, dreams she read me, and never knew
That nobler dreams were before her spread,
A fairer page for the eyes of blue
And a poem grander than all she read ;
That a living volume of dreams was there,
Which she alone could have read aright
Had the gold of her heart been like her hair,
And her soul as true as her eyes that night.
—Howard Hawthorne M'e e.

THE LEVEL AND SQUARE.

We meet upon the Level and we part upon the Square ;
What words of precious meaning those words Masonic are !
They fall like strains of melody upon our listening ears,
As they've sounded hallelujahs to the world three thousand years.

We meet upon the Level, though from every station brought—
The monarch from his palace and the peasant from his cot ;
For the king must drop his dignity when knocking at our door,
And the peasant is his equal as he treads the Checkered floor.

We act upon the Plumb—'tis the order of our Guide,
Upright we walk in virtue's way and lean to neither side,
To the All-Seeing Eye above this truth is clearly shown,
That we still try to honor God and give each man his own.

We part upon the Square, for the world must have its due,
We mingle with the multitude, a faithful band and true,
But the influence of our gatherings in memory is green,
And we long upon the Level to renew the happy scene.

There's a World where all are equal—we are hurrying toward it fast.
We shall meet upon the Level there, when the gates of death are passed ;
We shall stand before the Orient, and our Master will be there,
Our works to try, our lives to prove, by His own unerring Square.

When we meet upon the Level there we never shall depart ;
There's a mansion—'tis all ready for each trusting, faithful heart,
And an everlasting welcome from the host rejoicing there,
Who have met upon the Level and been tried upon the Square.

Let us meet upon the Level, then, while laboring patient here,
Let us meet and let us labor, though the labor is severe ;
Look, in the West the evening shadows bid us quick prepare
To gather up our working tools and part upon the Square.

Hands round, then, faithful Brotherhood, join in the golden chain—
We part upon the Square below to meet in Heaven again;
Each link that has been broken here shall be united there,
And none be lost around the Throne who've acted on the Square.
—ALBERT PIKE.

BETTER THAN GOLD.

BETTER than grandeur, better than gold,
Than rank and title, a thousandfold,
Is a healthy body and mind at ease,
And simple pleasures that always please.
A soul that another's joy can know,
A heart that can feel for another's woe,
With sympathies large enough to enfold
All men as brothers, is better than gold.

Better than gold is a conscience clear,
Though toiling for bread in humble sphere,
Doubly blest with content and health,
Untried by lusts and cares of wealth,
Lowly living and lofty thought
Adorn and ennoble a poor man's cot,
For mind and morals in nature's plan,
Are the genuine tests of a gentleman.

Better than gold is the sweet repose
Of the sons of toil when their labors close,
Better than gold is the poor man's sleep,
And the balm that drops on his slumbers deep,
Bring sleeping draughts to the downy bed
Where luxury pillows its aching head.
The toiler a simple opiate deems
A shorter route to the land of dreams.

Better than gold is a thinking mind,
That in the realms of books can find
A treasure surpassing Australian ore,
And living with the great and good of yore,
The sage's lore and poet's lay,
The glories of empires passed away;
The world's great dream will thus unfold
And yield a pleasure better than gold.

Better than gold is a peaceful home
Where all the fireside characters come,
The shrine of love, the heaven of life,
Hallowed by mother, or sister, or wife.
However humble the home may be,
Or tried with sorrow by heaven's decree,
The blessings that never were bought or sold,
And centre there, are better than gold.
—BY FATHER RYAN.

DRIFTING IN THE DARK.

I DRIFT across a midnight sea,
 The sail hangs hopeless from the mast;
And on the windward and the lea
 The long, black waves are creeping past.

The stars, the holy stars, no more
 Greet hopefully my anxious eye;
For ebon clouds are drifting o'er,
 In countless hosts, the blessed sky.

No beacon glimmers from the shore,
 If shore there be, or far, or near;
If on the rocks the breakers roar,
 'Twere sweeter sound than none to hear.

I strain my ear and long and vain,
 To hear the restless buoy-bell toll;
I only hear the pelting rain,
 And see the sullen waters roll.

But hark! There comes a mellow tone,
 Sweet, long and low; dies and swells,
And swells and dies, as it were blown,
 From some far place where sorrow dwells.

Oh, can it be the harbor bell—
 The harbor bell my prayer has sought?
Or Siren's songs whose fatal spell
 In music's sweetest strains is wrought?

I ask in vain, I do not know,
 God grant the night may soon be done!
Perchance the dawning day may show
 The harbor smiling in the sun.
—CHRISTIAN REGISTER.

PLAYIN' CHECKERS.

There's lots o' fun in winter time when
    woods is full o' haze
An' the blue smoke comes a-curlin'
    where the cabin fires blaze;
When the squirrel shakes the hick'ry
    nuts that tumble fur an' free;
But the best fun's playin' checkers by
    the chinyberry tree.

That takes you back to summer time—
    the village heaves in sight,
The sun a-silverin' the leaves an' burnin'
    'em with light!
The whole town roun' the grocery store,
    a-lookin' on to see
The boys a-playin' checkers by the
    chinyberry tree!

A pine box was the table—what they
    shipped the dry goods in;
It was kinder hacked an' whittled, but
    as 'riginal as sin!
With the "board" marked out in pencil,
    just as plain as plain could be,
For the boys that played the checkers
    by the chinyberry tree.

I use to stand an' watch 'em—jest a boy,
    with ragged hat,
Suspenders made o' cotton, an' me
    wearin' one at that!
It was most as good as swimmin', or as
    flyin' kites to me
To watch 'em playin' checkers by the
    chinyberry tree!

The Mayor come out to see 'em, an' the
    marshal left his beat;
The preacher, kinder solemn-like, come
    walkin' down the street
An' half fergot his sermons of salvation
    full and free,
As he watched that game o' checkers
    by the chinyberry tree!

You could hear the birds a-singin' in
    the meadows fur away.
The whistle o' the partridge an' the
    wranglin' o' the jay;
An' the trains rolled to the station jest
    as noisy as could be;
But they kept on playin' checkers by
    the chinyberry tree!

I guess they're still a-playin', though
    the years has rolled away,
An' the boy that loved to watch 'em is
    a-gettin' old an' gray;
But I see the light still shinin' on the
    meadow lands o' Lee,
An' in dreams I'm playin' checkers by
    the chinyberry tree!
        —Frank L. Stanton.

A NOTE OF HOPE.

Country's growin brighter,
    Hearts are feelin' lighter;
Everything is boomin' right along;
    Skies were never bluer;
    Friendship never truer,
And all the world melodious with song!

There is less of grieving;
    Hope is ever weaving
Rainbows when the tempest passes by;
    Stars with brighter shining;
    Sweeter roses twining;
And heaven, after all, not very high!
        —Constitution.

THE MYSTICAL RIVER.

There's a mystical river in the far-
    away
And it borders an unknown land,
And countless throngs, though un-
    aware,
Are walking along the strand.

A little child is drawing near,
    On the brink she takes her stand;
With a puzzled look in her serious eyes,
    As she watches a beckoning hand.

But a sweet voice calls, "Come over
    my child,"
She starts—and pauses no more,
But fixes her sweet eyes on the shadowy
    form
That stands on the other shore.

But hark! Hear that shriek that
    startles the air,
And there—tremblingly—stands a
    man,
With horror and fear in his eyes, as he
    looks
Across the unknown land.

Then 'tis o'er. A woman now slowly
  comes forth,
  Most slowly—and falters oft',
While dim eyes gaze as if to pierce
  The mystic veil. Then soft

A voice falls on the evening air,
  " And the weary are at rest,"
Then a sweet smile steals across her
    face,
  As she sinks to the river's breast.

Some sweet day in the far-away
  We'll all cross that shining strand,
And pass over the Mystical River of
    Death,
  And explore that Unknown Land.

"Where the wicked cease from trou-
    bling "
  And the world-worn soul opprest,
Will be lightened of all its burden,
  " And the weary will be ' at rest.' "
                    —NELLIE WOMACK.

DEATH.

A SPECTRE stood at my right hand,
  With aspect grim and drear,
Methought it said, " Come, quit this
    land,
  Thy dwelling is not here.
Thy home was built ere thou wast born,
  Or felt the throb of life ;
No sorrow there, no need to mourn,
  No more this endless strife."

Methought it breathed a clammy breath
  Upon my throbbing heart,
And coldly whispered, " I am Death !
  In life thou hast no part.
Come to thy home, I am the key—
  Thy master ; thou—my slave !
The worms and I thy friends shall be
  And share with thee—the grave."

Methought I gave a weary sigh,
  My eyes closed firm and fast ;
Yet weak'ning brain sent forth one cry :
  " Death ! Bring you peace at last ? "
My pulses stopped, slept then my mind,
  Became my being soul,
No sense remained of any kind,
  And Time had ceased to roll.
                    —NELLIE BLY.

WANTED.

A BARBER to shave the face of the earth.
A bed for the tick of a clock.
A timekeeper for a mill race.
A sure cure for a pig's stye.
A carpenter to put a roof on a water-shed.
A charter for a snow bank.
Agent to handle the spice of life.
Some one to spin a mountain top.
A tonsorial artist to shampoo the head of a river.
A detective to unravel a grass plot.
A doctor to cure a window pane.
An audience to see a horse fly.
A nurse-maid to rock the cradle of the deep.
A key to a fire lock.
A comb for a tow head.
A singer who can reach the high seas.
A man to find traces of a lost harness.
A lawyer to try a watch case.
A tailor to take the measure of a suit for libel.
A signal language for dumb waiters.
Some use for a dog's pants.
A pair of handcuffs for procrastination, " the thief of time."
A hand to go with an arm of the sea.
A necklace for a neck of land.
A pump for a well spring of information.
Some buttons for a coat of paint.
A commander to take charge of a courtship.
A machine to thrash " wild oats."
A harness-maker to build a harness for a night mare.

BEAUTIFUL THINGS.

BEAUTIFUL faces are those that wear—
It matters little if dark or fair—
Whole-souled honesty printed there.

Beautiful eyes are those that show,
Like crystal panes where heart fires
    glow,
Beautiful thoughts that burn below.

Beautiful lips are those whose words
Leap from the heart like the song of
  birds,
Yet whose utterance prudence girds.

Beautiful hands are those that do
Work that is earnest, brave, and true,
Moment by moment the long day
  through.

Beautiful feet are those that go
On kindly ministries to and fro—
Down lowliest ways, if God wills so.

Beautiful shoulders are those that bear
Ceaseless burdens of homely care
With patient grace and daily prayer.

Beautiful lives are those that bless—
Silent rivers of happiness,
Whose hidden fountains but few many
  guess.
—EXCHANGE.

ANTONY AND CLEOPATRA.

I AM dying, Egypt, dying,
  Ebbs the crimson life-tide fast,
And the dark Plutonian shadows
  Gather on the evening blast.
Let thine arms, O Queen, enfold me,
  Hush thy sobs and bow thine ear,
Listen to the great heart secrets,
  Thou and thou alone must hear.

Though my scarr'd and veteran legions
  Bear their eagles high no more,
And my wreck'd and scattered galleys
  Strew dark Actium's fatal shore.
Though no glittering guards surround
  me
  Prompt to do their master's will,
I must perish like a Roman,
  Die the great Triumvir still.

Let not Cæsar's servile minions
  Mock the lion thus laid low;
'Twas no foeman's arm that fell'd him,
  'Twas his own that struck the blow.
His, who pillowed on thy bosom,
  Turned aside from glory's ray;
His, who drunk with thy caresses,
  Madly threw a world away.

Should the base plebeian rabble
  Dare assail my name at Rome,
Where my noble spouse, Octavia,
  Weeps within her widow'd home,
Seek her; say the gods bear witness—
  Altars, augurs, circling wings—
That her blood with mine commingled
  Yet shall mount the throne of kings.

As for thee, star-eyed Egyptian,
  Glorious sorceress of the Nile,
Light the path of Stygian horrors,
  With the splendors of thy smile.
Give the Cæsar crowns and arches,
  Let his brow the laurel twine,
I can scorn the Senate's triumphs
  Triumphing in love like thine.

I am dying, Egypt, dying;
  Hark! the insulting foeman's cry,
They are coming! quick, my falchion,
  Let me front them ere I die.
Ah! no more amid the battle
  Shall my heart exulting swell;
Isis and Osiris guard thee!
  Cleopatra, Rome, farewell.
—GEN. WILLIAM HAINES LYTLE,
  U. S. A.

WE'S TWINNIES.

ROGER and I,
  We's twinnies!
When God opened up a bit of blue sky,
To let one little boy-angel by,
There was two slipped out, and that's
  just why
  We's twinnies!

Roger has blue eyes, and I has black,
Papa was going to send me back,
Mamma cried so, when he took that
  tack,
  We's twinnies!

More little dresses had to be made,
Two little chairs set out in the shade,
Two little childrens to be afraid,
  We's twinnies!

Papa comes home quick every night.
Roger's is left knee, mine is right,
We squeezes him up most awfully tight,
  We's twinnies!

And my wrecked and scattered galleys
Strew dark Actium's fatal shore.

CALIFORNIA

We puts our arms round his neck, just so,
He says he don't want to see us grow,
Won't be so cute when we're men, you know
　　We's twinnies!
　　　—ELIZABETH CHERRY HAIRE, *in Womankind.*

IN MEMORIAM.

DEAD!
And yet each moment of the day,
I feel your presence every way!
To me you are not dead, dear one—
Your life and mine have just begun!
If I am sad, if anxious care
Shadows my joy; if everywhere
Darkness appears—if not one star
Brightens my path anear, afar,
I need but feel that you are here
And grief gives way to you, my dear!
You're leading me, you know the way;
I'm nearer you each day, each day!

DAYS GONE BY.

OH the days gone by! Oh the days gone by!
The apple in the orchard and the pathway through the rye;
The chirrup of the robin and the whistle of the quail,
As he piped across the meadow, sweet as any nightingale;
When the bloom was on the clover and the blue was in the sky,
And my happy heart brimmed over, in the days gone by.
In the days gone by, when my naked feet were tripped
By the honeysuckle's tangles, where the water lilies dipped,
And the ripple of the river lipped the moss along the brink,
Where the placid-eyed and lazy-footed cattle came to drink,
And the tilting snipe stood fearless of the truant's wayward cry,
And the splashing of the swimmer, in the days gone by,
Oh the days gone by! Oh the days gone by!
The music of the laughing lip, the lustre of the eye;

The childish faith in fairies, and Aladdin's magic ring,
The simple, soul-reposing, glad belief in everything,
When life was like a story, holding neither sob nor sigh,
In the olden, golden glory of the days gone by.
　　　—JAMES WHITCOMB RILEY.

FATE.

Two shall be born the whole wide world apart,
And speak in different tongues and have no thought
Each of the other's being, and no heed;
And these o'er unknown seas to unknown lands
Shall cross, escaping death, defying wreck;
And, all unconsciously, shape every act
And bend each wandering step to this one end;
That one day out of darkness they shall meet
And read life's meaning in each other's eyes.

And two shall walk some narrow way of life
So nearly side by side that, should one turn
Ever so little space to right or left,
They needs must stand acknowledged face to face,
And yet, with wistful eyes that never meet,
With groping hands that never clasp, and lips
Calling in vain to ears that never hear,
They seek each other all their weary days
And die unsatisfied—and that is Fate!

YESTERDAY.

'TIS now alas, beyond recall,
　Lament it as we may,
No more around our feet shall fall,
　The light of yesterday.
It came as other days have come,
　Its smiles were kindly shed,
But, oh, its blossoms in our wake,
　Lie withered now and dead.

No sighs can breathe away our guilt
  Or bid the past return ;
If we have idly sown or failed
  This solemn truth we learn :
That every yesterday whose wreck
  Bestrews life's checkered way
Has worn amid the fleeting now,
  The raiment of to-day.

Then pluck each moment e'er it dies,
  The present is thine own,
But, oh, the future's hidden light
  Belongs to God alone.
Be thoughtful now ; to wisdom's son
  Give thou a ready ear,
'Twill make each yesterday a charm
  And save to-morrow's tear.

Each common deed our hands perform,
  Though small the act may be ;
Each thought unuttered in the soul,
  Lives on immortally.
It springs into a welcome flower
  To deck life's clover lea,
Or adds a cheerless thorn to swell
  The waste of memory.
        —L. L. KNIGHT.

SOME DAY.

"SOME day, somehow !" The hour is dead
  When I looked into loving eyes,
And kissed the whispering lips that said
  These words to me. And if the ties
Then made are broken ; if the breast
  Then warm with life, is pulseless now,
I still will think that God knows best,
  That we shall meet some day, somehow,
Until that time I still shall know
  That whereso e'er in Heavenly care
That pure and radiant soul may go,
  My thoughts may follow. Everywhere
I'll hear that voice so low and sweet,
  Just as I seem to hear it now ;
I'll hear the fall of fairy feet,
  I'll hear the words : "Some day, somehow !"
Upon the mantelpiece I see
The picture of a fair, sweet face,
And, though the lips are sealed, to me
  They speak with more than tender grace.

I question not the mystic spell ;
  But hark ! how clear the accents now !
'Tis not the language of farewell,
  'Tis trusting love's "some day, somehow !"
And so I fondly hope 'twill be,
  Not now, but some time ; after life
Is finished and eternity
  Dawns on the soul. The toil and strife
Of time once ended, then comes rest
  Such as we do not dream of now ;
And then will come to me the best
  Of all, my love, some day, somehow !
        —MINNEAPOLIS JOURNAL.

THE lights are growing dimmer—
  The day is nearly done.
I love the golden glimmer,
  From the slowly sinking sun ;
I love the silent shadows
  From the lurid waning west ;
The world is drawing closer
  To a haven sweet with rest.
        —AUBREY HARWELL.

WHAT WIVES ARE FOR.

IT is not to sweep the house and make the beds, and darn the socks, and cook the meat, chiefly, that a man wants a wife. If this is all he wants, hired servants can do that cheaper than a wife. If this is all, when a young man calls to see a young lady, send him into the pantry to taste the bread and cakes that she made ; send him to see the needlework and bed-making ; or put a broom in her hands and send him to witness its use. Such things are important, and the wise young man will quietly look after them.

But what the true man most wants of a wife, is her companionship, sympathy and love. The way of life has many dreary places in it, and he needs a companion with him. A man is sometimes overtaken with misfortune ; he meets a failure and defeat, trials and temptations beset him, and he needs one to stand by and sympathize. He has some stern battles to fight with poverty, with enemies, and with sin, and he needs a woman who, as he puts an arm around her, feels that he has something to fight for, will help him fight; who will put her lips to his ear and whisper words of counsel, and her hand to his heart and impart new inspiration.

All through storm and sunshine, conflict and victory, through adverse and favorable winds—man needs a woman's love. The heart yearns for it. A sister's and a mother's love will hardly supply the need. Yet many seek nothing further than housework. Justly enough, half of these get nothing more. The other half, surprised above measure, obtain more than they sought. Their wives surprise them by giving a nobler idea of marriage, and disclosing a treasury of courage, sympathy and love.

ALONE IN THE GLOAMING.

ALONE in the gloaming! How solemn the hour
When the daylight fades away:
Through shadowland gates, now standing ajar,
Flit phantoms, unknown to the day.

Alone in the gloaming; sadly, I gaze
Through the vista of bygone years:
Adown it its length, weird, appear silhouettes,
Which wring, from my heart, bitter tears.

The pleasures, the joy, beside the deep grief,
Which memory brings back to me—
Are few as the shells, strewn over the beach,
Compared with sands of the sea.

Alone in the gloaming, before me the world—
So nun-like, in mantle of gray—
Silently prays forgiveness of God,
For all evils done through the day.

Alone in the gloaming, the world must wait
Until smiles, sent down from heaven,
By moon and by stars, this message relate—
"Peace! all thy sins are forgiven!"

Alone in the gloaming, the Divine will,
With the world, I silently wait:
And pray that for me, may blessings, oh! God,
Come down through the Beautiful Gate.
—LOUISE MITCHELL.

LOOKING OFF UNTO JESUS.

O EYES that are weary when the heart is all sore,
Look off unto Jesus, and sorrow no more;
The light of his countenance shineth so bright,
That on earth, as in heaven, there need be no night.

Looking off unto Jesus, my ears cannot see
The troubles and dangers that throng about me;
They cannot be blinded with sorrowful tears,
They cannot be shadowed with unbelief fears.

Looking off unto Jesus, my spirit is blest;
In the world I have turmoil, in Him I have rest;
The sea of my life all above me may roar,
When I look unto Jesus I hear it no more.

Looking off unto Jesus, I go not astray;
My eye is on Him, and He shows me the way.
The path may seem dark as He leads me along,
But following Jesus I cannot go wrong.

Looking off unto Jesus, my heart cannot fear;
Its trembling is still when I see Jesus near;
I know that His power my safeguard will be,
"For why are ye troubled?" He saith unto me.

Looking off unto Jesus, O may I be found,
When the waters of Jordan encompass me round;
Let them bear me away in His presence to be—
'Tis but seeing Him nearer whom always I see.

Then, then shall I know the full beauty and grace
Of Jesus, my Lord, when I stand face to face;
I shall know that this love went before me each day,
And wonder that ever my eyes turned away!
—Exchange.

ORIGINAL WORDS OF "DIXIE."

They differ materially from the song as it is usually sung.

THE enduring popularity of "Dixie" is not confined to any one section of the country. It is as well known in New England and the northwest as it is in "Dixie Land."

There have been many versions of "Dixie." But few have seen the original. Following are the lines of the song as it was originally written, taken from an old magazine:

I wish I was in de land ob cotton,
Old times dar am not forgotten;
   Look away, look away, look away,
     Dixie land.
In Dixie land, whar I was born in,
Early on one frosty mornin',
   Look away, look away, look away,
     Dixie land.
Den I wish I was in Dixie.
Hooray! hooray!
   In Dixie land I'll took my stand,
   To lib an' die in Dixie.
   Away, away, away down South in Dixie;
   Away, away, away down South in Dixie.

Old missus marry "Will de weaber;"
William was a gay deceaber;
   Look away, etc.
But when he put his arms around 'er
He smiled as fierce as a forty-pounder;
   Look away, etc.
Den I wish I was in Dixie, etc.

His face was as sharp as a butcher's cleaber,
But dat did not seem to greab 'er;
   Look away, etc.
Old missus acted de foolish part,
And died for de man who broke her heart;
   Look away, etc.
Den I wish I was in Dixie, etc.

Now here's a health to de next old missus,
And all de gals dat want ter kiss us;
   Look away, etc.
But if you want to drive away sorrow,
Come and hear dis nig to-morrow;
   Look away, etc.
Den I wish I was in Dixie, etc.

Dar's buckwheat cakes and Ingen batter,
Makes you fat or a little fatter;
   Look away, etc.
Den hoe it down and scratch your grabble,
To Dixie's land I'm bound to trabble;
   Look away, etc.
Den I wish I was in Dixie, etc.
   —*From the* NEW YORK TIMES.

UNTO the editor's room he went,
                        bliss;
                    with
            stairs
        up
    strode
He
An interview, a word or two,
He
   came
      down
          stairs
             like
                this.
      —SYRACUSE POST.

WHAT A HORSE WOULD SAY IF HE COULD.

DON'T hitch me to an iron post or railing when the mercury is below freezing. I need skin on my tongue.

Don't leave me hitched in my stall at night with a big cob right where I must lie down. I am tied and can't select a smooth place.

Don't compel me to eat more salt than I want by mixing it in my oats. I know better than any other animal how much I need.

Don't think because I go free under the whip that I don't get tired. You would move up if under the whip.

Don't think because I am a horse that iron-weeds and briars won't hurt my mouth.

Don't whip me when I get scared at the street cars, or I will expect it next time, and may make trouble.

Don't trot me up hill, for I have to carry you and the buggy and myself too. Try it yourself some time. Run up hill with a big load.

Don't keep my stable very dark, for when I go out into the light my eyes are injured, especially if snow be on the ground.

Don't say whoa, unless you mean it. Teach me to stop at that word. It may check me if the lines break and save a runaway and a smash-up.

Don't make me drink ice water nor put a frosty bit in my mouth. Warm the bit by holding it a half minute against my body.

Don't forget to file my teeth when they get jagged and I cannot chew my food. When I get lean it is a sign my teeth want filing.

Don't ask me to "back" with blinds on, I am afraid to.

Don't run me down a steep hill for if anything should give way I might break your neck.

Don't put on my blind bridle so that it irritates my eye, nor so leave my forelock that it will be in my eyes.
—Our Dumb Animals.

WE MAY BE HAPPY YET.

Yet take good heart, though tempests lower,
And thy bright hopes all fade away,
Faith still exerts the gracious power,
To gild with radiance each day ;
So, take good heart—God reigns above—
His sun can neither wane nor set,
Let nature grow in grace and love—
We may be happy yet.

What though dark clouds obscure the light,
And sunny hours of day are past ;
What though the sable-shrouded night,
Is closing in all nature fast ;
We who have loved through doubts and fears,
And ne'er gave ear to sad regret,
Shall find some solace for our tears—
We may be happy yet.

What though unhappy years have past,
Since vows were laid on love's pure shrine,
Though severed wide, we meet at last,
Beyond the stormy verge of time ;
Now spirit-forms seem waiting near,
And their soft whisperings linger yet,
Though earth's sweet flowers are dead and sere,
We may be happy yet.

The stars that gem heaven's azure dome,
In whispers low speak peace to me ;
They tell of a delightful Home,
Across life's heaving, storm-tossed sea ;
And though on earth we meet with loss
Of kindred hearts, whom we have met,
We need not harbor thoughts morose—
We may be happy yet.

Ay, by the wandering birds that find
A home beyond the rolling wave,
Though oft the wind and storm combine,
To swallow them in some dark grave ;
By summer suns, that bright arise,
Through seas of tears, in which they set ;
By love's unfailing prophecies—
We may be happy yet.
—Luther G. Riggs.

THE SONG I NEVER SING.

As when in dreams we sometimes hear,
A melody so faint and fine,
And musically sweet and clear,
It flavors all the atmosphere

With harmony divine.
So, often in my waking dreams
I hear a melody that seems
Like fairy voices whispering
To me the song I never sing.

Sometimes when brooding o'er the years
My lavish youth has thrown away.
When all the glowing past appears
But as a mirage that my tears
Have crumbled to decay,
I thrill to find the ache and pain
Of my remorse is stilled again,
As forward bent and listening,
I hear the song I never sing.

A murmuring of rhythmic words,
Adrift on tunes whose currents flow
Melodious with the thrill of birds,
And far-off lowing of the herds
In lands of long ago.
And every sound the truant loves
Comes to me like the coo of doves,
When first in the blooming fields of spring,
I heard the song I never sing,

The echoes of old voices wound
In limpid streams of laughter where
The river Time runs bubble-crowned
And giddy eddies ripple round
The lilies growing there.
Where roses, bending o'er the brink,
Drain their own kisses as they drink.
And ivies climb and twine and cling
About the song I never sing.

An ocean surge of sound that falls
As though a tide of heavenly art
Had tempested the gleaming halls
And crested o'er the golden walls
In showers upon my heart.
Thus, with open arms and eyes
Uplifted toward the alien skies,
Forgetting every earthly thing,
I hear the song I never sing.
—JAMES WHITCOMB RILEY.

A GOOD PRAYER.

THY will be done. This is the prayer of every Christian. It is a lesson of a lifetime. It cannot be learned too soon. So we must keep repeating it from day to day and from year to year. Every repetition ought to deepen the impression made upon the heart, that God's will, not ours, is the thing to be done. Many a time we say, "Thy will be done on earth as it is in heaven," when we don't really mean it or understand fully what it means. How cheerfully those parents said in their morning prayer, "Thy will be done." At evening time, when a loved one has been taken away, how hard to feel submission to the very thing they prayed for in the morning! "Thy will be done" is easily said when everything is bright and cheerful in all our relations in the world; but when the beautiful flower is taken to bloom in a better land, far from the disturbing winds and storms of this life, it is hard to say, "The Lord gave, and the Lord hath taken away; blessed be the name of the Lord." But to say it in faith shows the Christian spirit that is childlike. There is a trust in God's wisdom and goodness and love expressed in this that is most honoring to him, and full of solace to a bleeding heart.

CHEAP PLEASURES.

DID you ever study the cheapness of some pleasures?" asks a writer. "Do you know how little it takes to make a multitude happy? Such trifles as a penny, a word, or a smile do the work. There are two or three boys passing along—give them each a chestnut, and how smiling they look, they will not be cross for some time. A poor widow lives in the neighborhood, who is the mother of a half-dozen children. Send them a half peck of sweet apples, and they will be happy. A child has lost his arrow—the world to him—and he mourns sadly; help him to find it or make him another, and how quickly the sunshine will play over his sober face. A boy has as much as he can do to pile up a load of wood; assist him a few seconds, or speak a kind word to him, and he forgets his toil and works away without minding it. You employ a man, pay him cheerfully, and speak a pleasant word to him, and he leaves your house with a contented heart, to lighten up his own hearth, with smiles and gladness. Pleasure is cheap. Who will not bestow it liberally? If there are smiles, sunshine and flowers about us, let us not grasp them with a miser's fist and lock them up in our hearts. No, rather let us take them and scatter them about us, in the cot of the widow, among the groups of children, in the crowded mart, where men of business congregate, in our families and elsewhere. We can make the wretched happy, the discontented cheerful, the afflicted resigned, at an exceedingly cheap rate. Who will refuse to do it.

KISS HER AND TELL HER SO.

You've a neat little wife at home, John,
 As sweet as you wish to see;
As faithful and gentle-hearted,
 As fond as wife can be;
A genuine home-loving woman,
 Not caring for fuss or show;
She's dearer to you than life, John,
 Then kiss her and tell her so.

Your dinners are promptly served, John,
 As likewise your breakfast and tea;
Your wardrobe is always in order,
 With buttons where buttons should be;
Her house is a cosy nest, John,
 A heaven of rest below;
You think she's a rare little treasure;
 Then kiss her and tell her so.

She's a good wife and true to you, John,
 Let fortune be foul or fair;
Of whatever comes to you, John,
 She cheerfully bears her share.
You feel she's a brave true helper,
 And perhaps far more than you know,
'Twill lighten her end of the load, John,
 Just to kiss her and tell her so.

There's a cross-road somewhere in life, John,
 Where a hand on a guiding stone
Will signal one "over the river,"
 And others must go on alone.

Should she reach the last milestone first, John,
 'Twill be comfort amid your woe,
To know that while loving her here, John,
 You kissed her and told her so.

GOD'S ACRE.

I LIKE that ancient Saxon phrase, which calls [is just;
 The burial ground God's Acre! It is just;
It consecrates each grave within its walls, [ing dust.
 And breathes a benison o'er the sleep-

God's Acre! Yes, that blessed name imparts [have sown
 Comfort to those, who in the grave
The seed, that they have garnered in their hearts, [their own.
 Their bread of life, alas! no more

Into its furrows shall we all be cast,
 In the sure faith, that we shall rise again [angel's blast
At the great harvest, when the arch-
 Shall winnow, like a fan, the chaff and grain.

Then shall the good stand in immortal bloom,
 In the fair gardens of that second birth; [perfume
And each bright blossom mingle its
 With that of flowers, which never bloomed on earth.

With thy rude ploughshare, Death, turn up the sod, [we sow;
 And spread the furrow for the seed
This is the field and Acre of our God,
 This is the place where human harvests grow!
  —HENRY W. LONGFELLOW.

THE OLD LODGE ROOM.

YES, the old lodge room, and who does not remember it, whether he is a member of any lodge or not? In every town the Masons, the Odd Fellows and other orders have had their halls and buildings, and how curiously and mysteriously you viewed them when a boy? About Masonry, especially, you had heard so much of "riding the goat," "climbing the greasy pole," and all that, that you had all kinds of weird and curious conceptions of both the Masons, and their lodge rooms. Your father was a Mason and an Odd Fellow, perhaps, yet you wondered if he was quite the same man up there, as he was at home and elsewhere? What did he do, and why did the Masons not leave the goat-riding and pole-climbing to their boys, were questions that puzzled your youthful mind. Occasionally they would meet in the old lodge room, and then you would watch those going in, and wonder if they were all Masons? Somehow you had a peculiar respect for those that went in, and you boys would get out your marbles and pretend to be at play close by, but all the time watching out for "the man with the sword," and trying to hear something from within! Once in a while some good man of the neighborhood would die, and how they would get together in the old lodge room and rap and knock; then put on white gloves and curious collars, and march down to the house where he died! Some would carry the Bible, square and compass, some carry long black sticks with crape on them, while the man with the sword was always on hand. You wondered what he had the sword for, and if that Bible was like other Bibles? When they buried the man that died, how they would strike a doleful bell, and how they would march around the grave, and drop pieces of green cedar in it, and throw up their hands, and say something about the Widow's Son. You wondered what it all meant, and if everybody that died were Widow's Sons!

After it was all over, and they had returned to the old lodge room, you somehow gazed at the old hall with wondering admiration and drew a conclusion that Masons were funny people, and that it all must mean something.

Perhaps you have since found out what it all meant, and that the old lodge room is dearer to you now than ever. Perhaps not; yet, around it are surely hallowed memories to all, and although in your case, it has only been a short while ago, your experience has been but a repetition of that of other boys almost

since time began. For it may be known when many of the Orders were founded, but in the language of the ancients, Masonry existed so long, in some form, that the knowledge of man "runneth not to the contrary." It is certain that in the days of Solomon the boys were viewing the old lodge room with like admiration and curiosity. And the necessity of the order, no matter how ancient its lodge rooms, was for a good and noble purpose, and even higher importance to the ancients than to the Masons of the present day.

It has, at all times, been a recognized fact that men require something higher and more binding upon them than the ordinary laws of the land, and which man-made and conflicting creeds do not satisfy. Men, who have no other principles but the fear of the civil law, find thousands of ways for evading its penalties. And, with the ancients, when their laws were few—often unjust, and frequently severe—without the temper of mercy, and often enforced by the iron hand of tyrants, the great Equity Court of Masonry was found to be a necessity for the promotion of simple justice, morality and true religion.

The criminal laws of all lands were, and are, for punishment only. Those of Masonry were, and are, for mercy, charity and reform. The laws of the land still are for the apprehension of open criminals, and apply to corporeal, rather than to mental, punishments. Those of Masonry appeal and apply to the mind and better nature, and inflict their penalties before, as well as after, the commission of the offence, when the individual's conscience is his jury and his God, his judge,

Almost every country has its peculiar laws, and although its subjects are presumed to know them, the fact is that it is an assumption, and a presumption, only. Love and duty are the well-known and universal laws of Masonry, the Fatherhood of God and the Brotherhood of man its dominion, and faith, hope and charity its simple code. Regardless of the changing laws of man, its edicts are those of the Grand Master, the Celestial Lawgiver of All.

There is beauty in the forest,
Where the trees are green and fair.

Page 53.

and all who assume the responsibilities of that Fathership and Brotherhood are required to meet on the same Level, to act upon the same Plumb, and to part upon one universal Square ; thus leaving their spirits, acts and deeds to be passed upon by the courts above, from which there is no appeal, and by the the Judge who knows the heart, as well as the laws by which it is judged.

It is no wonder, then, that an order with this record and code has challenged the respect and admiration of the world for its lodge rooms. It is no wonder that the boy of to-day relives and reacts the life of his fathers, and adds new links in the chain of love and devotion for the old lodge room. It is no wonder that the dear old lodge room, with all these associations clinging about it, finds a tender spot in all hearts, adds to the honor of being called a Mason, and makes every man, however bad, better by being one.

MY DAUGHTER'S LEARNED TO COOK.

We used to have old-fashioned things,
    like hominy and greens,
We used to have just common soup,
    made out of pork and beans ;
But now it's bouillon, consomme, and
    things made from a book,
And Pot au Feu and Julienne, since my
    daughter's learned to cook.

We used to have a piece of beef—just
    ordinary meat,
And pickled pigs' feet, spareribs, too,
    and other things to eat ;
While now it's fillet and ragout, and
    leg of mutton braised,
And macaroni au gratin and sheep's
    head Hollandaised ;
Escallops á la Versailles—á la this and
    á la that,
And sweetbread á la Dieppoise—it's
    enough to kill a cat !
But while I suffer deeply, I invariably
    look
As if I were delighted 'cause my daughter's learned to cook.

We have a lot of salad things with dressing mayonnaise,
In place of oysters, Blue Points fricasseed a dozen ways.
And orange Roley Poley, float and peach meringue, alas,
Enough to wreck a stomach that is made of plated brass !
The good old things have passed away in silent, sad retreat ;
We've lots of highfalutin' things, but nothing much to eat.
And while I never say a word and always pleasant look,
You bet, I've had dyspepsia since my daughter's learned to cook.
        —Court Challiss.

THE WORLD IS FULL OF BEAUTY.

There is beauty in the forest,
    Where the trees are green and fair ;
There is beauty in the meadow
    Where wild flowers scent the air ;
There is beauty in the sunlight,
    And the soft, blue beam above ;
O ! the world is full of beauty
    When the heart is full of love !

There is beauty in the fountain,
    Singing gayly at its play,
While rainbow hues are glittering
    On its silvery shining spray ;
There is beauty in the streamlet,
    Murmuring softly through the grove ;
O ! the world is full of beauty
    When the heart is full of love !

There is beauty in the moonlight
    When it falls upon the sea,
While the blue, foam-crested billows
    Dance and frolic joyously ;
There's beauty in the lightning gleams
    That o'er the dark waves rove ;
O ! the world is full of beauty
    When the heart is full of love !

There is beauty in the brightness
    Beaming from a loving eye ;
In the warm blush of affection ;
    In the tears of sympathy !
In the sweet, low voice whose accents
    The spirit's gladness prove !
O ! the world is full of beauty
    When the heart is full of love !

WHERE THE RIVER FLOWS.

There's music that dwells in the heart
    of the stream,
And a mystery breathes in its flow,
For I often look back, and sometimes a
    gleam
Of the castles I've built will flit to
    and fro,
    And fade
        Where the river flows.

And I've dreamed as I've watched it go
    flowing along
That a beautiful fairyland lay
Afar, in the mist of the hills where its
    song
Is born, and I've dreamed that some
    day
    I'd find
        Where the river flows.

Now I've travelled along by the river
    for years,
Till I've come close down to the sea,
And I've found there is laughter born
    often from tears,
Like the songs that rise from the
    mists, maybe,
    That float
        Where the river flows.

But there are tears, sometimes, ere the
    laughter dies;
There's a woeful shake of the head;
For some pass down where the water
    sighs,
And all pass out with the dead
    To the sea
        Where the river flows.
      —Walter M. Hazeltine.

A PRAYER OF THE HEART.

O God, lean downward to my couch
    this night—
This awful night of nights—and hear
    the prayer
That fain would struggle up the
    startled air,
To vex Thine ear, from my lips dumb
    and white
With pain. Lean down from heaven's
    own delight,
And lay Thy listening ear to my throat
    —where
The passionate words stop, voiceless
    in despair.
God, Thou canst hear and understand
    aright
All that my tortured heart would ask of
    Thee.
Put out the fires that leap along my
    veins,
And bids this beating of my pulses
    cease!
Take, take these maddening dreams
    away from me
And cool my eyes with tears like
    gentle rains. . . .
Hear Thou my wordless prayer!
God give me peace!
      —Ella Higginson.

HER NAME.

"I'm losted! Could you find me,
    please?"
Poor little frightened baby!
The wind had tossed her golden fleece,
The stone had scratched her dimpled
    knees,
I stooped and lifted her up with ease,
    And softly whispered a "Maybe!"

"Tell me your name, my little maid,
    I can't find you without it."
"My name is Shiney-Eyes," she said,
"Yes, but your last?" She shook her
    head,
"Up to my house 'ey never said
    A single fing about it."

"But, dear," I said, "what is your
    name?"
"Why, didn't you hear me tell you?
Dust Shiney-Eyes." A bright thought
    came:
"Yes, when you're good; but when they
    blame
You, little one—is't just the same
    When mamma has to scold you?"

"My mamma neber scolds," she moans,
    A little blush ensuing.
"'Cept when I've been a-frowing stones,
And then she says" (the culprit owns),
"Mehetable Sapphira Jones,
    What have you been-a-doing?"

"COME UNTO ME."

Oft when the tide of life runs low,
And brain and soul are sick with doubt,
And life seems full of grief and woe,
And mocking devils jeer and flout,
I turn unto my Lord in prayer;
I know His strength than mine is best,
And lo! A sweet voice thrills the air—
  "Come unto Me, ye weary laden,
    And I will give you rest."

Sometimes the night is very dark,
The way is rough and wounds my feet,
And life lies stretched out wan and
    stark,
The winds blow fierce and falls the
    sleet;
I fear, and fearing fain would fall
Beneath the shadows' dire distress,
But that I hear my Saviour call—
  "Come unto Me, ye weary laden,
    And I will give you rest."

And often when the waters roll
And surge and foam around me here,
And threaten to engulf my soul,
Roaring and rolling swift and near,
My strongest efforts seem in vain.
How can I 'scape, so hard oppressed?
And then I hear that voice again—
  "Come unto Me, ye weary laden,
    And I will give you rest."

Some days my burden bears me down,
I cannot see the far-off skies,
The grim, gray cross obscures the
    crown,
And in my heart hope faints and dies,
But leaps to life when, sweet and low,
With love and mercy full expressed,
These words across the silence go—
  "Come unto Me, ye weary laden,
    And I will give you rest."

Yea, Lord, I come to Thee in all
The evils that afflict my day,
And at Thy feet repentant fall,
For doubts that daunt and fears that
    slay
Give unto me, O give me more,
The strength to bear, the longing best,
Extend Thy shield my face before,
  For I indeed am weary laden,
    And come to Thee for rest!
          —Hamilton Jay.

THE GOOD OLD THINGS.

We used to have old-fashioned things,
  like hominy and greens;
We used to have just common soup,
  made out of pork and beans;
But now it's bouillon, consomme, and
  things made from a book,
And Pot au Feu and Julienne, since
  my daughter's learned to cook.

We used to have a piece of beef—just
  ordinary meat,
And pickled pig's feet, spareribs, too,
  and other things to eat;
While now it's fillet and ragout, and
  leg of mutton braised,
And maccaroni au gratin, and sheep's
  head Hollandaised.

The good old things have passed away,
  in silent, sad retreat;
We've lots of high-falutin things, but
  nothing much to eat.
And while I never say a word, and always pleasant look,
You bet I've had dyspepsia since my
  daughter's learned to cook.
          —Good Housekeeping.

A LIFE STORY.

He is too young to know it now;
But some day he will hnow.
          —Eugene Field.

Above her little sufferer's bed,
  With all a mother's grace,
She stroked the curly, throbbing head,
  And smoothed the fevered face.
"He does not know my love, my fears,
  My toil of heart and hand;
But some day in after years,
  Some day he'll understand;
    Some day he'll know
    I loved him so,
  Some day he'll understand."

A wild lad plays his thoughtless part
  As fits his childhood's lot,
And tramples on his mother's heart
  Oft times and knows it not.
He plays among his noisy mates
  Nor knows his truest friend;
His mother sighs, as still she waits,

"Some day he'll comprehend;
　　The day will be
　　When he will see,
Some day he'll comprehend."

The strong youth plays his strenuous
　　part;
　His mother waits alone,
And soon he finds another heart
　The mate unto his own.
She gives him up in joy and woe,
　He takes his young bride's hand,
His mother murmurs, "Will he know
　And ever understand?
　　When will he know
　　I love him so;
　　When will he understand?"

The strong man fights his battling days,
　The fight is hard and grim,
His mother's plain, old-fashioned ways
　Have little charm for him.
The dimness falls around her years,
　The shadows 'round her stand,
She mourns in loneliness and tears,
"He'll never understand,
　　He'll never know
　　I loved him so;
　　He'll never understand."

A bearded man of serious years
　Bends down above the dead,
And rains the tribute of his tears
　Over an old, gray head.
He stands the open grave above,
　Amid the mourning bands;
And now he knows his mother's love,
　And now he understands.
　　Now doth he know
　　She loved him so,
　And now he understands.
　　　　—SAM WALTER FOSS.

SOMETIME, SOMEWHERE.

SOMETIME, somewhere, in the eternal
　　plan,
　Will come a good to offset every ill,
As Nature's book is balanced; so to
　　man
　A balance perfect come there must
　　　and will;

This, then, our solace, when the way
　　is dark
　And only sorrows we are told to
　　share;
As came God's sunshine to the storm-
　　tossed Ark,
　'Twill come to us, sometime, some-
　　where.

Sometime, somewhere, in this world or
　　the next,
　And in some way, a perfect equipoise
Will come to souls by troubles now
　　perplext,
　And all our griefs find compensating
　　joys;
Go on, brave heart! if doing what you
　　can,
　Life's burdens, as they come, to fully
　　bear
Fear not! the justice that is due a man
　Will all be yours sometime, some-
　　where.
　　　　—CHARLES S. O'NEIL.

"THE FAMILY CLOCK."

IT has stood on the shelf this many a
　　year,
　Ticking the time away,
In the humble home where I was born
　In the flowery month of May.
It has stood like a faithful monitor
　Of family joys and cares,
Like the timepiece known in deathless
　　song,
"The old clock on the stairs."

It has witnessed scenes of joy and mirth
　Around the festive board,
When the deepening shadows fell a-
　　round,
　And the winds of winter roared.
But under the glow of the evening lamp,
　Warm hearts beat glad and free,
With never a thought of grief to come,
　Under the old roof-tree.

Its holds more secrets than I can guess,
　Or ever may hope to pen,
As it measures time with its friendly
　　hands
　Over and over again;

As it ticks away in its sheltered nook,
  With the same untroubled face,
One hasn't the heart to spy around,
  And the vanished past retrace.

What the future may have in store for us
  The family clock may know ;
Let us hope for the best as we used to do
  In our dreams of long ago.
When our friend on the shelf dealt out
    the hours
  Of childhood rare and sweet,
And the smiling earth looked beautiful
  In her bridal robes complete.

It is only a common thing, I know,
  Yet to me it is more dear
Then the famous clock in Strasburg
    town,
  That is noted far and near.
Though friends have met and friends
    have gone
  From my humble home to-day,
The family clock still holds its own,
  Ticking the time away.

MY SWEETHEART.

To me there is no other girl
  Half so dear as she,
Who always comes at eventide
  And sits upon my knee.
There's laughter in her sparkling eyes,
  There's sunshine in her hair ;
Of all the maidens that I know,
  Not one is half so fair.

Without her life would be to me
  Not half so sweet as now ;
And to her will, whate'er it be,
  Submissively I bow.
Whene'er she smiles my heart leaps up
  And throbs with fierce delight ;
Her tears, for me, whene'er they flow,
  Turn daytime into night,

I've loved her now for seven years,
  Since first I saw her face,
And to this maid each year has brought
  A new and charming grace.
What wonder, then, that I rejoice
  Whene'er this girl draws near,
And whispers when she kisses me :
  " I love you, papa, dear ! "
    —Trenton State Gazette.

THE MEN WHO LOSE.

Here's to the men who lose !
What though their work be e'er so nobly
    planned
  And watched with zealous care,
No glorious halo crowns their efforts
    grand ;
  Contempt is failure's share.

Here's to the men who lose !
If triumph's easy smile our struggles
    greet,
  Courage is easy then ;
The king is he who, after fierce defeat,
  Can up and fight again,

Here's to the men who lose !
The ready plaudits of a fawning world
  Ring sweet in victor's ears ;
The vanquished's banners never are un-
    furled—
  For them there sound no cheers.

Here's to the men who lose !
The touchstone of true worth is not suc-
    cess ;
  There is a higher test—
Though fate may darkly frown, onward
    to press,
  And bravely do one's best.

Here's to the men who lose !
It is the vanquished's praises that I
    sing,
  And this the toast I choose :
" A hard-fought failure is a noble
    thing,
  Here's luck to those who lose."
    —George H. Broadhurst.

APART WITH GOD.

Apart with God—how beautiful the
    thought
  From cares of earth to win such sweet
    release ;
To lay aside the vexing task, half-
    wrought,
  And by the green, o'ershadowed path
    of peace
Seek the white star-altar that the saints
  have sought.

Oh! precious is the quiet place of prayer,
  Where heaven and earth, where God
    and mortal meet;
To that dear spot come neither pain nor
    care,
And all about is like a garden sweet,
The flowers whereof shed healing on
    the air.

There, brother, bring your trial's vexing
    thorn,
  And God shall pluck it out and give
    you rest.
There bring your sin, and He whose side
    was torn
Shall cleanse your soul to be His pal-
    impsest,
New-written as your spirit is new-born.

None is forbid that blest communion—
    none.
  The hands that spanned the cruel
    cross so wide,
Thus would they clasp the troubled race,
    as one
  Lost brother, by love's anguish justi-
    fied,
Come, whosoe'er; behold! you are
    God's son!
           —JAMES BUCKHAM.

WHEN BABY WAS DEAD.

WHEN baby was dead,
And the golden rays of sunlight crept
  Into the quiet room, across the bed
Where he so gently, sweetly slept—
It seemed so strange not to hear him
    coo,
And catch at the light—like he used to
    do!

When baby was dead,
And mother's tear-scorched lips reached
    down
  To kiss the face, the eyes, the head,
And smooth the folds in the little night
    gown,
I would have bartered my soul to hear
    him coo,
And reach up his arms—like he used
    to do!

When baby was dead,
Ah, my God! what a moan was wrung
  From a broken heart as heavy as
    lead—
From lips where a baby song lately
    hung;
Ears strained to catch the tiny, soft coo,
And hear him laugh out—like he used
    to do!

When baby was dead,
I could see no joy in the air of gloom—
  Hope into outer darkness fled!
When God spoke soft through the deso-
    late room
A promise, some day we'd hear him coo,
And see him reach up—like he used to
    do!
          —EDWARD N. WOOD.

ARBITRARY ENGLISH LAN-
  GUAGE.

WE'LL begin with box, and the plural is
    boxes,
But the plural of ox should be oxen, not
    oxes.
The one fowl is goose, but two are
    called geese,
Yet the plural of moose should never be
    meese.
You may find a lone mouse or a whole
    nest of mice,
But the plural of house is houses, not
    hice.
If the plural of man is always called
    men,
Why shouldn't the plural of pan be
    called pen?
The cow in the plural may be called
    cows or kine,
But a bow if repeated is never called
    bine,
And the plural of vow is vows, never
    vine.
If I speak of a foot and you show me
    your feet,
And I give you a boot, would a pair be
    called beet?
If one is a tooth and a whole set are
    teeth,
Why shouldn't the plural of booth be
    called beeth?

If the singular's this and the plural is these,
Should the plural of kiss ever be nicknamed keese?
Then one may be that and three would be those,
Yet hat in the plural never be hose,
And the plural of cat is cats, not cose.
We speak of a brother and also of brethren,
But though we may say mother we never say methren.
Then the masculine pronouns are he, his, him,
But imagine the feminine she, shis and shim.
So the English, I think, you all will agree,
Is the greatest language you ever did see.
—COMMONWEALTH.

CHANGES.

WHOM we first love, you know, we seldom wed.
  Time rules us all. And life, indeed, is not
The thing we planned it out ere hope was dead.
  And then, we women cannot choose our lot.

Much must be borne which it is hard to bear:
  Much given away which it were sweet to keep.
God help us all! who need, indeed, His care,
  And yet, I know, the Shepherd loves His sheep.

My little boy begins to babble now
  Upon my knee his earliest infant prayer.
He has his father's eager eyes, I know,
  And, they say, too, his mother's sunny hair.

But when he sleeps and smiles upon my knee,
  And I can feel his light breath come and go,
I think of one (heaven help and pity me!)
  Who loved me, and whom I loved long ago.

Who might have been . . . ah, what I dare not think!
We all are changed; God judges for us best,
God help us do our duty, and not shrink,
  And trust in Heaven humbly for the rest.

But blame us women not, if some appear
  Too cold at times, and some too gay and light.
Some griefs gnaw deep; some woes are hard to bear.
  Who knows the past? and who can judge us right?

Ah, were we judged by what we might have been,
  And not by what we are, too apt to fall!
My little child—he sleeps and smiles between
  These thoughts and me. In heaven we shall know all!
—OWEN MEREDITH.

THE OLD HAND PRESS.

BATTERED and shattered,
  With ink all bespattered,
But still with the power to annoy and to bless,
  Loved by the editor,
  Cursed by the creditor,
Rumbling and stumbling—the old hand press!

  Gone are the editors,
  Patient, meek creditors,
Since the far day when it first saw the light.
  Age has but lengthened it,
  Riveted, strengthened it,
Made it a victor in many a fight.

  Stars from their setting fall;
  Men die, forgetting all;
Suns—they may vanish and light may grow less,
  But till Gabriel's horn shall blow,
  Ages unborn shall know
That it's still in the business—the old hand press.
—ATLANTA CONSTITUTION.

ROMANTIC MARRIAGES.

Marriage in the Old World is generally a matter of arrangement; is conducted, more or less financially, on the basis of what is called common sense. Marriage usually results in the New World from personal affinity, from some intense form of emotionalism, independent of material conditions or favoring circumstances. We Americans are more romantic, connubially, than any other people under the sun. We are gradually growing less so as the Republic ages, but we are still inclined to consult our feelings rather than our reason in choosing mates. Romance is an excellent thing in matrimony, but it may be carried too far in determining the question. When it survives matrimony, and is found to be a large ingredient in its composition after years of continuance, it is as beautiful as it is commendable. It is greatly enjoyed by the married, and warmly admired by their intimates. But, as a rule, the less dominant romance is in making a match, the larger is its influence after sobriety has set in. Young persons will seldom believe this, however, and they have to learn it therefore by painful experience. They declare that they love, and love is, in their partial opinion, sufficient warrant for any conjugal enterprise, even in the face of the most adverse fortune. Where love is, faith and hope are, and to the three combined everything desired is possible, and most things certain. They are in a state of ecstasy, and the hard world is moulded and mellowed by their enraptured vision.

They obstinately refuse to accept as true the assurance that wedlock must depend for its outcome on prosaic facts and figures, that it belongs as much to arithmetic as to sentiment; that love itself may not always withstand pinching penury and the trials it begets. Those who will tell them so are pronounced doubters and cynics, and their warnings pass like the breeze. Alas! how many couples have discovered, when too late, what terrible prophets those doubters and cynics have proved to be! They would not heed when they should have heeded, and the time has passed for regrets and contritions. But there are always new couples as confident and as obdurate as the old, and there will be while the years go on. Such couples are convinced beyond refutation that hearts and pulses that leap together are an earnest of the future, and a solid ground for co-operative housekeeping. Secular knowledge teaches otherwise. Leaping hearts and pulses guarantee nothing except their capacity to leap. And they often leap to no purpose, and on very slight provocation. Young men and women frequently wed without means and without prospects, without self-understanding and without forethought, yet never rue their precipitance or imprudence. But far more frequently they so wed and the result is grievous and irremediable. Not necessarily, either; not from discordant temperament or lack of individual adaptation, but from dire poverty and the ceaseless friction and irritability it involves. Those can hardly be healed, these might at least have been guarded against, might have been taken into account, which they never are when excessive romance defies the judgment.

—JUNIUS H. BROWNE, *in Harper's Bazar.*

MY MOTHER'S SONG.

When the thrushes cease their singing,
   and the wild bees leave the clover;
When the glory of the sunset fades,
   and leaves the heavens pale;
When above the hill and mountains
   misty shades of twilight hover,
And the discords of the daytime far
   away in distance fail;

When the ripe wheat gently rustles,
   and the timid aspens shiver,
And the west wind sighing softly,
   scent from sleeping flowers bring;
When the peewits cry together plaintively by the brook and river—
Then it is I hear the old song that my mother used to sing.

Round my neck I feel the pressure of
   her fingers warm and slender,
As in sleeping dreams and waking I
   have felt it many times,
Just as when of old I listened to that
   ditty, quaint and tender,
Till the boughs that waved above us
   caught the cadence of the rhymes ;

And my heart throbs loud and quickly
   as I hear it rising clearer ;
Youth is mine, its hopes and visions,
   dreams and plans are mine again ;
Earth is fairer, life is sweeter, ay, and
   heaven itself seems nearer
To me, as I list in fancy to that ne'er-
   forgotten strain.
                    —M. ROCK.

W'EN MA'S AWAY.

W'EN ma's away it seem's though
Th' sky gits dark an' folks must know
At sump'n's wrong ; an' nen it's chill
An' dreary home—th' house is still
An' creepy-like—
   We'en ma's away.

W'en ma's away they ain't no fun ;
I jest set roun' an' can't eat none,
An' feel my heart begin t' sink
At all th' accidents I think
Has happened sure—
   W'en ma's away.

W'en ma's away up to that place
Where nary angel's got a face
'S kind 's her's I b'leeve I'll die
An' foller her, 'cause I can't try
An' live alone—
   W'en ma's away.
              —ARTHUR CHAPMAN.

LEAD THOU ME ON.

"LEAd Thou me on," though hoping in
   the arms of doubting sleeps,
While 'cross the weary highway the
   deep'ning night time creeps—
The gleams of future promise will fill
   my drooping heart,
If Thou but lead me gently, the clouds
   of gloom will part !

"Lead Thou me on," my footsteps are
   stumbling, weak and drear,
'Midst thorns and bitter sweetness,
   'midst sorrow's burning tear ;
But o'er the aches and weeping comes
   a kiss of sweetest balm—
If Thou but lead me gently, the storms
   of life will calm !

"Lead Thou me on"—when softly
   clings the cloak of ending day,
When things I've loved aforetime, and
   lost, now fade away ;
"Lead Thou me on," when sleeping
   casts its arms around my soul,
And lead me gently, gently where life's
   billows cease to roll!
              —EDWARD N. WOOD.

A MISTAKE OFTEN MADE.

BOYS and young men sometimes start out in life with the idea that one's success depends on sharpness and chicanery. They imagine, if a man is able always to "get the best of the bargain," no matter by what deceit and meanness he carries his point, that his prosperity is assured. This is a great mistake. Enduring prosperity cannot be founded on cunning and dishonesty. The tricky and deceitful man is sure to fall a victim, soon or late, to the influences which are forever working against him. His house is built on the sand, and its foundation will be sure to give way. Young people cannot give these truths too much weight. The future of that young man is safe who eschews every phase of double dealing, and lays the foundation of his career in the enduring principles of everlasting truth.

LATTER DAY PREACHING.

I'M that disgusted, Sally Ann, in this
   here latter day,
About the way the preachers preach, I
   don't know what to say.
They've mighty nigh forsook the book
   when seekin' for a text,
An' goodness knows, fer I do not, what
   fad they'll take up next !

They use to preach of Jesus Christ,
  who died to save mankine,
But now they sermonize of things on
  quite another line.
The differ'nt "parties" they come in to
  be discussed and cussed,
An' now an' then a word is said of some
  "combine" or "trust."

The "World's Fair," was a common
  text, on which they all could soar—
From local preachers to D.D.'s—high
  in the heavens, shore!
An' if I ain't considerably off, I heard
  one once explain
"The 'fects of free love on the race,"
  an' how it proves a bane.

I guess they git the textes from the new
  translation, wife,
They may be good to p'int the way to
  the eternal life;
But then the old sweet words that tell
  God's kineness an' His love,
Have more effect to draw my thoughts
  to mansions up above!

HOW BEAUTIFUL.

How beautiful is rest,
After the long and wearying days of
  care,
When motionless the fervid summer
  air,
To feel that toil and striving all are
  done,
To watch the fields and hills at set of
  sun,
Type of that land by every nation blest—
  How beautiful is rest!

How beautiful is sleep:
After the fever leaves the throbbing
  veins,
To close the eyes tended by fond love's
  pains,
And 'neath the shadows of the earthly
  streams
To gently glide into the land of dreams,
Where memory and fond youth their
  visions keep—
  How beautiful is sleep!

How beautiful is love—
The heart that beats in sympathy with
  thine,
The smile that lights the earth with rays
  divine,
The song that soothes the soul in pain
  and woe,
The hand that clasps thine own when
  hot tears flow,
The tender tone, like music from above,
  How beautiful is love!

How beautiful is hope—
When breaking storm-clouds show the
  blue sky rifts,
After the snow melts and the vapor lifts,
When spring returns, and the white
  dove draws near
To dwell with us, type of the Spirit dear,
When rainbow arches crown life's moun-
  tain slope—
  How beautiful is hope!

How beautiful was peace,
When brothers met in strife that foes
  abhor,
On crimson fields of internecine war—
When fond hearts bled far o'er a shud-
  dering land,
While brave souls fled to join the seraph
  band—
When triumph tones proclaimed that
  war might cease—
  How beautiful was peace!

How beautiful is death!
After all care and pain and toil are o'er
To close the eyes upon this earthly shore,
Followed by memories of undying love,
Welcomed by guardian angels from
  above,
How tranquil to resign this laboring
  breath,
  How beautiful is death!
    —BOSTON TRAVELLER.

THE OL' BARLOW KNIFE.

THE long, long years have not effaced
  One bright hour of the past,
An' the mem'ry of that happy time
  I'll hang to 'til the last.

If I should mount the heights of wealth
  Beyond all sordid strife,
I'll not forget when dad bought me
  A bran' new Barlow knife.

I'd had the ager till I'd all
  But shook away my life,
An' dad, to get me swoller pills,
  Brought home that Barlow knife.
I seized it, pressed it to my heart,
  And to the woods, I strayed,
And there I read, 'ith bulgin' eyes,
  These signs—X C D—on the blade.

I never owned much property—
  Perhaps I never will—
A wife an' kids an' an ol' blind hoss
  Will 'ist about fill the bill—
'Cept a dog an' gun—but you
  Kin bet your precious life
I'd give the whole blame shootin' match
  For that 'ere Barlow knife.

O, time, turn back! O, days, return!
  If but for one brief hour!
An' let me be a tow-head boy
  An' feel agin the power
Of that good feelin' that I felt—
  The best in all my life—
When I set an' hummed an' whittled 'ith
  My bran' new Barlow knife!
          —CHICAGO HERALD.

FRANK L. STANTON.

THERE'S a feller down in Georgy, in ol'
  Atlanta town,
As is the best blamed song-bird in all
  them parts aroun';
The robin jes' ain't in it, an' ez fer the
  mockin' bird—
This feller down in Georgy beats the
  best one ever heard.

I never seed the feller, but they say he
  ain't so tall
Ez some folks what try awful hard, but
  jes' can't sing a tall;
He sings to us of meaders an' violets
  an' brooks,
An' bout the goodest fishin'-place an'
  cosy country nooks.

An' then he'll get so solemn-like an' sing
  of death an' sich,
An' make ez though he'd kilt a man—
  now, gee whiz! ain't that rich!
When I read his "dull" pieces, I'm sad,
  an' yet I laugh,
Fer I know his heart's so tender he
  couldn't kill a calf.

His "Summer-time in Georgy" is the
  piece I like the best;
But all his songs is good un's, an' I'm
  stuck on all the rest.
But his "Summer-time in Georgy" jes'
  makes yer feet keep time,
An' fills yer soul jes' plum chuck full of
  music, good an' prime.

An' talk about yer constancy—in love
  affairs, an' that—
Why he don't kere no more fer it 'n he
  does fer sayin' scat!
Fer every time he turns aroun' he loves
  a different girl,
An' tells about their feet an' eyes an'
  pretty hair in curl.

He'll talk 'bout lovin' Jenny, then switch
  off onto May—
An' the one he loves the best? I don't
  bl'eve he knows to-day—
But he ain't to blame fer that, fer its jes'
  a way o' his;
An' lovin' girls is proper—yer bet yer
  life it is!

But singin' 'bout his country life is Stan-
  tonses bes' holt,
An' when yer read them pieces yer feel
  spry, jes' like a colt,
But when he goes to singing 'bout not
  goin' back to Lea,
I don't know if he cries or not—I know
  how it 'fects me.

It's awful good of Stanton to sing jes'
  like he do,
An' make bad people better an' make
  'em good an' true.
He is jes' a natchul singer—he's got to
  sing or bust!
An' he'll keep on singin' till he "turneth
  back to dust."
          —JOHN D. SPENCER.

UNCLE EPH'S HORSE TRADE.

[Aunt Susan sends Uncle Eph to town to sell the cow. Meeting Farmer Johnson with a dun mule he makes a trade.]

UNCLE EPH.

"Come out hyah, Thomas 'Rastus, an' see wut daddy got—
Woa dar, you long-eared debbil, yo' legs too full ur trot!

Git out de way, you chillen, he mighty full ur fiah,
His mammy wus ur Mo'gan, ur jackus wus his siah.

Stop dat, you Gineral Jackson! (De voodoo's in dis mule!)
Say, chillen, whar yo' mammy? (I spec' I bin ur fool.)

Ob cose he summat spavin' an' stone blin' in one eye,
An' de ha'r all off in places—dat come a' right bimeby.

(Fo' de Lawd, dar Susan—now how I gwine ter 'splain
Urbout dis debblish hoss-trade—hit gwine go 'ginst de grain.)

Des look ur hyah, ol' 'oman, I's traded off de cow;
You bet I made ur bawgin an' dat youse boun' ter 'low.

De cow was mighty scrawny an' den she mos' was dry;
De price ur hay am risin'—dar's no green in my eye.

I met ol' Fa'mah Johnsing ur ridin' inter town,
I 'sarbed dis mule's fine action an' axed the gempmun down.

I led him foruds, backuds—his action mighty free,
His mouf I zaminated—his age des tirty-tree.

An' den I make ur offah—de cow fur Johnsing's mule.
He cussed urroun' ur little—I nebber wus ur fool.

So Johnsing dribe de cow off, wur kalin' doan' you see,
W'ile I come home ur ridin' ez big ez big kin be.

Des watch him trot, ol' 'oman, dat motion's Mo'gan true—
Fine blood gwine tell in muleses ez well ez hosses, too.

I needs him fur de plowin' w'en gyardenin' time come 'roun'
My back done got rheumatics an' I cyawn' spade de groun'.

SUSAN.

"You call dem bones ur hoss trade? You allus wus ur fool!
Tuck my cow an' traded fur ur knoc'-kneed, spavin' mule!

Dat blood do tell in mulesses; hit tells in niggahs mo'—
De Browns wus allus triflin,' an, Efrum, youse mo so.

I wucked ha'd all lars' summah w'en you wus loafin' roun'.
Spen'in' yo' lars' nickel in dem dramshops in de town.

Ur sweatin' an' ur gruntin' in dat ol' washin' tub
Ter buy dat Jussey heffah an' keep you all in grub.

Des come ur little closah, your triflin' lim' ob Ham!
Oom hoo! I smell de liquah. I knowed you hed ur dram.

You long-legged, tu'key-trottin,' black, good-fur-nothin' fool—
Ur tradin' off my heffah fur yo' match —ur spavin' mule!

Ef I des hed hot watah, I'd scal' you bofe, I 'clar;
You ringbone, knoc'kneed, triflin', ol' saddle-culled pa'r!

Des clam back in dat saddle an' fo' dat sun go down,
You hunts up ol' man Johnsing ez sho's yo' name am Brown,

An' gits dat Jussey heffah—I doan' cyah how hit's done ;
You tu'ns her in dat back ya'd urfo' de risin' sun !"

And Ephraim and the dun mule of Morgan blood descent,
Went galloping down the red road for Farmer Johnson's bent.

At five o'clock next morning, when the Shanghai rooster crowed,
The yellow Jersey heifer in Susan's back-yard lowed !
—JAMES EDWIN CAMPBELL.

COUNTRY EDITORS.

YOU say they ain't a set of men we care so much about ?
Unless we're after office—they're then the greatest out ?
An' when we want a little puff about our mules an' corn,
They're right convenient fer our use, the dullest of us l'arn !

Zeke Scobo said that he would bet the lizards on his fence
Wus smart as av'rige editors—of greater consequence ;
But when he sought to raise a school an' found the people glum,
An' had to wake 'em up with print— the editor was some !

An' Pokey Mason, he has preached agin 'em long an' loud,
An' swore the kit-an'-bilin' was a poor an' worthless crowd ;
But when he seed in print, the piece writ when his mother died
He's kind o' changed and come out squar' 'an holds to t'other side.

No sort o' 'sociation, seems, can move without the aid
Of them thar scrubby creeters now, 'at scribbles in the shade ;
An' as fer charity, I think it's formed a big combine
To never budge till editors shall come an' fall in line !

An' so the whole way round—'tis good fer country or fer town
To have a editor or two to boom or hold 'em down ;
An' blamed if I ain't one 'at holds to this opinion pat—
The feller 'at discounts the quill is crippled 'neath his hat.
—WILL T. HALE.

ACCOMPLISHED GIRLS.

A GIRL should learn to make a bed
To bake good biscuit, cake and bread ;
To handle deftly brush and broom,
And neatly tidy up a room.

A girl should learn to darn and mend,
To care for sick, the baby tend ;
To have enough of style and taste
To trim a hat or fit a waist.

A girl should learn to value time,
A picture hang, a ladder climb,
And not to almost raise the house
At sight of a little harmless mouse.

A girl should learn to dress with speed,
And hold tight lacing 'gainst her creed ;
To buy her shoes to fit her feet ;
In fact, above all vain deceit.

A girl should learn to keep her word,
To spread no farther gossip heard,
Home or abroad to be at ease,
And try her best to cheer and please.

A girl should learn to sympathize,
To be reliant, strong and wise ;
To ever patient, gentle be,
And always truly womanly.

A girl should learn to fondly hold
True worth of value more than gold ;
Accomplished thus with tender mien,
Reign, crowned with love, home's cherished Queen.
—NEW ORLEANS PICAYUNE.

DEFINITION OF HOME.

A PRIZE was offered by the London Tit Bits for the best answer to the question, "What is Home?" Here are a few of the answers which were received:

The golden setting, in which the brightest jewel is "mother."

A world of strife shut out, a world of love shut in.

Home is the blossom, of which heaven is the fruit.

The only spot on earth where the faults and failings of fallen humanity are hidden under the mantle of charity.

The place where the great are sometimes small and the small often great.

The father's kingdom, the children's paradise, the mother's world.

The jewel casket, containing the most precious of all jewels—domestic happiness.

Where you are treated best and you grumble most.

Home is the central telegraph office of human love, into which run innumerable wires of affection, many of which, though extending thousands of miles, are never disconnected from the one great terminus.

The centre of our affections, around which our heart's best wishes twine.

A little hollow scooped out of the windy hill of the world, where we can be shielded from its cares and annoyances.

O, PROMISE ME!

O, PROMISE me when shadowy sorrow
  Glooms dark upon life's leaden skies
On some forlorn and cheerless morrow
  The light of promise dawns and dies;
That though the world may all forsake me,
  Upon time's sombre, sunless sea,
Whatever grief may overtake me,
  I still may put my trust in thee!

O, promise me, when tears are falling
  Like rain upon life's sodden lea,
With waves of wold regret recalling
  The dreams of all I longed to be;
That thy sweet spirit may uphold me
  While saddening surges sweep the shore,
Thy constancy will still unfold me
  In loving kindness evermore!

O, promise me when faith is falling
  And shades of doubt are gathering fast,
And I can hear the woeful wailing
  Of dismal death's soul-chilling blast,
That thy dear eyes will shine upon me,
  Thy gentle hand will clasp my own,
And in the strength thy love hath won me
  That dark path I may tread alone!

O, promise me when all have perished,
  Ambition and its dazzling dreams,
Wild aspirations I have cherished,
  High hope and all its thousand themes;
That thou wilt keep thy pledge unbroken,
  Remembering through grief or glee,
Wi h every tender tie and token—
  O, promise me, O, promise me!
    —MONTGOMERY M. FOLSOM.

YEARS and years he spent at college,
Filling up his head with knowledge,
Learning Hebrew, Latin, Greek,
Growing wiser week by week;
But one thing he did not learn—
How his daily bread to earn.
Now his time he does employ
Hunting for a job, poor boy.
    —KANAS CITY JOURNAL

KEEP GOD ON YOUR SIDE.

THROUGH sorrow and anguish,
  Through trial and pain,
Or when joy sheds her brightness
  Like bountiful rain,
Whatever your station,
  Whatever betide,
In your Zionward journey
  Keep God on your side.

Put your resolute shoulder
  In time to the wheel,
And in life's urgent battle
  Be worthy your steel.
Be kindly, be honest,
  Be void of false pride,
And thus may you daily
  Keep God on your side.

As you cross over Jordan
  With billows cold,
As you near the great city
  Whose streets are of gold,

All sin may be vanquished,
All terror defied,
And your spirit triumphant
With God on your side !
—Mrs. M. A. Kidder, *in N. Y. Weekly.*

THE HASTY WORD.

To think before you speak is so wise an axiom that one would hardly think it needful to emphasize it by repetition. And yet in how many cases the hasty temper flashes out in the hasty word, and the latter does its work with the precision and the pain of the swift stiletto ! Singularly enough, the hasty word oftenest wounds those who love one another dearly, and the very closeness of their intimacy affords them opportunity for the sudden thrust. We know the weak points in the armor of our kinsman and our friend ; we are aware of his caprices, and ordinarily are tender and compassionate even of his vanities and small fancies and whims ; but there dawns a day when it is written in the book of fate that we shall be as cruel as we are loving. We are cold, or tired, or hungry. We are anxious over unpaid bills, or our expected letters have not arrived, or one of the children is ailing, and we dread the outcome of the malady. So politeness fails us, fortitude is vanquished, philosophy is in abeyance, and we say that which we repent in sackcloth and ashes. But though the hasty word may be forgiven, it is not at once forgotten. It has flawed the crystal of our friendship ; the place may be cemented, but there is a shadowy scar on the gleaming surface. Oh, if the word of haste had but been left unspoken ; if the strong hand of patience had but held back the sword as it was about to strike !

DRIFTING.

Drifting on the tide of years,
Drifting on 'mid hopes and fears,
Drifting on thro' this world of tears,
   Drifting onward each day.

Drifting away from the springtime of life,
On through the shadows of envy and strife,
Thro' a world with sin and temptation rife,
   Drifting onward each day.

Drifting on thro' sunshine and rain,
Smiling in gladness and moaning in pain,
Seeking balm for our wounds in vain,
   Drifting onward each day.

Drifting onward we weep o'er the bier
Of the loved and lost whom our hearts hold dear,
Adding fresh wounds to our hearts each year,
   Drifting onward each day.

Drifting on to a haven of rest
Where the ties of earth are renewed and blest,
And sealed for aye by Heaven's behest,
   Will drift into port some day.
      —Florence E. Smith.

A STUDENT'S LOVE LETTER.

The apiarist as well we know
  Will always like the B's,
The sailor never will outgrow
  His ardent love for C's.

The millionaire, with pockets full,
  His E's will ever prize.
Coquettish maidens find a joy
  In always making I's.

Surveyors, bound close by chain,
  Must in the L believe,
While preachers look out for the N,
  When one must sing or grieve.

Collectors take care of the O's,
  And farmers of the P's ;
The actors follow up the Q's,
  And ladies loves the T's.

Professors, men of letters grand,
  To all the Y's are true ;
And I, why don't you know, sweetheart,
  That I'm dead struck on U ?

IF I BUT KNEW.

If I but knew that somehow, sometime, I
Had dried one tear that dimmed a brother's eye,
Or slaked the thirst of parching fever's lips,
And led some soul through sorrow's dark eclipse,
Then I should feel life's mission had been true—
  If I but knew.

If I but knew some heart this side the dead
Had felt its burdens fall by what I said,
Or that one life had bloomed in noble deeds
Because I'd sowed somewhere some worthy seeds,
The thought would drive the clouds from o'er life's blue—
  If I but knew.

HOPE.

Hope has the power of soaring with a strong and untiring pinion from all that is dark and drear, into the radiant atmosphere of poetry. It takes us into a world of dreams, and causes the heart to wander amongst visions. It diverts the thought from the real to the ideal, and leads us amongst the picture-gleams of fancy to linger in the fairy realms of art. It hastens us into a visionary world, that we may have dreams of glory, power and fame. It unfolds a dazzling scroll, and shows us engraven on it an immortal name. Its holy task is to exhibit to us, even when care surrounds us, and we are treading along a harsh path, a time of dizzy joys, and to change into bright enchantment the stern realities of actual life. Nor do the strength of its dreams, the nobleness of its desires, and beauty of its thoughts, cease to actuate and influence our hearts even when life grows pale and wanes fast, when we turn our thoughts from earth to heaven, on the couch of sickness and weakness, and when the faint voice and fainter pulse speak in warning whispers of a time to die. It boldly walks along with us, prompting the spirit never to repine from the cradle to the grave.

We all hope. In every one of us that passion finds an object to feed upon. We all form some beautiful—we all sketch some fancy portrait, which we fondly cherish, and hope to find the fair original.—When hope first sheds its influence upon the heart, all one's roving thoughts are concentrated upon one object. A vacuum within is filled, of which we have never before known the extent. Heedless indifference to success in life forsakes one. A new stimulus succeeds; the mind revolves splendid success. All the alluring avenues of fame are spread upon before us. We burn to achieve some arduous enterprise which shall be worthy of the mind of man.

But strong as is the spell of hope to incite and inspire us, equally strong is it to elude and to deceive us. The fraud is sweet, but bitter pain and keen despair await to torment us upon our awaking and finding its chair broken and lying around us in glittering fragments. The heart that trusts the syren smile of hope drinks the most copious draught of pleasure while it grasps its soul-sought treasure; but when the mystic gleam departs, the heart sinks coldly, and too often breaks amidst the world's unkindness.

THE SOUTHERN MAMMY.

In the first dim dawn of Life's long years,
  She cradled the infant frame,
And wistfully watched with many fears
  The fluttering breath as it came.
'Twas mammy guided the toddling feet,
  And caught with its native sound
The name that, prattled in accents sweet,
  Is lisped the wide world round.

To mammy we ran with childish grief,
  And mammy taught us to sew,
As we stitched the hem in her gay 'kerchief,
  With fingers clumsy and slow.

Only a baby,
  Kissed and caressed;
  Gently held to a mother's breast.

Page 89.

To mammy, when clothes we rumpled
    or tore,
(For mother we dared not see,)
And mammy lessened the grievous sore
    Of pain on her generous knee.

We listened when mammy gave counsel
    quaint,
    As the pulse of our hearts beat fast,
"Honey, dars many would pass fur a
    saint
    Is wo'fs in de sheepskin at last."
When we gave to another a closer love,
    And we left the old home roof,
Ah! mammy prayed that the angels
    above
    Would tighten the golden woof.

No tenderer care could ever be known
    To nurture fair childhood's hours
Than doubled the love around us
    thrown
    Like the sun and the rain on flowers;
Nor mattered to us that the spirit's
    fold
    Of mammy was satiny jet,
Her love was pure as alchemic gold,
    And remains with her "chil'un"
    yet!

O, faithful heart! It is passing away—
    The name of those "chil'un" so
    dear,
But memory clings to the earlier day,
    And will cherish your virtues here;
And when Life's current flows swift to
    bear
    Our barque to Death's river, anon—
Among the white hosts of the ransom'd
    there
    Our "*mammy*" *shall beckon us on!*
        —INDA BARTON HAYS.

THE SEVEN AGES.

ONLY a baby,
    Kissed and caressed,
    Gently held to a mother's breast.

Only a child,
    Toddling alone,
    Brightening now its happy home.

Only a boy,
    Trudging to school,
    Governed now by a sterner rule.

Only a youth,
    Living in dreams,
    Full of promise life now seems.

Only a man,
    Battling with life,
    Shared in now by a loving wife.

Only a father,
    Burdened with care,
    Silver threads in dark-brown hair.

Only a graybeard,
    Toddling again,
    Growing old and full of pain.

Only a mound,
    O'ergrown with grass,
    Dreams unrealized—rest at last.
        —BOSTON TRAVELLER.

MR. TOMPKINS ON HIS BOARDERS.

COME, Mandy, get the fly screen out; I
    know they ain't no good—
A healthy fly will sure get in if oncet
    he's said he would.
But we can't take no chances; an' the
    city boarder's queer;
He allus wants his fly screens up while
    he's a-stayin' here.

I think we'd also better get a spinnin'-
    wheel or two,
An' set 'em in the drawin'-room, be-
    cause, 'tween me an' you,
We may get someone here who for
    antique things has a whim,
An' who will pay us twice its cost to
    take it home with him.

An,' by the way, ye'd better buy say
    twenty dozen eggs,
They does 'em up in lime these days an'
    sells 'em out in kegs.
Then every morn' I'll go out an' sort of
    strew 'em round
The coops an' haylofts, where they're
    sure by boarders to be found.

For I have noticed that the folks who
    come up here to stay
Thinks eggs is fresher laid if they have
    found 'em; an' I say,
Pack up the tablecloths, because these
    town folks think that we
Eat off a plain pine table without any
    cloth. Law me!

It makes me laugh to think of 'em.
    They call us "new" an' "green,"
But they're the very verdantest that
    ever I have seen.
An' every year when they come here—I
    know it is a sin—
But, Lord! how we poor country folks
    do take those fellows in!
        —HARPER'S BAZAR.

AN "OUT-OF-DATE" COUPLE.

WE are "so out of date," they say—
    Ned and I;
We love in an old-fashioned way,
    Long since gone by.
He says I am his help-mate true
    In everything;
And I—well, I will own to you
    He is my King.

We met in no romantic way
    'Twixt "glow and gloom;"
He wooed me on a winter day,
    And in—a room;
Yet, through life's hours of stress and
    storm
    When griefs befell,
Love kept our small home-corner warm,
    And all was well.

Ned thinks no woman like his wife—
    But let that pass;
Perhaps we view the dual life
    Through roseate glass;
Even if the prospect be not bright,
    We hold it true
That heaviest burdens may grow light
    When shared by two.

Upon the gilded scroll of fame,
    Emblazoned fair,
I cannot hope to read the name
    I proudly bear;

But happy in their even flow,
    The years glide by;
We are behind the times, we know—
    Ned and I.
    —E. MATHESON, *in Chambers's
      Journal.*

MY LITTLE GIRL.

OF course the little girl was just as
    much of mine as hers,
But somehow when our wedded life got
    full of pricks and burrs
I told her that she'd better take the little
    one and go
And stay a spell at Newton Creek along
    with Uncle Joe,
While I'd go off to some far land, and
    there I'd work and live
Until I'd quite made up my mind which
    one was to forgive.

I tell you pride's an awful thing when
    it gets into the heart;
I guess it was a thousand times I thought
    I'd rise and start
And go right after her, and that little
    maid of mine.
I never heard a word from them. She
    never wrote a line.
Then I had a spell of sickness and
    counted through my tears
And found I had not seen them both
    for more than fifteen years.

Oh, my pretty, laughing darling, she
    must be tall and fair!
How I'd rig her out in ribbons and
    feathers rich and rare!
I could almost feel my fingers upon her
    soft white brow;
That little sunny head of hers would
    touch my shoulder now.
Yet the strangest thing—in all my
    dreams she was a little child,
With the yellow curls of babyhood and
    big eyes, round and mild.

As soon as I was better I started on my
    way
And reached the town at noontime one
    hot and dusty day.

And near by, in the churchyard, I
  stopped to rest and wait,
There was a little baby's grave close to
  the mould'ring gate.
I pushed aside a straggling vine, kind
  o' curious—no more.
Great God, my little girl lay there, dead
  thirteen years before!
   —CLEVELAND PLAIN DEALER.

LAUGH.

LEARN to laugh. A good laugh is better than medicine. Learn how to tell a story. A well-told story is as welcome as a sunbeam in a sick room. Learn to keep your own trouble to yourself, The world is too busy to care for your ills and sorrows. Learn to stop croaking. If you cannot see any good in the world, keep the bad to yourself. Learn to hide your pains and aches under a pleasant smile. No one cares to hear whether you have the earache, headache or rheumatism. Don't cry. Tears do well enough in novels, but they are out of place in real life. Learn to meet your friends with a smile. The good-humored man or woman is always welcome, but the dyspeptic or hypochondriac is not wanted anywhere, and is a nuisance as well.

A LOST LIFE.

OH, for a glimpse of a natural boy,
  A boy with freckled face,
With forehead white 'neath the tangled
  hair
  And limbs devoid of grace,
Whose feet toe in, while his elbows
  flare,
  Whose knees are patched always,
Who turns as red as a lobster when
  You give him a word of praise,
A boy who was born with an appetite,
  Who seeks the pantry shelf
To eat his "piece" with resounding
  smack,
  Who isn't gone on himself.
A Robinson Crusoe reading boy,
  Whose pockets bulge with trash;
Who knows the use of rod and gun,
  And where the brook trout splash.

It's true he'll sit in the easiest chair,
  With hat on his tousled head;
That his hands and feet are everywhere—
For youth must have room to spread,
But he doesn't dub his father "old
  man,"
  Nor deny his mother's call,
Nor ridicule what his elders say,
  Or think that he knows it all.
A rough and wholesome, natural boy,
  Of good old-fashioned clay;
God bless him, if he's still on earth,
  For he'll make a man some day.
   —MRS. BAYNE, *in the Detroit Free Press.*

DO NOT THROW CUDGELS AT YOUR TOWN.

WHATEVER failings you may have, and
  heaven knows all have some,
That they should struggle day and
  night to try and overcome,
Ne'er stand within the market place,
  and as you coldly frown,
With all the strength that you possess,
  throw cudgels at your town.

Do not upon the corners stand and
  openly declare
Her merchants are the meanest men to
  be found anywhere,
For doing so, you only bring upon the
  town disgrace,
Besides, my friend, this is no way to
  build up any place.

What if the town hall is not as large as
  you, perhaps, desire;
The meeting house is over large for the
  height of the spire?
There is a better way, my friend, the
  town's good to advance,
Than throwing cudgels at her head
  whene'er you get a chance.

Do not unceasingly complain about her
  streets and squares,
The failures her officials have, the parson's talks and prayers,
And do not in an endless plaint your
  small opinion give
Of how much better things were done
  where once you chanced to live.

Do not throw cudgels at your town,
    because it is not right,
And if you do the chances are that
    most of it is spite,
If people do not look at things exactly
    as you do,
I would not be surprised to learn that
    the trouble is with you.

If things are not what they should be,
    and ought to be improved,
Roll up your sleeves and go to work,
    and have what's wrong removed:
But let me say, whatever line of action
    you pursue,
Do not destroy what you now have 'till
    you can build anew.
                    —Ex.

THE COUNTRY EDITOR.

THERE is no place so difficult to fill as that of a country editor. In cities a man who can do one department well, bothers himself about none other. Then he gets the knack of his specialty and continues at it. But the country editor must be good in all departments; he must be well read on all subjects; he must be able to discern the trend of the public mind, in politics, religious and social topics, he must discuss agriculture and anarchy with precision; he must be fluent on polemics and politics; he must write of the president and pumpkins; he must mind men of high degree and condescend to things of low estate; in short, he must be an "all around man." It is this that makes the position of a country editor so hard to fill. It is this training that makes the country editor such a splendid manager of a metropolitan daily. There is no place except in a country office, where such all-round training can be had.
                    —PRINTER'S CIRCULAR.

THANKSGIVING ON THE FARM.

YE may talk aboot yer spring time an'
    the merry month o' May,
Er Christmas, ef ye like it best, an' I'll
    not say ye nay;
But ez fer me, no time o' year hez sich
    a subtle charm
Ez Thanksgivin' in November, with the
    ol' folks on the farm.

Thar's dad, he's eighty-five, come June,
    er mebby eighty-six,
But chipper ez a two-year-old to argy
    polyticks;
Et allus does me good an' gives an appetizin' charm
To the stuffin' o' the turkey with the ol'
    folks on the farm.

Then thar's the dear ol' mother, with
    her sweet an' gentle face;
She sez 'taint no Thanksgivin' less her
    boy ez in his place;
An' while she's thar'—why, bless ye,
    'twon't need no other charm
To call me hum Thanksgivin' with the
    ol' folks on the farm.

An' when at night we gather round the
    pine log's ruddy glow,
An' watch the flickerin' shadders o' the
    firelight come an' go,
I dream 'at I'm a boy ag'in, an' life
    takes on a charm
An' lasts till next Thanksgivin' with the
    ol' folks on the farm.
                    —NEW YORK SUN.

WHEN SHE CAME HOME.

THE skies are bluer overhead,
Despite the summer that is dead,
The trees are now a brighter red—
    Since she came home.
Though sighing winds went over land
Of faded gold; though master hand
Gave sweeping touch to harping strings
And wooed the tearfulness of things—
Yet all the wistfulness and pain
That, passing, joined the sad refrain,
Stole sweetly, graciously away
To leave me happy on that day,
    When she came home.

PSALM OF LIFE.

TELL me not, in mournful numbers,
    Life is but an empty dream!
For the soul is dead that slumbers,
    And things are not what they seem.

Life is real! Life is earnest!
  And the grave is not its goal;
Dust thou art, to dust returnest,
  Was not spoken of the soul.

Not enjoyment, and not sorrow,
  Is our destined end or way;
But to act, that each to-morrow
  Find us farther than to-day.

Art is long, and Time is fleeting,
  And our hearts though stout and
    brave,
Still, like muffled drums are beating
  Funeral marches to the grave.

In the world's broad field of battle,
  In the bivouac of life,
Be not like dumb, driven cattle!
  Be a hero in the strife!

Trust no Future, howe'er pleasant!
  Let the dead Past bury its dead!
Act,—act in the living Present!
  Heart within, and God o'erhead!

Lives of great men all remind us
  We can make our lives sublime,
And, departing, leave behind us
  Footprints on the sands of time;—

Footprints, that, perhaps another,
  Sailing o'er life's solemn main,
A forlorn and shipwrecked brother
  Seeing, shall take heart again.

Let us, then, be up and doing,
  With a heart for any fate;
Still achieving, still pursuing,
  Learn to labor and to wait.
      —LONGFELLOW.

AUTUMN'S ARRIVAL.

O SIGNAL service officer—be careful
  what you do!
I've penned an ode on violets and
  honeysuckles, too;
But yesterday thermometers were 80,
  or about;
But now you've changed the business, for
    The
      Cold
        Flag's
          Out!

O signal service officer—be careful how
  you go!
But yesterday I penned an ode a hundred miles from snow;
But yesterday my overcoat the weather
  put to rout,
But now you've changed the business, for
    The
      Cold
        Flag's
          Out!

O signal service officer—just let up for
  a spell!
If you corner all the poets they will give
  the rebel yell!
We write to suit the weather, but you
  leave us all in doubt,
You've killed our autumn roses, for
    The
      Cold
        Flag's
          Out!
            —CONSTITUTION.

TO-DAY.

WAIT not the to-morrow, but forgive
  me now;
Who knows what fate to-morrow's
  dawn may bring?
Let us not part with shadow on thy
  brow,
With my heart hungering.

Wait not the morrow, but entwine thy
  hand
In mine with sweet forgiveness full
  and free;
Of all life's joys I only understand
  This joy of loving thee.

Perhaps some day I may redeem the
  wrong,
Repair that fault—I know not when
  or how,
Oh, dearest, do not wait—it may be
  long—
Only forgive me now.
      —THE ACADEMY.

THE OLD LADY SPEAKS.

JOHN'S in the legislature, and William's
  almost there.
And Richard—he's the sheriff, and
  Rufus he's the mayor;

Josiah takes the taxes—and says they're
  coming high ;
And Tom—he's out for Congress, and
  he'll get there by and by !
Mary married a lawyer, and Jenny is
  the wife
Of a revenue detective, in the moonlight
  of her life ;
And Maggie's being courted by the
  teacher over there,
And Molly's got a general that's almos'
  a brigadier !
And so the girls and boys are placed as
  well as well can be ;
It's a sort of a satisfaction to the old man
  and to me,
To sit here in the old home when the
  twilight shadows fall,
And see the children prosperin', and
  know we raised 'em all !
    —F. L. S.

HER HEART IS TRUE.

HER eyes are not as bright, perchance,
  As other eyes of blue ;
Her hair hath not a golden light,
  Nor cheeks a rosy hue,
But, then, she hath a treasure yet,
  That's far beyond all eyes of jet
Or even bluish tint coquette—
  Her heart is true.

She hath no jewels to adorn
  Her simple gown of blue ;
She hath no royal laces on
  Her gown of simple hue.
She wears a rosebud in her hair,
  Doth my dainty debonnaire,
And they love her everywhere—
  Her heart is true.

Perhaps you think she doesn't shine,
  When in the mazy dance,
With other faces more divine
  And smiles of debutants.
This by no means is the case,
  Her loving heart shines through her
    face,
And all forget the commonplace—
  Her heart is true.
    —AUBREY HARWELL.

FROM THE WORK SHOP "HOME."

A HUNDRED whistles flung their shrill, rasping voices across the city ; there was a lull—a few moments' utter stillness—and then there gradually arose and strengthened a roar of wheels, a beating of many horses' feet, a clanking and a rattling of chains, mingled with men's whistling, laughter, calling and oaths. It was six o'clock, and another day's wearisome toil was over ; another sweet, cool night was leaning her soft bosom to the earth, and soon tired bodies might lie down with outstretched arms and rest, and care-racked minds might lay all burdens and sorrows aside until another sun sailed over the distant mountains. I watched them coming home in twos and threes and fours. The merry, the sad ; the silent, the boisterous ; the good-natured, the surly ; the young and straight, the bent and old ; the man with the cheerful eyes and the one with the sullen brow—I watched them coming home. How gladly now the horses flung out their tired feet in each step that bore them nearer the stable ; how their nostrils swelled out, and their intelligent eyes flashed with eager expectation ! Here and there a dog sat up proudly on the seat beside a lenient master, or ran, leaping and barking for joy, at the horses' heads. The great sun, leaning his round, glowing face on the mountain line, set red gleams to dancing on that long line of dinner-pails, and on picks and shovels standing in the quiet places to rest until the morrow, and he set to flaming like burnished gold the windows of thousands of workmen's cottages—yea, God's own gold which the rich man never can steal from the poor ; and he made, too, the flowing river one moving sheet of hammered brass. Ah, me ! this hurrying, jostling, crowding home when the day's work is done ! It brings the tears to one's eyes to remember how few of them know what the word "home" means. Four walls, a silent supper, a few cold words, and then a lying down to sleep ; a weary rising to another day's toil, and a mad, hurried rush home again at night—and by and

by the end! Ay, the lonely, forgotten, inevitable end! O, how the dead, lying in their dark places, must strain their eyes for the sunlight, and their ears for the bird-voices, and their poor hearts for the love that they slighted on earth. O, you who go home, tired, when the whistles swell loud and shrill across the city, try to remember—just once—that there are tired hands and hopeless hearts waiting in the cottage, too, and that a careless look and a cold word make their burdens harder to bear. O, I wish you would go home to-night with a more cheerful face, and lay a kind, tender hand on the homemaker's arm, and say to her that you love her! It sounds old-fashioned, I know, but it is so little I ask of you—only that you try it once. Don't say it like a sentimental schoolboy, but with a simple, frank manliness that will bring tears to her eyes. Do—do—try it once. For I tell you that when you go "home" for the last time, it will not matter to you how much gold or how many jewels you have, nor how many days you have toiled early and late; but the sweetest thing to you in that hour will be the faithful hand-clasp of one who loves you, and for whom you made—in the tenderer and truer sense of the word—a home.
—ELLA HIGGINSON.

Across each man's pathway passes one woman whom, come good or evil, sorrow or joy, he never forgets to the last day of his life. So, well indeed, is it for him if that woman holds a good influence over him; for though their ways may lie far apart, he will feel her hand reach out to him in every care and burden; and clear as stars her remembered eyes will light him through every temptation.

LINES TO A SKELETON.

BEHOLD this ruin! 'Twas a skull,
Once of ethereal spirit full;
This narrow cell was life's retreat,
This space was thought's mysterious seat,

What beauteous vision filled this spot!
What dreams of pleasure long forgot!
Nor hope, nor joy, nor love, nor fear,
Have left one trace of record here.

Beneath this mouldering canopy
Once shone the bright and busy eye;
But start not at the dismal void;
If social love that eye employed—
If with no lawless fire it gleamed,
But through the dew of kindness beamed—
That eye shall be forever bright,
When stars and sun are sunk in night.

Within this hollow cavern hung
The ready, swift, and tuneful tongue;
If falsehood's honey it disdained,
And where it could not praise, was chained,
If bold in virtue's cause it spoke,
Yet gentle concord never broke,
This silent tongue shall plead for thee,
When time unveils eternity.

Say, did those fingers delve the mine?
Or with its envied rubies shine?
To hew the rock, or wear the gem,
Can little now avail to them.
But if the page of truth it sought,
Or comfort to the mourner brought,
These hands a richer meed shall claim
Than all that wait on wealth, or fame.

Avails it, whether bare or shod,
These feet the depths of duty trod?
If from the halls of ease they fled,
To seek affliction's humble shed;
If grandeur's guilty bribe they spurned,
And home to virtue's cot returned,
These feet with angels' wings shall vie,
And tread the palace of the sky.

THE GAME OF LIFE.

THIS life is but a game of cards,
  Which mortals have to learn;
Each shuffles, cuts, and deals the pack,
  And each a trump doth turn.

Some bring a high card to the top,
  And others bring a low,
Some hold a hand quite flush of trumps,
  While others none can show.

Some shuffle with a practised hand,
  And pack their cards with care,
So they may know when they are dealt,
  Where all the leaders are.

Thus fools are made the dupes of rogues,
  While rogues each other cheat,
And he is very wise, indeed,
  Who never meets defeat.

When playing, some throw out the ace,
  The counting cards to save;
Some play the deuce and some the ten,
  But many play the knave.

Some play for money, some for fun,
  And some for worldly fame,
But not until the game's played out,
  Can they count up their gain.

When hearts are trumps we play for love
  And pleasure rules the hour;
No thoughts of sorrow check our joy
  In beauty's rosy bower.

We sing, we dance, sweet verses make,
  Our cards at random play,
And while one trump remains at top
  Our game's a holiday.

When diamonds chance to crown the top,
  The players stake their gold,
And heavy sums are lost and won,
  By gamblers young and old.

Intent on winning, each his game
  Doth watch with eager eye,
How he may see his neighbor's cards,
  And beat them on the sly.

When clubs are trumps look out for war,
  On ocean and on land;
For bloody horrors always come
  When clubs are held in hand

Last game of all is when the spade
  Is turned by hand of Time,
He always deals the closing game,
  In every age and clime.

No matter how much each man wins,
  Or how much each may save,
The spade will finish up the game,
  And dig the player's grave.

THE CHOICE OF BOOKS.

EMERSON said: "A student's library dwindles down to a few books, the Bible, Plato, and Shakespeare." Horace Greeley, in his "Recollections of a Busy Life," says he had but few books, but those he had he read over and over again in his boyhood, that he went far and near to find a new book to read. Bacon said: "Some books are to be tasted, others to be swallowed, and some few to be chewed and digested." There is an old saying, "The man is known by the company he keeps." A man's books are his company, his consolation and his friend. Teachers and professors will tell very soon whether the students that come before them are out of families who associate with books. It makes a great difference whether students are from homes where books are considered the most essential furnishings in the family, where culture is hereditary, or from pioneer settlements which have not outgrown the hard struggle for livelihood. The culture that comes from books reaches through more than one generation and the inspiration spreads wider than the influence of a single individual. A good book is a perpetual teacher. A man or woman may be false to you, but a worthy book never deceives. There is no doubt that to a real seer, even the very face of a student and genuine lover of books, looks like the spirit of the books that he has read. How could it be otherwise, when the soul always impresses itself upon the body in which it lives? It is the light which shines through the eye in love or hate, in dream or purpose. The thoughts we think, and the feeling which fills our hearts become a part of the blood that courses in our veins.

The poets that we read quicken every impulse, open the eye of the soul in imagination and often unite the heart of the reader to the heart of the poet, as two lives moving on, hand in hand, in one common union of purpose, thinking the same thoughts, feeling with the same sympathy, breathing the common air of love, will grow to look alike.

Just so a sensitive soul becomes like the truth it gathers from the books it reads. Thus it is found from the spirit of each writer, a cosmopolitan in the world of thought and feeling. If a man is known by the company he keeps, the student may well be known by the books he reads. It is a great art to know how to buy books, and a library wisely selected is an evidence of culture and education that no man can borrow or buy. Money may pay for the books and the cases, but that fine instinct and judgment which are found only in the genuine lover of the best in human thought, are a priceless inheritance. To know books is an acquired and cultivated talent. "Good books," said Horace Mann, "are to the young mind what the warm sun and refreshing rain of spring are to the seeds which have lain dormant during the frosts of winter." "A little library growing larger every year is an honorable part of a man's history," said Beecher. "It is a man's duty to have books. A library is not a luxury, but one of the necessaries of life." A book is a record of things, acts or feelings and not the things themselves. In some instances books are the setting of gems. Some books are the scavenger's receptacle for his wares, and are to be avoided as a pesthouse. Books are the reflex of the minds of men and differ as the faces and character of their authors. Some books are the parents of our souls, or, rather, they are like Buddha, almost even like Christ, the saviour of intellectual life. Think as you step into your library that you are in the company of the choicest spirits that ever walked the earth, seers, philosophers, poets, and that here before you are the panoramas and the revelations of their inner life.

Said Dr. Johnson: "Read anything five hours a day and you will soon be a learned man." That should be taken with limitation, for in the days of Dr. Johnson the world was not flooded with cheap books. The books should be selected by winnowing as the wheat is selected from the chaff. Time is the stuff life is made of, and life is worth too much to be wasted on cheap books.

The soul should be fed on inspiration. . . . Every young man should be richer after reading a book, and more thankful because a teacher has spoken to you. Every young man should be educated in books, and he should own his own books, mark them, comment upon them, talk with them as with intimate friends. There is an aristocracy in books which should be cultivated. The souls of the writers will vitalize your own soul; they will lift you up into better manners, grander purpose, broader comprehension of man, principles, cause and effect, and God. A thinker should be married to his library; it should be the only creature of which his wife may be jealous. Books are the records of the acts, thoughts and feelings of mankind. They review to us the thoughts and remarks of the immortals. Books are the treasure-houses where the jewels of all time are preserved and the doors are opened only to students and thinkers.

—CLEVELAND PLAIN DEALER.

OLD MAUMA.

BLACK as the blackest of her race,
  Ill-featured, too—and yet
Her kindly voice, her smiling face,
  I never can forget.

* * * * *

When dreams enchant me, and the eyes
  Of memory perceive
Bright visions of the morn arise
  To bless the sight at eve;

How few there are of all the old
  Home pictures that appear,
But in the foreground I behold
  Her figure standing there!

She loved me well—my infant heart
  That gracious truth divined,
Ere yet her language could impart
  Such meaning to my mind.

My youthful joys she shared with me,
  My youthful sorrows shared;
She spared me heartache constantly,
  Herself, she never spared.

If lulled to sleep upon her knee,
  She nodded while I slept,
And when I laughed she laughed with me,
  And when I wept she wept.

Beset by visionary harms,
  Weary and seeking rest,
I knew no choice 'twixt mother's arms
  And Mauma's ebon breast.

What cared I that her skin was rough,
  And dusky brown of hue?
For me this truth was quite enough—
  The heart was warm and true.

I grew a man, she old and gray,
  And missed me from her side;
But many a day and oft, they say
  She called my name and cried.

And when she went, whose years were spent
  In servitude below,
Death from its sombre tenement
  Released a soul of snow.

* * * * *

Black as the blackest of her race,
  Coarse-featured, too—and yet
My second mother's kindly face
  I never can forget.
    —Whitemarsh Seabrook.

HOW GRANDMA DANCED.

Grandma told me all about it,
Told me so I couldn't doubt it,
How she danced—my grandma danced—
  Long ago;
How she held her pretty head,
How her dainty skirt she spread,
Smiling little human rose!
How she turned her little toes—
  Long ago.

Grandma's hair was bright and sunny,
Dimpled cheeks, too—ah! how funny!
Really quite a pretty girl,
  Long ago.
Bless her! why, she wears a cap,
Grandma does, and takes a nap
Every single day; and yet
Grandma danced the minuet
  Long ago.

Now she sits there rocking, rocking,
Always knitting grandpa's stocking,
(Every girl was taught to knit
  Long ago);
Yet her figure is so neat,
I can almost see her now
Bending to her partner's bow,
  Long ago.

Grandma says our modern jumping,
Hopping, rushing, whirling, bumping,
Would have shocked the gentlefolk
  Long ago.
No, they moved with stately grace,
Everything in proper place;
Gliding slowly forward, then
Slowly courtesying back again,
  Long ago.

A "POOR" RICH MAN.

On a summer morn—long faded
  Into distance of the Past—
In a chamber warm and shaded,
By an awful gloom pervaded,
  A " poor" rich man breathed his last.

'Mid the outside beauty lying
  Round his fair and stately home,
Sad and lonely, he lay dying—
Only summer winds were sighing,
  Only raindrops broke the gloom.

All around was wealth and splendor;
  Yet no weeper came to shed
Tears of sorrow, true and tender—
Such as only love can render—
  By his solitary bed!

Hirelings, set to watch, had slumbered
  As his dying breath he drew.
For they knew his hours were numbered,
And they cared not, nor were cumbered
  With Love's servings, kind and true.

(Love had stood, perchance, and waited
  To receive the dying breath,
Till the agony abated,
Till the spirit won, belated,
  Fled into the arms of death!)

With observance high and stately,
  He was borne unto his tomb;
And hired mourners, all sedately—
Who had laughed aloud so lately—
  Wore long faces full of gloom!

Bless her! why, she wears a cap,
Grandma does, and takes a nap
Every single day; and yet
Grandma danced the minuet
    Long ago.

— *Page 101.*

UNIV. OF
CALIFORNIA

While the muffled bells tolled slowly
　From the belfry overhead,
And the " De Profundis " holy,
Sung by voices melancholy,
　Sounded, for the silent dead !

Only when his head was covered
　With the earth all brown and cold,
Pitying eyes at last discovered,
One poor woman's form, which hovered
　O'er the silent, voiceless mold.

Only one he had forsaken
　And betrayed in her lost youth,
Came to mourn—as if o'ertaken
By her grief—as if to waken
　Him to honor, love, truth.

Yea, she wept as if despairing,
　With a heart by anguish torn,
While the idle crowd, uncaring,
Some with bitter jests unsparing,
　Mocked her! pallid and forlorn.
　　—J, H., *in Chambers's Journal.*

HER WISH.

I WISH my fairy would come to-day,
And brush the dust from these rooms
　away.

The cobwebs, too, on the ceiling high,
Empty traps with never a fly—

How horrid they look! upon my life,
The torment of every tidy wife!

I wish my fairy my place would take
In the kitchen, and let me see her bake.

For I'm so weary I really dread,
The thought of kneading a batch of
　bread.

Her husband heard her wish that day,
But scarcely heeding it hurried away.

At night he locked his office door,
And gladly entered his home once more.

As round the cosy room he glanced,
His eyes with pleasure fairly danced.

The firedogs of polished brass,
For burnished gold almost would pass.

His easy-chair was in its place—
Beside it beamed a smiling face.

No wonder that he turned to her,
Half husband and half worshipper,

And said : " Some fairy has had full
　sway
In every nook of our house to-day."

Forgotten were dust and cobwebs high,
And there was a light in somebody's
　eye ;

For the heaviest tasks that burden a
　wife
Grow light when they brighten another's
　life.
　　—EGBERT L. BANGS, *in Woman's
　　　Magazine.*

ONLY.

ONLY a woman with an aching heart,
　That sits in the firelight's blur,
And muses over the tangled threads
　That fate has woven for her.

Only a woman with hope all slain
　And buried within her breast,
That values life but a sad refrain,
　That only longs for rest.

Only a woman in woman's pride
　That smiles when her heart is dead ;
You cannot tell by her laugh and jest
　That her light in life has fled.

Only a woman that grieves alone
　Away from curious eyes ;
Grieves for those who sleep to-night
　Out under the summer skies.

Only a woman that fain would lay
　Her head by the dear one's side,
Rather than live her lonely life
　So weary the eventide.

NOTHING LOST BUT A HEART.

DRIFTING away from each other,
　Silently drifting apart,
Nothing between but the world's cold
　screen,
Nothing to lose but a heart.

Only two lives dividing
  More and more every day;
Only one soul from another soul
  Silently slipping away.

Only a man's heart striving
  Bitterly hard with its doom;
Only a hand, tender and bland,
  Slipping away in the gloom.

Nothing of doubt or wrong,
  Nothing that either can cure;
Nothing to shame, nothing to blame,
  Nothing to do but endure.

The world cannot stand still,
  Tides ebb and women change,
Nothing here that is worth a tear,
  One love less—nothing strange.

Drifting away from each other,
  Steadily drifting apart—
No wrong to each that the world can reach,
  Nothing lost but a heart.

THE TRUE WIFE.

OFTENTIMES I have seen a tall ship glide by against the tide, as if drawn by an invisible tow-line with a hundred strong arms pulling it. Her sails unfurled, her streamers drooping, she had neither side-wheel nor stern-wheel; still she moved on, stately, in serene triumph, as with her own life. But I knew that on the other side of the ship, hidden beneath the great bulk that swam so majestically, there was a little toilsome steam tug, with a heart of fire and arms of iron, that was tugging it bravely on; and I knew that if the little steam tug untwined her arms and left the ship, it would wallow and roll away, and drift hither and thither, and go off with the effluent tide no man knows where; and so I have known more than one genius high-decked, full-freighted, wide-sailed, gay-pennoned, but for the bare toiling arm and brave warm heart of the faithful little wife that nestled close to him so that no wind or wave could part them, he would have gone down with the stream and been heard of no more.

—O. W. HOLMES.

A WOMAN'S QUESTION.

Do you know you have asked for the costliest thing
  Ever made by the Hand above—
A woman's heart, and a woman's life,
  And a woman's wonderful love?

Do you know you have asked for this priceless thing
  As a child might ask for a toy,
Demanding what others have died to win,
  With the reckless dash of a boy?

You have written my lesson of duty out,
  Manlike you have questioned me;
Now stand at the bar of my woman's soul
  Until I shall question thee.

You require your mutton shall always be hot,
  Your socks and your shirts shall be whole;
I require your heart shall be true as God's stars,
  And pure as heaven your soul.

You require a cook for your mutton and beef;
  I require a far better thing;
A seamstress you're wanting for stockings and shirts—
  I look for a man and a king.

A king for a beautiful realm called home,
  And a man that the Maker, God,
Shall look upon as He did the first,
  And say, "It is very good."

I am fair and young, but the roses will fade
  From my soft, young cheek one day;
Will you love me then, 'mid the falling leaves,
  As you did 'mid the bloom of May?

Is your heart an ocean, so strong and deep
  I may launch my all on its tide?
A loving woman finds heaven or hell
  On the day she is made a bride.

THE SCRAP-BOOK.

I require all things that are grand and
  true,
All things that a man should be;
If you give this all I would stake my life
To be all you demand of me.

If you cannot do this, a laundress and
  cook
You can hire with little to pay;
But a woman's heart and a woman's
  life
Are not to be won that way.
  —N. O. TIMES-DEMOCRAT.

DISTANT.

IF you were only here to-night,
  And I were looking in your eyes,
I should not mind the autumn's blight,
  The wild night winds or sombre
    skies;
I should not mind the dreary rain
  That falls upon the sodden hill;
Your presence would have power to
    make
  My every pulse with summer thrill.

If you were here with me to-night,
  I would forget life's toils and tears,
The weary struggle without aim—
  The brooding shadows of the years.
To-night, if you were only here,
  Your dear eyes looking into mine,
Life's sorrows all would drop away,
  And living be a gift divine.

But we are miles and miles apart,
  And walking widely different ways,
You'll never know your words, dear
    heart,
  Make all the music of my days.
And so I sit alone to-night,
  In all the autumn wind and rain—
Ah me! ah me! does life hold naught
  But broken dreams and bitter pain?

THY NAME IS STILL THE MAGIC SPELL.

THY name is still the magic spell
  By which my heart is bound,
And memories glad of light and life
  Wake ever at the sound.

My heart beats quick whene'er I hear
  In praise, but ne'er in blame,
From any tongue, in any sphere,
  The mention of thy name.

When friends of yore come 'round me
    still
  They voice but praise of thee.
Full well they know that now, as then,
  Thou art all the world to me.

Long years, long years have passed
    since first
  My youthful heart was stirred,
But all its fount of feeling burst
  At sound of that dear word.

But still thy name, thy blessed name,
  My heart's aspiring fills.
Like some pure height in Heaven's own
    light
  Upon the distant hills,
Crowning the rugged path below,
  A type to human eyes,
How we may tread through toil and
    woe
  A pathway to the skies.

THE FIRST GRAY HAIR.

    AND thou hast come at last,
Thou baleful issue of the buried years—
    Sad fruitage of the past,
Root nurtured in a loam of hopes and
    fears;
I hail thee, but I hate thee, lurking
    there,
        Thou first gray hair!

    Thou soft and silken coil,
Thou milk-white blossom in a midnight
    tress!
    Out from the alien soil
I'll pluck thee in thine infant tenderness,
As the rude husbandman uproots the
    tare,
        Thou first gray hair!

    Of all the fleecy flock
Thou art the one to loathe and to de-
    spise;
    The cheat within the shock,
The mould that on the early harvest
    lies,
The mildew on the blossoms of the
    pear—
        The first gray hair!

And thou the Judas art,
The tattler of old Time, who doth betray
The weary, worn-out heart,
Ere yet we dare to dream of its decay ;
Thou art a hint of wreck beyond repair,
Thou first gray hair !

AN ALPHABETICAL WOOING.

Let others talk of L N's eyes,
And K T's figure, light and free,
Say L R, too, is beautiful—
I heed them not while U I C.
U need not N V them, for U
X L them all, my M L E.
I have no words when I would tell
How much in love with U I B.
So sweet U R, my D R E,
I love your very F E G ;
And when you speak or sing, your voice
Is like a winsome L O D,
When U R I-C, hope D K's,
I am a mere non-N T T.
Such F'E K C has your smile,
It shields from N E N M E.
For love so deep as mine, I fear,
There is no other M E D,
But that you love me back again—
O, thought of heavenly X T C !
So, lest my M T heart and I
Should sing for love an L E G,
T's me no more—B Y's, B kind,
O, M L E, U R, I C !

THE MORTGAGE.

We worked through spring and winter,
through summer and through fall,
But the mortgage worked the hardest
and the steadiest of them all ;
It worked on nights and Sundays, it
worked each holiday,
It settled down among us and it never
went away.

Whatever we kept from it seemed
almost as bad as theft ;
It watched us every minute and it ruled
us right and left.
The rust and blight were with us sometimes, and sometimes not ;
The dark-browed, scowling mortgage
was forever on the spot.

The weevil and the cut worm, they
went as well as came ;
The mortgage stayed forever, eating
hearty all the same.
It nailed up every window, stood guard
at every door,
And happiness and sunshine made their
place with us no more.

Till with failing crops and sickness, we
got stalled upon the grade,
And there came a dark day among us
when the interest wasn't paid ;
And there came a sharp foreclosure
and I kind o' lost my hold,
And grew weary and discouraged, and
the farm was cheaply sold.

And the children left and scattered
when they hardly yet were grown ;
My wife she pined and perished, and I
found myself alone.
What she died of was a "mystery,"
and the doctors never knew ;
But I knew she died of mortgage—just
as well s I wanted to.

If to trace a hidden sorrow were within
the doctor's art,
They'd a' found a mortgage lying on
that poor woman's heart.
Worm or beetle, drouth or tempest, on
a farmer's land may fall,
But for first-class ruination trust a
mortgage 'gainst them all.

HER PICTURE.

Thank God no change or pain can ever
come,
To that fair pictured face on yonder
wall,
With earnest eyes and lips forever
dumb,
That loved and trusted me through
all in all.

Full many a time, when filled with deep
unrest,
I watched it in the lamplight's quivering gleam
Until my soul with quiet was possessed,
And then it faded from me in a dream.

Sweet, gently curving mouth, that to me left
Its last smile in the last kiss that she gave,
Then closed to leave me utterly bereft,
Until we meet again beyond the grave.

Soft eyes, within the firelight's fitful glow,
I scarce can see you, sorrowful and deep;
And yet, in darkness, as in light, I know
That never weary is the watch you keep.

Sweet eyes, brown eyes, so tender and so kind:
I doubt if living eyes could ever be
To all my faults and failures half so blind,
Or half so fond, or pitiful to me.

Time cannot change those loving, earnest eyes,
So wishful for the love in mine they see;
Or watching o'er me in their sad surprise
And grieving for the grief that came to me.

Can you, then, blame me that I love this face,
That long ago became my dearest friend?
Or that I wish it, with its quiet grace,
To watch above me till I reach the end?

—F. H. CURTISS.

RUTH.

GLEAMS of the golden sunset are red in the orange trees,
And the breath of May comes soft and and sweet from the lips of the perfumed breeze;
And I sit here, my darling, and silently long for you,
While the dim day dies down the amber skies, and the stars are dark and few.

Why is it, I wonder, Ruth, that all we long for here
Seems never so sweet to our yearning hearts, never so bright and dear,

As when the long shades of the evening are silently closing in,
And the night comes down o'er the weary town, veiling its sorrow and sin?

Then all that we love seems nearer, and all that we loathe grows dim,
And the very birds tune sweeter songs as they chant their vesper hymn;
The great pure eyes of the holy stars are tender with Love's own dew,
And there comes no thought to me then, my Ruth, but the loving thoughts of you.

And I think it would be so easy if one could be always so,
To echo that sweet pure life above in our dim lives below;
To be noble and honest always, always earnest and true,
If one could be ever thus, Ruth, alone with the moon and you.

For the fears and the hopes and the terrors that make up this daily span,
Have surely but little to do after all with the marvellous life of man;
And empty and vain and unreal are the things that we live in and love;
For the soul that strives is the soul that lives the life of the Home above.

Yet I sometimes think, my darling when they tell me death is a sleep
That I would like to be lying there where the willows trail and weep;
But the fight must be fought, and the race be run, and the strife for duty striven,
Till the crest go down with the dying sun, and the weary soul be shriven.

But yet I think that a deeper truth lies hid in the pallid brow,
That the soul which hath faithfully sown the seed has gone a-reaping now;
And the feet which of late trod the furrowed fields, through the golden uplands roam,
And the grave and gate of death, my Ruth is the gate of the Harvest-Home.

There is something so strangely human
    in the wail of this restless sea !
I could almost think it was bearing,
    Ruth, a message from you to me :
For the ocean of suffering hems us
    round, and we never are wholly
    glad ;
And the songs that we sing and the
    tales that we tell are truest, being
    sad.

For we who sing of the joys and pains
    of the infinite human heart—
Ah ! Ruth, think not that we poets
    dwell in a fairy world apart :
But the song is ever the sweetest, Ruth,
    when the heart is breaking fast,
When the spirit wounds are yet un-
    healed, and the graves in our souls
    ungrassed.

Ah ! Ruth, my Ruth ; do you ever long
    sometimes when you sit alone,
For a glance from the eyes or a word
    from the lips you have made your
    own ?
Do you ever pray when the night comes
    down for the twin-soul far away ?
Ah ! pray for me, Ruth : I am sick and
    worn, and I have no strength to
    pray.

When, here by the wayside or there in
    the throng, we meet as we some-
    times do,
(For nothing of earthly distance lies un-
    travelled 'twixt me and you)
My heart leaps up with a wild lament
    to the bars of the sealed lips,
And I grope and stagger, with feeble
    feet through the shades of my life's
    eclipse.

And here by the shores of the viewless
    sea which between us spreads and
    flows,
So terrible in its passions' depth, its
    cruel and dread repose,
I stretch weak hands through the blind-
    ing mist, and shudder and pant and
    yearn ;
But the eyes that ache and the lips that
    long, feel only the tears that burn.

Ah well ! ah well ! there is work to be
    done somewhere in the world, I
    know ;
And if you will that I stand alone, the
    fight will be nobler so :
The crown comes not to the unpurged
    brow nor the palm to the coward
    hand,
And the little of life that we see on
    earth is so hard to understand !

But one truth lives though the whole
    world fail, and even you grow cold;
I love you still—I will love you still—
    with the faithful love of old.
Go on your way ! live down your heart !
    you cannot break the spell,
Love only can quench the spirit's thirst:
    I bid your time : Farewell !

FALLING LEAVES.

The leaves of autumn are falling :
    They are faded, and withered and
    torn ;
They shrink from the world and its
    tumult,
    Like souls that are weary and worn.

Not a light wind that weaves through
    the branches,
    But plucks the sear leaves from the
    spray,
But tosses, and tosses, and tosses,
    And twirls them and whirls them
    away.

They have flourished in beauty and
    freshness ;
    They have laughed in the beams of
    the sun ;
They have wept when the heavens were
    unwindowed ;
    They have sighed when the darkness
    begun.

Let them fall : it is well : let them perish;
    Their youth and their sweetness have
    fled ;
Never more will they waken in beauty
    From the limitless Land of the Dead.
    —Theo Carpenter.

WHEN DAY IS DONE.

When day is done the robins sing
  Their dulcet vesper lays;
When day is done the black bats wing
  Through all the dusky ways;
The crickets blow their flageolets
  More loudly than by day,
The crystal dew steals forth and wets
  Each blossom-bell and spray.

When day is done the western skies
  Become a sea of gold,
And holy, countless stars arise
  And pierce Heaven's curtain-fold;
The low winds sing a lullaby,
  And rock the flowers to sleep—
The moon climbs up the eastern sky,
  And bridges o'er the deep.

When day is done the mother lays
  Her babe upon her breast,
And while she dreams of other days
  Slow sings it unto rest.
When day is done the shepherd leads
  The lambs home to the fold;
When day is done our labor meeds
  Our willing fingers hold.

When day is done the toilers come
  With weary feet and slow,
Unto the peacefulness of home,
  Where life's best pleasures flow.
When day is done—life's little day,
  Which ends so quickly here,
God grant our weary feet may stray
  Unto His pastures dear.
      —E. B. Lowe.

MEMORIES OF HOME.

Murmuring night-winds sigh as they roam,
Wafting a message from my old home,
Whispering softly, gently and low,
Calling to mind the dear long ago.
Mem'ries awaken, start into life,
Bear me away from all sin and strife,
Filling my soul with a dream divine.
Mother! once more I'm a child of thine.

Thy tender face, with its lines of care,
Shaded by bands of soft, shining hair,
Bends low above me, thrills me with bliss,
As I remember thy good-night kiss.

Once more thy low, gentle voice I hear,
Sweetly its accents fall on my ear:
"Never, my boy, where'er you may roam,
Never forget thy mother at home."

Fondly sweet mem'ries crowd on my heart,
Mem'ries from which I would never part,
Bringing the scent of some homel flower
Growing close by the old ivied bower.
Often we sat there. The silvery moon
Beaming so softly. A song you'd croon,
Gentle and low, my head on your breast,
Soothed by its music, I'd sink to rest.

Gone! are the days of my childhood dear,
Gone! are the songs I so loved to hear,
Gone! is the sound of the voice so meek,
Gone! the sweet face with its furrow'd cheek.
Lonely I dream while my heart grows sore,
Sadly I think of the days of yore,
Never again can they come to me,
Mother! I would I could be with thee.
      —Frances Rawlins.

THE BEAUTIFUL LAND OF THE DEAD.

By the hut of the peasant where poverty weeps,
  And nigh to the towers of the king,
Close, close to the cradle where infancy sleeps,
  And joy loves to linger and sing,
Lies a garden of light full of heaven's perfume,
  Where never a teardrop is shed,
And the rose and the lily are ever in bloom—
  'Tis the beautiful land of the dead.

Each moment of life a messenger comes
  And beckons man over the way;
Through the heart-sobs of women and rolling of drums,
  The army of mortals obey.

Few lips that have kissed not a motionless brow,
A face from each fireside has fled,
But we know that our loved ones are watching us now
In the beautiful land of the dead.

Not a charm that we knew 'ere the boundary was crossed,
And we stood in the valley alone;
Not a trait that we prize in our darlings is lost,
They have fairer and lovelier grown;
As the lilies burst forth when the shadows of night
Into bondage at daybreak are led,
So they bask in the glow of the pillar of light,
In the beautiful land of the dead.

O, the dead, our dead, the beautiful dead!
Are close to the heart of eternity wed;
When the last deed is done and the last word is said,
We will meet in the beautiful land of the dead.

HOME, SWEET HOME.

THERE'S a beautiful realm in the faraway past
All lovely with sunshine and flowers,
And voices as sweet as songs of the birds,
Laugh away the bright, happy hours;
I can hear them now, come echoing back,
As I watch the starry dome,
And memory bells chime soft and low—
Home, Sweet Home.

There's a coming step! now a gentle hand
Rests lightly upon my brow—
A whispered word and the sweet caress
Call me back to the beautiful now,
To another real where flowers bloom,
From which nothing can tempt me to roam,
And my heart throbs chime with voices sweet:
Home, Sweet Home.

The voices loved so in that long ago,
And those which make music now—
The coming step and the hand whose touch
Lingers gently on my brow—
I hope to greet in that fadeless realm
Beyond the starry dome,
Where angel voices welcome breathe, to
Home, Sweet Home.
—THE BALTIMOREAN.

INDIAN SUMMER.

THERE is a season of the year when summer is past and autumn's approach recorded, known as Indian summer. The sun has ceased to pour forth its fervid heat and has dropped back to tropical climes. The frosts of autumn have robbed the leaves of their rich green hue and substituted in its place the golden tints of fall. Some of the leaves have been long-lived and held on to see their second childhood. Others have fulfilled their mission designed by the Creator, and one by one have fallen off and sunk to their mother earth.—Those that remain, lift their heads at the season's approach—and as old age of man—hope for a protracted existence. The hills, with few flowers here and there, still grapple with autumn's chill to retain their verdure. The fields, yellow with fruits, offer praises for their bounteous supplies for man's subsistence. The brooklet rustles along with nature's song, to bear earth's tears away to prevent its sadness. The birds perch upon some leafless limb and sing their spring-time songs. The dove has cooed to his side its mate, and sits basking in the warm sun rays. At eve the herd wind slowly along their homeward paths in search of shelter. The air is still at times, and again the cricket's chirp may be heard everywhere around. But what needs man to be sad to know this season—a second favor from Heaven—cannot last long?—There's nothing sad in fall save it may remind us of another misspent year. True, nature's register may have recorded thereon sad events,—

At eve the herd wind slowly along their homeward paths
in search of shelter.

— *Page 106.*

UNIV. OF
CALIFORNIA

probably the death of some father, mother, brother or sister,—but it was God's will. We should be thankful that they were not taken a year sooner. Soon winter's clouds will o'er-hover, the storms will come, the rain will beat and the winds will blow, yet the same favoring Hand rules all. If we live, we may expect the storms to pass, and the poetry of spring to cheer our hearts again. If we die, and die "the death of the righteous," we may expect to find our eternal spring-time in heaven.

WITHOUT AN E.

It is well known that the letter *e* is used more than any other letter in the English alphabet. Each of the following verses contain every letter in the alphabet except the letter *e*:

" A JOVIAL swain should not complain
    Of any buxom fair,
Who mocks his pain and thinks it gain,
    To quiz his awkward air.

" Quixotic boys who look for joys,
    Quixotic hazards run ;
A lass annoys with trivial toys,
    Opposing man for fun.

" A jovial swain may rack his brain,
    And tax his fancy's might ;
To quiz is vain, for 'tis most plain
    That what I say is right."
—NORTHAMPTON COURIER (*Eng*).

HOPE.

THERE is a star that shineth
    Above the thickest gloom,
And the sorrowing heart divineth
    Its light beyond the tomb.
With steady constant ray it gleams
    Upon the path of Youth,
And tingeth all its golden dreams
    With colorings of truth.

Far out upon the ocean
    Its cheering light is shed,
Yet hath no moral seen this star,
    The living nor the dead ;
But in the heart and in the soul
    Where death and danger cope,
Assuring with a firm control
    Doth shine this Star of Hope.
        —REAR ADMIRAL STEVENS.

GOD KNOWS BEST.

IN many troubles that perplex,
    And make us weary of this life,
If we should say, " I will not vex
    My soul no more with worldly strife,"
But, looking upward—"God knows best ;"
Unto His care leave all the rest.

Instead we strive with hands so frail
    To part the clouds upon our way.
Ah ! life give us no warrior mail
    Invulnerable to sorrow's sway ;
And when its darts pierce through our breast,
Teach us to feel that God knows best.

When in the throes of fiercest pain,
    And our weak spirits seek release,
And cry aloud to Him in vain,
    To succor or to still in peace,
Though granting not our wild request,
Teach us to feel that God knows best.

When like a serpent from its lair,
    With coils that kill all they embrace,
Sin springs upon us unaware,
    And poisons what was pure and chaste,
Though falling 'neath temptation's test,
Teach us to feel that God knows best.
        —EMMA CLARK WHITNEY.

THE MOTTO IN A WEDDING RING.

A LOVER gave the wedding ring
    Into the goldsmith's hand.
"Grave me," he said, "a tender thought
    Within this golden band."
        The goldsmith graved,
        With careful art,
    " *Till death us part.*"

The wedding bells rang gladly out,
    The husband said, " O wife,
Together we will share the grief,
    The happiness of life.
        I give to thee
        My hand, my heart,
    Till Death us part."

'Twas *she* that lifted now his hand
    (O love, that this should be !)
Then on it placed the golden band,

And whispered tenderly:
"Till Death us join,
Lo, thou art mine
And I am thine!

"And when Death joins we never more
Shall know an aching heart;
The bridal of that better love
Death has no power to part.
That troth will be
For thee and me
Eternity."

So up the hill and down the hill
Through fifty changing years
They shared each other's happiness,
They dried each other's tears.
Alas! alas!
That Death's cold dart
Such love can part!

But one sad day she stood alone
Beside the narrow bed;
She drew the ring from off her hand,
And to the goldsmith said:
"Oh, man, who graved
With careful art,
'Till Death us part,'

"Now grave four other words for me:
'*Till Death us join.*'" He took
The precious golden band once more,
With solemn, wistful look
And wrought with care,
For love, not coin,
"*Till death us join.*"
—ANONYMOUS.

TWILIGHT.

THE radiant colors in the west are
paling;
Fast fades the gold, and green and
crimson light,
And softly comes, each trivial object
veiling,
The all-ennobling mystery of night.

This is the hour of thought and silent
musing,
When poets' fancies tender buds unfold;
Like the sweet primrose of the twilight,
choosing
To spend on evening noonday's gift
of gold.

These blossoms hide within their deep
recesses
Treasures the wandering wind can
never seize;
Not all its inner wealth the flower con-
fesses,
Nor gives its choicest perfume to the
breeze.

What wizard's wand can charm the
secret sweetness
From the fair prison, where it lies
concealed?
What poet's lay can show in grand
completeness
The inmost heart, by human speech
revealed?

We twine the spell of rich harmonious
numbers,
We conjure up the graceful words in
vain;
Our lighter fancies waken from their
slumbers;
Without a voice the noblest thoughts
remain.

So dash the restless billows of the ocean,
But bring no tidings of the tranquil
deep;
Above, are endless tumult and commo-
tion;
Below, are silence and eternal sleep.
—CONSTANCE C. W. NADEN.

THE WESTWARD WINDOW.

I'M looking out the westward window,
Where the sun sinks slow to rest,
With lengthened shadows softly creep-
ing
Over hill and mountain crest;
The forests and the groves are vocal
With the songster's parting lay,
And redolent are all the woodlands
With the hue of parting day.

The streamlet murmurs down the hill-
side,
Flowing onward toward the sea,
And bears my spirit, on its bosom,
Forward toward eternity.
The cloud expanse is being gilded
With the crimson, purple, gold,
God's chariot through gates is passing.
Gorgeous with wealth untold.

I seem to hear the silent voices
  Out from yonder distant shore,
And friendly hands they seem to beckon,
  As they beckoned me of yore.
It's toward the east are the beginnings,
  Where our memories fondly dwell,
But westward are the souls aspiring
  Visions faith and hope foretell.

I'm looking out life's westward window,
  Where life's day is fleeting by,
Beyond the vision of life's present,
  Where the unseen we descry.
It's through the open westward gateway
  That I shall be passing soon,
Beyond the sun's rising and its setting,
  Where is high eternal noon.
    —Rev. J. B. Smith, D. D., *In Christian Inquirer.*

THE SWEET, SAD YEARS.

The sweet, sad years, the sun, the rain,
Alas, too quickly did they wane!
  For each some boon, some blessing bore;
Of smiles and tears each had its store;
Its checkered lot of bliss and pain.

Although it idle be and vain
  Yet cannot I the wish restrain
That I had held them evermore,
    The sweet, sad years!

Like echo of an old refrain
That long within the mind has lain,
  I keep repeating o'er and o'er,
" Nothing can e'er the past restore;
Nothing bring back the years again,
    The sweet, sad years."
      —Rev. Charles D. Bell.

WE CAN MAKE HOME HAPPY.

Though we may not change the cottage
  For a mansion tall and grand,
Or exchange the little grass-plot
  For a boundless stretch of land—
Yet there's something brighter, dearer,
  Than the wealth we'd thus command.

Though we have no means to purchase
  Costly pictures, rich and rare,
Though we have no silken hangings
  For the walls so cold and bare—
We can hang them o'er with garlands,
  For flowers bloom everywhere.

We can always make home cheerful,
  If the right course we begin,
We can make its inmates happy,
  And their truest blessings win;
It will make the small room brighter
  If we let the sunshine in.

We can gather round the fireside
  When the evening hours are long—
We can blend our hearts and voices
  In a happy social song;
We can guide some erring brother—
  Lead him from the path of wrong.

We may fill our home with music
  And with sunshine brimming o'er;
If against all dark intruders
  We will firmly close the door—
Yet should evil shadows enter,
  We must love each other more.

There are treasures for the lowly
  Which the grandest fail to find,
There's a chain of sweet affection,
  Binding friends of kindred mind—
We may reap the choicest blessings
  From the poorest lot assigned.
      —The Myrtle.

WHY?

Some men thirst while others drink,
Some men talk while others think,
  Why are these things so?
Some men smile while others swear,
Some men's heads have brains to spare,
While other's heads all run to hair—
  Why are these things so?

Bad men order; good men serve;
Mind grows thin where fattens nerve—
  Why are these things so?
Lies ride past in palace cars,
Truth all marked with bramble-scars,
Staggers on 'neath evil stars—
  Why are these things so?
      —Washington News.

A GOOD-BYE.

Farewell! How soon unmeasured distance rolls
  Its leaden clouds between our parted souls;

How little to each other now are we—
And once, how much I dreamed we two might be !
I, who now stand with eyes undimmed and dry,
    To say good-bye.

To say good-bye to all sweet memories,
Good-bye to tender questions, soft replies ;
Good-bye to hope, good-bye to dreaming too,
Good-bye to all things dear—good-bye to you,
Without a kiss, a tear, a prayer, a sigh—
    Our last good-bye.

I had no chain to bind you with at all,
No grace to charm, no beauty to enthrall ;
No power to hold your eyes with mine, and make
Your heart on fire with longing for my sake,
Till all the yearnings passed into one cry :
    " Love, not good-bye ! "

Ah, no—I had no strength like that, you know,
Yet my worst weakness was to love you so !
So much too well—so much too well—or ill—
Yet even that might have been pardoned still—
It would have been had I been you—you I !
    But now—good-bye.

How soon the bitter follows on the sweet !
Could I not chain your fancy's flying feet ?
Could I not hold your soul—to make you play
To-morrow in the key of yesterday—?
Dear—do you dream that I would stoop to try—
    Ah, no—good-bye !

A METAMORPHOSIS.

OH, he preached it from the housetops, and he whispered it by stealth !
He wrote whole miles of stuff against the awful curse of wealth :
He shouted for the poor man, and he called the rich man down,
He roasted every king and queen who dared to wear a crown.
He hollered for rebellion, and he said he'd head a band
To exterminate the millionaires, to sweep them from the land.
He yelled against monopolies, took shots at every trust,
And swore he'd be an Anarchist, to grind them in the dust,
He stormed, he fumed, he ranted, 'till he made the rich men wince ;
But an uncle left him money, and he hasn't shouted since.
—NEW ORLEANS TIMES-DEMOCRAT.

WHAT PEOPLE CALL DEATH.

THE holiest (and what should be the happiest) hour is that when a spirit is struggling to free itself from its wall of clay—to unfetter its wings and spring forth into a newer and higher life like a new-born butterfly from its clayey shell. But those who are left behind—to whom the departing spirit was a part of his life in the bonds of sweetest love—feel the strain upon each fibre of their being until it seems the departing spirit takes with it the airy life, and all which endears the world and makes a life here desirable. And when, at last, the struggle is over, and the spirit is at rest, there comes a loneliness which is in itself an evidence that *something* has departed from the temple—the casket, for that which was a house to the spirit still remains, but that which animated it has gone—we know not where or how but as it is revealed to us by the " Master of Life ! "

In vain they look up where the stars are shining ; they see nothing but those blazing worlds—they look into earth, but see nothing but the elements of which the material covering of the spirit was composed.

In vain would worldly wisdom seek to solve the problem.

But a science which is infallible—the acme of all science—the science of life—which comes from the highest reason, declares the immortality of the soul, and that the dear one departed still lives; that the darling you love yet lives to be loved, and in the eternity of which the present life is the vestibule toward which all are hastening, will again be united in a stronger, a holier, love than that which has growth on earth.

Truly hath eye not seen, nor hath ear heard, nor hath it entered into the heart of man to conceive, the glory of that home prepared for those who love God. So when a loved one departs to enter before you the "house of many mansions," there ought not to be that sorrow, that despair, which so often is seen.

It seems proper and reasonable that the freed spirit would see the grief of friends, and that such knowledge may, although blessed with knowledge that "sorrows are blessings," sympathize with the sufferings of those left behind.

It is more than mere speculation or theorizing to speak of the glory of that eternal home, of the employments and the scenery of the "other land"—for we believe that aspirations will be answered, and the longings of the student to learn more of the laws which govern the universe—which this short span of life only permits a knowledge compared only as is one grain to a thousand worlds—will be gratified; that the lover of humanity shall, when this life shall have ceased, continue to visit the afflicted, and aid in the thousand means to better the condition of his fellows; that the inventor shall employ his talent to the devising means to accomplish results through utilizing hitherto hidden powers of nature for the benefit of God's kingdom and the glory of His name.

Away, then, the pall, the clouds of despair, and let the sunshine of God's promises illuminate sorrowing hearts.

Death is beautiful, it is natural, and as we shall learn to live aright, shall we learn to die aright, when all of God's dear humanity will arise and sing joy songs—and none but shall exclaim when that auspicious time shall come when the grand ultimate of *this* life shall have been attained: "Oh! death, where is thy sting! oh! grave, where is thy victory!"

MEMORY.

MEMORY! Thy voice we hear,
 Sweet as the vesper bell:
Solemn and low, yet clear,
 As of the past ye tell!
Sounding the sweet refrain—
Life was not lived in vain!

Memory! Unfold the past!
 Throw open wide the door!
E'en though in shadow cast,
 Yet would we see once more,
Unstained by soil or rust,
Those who've returned to dust!

Memory! Alas, the tone
 Changes, for now again
Wrung from the heart, a groan,
 Tells of a bitter pain!
Shows by the falling tear
Mem'ry's not always dear!

Memory! Enough! I pray
 Thou wilt be silent now!
No more return! Away!
 See'st thou this furrowed brow?
These lines show care and woe!
Canst thou efface them? No!
 —DR. HOWARD W. LONG.

ROCK ME TO SLEEP, MOTHER.

BACKWARD, turn backward, O Time, in your flight,
Make me a child again just for to-night;
Mother, come back from the echoless shore,
Take me again to your heart as of yore;
Kiss from my forehead the furrows of care,
Smooth the few silver threads out of my hair;
Over my slumbers your loving watch keep;—
Rock me to sleep, mother,—rock me to sleep!

Backward, flow backward, oh, tide of
 the years !
I am so weary of toil and of tears,—
Toil without recompense, tears all in
 vain,—
Take them, and give me my childhood
 again !
I have grown weary of dust and de-
 cay,—
Weary of flinging my soul-wealth away;
Weary of sowing for others to reap ;—
Rock me to sleep, mother, rock me to
 sleep !

Tired of the hollow, the base, the untrue,
Mother, O mother, my heart calls for
 you !
Many a summer the grass has grown
 green,
Blossomed and faded, our faces between :
Yet, with strong yearning and passionate pain,
Long I to-night for your presence again.
Come from the silence so long and so
 deep ;—
Rock me to sleep, mother,—rock me to
 sleep !

Over my heart, in the days that are
 flown,
No love like mother-love ever has
 shone ;
No other worship abides and endures,—
Faithful, unselfish, and patient like
 yours ;
None like a mother can charm away
 pain
From the sick soul and the world-weary
 brain.
Slumber's soft calms o'er my heavy lids
 creep ;—
Rock me to sleep, mother,—rock me to
 sleep !

Come, let your brown hair, just lighted
 with gold,
Fall on your shoulders again as of
 old ;
Let it drop over my forehead to-night,
Shading my faint eyes away from the
 light ;

For with its sunny-edged shadows once
 more
Haply will throng the sweet visions of
 yore ;
Lovingly, softly, its bright billows
 sweep ;—
Rock me to sleep, mother,—rock me to
 sleep !

Mother, dear mother, the years have
 been long
Since I last listened your lullaby song ;
Sing then, and unto my soul it shall
 seem
Womanhood's years have been only a
 dream.
Clasped to your heart in a loving em-
 brace,
With your light lashes just sweeping my
 face,
Never hereafter to wake or to weep ;—
Rock me to sleep, mother,—rock me to
 sleep !
—Elizabeth Aker.

KEEP ME AWAKE, MOTHER.

Forward ! Oh, forward ! time stays
 not his flight,
I'm older, and wiser and sadder to-
 night,
And mother, dear mother, I see thee
 no more,
But watch me, oh watch me, again as
 of yore,
And let me not slumber, but gaze on
 life's cares
With a look of defiance a warrior
 wears,
Once more to thy bosom a weary one
 take,
But keep me awake, mother, keep me
 awake.

I'm tired of earth, and I'm weary of
 life,
It's unfulfilled hopes and its profitless
 strife,
But still must I onward, my destiny
 calls,
Tho' troubles surround me and danger
 appals,
My life path is covered with gloom and
 decay,

But let me not falter, or sleep by the way,
For virtue and honor a name let me make,
And keep me awake, mother, keep me awake.

Oh, give me stern power of frame and of soul,
To master the troubles that over me roll,
And let me not murmur, tho' waking I be,
For those whom I see not, and never may see,
And let me plant trees, tho' they flourish and bloom
When I am asleep in a far-away tomb,
For those who are coming some care let me take,
And keep me awake, mother, keep me awake.

The dreams of my childhood have faded or flown,
The objects I cherished repulsive have grown,
And all things seem fleeting, no pleasure endures,
But mother, dear mother, the same lot was yours,
Such dreaming, such mourning, such hoping and trust,
Such crumbling of dainty air-castles to dust,
As bravely as thou didst, my part let me take,
And keep me awake, mother, keep me awake.

Awake to my duties, awake to my trust,
Let me do my task bravely, if toil I must,
But sometimes, oh, sometimes, in dreams let me be
The child again, mother, that slept on your knee ;
Wipe out for a moment my story of life,
Its struggle, its sorrows, its follies and strife,
Some season of pleasure, of rest, let me take,
Then wake me, my mother, and keep me awake.

And mother, dear mother, when life's nearly o'er,
And God bids me cross to the "echoless shore,"
My last task is done, and my busy brain still,
And I have no longer a power or will,
Oh, then, blessed spirit, oh, then, hover near,
And smooth from my brow the dark shadows of fear.
Then linger near, mother, to watch and to weep,
Then "rock me to sleep, mother, rock me to sleep."
—Mrs. M. W. Stratton.

MAN, THE KICKER.

In winter, when the cold winds blow,
  Man kicks.
He doesn't like the ice and snow,
He hates to see the mercury go
To zero ; if it falls below
  He kicks,
  Oh, how he kicks !

In summer, when the sizzards siz,
  Man kicks,
He groans : "Oh, Lord, how hot it is!"
As if no misery equalled his.
Then, as he wipes his streaming phiz
  He kicks.
  Oh, how he kicks !

And so it is, if cold or hot,
  Man kicks.
He's never pleased with what he's got,
But growls and fumes, and swears a lot,
And whether it is right or not
  He kicks,
  Oh, how he kicks !
—Somerville Journal.

GIVE A KIND WORD WHEN YOU CAN.

Do you know a heart that hungers
  For a word of love and cheer ?
There are many such about us,
  It may be that one is near.

Look around you! If you find it,
  Speak the word that's needed so,
And your own heart may be strength-
    ened
  By the help that you bestow.

It may be that some one falters
  On the brink of sin and wrong,
And a word from you might save him—
  Help to make the tempted strong.
Look about you, O my brother!
  What a sin is yours and mine
If we see that help is needed
  And we give no friendly sign!

Never think kind words are wasted—
  Bread on waters cast are they,
And it may be we shall find them
  Coming back to us some day;
Coming back when sorely needed
  In a time of sharp distress;
So, my friend, let's give them freely;
  Gift and giver God will bless.
              —THE HOUSEHOLD.

OF THE OLD BACK STAIR.

OF all the sports of childhood,
  I know of none so rare
As sliding down the banisters
  Of
    the
      old
        back
          stair.

I remember well the circus,
  And the fun it used to bring:
While watching fearless riders
  Dashing around the ring.
But this jolly old attraction
  Could never near compare
To sliding down the banisters
  Of
    the
      old
        back
          stair.

Then I recollect the barn loft,
  Chucked full of clover hay;
Mother used to send us there
  To pass a rainy day.
But I often stole away from that
  And while mother wasn't there,
Be sliding down the banisters
  Of
    the
      old
        back
          stair.

I have grown to manhood now,
  And often wander home;
The old folks always welcome me—
  They're glad to have me come;
But, while they're not looking
  I'm tempted, I declare,
To slide down the banisters
  Of
    the
      old
        back
          stair.

LOVER'S LIMIT.

I'D swear for her,
I'd tear for her,
The Lord knows what I'd bear for her;
  I'd lie for her,
  I'd sigh for her,
I'd drink a fountain dry for her;
  I'd "cuss" for her,
  Do "wuss" for her,
I'd kick up a thunderin' fuss for her;
  I'd weep for her,
  I'd leap for her,
I'd go without my sleep for her,
  I'd fight for her,
  I'd bite for her,
I'd walk the streets all night for her;
  I'd plead for her,
  I'd bleed for her,
I'd go without my "feed" for her;
  I'd shoot for her,
  I'd boot for her,
A rival who'd come to sue for her;
  I'd kneel for her,
  I'd steal for her,
Such is the love I feel for her,
  I'd slide for her,
  I'd glide for her,
I'd swim 'gainst wind and tide for her;
  I'd try for her,
  I'd cry for her,
But—hang me if I'd die for her.
  N. B.—Or any other woman.

AFTER HIAWATHA.

"SHOULD you ask us why this dunning,
Why these sad complaints and murmurs,
Murmurs loud about delinquents
Who have read the paper weekly,
Read what they have never paid for,
Read with pleasure and with profit,
Read of Church affairs and prospects,
Read of news both home and foreign,
Read the essays and the poems,
Full of wisdom and instruction,
Should you ask us why this dunning?
We should answer, we should tell you:

"From the printer, from the mailer,
From the kind old paper maker,
From the landlord, from the carrier,
From the man who taxes letters
With a stamp from Uncle Samuel—
'Uncle Sam' the rowdies call him;
From them all there comes a message,
Message kind and firmly spoken,
'Please to pay us what you owe us.'

"Sad it is to hear such message,
When our funds are all exhausted,
When the last bank note has left us,
When the gold coin all has vanished,
Gone to pay the paper-maker,
Gone to pay the toiling printer,
Gone to pay the landlord tribute,
Gone to pay the nimble carrier,
Gone to pay the faithful mailer,
Gone to pay our Uncle Samuel—
'Uncle Sam' the rowdies call him.

"Would you lift a burden from us?
Would you drive a spectre from you?
Would you taste a pleasant slumber?
Would you have a quiet conscience?
Would you read a paper PAID FOR?
Send us money—send us money—
Send us money—*send us money*—
SEND THE MONEY THAT YOU OWE US!"
—THE LUTHERAN.

SOME DAY.

SOME day when the flowers have faded,
  And the summer days have gone,
When the heart of love is shaded,
  As you wait in tears alone,
Let the rays of sunshine cheer you,
  While the birds sing songs of glee;
Keep life's roses ever near you,
  And the future bright shall be.

Some day your friends will leave you,
  With the warm, true love they gave—
It may be death that has bereft you,
  And you stand beside their grave.
Do not let your heart grow weary,
  In the gloom of earth's dark night;
Look beyond those hours so dreary,
  And behold the dawn of light.

Some day, when your age is nearing,
  And your hair has turned to gray,
When life's prospects are not cheering,
  As you dream of childhood's day,
Do not turn away in sorrow,
  With a heart grown cold through care;
Watch and wait for a to-morrow
  When the sky is calm and fair.

Some day, when love is bringing
  You so near the heavenly throne,
And you hear the angels singing,
  While a kind, dear voice says, Come!
Do not wait this side the river,
  Through the long, dark hours of night;
Go to One who is life's giver
  In the world of glorious light.

HELPING ON THE TRACK.

DID you ever see a locomotive off the track? Isn't it a pitiable sight? What was the embodiment of beauty, power and usefulness, at once becomes a useless and helpless mass by getting off the track. It is just so with men who make mistakes by running too fast, or doing something wrong that throws them off the track.

Like the locomotive perhaps, they are built strongly, work well, of the proper material, and ordinarily well balanced; yet, they sometimes get off the track. Perhaps it was the first time in life, perhaps it was the fault of the defective track, or of some unexpected condition; yet, like the locomotive, they get off the track and are rendered helpless; and without the aid of others, their lives are ruined by once going wrong. Alas, that there are so many men and women in this condition, and so few who will see the condition and will lend a helping hand towards getting them back! It is just here the world needs help. Sympathy is good, but it is not the remedy. Charity is good, but it will often not be needed if the individual be only again placed on the track. He could then help himself, and if placed on some side track even, might again work himself to the main line. But without aid at this juncture, like the locomotive, his life is wrecked no matter how good his past, or what the possibilities of the future. The world is full of such cases, and men are apparently less thoughtful of the human, than of the locomotive wrecks. Everywhere we find men and women wrecked by first one course and then another, who were really in fine condition for good and useful lives had they only been given a little lift, a kind word, and fresh encouragement in this time of need. Like the locomotive, human nature can withstand and recover from almost any blow, so long as they are on the track and can help themselves. But when once off, their power for recovery is gone. It is then they need help, and then a little help counts most. Perhaps it was their fault for being off, perhaps an accident; it may have been for the want of judgment, or even the wilful violation of orders. Yet, the damage is done, and it is now no time for abuse, lecturing or scolding. Help back the wrecked, clear the track for others, and in most of cases the scolding and lecturing may be dispensed with; for renewed effort, new success and renewed help to others, will be the willing coin repaid.

It is so easy to make a mistake—and who does not make them, and occasionally get off the track? Who is perfect, and without the need of the help of God and man? The best men and engines go wrong, and many of them have been off the track, and had they not been helped back, how fruitless would have been their lives? And it is so much better and easier to help a man, woman or child back on the track, than it is a locomotive. Many a boy has been helped back by a dime, a good example, or proper directions; many a woman has been helped back by a kind word and good advice; many a man has been helped back and sent on his way rejoicing—a living helper for others —by a lift that may have been given in a thousand ways. Oh, that people would think more of, and try the harder to help others back to the right track! It would do so much to enable the helpless to help themselves, and leave so much more of charity and sympathy for those who really cannot help themselves. It is well and better late than never; yet the real and best help is that which enables people to help themselves. This is capital doubly invested, for ingratitude rarely exists in the heart of the helped, and compound interest is always the return to humanity.

We have lots of men who endow colleges, build asylums, and found noble charities, and for such works go out the thanks of man, and the blessings of God. They are all good and necessary. Yet, what we most need to make their work better and more complete, are wrecking crews all along the tracks of life. Helping on the track is the work and mission of all, and many more would be the self-helpers, as well as the helpers of others, were they only helped back on the track! How many of the best men, and best helpers, are those who, at some time in life, were themselves helped back on the right track! Such are, indeed, the best helpers of humanity. Yes, it is here that is the true field of the reformer. It is here that most is accomplished by least. It is here we need the wrecking crews and the life-savers. It is here the crews can best accomplish their work for God and man, and best recruit their numbers for the helping of others.

OUR LIVES.

Our lives are like the autumn leaves
That fall upon life's troubled stream;
Some darkly circle by the shore,
Some brightly on its bosom gleam;

And many crushed into the dust
 By this world's unrelenting pride,
Shall be enwreathed in glory's crown
 By seraphs on the other side.

For souls there are whose darkening
    fates
 Have never known the power of
    love—
That, like the stars unknown to earth,
 Shall gem God's firmament above.
There shall they find the missing chords
 Sought vainly in this vale of tears,
And in the golden sunlight bask
 That fills the long, eternal years.

And what enchanting strains of joy
 Fall like sweet music on life's sea,
When we can say I've done to men
 As I would have them do to me,
And though in poverty we dwell,
 We're richer far than ermined kings,
For when we feel that angels smile,
 And hear the rustling of their wings.

And it is this which constitutes
 The spirit wealth in that grand life
Which opens wide the doors of truth,
 When we have done with sin and
    strife ;
And he whose treasures have been laid
 But to enhance his mortal need,
Must, when we seek that unknown
    bourne,
 Himself find destitute indeed.

SITTING IN SILENCE.

I'M sitting to-night in silence,
 Thinking of the years before,
When the future shall be the present,
 And the present be no more ;
When the friends I've loved and cherished,
 The little while here I be,
Shall have lived like me, and perished
 In the waves of death's dark sea.

I'm sitting to-night in silence,
 Thinking of the days of yore,
When the past was then the present,
 And the present then before ;
When the youthful dreams of fancy
 Were sweet as the morning's dawn,
And the wily hand of fortune
 Did beckon me gently on.

I'm sitting to-night in silence,
 Thinking of the weary years
I've wandered along with sorrow,
 And a traveller been with tears ;
But sweet is the consolation
 There's a place of rest above,
Where the dreams are more than fancy
 And the ruling law is Love.

So I'm sitting to-night in silence,
 Thinking of the years before,
When the future shall be the present,
 And the present be no more ;
When the friends I've loved and cherished,
 The little while here I be
Shall have lived, like me, and perished
 In the waves of death's dark sea.
         —JOSEPH W. HUMPHRIES.

FATE.

DOWN the stream of Life we're drifting,
 Slowly, surely, moving ever.
Childhood's shores we've passed already,
 To return, ah never, never !
And we fancied that the currents
 All through life, would bear us on
Close together and the parting
 Would but come when life was done.

Now, although you do not see it,
 Now, although you do not heed,
I with anguish see you drifting,
 Ever with increasing speed,
From my side ; and though your voice
    has
 All the fond, sweet tones of yore,
Faintly, now, I seem to hear them,
 As from some far-distant shore.

Oh, I cannot, cannot stay you !
 Yet I will not let you go !
By the past and all its memories,
 Do not, do not leave me so !
And once again we move together,
 And once again our hands we press,
And each one's thoughts is all the
    other's
 And every look is a caress.

But I know it all is fleeting ;
 'Tis but one long, last farewell,
Now I know that it is fated,
 And my anguish I must quell.

Can't you see the rolling waters,
  Separating you from me ?
Can't you see that you are drifting
  Out into the open sea ?

I must stay here in the shadow ;
  Along the shore my current flows ;
Crowds of smiling friends await you,
  Oh, never may the winter's snows
Upon you fall. May softest showers
  Refresh you, and may the sky
Be always fair and bright above you ;
  You are drifting on. Good bye !
        —ELENOR SPINNEY.

FRIENDSHIP.

IF you have a friend worth loving,
  Love him. Yes, and let him know
That you love him, ere life's evening
  Tinge his brow with sunset glow,
Why should good words ne'er be said
Of a friend—till he is dead ?

If you see the hot tears falling
  From a brother's weeping eyes,
Share them ; and by kindly sharing
  Own your kinship with the skies.
Why should any one be glad
When a brother's heart is sad ?

If your work is made more easy
  By a friendly, helping hand,
Say so. Speak out brave and truly
  Ere the darkness veil the land :
Should a brother workman dear
Falter for a word of cheer ?

Scatter thus your seeds of kindness,
  All enriching as you go—
Leave them. Trust the Harvest Giver,
  He will make each seed to grow.
So, until its happy end,
Your life shall never lack a friend.
    —RELIGIOUS HERALD, *Hartford.*

THE BEAUTIFUL STEER.

OH, the steer, the beautiful steer,
  Kicking the flies from the points of its ear,
Flapping his tail in its rolicsome glee,
Hopping about like a Snake River flea,
    Bellowing !
      Roaring !
        Thundering along !
Filling the air with its steerical song,
Till the rumble from its lung-laden pits,
Scared timid jackrabbits and wolves into fits.
To me there is nothing on earth half so dear
As the long-horned, slim-bodied Texican steer.

How often I wish that I was a steer,
With a long, shiny horn at the butt of each ear,
With a clear, fearless eye and a tapering tail
That would snap like a whip in the maddening gale.
    How I'd beller !
      And roar !
        And paw up the ground !
And lope over the hills with a thundering sound,
And snort like a terrier, and hump up my back
When I saw the wild cow-boy pursuing my track,
And I'd laugh at his oaths as he fell to the rear,
Oh, I'd be a Jo-dandy if I was a steer !

I once roped a beautiful steer—but I fell
From my pony with ear-piercing yell !
Fell with the lariat fast to my wrist !
Fell to be dragged through the grass wet with mist.
    Bumping !
      Rolling !
        Grunting I went !
A full mile a minute or I don't want a cent.
The gravel and grass yanked the hide from my nose,
And ruined a pair of forty-cent hose ;
Aye, even my bustle was thrown out of gear
By the frolicsome freaks of that beautiful steer.
    —WESTERN COW-BOY-GIRL.

CHOOSE YOUR FRIEND WISELY.

CHOOSE your friend wisely,
  Test your friend well ;
True friends, like rarest gems,
  Prove hard to tell.
Winter him, summer him,
  Know your friend well.

Oft, bosom companions
  Are dangerous things,
Rifling your honey,
  But leaving their stings ;
Creeping and crawling,
  Like bees without wings.

Leave not your secrets
  At every man's door,
High tides will shift them,
  Like sands on the shore—
Sift them, and shift them,
  Now higher, now lower.

Take advice charily ;
  Many a man
Dates back his ruin
  To change of his plan.
Choose your friend wisely,
  And well, if you can.

MUSINGS IN THE TWILIGHT.

In the twilight alone I am sitting
And fast through my memory are flitting
  The dreams of youth ;
The future is smiling before me,
And Hope's bright visions float o'er me ;
  Shall I doubt their truth ?
I know that my hopes may prove bubbles
  Too frail to endure,
And thick-strewn be the cares and the troubles
  That life has in store.

But 'tis best we know not the sorrow
That comes with a longed-for to-morrow,
  And the anguish and care ;
If the veil from my future were lifted,
Perhaps at the sight I had drifted
  Down into despair ;
If I knew all the woes that awaited
  My hurrying feet,
My pleasure might oftener be freighted
  With bitter than sweet.

And yet, though my life has been lonely,
Some flowers I have plucked that could only
  From trials have sprung ;

Some joys I have known that did borrow
Their brightness from contrast with sorrow
  That over me hung ;
For the moonbeams are brighter in seeming
  When clouds are gone by,
If only a moment their gleaming
  Be hid from the eye

Sad indeed would be Life's dewy morning
If, all Hope's bright promises scorning,
  O'erburdened with fears,
We saw but the woe and the sorrow
That would come to our hearts on the morrow,
  The sighs and the tears.
So 'tis best we may not discover
  What Fate hath in store,
Nor lift up the veil that hangs over
  What lieth before.

WHERE MOTHER USED TO SIT.

In Memory's silent studio hang
  Some pictures ne'er will fade,
Pictures of songs that dear ones sang,
  And treasured words they said.
Then there are bits of old farm life, and
  woods where glad birds flit,
But none are dear's the quiet porch
  where mother used to sit.

The shade on summer afternoons
  Would linger coolest there ;
In twilight dim the insects' croons
  Made twilight tenderer ;
And, like some wordless psalmody, the
  moonshine fair would flit
Among the vines that decked the porch
  where mother used to sit.

And when she'd sing I half-way thought
  The angels hovered near ;
A boyish fancy, but it wrought
  A kind of sacred cheer ;
And how I'd like to dream once more
  —have angels round me flit—
As when I played about that porch
  where my mother used to sit !
    —Will T. Hale.

WHAT CAN YOU DO?

ON one occasion the writer was present when a young man presented himself to the manager of a show and said he wanted to be employed to go with the show. "All right," said the manager, "we wish to add some new features—what can you do?" This question startled the young man, who stood for a moment in silence, and then replied by the question, "What do you want me to do?" "I want you to do what you do best, said the manager. "Well," said the youth, "I can do 'most anything;—what do you pay for good men?" "We don't pay for good men, we pay for services," said the manager,— "What specialty have you?" "Oh," said the young man, growing redder in the face, "I—I don't do no tricks, but thought you might want an all-'round man to go with you, to learn and help you out." "That's it," said the showman.— "No, we are not teaching the show business, wish none but specialists, and have plenty of attachés that are better than you would be. I am the only all-'round man the show has, and I spent twenty years in the business before I could get that position," The young man hung his head in despair, walked off and is still in search, doubtless, of a job, that he has never learned to do, and is wondering why it is that others can get good jobs, at good wages, while he cannot do so.

How applicable to the case of the average young man is this instance! "What can you do?" is a question most of them have never asked themselves, nor will they do so, until they are informed by parties to whom they apply for jobs that they are not teaching, but practising, their business, and wish none but specialists in it. Young man, "What can you do?" What have you studied, and what is your specialty? Parents, what can your sons and daughters do, that they may earn livings, and demand of the individual, or the world, good jobs, or good wages? You may have sent them to school, that is a part of your duty, but it is only a means to an end, and will not answer the question, What can your boy or girl do? Are you teaching them a trade? Are you schooling them in the line of business they are to follow? If not, who is to do so? Will it ever be done, before they are faced with the questions, "What is your specialty?" "What can you do?" This is the question of all questions, and will be sure to present itself. People having jobs to give will remind your boys that it is men with specialties wanted; and that they spent one, two, five, or twenty years to earn the position they apply to fill. Young men, what are you going to do about it? Have you a trade, a specialty?— What can you do? Who do you expect to teach you, and when will you begin? The world is full of men without specialties, and they are "hewers of wood and drawers of water," at from fifty cents to one dollar per day. Do you wish to compete with them? How will you help it, if you do not learn a trade, or master some specialty? Can you expect to receive more than they, when you can earn, or produce, no more? No matter about your goodness, or family connections, you will be reminded that it is your SERVICES, and not these, the employer wishes. If they were demanded, perhaps you might be in the fight, but it is services desired; something which your employer can pay wages for, and still have a profit left him, after doing so. In order to be valuable to yourself, you must be more valuable to your employer. Are you asking yourself, What can you do well? Are you learning a trade and preparing for the future? If not, rest assured that you will also be puzzled by the same question: "What can you do?"

MY FIRST SWEETHEART.

SHE'S rather faded now, and thin.
  Her shining locks are not so glossy;
She's lost the dimple in her chin,
  Her air's subdued instead of saucy.
She's paler, too; the wild rose bloom
  That used to make her such a beauty
Has faded, to make standing room
  For lines marked out by care and duty.

Her hand is not so plump and white
  As on the day when first I pressed it ;
But baby hands have clasped it tight,
  And baby lips in love caressed it.
A firm, warm hand to shield and guide
  The little lives that must come after ;
A tender heart to hold and hide
  The baby love and baby laughter.

I often see her pass this way,
  Her bright-eyed children trooping
    'round her,
Oh, for the wasted yesterday,
  Ere yet another year had found her !
It might have been. Within my breast
  The secret grieving long hath tarried ;
I wonder if she sometimes guessed
  The reason why I never married.
    —BACHELOR BRAG.

WAIT TILL TROUBLE COMES.

WE sit down, wayworn and weary,
  And think of the days to be,
And forget there's a silver lining,
  To all the clouds we see.
We fret over care and trouble
  Before it is begun,
And think of stormy weather ;
  We forget the warm bright sun.

It were better to wait, my brother,
  Till the trouble and care is here ;
Why should we cloud the sunshine
  When the day is bright and clear
By dreading what may await us ?
  Better to laugh and sing,
And bid the bird of foreboding
  From these hearts of ours take wing.

What was the sunshine made for,
  If not to make us glad ?
We are doing wrong to waste it
  In repining, idle and sad.
We are doing wrong to squander
  The sunshine of to-day
In foreboding that to-morrow
  The sky may be cold and gray.

Then I pray be wise, my brother,
  As you climb the hill of life,
Enjoy the time to the utmost
  That is free from care and strife.
Thinking only of blight and failure
  We sow no seed-time grain ;

Make use of to-day's glad sunshine,
  And for to-morrow's rain.

To-day is ours, but to-morrow,
  Perhaps, we may never see ;
Then why should we borrow trouble
  For a time that may not be ?
Leave to the future, brother,
  The trouble it may bring :
In the sunshine that God gives us
  Be glad of heart and sing,

THE PRAYER OF A BETROTHED.

[A lady, over the signature of "Inez," portrays her thoughts in the following most beautiful verses on the eve of her marriage :]

FATHER, I come before Thy throne,
  With low and bended knee,
To thank Thee with a grateful tone
  For all Thy love to me.
Forgive me if my heart this hour
  I give not all to Thee ;
For deep affection's mighty power
  Divides it now with Thee.

Thou knowest, Father, every thought
  That wakes within my breast,
And how this heart has vainly sought
  To keep its love suppressed :
Yet when the idol, worshipped one,
  Sits fondly by my side,
And breathes the vows I cannot shun,
  To me, his destined bride—

Forgive me if the loving kiss
  He leaves upon my brow
Is thought of in an hour like this
  And thrills me even now,
He's chosen me to be his love
  And comforter through life ;
Enable me, oh, God, to prove
  A loving, faithful wife.

He knows not, Father, all the deep
  Affection I control—
The thousand loving thoughts that
    sweep
  Resistless o'er my soul—
He knows not each deep fount of love
  That gushes warm and free ;
Nor can he ever, ever prove
  My warm idolatry.

Then guard him, Father;—'round his
    way
Thy choicest blessings cast,
And render each successive day
    Still happier than the last:
And, Father, grant us so to live
    That when this life is o'er
Within the happy home you give
    We'll meet to part no more.
                —RICHMOND DISPATCH.

ALONE.

SINCE she went home—
Longer the evening shadows linger
    here,
The winter days fill so much of the year,
And even summer winds are chill and
    drear
        Since she went home.

Since she went home—
The robin's note has touched a minor
    strain,
The old glad songs now breathe a sad
    refrain,
And laughter sobs with hidden, bitter
    pain,
        Since she went home.

Since she went home—
How still the empty rooms her presence
    blessed;
Untouched the pillow that her dear
    head pressed:
My lonely heart hath nowhere for its
    rest,
        Since she went home.

Since she went home—
The long, long days have crept away
    like years,
The sunlight has been dimmed with
    doubts and fear,
And the dark nights have rained in
    lonely tears,
        Since she went home.
                —ROBERT J. BURDETTE.

THE OLD-TIME CIRCUS CLOWN.

I WONDER where's the circus clown,
    with all his fun an' noise—
The feller who just ruled the ring when
    you an' me was boys?

There's lots o' funny fellers now that
    travel with the show;
But where's the old-time circus clown
    we all knowed long ago?

I remember, like 'twas yesterday, his
    every smile and frown—
The capers that he cut up when the
    circus come to town;
How the old ring-master nagged him;
    all his frolic an' his fuss;
Jest the best thing in the circus—was
    the old-time clown to us!

When he smiled we fell to laughin';
    when he laughed we give a shout!
We was always watchin' for him and a-
    follerin' him about;
He use to come so reg'lar that we
    knowed him, up and down;
He was sociable an' friendly—was the
    old-time circus clown.

We would jump behind his wagon when
    he wasn't tellin' jokes,
An' he'd give a grin o' welcome; maybe
    ask us how's the folks.
He knowed the little boys and gyrls
    from Billville clean to Brown,
An' they loved him—every one o' them
    —the old-time circus clown.

I wonder where he's gone to now? The
    circus comes along,
An' the steam pianner's playin' off a
    screechy sort o' song;
There's half a dozen painted chaps in
    every street parade;
But their fun is mighty solemn to the
    fun the old clown made!

I wonder what's become o' him? I
    guess they've laid him by;
Warn't use to three-ringed circuses an'
    women kickin' high;
He kinder saw his time was up; the
    circus light growed dim,
An' he couldn't see the faces of the old
    boys cheerin' him.

He's gone, an' gone forever, but on
    every circus day,
When I sit with all the children where
    the new clowns prance an' play,

My old eyes grow right misty, an' a tear
  comes tumblin' down
From an old-time circus feller for the
  old-time circus clown !
    —Frank L. Stanton.

FAILURE.

Up the white walls the shadows steal
    apace ;
Fast slips the day, the day that prom-
    ised fair ;
At morn I rose with flushed and eager
    face,
And to the hillside turned to toil my
    share.
But at the gate I paused to pull a rose,
  Then idled where the goldfish glance
    and gleam ;
And Lise and Lettice call me from the
    slope,
  Beneath the myrtles there to lounge
    and dream.
And so with laugh and jest the morning
    sped ;
  Ere I could guess it it was afternoon.
" And why go now ? Stay yet awhile,"
    they said,
  "To-morrow toil ; to-day is all too
    soon."

Thus with my life ; a youth that prom-
    ised fair,
  The world's broad highway for my
    eager feet ;
And pleasure wooed me from the noon-
    day glare,
  And old age finds me with no task
    complete.
          —Exchange.

STUB ENDS OF THOUGHT.

Cupid claims all or nothing.
Stinginess is perverted economy.
Work is an investment ; rest the
dividend.
The devil has a claim on every man's
heart.
Beauty must be known to be appre-
ciated.
Men may make creeds, but they can't
make religion.

An ounce of action is better than a
pound of sentiment.
Two souls with but a single thought,
want that thought doubled.
The tongue was not made to tell
everything the eyes see or ears hear.
If you know what laws have to be
passed to restrain a man, you know the
man.
The surest way to please is to forget
one's self and think only of others.
The one thing that man dislikes to
do is often just the thing that stands in
his way.
There is only one real failure of life
possible, and that is not to be true to
the best one knows.
One reason why some people never
get religion, is because they do not want
to get enough to spoil them for the
world.
The guardians of the soul are pure and
beautiful thoughts, sympathy, sincere
and loving, is the key which unlocks
the every heart.
A man doesn't get much done when
working around the house. Every few
minutes he is reminded of something for
which he must scold his wife, and that
takes time.
          —Atchison Globe.

MY SWEETHEART.

'Twas a quaint rhyme scrawled in a
    spelling-book,
And handed to me with a bashful look,
By my blue-eyed sweetheart so fondly
    true,
In the dear old school days long years
    ago—
  "If you love me as I love you,
  No knife can cut our love in two."

That "Saunders' Speller," so tattered
    and torn,
Has always a halo of romance worn,
And never a poet with honeyed pen
Has written so precious a rhyme since
    then—
  "If you love me as I love you,"
  Ah, dear, you know I did—I do.
I've kept it safely for many a year—
This dog's-eared, shabby, old spelling-
    book dear,

And now, as I hold it within my hand,
Again in the school-room I seem to stand—
　Reading once more with rapture new—
　" If you love me as I love you."

How some foolish saying from out the past,
Like a rose-branch is over the pathway cast,
And the time of flowers, we still remember,
Till winds blow cold in the bleak December.
　God grant it may always be true—
　" That you love me as I love you."
　　　　　—CAROLYN L. BACON.

SOMEBODY ELSE.

WHO's Somebody Else? I should like to know,
Does he live at the north or south?
Or is it a lady fair to see
　Whose name is in every one's mouth?
For Meg says, " Somebody Else will sing,"
Or " Somebody Else can play,"
And Jack says, " Please let Somebody Else
　Do some of the errands to-day."

If there's any hard or unpleasant task
　Or difficult thing to do,
'Tis always offered to Somebody Else—
　Now, isn't this very true?
But if some fruit or a pleasant trip
　Is offered to Dick or Jess,
We hear not a word about Somebody Else.
　Why? I leave you to guess.

The words of cheer for a stranger lad,
　This Somebody Else will speak,
And the poor and helpless who need a friend
　Good Somebody Else must seek.
The cup of cold water in Jesus' name,
　Oh, Somebody Else will offer,
And words of love for a broken heart
　Brave Somebody Else will proffer.

There are battles in life we only can fight,
　And victories, to win,
And Somebody Else cannot take our place.
　When we shall have " entered in ; "
But if Somebody Else has done his work
　While we for our ease have striven,
'Twill be only fair if the blessed reward
　To Somebody Else is given.
　　　　　—UNION SIGNAL.

THE FIRST TELEGRAPHIC DISPATCH.—Henry J. Rogers was the telegraph operator who received the first dispatch sent over wire. He lived in Baltimore, and worked with Professor Morse in establishing the original line from Washington to Baltimore, and when the line had been completed, in 1844, sat down at his instrument in the Washington office. Professor Morse, being in Baltimore, sent to President Polk the message :

" What God hath wrought."

Mr. Rogers, in reply, sent the following :

" Hail ! thou beauteous stranger of the grove—
Thou messenger of spring !
Now, heaven rejoices,
And woods thy welcome bring."

REGRET.

O, THAT word Regret !
There have been nights and morns
　when we have sighed
" Let us alone, Regret ! We are content
To throw thee all our past, so thou wilt sleep
For aye." But it is patient and it wakes ;
It hath not learned to cry itself to sleep,
But 'plaineth on the bed that it is hard.

We did amiss when we did wish it gone
And over ; sorrows humanize our race ;
Tears are the showers that fertilize this world ;
And memory of things precious keepeth warm
The heart that once did hold them.

　　　　　　They are poor
That have lost nothing ; they are poorer far

Who, losing, have forgotten; they are most poor
Of all, who lose and wish they might forget.
For life is one, and in its warp and woof
There runs a thread of gold that glitters fair,
And sometimes in the pattern shows most sweet,
Where there are sombre colors. It was true
That we have wept. But O! this thread of gold,
We would not have it tarnished; let us turn
Oft and look back upon the wondrous web.
And when it shineth sometimes we shall know
That memory is possession,

I.

When I remember something which I had,
But which is gone, and I must do without,
I sometimes wonder how I can be glad,
Even in cowslip time when hedges sprout;
It makes me sigh to think on it, but yet
My days will not be better days should I forget.

II.

When I remember something promised me,
But which I never had, nor can have now,
Because the promiser we no more see
In countries that accord with mortal vow;
When I remember this, I mourn—but yet
My happier days are not the days when I forget.

THE TRAMP.

THE so-called modern civilization has brought with it the tramp. When the world was younger—and it is now said to really be over 20,000,000 years old—this individual was unknown, unless we recognize him as the prodigal. But at the present day the tramp and his counterpart, the millionaire, are everywhere with us. Many of them—at least, of the tramps—deserve better fate, and at least merit a consideration and recognition among the conditions of men. For, say what you will, circumstances and conditions have done much to make the tramp, and many of them are heroes rather than the despised of men. Many of the more fortunate would bear life's burdens with less fortitude and philosophy than does the tramp. For while there are many undeserving of their class, there are also many suicides and drones who are not tramps because of their want of materials that make the hero, in spite of ill luck, hardships and all there is in life that is discouraging. Such are many of the Dusty Roads, Willie Raggles and Weary Walkers that you meet. Many of them are carrying loads, bearing burdens,—within and without,—and standing up continually against adversities that you would have long since gone down under.

But few people would be tramps from choice, and many that are tramps, are so because they voluntarily refuse to do inhumane things, and dirty work that perhaps made millionaires of their contemporaries.

After all, tramps are human beings—brethren of the same brotherhood, and sons of the same Fatherhood. However little you think it, they were once mothers' dimpled-armed darlings. They once had their hair combed; were perhaps, Sunday school models, and actually indulged in what now seems to be a needless luxury—soap. And what if they do go without this one of the many luxuries now? You should remember it is not the luxury clauses of tariff bills they are interested in, and besides, that a change of conditions make many things luxuries that may have been very commonplace. If it is said that he produces but little, may it not also be said that he consumes but little? In fact, could he cost humanity much less to support him? He is surely not very extravagant in dress; for, like the goat, what he eats is about all he gets. On the principle that the horse is worth more than the colt, I have always had an idea that a tramp was worth more than a dude, yet you can clothe a regiment of tramps for the cost of one dude. And, if their stories are to be believed, they don't average but one or two meals a week!

In their better days, the tramps had friends and means. When fortune and luck were with them, they thought and did very much as you do now.

When the tide of adversity set in against them, how do you know what they had to withstand, or that you could have been a better hero against their adversities? Indeed, amid the whirlpools of life, may not the mills of the Gods grind you as severely as they have them?

In the new order of things, may not the millionaire yet become the tramp, and the tramp, the millionaire? There is no telling, for the law of compensation is wonderful in its workings, and "There's a destiny that shapes our ends, rough hew them as we may."

The average tramp acts his faith in God, if he has none; accepts the situation, bids defiance to adversities and gets happiness out of life in spite of them. Do you? It takes a hero to do this, and more heroism than the average man, who laughs at the tramp, ever possesses. No one knows this so well as the man, whose cup has been filled to the brim with sorrow or misfortune. Perhaps it is no real fault of his, but that he has been judged by some one act, or mistake of his life. Perhaps he took some choice of evils, and is patiently paying the penalties; or, perhaps he is an outcast for his loyalty to a friend, or is suffering for the acts of another.—Who knows?

And who would not be condemned were he judged by some unguarded word or act of his life? Who, in fact, if he were judged by some parts of his life would not sleep in more ignominious places than the tramp's barn or haystack? In the barn or haystack the tramp bears his own burdens, and perhaps accepts them with honor and a clear conscience in preference to a more public charity, or a palace gotten at the expense of others. In such he "Folds his mantle about him, and lies down to pleasant dreams!" Alas, alas, how many in gilded palaces and high places would give the world if they could call back the word, or deed, and accept the tramp's place and peace! Some time, way back, Jesus said something about throwing rocks, and the condemnation was so great that his hearers had other business than casting stones! Is it not as true to-day, and who of us can truly say "Forgive us our debts, as we forgive our debtors?" Indeed the tramp is not the only sinner, if they are the greatest sinners, and experience teaches, that after all, mankind is much alike. They may not be dressed alike and may have different wants, tastes and wishes, yet they have much of the same human nature. Their fortunes often turn on a pivot, or the throw of a dice, yet the turn of the pivot or the throw of the dice neither makes the millionaire a gentleman, nor the tramp a thief. They are both much the same by nature as they were before; and as a rule there is much more of good, than bad, in all. It is said there is honor among thieves. There is surely none the less honor among tramps, who like comrades, share each other's sorrows and divide each other's hand-outs. Many that are now considered gentlemen, are simply tramps in better luck; and beneath the ragged coats of many of those still tramps, beat great big hearts that are warm and true; and it is but simple justice to say of them that upon a fair divide of this world's goods, there would be fewer tramps as well as fewer millionaires; and that,

"There's many a one forsaken here,
Despised by man and banned,
Who, when all his deeds are reckoned,
Will be found at God's right hand."

A MAIDEN'S LOVE.

THE first experience in love is a glorious peep at heaven; and there is no sweeter or tenderer or a more soul-bewitching and soul-enchanting emotion that the one experienced by the young and pure and ardent and blushing maiden when she tremblingly opens for the first time in life the sacred door of her heart, and bids her chosen one to enter the hallowed treasury of her God-given wealth, and enjoy the uncounted riches of her inexhaustible vaults of devotion. Human nature has no essence more pure, the world knows nothing more chaste, Heaven has no feeling more holy than the nascent affections of a virgin's soul. To her life is rosy tinted, and earth seems bathed in the fragrance shaken out of the flowers of Paradise, and scattered down by the hands of Peri, The scenes which are then unfolded, break as beautifully upon her rapture-dazzled vision of the corruscant glories of shattered, autumnal sunsets. And while the inception of this feeling at first comes as faintly as the silver lustre of a glimmering star through a bower of spring foliage, and makes an impression almost as "slight as the shadow cast by a rose-leaf upon marble," still it comes in the beauty of its own sweet faith to stay and to build its everlasting fires of devotion upon the new-found shrine of idolatrous worship. And while the light of this Heaven-kindled fire rises as gradually as the sunbeams, when morning's crimson fingers first touch and awake them, and start them out to kiss the dewdrops from the flowers, yet it continues to spread and grow and glow until every chamber of the bosom is filled with flames of celestial beauty, and then, breaking out of the open windows of affectionate demonstration it goes unrestrainedly forth to show the pathless and glorifying light of its own eternity of rapture.

"WHEN THE DEVIL WAS SICK."

A MAN who had delved in the lore of
   the ages,
And could tell you the weight of the
   stars,
Who had added wise words unto Science's pages
And written an essay on Mars,
Arrived at the startling conclusino, one
   day,
That lawyers who plead and preachers
   who pray,
And doctors who claim to subdue
   people's ills
With scalpels and nostrums and poisonous pills,
Were nothing but swindlers, each in
   his way.

But the man who had delved in the lore
   of the ages,
And studied the far-away stars,
Who had earned the proud right to be
   classed with the sages,
One day got in front of the cars!
They picked him up tenderly; put him
   to bed,
And, as he lay groaning and moaning,
   half dead,
A preacher came in and knelt down
   at his side
And called on the God that the sage
   had defied.
And he heartily joined in the prayers
   that were said.

Yet the man who had delved in the lore
   of the ages,
And could name all the stars in the
   sky,
Who had added wise words unto Science's pages,
Was not quite ready to die!
He summoned a surgeon and patiently
   lay
While the "brute of a butcher" was
   sawing away;
He took all the poisons they gave
   him to take,
Forgetting that "doctoring's only a
   a fake"—
And arose and hobbled away, one day.

Now the man who has delved in the
   lore of the ages
And can tell you the names of the
   stars,
Who has earned the proud right to be
   classed with the sages
And was knocked galley west by the
   cars—

Who prayed when he thought he was
 going to die,
Who, ill, sent for him of whom, well, he
 fought shy,
 Has hired a lawyer to take up his
  case—
 To sue for the damages done to his
  face
And the leg that he lost when the train
 went by.

—S. E. KISER *in Cleveland Leader.*

QUITS.

SAID a young and tactless husband
 To his inexperienced wife,
"If you would but give up leading
 Such a fashionable life,
And devote more time to cooking—
 How to mix and when to bake—
Then perhaps you might make pastry
 Such as mother used to make."

And the wife, resenting, answered
 (For the worm will turn, you know),
"If you would but give up horses
 And a score of clubs or so,
To devote more time to business—
 When to buy and what to stake—
Then perhaps you might make money
 Such as father used to make."

—G. S. T. *in Brooklyn Life.*

THE BLUE AND THE GRAY.

[An olive-twig dropped by a Massachusetts soldier upon a Confederate's grave.]

ON many a slumbrous hill they lie,
 In many a peaceful valley ;
Unheard the surging battle-cry,
 Unheeded rout or rally.

The same old sun shines brightly down,
 The same pale moonbeams quiver ;
And piney spindles still are blown
 Along the sighing river.

Alike they sleep, the Blue, the Gray,
 And tears still rain above them ;
And long as day shall follow day
 Our hearts will bleed which love
  them.

Alike they fought, alike they fell,
 In conflict grim and gory ;
And many an unborn tongue shall tell
 The fratricidal story,

When friend met friend with shot and
 shell,
When brother strove with brother,
And blood, which crimsoned hill and
 dell,
 Flowed from a common mother.

Oh, ne'er while swerveless hands of
 time
 Are 'round its dial sweeping,
Shall bugle blast or brazen chime
 Call forth to such a reaping.

Ay, evermore shall palm and pine
 Stand firm through tempest weather ;
For when we next fall into line,
 We'll breast the storm together.

Then let them rest, the Blue, the Gray,
 Upon her breast who bore them,
While, hand in hand, we spread to-day,
 A flowery mantle o'er them.

And, as we greet each fallen Brave
 In accents true and tender,
Above each hallowed mound we'll wave
 Our Banner's triple splendor.

One Flag is ours ! one fame ! one fate !
 And naught the ties shall sever,
Which bind us firmly, State to State,
 One Union ! one forever !

—S. P. DRIVER.

SHADOWS AND SUNSHINE.

IN the golden years of life's fair morn—
 So long ago—when I was but a little
  child—
There were no clouds athwart the
 azure arch
That drooped above the sunny days,
 and filled
The silver nights with waves of limpid
 light ;

Or, if there were, I saw them not, by reason of
The golden shine that flooded all the happy days,
Wherein no shadow wove its bordering of dusky hues ;
And I was satisfied, and thought for aye and aye
The sky would be one cloudless canopy of sapphire light,
And—I did not know what shadows were !
The golden years went hurrying by,
With the noiseless flight of phantom feet,
And a tremulous fleck, like a dusky plume,
Flickered a moment across the day,
And then was lost within a flood of gold.

And the sunny heart, that ne'er had found
One single shadow bordering its sky,
Grew tremulous with nameless fear,
And sought to find the meaning of the transitory gloom
That cast its dusky shadow athwart the royal day.

And the startled eyes were lifted to the overhanging skies
As if the weird solution were hidden in their blue,
And lo ! a tiny cloud—no bigger than a baby's palm—
Hung, like a bit of dusky down, a-tremble in the air,
That swept along the fair horizon's golden rim.

And from that cloudlet's garnered duskiness
A mystic *something* fell and furled its sombreness within my heart ;
And—it seemed the world was at an end ah ! me,
And that was *ages long ago*, it seems,
And I have learned too sadly since that time
What clouds and shadows really are !

And I lost the childish wistfulness
That wished the sun might shine for aye and aye ;
For along the sad years' hurrying flight
There came a time when I was grateful for the dewy eves,
For the sunlight hurt me like a knife,
And my eyes were dry and burning in the hot glare of the day ;
And I was glad for every night that fell,
Like Elam's grateful shade, across the weary day.

And thus I learned that constant sunshine is not well,
And I have learned to bless the frequent clouds,
From filmy fleck, with curling edge, like fringe of gold
Turned toward the setting sun, to sombrest cloud
That shuts out all the golden light of day.

And if I could, I would not have my sky
One cloudless arch of sapphire light ;
For *cloudless sunsets* are not half so beautiful and grand
As those whose funeral fires are lit
By brands from burning wrecks of clouds.

And to the shadows of noon—the clouds that swept life's zenith sky—
I pray may hover toward its slanting west
With just enough of sombreness to make
Life's *sunset* one of grandeur and sublimity,
And beautiful as grand !
—AMANDA ELIZABETH DENNIS.

TRUST ME, DARLING, I'LL BE TRUE.

'TWAS the sweetest of all moments,
Greatest joy my heart e'er knew,
When my own dear sweetheart whispered,
" Trust me, darling, I'll be true."

We were out amidst the moonlight,
He was standing by my side,
When he asked me, " Would I love him,
Would I be his own sweet bride ? "

And I felt that I could trust him,
　For in his eyes of tenderest blue,
I could read the self-same sentence,
　"Trust me, darling, I'll be true."

Then his arms stole gently 'round me,
　Say, dear friends, what could I do?
He bent his head and softly kissed me,
　Whispering, "trust me, darling, I'll be true."

Then the little stars looked brighter,
　Seemed to know my secret too;
Twinkled, that the sky believed him,
　When he whispered, "I'll be true."

On my hand now brightly sparkles,
　Ring of purest sapphire blue,
Placed there by the one that whispered,
　"Trust me, darling, I'll be true."

A WISH FOR MY FRIEND.

I WISH that not a line of care
May fall upon thy brow so fair;
Nor sadness mark its footprints there,
　　Thy bliss to sever.

Though I thy face no more may see,
My wish, dear friend, shall ever be,
That pure, and true, and full, and free
Life's brightest joys may bloom for thee,
　　And wither never.

And still I have a wish more dear,
That when the night of death draws near,
And this bright world grows dim and drear,
　　And life is riven,—

That you may have a mansion where
The sky is always bright and clear;
For those we loved the most are there,
I wish that you with them may share,
　　The bliss of heaven.
　　　　—J. S. MASON.

MIXED METAPHOR.

'TWAS midnight, and the setting sun,
　Was slowly rising in the west,
The stagnant waters swiftly run,
　And lulled the peacock in her nest;
While pensive goose and playful cow,
　Lightly skipped from bough to bough.

'Twas Spring, Summer's oppressive heat
　Bowed the tenants their seed to sow,
Autumn rains incessantly beat,
　The earth was all wrapped in snow;
While thirsty fields and feathered train
All bounteously teemed with grain.

'Twas far out on a train of cars,
　Far on a firm and leaky bark,
Sailing around, among the stars,
　Beneath the shades of Highland Park;
While the joyful, loud death-knells rung,
To the sweet songs the cat-fish sung!

THY HOLY MEMORY.

MY soul thy secret image keeps,
　My midnight dreams are all of thee,
For nature then in silence sleeps,
　And silence broods o'er land and sea;
O, in that still, mysterious hour,
　How oft from waking dreams I start
To find thee but a fancy flower,
　Thou cherished idol of my heart.
Thou hast each thought and dream of mine,
　Have I in turn one thought and dream of thine?

Forever thine my dreams will be,
　Whate'er may be my fortunes here;
I ask not love—I claim from thee
　Only one boon, a gentle tear;
May e'er blest visions from above
　Play lightly 'round thy happy heart,
And the glad beams of peace and love
　Ne'er from thy glowing soul depart.
Farewell! My dreams are all of thee,
Hast thou one tender thought of me?

My joys like summer birds may fly,
　My hopes like summer blooms depart;
But there's one flower that cannot die,
　Thy holy memory in my heart.
No dews that one flower's cup may fill,
　No sunlight to its leaves be given,
But it will live and flourish still
　As deathless as a thing of heaven.

My soul greets thine unasked, unsought,
Hast thou for me one gentle thought?

Farewell! farewell! my far-off friend!
Between us broad, blue rivers flow,
And forests wave and plains extend,
And mountains in the sunlight glow;
The wind that breathes upon thy brow
Is not the wind that breathes on mine;
The star beams shining on thee now
Are not the beams that on me shine;
But memory's spell is on me yet—
Can'st thou the holy past forget!

The bitter tears that thou and I
May shed, when'er by anguish bowed,
Exalted to the noontide sky
May meet and mingle in the cloud;
And thus, my dearest friend, tho' we
Far, far apart must live and move,
Our souls, when God shall set them free,
Can mingle in the world of love,
This were an ecstasy to me—
Say, would it be a joy to thee?

DARLING.

WE walked through a fragrant moon-lit way,
My love and I, in the sweet June weather,
The eyes of the flowers that watched the day
Had folded their dewy lids together;
The noise of the day, and its toil and strife,
The calm of the night had caused to cease;
All the world seemed living its dreaming life,
And over my soul stole its perfect peace.

My love bent down his stately head
And whispered too low for the flowers to hear:
'Twas but one word, yet my cheeks grew red,
And my heart's quick throbs I could almost hear—
'Twas the one word "Darling"—yet by it I knew
The best of life that a woman knows,

The silence echoed it through and through,
From the stars in the sky e'en down to the rose.

When June again its blossoms shed
My love and I by the altar stood,
When the words that made us one had been said,
My love spoke low, but I understood,
And with that "Darling" a vision blest,
Of the coming years stretched long and fair;
My heart had found love's perfect rest,
For peace had taken its dwelling there.

But when another June time came,
I cannot tell if the world were fair,
For my love and I, and one whose name
E'en brought a chill to the summer air,
Walked slowly down to a darkling tide,
Where "Darling" I heard with my love's last breath,
And there I knew our ways must divide,
I must walk alone, while he crossed with death.

And when on his mute lips my kisses fell,
I whispered low, 'twas but one word,
But I gave him back his last farewell
And I think that surely his soul must have heard.
So I calmly wait through the Junes that are
For a brighter June that is yet to be,
When into his home, that lies afar,
With "Darling" my love shall welcome me.
—CHICAGO INTER-OCEAN.

THE LILIES OF THE FIELD.

THE Saviour's flowers! How pure and fair,
Those simple "Lilies of the Field";
How sweet an incense to the air
Their fragrant, snow-white blossoms yield!

Not Solomon in glory bright,
In gorgeous and in gold array,

Was such a fair and wondrous sight
  As in their modest beauty they !
They weave not the white robes they
    wear ;
They toil not, neither do they spin ;
No burdens like frail man they bear,
  For—unlike him—they know not sin.

Oh, emblems fair, oh, emblems sweet,
  Of Christian humbleness of heart !
May we, as pure, at Heaven's feet
  Sit low and " choose the better part."

That to the " meek in heart " alone
  Is by the Great Redeemer given ;
That brings us kneeling to His Throne,
  Throws wide the Golden Gates of
    Heaven.
              —CHAMBERS'S JOURNAL.

O LOVING HEARTS.

O LOVING hearts ! not prized when they
    were ours,
Now lost to all but mem'ry and to grief.
Could we recall them, or those vanished
    hours
When they were with us, it were some
    relief
To those who mourn, who mourn, alas !
    too late
            For loving hearts.

We sigh and mourn and sicken—yet no
    hand
Is stretched to aid us, and no kindly
    voice
In gentle accents speaks of home. We
    stand
Aghast to feel and know we should
    rejoice—
If death would summon us—for all is
    past,
            O loving hearts !

Remorse ! Ah, yes, in that we think
    and feel
And seek to find relief—but all in vain
Our sorrow for the past. Some wounds
    we cannot heal.
Our wearied hearts may pant, but not
    complain ;
We may not speak—we only sigh too
    late
            For loving hearts !

They once were ours, those loving
    hearts now lost.
(To all save mem'ry but a mocking
    dream.)
They come to haunt us, when too sadly
    lost
Upon our sleepless couch. We fain
    would deem
They once again were with us, but too
    late,
            O loving hearts !

Ye may not hear us, and ye may not
    know
Of our wild heart-beats, and our useless
    tears.
They should have come before ; the
    tears that flow
Are acrid now—they cannot calm our
    fears,
Nor ease our troubled hearts. All, all
    is past,
            O loving hearts !

THEY MET AND KISSED AND PARTED.

THEY met and kissed and parted
  (He didn't please her dad,
Nor she his ma) and all the world
  Cried out, " How very sad ! "
But thus to part 'twas better
  Than too late to wish they had,
For she'd a temper of her own,
  And he'd one just as bad,
And so that they should marry
  A kindly fate forbade :
For think how dreadful 'twould have
    been
  When both of them got mad !
Ah ! lucky spooney maiden,
  Ah ! lucky spooney lad,
To meet and kiss and part before
  Too late to wish you had !

" MY ANGEL LOVE."

I GAZED down life's dim labyrinth,
  A wildering maze to see,
Crossed o'er by many a tangled clew,
  And wild as wild could be.
And as I gazed in doubt and dread,
  An angel came to me.

I knew him for a heavenly guide,
　I knew him even then,
Though meekly as a child he stood
　Among the sons of men—
By his deep spirit loveliness,
　I knew him even then.

And as I leaned my weary head
　Upon his proffered breast,
And scanned the peril-haunted wild
　From out my place of rest,
I wondered if the shining ones
　Of Eden were more blest.

For there was light within my soul,
　Light on my peaceful way,
And all around the blue above
　The clustering starlight lay,
And easterly I saw upreared
　The pearly gates of day.

So, hand in hand, we trod the wild,
　My angel love and I—
His lifted wing all quivering
　With tokens from the sky.
Strange my dull thoughts could not divine
　'Twas lifted but to fly!

Again down life's dim labyrinth
　I grope my way alone,
While wildly through the midnight-sky
　Black hurrying clouds are blown,
And thickly in my tangled path,
　The sharp bare thorns are sown.

Yet firm, my foot, for well I know
　The goal cannot be far,
And ever, through the rifted clouds,
　Shines out one steady star,
For when my guide went up, he left
　The pearly gates ajar!
　　　—Mrs. Emily C. Judson.

"STONE THE WOMAN—LET THE MAN GO FREE."

Yes, stone the woman—let the man go free!
Draw back your skirts lest they perchance
May touch her garments as she passes;
But to him put forth a willing hand
To clasp with his that led her to destruction
And disgrace. Shut up from her the sacred
Ways of toil, that she no more may win an
Honest meal; but ope to him all honorable
Paths, where he may win distinction,
Give to him fair, pressed down measures of
Life's sweetest joys. Pass her, O maiden,
With a pure, proud face, if she puts out
A poor, polluted palm; but lay thy hand in
His on the bridal day and swear to
' cling to him
With wifely love and tender reverence,
Trust him who led a sister woman
To a fearful fate.

Yes, stone the woman—let the man go free!
Let one soul suffer for the guilt of two—
It is the doctrine of a hurried world,
Too out of breath for holding balances
Where nice distinctions and injustices
Are calmly weighed. But ah, how will it be
On that strange day of final fire and flame,
When men shall stand before the one true
udge? Shall sex make then a difference in Sin? Shall He, the searcher of the hidden
Heart, in His eternal and divine decree,
Condemn the woman and forgive the man?

OVER AND OVER AGAIN.

Over and over again,
　No matter which way I turn,
I always find in the Book of Life,
　Some lesson I have to learn.
I must take my turn at the mill,
I must grind out the golden grain,
I must work at my task with a resolute will,
　Over and over again.

We cannot measure the need
　Of even the tiniest flower,

Nor check the flow of the golden sands
That run through a single hour;
But the morning dews must fall,
The sun and the summer rain
Must do their part, and perform it all
    Over and over again.

    Over and over again
The brook through the meadow flows,
And over and over again
The ponderous mill-wheel goes.
Once doing will not suffice,
Though doing it be not in vain;
And a blessing failing us once or twice
May come if we try again.

The path that has once been trod
Is never so rough to the feet;
And the lesson we once have learned
Is never so hard to repeat.
Though sorrowful tears may fall,
And the heart to its depths be driven
By the storm and tempest, we need them all
To render us meet for heaven.

JOHN'S WIFE.

IF I say "Yes" to thee, John, can I
    thy love retain?
For I'm no beauty, dear; there's plenty
    call me plain.
Lilies and roses don't blend their tints
    in my face;
I have no witching blue eyes, no wonderful grace;
But I have health, and truth, and youth,
    and I love no other but thee;
John, thou must take me all in all, or
    else thou must let me be.

I am no scholar, John; of art I could
    not speak;
I could not pose or dress, and look like
    an ancient Greek;
I'm not æsthetic at all; I do not paint
    or play;
Nor could I write tale or poem, no
    matter what the pay:
But I can keep the house-place bright,
    I love no one but thee;
John, thou must take me all in all, or
    thou must let me be.

Come to my heart, dear girl! Give me
    that sun-browned hand.
Fairer art thou to me than the fairest
    in the land.
Dear little womanly woman! Love
    shall be my share.
Love is better than witching eyes or
    sunny hair;
Love is better than beauty or wit, love
    is better than gold;
For love is not found in the market-place; love is not bought and sold.

THANK GOD FOR SUNDAY.

SUNDAY, when all the world rests from its labors and the tired, care-worn opens his eyes, his first thought is, "Thank God for Sunday."

The poor laboring man toils from early Monday morning until Saturday night, that the wife and little ones that cluster around his humble hearth shall have a sufficiency of the staff of life. Next to the thought of his dear ones is that of the one day of rest ordained and set apart by the great God, and he toils on to that haven of rest, and, as the day approaches his soul is rekindled with life, as the foot-sore soldier is revived on his long march by the soul-stirring music—and when, at last, the slow hours and days of incessant work have tolled off the weary work-days, a bright, happy, joyous feeling pervades his own and the hearts of those dependent upon him.

The mechanic, while toiling through the six days of labor, looks forward to Sunday with a relish quickened by the thought that on that day he may enjoy the quiet of his home and rest from his labors. The innermost recesses of his heart give thought and expression to "Thank God for Sunday." As he steps without the threshold of his workshop on Saturday evening his steps are brisker, and his heart lighter, and a perfect happiness pervades his being—to-morrow is Sunday and he can rest and worship God according to the dictates of his own conscience, with the dear wife and children around him in an unbroken circle.

Come to my heart, dear girl! Give me that sun-browned hand.
Fairer art thou to me than the fairest in the land.
—Page 134.

UNIV. OF
CALIFORNIA

"Thank God for Sunday" is the mental expression of the merchant and professional man as he quits his place of business Saturday night. The lawyer lays aside his books and briefs; the merchant closes the pages of his ledger and cash book; the physician leaves his office, but it is with the thought that his professional skill may be required on the morrow—for none are exempt from sickness on Sunday. Yet he feels that work is over—to-morrow will be Sunday.

All classes "Thank God for Sunday"—all feel a higher, purer, better feeling pervading their hearts—all hearts are turned more nearly to God, and they feel that for all His love and kindness years of devotion would not remove the debt. All look forward to Sunday with more or less pleasure. The day seems brighter and purer than other days, there seems to be a peculiar charm about it that is irresistible, and all " Thank God for Sunday."

KISS ME, DARLING.

Kiss me, darling, if you love me,
  Thrill me with a sweet caress ;
Happy—happy are the mortals,
  Whom with lips you deign to bless,
Fold your soft white arms around me,
  Press me closer—tighter—love ;
Joys like this are sunbeams straying
  From celestial lights above.

Kiss me, darling, if you love me.
  Life can yield no sweeter joy ;
For your lips will bring to me, love,
  Happiness with no alloy.
Let others paint the joys of Heaven,
  Their highest aim or hope of bliss ;
But for me, oh ! kiss me, darling,
  Angels knew no joy like this.

Kiss me, darling, if you love me,
  Press me closer to your breast ;
O'er my face your soft hair shower,
  In your arms let me find rest.
Lip to lip, with heart throbs mingling,
  Faint in this maddening bliss ;
Cling still closer—nearer—darling,
  In a lingering, loving kiss.

THE OLD PLAY-GROUND.

I sat an hour to-day, John,
  Beside the old brook stream,
Where we were schoolboys in old time,
  When manhood was a dream ;
The brook is choked with fallen leaves,
  The pond is dried away ;
I scarce believe that you would know
  The dear old place to-day.

The school-house is no more, John,
  Beneath our locust trees,
The wild rose by the window side
  No more waves in the breeze ;
The scattered stones look desolate,
  The sod they rested on
Has been ploughed up by stranger hands,
  Since you and I were gone.

The chestnut tree is dead, John ;
  And, what is sadder now,
The broken grapevine of our swing
  Hangs on the withered bough ;
I read our names upon the bark,
  And found the pebbles rare
Laid up beneath the hollow side,
  As we had piled them there.

Beneath the grass-grown bank, John,
  I looked for our old spring
That bubbled down the alder path
  Three paces from the swing ;
The rushes grow upon the brink,
  The pool is black and bare,
And not a foot, this many a day,
  It seems, has trodden there.

I took the old blind road, John,
  That wandered up the hill ;
'Tis darker than it used to be,
  And seems so lone and still.
The birds sing yet among the boughs
  Where once the sweet grapes hung,
But not a voice of human kind
  Where all our voices rung.

I sat me on the fence, John,
  That lies as in old times,
The same half panel in the path
  We used so oft to climb ;
I thought how o'er the bars of life
  Our playmates had passed on,
And left me counting on this spot
  The faces that are gone.

NO TIME FOR HATING.

Begone with feud ! away with strife ;
  Our human hearts unmating !
Let us be friends again ! This life
  Is all too short for hating !
So dull the day, so dim the way,
  So rough the road we're faring—
Far better wend with faithful friend,
  Than stalk alone uncaring !

The barren fig, the withered vine,
  Are types of selfish living ;
But souls that give, like thine and mine,
  Renew their life by giving,
While cypress waves o'er early graves,
  On all the way we're going,
Far better plant, where seed is scant,
  Than tread on fruit that's growing.

Away with scorn ! Since die we must
  And rest on one low pillow ;
There are no rivals in the dust—
  No foes beneath the willow.
So dry the bowers, so few the flowers,
  Our earthly way discloses,
Far better stoop where daisies droop
  Than tramp o'er broken roses.

Of what are all the joys we hold
  Compared to joys above us !
And what are rank, and power and gold,
  Compared to hearts that love us ?
So fleet our years, so full of tears,
  So closely death is waiting ;
God gives us space for loving grace,
  But leaves no time for hating.
          —A. J. H. Duganne.

TILL DEATH US PART.

"Till Death us part."
  So speaks the heart,
When each to each repeats the words
    of doom ;
  Thro' blessing and thro' curse,
  For better and for worse,
We will be one, till that dread hour
    shall come.

Life, with its myriad grasp,
Our yearning souls shall clasp,
By ceaseless love, and still expectant
    wonder ;
In bonds that shall endure,
Indissolubly sure
Till God in death shall part our paths
    asunder.

Till Death us join,
  O voice yet more divine !
That to the broken heart breathes hope
    sublime :
  Thro' lonely hours
  And shattered powers
We still are one, despite of change and
    time.

  Death, with his healing hand,
  Shall once more knit the band
Which needs but that one link which
    none may sever ;
  Till, thro' the Only Good,
  Heard, felt, and understood,
Our life in God shall make us one for-
    ever.

MY MOTHER.

My mother—how these hallowed words
  My heart with rapture thrill,
Charming from memory's magic chords,
  Their tenderest music still !
Down the dim vista of the years,
  My path I oft retrace,
Till, through a shining mist of tears,
  I see my mother's face.

Her soulful eyes, her pallid cheek,
  Her dark hair streaked with gray,
Her mouth, I never knew to speak
  Save in a winning way,
Her modest mien, her gentle grace,
  Her form, so fine and fair,
The sunshine of her smiling face—
  All, all again are there !

I feel the tender hand she laid
  Upon my curly head,
I see her kneel beside my bed,
  And hear the prayer she prayed ;
I feel again her " good-night " kiss,
  And hear—the crowning joy
Of childhood's happy days was this—
  Her fond : " God bless my boy ! "

The path that leads to manhood's prime,
  In fancy I retrace,

Back to that sacred hour of time,
　When last I saw her face;
　I see her on the threshold stand,
　Tears gathering in her eye,
　I feel the last clasp of her hand,
　I hear her last "good-bye!"

My mother! Many a year
　God called her home to rest;
Sweet violets grow, and roses blow,
　Above her mouldering breast;
Yet on me smiles her image still,
　From memory's golden frame,
And still my heart-strings throb and thrill,
　At mention of her name.
　　　　—CHARLES W. HUBNER.

MY HUSBAND.

WHO took me from my childhood's home
To love me for myself alone,
And for my sacrifice atone?
　　　　My husband!

Who grumbled at the poor beefsteak,
And bade me better coffee make,
And told me greater care to take?
　　　　My husband!

Who swore because the baby cried,
And to the spare room quickly hied,
While I to quiet, vainly tried?
　　　　My husband!

Who tore the buttons off his shirt,
And said I could these ills avert
If I was more on the alert?
　　　　My husband!

Who bade me rise the fire to make,
While he another nap should take,
Although I'd been all night awake?
　　　　My husband!

Who, when I ask for half a crown,
Knits up his brows into a frown,
And asks me where the other's gone
　　　　My husband!?

And when I see my mother dear,
Who tried my lonely lot to cheer,
Who says she's dreadfully, dreadfully queer?
　　　　My husband!

Who stays out till late at night,
And then comes home so very tight
That I nearly die of fright?
　　　　My husband!

Who breaks the china, slams the door,
Leaves all his clothes upon the floor,
And swears it's all a dreadful bore?
　　　　My husband!

And who do I, for his dear sake,
Of every sacrifice partake,
Lest I his confidence should shake?
　　　　My husband!

LIVING THE PAST.

CHRISTMAS eve. Outside the night is clear and cold, with a great moon swinging adown the sky and all God's silver eyes watching, watching. The whole day long heaven's white snow blossoms have fallen—sadly and ceaselessly, like the tears of women—and piled themselves into soft banks over the fields and meadows, across the pasture lands and the fallow places, and against the hedges; they have bent down the boughs of the strongest firs and pines, and nestled around the tree trunks, warming with their very coldness; they have kissed and fallen away from the last roses and chrysanthemums out in the gardens, and they have clung to the drooping branches of the weeping willow over the well; yea, they have covered over—all those sweet snow flowers—every lonely grave that a while ago was green on the hill that slopes to the river. The night is like a great diamond lying on some restless woman's breast, glistening anew with each breath that flutters from her lips; but the night's breath is colder and crueler than was ever the breath of woman, and its heart beats with varied passions, too strong and lion-like to be controlled. Past my window the footsteps go, this way and that way—the footsteps of the countless people who live in my world, and who know the same hopes, ambitions, loves, failures, sins—footsteps of the old and the young, the gay and the lonely, the happy and the sorrowful, the eager and the hopeless. Ah, me! you can read every soul if you only listen to the steps that go past your window. And how they crisp to-night as they press the sparkling snow! And oh! how some of them falter and stumble for the need of a strong hand to guide them—and how often do you and I reach out that hand? I wonder if they haunt you to-night as they go past. They haunt me, for with them are mingled the footsteps of many who are dead, and to whom I might have reached a helping hand. I hear them more plainly than any others. Dead, sorrowful eyes look at me, too, from out the past. Is there not one dead to whom you, also, might have been more kind and tender? Heigho! my room has grown dim and shadowy and the fire is low. The rest of the house is bright and ringing with Christmas cheer; but you and I, love, we will stay here in this quiet place together. Have not all our Christmas eves been so spent, just we two, alone and happy in our great love, heeding not and caring not for the passionate, foolish world about us? Do you remember, dear, how one dull Christmas we were separated, and you wrote me that you leaned out your window in the midnight with the snow falling upon your brow and listened to the glad, soft bells while you thought of me? Come closer, dear heart! Somehow, to-night I seem to want you so—I seem to need you so—my very heart aches to have you closer. It is almost as if I knew you could not come; but you can, love. Come closer—closer yet—kneel down beside me as you used to do, and lay your cool fingers upon mine and lean your cheek on my breast—it is only so that I understand heaven. Do you remember that your gift to me was always a bunch of white flowers, and how once you could find only one pale rosebud? How I loved you! How I do love you—kind heaven! I have been dreaming, alone in the dark. I have been living again the past, and I had forgot that the snow blossoms are white on your grave, too, this night.

—ELLA HIGGINSON.

LIFE, A TANGLED SKEIN.

LIFE is but a tangled skein,
  Full of trouble, toil, and travail,
Knots that puzzle heart and brain,
  We must study to unravel:
    Slowly, slowly,
    Bending lowly
O'er our task and trusting wholly
Unto Him, whose loving hand
Helps us smooth each twisted strand.

In our hands at early morn,
  And at night when darkness lingers,
Still the distaff must be borne,
  While the thread slips through our fingers,
    Lightly, lightly,
    Twisting tightly
Colors that shall gleam out brightly
When the fabric feels the stain
Of misfortune, grief and pain.

He who lacks of skill or thought
  Is in awkwardness betraying,
Will the lines of grace distort,
  By the friction surely fraying
    Thread so tender,
    Fine and slender
Stand accused as an offender,
And himself alone must blame
Nor the knot that caused him shame.

Some may wind a silken thread,
  Soft and smooth and beautiful;
Other flax may hold instead,
  Or the coarse and shaggy wool;
    But if ever
    Our endeavor
From the stains of sin to sever,
We may weave them bright and fair
In the robes that angels wear.

Life's a complex skein indeed,
  Full of trouble, toil and travail,
More than human help we need
  All its mazes to unravel.
    Slowly, slowly,
    Bending lowly
O'er our task, and trusting wholly
In God's love we patience gain
As we wind the tangled skein.

THE SWEET LONG AGO.

GOLDEN memories float before us
    Of the sweet, sweet long ago,
Of a rosy, happy childhood,
    Still our fancies are aglow.

When we wandered to the wildwood,
    Gathering flowers of rarest sheen,
Memory yet inhales their fragrance,
    Though long years have rolled between.

"John Jump-ups" (thus we called them)
    In our pathway grew so bright,
Looked as though they caught their radiance
From the rainbow's blended light.

Graceful ferns in beauty waving,
    Kissed by every passing breeze,
Seemed as making their obeisance;
    To the foliage of the trees.

While the foliage of the forest
    Seemed to rustle as with joy
At the merry, ringing laughter
    Of each happy girl and boy.

Moss-clad rocks with honeysuckles,
    Overhung most strangely sweet,
Greeted then our childish vision,
    Making rural scenes complete.

Happy childhood, happy childhood,
    We in fancy live it o'er,
Gathering pebbles by the streamlet,
    Washed by wavelets on the shore.

And we seem to hear the music
    Of the murmuring streamlet's flow,
As it rippled o'er the pebbles
    In the sweet, sweet long ago.

And the winding path we see it,
    Leading to a homestead dear,
Linked with many a fond remembrance,
    Many a sigh, and many a tear.

For within its sacred precincts
    Once a happy family dwelt,
Father, mother, sisters, brothers,
    Round the same old hearthstone knelt.

Father, yet I seem to hear him,
    As he read with trembling breath,
From the Book he so much valued:
    "Be thou faithful unto death."

Mother's voice I seem to hear it,
    As she softly, sweetly sung:
"Jesus ready stands to save you;"
    This she sang when I was young.

Since the halcyon days of childhood
    Many weary years have fled,
Sisters, brothers, they are scattered—
    Father, mother, they are dead.

Hark! I seem to hear the music,
    Echoing from the other shore,
"Jesus ready stands to save you
    Full of pity, love and power."

If we but accept the Saviour,
    On His mercy but rely,
We at last shall meet our loved ones
    In the sweet, sweet by-and-by.

NEVER MIND WHAT "THEY" SAY.

DON'T worry nor fret
    About what people think,
Of your ways or your means—
    Of your food or your drink.
If you know you are doing
    Your best every day,
With the right on your side,
    Never mind what "they" say.

Lay out in the morning
    Your plans for each hour,
And never forget
    That old time is a power.
This also remember
    'Mong truths old and new—
The world is too busy
    To think much of you.

Then garner the minutes
    That make up the hours,
And pluck in your pilgrimage
    Honor's bright flowers.
Should grumblers assure you
    Your course will not pay,
With conscience at rest,
    Never mind what "they" say.

Then let us, forgetting
    The insensate throng,

That jostles us daily
  While marching along,
  Press onward and upward,
  And make no delay—
  And though people talk,
  Never mind what " they " say.

LIGHT.

I STOOD on the bridge at sunset,
  And the river went rushing along,
  And I listened with a strange, sweet pleasure,
  To its wild but mournful song.

As I gazed at the heaving water,
  Surging beneath my feet,
  I thought of the trials, the troubles,
  I had not the strength to meet.

A strange unquiet stole o'er me ;
  A nameless longing for rest ;
  Then I thought of the Heavenly Father
  Who doeth all for the best.

A flash of light came o'er me
  Like the light of the bursting dawn,
  And all the pain and weariness,
  Like the summer rain was gone.

The sun had sunk behind the hills,
  The stars were shining clear and bright,
  The river still sang mournfully,
  But all within was bright.

NIGHT SCENES IN ——.

A FEW stars yet linger in the heavens. The moon has blushed in shame at the world of sin and corruption, and hid its face. The lamps, worn, weary and sorrowful, burn along the streets. The clock in the steeple has already tolled ten. Mark the hurried steps of yon innocent maiden, as she wends her way homeward. Ah, unknown to the wickedness of the world, she is permitted to spend late evenings with her friends ; and now she wends her way homeward alone. But note the closely muffled female hurrying rapidly up the pavement. Her children are doubtless unattended and uncared for. Her husband,—oh, heaven knows where he is—home has no attractions for him. He is a reveller—friendless and penniless—to occupy *waste* space in some one's graveyard. Issuing from yonder cellar is a band of drunken revellers, who have disgraced the very name of man, by vexing the ear of night with ribald songs and jests ; wasting, probably, the hard earnings which has taken some industrious parent years to collect. Wandering through life without aim, without object, and almost without chance of salvation. Having no tear for the wretched, no hope for the despairing, no balm for the suffering. Decay and death are already written upon their countenances, and the last anchor of hope has been cast and foundered in the pit of perdition. To the right you behold one of a different order. The opera dress proclaims that she has also passed the night from home. Her cheek is flushed and her features fair ; but the dimmed eyes portray that early decay has commenced its ravages on her fair form. Sin had set its lasting stain upon her brow, and lovely, as it is, shame has blushed thereon until it has blushed itself to death. There's another ; the heavy black cross, however, portrays her Catholic faith. A little further on, you may behold a young man with downcast looks and staggering gait. This staggering is not caused, however, by intoxication. He, and the lads that are following behind him, have spent their first night at the gambling-table. They are making good progress in the science their teachers taught them. The pallor on their faces shows that the hell of earth has given them a foretaste of their hell below. Soon their fair and elastic forms will be the prey of disease, and their fortunes the fees for their instructors. Soon their parents and relations will have to bear their loss as going to an early grave, " unwept, unhonored, and unsung ! " But you ask yourself, is there *nothing* but corruption and unholiness in this world of sin ! Ah, yes, my reader ; there is to God's chosen ones. Their fortunes may be rent, the cares of life may cluster thickly around them but, "sleep comes unbidden to the hard couch of poverty,

BOOK NO. 15

Your glances seemed drawing
My soul through my eyes.

while downy pillows of the desolate woo the gentle goddess in vain, and drugs and opiates purchase the fevered slumber that is not rest, nor even forgetfulness, but a heavy *stupor*, peopled by the spectres of conscience." Yes, "there's a silver side to every cloud," and those who make their dark side here by obeying the laws of nature and the commands of God, will see their "silver side " in Heaven.

A TOUCHING POEM.

One day, while *en route* to Macon from Augusta, the Ford Troupe were entertained upon the cars by a little deaf and dumb girl, the daughter of a well-known Georgia gentleman. Finally, at the solicitation of her father, the little girl recited, by gesture, the Lord's Prayer." This she did kneeling, and in a manner which made every sign expressive, and deeply touched the looker-on. Mr. Barton Hill, the actor, immediately wrote out the following and handed it to the child's father:

TO A. E. E.

AGNES—sweet lamb of innocence !
Ethel—ethereal dove !
Sent for the worship of mankind
  From the bright realm above.

Borne on an angel's wing to earth,
  And then to " Alba " given,
To show how pure and white a soul
  Can crystallize in Heaven.

God would not let thee hear the woes
  That desolate our land ;
Nor suffer thee to speak with man,
  Lest thou should understand

How poor, how weak, we mortals are ;
  How we abuse our powers,
What miseries our crimes inflict
  On this sad earth of ours.

Therefore, he blessed thee with a soul
  Only to angels given,
And left two senses as a pledge
  Of thy return to Heaven.

Lips that refuse to speak on earth
  The language of the saints,
And ears that must not listen to
  Mortality's complaints.

When thy pure mission is fulfilled
  And thou return'st above,

To nestle at the Saviour's feet,
  Thou minister of love,

Surely the whole immortal sphere
  With melody shall ring,
For thou shalt speak with angels then
  And hear the seraphs sing.

Enough for us to see thine eyes,
  That make the planets pale,
To hear the rippling, joyous laugh
  That thy pure thoughts exhale ;

To watch thy waving, golden hair,
  Tinged with the setting sun,
And note how true a heart can speak,
  Taught by the holy One !

Dumb ? When the very soul inspired
  Beyond the powers of speech,
Can utter the Lord's Prayer in tones
  That language cannot reach.

Dumb ? When thy little hands are clasped
  In eloquence of prayer,
And every glance ascends to Heaven
  Entreating for us there !

Dumb ? When these fingers can express
  " Forgive," " Thy kingdom come ! "
Thou hast thy faculties in full,
  And we are deaf and dumb.
      —BARTON HILL.

THE ECSTASY OF KISSES.

YOU kissed me ! my head
  Dropped low on your breast,
With a feeling of shelter
  And infinite rest ;
While the holy emotions
  My tongue dare not speak
Flashed up in a flame
  From my heart to my cheek.
Your arms held me fast—
  Oh, your arms were so bold,
Heart beat against heart
  In your passionate fold.
Your glances seemed drawing
  My soul through my eyes,
As the sun draws the mist
  From the seas to the skies,
Your lips clung to mine
  Till I prayed in my bliss

They might never unclasp
  From the rapturous kiss.

You kissed me! my heart
  And my breath and my will
In delirious joy
  For a moment stood still.
Life had for me then
  No temptations, no charms,
No visions of happiness
  Outside of your arms.
And were I this instant
  An angel, possessed
Of the peace and the joy
  That are given the blest,
I would fling my white robes
  Unrepentingly down,
I would tear from my forehead
  Its beautiful crown,
To nestle once more
  In that haven of rest,
Your lips upon mine,
  My head on your breast!

You kissed me! my soul
  In a bliss so divine,
Reeled and swooned like a drunkard
  Foolish with wine;
And I thought 'twere delicious
  To die there, if death
Would but come while my lips
  Were yet moist with your breath,
If my heart might grow cold
  While your arms clasped me round
In their passionate fold.
  And these are the questions
I ask day and night:
  Must my lips taste no more
Such exquisite delight?
  Would you care if your breast
Were my shelter as then,
  And if you were here
Would you kiss me again?

COLONEL BLUEGRASS, KENTUCKY.

You may boom each foreign noble with
  his epaque pedigree,
All the titled importation Anglo-maniacs love to see,
Swing the censer low before them, bow
  the head and bend the knees.
But from joining in the worship, well,
  excuse me if you please.
Oh, a true man as God made him is
  the heir I admire,
And upon this broad, green earth—
For brains, valor, build and birth,
  Col. Bluegrass of Kentucky, beats
  them all from word to wire.

In the desert of Sahara I would know
  him at a glance,
So like Hamlet at a funeral and Mercutio at a dance,
With his Bourbonesque complexion,
  and his bills like crying babies,
And that horror of cold water entertained by dogs with rabies.
Yet he's certain not to turn his back
  upon a friend or foe,
Has a pistol in one pocket,
And is careful not to knock it
  Against the whiskey bottle on the
  other side, you know.

The stud book is the Bible which he
  quotes from day and night,
He would turn back for a horse-race
  were sweet Heaven itself in sight,
He's not up to date with "Trilby," but
  his equine lore's sublime.
He can give the favorite's pedigree from
  B C to our time,
When it comes right down to horse
  talk, oh, he marches with the
  band—
Pshaw, you've seen him at the track,
  Yelling like a maniac,
Or looming up serenely in the judge's
  crowded stand.

He's a sworn knight of the ladies and
  bows low at beauty's shrine,
Takes his hat off to a petticoat that
  hangs upon the line,
Put him on some desert island with the
  homeliest girl on earth,
He would flirt to keep his hand in and
  make love for all he's worth.
Though his fancy's queen is lovely,
  yet he blushes as he says,
That he often strays from her,
For this reason I infer,
  That a lover like a gourmand tires
  of quail for thirty days.

He makes his house a free hotel and
    welcomes rich and poor,
Always keeps the latch-string hanging
    on the outside of the door,
There the whiskey jug's unfailing as the
    widow's cruse, they say,
And the wily game of poker holds its
    own both night and day.
There the red-faced politicians meet
    to fix their fences tight,
While the young folks bill and coo,
    As their elders used to do,
And the music of the foxhounds is
    blown in from out the night.

Yet with all his imperfections, he is
    reverent and sincere,
Asks the preacher out to dinner every
    Sunday in the year,
And upon these grand occasions he as-
    sumes a solemn air,
But his language is less picturesque—
    because he doesn't swear.
He converses on the Bible in a most
    impressive tone—
Moses and the promised land,
    Aaron's rod and Gideon's band,
While the doctrine of election he
    considers quite his own.

Honest gentleman, God bless him, with
    his bluff but kindly ways,
Clinging to the good traditions of the
    homespun yesterdays,
With his virtues not post mortem, and
    his faults so few, I think
The kind recording angel does not set
    them down in ink.
He's Dame Nature's pet edition, may
    he stay in fruit fore'er,
For upon this broad, green earth,
    For brains, valor, build and birth,
Col. Bluegrass, of Kentucky, breaks
    the record every year.
        —Elma Sydem Miller.

WEEP NOT FOR THE PAST.

Weep not for the past,—'tis a dream
    that has fled,
Its sunshine has vanished, its garlands
    are dead ;
Deep, deep in its shadows bright hopes
    are laid low,
Oh ! call them not back to the land
    whence they go.

They came as the light that may gleam
    from on high,
From the raving of some spirit that
    passes us by ;
So gently—we deemed that the fetter
    of earth
Had fallen away for a holier birth ;
And they passed—but a voice lingers
    yet on the ear
In accents that fall from some sunnier
    sphere ;
Weep not, child of sorrow, for hopes
    that were thine,
Unblest are the gifts of an unhallowed
    shrine,
Thy idol was earthly—thy life-star has
    set.
Bright stars are in Heaven that beam
    for thee yet !

Weep not for the past, though it hold
    in gloom,
Loved forms that have sunk to their
    rest in the Lamb—
Fond voices that rang in the laugh of
    the song,
And faces that smiled as they flitted
    along ;
Oh, call them not back ! for they went
    in their mirth,
Ere their hearts had been chilled by
    one frost of this earth,
And 'tis sweet to lie down with the
    song yet unsung,
And wake its first notes in a heavenly
    tongue !

Then yield not to sorrow, life has not a
    day
That gives not some sunbeam to lighten
    our way,
But call from the past, from each
    blessing that dies
A gem to illumine the crown for the
    skies.
The future is o'er us ;—the present is
    ours,
To shroud it in sadness or gild it with
    flowers,
To sink on life's ocean, or find on its
    wave
A halo that wakes e'en the gloom of the
    grave !

DREAMING.

Oh, tell me not 'tis vain to dream,
  While the hours are fleeting past ;
The golden moments sweeter seem,
  And joys the longer last.
We quaff imagination's fount,
  When, lo ! all Nature smiles,
And free from every worldly care,
  We rove 'mid dreamland aisles.

Ah ! ye, who never pause to note
  The beauty of life's day ;
Who never pluck the blossoms fair,
  That bloom along the way.
Oh, do not chide the dreamer,
  Who, culling from the hours,
Would gather for life's harvest
  The soul's pure fadeless flowers.

'Tis but a dream, the life we live,
  And we must wake at last,
When all the happy hours are o'er,
  And all our joys are past ;
'Tis but a dream, and yet how true
  The fleeting moments seem,
While sadly on the life-sands drift,
  In Time's dark pulseless stream.

AUTUMN.

Again the golden dawn has flushed with magnetic splendor the eastern sky, and tipped with prismatic tints the towering boughs of the ancient oak, that rises majestically far above the level of the terra firma that laves the base.

All seems life and pleasure, the little birds have begun their matin songs, man and beast seem to enjoy the pleasures that earth bestows, the eagle's shrill scream is reverberating from hill to dale, as it spreads its pinions and soars toward the eastern horizon.

Again the green cloak of summer has been exchanged for the golden months of autumn, the laurels have bloomed on the hill-tops, the fireflies have twinkled in the evening grass, and many who watched the lengthening rays of the brilliant orb of day as it sank slowly behind the western hills, and numbered with the past another summer, will sleep their last and peaceful sleep, beneath the damp, cold sod, ere the spring will again clothe the earth in verdure.

The loveliest season of the year is here—not the season of " wailing winds and naked woods," dead flowers, and brown meadows, but that of beauty, joy and hope's fruition. Now the skies are as " blue as Italy's own," and the mellow sunlight quivers through foliage more gorgeous than departed summer's brightest tints.

Welcome its bright skies, its brilliant drapery, its crisp bracing air. Now may the tired lungs inhale great draughts of health, and the relaxed frame grow strong and vigorous. Now the city's thoroughfares begin to be thronged with gay parties just returned from their summer flitting. At the sea side, among the mountains, or the country, they have been seeking health and recreation. And while gathering strength and vitality for the winter's labor or dissipation, let us hope that some atom of worldly selfishness and greed has fallen away to give place to better thoughts and nobler impulses.

There is nothing saddening in the autumn time, save that it may remind us of another misspent year. It is not alone the season of decay and death, but also that of perfected life and fulfilled promises. The harvest has been gathered—orchards have yielded their lucious fruits ; barns and garners are filled ; man, bird and beast are busy storing earth's bounties for future subsistence. All is busy, joyous life. The squirrel, frisking and chattering over his winter's hoard, is not more blithe than the laborer, whose cheering song and ringing shout still echoes in the deserted fields. Yes, the season is bright, but it has its chilling storms. Days when drenching rains fall and wild winds beat against our windows, we know that the Frost-king will soon rule this fair realm. We know, too, that another spring will clothe the earth with verdure, therefore we look forward hopefully.

" The tiny leaflet has preceded the bud, the bud has become the flower, and this in turn the perfect fruit."

Some buds have been blighted—some fruit blasted, but each has fulfilled the

Autumn.

UNIV. OF
CALIFORNIA

purpose of its existence, and now their rest approaches.

We, too, have lived our lives; to some purpose, if diligent stewards; to none if unfaithful. To many the autumn has not yet come, but others are waiting for that winter which men call death. Beyond this is the glad awakening in the Land where winter never comes. And so we are content to work and wait knowing that, whether here or there, our Father's loving, protecting care is over all.

MY FATHER'S GRAVE.

Is there a spot on this wide earth,
On this bright land that gave me birth,
More hallowed than this spot of earth—
My dear, dear. Father's grave?

That pretty flower, it bows its head
As lowly as the sleeping dean;
The grass in morning bends its head
Above my Father's grave.

I planted it one evening there,
I nursed it with a mother's care,
I knew it would bloom in beauty there,
Above my Father's grave.

My Father sleeps his last long sleep;
The angels 'round their vigils keep;
Then I will not for Father weep,
For he has gone to God.

The daughter will no longer mourn
For one who from this world has gone
We'll meet together some bright morn—
We'll meet above in heaven.

SO MUCH OF LIFE BEHIND ME LIES.

So much of life behind me lies,
My heart grows faint with sorrow,
That each to-day the swifter flies,
And sooner comes each morrow.

I marvel much that once I deemed
Time's azure wings were leaden;
And on life's boundless ether seemed
Youth's ecstasies to deaden.

While now my precious days glide on,
Than all fleet symbols faster;

With fortune gay, scarce quicker gone,
Than glooming with disaster.

It is not that my life has brought
Of its young dreams fruition!
Its warp, alas! is thick in-wrought
With crossing of ambition.

Not that my days have all been good—
I mourn them few and fleeting;
Meagre, I own, their gains that would
Be worth their poor repeating.

And this a double worth bestows
On hours as yet unsquandered;
Priceless to him the sunset grows
Who the long day has wandered

A wanderer and a loiterer I,
From whom life's shadows lengthen;
Above me shine the summits high,
Around me fetters strengthen.

I cannot reach their golden crests,
The while I strive receding;
My soul, impatient while it rests,
Weeps o'er each moment speeding.

So much to do, so far to climb,
So little learned at fifty!
Ah! youth is prodigal of time,
Age only makes us thrifty.

The silver gleams that in our locks
Are sunset's pale fore-glances,
Teach us that deeds, not beating clocks,
Mark fitly Time's advances.

What's then to do, since Time will run,
And graves end earth's ambitions?
This first, this only, is well done—
To live for heaven's fruitions.

FACES AT THE FIRE.

I PASSED a window in the dusk of the evening. A broad stream of light flows across the darkening street, and shines against the opposite wall. The blaze flashes in my eyes, and, but for an instant, unconsciously I turn aside to meet it. I catch but a glimpse of the interior of a home, but it is enough.

Through a screen of green leaves, I see a group of merry faces by the fire, cheerful blaze making "a sunshine in the shady place." The light flashes upon the features of a beautiful girl, with a laughing child upon her knee; a little ruddy fellow is crouched at her feet, and a cheerful-looking old dame, in spectacles, busy at her knitting, from which for a moment she looks up to watch the gambols of the youngsters, occupies the further side of the hearth. There is another figure, that of a man with his back toward me, on the opposite side, doubtless the fire brightens his face, too, but the faces of the women and the children are enough. What is a cheerful fireside without them! They are the precious jewels which glitter and shine around the happy hearths, and make light and beauty there even in the saddest hour. Like white flowers in the dusk, they cheer and hallow it—they speak of the thousand hopes and joys which cluster about a home—they are the emblems of virtue, cheerfulness, beauty, and divine comfort.

Burke has said that "to love the little platoon we belong to in society is the germ of all public affections." Yes, unless the faces shine by the fire, they will shine nowhere else. If we feel not warmed by the fire which glows about the hearthstone—we mean the affection and love which are its true moral glow —how can we feel less affection and sympathy for those who compass us about in ever-widening circles in the outer world! All genial warmth emanates from the home; it is there the affections are first moved, and there the heart is first attuned to human sympathy.

You see that child laughing in the full glow of firelight—it is drinking in impressions which will last its life out. The little child is formed by love, its character is moulded by love, its future is determined by love:

> "Ah! how skilful grows the hand
> That obeyeth love's command,
> It is the heart, and not the brain,
> That to the highest doth attain;
> And he who followeth love's behest,
> Far exceedeth all the rest."

HOME.

I ASK what constitutes a home? Is it the mere dwelling-place where our parents and friends reside? Is it this accompanied by the additions and improvements that our rank and station require? It is all this and something more. It is a possession common to all. The outcast, as well as the prince, has some endearing spot which he cherishes in his memory and calls it "home." He may be asked to describe it, and he will mention the cottage, or the hut, the garden, the "old oaken bucket," and numerous other things—but here he will stop. You ask him, is *that* what he cherishes? Are there not thousands of cottages with wells and gardens near by, and why should he admire this one so particularly. He will answer "Because it's home!" This is all he will say—he has yet left "home" undefined. Nor, my reader, is it an easy object to define. The heart is bound there by a transparent cord which cannot be described. And true, some of our homes are more comfortable than those of others, but "home" does not depend upon gaudy appearances or unnecessary comforts. There can be no place on earth more charming than the cottage. King's palaces have not the real unspeakable attractions that these possess. The neat dwelling, the plain whitewashed paling, the lovely shade, the pure fresh air, all serve to make up its attractions. Then how necessary is it that we should strive to make these improvements to make home attractive? How important it is that we should add these things which, though in themselves small, yet serve and knit the ties of home in closer compact. It has been said that home is a realm for its possessor: and though the rain and wind may enter there, the law nor the king cannot! And what is best of all is it united circle! Genial warmth emanates there, and there the affections are first moved and the heart attuned to human sympathy. There the father is king of all his realm, and the mother queen of all. There may have been sadnesses to mar the pleasures, there may be a chair whose vacancy tells of some departed father or mother, brother or sister; yet, its ties by these circumstances are only made the stronger. And blessed be the unchanging type which "home" represents! Our lives may be a sea of trouble, nipped by the waves of care and sorrow, age may plough deep furrows in tinted cheeks, and time change jetty ringlets into snowy white; yet, the one eternal home still awaits us. We must leave our earthly homes, though beautiful and attractive they be. But glorious consolation it is to know that though dear ones have left us, and though spots that we cherished as "home" are blotted from memory's page, there yet remains a universal "home, home, *sweet* home!"

GOOD-NIGHT.

IF I could only lay me down to rest,
   Crossing my weary hands upon my breast,
And shut my troubled eyes without a fear,
   Knowing that they would never open here—
How blissful it must be, both worlds in sight,
   To say my tired good-night.

If only, from the fretting cares of Time,
   To truths eternal I at once may climb,
No longer count the graves whereon I tread,
   But in one moment be all comforted—
If such could be, what joy, in upward flight,
   To sing my tired good-night.

I watch the sweetest flowers throughout the morn,
   I look, and lo! at noontide they are gone,
The wings of sorrow are forever spread;
   I weep, but weeping brings not back my dead,
If God would but reveal the breaking light,
   How sweet to say good-night.

This flooding tide of yearnings will not cease;
   I cannot reach to touch the lips of Peace;
Nor can I gather to my sobbing heart
   The white-winged angels God has set apart,
Yet haply I may find them *all* in sight
   After some tired good-night.

What wonder, then, that I should long to rest,
   Crossing my weary hands upon my breast;
To shut my troubled eyes without a fear,
   Knowing that they would never open here;
To say to earth, with heaven alone in sight,
   My rapturous good-night.

YOUNG men, build strongly in youth your ship of character. Mark how the shipwright does his work; so when you are launched upon the sea of life—often more stormy than the ocean—when business, cares and temptations, with all the world's allurements beset you, you may, like a well-constructed vessel, withstand the tempest, and accomplish your voyage of life with profit and safety.

LAUGH.

THE world loves the man who laughs. He is welcomed everywhere, even at a funeral. His sympathy for you in time of sorrow you cannot question, yet you see laughter lurking behind his sorrowful face, and you bless him for it, while your burden grows lighter. The sweetest music in this world is human laughter. It rises higher, swells grander, is more nobly beautiful than any deep-toned peals that ever sounded from gilded chancel to tall steeple. It is to the harmonies of life what a beautiful woman is to the earth's material things. You laugh, and the sunshine bursts through every cloud; laugh, and you hear the birds singing; laugh, and you catch the odors of the flowers; laugh, and to you comes the nameless beautyl of springtime and harvest; laugh, and echoes laugh back to you from every human heart; laugh, and you lift yourself above kings and emperors, and hold converse with the gods; laugh, and you catch the spirit of the morning, the afternoon and the soft twilight. One peal of honest laughter is of more benefit to mankind than every sneer that ever came from lips of cynic since cynics appeared upon the face of the earth.

TO THOSE WHO FAIL.

COURAGE, brave heart, nor in thy purpose falter;
  Go on and win the fight at any cost.
Though sick and weary after heavy conflict,
  Rejoice to know the battle is not lost.

The field is open still to those brave spirits
  Who nobly struggle till the strife is done,
Through sun and storm, with courage all undaunted,
  Working and waiting till the battle's won.

The fairest pearls are found in deepest waters,
  The brightest jewels in the darkest mine,
And through the very blackest hour of midnight,
  The star of hope doth ever brightly shine.

Press on! Press on! The path is steep and rugged,
  And storm-clouds almost hide hope's light from view;
But you can pass where other feet have trodden;
  A few more steps may bring you safely through.

The battle o'er, a victor crowned with honors;
  By patient toil each difficulty past,
You then may see these days of bitter failure,
  But spurred you on to greater deeds at last.
      —CHAMBERS'S JOURNAL.

REGRET.

IF I had known, O loyal heart,
  When hand to hand we said farewell,
How for all time our paths would part,
  What shadow o'er our friendship fell,
I should have clasped your hand so close
  In the warm pressure of my own
That memory still might keep its grasp,
    If I had known.

If I had known, when far and wide
  We loitered through the summer land,
What presence wandered by our side,
  And o'er you stretched its awful hand,
I should have hushed my careless speech
  To listen well to every tone
That from your lips fell low and sweet,
    If I had known.

If I had known, when your kind eyes
  Met mine in parting, true and sad—
Eyes gravely tender, gently wise,
  And earnest rather more than glad—
How soon the lids would lie above,
  As cold and white as sculptured stone,
I should have treasured every glance,
    If I had known.

If I had known, how from the strife
  Of fears, hopes, passions, here below,
Unto a purer, higher life
  That you were called, O friend, to go,
I should have stayed all foolish tears,
  And hushed each idle sigh and moan,
To bid you a last, long godspeed,
    If I had known.

If I had known to what strange place,
  What mystic, distant, silent shore,
You calmly turned your steadfast face,
  What time your footsteps left my door,
I should have forged a golden link,
  To bind the heart, so constant grown,
And keep it constant ever there,
    If I had known.

If I had known that, until death
  Shall with his finger touch my brow,
And still the quickening of the breath
  That stirs with life's full meaning now—

So long my feet must tread the way
 Of our accustomed paths alone,
I should have prized your presence
    more,
  If I had known.

If I had known how soon for you
 Drew near the ending of the fight,
And on your vision, fair and new,
 Eternal peace dawned into sight,
I should have begged, as love's last
    gift,
 That you before God's great, white
    throne
Would pray for your poor friend on
    earth,
  If I had known.
—CHRISTIAN REID, *in Providence Journal.*

THE SOUL'S FLIGHT.

WHEN coldness wraps this suffering
    clay,
 Ah, whither strays the immortal
    mind,
It cannot die, it cannot stay,
 But leaves its darkened dust behind.
Then, unembodied, doth it trace
 By steps each planet's heavenly way,
Or fill at once the realms of space,
 A thing of eyes, that all survey?

Eternal, boundless, undecayed,
 A thought unseen, but, seeing all,
All, all in earth, or skies displayed,
 Shall it survey, shall it recall:
Each fainter trace that memory holds,
 So darkly of departed years,
In one broad glance the soul beholds,
 And all that was at once appears.

Before Creation peopled earth,
 Its eyes shall roll through chaos back;
And when the furthest heaven had
    birth,
 The spirit trace its rising track,
And where the future mars or makes,
 Its glance dilate o'er all to be,
While sun is quenched or system
    breaks
  Fixed in its own eternity.

Above or Love, Hope, Hate, or Fear,
 It lives, all passionless and pure;
An age shall fleet like earthly year—
 Its years as moments shall endure.
Away, away, without a wing,
 O'er all, through all, its thoughts
    shall fly,
A nameless and eternal thing,
 Forgetting what it was to die.
                              —BYRON.

FROM SOFA TO HAMMOCK.

DEAR parlor sofa, fare thee well,
 A long and fond adieu,
The hammock days have come and so
 We say farewell to you.
We say farewell to you and sigh
 To think of all the beaux
We had and—coal was awful high—
 None ventured to propose.

Ah, no, they'd simply talk and smile
 And sigh and hesitate,
And pa kept scolding all the while
 Because gas bills were great.
But none got down to business and
 Brought matters to a close,
Although mamma and I have planned,
 None of them have proposed.

And pa he often threatened to
 Apply to them his boot,
And sought to hang within their view
 This motto : "Pop or scoot !"
But after all the coal they burned—
 We say it with regret—
Another summer has returned
 And finds us single yet.

Now that we greet the gentle spring
 And chilly winds are gone,
We'll once more in the hammock swing
 At even on the lawn,
Where some one may, ere summer's
    o'er,
 Propose and make us glad,
And if they don't we're very sure
 Poor pa will just go mad.
                       —CHICAGO HERALD.

A BEAUTIFUL EXTRACT.

IT was night. Jerusalem slept as quietly amid her hills as a child upon the breast of its mother. The noiseless sentinel stood like a statue at his post, and the philosopher's lamp burned dimly in the recess of his chamber. But a moral darkness involved the nation in its unenlightened shadows. Reason shed a faint glimmering over the minds of men—like cold and insufficient shining of a distant star. The immortality of man's spiritual nature was unknown, his relation to Heaven undiscovered, and his future destiny obscured in a cloud of mystery. It was at this period that two forms of ethereal mould hovered about the land of God's chosen people. They came like sister angels, sent to earth on some embassy of love. The one of majestic stature and well formed limb, which her drapery scarcely concealed, in her erect bearing and steady eye, exhibiting the highest degree of strength and confidence. Her right arm was extended in an impressive gesture upward, where night appears to have placed her darkest pavilion; while on her left reclines her delicate companion, in form and countenance the contrast of the other. She was drooping like a flower moistened by refreshing dews, and her bright and troubled eyes scanned them with ardent but varying glances. Suddenly a light like the sun flashed out from the Heavens and Faith and Hope hailed, with exciting songs, the ascending Star of Bethlehem. Years rolled away; and a Stranger was seen at Jerusalem. He was a meek, unassuming man, whose happiness seemed to consist in acts of benevolence to the human race. There were deep traces of sorrow on His countenance, though no one knew why he grieved, for He lived in the practice of every virtue and was loved by all the good and wise.

By and by it was rumored that the Stranger worked miracles: that the blind saw, the dumb spoke and the dead arose, the ocean moderated its chafing tide, the very thunder articulated. He was the son of God. Envy assailed Him to death.

Thickly guarded he slowly ascended the Hill of Calvary. A heavy cross bent Him to the earth. But Faith leaned on His arm, and Hope, dipping her pinions in His blood, mounted to the skies.

A NAME IN THE SAND.

Alone I walked the ocean strand,
A pearly shell was in my hand;
I stooped and wrote upon the sand
 My name, the year, the day,
As onward from the spot I passed,
One lingering look behind I cast;
A wave came rolling high and fast,
 And washed my line away.

And so, methought, 'twill quickly be,
With every mark on earth from me,
A wave of dark oblivion's sea,
 Will sweep across the place.
Where I have trod the sandy shore
Of time, and been, to be no more—
Of me, my day, the name I bore,
 To leave no track or trace.

And yet with Him who counts the sands,
And holds the waters in His hands,
I know a lasting record stands
 Inscribed against my name.
Of all this mortal part has wrought,
Of all this thinking soul has thought,
And from these fleeting moments caught,
 For glory or for shame.
—George D. Prentice.

Good-Night.—How tenderly and sweetly falls the gentle "good-night," into loving hearts, as members of a family separate and retire for the night. What myriads of hasty words and thoughtless acts, engendered in the hurry and business of the day, are forever blotted out by its benign influence. Small token indeed; but it is the little courtesies that make up the sum of a happy home. It is only the little courtesies that can so beautifully round off the square corners in the homes of laboring men and women. The simple "I thank you," for a favor received, will fill with happiness the heart of the giver. True wealth is not counted by dollars and cents, but by the gratitude and affection of the heart. If a home be happy, whether the owner possesses a patch of ground of one or a thousand acres, they are in the end wealthy beyond mathematical calculations.

Then how much more lovingly are the sable folds of night gathered around the happy homes; how much more confidently do its members repose their weary bodies in the care of Divine goodness, soothing their overtaxed minds to the realities of a beautiful dreamland; awakened, refreshed and invigorated for the coming day's labor, by having bid their loved ones an affectionate "good-night." And if, during this life, we have faithfully attended to all these little courtesies, these little souls need, if we have guarded carefully all "God's hearts" placed in our keeping, at the close of its brief, yet eventful day, how much easier to bid all our dearly beloved ones a final "goodnight."

THE OLD CEMETERY.

Way down in the balmy, sweet Sunny South,
 Where flowers have continuous springs,
And where the birds nature's glad songs repeat,
 Is the spot 'round which mem'ry clings,
And to which my mind gently steals away—
 Leaves me sad tho' the world be gay.

Oh, how often have I lonely wander'd
 Over that sweet and sacred spot;
While the moments were silently number'd
 And the sad thoughts were half forgot,
As I pluck'd wild flowers sent to bestow
 Tokens from those sleeping below.

Then, their messages I did not receive
 Which those sad, sweet messengers bore,
Nor, in my dreams, could I scarcely conceive
 The joys of the songs, by the score,
Sung by the songsters in happy refrain,
 And oft repeated o'er again.

Yet, now as I wander in lands unknown,
 Among the festive and the gay;

Halts my weary mind and turns from the scenes,
And like a wand'rer steals away
Where the jasmine and arbutus entwine
 That sacred spot of sunny clime.

And there on the Meherrin's rugged banks,
 Where the holly and tulips grow,
And like living spires, heavenward pointing,
 The flights of those sleeping below:
There, it builds its castle, pitches its tent,
 And, with folded wings, is content,

That castle fair is neither built with hands,
 Nor has it size, or shape, or form;
It is neither of earth, or wood, or stone,
 And yet it is to my mind a home
Dearer by far than all the joys it brings,
 And brighter than the realms of kings.

There, methinks, "In the sweet by and bye,"
 We shall meet, know as we were known,
Children, parents and friends each other greet,
 Thence gather to the Great White Throne,
Both the living, and those beneath the sod,
 To spend eternity with God.

FAREWELL.

Farewell,—solemn word of regret,
 A shade cast o'er the parting rays,
Of a sun that's forever set,
 Tho' it gladdened happier days.

Farewell: My heart feels its smarting,
 Tho' it welcomed its destined knell,—
Gives back the token of parting,
 As dies the echo of "Farewell."

Be it so, and the past forgot,
 Tho' my heart should break in the spell;
For, dear, if I could, I would not
 Call it back again. Hence, Farewell.

And with "Farewell," a joyful hail—
  Joyful and multiplied in scores ;
For though my cheerless life should fail,
  May happiness double, in yours.

Friendship you ask ; friendship you
    get ;
  Friendship that is pure, true and
    tried ;
Just as deep as the ocean set,
  Just as boundless as it is wide.

And through life, whate'er be thy 'state,
  Whate'er befall, whate'er withstand—
Whether bad or good be thy fate,
  I am thine, only to command.

THE LIGHTNING AGE.

What's the world a-coming to, a feller'd like to know,
When they're making ice to order an'
  manufacturin' snow ?
The cities—they'r gone out o' sight ; it
  'pears jus' like a dream,
For when they have a cloudy night
  they run the stars by steam !
An' here's the lightnin', with a song,
  proclaimin' it is boss,
An' all the street cars skimmin' long
  without a mule or hoss !
An' here's that ringin' telephone, which
  never seems to tire,
But takes a man's voice, free of charge,
  across six miles o' wire.
An' the blessed phonygraf, which
  makes your memory vain,
An', like a woman, when you talk,
  keeps talkin' back again !
Lord ! how the world is movin' on beneath the sun an' moon !
I can't help thinkin' I was born a hundred years too soon ;
But when I go—praise be to God !—it
  won't be in the night,
For my grave will shine like glory in a
  bright electric light !

THERE ARE—

Beautiful words never spoken,
  Whispers of cheer that might save
Hearts drifting, wearily broken,
  Down to the night of the grave.

Silence more deadly than passion,
  Glances that slander can send,
Fram'd in the world's devilish fashion,
  To murder the heart of a friend.

Looks, spotless virtue impeaching,
  Souls lying crush'd on the plain,
With tear-frozen eyelids beseeching
  The touch of love's sunlight again.
Burdens to bear for the weaker,
  Jewels to dig from God's mine ;
And gems, fairer still, to the seeker
  In the angels' tiara that shine.

Within us, the soul's silent treasure
  Waiting the kiss of the light ;
Sweet scented blossoms of pleasure
  Our fingers may cull from the night.
Fruits shining ripe on toil's mountains,
  Pearls that sleep under life's sea ;
Music in God's laughing fountains
  Undream'd of by you or by me.

Larks singing down in love's meadow,
  Throstles that pipe by the hill ;
Out of time's darkness and shadow,
  Whispers that comfort and thrill.
Voices within ever singing,
  Melody soften'd by tears,
And the phœnix of hope at last spring-
    ing
  Serene from the ashes of years.
    —J. R. Parke, *in Detroit Free Press.*

A PRINTER'S LOVE LETTER.

Can you read it, Girls ?

An S A now I mean 2 write
  2 you, sweet K T J,
The girl without a ¶,
  The belle of U T K.

I 1der if you Ntertain
  The calm I D A bright
That 8T miles from you I must,
  M—— this chance to write.

& 1st, should N E N V U,
  B E Z, mind it not ;
If any friendship show, B sure
  They shall not be 4got.

From virtue never D V 8,
  Her influence B9,
Alike induces tenderness
  Or 4otude divine.

& if you cannot cut a —
  Or cause an !,
I hope you will put a .
  2 I ?

R U for an Xation, 2,
  My cousin, heart & 🖙 ?
He offers in a ¶
  A ⅜ broad of land.

He says he loves U 2 X S,
  U 'r virtuous and Y's ;
In X L N C, U X L,
  All others in his I's.

This S A until I C U,
  I pray U to X Q's,
And do not burn in F I G
  My quaint and wayward muse.

Now, fare U well, dear K T J,
  I trust that U R true,
When this U C, then U can say,
  An S A, I O U.
    —MARION COMMONWEALTH.

GRAMMAR SCHOOL EXTRAORDINARY.

TEACHER—Parse man.
Pupil—Man is a common noun of the feminine gender. What is that, sir ? Man is a common noun of the feminine gender—common 'cause he can be bought cheap ; and feminine gender because he's always got woman on the brain, 8th person, 'cause his wife and six children come first—is in the objective case and governed by a woman. Go to your seat and put a wet cloth on your head. Next, parse woman. Woman is a female noun of the masculine gender. Mercy on us ? What do you say, sir ? She's a female noun of the masculine gender—masculine 'cause she wears the breechaloons and is determined to vote ; she's compound of cotton, whalebone, starch, smiles, sunshine and thunder-clouds—is in the first person, 'cause she's always the person speaking ; plural number, 'cause she makes more noise than half a dozen parrots—is in the objective case and governed by the fashions. Sit down and rinse your mouth with prophylactic fluid. Next, parse boy. Boy is an uncommon noun of the goslin gender and female persuasion. Thunder and boot-jacks ! What's that, sir ? Boy is an uncommon noun of the goslin gender and female persuasion - uncommon 'cause he's hard to find nowadays ; 'cause he soon enters the threshold of goosehood ; female persuasion, 'cause he's always got the heart-sick about some female ; first person big Ike ; singular number, 'cause there's nobody but himself ; in the objective case and governed by embryo moustache, Scheidam schnapps, and the length of his daddy's purse. Go home, sir, and bathe your feet in mustard. Parse girl. Girl is an angelic noun of the bicycle gender, and masculine tendencies. Save us from sudden death ! These boys will never be raised. How is that, sir ? Girl is an angelic noun cause she paints her cheeks and loves inguns ; she's compounded of cosmetics, flowers, fuss and feathers ; is of masculine tendencies, cause she wears shirt bosoms, high collars, and always has her head full of boys ; singular number cause the boys are afraid of them, and matrimony is played out, third person, cause she's much spoken of; in the objective case and governed by a gipsy bonnet. Next, parse fashion. Fashion is a tyrannical noun of the common gender, Catfish and blunderbusses ! What's that, sir ? Fashion is a tyrannical noun, 'cause it must be obeyed and laughs at a poor man's purse ; common gender, 'cause all people must bow to it ; it is compounded of flounces, flimsies, ruffles, scuffles, bubbles, ruffs, cuffs, snuffs, higgles, giggles, sniggles, curls, furls, heirs, snares, fuss and feathers. It was once in the objective case and governed by Eugenie, but is now in the nominative case independent. Go home, sir, and go to bed. Next, parse baby. Baby is an obstreperous noun of the neuter gender. Moses and the prophets, save us from destruction ! What do you say, you little imp ? Baby is a musical noun 'cause it sings a soft tune between midnight and day, specially of a cold night—it is neuter gender 'cause

it is neither male nor female till it is big enough to wear breeches. It weighs according to size and measures according to proportions ; compounded of milk and lungs, and especially of lungs ; grows at a rapid rate. It is also of the spoilt gender, 'cause it is allowed to put its foot in the gravy whenever it pleases ; is in the objective case and governed by candy and sugar-plums.

Go home, sir, and tell your mother to rock you to sleep. Parse matrimony. Matrimony is an ancient noun, defunct gender. Hear him ! You little vagabond, what do you say ? Matrimony is of the defunct gender, 'cause its played out. Girls are as plentiful as blackberries, but they've got nothing. Matrimony is compounded of the words mate and money, but when there's a match nowadays, it is nothing without the money. Third person cause it is spoken of much by the girls. In the objective case and governed by the spondulix of the girl's daddy.

THE BOSTON GIRL.

SHE thinks she has a mission
In the field of erudition,
And goes in for education with an energy intense ;
She went through a female college
And exhausted all its knowledge,
And nearly crazed the teachers by her mental vehemence.

In striving for more culture,
She is keener than a vulture,
And will never know contentment till she's conquered all the fates,
And has grappled with the giants
And in every field of science ;
For the thornier the path she treads the more it fascinates.

She believes in evolution,
And in every revolution
Which science has effected in the minds of those who think ;
And though 'tis now above her,
There's a chance she may discover
That unrevealed connective tie that's called the missing link.

In all matters literary,
There was never yet a fairy
Who could put a girdle round the earth's great intellectual stores,
With such well-assured conviction
As will brook no contradiction,
That to every secret chamber she has opened all the doors.

She's a special friend of Lowell's
She has realized with Howells,
And unlocked a fund of humor with Dr. Holmes' key ;
And as she is no laggard
She's caught on to Rider Haggard,
And devoured all the pages of the much-entrancing "She."

She is up in Anglo-Saxon,
And can furnish all the facts on
Th' orthography so staggering which reigned in Chaucer's time ;
And can follow down the ages
Till she strikes the modern pages
That are lurid with the fervid light of Ella Wheeler's rhyme.

And of course it is no bother
For her to be an author ;
She's at home with odes and sonnets, and with epigrams can cope ;
She can turn off little lyrics,
And most precious panegyrics,
And no doubt could earn her living writing puffs for Pears's soap.

She is high in metaphysics,
And in that better physics
Which treats of blocks and pulleys, and inertia and force ;
And on the screw and lever
One would never—hardly ever—
Find a person to deliver a more practical discourse.

Mathematics are no terror :
She can solve without an error
The knottiest of problems that the text-books now display ;
All the 'ometries are captive,
To her intellect adaptive,
As also is arithmetic and likewise algebra.

She's not rigidly religious
But her knowledge is prodigious
Of theology, theosophy, and all the
    worn-out creeds ;
And the doctrine of probation
After death and condemnation
She could settle if they'd let her take
    the way that reason leads

Paganism, Gnosticism,
    Pantheism, Brahmanism
Judaism, and to each schism that was
    ever known to be,
She has taken up in study,
    With a brain that's never muddy,
And has listened to the doctrines of
    Mohini Chatterjee.

She can read both Greek and Latin
    French and German she is pat in,
While Spanish and Italian she has mar-
    shalled into line ;
And with really more than man's
    grit
She has conquered even Sanscrit,
And the oriental languages make part
    of her combine.

Should she feel communicative,
    She could talk to any native
In any part of Christendom in his own
    native tongue ;
And could give him information
    From the budding of creation
Down to the very moment of the times
    as yet unsung.

She's the product of the century,
    And if I thought to venture a
Remark about her usefulness in this
    enlightened year,
I should say—with all who knew
    her—
That I thought all praise was due
    her
For expanding and developing the
    bounds of woman's sphere.
    —BOSTON ADVERTISER.

TO GROWN-UP LANDS.

GOOD-MORROW, fair maid, with lashes brown,
Can you tell me the way to Womanhood Town ?
O, this way and that way—never stop,
'Tis picking up stitches grandma will drop,
'Tis kissing the baby's troubles away,
'Tis learning that cross words will never pay,
'Tis helping mother, 'tis sewing up rents,
'Tis reading and playing, 'tis saving the cents,
'Tis loving and smiling, forgetting to frown—
O, that is the way to Womanhood Town.

Just wait, my brave lad, one moment, I pray,
Manhood Town lies where—can you tell me the way ?
O, by toiling and trying we reach that land—
A bit with the head, a bit with the hand—
'Tis by climbing up the steep hill Work,
'Tis by keeping out of the wide street Shirk,
'Tis by always taking the weak one's part,
'Tis by giving mother a happy heart,
'Tis by keeping bad thoughts and actions down—
O, that is the way to Manhood Town.
And the lad and the maid ran hand in hand
To their fair estates in Grown-Up-Land.
    —PHILADELPHIA RECORD.

THE LANGUAGE OF PRECIOUS STONES.

THE quality of turquois imparts a prosperity in love.

Chrysolite was used as an amulet against evil passions and despondency.

The opal imparts apprehension and insight, and is the emblem of unrealized hope.

Conjugal felicity was symbolized by the sardonyx, which it was believed to insure.

The topaz was thought to promote fidelity and friendship and to calm internal passions.

The diamond has the mystic symbolism of light and purity, faith and uprightness of character.

The properties of the amethyst are to calm the passions of the body and prevent drunkenness.

The bloodstone was thought by the ancients to impart courage, prudence, fortitude and stability of character.

The moonstone was the emblem of the merchant prince, and signified well-directed industry and the arts of peace.

Garnet or carbuncle represents constancy of purpose and fidelity to duty. It is pre-eminently the soldier's gem.

The ruby was thought to guard against unfriendliness, and particularly that form so common in antiquity—poisoning.

The sapphire signifies modesty and charity of opinion, and was thought to possess the power of breaking the spells of magic.

The agate or chalcedony represents physical prosperity, and it is the stone of the athlete and physician, and imparts longevity and health.

The emerald symbolizes truth, and was believed to secure good faith and happiness in friendship and home. It was also the appropriate emblem for judge or lawyer.

UNDER A CRAZY QUILT.

HE slept and dreamt that the kangaroo
  Had given a fancy ball ;
The elephant came with the festive gnu,
  The mouse with the ostrich tall,
A funny giraffe that did nothing but laugh,
  Dropped in with a centipede ;
And a cricket and flea, that had just been to tea,
  Waltzed round with remarkable speed.

A wasp and a bumble-bee had a chat
  Just over his little nose ;
And a boa constrictor upon the mat
  Dressed up in his Sunday clothes.
A crow and raccoon, in a fire-balloon,
  Paused over his bed to sing ;
And a neat armadillo crept up on his pillow
  To dance the Highland fling.

Then all, ere they left, made a graceful bow,
  And out in the moonlight sped,
Except a ponderous brindle cow
  Which stopped to stand on its head.
The little boy woke and grinned at the joke,
  Sprang out of the bed with a tilt,
"I can dream it all over," said he,
  " while they cover
Me up in this crazy quilt."
      —FARM AND GARDEN.

GRANDMA'S BIRTHDAY.

I SEE a figure quaint and fair,
  In silken gown and kerchief white,
And dainty cap, on snowy hair ;
  A gentle face, with eyes so bright,
That seem to muse o'er times now flown,
  In the fond, lingering, dreamy way
Of those who many years have known,—
  For Grandma's eighty-six to day.

For six-and-eighty changeful years
  The web of life she's bravely wove,
And watched with smiles or starting tears
  The mingled threads of grief and love
That crossed each other here and there,
  With now a scarlet line of pain,
And then of faith and patience fair,
  That seemed to make the pattern plain.

And when, sometimes, a thread would break,
  So swiftly time, the shuttle, flew,
The tangled ends did slowly make
  A figure straight and smooth and true.
Now, looking back, with wisdom meet,
  She sees what then she dimly knew,—
Each thread was needed to complete
  This beauteous web of varied hue.

And now, in life's sweet twilight hour,
  Untouched alike by joy or pain,
Old memories rise with wondrous power,
  And in the past she lives again.

Her youthful locks of raven-hair
  Old Time has turned to snowy white;
  It only makes her look more fair,—
    He could not make her smile less bright.

To see her quick and sprightly ways,
  One well might think, in very truth,
  She'd found the spring that poets praise,
    The fountain of eternal youth.
The fable must be true, in part,
  For though long years their course have rolled,
  She's kept her fresh and youthful heart,
    And so she never can grow old.
      —Nellie K. Kellogg.

A GAME OF EUCHRE.

The game was euchre, and we two
  Were partners, Beatrice and I.
A darling maid; the roses hue,
  Her cheeks were, and her eyes of blue
  Were clearer than the sky.

It was my deal; the trump, the jack
  Of hearts; one look I send
To Beatrice; she sends one back;
That of trump-cards she had a lack,
  Was what I thought it meant.

The trump was passed; I was not slow
  To take it when my cards I'd scanned.
"I'll take your highest trump, although—"
And this I whispered very low—
  "I'd like to take your hand!"

She smiled; bright pink her cheeks became—
  I knew she saw my little fun;
But she was new unto the game.
And so, quite puzzled, did exclaim:
  "Of hearts I have but one."

"Then will you give me that?" I said;
  My meaning quickly she inferred;
The pink turned into deepest red,
Then o'er her face a wee smile spread—
  A low, faint "Yes" I heard!
      —Henry Talcott Mills.

THE SPINNING WHEEL.

In country houses long years ago,
  The spinning wheel went round and round,
And those who heard it will always know
  Its solemnly quaint and droning sound.

The soft, white wool from the spindle ran
  Into a thread so fair and fine,
That it always baffled the boy or man
  Who tried to watch its even line.

For the wheel was given a curious twirl—
  Some magic prompted its humming snore;
Yet it did not trouble the country girl,
  Who learned its art on the kitchen floor.

I see her still step to and fro,
  Fulling each roll in the deftest way;
And singing some air to make it go,
  With strange delight through the toilsome day.

On the burdened spindle the white thread grew
  Just as her cunning foresight planned;
And it was wondrous to see how true
  The swift yarn followed her guiding hand.

'Twas a charming picture in summer days,
  But the wheel to rack and ruin has gone,
And the pretty spinner's grandchild's face
  Is seen "croquet"-ing upon the lawn.

Hushed is that solemn, droning sound—
  Its art is now forgotten lore;
So the spinning wheel no more goes round
  On summer days by the kitchen door.
      —Joel Denton.

A WOMAN'S NAY.

No, Impudence, you shan't have one!
How many times must I refuse?
    Away!
    I say!
Or else you'll sure my friendship lose.
I cannot bear such forward fun,
So, quick, begone! If not, I'll run!

Why, now I'll have to be severe—
No, not a kiss to you I'll give—
    Take care—
    I swear
I'll tell papa sure as I live!
I never saw a man so queer!
But are you certain no one's near?

SHE WAITED BY THE RIVER.

They sat by the side of the stream
  That quietly rippled below;
He thought he must be in a dream—
  How quickly the moments did flow!
He ventured his arm 'round her waist,
  All under the moon's silver light;
He thought it would not be misplaced,
  And found that he thought about right.

He mused: Do I dare steal a kiss?
  And upon it his mind was so bent,
Though he feared she might take it amiss,
  He took one without her consent.
She gave a quick toss of her head;
  He tremblingly thought he'd done wrong;
"My dear, are you angry?" he said.
  "Yes; because you have waited so long!"

BLISS INTERRUPTED.

ACT I.

Lovers swinging in a hammock,
  Close together in the dark;
Small boy, hiding in the grapevines,
  Chuckles, while the lovers spark.

ACT II.

Lovers, of the world unconscious—
  (Next week she will be his wife)—
(Small boy, weary of their spooning,
  Calls to mind his brand-new knife.

  *   *   *   *   *

ACT III.

Lovers in a heap together—
  Neither injured much, let's hope,
Then the youth profanely mutters:
  "Damn the boy that cut that rope!"

"SOME DAY."

She came, I knew not whence or how,
  In the sweet past; I only know
I loved her then—I love her now,
  No wonder that I loved her so,
    For then my dearest, bright-eyed May
  Had promised to be mine—
    "some day!"
Her look sustained my heart, and cheered;
Her words my wounded spirits healed,
The human mortal disappeared
  And God's own angel stood revealed;
For I was hers, and she was mine—
  Forever hers! forever mine!

  *   *   *   *   *

But ah! with ceaseless Time, came Death
And plucked the sweetet flowers God gave
To me, and now, alas! the wreath
  Lies mouldering in the silent grave;
But this sweet hope within me lies—
  In the brignt realm of Paradise
I'll meet my darling, and I pray
She will be mine again—some day!

                —Mashile.

WOMAN'S RIGHTS.

To be the little children's truest friend,
  To know them in their ever changing mood;
Forgetting self, to labor to the end
  To be a gracious influence for good.

To be the ladies of creation's lords,
  As mothers, daughters, sisters or as wives;
To be the best that earth to them affords,
  To be to them the music of their lives.

The right in strength and honor to be free ;
In daily work accomplished, finding rest ;
The right in "trivial round" a sphere to see ;
The right, in blessing, to be fully blest.

Right to be perfect, right to be pure,
Right to be patient and strong to endure ;
Right to be loving—right to be good—
These are the rights of the true womanhood.

THE WEDDING.

Two rivers wandered o'er the lea,
Unlike as like can ever be—
The one a deep and sturdy stream
With measured flow bespeaking power ;
The other danced with sunny gleam
And curt'sied to each nodding flower.

My fancy gave them form divine—
For fancy oft may thus incline—
The one a man profound and staid,
With purpose firm that told of might ;
The other seemed a blithesome maid
That lived to love—a cheery sprite.

Those rivers merged beyond the lea,
And thus together sought the sea.
Nor earthly power could disunite
Their mingled waters as they sped,
Since nature's priest performed the rite
By which those streams for aye were wed.

SOMEBODY'S SUNBEAM.

SOMEBODY crawls into mamma's bed
Just at the break of day,
Snuggles up close and whispers loud,
"Somebody's come to stay."

Somebody rushes through the house—
Never once shuts a door ;
Scatters her playthings all around
Over the nursery floor ;

Climbs on the fence and tears her clothes—
Never a bit cares she ;
Swings on the gate and makes mud-pies ;
Who can somebody be ?

Somebody looks with roguish eyes
Up through her tangled hair ;
"Somebody's me," she says ; "but then
Somebody doesn't care."

A QUEER MARRIAGE CEREMONY.

A COLORED pair named Jim and Bet, called upon a country squire to be united, "for better or worse." Having had some notice of their coming, he prepared and actually used the following unique ceremony :

"Jim, will you take Bet
Without any regret,
To love and to cherish,
Till one of you perish,
And is laid under the sod ;
So help you God."

Jim having given the usual affirmative answer, the Squire turned to Bet :

"Bet, will you take Jim
And cling to him
Both out and in,
Through thick and thin ;
Holding him to your heart,
Till death do you part ? "

Bet modestly acquiesced, and the newly married couple were dismissed with

"Thro' life's alternate joy and strife,
I now pronounce you man and wife."

TRUST IN GOD, AND DO THE RIGHT.

COURAGE, brother, do not stumble,
Though thy path be dark as night ;
There's a star to guide the humble,
"Trust in God, and do the right."

Let the road be rough and dreary,
And the end far out of sight ;
Foot it bravely, strong or weary,
"Trust in God, and do the right."

Perish policy and cunning,
  Perish all that fears the light;
Whether losing, whether winning,
  " Trust in God, and do the right."

Trust no party, sect or faction,
  Trust no leaders in the fight;
But in every word and action
  " Trust in God, and do the right."

Trust no lovely forms of passion;
  Friends may look like angels bright,
Trust no custom, school, or fashion;
  " Trust in God, and do the right."

Simple rule and safest guiding,
  Inward peace and inward might,
Star upon our path abiding—
  " Trust in God, and do the right,"

Some will hate thee, some will love thee,
  Some will flatter, some will slight;
Cease from man, and look above thee—
  " Trust in God, and do the right."
    —NORMAN MCLEOD.

MRS. LOFTY AND I.

MRS. LOFTY keeps a carriage,
  So do I;
She has dapple-grays to draw it,
  None have I;
She's no prouder with her coachman
  Than am I,
With my blue-eyed, laughing baby,
  Trundling by.
I hide his face lest she should see
The cherub boy and envy me.

Her fine husband has white fingers,
  Mine has not;
He could give his bride a palace—
  Mine, a cot;
Hers comes home beneath the starlight,
  Ne'er caresses she;
Mine comes in the purple twilight,
  Kisses me,
And prays that He who turns life's sands
Will hold His loved ones in his hands.

Mrs. Lofty has her jewels,
  So have I;
She wears hers upon her bosom,
  Inside I;

She will leave hers at death's portal,
  By and by;
I shall bear my treasure with me
  When I die;
For I have love, and she has gold;
She counts her wealth—mine can't be told.

She has those who love her—station,
  None have I;
But I've one true heart beside me—
  Glad am I.
I'd not change it for a kingdom,
  No, not I.
God will weigh it in His balance,
  By and by,
Then the difference He'll define
Twixt Mrs. Lofty's wealth and mine.
    —MRS. C GILDERSLEEVE.

THANKSGIVING.

FAIR Autumn spreads her fields of gold,
  And waves her amber wand;
See earth its yellow charms unfold
  Beneath her magic hand.

Unrivalled beauty decks our vales,
  Bright fruitfulness our plains;
Gay health and cheerfulness prevails,
  And smiling glory reigns.

Beneath the sickle, smiling round
  And in destruction fair,
The golden harvest strews the ground,
  And shuts the labored year.

Man drops into refreshing rest,
  And smoothes his wearied brow;
With rural peace the herds are blest,
  And nature smiles below.

To Thee, great liberal source of all,
  We strike our earthly lyre;
Till fate our rising soul shall call,
  And angels from the choir.

The splendor that enchants our eyes
  Remind us of Thy name;
The blessings that from earth arise
  The generous hand proclaim.

The plenty round our meadows seen
  Is emblem of Thy love;
And harmony that binds the scene,
  The peace that reigns above.

BEAUTIFUL HANDS.

WE have read this beautiful incident: There was a dispute among three ladies as to which had the most beautiful hands. One sat by a stream and dipped her hand into the water and held it up, another plucked strawberries until the ends of her fingers were pink, and the other gathered violets until her hands were fragrant. An old, haggard woman passing by asked, "Who will give me a gift, for I am poor?" All three denied her; but another who sat near, unwashed by the stream, unstained with fruit, unadorned with flowers, gave her a little gift and satisfied the poor woman. And then she asked them what was the dispute, and they told her, and lifted up before her their beautiful hands. "Beautiful, indeed," said she when she saw them. But when they asked her which was the most beautiful, she said, "It is not the hand that is washed clean in the brook, it is not the hand that is tipped with red, it is not the hand that is garlanded with fragrant flowers, but the hand that gives to the poor is the most beautiful." As she said these words her wrinkles fled, her staff was thrown away, and she stood before them an angel from heaven with authority to decide the question in dispute. And that decision has stood the test of all time.

HOW FATHER CARVES THE DUCK.

WE all look on with anxious eyes
   When father carves the duck,
And mother almost always sighs,
   When father carves the duck.
Then all of us prepare to rise
And hold our bibs before our eyes
And be prepared for some surprise,
   When father carves the duck.

He braces up and grabs a fork,
   Whene'er he carves a duck,
And won't allow a soul to talk
   Until he carves the duck.
The fork is jabbed into the sides,
Across the breast the knife he slides,
While every careful person hides
   From flying chips of duck.

The platter's always sure to slip,
   When father carves the duck,
And it makes all the dishes skip—
   Potatoes fly amuck.
The squash and cabbage leap in space,
And father mutters Hindoo grace,
   Whene'er he carves a duck.

We have all learned to walk around
   The dining-room, and pluck
From off the window-sills and walls
   Our share of father's duck,
While father growls, and blows and jaws
And swears the knife is full of flaws;
And mother jeers at him, because
   He cannot carve a duck.
               —A. T. S.

THE LITTLE WOMAN.

DON'T talk to me of Olympus maids,
   "Divinely tall and fair"—
Of Cleopatra's imperial form,
   Of Juno's stately air.
Those mighty dames, with redoubted names,
   May erst have held their sway:
'Tis the little woman—bless her heart!
   Who rules the world to-day.

With her wilful, witching, winsome ways,
   Her artful, artless smiles—
Her airy grace, and her fairy face—
   Her wisdom, wit and wiles,
She mocks the pride and she sways the strength,
   She bends the will of man,
As only such a despotic elf—
   A little woman—can.

Though her pathway may lead thro' the darkest ways,
   She always finds a light;
Though her eyes be dazzled by fortune's rays,
   She's sure to see aright;
Though her wisdom be of no special school,
   Her logic, "just because,"
The first has settled a kingdom's fate,
   The last has made its laws.

'Tis the little woman that goes ahead
   When men would lag behind,

The little woman who sees her chances,
And always knows her mind—
Who can slyly smile as she takes the oath
To honor, love, obey,
And mentally add the saving clause
In a little woman's way!

Would the diamond seem such a perfect gem
If it measured one foot round?
Would the rose-leaf yield such a sweet perfume
If it covered yards of ground?
Would the dewdrops seem so clear and pure
If dew like rain should fall?
Or the little woman seem half so great
If she were six feet tall?

'Tis the hand as soft as the nestling bird
That grips the grip of steel;
'Tis the voice as low as the summer wind
That rules without appeal,
And the warrior, scholar, the saint and sage,
May fight and plan and pray,
The world will wag till the end of time
In the little woman's way.
—MARY C. BARNES.

HER PROPOSAL.

SHE gently took his passive hand,
And tenderly she placed
Her arm, without a reprimand,
About his willing waist.

She drew him close; a reverent kiss
Upon his brow she pressed,
He yielded, and a new-found bliss
Set all her fears at rest.

Then in a wild, impassioned way,
Her love for him she told,
And begged of him that he would say
She'd not been over bold.
Without him all her life, she said,
Would be a desert drear;
If he said "No," she'd never wed—
At least till next Leap Year.

Blushing, he heard her bravely through,
And then he cooed: "Oh, la!

This is so awful sudden, Sue!
You'll have to ask my ma!"

RICE-THROWERS AT WEDDINGS.

IN the days of the Shang dynasty, some 1,500 years before Christ, there lived in the province of Shansi a most famous sorcerer called Chao. It happened one day that a Mr. P'ang came to consult the oracle and Chao, having divined by means of the tortoise diagram, informed the trembling P'ang that he had but six days to live. Now, however much we may trust the sagacity and skill of the family physician, we may be excused if, in a matter of life and death, we call in a second doctor for a consultation, and in such a strait is not to be wondered at that P'ang should repair to another source to make sure that there was no mistake. To the fair Peach-blossom he went, a young lady who had acquired some reputation as a sorceress, and to the tender feminine heart unfolded the story of his woe. Her divination yielded the same result as Chao's; in six days P'ang should die, unless by the exercise of her magical powers, she could avert the catastrophe. Her efforts were successful, and on the seventh day great was Chao's astonishment, and still greater his mortification and rage, when he met P'ang taking his evening stroll, and learned that there lived a greater magician than he. The story would soon get about, and, unless he could put an end to his fair rival's existence, his reputation would be ruined. And this is how Chao plotted against the life of Peachblossom. He sent a go-between to Peachblossom's parents to inquire if their daughter was still unmarried, and receiving a reply in the affirmative, he befooled the simple parents into believing that he had a son who was seeking a wife, and ultimately he induced them to engage Peach-blossom in marriage. The marriage cards were duly interchanged; but the crafty Chao had chosen the most unlucky day he could select for the wedding, the day when the "Golden Pheasant" was in the ascendant. Surely as the bride entered the red chair the

spirit bird would destroy her with his powerful beak. But the wise Peachblossom knew all these things and feared not. "I will go," she said; "I will fight and defeat him." When the wedding morning came she gave directions to have rice thrown out at the door, which the spirit bird seeing made haste to devour, and while his attention was thus occupied Peachblossom stepped into the bridal chair and passed on her way unharmed. And now the ingenious reader knows why he throws rice after the bride.
—CHINESE TIMES.

MAN AND HIS SHOES.

How much a man is like his shoes!
For instance, both a soul may lose;
Both have been tanned; both are made tight
By cobblers; both get left and right,
Both need a mate to be complete;
And both are made to go on feet.
They both need healing; oft are sold,
And both in time will turn to mold.
With shoes the last is first; with men
The first shall be the last; and when
The shoes wear out they're mended new;
When men wear out they're men dead too!
They both are trod upon, and both
Will tread on others, nothing loath.
Both have their ties, and both incline,
When polished, in the world to shine;
And both peg out. Now, would you choose
To be a man or be his shoes?
—BOSTON COURIER.

GROWING OLD GRACEFULLY.

SOFTLY, O softly, the years have swept by thee,
 Touching thee lightly, with tenderest care;
Sorrow and death they have often brought nigh thee,
 Yet they have left thee but beauty to wear;
Growing old gracefully,
 Gracefully fair.

Far from the storms that are lashing the ocean,
 Nearer each day to the pleasant Home-light;
Far from the waves that are big with commotion,
 Under full sail, and the harbor in sight;
Growing old cheerfully,
 Cheerful and bright.

Past all the winds that were adverse and chilling,
 Past all the islands that lured thee to rest,
Past all the currents that lured thee unwilling,
 Far from thy course to the Land of the Blest;
Growing old peacefully,
 Peaceful and blest.

Never a feeling of envy nor sorrow
 When the bright faces of children are seen;
Never a year from the young would'st thou borrow—
 Thou dost remember what lieth between;
Growing old willingly,
 Thankful, serene.

Rich in experience that angels might covet,
 Rich in a faith that hath grown with each year,
Rich in a love that grew from and above it,
 Soothing thy sorrows and hushing each fear:
Growing old wealthily,
 Loving and dear.

Hearts at the sound of thy coming are lightened,
 Ready and willing thy hand to relieve;
Many a face at thy kind word has brightened—
 It is more blessed to give than receive;
Growing old happily,
 Ceasing to grieve.

Eyes that grow dim to the earth and
  its glory
Have a sweet recompense youth cannot know;
Ears that grow dull to the world and
  its story
Drink in the songs that from Paradise
  flow;
Growing old graciously,
  Purer than snow.

"AH me," exclaimed the henpecked
  man,
  "When all is said and done
'Tis better to have loved and lost,
  Than to have loved and won!"

HOME RANCH ACROSS THE BIG DIVIDE.

Now, cowboys, give attention and list'n
  to what I say:
I'm out upon the round-up gathering
  every stray,
And though you've broke the hobbles
  and dragged the picket-pin,
And quit the feats of bucking to follow
  the paths of sin,
I'll haze you in the narrow trail, where
  safely you can ride—
It leads up to the Home Ranch, across
  the big divide.

You need not carry fodder, for you'll
  be sure to find
The very best of feed grows there, and
  peace unto your mind.
The Round-up Boss has promised to
  watch the trail of all—
Of every stray and maverick that answers to His call;
And range replete with plenty, where
  dangers ne'er betide,
You'll find up at the Home Ranch,
  across the big divide.

You're not the only ones that are straying from the herd,
For sinners' names are legion who need
  God's holy word;
So come and join some outfit, no matter
  what the brand,
For any one will lead you up to the
  Holy Land.

If with sincere repentance to do God's
  will you've tried,
You are solid at the Home Ranch,
  across the big divide.

There are so many trails in this degenerate day,
If you should hunt for landmarks you'll
  surely lose your way;
So hit the breeze on the first one that
  leads you to the right,
Put your trust in Heaven above, use
  everybody white.
Come now and shed your folly and
  every grain of pride—
You'll wind up at the Home Ranch
  across the big divide.

Don't fall into temptation, but leap it
  wide and clear,
As oft you've jumped the washout behind the Texas steer,
And when weak souls are drifting and
  parting from the herd,
Just tell them of the wind-break found
  in God's holy word.
He'll stay with every promise on which
  you have relied,
He'll redeem them at the Home Ranch,
  across the big divide.

God has made these promises—he
  makes them unto you;
While he gathers up the big herd He
  takes skim-milkers, too.
If beef steers in Chicago are only big
  and fat,
What if they ranged on the Rio Grande
  or skim-milked on the Platte.
So, boys, tie down these precepts and
  don't you let them slide,
But strike out for the Home Ranch,
  across the big divide.

If you do unto others as you'd have
  them to you do,
When they skip and pull their freight,
  pray that they may wind up true.
If you forgive your enemies and act
  upon the square,
When you reach the Grand Corral He
  will gladly meet you there.
God, I know, is merciful, when our
  weak souls are tried—
He close-herds at the Home Ranch,
  across the big divide.

And now from deeds of evil come break
   the sinful spell,
And hasten to the round-up at the
   Home Corral.
When death, the tireless chop-horse,
   will cut you from the band,
He'll run you in the bunch where good
   cow-punchers stand.
An eternity of joy, with dear friends at
   your side,
Awaits you at the Home Ranch, across
   the big divide.
             —GRANT C. THURSON.

WHAT MATTERS IT?

WHAT matters it, my curious friend,
   where lies
Our heavenly harbor and our land of
   rest?
Whether it be beyond the azure skies
   Or in some lower world, God know-
   eth best,
It offers safety from our cares, and so
What matters whether it be high or
   low,
It offers rest, what more should mortals
   know?

Rest from the weariness of burdened
   days,
   Of bitter longings and of evil hours,
Of duties leading us through darkened
   ways
   And into efforts far beyond our
   powers,
Of dark temptations into secret sin,
Of constant labor, earth's poor gauds
   to win,
Of spirits deafened by the strife and
   din.

It matters nothing as to when or where
   We find the haven and the welcome
   home;
Let curious doubt give place to trusting
   prayer,
   And no weak soul through specula-
   tions roam
To seek for sealed-up secrets, hidden
   things;
Enough for us, if on eternal wings,
We reach the country of those better
   things.

Vex not thy spirit, O aspiring man,
   But live thy days as earnest workers
   must,
Nor try to pierce thy God's mysterious
   plan
   Which obligates thee to a life of
   trust.
Some day, some where, while countless
   ages roll,
Thy hungry heart shall comprehend the
   whole,
The veil be parted for thy thankful
   soul.
   —I. EDGAR JONES, *in London Echo.*

THE DIFFERENCE.

TENNYSON could take a worthless sheet of paper and by writing a poem on it, make it worth $5,000. That's genius. The millionaire could write fewer words on a similar sheet and make it worth $50,000. That's capital. The United States government can take an ounce and a quarter of gold and stamp on it an eagle bird and? "Twenty Dollars." That's money. The mechanic can take material worth $30 and make it into a watch worth $100. That's skill. A merchant can get an article worth 25 cents and sell it for $1. That's business. A woman can purchase a comfortable bonnet for $5, but prefers to pay $10 for one. That's foolishness. The ditch digger works ten hours a day and shovels out three or four tons of earth for $1. That's Labor.

DON'T SCOLD.

MOTHERS, don't scold. You can be firm without scolding your children; you can reprove them for their faults; you can punish them when necessary, but don't get into the habit of perpetually scolding them. It does them no good. They soon become so accustomed to fault-finding and scolding that they pay no attention to it. Or, which often happens, they grow hardened and reckless in consequence of it. Many a naturally good disposition is ruined by constant scolding, and many a child is driven to seek evil associates because there is no peace at home. Mothers, with their many cares and perplexities, often fall into the habit unconsciously; but it is a sad habit for them and their children. Watch yourselves, and don't indulge in this unfortunate and often unintentional manner of addressing your children. Watch even the tones of your voice, and, above all, watch your hearts; for we have divine authority for saying that "out of the abundance of the heart the mouth speaketh."

SHE WAS WILLING.

He clasped her hand, gazed in her eyes
    With tenderest devotion;
" Oh, darling, will you share my lot?"
    He said with marked emotion.

She looked him sweetly in the face,
    Then fingered with her bonnet.
And answered "Yes, indeed, I will,
    If there's no mortgage on it."

TO AN INQUIRER.

Forget thee! Ask the violet blue,
    In yonder flowery bed,
If it forgets the pearly dew
    That trembles on its head.
Forget thee! Ask the vesper star
    That glides the evening skies,
If, in the blazing amplitude,
    It ever forgets to rise.

Forget thee! Ask the bird of flight,
    With rich and glossy wing,
If it forgets the moorland green
    Of sweet and early spring.
Forget thee! Ask the blushing rose
    That opens its petals fair,
If it forgets the rain that throws
    Its fragrant moisture there.

Forget thee! Ask the blighted heart,
    Bereft of every friend,
If it forgets the holy spot
    Where weeping willows bend.
Forget thee! Ask the mother now,
    With sad and tearful eyes
If she forgets her cherub's brow
    So guiltless in the skies.

Forget thee! Ask the harping throng
    That fill the courts on high,
If they forget to sing their song
    Of triumph through the sky.
Forget thee! Ask the child of light,
    Wreathed with undying flowers,
If he forgets the wreathlet bright
    Culled from celestial bowers.

Forget thee! I can never forget
    A face so sweet as thine;
Thine image is forever set
    Within this heart of mine;
And when 'neath other skies I be,
    And brave the ocean's foam,
I'll never, love, forget thee,
    In that celestial home.

MY VANISHED PAST.

I will write on the tomb of my vanished past
    This is the "nevermore";
Here lies the sunshine too bright to last,
    This was the golden shore.

This was the land of the poet's song,
    This was the artist's dream;
Here were the flowers love dwelt among,
    Here was life's fairest gleam;

This was a heaven come down below,
    And it was left God's smile;
Yet now must the green grass over it grow,
    It lived such a little while—

Such a little while, like an island bright,
    That has risen far out at sea,
Which on some morrow we find the night
    Has changed to a memory.

A memory mine, one that sadly thrills;
    And ofttimes I wearily pray
That it may again, if it be God's will,
    Come back to my life some day.

But it cannot come. Oh, my dead, dead past!
    You are silent forever and still!
But the sunset glories that fade so fast
    Shall arise o'er the top of the hill;

And I'll touch the stone with gentle hand,
    And train o'er it flowers fair,

He clasped her hand, gazed in her eyes
With tenderest devotion.

—*Page 16*

CALIFORNIA
TO
WIND
AEROLITE

For I think, when I wake in that other land,
Perhaps you will meet me there.

THE EVOLUTION OF THE BOOK.

SOME one has truly said, "Of the making of books there is no end." Yet, if this was said of the past, what may be said of the present? Solomon said "Oh, that mine enemy would write a book!" Had he lived now, oh, how he could have produced the written evidence against his enemies! In the days of Solomon, however, it was more trouble and expense to write books than at present, and the word book was not limited to bound volumes as we now understand it. Then, most any thousand-word article was the subject-matter for a book. Yet we can but admire the wisdom, and be amazed at the foresight of their seeing thus early the great evolution in the future possibilities of the book. It was but little short of prophecy, for the world was then really in the age of pamphlet, and the full developed book was yet to come. The hustings was then the training ground, and the Orator the teacher. Paper and the real art of book-making had not yet been discovered. Types and printing-presses were still things of the future. Yet, the prophecy was fulfilled as gradually the circular followed the pamphlet, the annual followed the circular, the quarterly followed the annual, the monthly followed the quarterly, the weekly followed the monthly, the daily followed the weekly, and all stimulated a demand for knowledge, and opened up a way for the book. It was but another case of the survival of the fittest, for in the early days existing knowledge was too much confined to the few. It depended too much on the great wealth, favoritism, and great time for research. Such books as they had were too rare, and placed too great a premium on the monopoly of intelligence, which dispensed its information too sparingly upon the people who almost worshipped the orators as demi-gods, as they cried out for drippings from their stores of learning. New demands, however, gradually created new orators and teachers and new supplies of information as the parchment pamphlet gradually made way for the coming book. In the wake of the great Reformation which followed, were the remains of thousands of orators and teachers, who had been outstripped by their scholars, and fell by the wayside. The scholars, in turn, took up the battle-cry of the book as the greatest and longest revolution of the world went on, and neither stopped for generations nor centuries, but was continued by sire and son from Solomon to the present day.

In the course of time came the printing-press, stereotyping and typesetting machines, and there were not only the pamphlet, but the newspaper,—which is but the weekly, or daily, book. With their coming the mist of ignorance, doubt and superstition gradually vanished like fogs before the rays of the greater light. They heralded not only the victory of the book, but the triumph of light over darkness ; for what could have only been seen by the few, was now made visible to all. It broke up the monopoly on learning, threw many of the orators out of a job, and supplied the teacher with newer and better modes of teaching. It brought intelligence to the masses, and gave the man, who didn't have the time to spend in hearing, the opportunity to read ; and with it, the choice to discard what was false. Perhaps with this came the greatest victory, though it may have taken years to recognize it, if indeed, it is yet realized. The past always had associated with it fable, legend and myth, and with which it was loath to part. Imagination, and the assumptions of second childhood, have always had much to do with early history and literature, and illiteracy is indeed the first cause of the orator, and wherever he has been in great demand, it was to supply the wants of a less informed constituency. It was especially so in the early days, and to the records of which still cling many things both shocking to intelligence and unwarranted by literal truth. The book and newspaper have brought to the individual the opportunity to find the truth, and without offending a weaker brother who accepts almost anything as true and sacred, because it was connected with the past. On this line, at least, the evolution of the book still has much before it.

In the earlier days, however, only the best books were printed. The publisher was not only more discriminating, but the price made the public more so. Yet, what were published, were eagerly sought as mankind read the pros and the cons, and called for more! Like other demands, the supply came. As the costs and prices cheapened, whether enemies of Solomon or not, people wrote books. A new way had been discovered for a man with an idea to have his say, and as many had ideas, they wrote books! And this book-making went on and on until the shelves and libraries were filled in spite of the flood-gates of the second-hand book-stores. Some of them were good, some bad, and many indifferent. Yes, many indifferent, is hardly the expression for it; for through the rivalry of publishers and authors the world has truly been afflicted with a lot of trash, scarcely worthy of being called books. For after the victory of the book had been won, it became popular to write a book, and even fools rushed in, in mad rivalry to have their say; and it is almost debatable if the art of book-making has not been abused, and the pendulum allowed to swing too far.

The Orators, who could not find audiences, felt they must reach the public in another way. The bump-headed individual, imagined the bumps were put on his head for a purpose, and that he must tell the world what he knew. The love-maddened youths rushed into print, and spoiled what would have been lots of good memorandum pads. The politician re-thrashed the straw of political economy, and other things, and by a book expected to become a statesman. The minister who had the qualifications of a long face and two D's, had tired out one or two congregations of hearers, felt specially called to a congregation of readers; while many who had proven failures in the real, turned to the revelries of fiction, and trusted the imagination to supply what nature had apparently forgotten. Is it any wonder that the world was disappointed at the results, and that such products were nothing but gush?

The newspapers have served as a safety-valve by which the public has been spared many showers of gush. For while spite, and a desire to purchase a step-ladder by which to gather crops of greatness, have sold many printing presses and fonts of type, they are dangerous and expensive tools to the novice, and their expense, like the "ten-cents a line" notice, have made many an editor unpopular but have spared the world many distortions of words, and combats of ink. Yes, there is nothing like a little cost to quell the gusher.—It beats turning the hose on mad and ambitious dogs,—and all well-regulated editors have long since learned this. Yet, the full-blown gusher must gush, and in the present state of the book-trade, it is cheaper to print a book than to buy a press, and own an editor. Besides, it is more fashionable to be "an author," and an owned Editor is, after all, a poor stick! So, while the evolution of the book has already evolved much, it must continue to evolve, as there are still many who have not had their say, or gathered their crops of greatness! Yet, there are but few people who can really write a book that will find many readers; though there are many like the old lady who was told by the boarding-school teacher that he feared her daughter needed capacity: Does she?" said the good woman, wiping her spectacles, "well, she is my daughter, and she shall have what she wants, so if she needs it, send and get it for her and charge it in the bill."

If the evolution of the book continues, the publisher, as well as the teacher, may have large orders for "Capacity!"

MAN IN THE MOON.

SAID the raggedy man, on a hot afternoon,
  My!
    Sakes!
      What a lot of mistakes
Some little folks make on the man in
    the moon!
But people that's been up to see him,
    like me,
And call on him frequent and intimately,
Might drop a few facts that would interest you
  Clean
    Through!—
      If you wanted 'em to—
Some actual facts that might interest
    you!

O, the man in the moon has a crick in
    his neck!
  Whee!
    Whim!
      Ain't you sorry for him?
And a mole on his nose that is purple
    and black,
And his eyes are so weak that they
    water and run,
If he dares to dream even he looks at
    the sun—
So he jes' dreams of stars, as the
    doctors advise—
  My!
    Eyes!
      But isn't he wise—
To jes' dream of stars, as the doctors
    advise!

And the man in the moon has a boil on
    his ear—
  Whee!
    Whing!
      What a singular thing!
I know! but these facts are authentic,
    my dear—
There's a boil on his ear, and a corn on
    his chin—
He calls it a dimple—but dimples stick
    in—
Yet it might be a dimple turned over,
    you know!
  Whang!
    Ho!
      Why, certainly so!—
It might be a dimple turned over, you
    know!

And the man in the moon has a rheumatic knee!
  Gee!
    Whiz!
      What a pity that is!
And his toes have worked round where
    his heels ought to be—
So whenever he wants to go north he
    goes south,
And comes back with porridge-crumbs
    all round his mouth,
And he brushes them off with a Japanese fan,
  Whing!
    Wham!
      What a marvellous man!
What a very remarkable, marvellous
    man!

And the man in the moon, sighed the
    raggedy man!
  Gits!
    So!
      Sullonesome, you know—
Up there by hisse'f sence creation began—
That when I call on him and then come
    away,
He grabs me and holds me and begs
    to stay—
Till—well! if it wasn't fer Jimmy-cum-jim,
  Dadd!
    Limb!
      I'd go pardners with him—
Jes' jump my job here and be pardners
    with him!
    —JAMES WHITCOMB RILEY.

"THE EYES THAT CANNOT WEEP."

THE saddest eyes are those that cannot
    weep;
  The loneliest breast the one that sobbeth not,
The lips and mind that are more
    parched and hot
Are those that cannot pray, and cannot sleep;—
It is the silent grief that sinketh deep,

To weep out sorrow is the common lot,—
To weep it out and let it be forgot,—
But tears and sobs are after all but cheap,
We weep for worries, frets and trifling cares,
For toys we've broken, and for hopes that were,
For fancied woes of passion, love-affairs;
But only One can raze the breast of her
Whose hurt for fruitless moans has gone too deep.
Pity, O God, the eyes that cannot weep.
—ELLA HIGGINSON.

DEAD LEAVES WHISPER.

THERE is no song within the wood,
　The trees are silent ever;
The land hath lost its ancient good,
　And spent with their endeavor,
The dead leaves whisper, sweet and low,
The happy thoughts of long ago!

There is no joy in street or lane,
　No raptured voices calling;
The weary earth grown old again
　While all her leaves are falling—
And still they whisper, sweet and low,
The happy thoughts of long ago!

There is no present, but the past
　Breaks out in sudden yearning:
The loveliest leaves of life are cast
　When all the heart is burning—
The dead leaves whisper, sweet and low
The happy thoughts of long ago!
—FRED G. BOWLES *in St. Paul's.*

FOUR-LEAF CLOVER.

I KNOW a place where the sun is like gold,
And the cherry blooms burst with snow,
And down underneath is the loveliest nook,
Where the four-leaf clovers grow.

One leaf is for hope, and one is for faith,
　And one is for love, you know,
And God put another one in for luck—
　If you search you will find where they grow.

But you must have hope, and you must have faith,
You must love and be strong—and so—
If you work, if you wait, you will find the place
Where the four-leaf clovers grow.
　　　　　—ELLA HIGGINSON.

THE BRAVEST OF BATTLES.

THE bravest battle that ever was fought,
　Shall I tell you where and when?
On the maps of the world you'll find it not;
'Twas fought by the mothers of men.

Nay, not with cannon or battle shot,
　With sword or nobler pen;
Nay, not with the eloquent word or thought
From mouth of wonderful men,

But deep in a walled-up woman's heart—
Of woman that would not yield,
But bravely, silently, bore her part—
Lo, there is the battle-field!

No marshalling troop, no bivouac song,
No banner to gleam and wave!
But, oh, these battles, they last so long—
From babyhood to the grave!
　　　　　—JOAQUIN MILLER.

THE OLD FOLKS AT HOME.

WHEN, in late autumn we attempt to take up one of the plants which have grown luxuriantly in a garden bed, we find the danger to its life, in transplanting, is not so much the injury which its large roots are likely to receive, as the smaller ones, which are like little fingers reaching everywhere. There is a strange likeness to this in the uprooting of a life which has for years been lived in one home. There is nothing sadder than to see the old father and mother give up their independent life and become inmates of a new home with their children. This change is often, if not always, urged by sons and daughters from the purest motives. They feel that the care of housekeeping, the oversight of a home, are too great burdens for father and mother. "Come and live with us," they say, "and take life easy." But few, indeed, are the parents who can adjust themselves to the new relations, and they find after a few months that they have a peculiarly homeless feeling. They seem to fit in nowhere. They miss the old neighbors and all the little nameless associations which helped to fill up the measure of their days. They realize, as they never did in the old home, to which they gave tone and direction, how strongly the tide of young life flows on and leaves them behind, and unless their faculties are greatly impaired they are filled with sadness. They have nothing to do. Grandma can knit, and grandpa can do some trifling things, but there is nothing to satisfy them. It is no one's fault; it is in the nature of things that this should be so; and so it seems that that there should be less confidence in the appeals of children for their parents to break up the old home before necessity compels them to do so. In our modern homes there are not many "corners built for old age," and possibly old age is not content in a corner. However this may be, it certainly appears reasonable that so long as old people are able to carry on the home, it is kindest and wisest to leave them in it."

THE REASON.

SOMETHING has changed him; yesterday
 He passed me frowning, scarcely bowed,
And almost looked the other way,
 A careless stranger in the crowd.

But now? What grasp of cordial hand!
What cheery laugh, what genial tone!
'Mid eddying throngs we pause and stand
As if Broadway were ours alone.

Dear fellow! One word tells the tale;
 'Tis not the world of yesterday!

His heart gives every comrade hail;
 His wife is coming home to-day!
—MARGARET E. SANGSTER.

WHEN SAM'WEL LED THE SINGIN'.

OF course I love the house o' God,
 But I don't feel to hum there
The way I uster do, afore
 New-fangled ways had come there.
Though things are finer now, a heap,
 My heart it keeps a-clingin'
To our big, bare, old meetin'-house,
 Where Sam'wel led the singin'.

I 'low it's sorter solemn like,
 To hear the organ pealin';
It kinder makes your blood run cold,
 An' fills ye full o' feelin'.
But, somehow, it don't tech the spot—
 Now mind, ye, I ain't slingin'
No slurs—ez that bass viol did,
 When Sam'wel led the singin'.

I tell ye what, when he struck up
 The tune, an' sister Hanner
Put in her pretty treble—eh?
 That's what you'd call sopranner—
Why, all the choir, with might an' main,
 Set to, an' seemed a-flingin'
Their hull souls out with ev'ry note,
 When Sam'wel led the singin'.

An', land alive, the way they'd race
 Thro' grand old "Coronation"!
Each voice a-chasin' t'other round—
 It jes' beat all creation!
I allus thought it must 'a' set
 The bells o' heaven a-ringin'
To hear us "crown Him Lord of all,"
 When Sam'wel led the singin'.

Folks didn't sing for money then;
 They sung because 'twas in 'em
An' must come out. I uster feel—
 If Parson couldn't win 'em
With preachin' an' with prayin' an'
 His everlastin' dingin'—
That choir'd fetch sinners to the fold,
 When Sam'wel led the singin'.

A SONG FOR THE FUTURE.

SING sweetly a song for the days that are gone,
 They were merry and glad and free;

And O for the days that are yet to dawn,
And the joys that are yet to be!

Fair is the east when the morning shines,
And the glad earth awakes from rest;
But lovelier far, when the day declines,
Is the glory that fills the west.

To-morrow will come, with a brighter light
Than yesterday ever knew,
For a pleasure unknown and a new delight
Will gladden it through and through.

Then sing for the light-hearted, by-gone times,
They were merry and gay and free;
But, O sing in fuller and happier chimes
Of the joys that are yet to be.
—D. H. Morehead.

THE NEW CHURCH ORGAN.

They've got a bran-new organ, Sue,
For all their fuss and search;
They've done just as they said they'd do,
And fetched it into church.
They're bound the critter shall be seen,
And on the preacher's right
They've hoisted up the new machine,
In everybody's sight.
They've got a chorister and choir,
Agin my voice and vote;
For it was never my desire
To praise the Lord by rote.

I've been a sister, good and true,
For five-an'-thirty year;
I've done what seemed my part to do,
And prayed my duty clear
I've sung the hymns, both slow and quick,
Just as the preacher read,
And twice, when Deacon Tubbs was sick,
I took the fork and led!
And now their bold, new-fangled ways
Is comin' all about,
And I, right in my latter days,
Am fairly crowded out.

To-day the preacher, good old dear!
With tears all in his eyes,
Read: "I can read my title clear
To mansions in the skies."
I al'ays liked that blessed hymn—
I 'spose I always will;
It somehow gratifies my whim,
In good old Ortonville;
But when that choir got up to sing,
I couldn't catch a word;
They sang the most dog-gondest thing
A body ever heard.

Some worldly chaps was standin' near,
An' when I seed 'em grin,
" I bid farewell to every fear,"
An' boldly waded in.
I thought I'd chase their tune along,
An' tried with all my might,
But though my voice is good and strong,
I couldn't steer it right.
When they was high, then I was low,
An' also contrarywise,
An' I too fast, or they too slow,
" To mansions in the skies."

An' after every verse, you know,
They played a little tune;
I didn't understand, and so,
I started in too soon.
I pitched it pretty middlin' high—
I fetched a lusty tone;
But oh, alas! I found that I
Was singing there alone!
They laughed a little, I am told,
But I had done my best,
" And not a wave of trouble rolled
Across my peaceful breast."

And Sister Brown—I could but look—
She sits right front of me;
She never was no singin' book,
An' never went to be;
But then she's al'ays tried to do
The best she could, they said,
She understood the time, right through,
An' kept it with her head;
But when she tried this mornin', oh,
I had to laugh, or cough;
It kept her head a-bobbin' so
It e'en a' most came off.

An' Deacon Tubbs—he all broke down,
As one might well suppose;
He took one look at Sister Brown,
An' meekly scratched his nose;

He looked his hymn right thro' an' thro',
   And laid it on the seat,
An' then a pensive sigh he drew,
   An' looked completely beat.
An' when they took another bout,
   He didn't even rise,
But drawed his red bandana out,
   " An' wiped his weepin' eyes."

I've been a sister good an' true
   For five-and-thirty year;
I've done what seemed my part to do,
   An' prayed my duty clear;
But death will stop my voice, I know,
   For he is on my track;
An' some day I to church will go,
   An' never more come back;
An' when the folks get up to sing—
   Whene'er that time shall be—
I do not want no *patent* thing
   A squealin' over me.
            — W. C. CARLETON.

TO A MOCKING-BIRD.

HAST ever heard the skylark's deathless note,
   As with ambitious wing,
And more ambitious song, he seemed to float
   Almost where angels sing!
As though he sought to steal some heavenly strain
To fill the measures of his own refrain!

Hast thou had teaching from the nightingale,
   Hymning the list'ning moon?
Or slyly covert in some secret vale,
   Conned o'er the thrush's tune?
And caught the rich, full throated gush he flings
Into the orchestra that April brings?

To learn the bul-bul's note, o'er Persia's sands
   Hast thou unwearied flown,
Or snatched from the fair Australian strands,
   The bell-bird's vibrate tone,
That thou can'st blend its lingering, silver thrill
With parodies of jay and whippoorwill?

Do orioles from verdant Chesapeake,
   And crested cardinal,
With linnets from the Severn, come to seek,
   Obedient to thy call?
If they can give thee one new music thought,
Who ev'ry note from ev'ry land hast caught?

Or hast thou been where music fountains start,
   'Neath mystic, mythic skies?
And drank too deeply, that from out thy heart
   Such glorious melodies
Leap gushing—gurgling—in tumultuous throng
Until the quivering tree-tops drip with song?

Methinks the rarest choirs of fairyland
   Attuned each choicest chord;
Then sent the master songsters from each land,
   And bade them teach thee, bird!
Who, having taught, bewildered gathered round
And marvelled where such wondrous song was found.

God bless thee, Southland bird! God bless thy lay;
   Like music in a dream,
It floats from old Potomac's cliffs away
   To Colorado's stream;
From where Virginia's mountain torrents roar,
To where the warm Gulf laps the Texas shore;

Where Creole maids their loved and lost ones weep
   Among the cypress glades;
Or Carolina's blue-eyed daughters keep
   Beneath magnolia's shades
The darling graves where rest their darlings dead,
And lay camelias o'er the sleepers' head!

And everywhere thy joyous medleys ring
   The weary mourners smile,

And saddest hearts grow bright to hear
  thee sing,
Sweet music—king, the while
They breathe, "God bless thee," thou
  that dost belong
To us, O bird of universal song!
—Gen. E. G. Lee.

SOMEBODY'S MOTHER.

The woman was old, and ragged and
  gray,
And bent with the chill of the winter's
  day;
The streets were white with a recent
  snow,
And the woman's feet with age were
  slow.

At the crowded crossing she waited
  long,
Jostled aside by the careless throng
Of human beings, who passed her by,
Unheeding the glance of her anxious
  eye.

Down the street, with laughter and
  shout,
Glad in the freedom of "school let
  out,"
Come happy boys, like a flock of sheep,
Hailing the snow, piled white and deep,
Past the woman, so old and gray,
Hastened the children on their way.

None offered a helping hand to her,
So weak, so timid, afraid to stir,
Lest the carriage wheels or the horses'
  feet
Should trample her down in the slippery
  street.

At last came out of the merry troop
The gayest boy of all the group;
He paused beside her, and whispered
  low,
"I'll help you across, if you wish to
  go!"

Her aged hand on his strong young
  arm
She placed, and so, without hurt or
  harm,
He guided the trembling feet along,
Proud that his own were firm and
  strong;

Then back again to his friends he went,
His young heart happy and well content.

"She's somebody's Mother," boys, you
  know,
For all she is aged, and poor and low,
And some one sometime may lend a
  hand,
To help my mother—you understand—
If ever she's poor, and old, and gray,
And her own dear boy is far away."

"Somebody's Mother" bowed low her
  head
In her home that night, and the prayer
  she said
"May God be kind to that noble boy,
Who is somebody's son, and pride, and
  joy."

Faint was the voice, and worn and
  weak,
But heaven lists when its chosen speak;
Angels caught the faltering word,
And somebody's Mother's prayer was
  heard.

WHAT I LIVE FOR.

I live for those who love me,
  Whose hearts are kind and true;
For the heaven that smiles above me
  And awaits my spirit too;
For all human ties that bind me,
For the task by God assigned me,
For the bright hopes left behind me,
  And the good that I can do.

I live to learn *their* story
  Who've suffered for my sake;
To emulate their glory,
  And follow in their wake:
Bards, patriots, martyrs, sages,
The noble of all ages,
Whose deeds crowd History's pages,
  And Time's great volume make.

I live to hold communion
  With all that is divine;
To feel there is a union
  'Twixt Nature's heart and mine;
To profit by affliction,
Reap truths from fields of fiction,
Grow wiser from conviction,
  And fulfil each grand design.

I live to hail that season
  By gifted minds foretold,
When men shall live by reason,
  And not alone by gold ;
When man to man united,
  And every wrong thing righted,
The whole world shall be lighted
  As Eden of old.

I live for those who love me,
  For those who know me true,
For the heaven that smiles above me,
  And awaits my spirit too ;
For the cause that lacks assistance,
For the wrong that needs resistance,
For the future in the distance,
  And the good that I can do.
    —F. LINNÆUS BANKS.

THE EXILE'S SONG.

OH ! bear me back to my native shore,
  O'er the circling ocean's foam ;
And ere I die, let me gaze once more
  On my father's humble home.
Oh ! bear me back to the greenwood's
    shade,
  To the well-known chestnut tree—
To the quiet vale, and the sunny glade,
  The haunts of my childish glee.

My spirit pines for the breezy hills,
  Far off in my own bright land ;
For the warblings that gush from its
    lonely rills,
  And the joyous household band.
Kind faces met by the fireside's gleam,
  When arose the evening hymn ;—
But their spells are gone, like a passing
    dream,
  Their memories vague and dim.

I list to the billows' thundering sound,
  As their surges break in the bay ;
I watch them fringing the cliffs around
  With a beautiful girdle of spray.
But nor bark, nor ship, to the wander-
    ing breeze
  Their cloud-like sails unroll,
And the anthem sublime of the swelling
    seas,
  Like a death-song thrills my soul.

On the mountain-tops the wild deer
    springs
  In happiest freedom by ;
And the proud eagle soars on his golden
    wings
  To the crystalline dome of the sky ;
And the midnight wind unchained
    sweeps past
  O'er mount and forest dell—
But o'er ME there's a strange dull feel-
    ing cast,
  With a power I may not quell.

Then bear me back to my native shore,
  O'er the circling ocean's foam !
And ere I die, let me gaze once more
  On my father's humble home.
Oh ! bear me back to the greenwood
    shade,
  To the well-known chestnut tree—
To the quiet vale, and the sunny glade,
  The haunts of my childish glee !
    —ROBERT CHARLES WELSH.

THE KNOT OF BLUE AND GRAY.

UPON my bosom lies
  A knot of blue and gray ;
You ask me why. Tears fill my eyes
  As low to you I say :

I had two brothers once—
  Warm-hearted, bold and gay ;
They left my side—one wore the blue,
  The other wore the gray.

One rode with Stonewall and his men
  And joined his fate to Lee,
The other followed Sherman's march
  Triumphant to the sea.

Both fought for what they deemed the
    right ;
  And died with sword in hand,
One sleeps amid Virginia's hills
  And one in Georgia's sand.

The same sun shines upon their graves,
  My love unchanged must stay ;
And so upon my bosom lies
  The knot of blue and gray.

RECIPE FOR A GOOD HUSBAND.

SPEAKING of recipes, I have one which was sent me the other day, entitled, " How to Cook a Husband." I can't say why my unknown friend sent this particular recipe to me, since I am well known to have no such commodity in my larder. But, because I have no personal use for the information is no reason why others may not find it very valuable. And so I append it hereto with great pleasure:

"A good many husbands are utterly spoiled by mismanagement. Some women go about as if their husbands were balloons and blow them up. Others keep them constantly in hot water; others let them freeze by indifference and carelessness. Some keep them in a stew by irritating ways and words. Others roast them. Some keep them in pickle all their lives. It cannot be supposed that any husband will be tender and good if managed in this way, but they are really delicious when properly treated. In selecting your husband do not go to market for him, as the best are always brought to your door. It is far better to have none, unless you will patiently learn how to govern him.

"See that the linen in which you wrap him is properly washed and mended, with the required number of buttons and strings tightly sewed on. Tie him in the kettle by a strong silk cord called 'comfort,' as the one called 'duty' is apt to be weak. They are apt to fall out of the kettle, and be burned and crusty on the edges, since, like crabs and lobsters, you have to cook them while alive. If he sputters and fusses do not be anxious—some husbands do this until they are called done. Add a little sugar in the form of what confectioners call kisses, but no vinegar or pepper on any account. A little spice improves them, but it must be used with judgment. Do not stick any sharp instrument into him to see if he is becoming tender. Stir him gently, watching the while lest he adhere to the kettle, and so become useless. You cannot fail to know when he is done. If this treatment is closely followed you will find him all that is desirable; but do not be careless with him and keep him in too cool a place."

That certainly is a recipe in which there is sound sense as well as sentiment. I commend it to the consideration of young wives. I wish some one would send me the companion-dish to this one; I think some information is needed in regard to "how to cook a wife." I know more than one good wife who is spoiled from bad treatment.

RETROSPECTION.

It is saddest of folly to live in the past
    And shut out the light of the day that is beaming,
For the spirit will pant, where the shadows are cast,
    For the rays that perchance through the crannies are streaming.
As well may the captive who freedom regains
    Rebel 'gainst the edict that opens the gates,
And go forth into life bewailing his chains
    Leaving hope still entombed by the bars and the grates,
As for one well along in the battle we fight
    From the breast to its sequence, the echoless grave,
To turn as if scorning, from all that is bright,
    And cringe to the past, as but memory's slave.
Ah! 'tis only suggestive of mould and decay,
    This life in a circle—forever returning,
With torch that should blaze with flame of to-day,
    To be lit from the embers of yesterday's burning.
There are cinders enough in the air, Heaven knows,
    Take life as we may, as we journey ahead,
And he is the wisest who no back glance throws
    To take count of the milestones or number the dead.
Ah, the pillar of salt that Lot left in his flight
    As a warning to all who should turn in the track,

Would be melted away in the desert to-night,
By the tears that are born to the eyes that look back.
—S. A. JONAS.

MEASURING THE BABY.

We measured the riotous baby
 Against the cottage wall;
A lily grew on the threshold,
 And the boy was just as tall;
A royal tiger lily,
 With spots of purple and gold,
And a heart like a jewelled chalice,
 The fragrant dew to hold.

Without, the bluebird whistled
 High up in the old roof trees,
And to and fro at the window
 The red rose rocked her bees;
And the wee, pink fists of the baby
 Were never a moment still,
Snatching at shine and shadow
 That danced on the lattice sill.

His eyes were wide as bluebells,
 His mouth like a flower unblown,
Two little bare feet, like funny white mice,
 Peeped out from his snowy gown;
And we thought with a thrill of rapture,
 That yet had a touch of pain,
When June rolls around with her roses,
 We'll measure the boy again.

Ah, me! in a darkened chamber,
 With the sunshine shut away,
Through tears that fell like bitter rain,
 We measured the boy to-day;
And the little bare feet, that are dimpled
 And sweet as a budding rose,
Lay side by side together
 In the hush of a long repose.

Up from the dainty pillow,
 White as the risen dawn,
The fair little face lay smiling,
 With the light of heaven thereon;
And the dear little hands, like rose-leaves,
 Dropped from a rose, lay still,
Never to snatch at the sunshine
 That crept to the shrouded sill.

We measured the sleeping baby
 With ribbons white as snow,
For the shining rosewood casket,
 That waited him below;
And out of the darkened chamber
 We went with a childless moan—
To the height of the sinless angels
 Our little one has grown.
—EMMA ALICE BROWN.

IN THE TWILIGHT.

As we grow old, our yesterdays
 Seem very dim and distant;
We grope, as those in darken'd ways
 Through all that is existent;
Yet far-off days shine bright and clear
 With suns that long have faded,
And faces dead seem strangely near
 To those that life has shaded.

As we grow old our tears are few
 For friends most lately taken;
But fall—as falls the summer dew
 From roses lately shaken—
When some chance word or idle strain,
 The chords of memory sweeping,
Unlock the flood-gates of our pain
 For those who taught us weeping.

As we grow old our smiles are rare
 To those who greet us daily,
Or if some living faces wear
 The looks that beam so gayly
From eyes long closed, and we should smile,
 In answer to their wooing,
'Tis but the past that shines the while
 Our power to smile renewing.

As we grow old our dreams at night
 Are never of the morrow;
They come with banish'd pleasure bright,
 Or dark with olden sorrow:
And when we wake the names we say
 Are not of any mortals,
But of those in some long dead day
 Passed through life's sunset portals.

THE OLD OAKEN BUCKET.

How dear to this heart are the scenes of my childhood,
 When fond recollections present them to view!

The orchard, the meadow, the deep-
    tangled wildwood,
And every dear spot which my in-
    fancy knew;
The wide-spreading pond, and the mill
    which stood by it,
The bridge and the rock where the
    cataract fell;
The cot of my father, the dairy house
    nigh it,
And e'en the rude bucket which hung
    in the well;
The old oaken bucket, the iron-bound
    bucket,
The moss-covered bucket which hung
    in the well.

The moss-covered vessel I hail as a
    treasure;
For often, at noon, when returned
    from the field,
I found it the source of exquisite pleas-
    ure,
The purest and sweetest which nature
    can yield.
How ardent I seized it, with hands that
    were glowing!
And quick to the white-pebbled bot-
    tom it fell;
And soon, with the emblem of truth
    overflowing,
And dripping with coolness, it 'rose
    from the well.
The old oaken bucket, the iron-bound
    bucket,
The moss-covered bucket arose from
    the well,—

How sweet from the green mossy brim
    to receive it,
As poised on the curb it inclined to
    my lips,
Not a full blushing goblet could tempt
    me to leave it,
Though filled with the nectar that
    Jupiter sips.
And now, far removed from the loved
    situation,
The tear of regret will intrusively
    swell,
As fancy reverts to my father's planta-
    tion,
And sighs for the bucket which hangs
    in the well.

The old oaken bucket, the iron-bound
    bucket,
The moss-covered bucket, which hangs
    in the well.
    —SAMUEL WORDSWORTH.

THE OLD, OLD HOME.

WHEN I long for sainted memories, like
    angel troops they come,
If I fold my arms and ponder on the
    old, old home,
For the heart hath many passages
    through which the feelings roam,
But its middle aisle is sacred to the old,
    old home.

CHORUS.

Oh! the old, old home! oh, the old, old
    home!
But its middle aisle is sacred to the old,
    old home.

Where infancy was sheltered, like rose-
    buds from the blast,
And childhood's brief elysian in joy-
    ousness passed;
To that sweet spot forever, as to some
    hallowed dome,
Life's pilgrim bends his vision on the
    old, old home.

CHORUS.

Oh! the old, old home!
Life's pilgrim bends his vision on the
    old, old home.

There a father sat, how proudly, by
    that hearthstone's rays,
And told his children stories of his early
    manhood days,
And one soft eye was beaming, from
    child to child 'twould roam,
Thus a mother counts her treasures in
    the old, old home.

CHORUS.

Oh! the old, old home!
Thus a mother counts her treasures in
    the old, old home.

The birthday gifts and festivals, the
    blended vesper hymn,
One dear one who was hymning it is
    with the seraphim,

The fond good nights at bed-time ; how
    quiet sleep would come
And fold us all together in the old, old
    home.

        CHORUS.
Oh ! the old, old home !
And fold us all together in the old, old
    home.

Like a wreath of scented flowers, close
    entwined each heart,
But time and change in concert each
    have blown the wreath apart,
Yet faithful, sainted memories, like
    angels ever come,
If I fold my arms and ponder on the
    old, old home.

        CHORUS.
Oh ! the old, old home !
If I fold my arms and ponder on the
    old, old home.
        —REV. P. ROBERTS.

OLD CHURCH BELLS.

    RING out merrily,
    Loudly, cheerily,
Blithe old bells, from the steeple tower ;
    Hopefully, fearfully,
    Joyfully, tearfully,
Moveth the bride from her maiden
    bower.

Cloud there is none in the bright sum-
    mer sky,
Sunshine flings benisons down from on
    high ;
Children sing loud as the train moves
    along,
" Happy the bride that the sun shineth
    on."

    Knell out drearily,
    Measure out wearily,
Sad old bells, from the steeple gray ;
    Priests chanting lowly,
    Solemnly, slowly,
Passeth the corpse from the portal to-
    day.

Drops from the leaden clouds heavily
    fall,
Dripping over the plume and the pall ;
Murmur old folks as the train moveth
    along,
" Happy the dead that the rain raineth
    on."

    Toll at the hour of prime,
    Matin and vesper chime,
Loved old bells, from the steeple high—
    Rolling like holy waves
    Over the lowly graves,
Floating up, prayer fraught, into the
    sky ;

Solemn the lesson your lightest note
    teaches
Stern is the preaching your iron tongue
    preaches ;
Ringing in life from the bud to the
    bloom,
Ringing the dead to their rest in the
    tomb.

    Peal out evermore—
    Peal as ye pealed of yore,
Brave old bells on each Sabbath day ;
    In sunshine and gladness,
    Through clouds and sadness,
Bridal and burial have both passed
    away.

Tell us life's pleasures with death are
    still rife ;
Tell us that death even leadeth to life ;
Life is our labor and death is our rest,
If happy the living, the dead are the
    blest.

SHE KISSED ME GOOD-NIGHT.

AT the little front gate we lingered,
    A dear little loved one and I,
Each wishing the moments would linger,
    For the hour of parting drew nigh ;
Her head it was close to my shoulder,
    Could mortal ask much more of fate ?
That the trusting look in loving eyes,
    She kissed me good-night at the gate.

She's a dear little winsome fairy,
    With cheeks as red as roses,
And a merry sparkle in those eyes
    Wherein her soul reposes ;
And when life's skies are clouded o'er,
    Anxiously I'll fondly watch and wait,

For cheering words will come from lips
That kissed me good-night at the
   gate.

There's a happy time coming, presently,
  When we shall married be,
And we'll pass our life in joyousness,
  In a dear little home by the sea ;
And if she be called to heaven first,
  For me she will fondly wait,
And meet me at the tryst above,
  And kiss me at heaven's gate.

THE OLD SPINNING WHEEL.

How well we remember the old spinning wheel ! What happy memories come to us as we call back the scenes of our early childhood, in which the old wheel, " with its great rim and little head," bore so conspicuous a part. We can almost hear again its whirr, whizz, and see the long slender thread shape itself, as the nimble feet of sister walked to and fro, and her dexterous fingers drew out the carded " roll " and twisted it, and then ran it up on the spindle.

Then came the reeling. Ah, that was the interesting part of it all. How patiently we waited till the spindle was full, and we could see it reeled off into skeins. What a wonderful piece of machinery that old reel was in our childish estimation. That round wheel " with its notches all around it," and a spring that would snap at every forty rounds. How fast sister would make it go round. How, again and again, we would try in vain to count the times.

Indeed what a continued round of pleasure that old-fashioned family cloth-making business was, to " us boys," anyway ! What a day of enjoyment the sheep-washing day was. First, there was the pen-building. That gave us a full day of enjoyment, to begin with, as it took a whole day for the men and our big brothers to build the pen. Of course we were too small to lift the rails, but we were large enough to go fishing, and there was just where the fun came in. How well we remember once, when brother Frank stood watching us getting our poles ready with a look so sad that we remember it still, as, swallowing the great lump in his throat he said, " I wish I hadn't grown big."

But that day at the river, when the sheep were washed ! What a day that was for us boys, to be sure ! There would be the sheep of from two, to half a dozen farms, all to be taken into the river. Even the lambs needed washing, in the estimation of the boys, and what fun it was to do it.

Nor was it always without its serious side either. We remember the first time we undertook to wash a big sheep. It seemed so easy, that we knew we could handle any sheep in the pen, if we could only get him into the water, and Henry Jackson, our great big neighbor, volunteered to take one in for us. Poor Henry ! He died of consumption long, long ago, and we have fully forgiven him ; but we believe even yet that he did it on purpose to have some fun at our expense. He selected one of the biggest in the pen, and took him out where the water was fully up to our arms. Then we took him in charge, but alas ! the water was too deep. A few steps more and the sheep was master of the situation. Hoisting all sail he immediately headed for the other shore, and we were left to the alternative of hanging on to his wool, and being towed across, or letting go and being drowned. We preferred the former ; and by the time we reached the shore, we had reached the decision to fight it out on that side, if it took us all summer. And we did, compelling the sheep to turn about and tow us back again.

But, oh dear ! The record of all that the memory of the old spinning-wheel brings to us would be too long for a newspaper article. There was a visit to the carding-machine, which of course gave us another day of exquisite pleasure. There was coloring day, when mother, wise woman that she was, to understand all about such things— would change the pure white yarn into a dozen different hues. Then the weaving, where we could sit for hours and watch the shuttle fly from side to side, and the thousand threads shape themselves into the soft warm fabric. Then the woman to sew, and when the winter blasts came roaring over the Canadian hills, they found us all clothed in our new, warm winter garments, ready to give them battle.

But all that has changed. The men of those days have passed into the Great Beyond, and the boys have either become gray-haired men, like ourself, or they too have taken up the line of march to the unknown country. We do not know what has become of the old spinning-wheel, and its companion the reel, but we do know that, poor as we are, if we had them to-day, a thousand dollars would not purchase them. You may call it mere sentiment, or regard it as you will, but the memories they would bring to us would be more precious than gold.

THE DOVE.

A COMPANION TO POE'S RAVEN.

ONCE upon a summer evening,
As I lay reposing, dreaming,
While the twinkling stars were beaming,
And their light was faintly gleaming
    Through the window of my room,
Suddenly beside my pillow,
Like the murmur of a billow,
Or the sigh of weeping willow,
'Mid the shadow and the gloom,
There was heard a gentle sound,
Floating on the air around,
    As an echo from above;
And I, walking, saw a dove
Perched upon the whitened head
Of a statue near my bed,
And it seemed with soft, low cooing
My lone heart to soothe with wooing,
Like an angel from the sky,
Or a spirit hovering nigh.

While I lay entranced and dreaming,
Startled by the echo seeming
    To be whispered from above,
In the starlight faintly gleaming,
With its form of beauty beaming,
    I beheld the snowy dove:
With a thrill of wonder, gazing
On the visitor, amazing,
    I demanded : " Who are you ? "

And the gentle bird of whiteness,
With its snowy robe of brightness,
    Answered with a coo :
" I am sent," he said, " from Aiden,
By a fair and lovely maiden,
    With a message unto thee ;
I am come to soothe thy sorrow,
Bid thee from despair to borrow
    Hope that thou her face shall see ;
For thy cherished one is living,
And her thoughts to thee is giving,
    On a bright and distant shore ;
And I come, her carrier dove,
With a message from thy love,
    Who is thine for evermore."

By this joyful news excited,
Raptured, ravished and delighted,
    I, the snowy bird addressing,
Asked, with earnest voice inquiring,
What my soul was most desiring,
    That her name to me expressing,
He would set my heart at rest—
Still the tumult in my breast,
And assure me that MY maiden,
In the distant fields of Aiden
    Waited for me on that shore—
    Would be mine for evermore.
Then I spoke with greater fervor,
I, the maiden's ardent lover :
    " Does my own departed live ? "
(To the bird of whiteness listening
While my eager eyes were glistening,
    For the answer he should give) ;
" Tell me, O thou carrier dove,
Of my absent, cherished love,
    Whom I knew in days of yore,
Has she passed the shining portal
Of the blessed land immortal,
    Going through the golden door ?
Does she move in light and splendor,
Do the graces all attend her,
    On that fair and distant shore ? "

Words and tones and looks revealing,
All my depths of inward feeling,
Moved, affected by my pleading,
And my anxious question heeding,
Thus the dove, my soul discerning,
Answer made, these words returning :
    " In the distant fields of Aiden,
    On a bright, Elysian shore,
    Dwells a fair and lovely maiden,
    And her name is Elinore ;

'Mid the flowers about her blooming,
'Mid the odors sweet perfuming
　All the balmy air around,
She, arrayed in robe of whiteness,
Walks an angel in her brightness,
　With a wreath immortal crowned."
Then the bird, his wings unfolding,
Left me, as I lay beholding,
　Filled with transport and delight;
With a soft, sonorous coo,
Nodding, bidding me adieu,
Through the open window flew
　Out into the gloomy night.
But the bright, enchanting vision
Of the distant fields Elysian,
　And my cherished Elinore,
As a fair and lovely maiden,
Dwelling in the land of Aiden,
　Is my light for evermore.
There shall I, my loved one greeting,
At our future, early meeting,
　On that distant, radiant shore,
With ecstatic joy and gladness,
Free from parting, pain and sadness,
　Clasp again my Elinore,
　Call her mine for evermore!
　　　—Rev. J. H. Martin, D. D.

THE BLUE AND THE GRAY.

By the flow of the inland river,
　Whence the fleets of iron have fled,
Where the blades of the grave-grass
　　quiver,
　Asleep are the ranks of the dead;
　　Under the sod and the dew,
　　　Waiting the judgment day;
　　Under the one, the Blue,
　　　Under the other, the Gray.

These in the robings of glory,
　Those in the gloom of defeat;
All with the battle blood gory,
　In the dust of eternity meet;
　　Under the sod and the dew,
　　　Waiting the judgment day,
　　Under the laurel, the Blue;
　　　Under the willow, the Gray.

From the silence of sorrowful hours
　The desolate mourners go,
Lovingly laden with flowers
　Alike for the friend and the foe;
　　Under the sod and the dew,
　　　Waiting the judgment day,
　　Under the roses, the Blue;
　　　Under the lilies, the Gray.

So, with an equal splendor,
　The morning sun-rays fall,
With a touch impartially tender,
　On the blossoms blooming for all;
　　Under the sod and the dew,
　　　Waiting the judgment day;
　　Broidered with gold, the Blue;
　　　Mellowed with silver, the Gray.

So, when the summer calleth,
　On forest and field of grain,
With an equal murmur falleth
　The cooling drip of the rain;
　　Under the sod and the dew,
　　　Waiting the judgment day;
　　Wet with rain, the Blue;
　　　Wet with tears the Gray.

Sadly, but not with upbraiding,
　The generous deed was done;
In the storm of the years are fading
　No braver battle was won;
　　Under the sod and the dew,
　　　Waiting the judgment day;
　　Under the blossoms, the Blue;
　　　Under the garlands, the Gray.

No more shall the war-cry sever,
　Or the winding rivers be red;
They banish our anger forever
　When they laurel the graves of our
　　dead,
　　Under the sod and the dew,
　　　Waiting the judgment day;
　　Love and tears for the Blue,
　　　Tears and love for the Gray.
　　　—M. E. P. Finch.

CHILDHOOD.

Dear wonderland of childhood,
　Could we but return to thee,
Could we live among the fairies
　In a sort of ecstasy,

Could we laugh and sing and prattle
　Happy, all the livelong day,
Making playthings of the shadows,
　When they keep the sun away,

Could some magic wand transport us
　To the land of long ago,

We would ask the elves to teach us
  How to live yet not to grow.

IDAHO.

IDAHO, "Gem of the Mountains,"
  Fair as e'er land could be,
With Nature's spires heav'nward pointing
  Beautiful beyond degree ;
With skies as bright as heaven's own light,
  With air as pure and free !

CHORUS.

Idaho, "Gem of the Mountains,"
  The pride of land and sea,
With skies as bright as heaven's own light,
  With air as pure and free.

Thy veins are traced in golden seams,
  Thy ribs of rock and steel,
Thy limpid, flowing, crystal streams
  Gladden the hill and field—
With acres wide as ocean's tide,
  And as ready to yield.

With homes of love will'd from above,
  Bourn for the chosen few ;
Thy sons are bold for deeds untold,
  And are as brave as true ;
And daughters fair with graces rare
  As men or gods e'er knew !

Fair Idaho—the red man's choice
  Of all Nature's bequest—
The jewel in the Nation's crown,
  Of heav'n and earth all blest ;
In the galaxy of the states
  Thou excellest the rest !

FOR LOVE'S SAKE ONLY.

IF thou must love me let it be for naught,
  Except for love's sake only. Do not say—
  " I love her for her smile—her look—her way
Of speaking gently—for a trick of thought
That falls in well with mine, and certes brought
  A sense of pleasant ease on such a day."
For these things in themselves, Beloved, may
Be changed, or change for thee—and love so wrought
May be unwrought so. Neither love me for
  Thine own dear pity's wiping my cheeks dry—
Since one might well forget to weep who bore
  Thy comfort long, and lose thy love thereby ;
But, love me for love's sake, that evermore,
  Thou mayst love on through love's eternity.
—ELIZABETH BARRETT BROWNING.

THE KING'S KISS.

" How long," he asked, " will you remember this—
" How long ? " Then downward bent
His kingly head, and on her lips a kiss
Fell like a flame—a flame that sent
  Through every vein
  Love's joy and pain ;
" How long," he asked, " will you remember this ? "

" How long ? " She lifted from his breast her cheek
  Red with sacred love,
Yet when her redder lips essayed to speak,
  And when her heart did move
    To answer grave and sweet,
    Somehow a smile unmeet
Broke waywardly across red lips and cheek.

" How long, how long will I remember this ?
  Say you," she murmured low—
" Say you,"—and while she trembled with her bliss,
  That smile went to and fro
    Across her flushing face,
    And hid a graver grace—
" Say you, how long will you remember this ? "

He bent above her in that moment's
    bliss,
He held her close and fast;
"How long, how long will I remember
    this?
Until I cross at last,
    With failing, dying breath,
    That river men call Death—
So long, so long, will I remember this."

But, when apart they stood, did he re-
    member
His words that summer day?
Did he remember through the long
    December
The warmth and love of May,
    The warmth and love and bliss,
    The meaning of that kiss,
When kingdoms stood between—did he
    remember?

Ah, who can say for him? For her we
    know
The king's kiss was her crown;
For her we know no agony of woe,
    No other smile or frown,
    Could make her heart forswear
    That summer morning there,
Beneath the forest trees of Fontainbleau.
                    —DORA PERRY.

UNTO DEATH.

O, OFTTIMES in the twilight
    I am sitting silently,
When the glory of the sunlight
    Leaves its impress in the sky;
And a low voice seems to whisper,
    With passion in each breath,
"I will love thee, love, forever;
    You may trust me unto death!'"

And I live upon the echo
    Of that passionate refrain;
And my hope is firm and steadfast
    I shall hear it once again,
Though years may pass and vanish,
    And life grow worn and cold,
I am waiting the re-utterance
    Of those pleading words of old.

It may be an illusion,
    A myth, a fancy bare;
But it keeps my heart from breaking,
    And my life from much despair,

And as long as life shall linger
    Comes the echo of each breath,
"I will love thee, love, forever;
    You may trust me unto death!"
                —TINSLEY'S MAGAZINE.

WHAT IS A YEAR?

WHAT is a year? 'Tis but a wave
    Of life's dark rolling stream,
Which is so quickly gone that we
    Account it but a dream;
'Tis but a single earnest throb
    Of Time's old iron heart,
As tireless now and strong as when
    It first with life did start.

What is a year? 'Tis but a turn
    Of time's old brazen wheel,
Or but a page upon the book
    Which death must shortly seal;
'Tis but a step upon the road
    Which we must travel o'er;
A few more steps and we shall walk
    Life's weary road no more.

What is a year? 'Tis but a breath
    From Time's old nostrils blown;
As rushing onward o'er the earth
    We hear his weary moan;
'Tis like a bubble on the wave
    Or dew upon the lawn,
As transient as the mist of morn
    Beneath the summer's sun.

What is a year? 'Tis but a type
    Of life's oft-changing scene;
Youth's happy morn comes gayly on
    With hills and valleys green;
Next summer's prime succeeds the
    spring
    With flowers everywhere;
Then comes old winter—death and all
    Must find their level there.

SMALL THINGS.

SOME one has asked where all the pins and hairpins go? But so far as heard from no one has heard where such things come from. Of course they first come from the factories; but everybody uses small things, but who buys them, is the question? Take matches, toothpicks and pins, for instance, and who supplies them? If a record were kept of the actual purchasers of such things, it would be surprising how few of mankind does the purchasing of such things of universal use. And the straw is no surer to tell the way the wind blows, than are small things to demonstrate real character. It is like dinner-table manners,—there the hog in nature crops out. For it takes a real gentleman not to let his appetite get the better of him, and to do as he would be done by, in investing in pins, toothpicks, and matches! No one expects to be watched on such things, because "it is small."—Yes, small, and it just takes small traps to catch small game! It is really surprising sometimes what big game are, however, found in these little traps. Great big people, whom you would think couldn't get in them. Yet, they know their size trap, and walk right in!

A GENTLEMAN DEFINED.

LONDON Tid Bits offered a prize for "the best definition of a gentleman." The winning definition is as follows:
A knight whose armor, whose weapon is courtesy.
The following are some of the definitions sent in:
A gentleman is one who combines a woman's tenderness with a man's courage.
The mirror of mannerly manhood.
A man who does his best to do the best.
A man whose money mars not his manners.
Is one who wherever he may be, remembers what he is.
The quintessence of true manliness.
The embodiment of male perfections.
A happy result of the combined efforts of nature, preceptors, and—the tailor.
One whose merits are patent as well as his shoes.
Manly, honest, generous, pure, a gentleman—rich or poor.

A man both cultured and refined, who always has it in his mind, and acts upon it always, too, to do as he'd have others do.
A human magnet.
A man who gracefully recognizes the rights of others.
Nature's finishing touch.
The crown of man's accomplishments.
A planet in humanity's constellation.
A gentleman is a person who perfectly combines self-forgetfulness with self-respect.
A compound of various good qualities that embellish mankind.
A human brilliant very frequently unpolished.
One who acts with equal courtesy and consideration to all men, be they prince or peasant.
Man's truest model, with "honor" for its base.
A gentleman is one who realizes that there are others beside himself.
Honor personified.
One who knows what honor is and acts up to it.
A man who treats others with considerable kindness and respect because he can't help it.
A man who has a great capacity for doing right.
A man who does unto others as he would they should do unto him.
He whose first consideration is for the feelings of others.

WEARINESS.

I AM weary of life and its struggles, I
   am weary of love that is vain—
Of watching and waiting and wishing,
   and longing and passion and pain.
I am weary of dreams that all vanish
   like mists in the desolate air,
Of taking a love in my spirit, to burn
   and to torture me there.

I am weary of great aspirations that
   shatter like rose-petals shed,
Of garlands I weave for the banquet
   that change into thorns on my head.

Of all of the fancies and phantoms that
    mock at my desolate heart—
Of beauty that dies and ambitions that
    never can melt into art ;
Of the cant of the pitiless Christian, who
    talks of his God and his Heaven,
While souls by his merciless hatred are
    broken and tender hearts riven,

I am weary, so weary, of looking down
    deep into my sin-spotted soul,
Of fighting the demons of passion too
    great for my will and control ;
And weary of prayers that unanswered
    die unheard, unechoed away—
And weary of midnights that linger to
    the noon of the desolate day.
                                —B. W. B.

THE ENGINEER'S SIGNAL.

THE rush and the roar of the rattling
    train
Is heard at midnight again and again,
As it sweeps along with fearful speed
Over the bridges and through the
    mead—
Waking the echoes far and wide,
Startling the sleepers on every side,
Flitting and fleeting, and steaming on
Till it reaches the edge of Providence
    town.

'Tis at Elmwood crossing, and hark !
    on the air,
A sharp, quick whistle, distinct and
    clear,
Rouses the passengers on the train,
As the engine repeats the shrill refrain ;
'Tis not the signal for " Down with the
    Brakes ! "
Nor " Danger Ahead ! " that rudely
    awakes
The drowsy slumberers in the rear,
And starts the question with anxious
    fear—

What does it mean, that singular
    sound ?
And as the inquiry passes around,
They are told it is Guild, the engineer,
Who speaks to his wife in yon cottage
    there,
And says in this strange but significant
    strain :
" All is well, my love, and I'm off
    again ! '

And thus he had spoken for many a
    year,
To the loved one who watched and
    waited to hear
Her husband's salute in the sonorous
    steam,
Then retired to rest—but only to dream
That the same mystic greeting a hun-
    dred times o'er
Seemed to say to the heart as she stood
    at the door
" I'm safe, darling wife ; for God's wing
    is outspread
Alike o'er the engineer's cottage and
    head."

But why is the watcher waiting in vain
To catch the first sound of the Stoning-
    ton train ?
It comes not ; as moments like hours
    drag by,
" Oh God ! " she exclaims, in an ago-
    nized cry,
"My husband ! where is he ? And why
    this delay ? "
Alas ! she knows not that miles back
    on the way,
Crushed, mangled, and burning, but
    true to his trust,
His hand on the throttle—his face in
    the dust—

The wreck of the engine piled over his
    head,
The engineer's lying—is dying—is dead!
Ah ! heart-stricken wife, you shall never
    again
Hear the greeting of love from the
    swift-rushing train ;
'Twill still pass the crossing ; you'll
    hear it at night,
And see through the windows the glare
    of the light ;
But you'll waken to weep, for the
    whistle no more
Shall give its glad signal at Guild's
    cottage door.

GOBLETS AND GLASSES AND MUGS.

Talk not of goblets made of gold
  In Duke of Alva's reign ;
Nor how your fathers lorded them,
And Spanish nobles hoarded them
When reckless rovers boarded them
  With lust for golden gain !
They're only put up there for show,
  So cease you to explain.
Your ancestors oft caught for them
The deuce from those who sought for them —
Who cursed and swore and fought for them —
  Upon the Spanish Main !

And, pouf! for all your famous glasses
  Lined on the sideboard there !
'Twas Fashion who first vaunted them,
  At once her fools all wanted them,
In glass shops hourly haunted them
  To find some cut more rare !
Though champagne fill them to the brim,
  They're less to me, I swear,
Than those poor fools who keep o'er them
A nightly vigil ; weep o'er them,
And, lastly, fall asleep o'er them,
  Beneath some dinner chair !

So, ho ! my Gretchen, buxom lass,
  I want no tricky wine,
But amber nectar cling to me,
Whose rich bouquet shall bring to me,
Whose spirit-love will sing to me
  From out the mug divine !
So here's your toll—a kiss—away,
  You Hebe from the Rhine !
No goblet's gold means cheer to me,
Let no cut glass get near to me !
Go, Gretchen, haste the beer to me,
  And put it in the stein !
—Pacific Wine and Spirit Review.

ENDURANCE.

How much the heart may bear, and yet not break !
How much the flesh may suffer, and not die !
I question much if any pain or ache
  Of soul or body brings our end more nigh,
Death chooses his own time ; till that is sworn
  All evils may be borne.

We shrink and shudder at the surgeon's knife,
  Each nerve recoiling from the cruel steel,
Whose edge seems searching for the quivering life ;
  Yet to our sense the bitter pangs reveal
That still, although the trembling flesh be torn,
  This also can be borne.

We see a sorrow rising in our way
  And try to flee from the approaching ill ;
We seek some small escape ; we weep and pray ;
  But when the blow falls, then our hearts are still ;
Not that the pain is of its sharpness shorn,
  But that it can be borne.

We wind our life about another life ;
  We hold it closer, dearer, than our own,
Anon it faints and fails in deadly strife,
  Leaving it stunned and stricken and alone ;
But, ah ! we do not die with those we mourn ;
  This also can be borne.

Behold ! we live through all things— famine, thirst,
  Bereavement, pain ; all grief and misery,
All woe and sorrow ; life inflicts its worst
  On soul and body—but we cannot die.
Though we be sick and tired and faint and worn—
  Lo ! all things can be borne !

—E. A. Allen.

DYING WORDS OF NOTED MEN.

It is well.—Washington.
I must sleep now.—Byron.
Thy will be done.—Donne.
Is this your fidelity?—Nero.
Then I am safe.—Cromwell.
Let the light enter.—Goethe.
And is this death?—George IV.
God's will be done.—Bishop Kerr.
God will save my soul.—Burghley.
Lord, take my spirit.—Edward VI.
Lord, make haste.—H. Hammond.
Lord, receive my spirit.—Cranmer.
The artery ceases to beat.—Haller.
Don't give up the ship.—Lawrence.
It is the last of earth.—J. Q. Adams.
God preserve the emperor.—Haydn.
I am about to die.—Samuel Johnson.
Independence forever.—John Adams.
Give Dayrolles a chair.—Chesterfield.
I shall be happy.—Archbishop Sharp.
Don't let poor Nellie starve.—Charles II.
I have endeavored to do my duty.—Taylor.
I thank God I have done my duty.—Nelson.
I feel as if I were myself again.—Walter Scott.
An emperor should die standing.—Vespasian.
The best of all is, God is with us.—John Wesley.
Clasp my hand, my dear friend, I die.
It matters little how the head lieth.—Raleigh.
I'm shot if I don't believe I'm dying.—Thurlow.
I loved God, my Father, and liberty.—De Staël.
A dying man can do nothing easy.—Franklin.
My beautiful flowers, my lovely flowers.—Richter.
James, take good care of the horse.—Winfield Scott.
Many things are becoming clearer to me.—Schiller.
I feel the daisies growing over me.—John Keats.
What, is there no bribing death?—Cardinal Beaufort.
Taking a leap in the dark. O, mystery!—Thomas Paine.
Let the earth be filled with His glory.—Earl of Derby.
There is not a drop of blood on my hands.—Frederick V.
I am taking a fearful leap in the dark.—Thomas Hobbes.
Don't let that awkward squad fire over my grave.—Burns.
Here, veteran, if you think it right, strike.—Cicero.
My days are past as a shadow that returns not.—R. Hooker.
I thought that dying had been more difficult.—Louis XIV.
O Lord, forgive me specially my sins of omission.—Usher.
Let me die to the sounds of delicious music.—Mirabeau.
It is small, very small, alluding to her neck.—Anne Boleyn.
Let the earth be filled with His glory.—Bishop Broughton.
Let me hear those notes so long my solace and delight.—Mozart.
To die for liberty is a pleasure and not a pain.—Marco Bozzaris.
We are as near Heaven by sea as by land.—Sir Humphrey Gilbert.
I resign my soul to God: my daughter to my country.—Jefferson.
I would not change my joy for the empire of the world.—Philip Sidney.
Farewell, Livia, and ever remember our long union.—Augustus Cæsar.
I have sent for you to see how a Christian can die.—Addison to Warwick.
Into thy hands, O Lord! I commend my spirit.—Christopher Columbus.
This is the last flickering of a lamp that has long been burning.—Gen. Wool.
I want nothing, and I am looking for nothing but Heaven.—Phil. Melancthon.
I have seen all things, and all things are of little value.—Alexander Severus.
Remorse! Remorse! Write it! Larger! Larger!—John Randolph.
We are all going to Heaven, and Vandyke is of the company.—Gainsborough.
Gentlemen of the jury, you will now consider your verdict.—Lord Tenterden.

I thank God that I was brought up in the Church of England.—Bishop Gunning.

O Liberty, Liberty, how many crimes are committed in thy name!—Mme. Roland.

Let us cross over the river and rest under the shade of the trees.—Stonewall Jackson.

Crito, we owe a cock to Esculapius; pay it soon, I pray you, and neglect it not.—Socrates.

I am dying out of charity to the undertaker who wishes to earn a lively Hood.—Hood.

"Throw up the window that I may once more see the magnificent scene of nature.—Rousseau.

Soul, thou hast served Christ these seventy years, and art thou afraid to die? Go out, go out!—Hilary.

If I had strength enough to hold a pen, I would write how easy and delightful it is to die.—William Hunter.

I pray you to see me safe up, and for my coming down let me shift for myself.—Sir Thomas More on the scaffold.

My soul I resign to God, my body to the earth, and my worldly possessions to my relatives.—Michael Angelo.

When you wish to know what to do, ask yourself what Christ would have done in the same circumstances.—Horace Mann.

I had provided for everything in my life except death, and now, alas! I am to die, though entirely unprepared.—Cæsar Borgia.

Had I but served my God with half the zeal I served my king he would not have given me over in my gray hairs.—Cardinal Wolsey.

It will not be long before God takes me, for no mortal man can live after the glories which God has manifested to my soul.—Toplady.

Lord, enlighten and soften the hearts of my executioners. Adieu, forever, my dear children, I go to join your father.—Marie Antoinette.

Be of good comfort, brother, for we shall this day light such a candle in England as, by God's grace, shall never be put out.—Latimer to Ridley.

Do not weep for me, nor waste your time in fruitless prayers for my recovery, but pray rather for the salvation of my soul.—Isabella of Aragon.

I have lived long enough, and I am thankful I have enjoyed a happy life; but after all, look on this life as nothing better than vanity.—John Locke.

I am perfectly resigned. I am surrounded by my family. I have served my country. I have reliance upon God, and I am not afraid of the devil.—Grattan.

What is the matter with my dear children? Have I alarmed you? Oh, don't cry. Be good children and we will all meet in Heaven.—Andrew Jackson.

I am going the way of all flesh. I am satisfied with the Lord's will.—Jack Newton.

My country! O, how I love my country.—William Pitt, the younger.

Thank God, I can lay my hand upon my heart and say, that since I came to my estate, I have never intentionally done wrong to any one.—Francis Marion.

Here is a book (the Bible) worth more than all others ever printed; yet it is our misfortune never to have found time to read it. I trust in the mercy of God. It is now too late.—Patrick Henry.

Not one foot will I flee so long as breath bides within my breast, for he who shall see both sea and land this day shall end the battles or my life. I will die King of England.—Richard III.

Father in Heaven, though this body is breaking away from me, and I am departing this life, yet I know that I shall forever be with Thee, for no one can pluck me out of Thy hand.—Martin Luther.

I shall die regretting; I have always desired the happiness of France, I did all in my power to contribute to it. I can say with truth that the first wife of Napoleon never caused a tear to flow.—Josephine.

Lockhart, I may have but a moment to spend with you. My dear, be a good man, be virtuous, be religious, be a good man; nothing else will give you

any comfort when you come to lie here.
—Walter Scott.

Thy creatures, O Lord! have been my books, but Thy Holy Scriptures much more. I have sought Thee in the courts, fields and gardens, but I found Thee, O God! in Thy sanctuary—Thy temple.
—Lord Bacon.

I have meditated upon the state of the Church, the spouse of Christ. I have fought against spiritual wickedness in high places, and I have prevailed; I have tasted of the heavenly joy, where presently I shall be! Now, for the last time, I commit soul, body and spirit into His hands. Now it has come.—John Knox.

HOW SWEET 'TIS TRUE.

That the hand, instrument of the will,
Emblem of strength and duty, can grasp
The hand of friend, firmest evidence
Of being living, feel the thrill
Of friendship warm and love intense,
Say sad farewell or glad greeting,
To those you love and who love you—
　　How sweet 'tis true!

That the eye, window of the soul,
Mirror of the mind, can catch
The image of those loved, essence
Of the thing, or self seen, the whole
Of its beauty, grace and presence;
And photograph the limpid sky,
The wonder world for you and I,
And all who love and who love you—
　　How sweet 'tis true.

That the lips, lovely lutes of love,
Framed like Cupid's bow, can voice
The thoughts of mind, the positive part
Of intelligence given from above;
Of desires that echo from the heart,
And softly touch softer lips to press
Love's fondest kiss in fond caress
On lips you love that, too, love you—
　　How sweet 'tis true!
　　　　—G. Edmund Hatcher.

WOMAN.

Empress of creation, Woman! Unto
　thee my harp is strung.
Lay thy tender lips upon it; else in vain
　this song is sung.

Woman must interpret woman; for this
　truth the poet knows:
He, who gives the rose his pencil, needs
　to dip it in the rose!

How shall I begin to praise thee?
　Teach my silent muse to sing,
For thy virtues disconcert me, like the
　riches of the spring.
Who can mirror back thy beauty? Let
　him catch the morning's ray,
And across the snowy canvas limn the
　glory of the day.

Back into the grim old garden, ere the
　cares of earth began,
And the lower creatures mated mocked
　the loneliness of man;
Lo, the mystic light of heaven wraps
　the sleeping in its gleam,
And the world's imperial woman wakes
　the blossom of his dream!

Unto man in every sorrow she has been
　his solace sweet;
Lighting up the soul within him; piloting his weary feet;
Flooding all his path with perfume,
　sweeter than the clover lea;
Putting all his cares to slumber, lulled
　by love's sweet minstrelsy.

Woman! to thy tender keeping God
　has given this command:
Rear the childhood of the nation; nurse
　the young hope of the land;
Teach the principles of virtue; lift the
　manly brow of youth,
Till it scorns each baser laurel for the
　triumph of the truth!

Never leave thy little kingdom; never
　sacrifice the crown,
Though your realm is but a cottage,
　keep it ever, 'tis thine own.
Let no trespasser invade it; from its
　door let hate be hurled,
From the teachings of the fireside rule
　the forums of the world.

'Tis thy mission to be gentle; meek in
　spirit, undefiled,
For the nation's growth is rooted in the
　nurture of the child.

Woman,
Unto man in every sorrow she has been
His solace sweet.

—*Page* 190

She who rears a goodly offspring gathered at her pious knee,
Reigns the queen of the republic; guards the courts of liberty.
—L. L. KNIGHT.

PROCRASTINATION.

I SAID, "To-morrow!" one bleak winter day,
"To-morrow I will live my life anew."
And still "To-morrow" while the winter grew
To spring, and yet I dallied by the way,
And sweet dear Sins still held me in their sway.
"To-morrow!" I said, while summer days wore through;
"To-morrow!" while chill autumn round me drew;
And so my soul remained the sweet Sins' prey.

So pass the years, and still, perpetually,
I cry, "To-morrow, I flee each wile;
To-morrow, surely, shall my soul stand free,
Safe from the siren voices that beguile!"
But death waits for me with a mocking smile.
And whispers, "Yea! To-morrow, verily!"
—PHILIP BOURKE MARSTON.

THE BATTLE-SCARRED BOY.

WE put him to bed in his little nightgown,
The most battered youngster there was in the town;
Yet he said, as he opened his only well eye,
"Rah, rah, for the jolly old Fourth of July!"

Two thumbs and eight fingers with lint were tied up,
On his head was a bump like an upside-down cup,
And his smile was distorted and his his nose all awry,
From celebrating the glorious Fourth of July.

We were glad; he had started abroad with the sun,
And all day had lived in the powder and fun,
While the boom of the cannon roared up to the sky
To salute Young America's Fourth of July!

I said we were glad all the pieces were there,
As we plastered and bound them with tenderest care,
But out of the wreck, came the words, with a sigh:
"If To-morrow was only the Fourth of July!"

He will grow all together again, never fear,
And be ready to celebrate freedom next year.
Meanwhile all his friends are most thankful there lies
A crackerless twelvemonth 'twixt Fourth of Julys.

We kissed him good-night on his powder specked face,
We laid his bruised hands softly down in their place,
And he murmured, as sleep closed his one open eye:
"I wish every day was the Fourth of July!"
—GOOD ROADS.

AT THE BABY'S BEDTIME.

THIS is baby's bedtime;
My little one comes to me,
In her snowy little night-gown,
And kneels down at my knee;
And I fancy a sweet child angel
Is for a time my guest,
As she says her little prayer over,
With her hands upon her breast.

"Now I lay me," she whispers
In low voice, "down to sleep;
I pray the Lord"—and the blue eyes
Half close—"my soul to keep;
If I should die"—Oh! the shiver
At my heart—"before I wake,

I pray the Lord "—and the eyelids
    Droop low—" my soul to take."

Then I lift up the little one, clasping
    Her close to my loving heart,
And give her warm, good-night kisses
    Till the closed lids break apart,
As the leaves do a folding flower;
    And the violets of her eyes
Look up in their drowsy fashion,
    And smile at me angel-wise.

"Dood-night" she whispers me softly,
    And sleepy, with a kiss,
That lingers with me in slumber,
    And stirs my heart with bliss,
As I think of the little one dreaming
    With her head against my breast,
Till my sleep is full of rapture
    As her dreaming is of rest.
            —EBEN E. REXFORD.

MY MUSICAL MAID.

"She made a swan-like end, fading in music."

IN the hush of the stars she was singing,
    With a voice that was drifting above;
And my heart with the chorus was ringing,
    Sweet attuned to the lay of her love.
And I stole to the lattice with lightness
    Of a zephyr 'mid leaves of the glade;
And, beneath me—an angel in whiteness!—
    Beamed the face of my Musical Maid.

Ah! she sang of a ship, and a lover—
    Of a beautiful, vanishing face—
Ne'er returning the dark billows over,
    To a sweetheart's delicious embrace.
And the music was touched with such meter,
    That a tear from my eye would exhale;
For the notes quivered sweeter and sweeter
    From the throat of my sad nightingale.

And she trilled, and she crooned, and she warbled,
    Like a lark that, imprisoned, will long
For an ether, untrod and unmarbled,
    Where her mate flies to God with a song.

And she chirped, and she piped, and she fluttered
    All her dimples and laces to love;
Till my hand on my bosom, I uttered:
    "Hither fly to thy home, little dove!"
Oh, she heard, and she smiled and awakened
    All her dark, dreamful tresses for me;
And I called her my own, unforsaken,
    Little darling of sweet minstrelsy.
Lo! she saw, and her eyes were uplifted
    With a gray, solemn splendor to mine,
As her soul-light in silver was sifted
    Thro' their long, dreamy lashes divine.

Still she sang, and she hummed, and she whistled,
    Till the voice of the lyre was mute;
For the rhythm, thro' her spirit that mistled,
    More sweet than the dream of the flute.
Still a-blushing, cadencing and chanting,
    Till her lips of red rose were aglow
From the warmth of a soul that was panting
    For a chord which the seraphim know.

Ah, that voice! not the coo of the lisper
    Half so soft as its purl and its stream;
It was sweet as the drift of a whisper
    Down the vale of violet dream.
It was blithesome, elastic, capricious—
    In its depths was the home of a prayer!—
It was rich, it was fragrant, delicious
    As the beamy blue braid in her hair.

It was mellow, melodious, magnetic,
    Like the song of the swan when it dies;
It was pretty, poetic, pathetic,
    Like the light and the love in her eyes.
And I called her my charmful canary—
    Little bird that had stolen a tune
From the lips of a musical fairy,
    In the beautiful mist of the moon.

And I sighed—yea, I smiled and I sorrowed
    At the close of the suave symphony;

And her heart from her bosom I borrowed
To repeat still its sweetness to me;
For, in hush of the star silence, had her Soul touched mine in that sweet serenade;
And I twirled a red kiss thro' the shadow
As a rose for my Musical Maid.
—Joseph Lee May.

SNAP SHOTS.

Civilization begins with soap.

The man who expects to lose rarely wins.

A really good talker is one who never talks too much.

It is the guilty man who cannot afford to be suspected.

Some people marry for life and others just for a honeymoon.

A good way to help people is to refuse to speak unkindly to them.

"Every dog has his day," and then wants somebody else's day.

Don't make your home a half-way house between your office and your club.

No useful man has time to go back and rub out his unfortunate foot prints.

A little learning is dangerous, but downright ignorance is even more disastrous.

It is not what people know, but what they think they know that is so dangerous.

Any man who has opinions of his own is suspected of being hardheaded by somebody.

The jumping-off place is not always precipitous. It is sometimes a graceful and gradual incline.

There are some mortals who are never happy save when they have some hurt feelings to enjoy.

The greatest slaves on earth are the mortals who always follow their own inclination.
—Dallas-Galveston News.

THE MOTHER AT HOME.

The mother is the heart of home. She it is who determines its characteristics and diffuses through it that subtle atmosphere which every sensitive person can feel when introduced into the home circle and from which can quickly be inferred the ruling spirit of the home. There can be no doubt that the most effective training for children is the training of example, and this truth the mother needs constantly to bear in mind. How can the impatient, querulous, fault-finding mother teach patience and kindness and good temper? How can the vain mother, greatly absorbed in keeping up with the pomps and vanities of life, eager for place and show, teach her children the true principle of a happy life? How can the selfish mother teach generosity or kindness, or he discontented mother teach contentment?

OLD-TIME MUSIC.

We love the old-time music, the music of long ago.
The thrilling tones of memory that come all soft and low:
They set the heart a-quivering, and the tears all aflow,
A-listening to the old tunes and the music of the bow.

We love the old fiddle tunes jes' without the classic rig,
The old-time jocund reel, and the hornpipe and the jig—
"Billy in the Low Grounds," and "Old Mollie Har"—
"Jinnie, put the kittle on," and "Stop dat knockin' dar";

"Chickens in de bread-tray," a scrachin' out dough,
"Arkansaw traveller," and "Old Rosin o' the bow!"
And hand in hand we swing, and partners change once more,
And dance the merry dance of youth on the old puncheon floor.

We love the old fiddle tunes, and its music soft and low,
The old-time airs get new music from the bow;
"Ben Bolt," "sweet Alice;" dear old "Annie Laurie," too;
"The Last Rose of Summer," "Highland Mary" 'neath the dew;

The banks and the braes of sweet old
    "Bonnie Doon "—
Oh, the melody and sweetness of the
    old-fashioned tune!

We love the old fiddle tunes, though
    classic's now the fad;
And we hanker arter old airs played
    by the dear old dad,
And we feel the tears a-droppin' when
    the music's soft and low—
For dear old dad's in heaven, and on
    earth silent's his bow.

VIOLIN AND SONG.

[Whitcomb Riley's Favorite Poem.]

HE'D nothing but his violin,
    I'd nothing but my song,
But we were wed when skies were blue
    And summer days were long;
And when we rested by the hedge,
    The robins came and told
How they dared to woe and win
    When early spring was cold.
We sometimes supped on dewberries,
    Or slept among the hay,
But oft the farmers' wives at eve
    Came out to hear us play
The rare old tunes, the dear old tunes,
    We could not starve for long,
While my man had his violin
    And I my sweet old song.

The world has aye gone well with us,
    Old man, since we were one;
Our homeless wandering down the
    lanes,
    It long ago was done.
But those who wait for gold or gear,
    For houses and for kine,
Till youth's sweet spring grows brown
    and sere,
    And love and beauty tine,
Will never know the joy of hearts
    That met without a fear,
When you had but but your violin,
    And I my song, my dear.
                    —THE VOICE.

RUTH.

"INTREAT me not to leave thee,
    Intreat me not," she said,
And on Naomi's bosom,
    Weeping, she bowed her head.

"Whithersoe'er thou goest,
    There I will follow thee;
And wheresoe'er thou lodgest
    There shall my lodging be;

"Henceforth, beloved mother!
    Thy people shall be mine;
All other gods forsaking,
    I'll know no God but thine;

"I'll die where'er thou diest,
    And there will buried be;
Bear witness, Lord! death only
    Shall sever me from thee!"

O golden words! the token
    Of love and faith sublime,
That still, with matchless splendor,
    Illume the scroll of time;

Thereon are writ the records
    Of words and deeds, that prove
The beauty and the glory,
    The might of woman's love;

But of them all the dearest,
    The holiest still you are—
Amid their galaxy's splendors,
    The bright and morning star!

When spake this Moab woman
    She touched with tender breath
The harp that slept in silence
    Till waked by Love and Faith;

That touch divine endowed it
    With their immortal youth—
Breathe on the strings: "Naomi!"
    And they will murmur "Ruth."

A QUESTION.

IF we could go back just a little
    And take up the thread of the years,
And weave it to good with the wisdom
    We've learned by our sins and our
    tears;

If we could go back just a little
    Beyond the first sinking to shame,
Bearing all the dark lessons of passion,
    I wonder would life be the same?

I wonder if we would live over
    The soiling, sweet rapturous hours,

Ruth and Naomi.
"Whithersoe'er thou goest,
There I will follow thee."

When Lust held the glass of the banquet,
And Hell burned in odors of flowers?

I wonder if we would take kisses
From lips that seared scars to the soul—
I wonder if we would lie fettered
By vice in the Demon's control?

I wonder if we would drink nectar
When poison was hid in the taste?
I wonder if we would live over,
The evil, the baseness, the waste?

Would we throw down our purest ambition,
Our faith and our love, and our trust,
Like husks to be trodden and trampled
In the burning and desolate dust?

Would we take the new life and so use it
As to fill it with beauty and truth,
Or again play the spendthrift of Heaven
With the jewels of power and youth.

THEOLOGY AND RELIGION.

THEOLOGY and religion are closely related, but they are not identical. Theology is the science of God's existence, nature, attributes and relations. Religion embraces the duties which devolve upon man by virtue of his relations to God, as his Creator, Father and Friend. Theology is intellectual; religion is spiritual. Theology is thought; religion is feeling; the one is mental; the other emotional. Theology belongs to the head, religion to the heart; theology is concerned with creeds, religion with life. We get our theology very largely from men; our religion from God. Our theology is human; our religion is divine. We may have a narrow theology and a broad religion, as a man's heart may be larger than his head. Theology is science; religion is love. Theology is what we think of God; religion is the very life of God in the soul of man. Theology springs from the relations of the intellect to a certain class of truths; religion grows out of the relation of man to God.

Theology is theoretical; religion is practical. Religion is related to theology just as the emotions are related to the intellect and feeling is connected with thought. Rational love depends on knowledge, and religion, which is love for God, in part depends on our theology, which is our knowledge of God. It is true that religion is intuitional and theology is logical, but it is the office and function of logic to define, enlarge and apply the truths given by the intuitions. This fact is recognized in all philosophy and science. Feeling responds to thought, love springs up under the light of knowledge, and gratitude is awakened by the manifestation of goodness, kindness and benevolence. Theology, as it teaches us the love of God for man, reveals to our intellects His practical benevolence toward us, enkindles our love, and awakens our gratitude to Him, which causes our thanksgiving, worship and obedience—and this is religion. We cannot have feeling without thought, for the mind is a unit. Love without a knowledge of the object loved, and gratitude without a conscious knowledge of favors conferred, are impossible. To give us the knowledge of God in His practical relation to man is the function of theology. It thus presents the conditions of all rational religion. Before we can truly worship God we must know Him. This knowledge is theology, and the worship that springs from it is religion.

The great function of the pulpit is to teach theology, and thus by a natural and philosophical process promote the growth of religion. This shows the practical relation of the two in the life-work and growth of the church. A man's religion will receive color from his theology, as feeling takes on the hue of thought, and as the practical receives the cast of the ideal thoughts become things. Knowledge is power. Ideas become forces, and theology is changed into religion. The richer and sweeter the theology we believe the brighter and purer the religion we live. The Wise Man taught that "as a man

thinketh so is he." We cannot rise above our ideals. Life is very largely what we plan to make it. A successful life is always the embodiment of rational thought. To act wisely we must think correctly and in wisdom plan the life w live. A rational Christian life must be rooted and grounded in a rational Christian theology. We cannot build a living Christian church upon Buddhism, Pantheism or Agnosticism. Christian life and character can only be builded upon faith in Christian doctrine.
—The Universalist.

EASTER.

Without the Easter morning this would be a dark and dreary world. It is true that after the desolateness of winter we have the warmth and verdure of spring. The streams are released from their icy fetters ; the branches that were bare and brown renew their waving foliage ; the robins which left with the first chill of autumn, come back to greet us with their happy song ; the fruit trees once more put out their fragrant blossoms, and the lawn and meadow are carpeted again with living green. Then follow the long bright summer and the golden harvest, and we half forget the bleak winds, and the biting frost that spread over the earth its fatal mantle and laid away all that was bright and lovely to decay and death. And when the winter once more comes creeping in with its blighting touch, we recall the vernal succession and wait with a patient spirit for the promised return of song, and leaf, and flower, and fruit. We hope because our eyes have seen the change in each revolving year. The spring may have been delayed and the icy fingers may have mocked our eagerness, and have been long and late in releasing the frozen earth from their deadly grasp, but all this seeming reluctance has had its end, and the brightness and beauty have not only been all the more welcome, but have come in with swifter feet when called to a new life by the impatient sun.

The eyes, unaccustomed to weeping, see the lesson thus written upon the revolving seasons, and the hearts which have never been wrung with the anguish of bereavement, accept the assurance thus given that new life shall follow the dreariness of decay. But when the sorrow comes with its blinding tears and ties that made the heart's sweetest comfort have been rudely severed, the stars go out one by one behind the gathering clouds, and to the eye of sense there is no hope above the hiding grave. The child has fallen asleep in its mother's arms to a lullaby from the spirit land, and she cannot bring back the lost color to its pallid cheek. She wraps the stiffened form in the daintiest robe, and hides it in a silken casket, and lays it away to its rest. It is winter with her now, the chill is in her heart, and verdure and bloom have all gone out of her life. The flowers may blossom again about her home and the birds sing once more beneath her windows, but will this one bud so dear to her find some spring-time for its return ?

Friends walk together in sweet converse along the path of life, "two souls by love together knit, two hearts that beat as one," until they come to the dividing of the way. One fades from the path into the land of silence, and the other with bitter moans and faltering feet, as if the strength had all gone out of the tottering limbs, goes on alone. The spring in the natural world may come ever so early after the desolate winter, but it does not bring the glad sunshine to the aching heart. When the frozen turf hid beneath its covering so brown and bare no one that was fondly loved and longed for the future seemed bright with the promise of returning verdure. But when the form of one so fondly cherished lies buried in its icy clasp, the assuring voice seems but a mocking echo. The fierce December blasts howl their hoarse dirges above the hiding tomb, and there comes from neither earth nor the brooding heavens any answer to the agonizing cry. The voices of nature make sweet harmony for one whose happy spirit is attuned to the music they sing, but they cannot restore the lost chord when the heart's strings have been rudely jarred or broken.

Into a life burdened at every step with griefs that find so little of help or comfort in the visible world about us there comes with the Easter anthem not only a blessed hope, but a positive assurance that answers every question of the aching heart. The old inquiry that springs so often to the lip, "If a man die shall he live again?" does not wait for a reponse at the portals of the hiding tomb. It has been answered by One who burst the bars of death, bringing life and immortality to light, and leading captive the blighting frost that makes the hopeless winter for those who have been bereaved. The seal of the sepulchre has been broken and the hiding stone forever rolled away. The resurrection is not something to be revealed, but a fact accomplished. There comes to all the children of men this day an invitation within which is bound up a new life for a lost and dying world. "Come see the place where the Lord lay!" has in it the pledge of an open tomb for all that have been laid away to the last slumber any may know.

"He is not here; He is risen," has in it the prophecy and pledge that every eye now closed shall open once more to the light of a new and brighter day. The first fruits are an earnest of the harvest, but here we have the ground of a still surer faith, for He, whose rising we commemorate this day, has promised that He will bring with Him when the call is issued all that have fallen asleep in this blessed hope. The new life is no longer a theory; it has had its beginning and there is to be no after break in the glad procession. The eternal spring-time has come to gladden every grief-stricken mourner, and it has come to stay. It gilds with a perpetual rainbow every mound that hides man's mouldering dust, and throws its brilliant hues over the waves which have closed above those who are buried at sea. All shall hear that potent Voice and come forth to the general assembly of the race. Not one of all who have looked even for one brief moment on the light of an earthly day shall be missing when the roll is called.

There is both a blessed comfort and a solemn warning in the Easter chimes. When the hour shall come the mother will clasp her little one again, not as of old with the wan face and the cold, unanswering lips, but to see the look of love in its beaming eyes, and to feel the warmth of the welcome kiss, and the clasp around her neck of the tiny arms. Those who were sundered on earth by the parting ways will come to the glad reunion that has no separating hour. We look heavenward now for those who have left us on earth, and too often think of them as mystic shadows to whom we may not speak. There will come a day when hand may clasp hand and we may hold our beloved once more in our fond embrace. There is a word of warning, but it does not take from the harmony of the Easter anthem. Some may go out of the world never having had any sympathy with the theme we celebrate to-day. Will there be no shame on the face now turned only toward the dark side of life when it greets that coming day? The story of the hour gives us an assurance of a Divine Helper, so that we may even now begin to rise from the depths of our low estate toward a new and better life. He who broke the bands of death can sever for us the bondage of evil habits, impure desires and unholy affections, and give us the happy freedom of the Easter holiday.

PAST AND PRESENT.

WHAT man forgets that boyhood woe,
   That season of distress,
When life, it seemed, could never know
   A taste but bitterness?
What angry thoughts came surging then,
   What torrents of despair
Beat o'er his shattered spirit, when
   His mother cut his hair!

And trouble never ends; for now
   You notice with a sigh

That baldness slight, that heightening brow,
That comes on as years steal by.
And, mentally, once more you writhe,
And 'gainst your fate declare,
When Father Time take down his scythe
And starts to cut your hair.
—PHILANDER JOHNSON.

THIS LITTLE WIFE OF MINE.

I COULD not write a sonnet to the deep blue of her eye,
Nor praise her rippling golden locks unless I wrote a lie.
Her figure is not Venesque; she's not divinely tall;
She has not got two Cupid lips to hold my heart in thrall;
I don't imagine I'm an oak and she an ivy vine—
Although her tendrils hold my heart—
This little wife of mine.

I wouldn't dare compare her voice to music of the spheres;
There is nothing very shell-like in the make-up of her ears;
She hasn't got a dimple, making mischief, in her chin,
Because her eyes betoken she is "average" in sin;
I don't imagine she's a saint—of halo there's no sign;
She's a just a daughter of the earth—
This little wife of mine.

I did not wed a picture. Let me give the dear her dues:
She's good at getting dinner, and a queen at chasing blues;
There s a sure cure for each heartache in the magic of her touch..
She is common sense incarnate and a needed moral crutch;
How very dear she is to me, you may readily divine,
For I've two reduced editions of
This little wife of mine.
—HARRY HARDIE.

CHILDHOOD'S SONG.

THE fire upon the hearth is low,
And there is stillness everywhere;
Like troubled spirits here and there,
The firelight shadows fluttering go.
And as the shadows round me creep
A childish treble breaks the gloom,
And softly from a farther room
Comes: "Now I lay me down to sleep."

And somehow, with that little prayer,
And that sweet treble in my ears,
My thoughts go back to distant years
And linger with a dear one there;
And, as I hear the child's amen,
My mother's faith comes back to me,
Couched at her side as I seem to be,
And mother holds my hands again.

Oh, for an hour in that dear place!
Oh, for the peace of that dear time!
Oh, for that childish trust sublime!
Oh, for a glimpse of mother's face!
Yet as the shadows round me creep,
I do not seem to be alone—
Sweet magic of that treble tone—
And "Now I lay me down to sleep."
—CHICAGO NEWS.

THE FALLING STAR.

A LITTLE maid by the window-bar
Stood eagerly watching a falling star;
She clapped her hands with a quick delight,
But grew demure as it passed from sight.

One moment still as the star, now dead,
The next she lifted her curly head,
And said with an earnestness none could doubt,
"I fink it's a tandle dat Dod blew out!"
—WILLIAM H. HAYNE.

WITH THE BABY IN HER ARMS.

HOPEFUL, happy, halcyon days
Where those when Elsie, my wife,
Lent a subtle, softening color
To my erstwhile vapid life.
Lovely she was as an houri,
With a wealth of varying charms,
But I always thought her sweetest
With
   the
      baby
         in
           her
             arms.

Why are joys so evanescent,
  Changed so quickly into pain,
As the brightest dawns of April
  Are but harbingers of rain?
Lost to me—aye, lost forever
  Are her many, many charms,
For she's sleeping 'neath the daisies
  With
    the
      baby
        in
          her
            arms.

Yet I picture her in heaven,
  Waiting patiently till I
Quit this vale of disappointment
  For that mansion in the sky,
And methinks I hear her calling:
  "Dearest one, fear no alarms,
I will meet you at the portal
  With
    the
      baby
        in
          my
            arms."
—A. L. BROWN.

ST. PATRICK'S DAY.

ONE day to touch the golden strings
  Of Erin's harp again,
One day when Erin's music sings
  Defiance unto pain.
One day when Irish fingers twine
  The shamrock and the rose,
And red lips smile and bright eyes shine
  And love and laughter glows.

One day to dream the land is free
  From fetter and from chain,
One day to dream that out the sea
  O'Donohue again
Rides from the realm of love and youth,
  With that wild monologue
That sings of justice and of truth
  From lands of Tirn-a-nhoge.

One day to dream that Carolyn
  Walks Irish vales along,
And glads the young birds with the din
  Of Gaelic battle song,

One day to dream the old sod blessed
  From laughing lakes to seas,
One day to soothe the patriot's breast
  With glorious memories.

And, best of all, one day to dream
  Of happy years to come,
When Freedom's blazing torch shall gleam
  And Peace make Erin home.
One day to wake again the song
  Of Tara's harp of gold,
And spread, a happy land along,
  The grace of days of old.

One day for patriot hope and pride,
  One day for living trust
That sometime hatred shall have died
  And power shall be just.
One day to set the shamrock bloom
  In reverence apart,
To share each rich and rare perfume
  Of flowers of the heart.
—HOWARD HAWTHORNE M'GEE.

SUNDAYS LONG AGO.

OF all the memories of the past that flood me with their roseate glow,
There's none that's half so sweet as one—the Sundays of the long ago.
The Sundays in the little town, that unromantic little place,
Without a vestige of romance, without a single touch of grace;

Except the romance of our hearts, the grace that lent its regal glow
To pure young lives and made all sweet—the Sundays of the long ago.
How well I see the old white church, with its square pillared portico
And tottering steeple where'n we met on Sundays of the long ago.

I see the bright-eyed girls and boys, with hair all prim and faces bright,
At Sunday school, and hear the songs we never sung exactly right.
I see the teacher's gentle eyes, and feel my heart again rejoice,
As first love crept into my soul in echo to her tender voice.

And then, the drowsy sermon's tone
rings musical adown the years,
And all the sleepy deacons nod their
heads through gleaming mists of
tears.
And then, the walking home with her—
the long talk standing at the gate,
The dreams of happy days to come, the
prattled prophesies of late.

The long, sweet, fragrant afternoons,
the still, soft nights when mother
sang,
And from the blossomed locust trees
the katydid's shrill treble rang.
And then the good-night prayers and
then the dear, unbroken, childish
sleep ;
he pure, clean, happy dreams that
would into our slumbers creep,

And all the perfect trust and faith that
only children ever know,
All these are mine when I live o'er the
Sundays of the long ago.
—HOWARD HAWTHORN M'GEE.

THE GARDEN OF DREAMS.

WHO could dispense with that garden
fair,
The lotus-flowered garden of dreams ?
Never a life is too homely or bare
To cherish a fragrant spot somewhere,
Budding to open in promises rare
In the magical garden of dreams.

How could we live and not yield to
despair,
Bereft of the garden of dreams ?
The fever of living, the pangs of care,
The hopes deferred, all the sorrows we
bear,
Forgotten, are charmed to sleep in the
air
Of the magical garden of dreams.

The coveted things of life are there,
In the tranquil garden of dreams.
Instead of our one little life of care,
There we live many lives ideal and
fair,
Great aims uplift us, all things we dare
In the magical garden of dreams.
—ELIZABETH BARTON.

THE NEW YEAR.

NEW YEAR'S DAY is a combination of all the holidays. It is all in one. It is a day of thanksgiving and praises for the blessings of the past, and the joyous gateway of the future year. It is the day of all days for striking balances, proving accounts, whether those accounts be religious, social or business ones, and for calculations as to the progress made during the past twelve-month.

Reader, how stand the balances with you to-day ? Have you made satisfactory progress during the past year ? Are you morally, a better man or woman, to-day, than you were a year ago ? In business, how does your balance stand ? Have you prospered or retrograded ? Is the balance sheet for, or against you? Be just to yourself, make the claculation and settle the question for yourself. In social matters, are you better to-day than a year ago ? Have you done your duties in the various spheres of life and made others happier and better by reason of your past year's efforts ? Is your conscience easy, and does it approve your actions during that unit of life ? These are sad and stern questions that do, or should, present themselves to every one. Their answers are with God and the individual, and he alone must be responsible for their verity whether they be true or false.

The holiday season has brought many merry peals of laughter, many songs, of gladness, and in some instances, thoughts that were sweetly sad. To but few indeed was their gladness unmingled with sadness. Many prodigals have returned to their former firesides, and many hearts which were drifting apart, have been once more brought together and their unions were all the sweeter by virtue of mistaken differences. Yet, in but few households have there not been at least one vacant chair. Hence bitter memories cluster, and once more have caused the eyes to be filled with tears at those vacant chairs, empty cradles, broken vows, shattered prospects of gain, and all that has been wrecked in the voyage of life have come again over the threshold from the past, and filled up the hours with their ghastly presence and sad refrain. Even during the gayety of the holiday season, no voice of entreaty, no severity of rebuke will drive these phantoms back to their hiding places. Even the cheering blaze from the yule log around the fireside, will not drive those recollections from the remembrances of its members. Yet, with them come occasions for joy and cheer. Those departed, while they have missed something of earth, have enjoyed more of heaven. Their going in advance may be the means of opening the way to others and eventually the sweet memories of the past may cause better resolves, better lives and eventually a united household in a better land. At any rate, it becomes us all to leave the past with God, and to look well to the future. That, if it ever comes to us, we may improve by the lessons of the past. All have made mistakes, all have "done those things which we ought not to have done, and left undone those things which we ought to have done."—To this charge must the human race plead guilty. Perhaps the old year carries with it some regrets in this direction. What year does not? Yet, does its balance-sheet not show more joys than sorrows? Many good deeds than bad ones? Has it not, after all, been a year of happiness and progress? Then let us bid it adieu with a tear of regret, and with a hope that its successor may be a still more profitable and happy one.

MASTER RALPH'S OPINION OF GRANDMOTHERS.

Grandmothers are very nice folks;
 They beat all the aunts in creation;
They let a chap do as he likes,
 And don't worry about education.

Grandmothers have muffins for tea,
 And pies, a whole row in the cellar;
And they're apt, if they know it in time,
 To make chicken-pies for a feller.

And if he is bad now and then,
 And makes a great racketing noise,

They only look over their specks,
 And say, "Ah, those boys will be boys!"

Quite often, as twilight comes on,
 Grandmothers sing hymns, very low,
To themselves, as they rock by the fire,
 About heaven and when they shall go.

And then a boy, stopping to think,
 Will find a hot tear in his eye,
To know what will come at the last;
 For grandmothers all have to die.

I wish they could stay here and pray,
 For a boy needs their prayers every night;
Some boys more than others, I s'pose;
 Such as I need a wonderful sight.
  —Christian Advocate.

A BEAUTIFUL PICTURE.

The world loves the lover, and is prone to admire and comment on the happiness of a newly married couple. At the celebration of the union of two plighted hearts, scarcely is the service over before friends vie with each other to be the first to grasp their hands and extend congratulations and wish happy voyages through life. They are the hero and heroine of the occasion, and from which time is their happiness noted and watched with almost jealous admiration. A few months, however, passes, and they take their places in life with the great herd of humanity, and their identity is almost forgotten, or overlooked in the crowds that press onward in their footsteps.

It is both pleasant and proper to give young plighted hearts, joined together for the voyage of life, a good and happy send-off. It is a pleasure to their friends, in which the public shares, to see them go cheerfully and happily down the stream of life, a blessing to each other, and a joy to those around them.

Yet, perhaps the prettiest picture in their lives is to see them "Sweethearts" still in old age, sharing each other's burdens and dividing each other's cares. Such may be the cause of occasional unholy jests, or excite the rivalry o. some younger heart; still a more sober reflection brings almost tears of joy to the observer, and a desire of emulation to the younger lover. The example makes its impression upon all, and breathes a holiness about it that betokens of a still happier immortality. It demonstrates that that match was made in heaven, and that their plighted love and affections were so strong and enduring that they were enabled to withstand the wear and test of years; and while, like the wedding-ring upon her wrinkled finger, it is worn by time and use, it is all the brighter for the wearing.

DAD'S OLD GRINDSTONE.

UNDER a spreading russet bough,
  Uncared for an' alone,
Through summer's sun an' winter's snow
  Has stood dad's ol' grindstone.
An' I in fancy see it now
  Almost with weeds o'ergrown.

How well I recollect each morn
  That dad would call to me,
At break of day, to come an' turn
  The stone beneath the tree;
An' every whirl she 'ud squeak and groan,
  An' much exerted me.

My hands would blister, peel an' tear,
  But I made ne'er a face;
'Twas better to be blistered there
  Than on some other place.
So while the lark songs filled the air
  The grindin' went apace.

I steal from town life oft in ruth
  An look the old scenes through,
And though it sounds a bit uncouth
  I find these words come true,
"The work I dreaded so in youth
  I now would gladly do."

I'm turning now the stone of life,
  A-grinding fortune's blade,
With nicks and cracks extremely rife
  An' ruther poorly made,
An' oft the stone squeaks in the strife,
  Like dad's beneath the shade.
      —BOSTON ADVERTISER.

THE LITTLE ARM-CHAIR.

NOBODY sits in the little arm-chair;
  It stands in a corner dim;
But a white-haired mother gazing there,
  And yearningly thinking of him—
Sees through the dusk of the long ago
  The bloom of her boy's sweet face,
As he rocks so merrily to and fro,
  With a laugh that cheers the place.

Sometimes he holds a book in his hand,
  Sometimes a pencil and slate,
And the lesson is hard to understand,
  And the figures hard to mate;
But she sees the nod of his father's head,
  So proud of the little son,
And she hears the word so often said,
  "No fear for our little one."

They were wonderful days, the dear sweet days,
  When a child with sunny hair
Was hers to scold, to kiss, and to praise,
  At her knee in the little chair.
She lost him back in the busy years,
  When the great world caught the man,
And he strode away past hopes and fears
  To his place in the battle's van.

But now and then in a wistful dream,
  Like a picture out of date,
She sees a head with a golden gleam
  Bent over a pencil and slate.
And she lives again in the happy day,
  The day of her young life's spring,
When the small arm-chair stood just in the way,
  The centre of everything.
    —MARGARET E. SANGSTER, *in Harper's Bazar*.

A CHANSONNETTE.

I SAW two silv'ry clouds, love,
  Come sailing one by one,
As spirits soft that moved aloft
  On toward the setting sun.
Methought in fancy's dream, love,
  That they were you and I
Thus gliding on to love-land
  Beyond the blushing sky.

Then floating side by side, love,
  And ling'ring on the way

To greet the star, that from afar
   Stole forth to steal the day,
Still closer e'er they drew, love,
   Until the day was done,
When fading into love-land
   The two were only one.
          —CLIFFORD HOWARD.

THE VIRGIN'S REFRAIN.

My lover leaned over in silence
   And toyed with my kerchief of lace,
While the passion that burned in my bosom
   Flamed up in a blush to my face.
There was no one to hear us but Cupid,
   So artlessly aiming his dart,
To see there was no one but Cupid,
   So he folded me close to his heart.

My hand fluttered up to his shoulder,
   To his neck and around it and lay
Caressing his dear silken tresses,
   But never a word did we say.
And still in that eloquent silence—
   I tremble with passion divine—
As light as the thistle-down falling
   The lips of my dear one touched mine.

He touched them and pressed them, and clinging
   Close, close in a rapturous kiss,
He drew, as a bee draweth honey,
   My soul till it fainted with bliss,
And it passed in his keeping forever,
   To have and to hold as his own,
Till the earth is a handful of ashes,
   By the winds of eternity blown.
          —CHICAGO TIMES.

ONE BY ONE.

One by one the shadows cast themselves across the road,
One by one the sorrows, of this life, increase the load
Of the weary, dreary burden clinging closer, day by day,
As the flickering light of childhood softly fades away.

One by one the pleasures, once so fraught with light,
Droop and die in sadness at the fast approach of night;
One by one the sweetest notes of youth's melodious chime,
Becomes a tender echo in the memory of that time.

One by one the threads of Hope will guide my faltering feet,
Toward the silent river with its flowers blooming sweet;
One by one the scourgings of the father's chastening rod,
Marks out plain the pathway that will lead me up to God.

One by one new pleasures break forth where I can see,
One by one sweet messages come floating down to me;
One by one the hours take me closer to the shore,
Where one by one dear loved ones await me at the door.
          —EDWARD N. WOOD.

WOMAN.

She's warm, she's cold, she's pleasing, vexing,
An open book and a thing perplexing;
She will give you joy, she will cause you sorrow
With a smile to-day and a frown to-morrow;
She'll bring despair, then hope restore you,
She'll be your slave and she'll lord it o'er you.
Responsive, shy, forgiving, spiteful,
An inconsistency delightful;
Repelling, now, anon caressing,
Man's greatest plague, his chiefest blessing,
And though beneath himself he's classed her,
And calls himself her lord and master,
She casts him off and closer binds him,
And 'round her little finger winds him.
          —NEW YORK PRESS.

LOVE HAS ITS WAY.

"I'll never wed for love alone,"
   A haughty maiden said,
"The man who claims me for his own
   In paths of fame must tread.

He must have ships upon the main,
   And be of proud degree,
Or I shall treat with high disdain
   His words of love for me."
Ah, haughty maiden, have a care
Lest wealth and fame prove but a
   snare.

A lover came this maid to woo,
   A youth quite fair to see ;
His love was strong, his heart was true,
   But yet no gold had he.
Unknown to fortune or to fame,
   In humble paths he trod ;
His only wealth an honest name,
   The noblest gift of God.
Ah, haughty maid, bethink thee well
The power of love no tongue can tell.

The maiden listened, first with scorn,
   To his soft tales of love,
But soon more beauteous seemed the
   morn,
   More bright the stars above,
For love had lit the tiny flame
   That slumbered in her breast.
What cared she now for wealth or fame,
   Since love her soul possessed ?
The haughty maid had learned to know,
'Tis love that makes the flowers grow

Though great its might, the power of
   gold
True love can never buy,
And yearning hearts are not consoled
   By fame or lineage high.
'Tis love alone that rules the heart,
   And so 'twill be alway ;
When Cupid sends his shining dart,
   Love always wins the day.
And happiness is always found
Where love and tenderness abound.
   —PICAYUNE.

A BENEDICTION.

How can I cease to pray for thee ?
   Somewhere
In God's great universe thou art to-
   day,
Can He not reach thee with His tender
   care ?
Can He not hear me when for thee I
   pray ?
What matters it to Him who holds within
The hollow of His hand all worlds, all
   space,
That thou art done with earthly pain
   and sin ?
Somewhere within His ken thou hast
   a place,
Somewhere thou livest and hast need
   of Him ;
Somewhere thy soul sees higher
   heights to climb ;
And somewhere still there may be
   valleys dim
That thou must pass to reach the
   hills sublime.
Then all the more because thou canst
   not hear
Poor human words of blessing, will I
   pray.
Oh, true, brave heart ! God bless thee,
   wheresoe'er
In His great universe thou art to-day !
   —JULIA C. R. DORR.

BEING IN DEBT.

AMONG the many good things which Horace Greeley wrote is the following vivid article on the misery of being in debt.

To be hungry, ragged and penniless is not pleasant, but this is nothing to the horror of bankruptcy. All the wealth of the Rothschilds would be a poor recompense for a five years' struggle with the consciousness that you had taken the money or property of trusting friends—promising to return or pay for it when required, and had betrayed their confidence through insolvency.

I dwell on this point, for I would deter others from entering that place of torment. Half of the young men in the country, with many old enough to know better, would " go into business " —that is, into debt—to-morrow, if they could. Most poor men are so ignorant as to envy the merchant or manufacturer whose life is an incessant struggle with pecuniary difficulties, who is driven to constant borrowing, and who, from month to month, barely evades that insolvency which sooner or later overtakes many men in business ; so that it has been computed that but one in twenty of them achieves a pecuniary success.

For my part,—and I speak from sad experience,—I would rather be a convict, a slave, than to pass through life under the harrow of debt. Let no young man misjudge himself unfortunate or truly poor, so long as he has the full use of his limbs and faculties, and is substantially free from debt. Hunger, cold, rags, hard work, contempt, suspicion, unjust reproach, are disagreeable, but debt is infinitely worse than them all. And, if it had pleased God to spare any or all of my sons to be the support and solace of my declining years, the lesson which I should have most earnestly sought to impress upon them is: "Never run in debt! Avoid pecuniary obligations as you would pestilence or famine. If you have but sixpence, and can get no more for a week, buy some corn, parch it, and live on it, rather than owe any man money!"

Of course, I know that some men must do business that involves risks, and must give notes and other obligations; and I do not consider him really in debt who can lay his hands directly on the means of paying, at some little sacrifice, all he owes; I speak of real debt—that which involves risk or sacrifice on the one side, obligation and dependence on the other—and I say, from all such let every youth humbly pray God to preserve him evermore!

THE SWEETEST PART OF LIFE.

You may talk about a feller
   When he's in his courtin' days,
And I know he's mighty meller
   And has awful calfish ways,
But that feller then's a-livin'
   'Way ahead of you or I—
Not a sixpence is he givin'
   What's a comin' by and by.

And the future has no shadder
   For a feller in his state:
He's a-climbin' Cupid's ladder,
   Not for fame, but for a mate;
And he has no thought of stoppin'
   Till the proper one he's found,
And the question he's a-poppin'
   As he goes from 'round to 'round.

He's not doin' much at savin'
   Of the little that he makes—
There are other things he's cravin'
   More than large and bulky stakes;
Plenty of love within a cottage
   Will do them to begin—
Not knowin', on sich pottage,
   He will grow uncommon thin.

But let's not disturb his dreamin',
   It's the sweetest part of life,
When you're hustlin' and a-schemin'
   For to try and get a wife—
And you're mighty shore to find her
   If you'll keep on lookin' 'round,
For there's plenty of them kinder
   Jest a-waitin' to be found.

And my advice to ev'ry feller
   Of the single harness kind
Is to find one and to tell her
   What's a weighin' on his mind,
And my all's agin a shillin'
   That he'll always bless the day
When she told him she was willin'
   To be his'n right away.
         —SAM BEAN.

WE'VE ALL BEEN THERE BEFORE.

When troubles come to torture you
   In this dark world of woe,
And disappointments grimly rise
   Whichever way you go,
Don't be cast down or faint of heart,
   Or chafe at trials sore—
You're not the first to suffer, for
   We've all been there before.

When to some fair young maid you make
   The offer of your hand,
And tell her that unbounded love
   Is more than house or land,
Don't think that earth has grown so dark
   'Twill never brighten more—
Remember when she laughs at you
   We've all been there before,

If at the races you "put up"
   The last ten that you possess,
And find you have to foot it home
   Without a cent to bless

Don't curse your luck as something
    strange,
  Or seek the jockey's gore—
You're no worse off than other men
  Who've all been there before.

If in some cosy little flat
  A fair girl lives alone,
Who, thro' some subtle reasoning,
  You think is all your own,
Don't take it hard if some cold day
  You find your dream is o'er ;
It's hard, but " there are others," and
  We've all been there before.

In fact when luck has "cut you dead,"
  When fate is hard and stern,
And for the unattainable
  You yearn and yearn,
Be sure you have our sympathy—
  Just that and nothing more—
For we've been there before, dear boy,
  We've all been there before.

A BLAMED SIGHT WORSE.

A BACHELOR, old and cranky,
  Was sitting alone in his room,
His toes with gout were aching,
  And his face was o'erspread with
    gloom.

No little ones' shouts disturbed him,
  From noises the house was free—
In fact, from the attic to cellar
  Was quiet as quiet could be.

No medical aid was lacking,
  The servants answered his ring,
Respectfully heard his orders,
  And supplied him with everything,

But still there was something wanting—
  Something he couldn't command—
The kindly words of compassion,
  The touch of a gentle hand.

And he said, as his brow grew darker,
  And he rang for the hireling nurse,
" Well, marriage may be a failure,
  But this is a blamed sight worse ! "
    —BOSTON COURIER.

HE HAS NOT LIVED IN VAIN.

He has not lived in vain, who leaves
  A single soul the lighter ;
Whose walk through life hath made
    this world
  To any one the brighter.

He has not lived in vain, if one
  Shall sorrow at his going,
Or hope shall brighten from the spark
  He kindled into glowing.

He has not lived in vain, if, when
  Death's hand his heart shall chill,
The beggar feels there is a void
  No other man can fill.

He has not lived in vain, if on
  The midnight air shall fall
The wailing howl of the faithful dog
  That has missed his master's call.

He has not lived in vain, if there
  Shall be a man to mourn him,
When they return, who to the grave,
  In duty's name have borne him.

He has not lived in vain, if we,
  Who piled the earth above him,
Admit he had a single trait
  That made his fellows love him.
    —S. A. JONAS.

HANG UP THE BABY'S STOCKING.

HANG up the baby's stocking,
  Be sure you don't forget.
For the dear little dimpled darling
  Has never seen Christmas yet.
But I've told her all about it,
  And she opened her big, blue eyes,
And I'm sure she understands it—
  She looked so funny and wise.

"Dear, dear, what a tiny stocking !
  It doesn't take much to hold
Such little pink toes as baby's
  Away from the frosts and cold,
But now for the baby's Christmas,
  It never will do at all,
For Santa wouldn't be looking
  For anything half so small.

"I know what we'll do for the baby,
 I've thought of the very best plan:
We ll borrow a stocking of grandma,
 The longest and best that we can;
And you'll hang it by mine, dear mother,
 Right here in the corner—so;
And you'll write a letter to Santa,
 And fasten it on to the toe.

"Write: 'This is the baby's stocking
 That hangs in the corner here;
You never saw her, Santa,
 For she only came this year,
But she is the blessedest baby!—
 And now before you go,
Just cram her stocking with goodies,
 From the top clear down to the toe.'"
                    EMEL JAY

NOT FOUGHT FOR.

MY dear boy, men have fought, bled, and died, but not for beer. Arnold Winkelried did not throw himself upon the Austrian spears because he was ordered to close his saloon at nine o'clock. William Tell did not hide his arrow under his vest to kill the tyrant because the edict had gone forth that the free-born Switzer should not drink a keg of beer every Sunday. Freedom did not shriek as Kosciusko fell over a whiskey barrel. Warren did not die that beer might flow as the brooks murmur, seven days a week. Even the battle of Brandywine was not fought that whiskey might be free. No clause in the Declaration of Independence declares that a Sunday concert garden, with five brass horns, and one hundred kegs of beer, is the inalienable right of a free people and the cornerstone of good government.

Tea—mild, harmless, innocent tea; the much-sneered-at temperance beverage, the feeble drink of effeminate men and good old women—tea holds a higher place, it fills a brighter, more glorious page, and is a grander figure in the history of this United States than beer. Men liked tea, my boy, but they hurled it into the sea in the name of liberty, and they died rather than drink it until they made it free. It seems to be worth fighting for, and the best men in the world fought for it. The history of the United States is incomplete with tea left out. As well might the historians omit Fanueil Hall and Bunker Hill, as tea. But there is no story of heroism or patriotism with rum for its hero.

The battles of this world, my son, have been fought for grander things than free whiskey. The heroes who fall in the struggle for rum, fall shot in the neck, and their martyrdom is clouded by the haunting phantoms of the jim-jams. Whiskey makes men fight, it is true but they usually fight other drunken men. The champion of beer does not stand in the temple of fame; he stands in the police court. Honor never has the delirium tremens; glory does not wear a red nose; and fame blows a horn but never takes one.
                —R. T. BURDETTE.

OUR LITTLE BOY 'AT'S GONE.

A SIGHT of help he was—our boy 'at went,
 Pudgin' aroun' with knee trousers on!
But what was more than all his workin' meant,
 He seemed to be our sunshine, now he's gone.
He'd go to take the cows to pasture, morns,
 An' seems I hear his tiny whistle now,
As I go out an' walk about the barns,
 Or take the team afield and try to plow.

About the house he kept a sight of noise,
 Singin' or trampin' at his boyish will,
It did not seem with health jest like my boys,
 His voice could hush so quick an' be so still.
But he weren't sick much more'n a week, I b'lieve,
 An' kept his little senses durin' all;
An' didn't grumble because he had to leave,
 But lay there still list'ning for a call.

That evening that I never will forget,
  He lay beside the window an' looked out.
I sorter hoped 'at God would spare him yet,
  An' give us back his noisy step an' shout,
But sudden-like he gazed intent ahead,
  While crooned the katydid jest out the door
An',—" Angels, mammy. See 'em pap!" he said,
  An' then was still and never said no more.

Now, sometimes standin' by the meader bars
  Waitin' the cows, all lonesome an' forlorn,
The heavens twinklin' with the cur'ous stars,
  The breezes whisperin' 'mongst the rustlin' corn,
I wish the rustle was of angels' wings
  The stars the guidin' lamps of seraphs, come
To waft us after all our sorrowings
  Where we'n our boy'll be again at home.
—MEMPHIS COMMERCIAL-APPEAL.

SHE WOULD BE A MASON.

THE funniest thing I ever heard,
The funniest thing that ever occurred,
Is the story of Mrs. Mehitable Byrde,
  Who wanted to be a Mason.

Her husband, Tom Byrde, a Mason true—
As good as any of you;
He is Tyler of Lodge Cerulean Blue,
And tyles and delivers the summons due,
And she wanted to be a Mason too,
  This ridiculous Mrs. Byrde.

She followed him around, this inquisitive wife,
And nagged him and teased him half out of his life;
So to terminate this unhappy strife
  He consented at last to admit her.

And first, to disguise her from bonnet and shoon,
This ridiculous woman agreed to put on
His breech—ah! forgive me—I meant pantaloons;
And miraculously did they fit her.

The lodge was at work on the Master's degree,
The light was ablaze on the letter G;
High soared the pillars J. and B.
The officers sat like Solomon, wise;
The brimstone burned amid horrid cries;
The goat roamed wildly through the room;
The candidate begged them to let him go home;
And the devil himself stood up in the east,
As broad as an alderman at a feast,
When in came Mrs. Byrde.

Oh, horrible sounds! oh, horrible sight!
Can it be that Masons take delight
In spending thus the hours of night?
Ah! could their wives and daughters know
The unutterable things they say and do,
Their feminine hearts would burst with woe!
But this is not all my story.

Those Masons joined in a hideous ring,
The candidate howling like everything,
And thus in tones of death they sing
  (The candidate's name was Morey):

" Blood to drink and bones to crack,
Skulls to smash and lives to take,
Hearts to crush and souls to burn,
Give old Morey another turn,
  And make him grim and gory."

Trembling with horror stood Mrs Byrde,
Unable to speak a single word.
She staggered and fell in the nearest chair
On the left of the Junior Warden there,
And scarcely noticed, so loud the groans,
That the chair was made of human bones.

Of human bones! On grinning skulls
That ghastly throne of horror rolls,
Those skulls, the skulls that Morgan
    bore ;
Those bones, the bones that Morgan
    wore ;
His scalp across the top was flung,
His teeth around the arms were strung,
Never in all romance was known
Such usage made of human bone.

There came a pause—a pair of paws
Reached through the floor, upsliding
    doors,
And grabbed the unhappy candidate!
How can I, without tears relate,
The lost and ruined Morey's fate?
She saw him sink in a fiery hole,
She heard him scream : "My soul! My
    soul!"
While roars of fiendish laughter roll,
And drown the yells for mercy.

The ridiculous woman could stand no
    more,
She fainted and fell on the checkered
    floor,
'Midst all the diabolical roar.
What then, you ask me, did befall
Mehitable Byrde? Why, nothing at all.
She dreamed she'd been in a Mason's
    hall.
    —TIDINGS FROM THE CRAFT.

BE GOOD TO YOURSELF.

THIS is a common admonition, and it is full of important meaning. A man should take as good care of himself as he does of his horse ; but how few do this! If you do not take care of yourself, no one can take care of you. Take care of your body. Consider its needs. "Make up your mind firmly not to abuse it. Eat nothing that will hurt it ; wear nothing which distorts or pains it. Do not overload it with victuals, or drink, or work. Give yourself regular and abundant sleep. Keep your body warmly clad. At the first signals of danger from any of the thousand enemies which surround you, defend yourself. Do not take cold ; guard yourself. against it ; if you feel the first symptoms, give yourself heroic treatment ; get into a fine glow of heat by exercise. This is the only body you will ever have in this world. A large share of pleasure and pain of life will come through the use you make of it. Study deeply and diligently the structure of it, the laws which govern it, the pains and penalties which will surely follow the violation of every law of life and health."

Glorify God in your body, and let your body be a temple of the Holy Ghost, that God may dwell in you and walk in you.

I'M GROWING OLD.

MY days pass pleasantly away ;
    My nights are blessed with sweetest
        sleep ;
I feel no symptoms of decay,
    I have no cause to mourn or weep ;
My foes are impotent and shy,
    My friends are neither false nor cold ;
And yet, of late, I often sigh—
    I'm growing old !

My growing talk of olden times,
    My growing thirst for early news,
My growing apathy of rhymes,
    My growing love for easy shoes,
My growing hate of crowds and noise,
    My growing fear of taking cold,
All whisper in the plainest voice,—
    I'm growing old !

I'm growing fonder of my staff ;
I'm growing dimmer in the eyes ;
I'm growing fainter in my laugh ;
I'm growing deeper in my sighs ;
I'm growing careless in my dress ;
I'm growing frugal of my gold,
I'm growing wise ; I'm growing—yes—
    I'm growing old !

I see it in the changing taste ;
    I see it in my changing hair ;
I see it in my growing waist ;
    I see it in my growing heir ;
A thousand signs proclaim the truth,
    As plain as truth was ever told,
That even in my vaunted youth
    I'm growing old !
        JOHN G. SAXE.

YESTERDAY.

THAT which has passed is yesterday. Into the shades of an inexorable past have slipped the joys and sorrows, the tears and smiles, the days of abundant prosperity, as well as the days in which we warred with misery and tugged with distress and adversity—all have gone. They are dead and buried with the past, but to them memory erects a monument, indestructible and lasting, which fadeth not away. Dear remembrance! No, it is not always dear remembrance. Upon memory's page there oftentimes appears unpleasing blots—unsightly stains which cannot be forgotten, but which mock and jeer and scoff until we, too, belong to the things of yesterday. When you take a retrospective view, does there not loom up before you in living letters of fire your past actions? and does not your bad deeds obscure the good with a dazzling, overpowering light? In memory's scales do you balance with the good or the bad you have done? You must make answer, and, to yourself and to your God, you are accountable. Has the world been better or worse for your having lived in it? That's the question.

How sweet at times are the pleasures of memory! But, are not the pricks and wounds of conscience, too, harrowing, as an unwelcome thought obtrudes itself upon you? Yes, you say it is so. "A wound is made that healing leaves a scar." There are many things you well remember; there are some you cannot but would fain forget.

Time, with its golden opportunities, has come and gone and with it went away our broken resolutions, our unfulfilled promises, our opportunities unimproved. Memory brings before us the scenes of the past, and there rushes upon us the thoughts of other days. Upon the kindly wings of remembrance we go back to the scenes of innocence and childhood, when a fond loving mother sang us to sleep with the sweetest, tenderest lullaby we have ever heard. Nowhere in the world again will you ever hear such sweet and heavenly music as that your mother used to sing when bending over you, her infant child, she rocked you to sleep. Have you forgotten it? No, God be thanked, you remember it as if it were indeed yesterday and they—the songs your mother used to sing, will be the songs of your life. You have listened now, in the latter part of your life, to earth's sweetest music, but how did it compare to mother's song? You say there is no comparison. The songs which came from the loving heart of your mother was music of heaven—love's music. Love is an attribute of God Himself, which is reflected in the heart of the best friend you ever had—your mother.

You grew to be a boy—romping, mischievous, playful. Will you ever forget the first time you put on the little knee pants? How proud you were! Then came tops and marbles and other youthful games, and how you did love to play! You liked to play ball, too, and would run about in boyish glee with your other companions. You greatly liked the little boy just across the street from where you lived. He was a brave little fellow, and had the prettiest little dog in the world, you thought. You thought your companion was brave, for he would slip off from his mother and go in bathing in the little creek not far away with the other boys. You were asked to go with them, too, but you refused because you were afraid mother would not like for you to go. At last you reluctantly consented when the boys proposed to go to the creek again. You could not resist the cruel thrusts which the boys gave you about being tied to your mother's apron strings. Don't you remember when you returned home and mother asked you where you had gone to and you said over to Johnnie's to play ball. My son, why is your head wet? You told her, and it was the first story you had ever told, that you had been running and washed your head and face over to Johnnie's to cool off. Aye, my boy, that was the hardest thing you ever tried to do—tell your mother the first lie. Mother seemed to be satisfied and you went from her presence to a quiet place by yourself to think over what you had done. It almost made you cry, but soon the boys came over to see you and you forgot it all.

One day your mother sent for you and said you must go to school and make a man. You thought that was fine, and with your books all strapped and ready you started for the little village school just over the way. It was a little cabin situated on a small hill surrounded by a grove. You entered the door, and the tall schoolmaster with his spectacles and ferule greeted you. Somehow or other you did not like his looks and was at first a little afraid of him, but that soon wore off when you had taken your seat. You were displeased at the strange girls and boys because they stared at you so hard, but at recess you soon became acquainted with each other and became friends. The school days came and passed. You played your boyish pranks and were a leader in mischief. You learned your lessons though and were considered a bright boy, which made you feel proud. Years passed and the time came for you to leave the village school and go to college—go off to school. How glad you were! You took your departure after bidding the friends of your boyhood good-bye. Like a bright and interesting page in the past history of your life stands forth the four years which you spent at college. You graduated with distinction and took a degree—yes, "that proud entrance upon our American life which begins with the baccalaureate degree." You remember it all now. You went home—to that home you loved so well, to receive the glad embrace of father and mother. Your sweet sister and manly brothers, too, greeted you so gently and so kindly. You were glad to reach home. To-day as you think of it what pleasant thoughts rush upon you! Then—why are you so sad? Yes, that home has gone long years ago—desolated, wasted, and those who made it happy forever departed.

Yes, you went home after graduating from college. They tried to make it pleasant for you—mother, father, sister and brothers, all had a regard for your pleasure and comfort, but you were not satisfied. You wanted to make your own way in the world. They consented to let you go to the city. Don't you remember when standing upon the little porch of your home you bade your dear mother and father, your brother and sister, farewell? It was a tender and tearful farewell, but you felt that you must go and you did go. Yes, and you cannot forget it. It is imperishable in your memory. It comes to you now after ceaseless rocking of the waves of many years. That old home has been a guide to point you to God and to heaven.

Yes, you left the old home and stepped out into the cold, unsympathetic world. You went to the city full of bustling activity. You entered upon an active life—the practice of your cherished profession—law. You set out to make your fortune. Have you made it? Have you accomplished all that you set out to accomplish? Those air-castles you built in your youth, did you people them? Are you the man to-day that you thought you would be when a boy?

When you left the old home there were others who claimed your thoughts beside the old folks at home. How could you leave behind that pretty girl whose image was quartered in your heart? Of course she was pretty, for you often told her so, and you meant it. Those mischievous black eyes, that shining black hair, indeed she was a fairy as she tripped along, lovely as spring. Don't you remember when sitting by her side you whispered to her the old, old story which sounds sweeter every time it is repeated? Now she is your wife whom you love better than you love your own life. You are the father of a family, and to-day you have fallen into this reverie—this day-dream of yesterday, from which awake.

—KATIE WARD.

WHEN THE DAWSONS MOVED AWAY.

OF all the childish memories that linger with me yet
Amid the busy scenes of life there's one I can't forget ;
It rises oft before me spite of years that intervene,
And recollection wafts me back unto that olden scene ;
I see two frowsy little boys a-standing hand in hand,
With tears a-trickling down their cheeks to vanish in the sand ;
No matter what's in store for me I'll ne'er forget the day,
In the middle of the summer, when the Dawsons moved away.

They lived across the alley, and from early morn till night
We scaled the fence between us, now to play and now to fight :
Sometimes they sent me motherward with garments sadly torn,
And I would send Jim Dawson home of plumage often shorn ;
We averaged ten spats a day ; it made no difference,
The stars would always find us side by side upon the fence,
And there we'd sit and spin our yarns, tremendous yarns were they,
And that is why I blubbered when the Dawsons moved away.

There was little Jennie Dawson with the freckles on her face,
A million more or less, but in my eyes they lent her grace.
We'd wander down the alley to the ancient oaken tree,
And there I'd tell her modestly how dear she was to me ;
Her blushes hid her freckles for a moment, and her hand
Would touch mine in a timid way, and I would understand ;
But the fleeting dream was broken forty years ago to-day,
When to the new and golden West the Dawsons moved away.

I've wondered often where they are and what's become of Jim,
His father used to say he'd make a Congressman of him ;
And there was Tom, the oldest boy, whose hair was fiery red,
"I'll make a minister of Tom," his mother often said ;
And Ben, the little cripple, now his sad white face I see,
He used to at the window sit and watch and wait for me ;
But most of all I think of her, though I am old and gray,
For love is just as strong as when the Dawsons moved away.

The old folks must be sleeping now toward the setting sun,
And on the children's heads to-day old Time his work has done ;
He's frosted mine, he's frosted theirs, with an unsparing hand,
And 'twixt us lie this summer night a thousand leagues of land ;
Old forms and faces fill my mind despite life's ebb and flow,
And I feel again the kisses that she gave me long ago ;
But still a sorrow finds my heart, though I am old and gray,
When I recall the morning when the Dawsons moved away,
—T. C. HARBAUGH.

DOT LONG-HANDLED DIPPER.

DER poet may sing of "Der Oldt Oaken Bookit,"
Und in schveetest langvitch its virtues may tell ;
Und how, vhen a poy, he mit eggsdasy dook it,
Vhen dripping mit coolness it rose vrom der vell.
I don't take some schtock in dot manner of trinking !
It vas too mooch like horses and cattle, I dink,
Dhere vas more satisfactions, in my vay off drinking,
Mit dot long-handled dipper dot hangs py der sink.

"How schveet vrom der green mossy
  brim to receive it—"
Dot vould soundt pooty goot—eef it
  only vas true—
Der vater schbills ofer, you petter pe-
  lieve it!
Und runs down your schleeve; und
  schlops indo your shoe.
Dhen down on your nose comes dot old
  iron handle,
Und makes your eyes vater so gvick
  as a vink.
I dells you dot bookit it don'd hold a
  candle
To dot long-handled dipper dot
  hangs py der sink

How nice it musd been in der rough
  vinter vedder,
Vhen it settles right down to a coldt,
  freezing rain,
To haf dot rope coom oup so light as a
  feddher,
Und findt dot her bookit vas proke
  off der chain,
Dhen down in der vell mit a pole you
  go fishing,
Vhile into your back cooms on old-
  fashioned kink;
I pet you mine life all der time you vas
  vishing
For dot long-handled dipper dot
  hangs py der sink.

Dhen gief oup der bookit und pails to
  der horses;
Off mikerobes und tadpoles schust
  gife dhem dheir fill!
Gife me dot pure vater dot all der time
  courses
Droo dose mains from der standpipe
  dot nefer knows ill;
Und eff der goot dings off dis vorld I
  gets rich in,
Und friends all aroundt me dheir
  glasses schall clink,
I schtill vill remember dot oldt counc-
  try kitchen,
Und dot long-handled dipper dot
  hangs by der sink.

FATHERS AND DAUGHTERS.

No matter how stern he may be to others, a father has a peculiarly tender feeling for his daughter, and even though the spring is hidden the child knows where to find it. This being so, a father has great influence upon a daughter's character, but too often he fails to recognize the fact and to accept the responsibilities which it brings. Surely this is a mistake. I believe there are elements of womanly character which a father can develop even better than a mother can.

Take, for example, that most admirable quality in women, a businesslike accuracy in money matters. The father who gives his daughter while still a little child her tiny allowance, paying it regularly at a stated time, and requiring her to render an account of how the pennies go, is laying the foundation of business honor and accuracy in the child. This course pursued throughout a girl's home life, increasing the allowance as the years go on, until she can be trusted to manage her personal expenses entirely, produces excellent results. Business honor becomes second nature to her, while foolish extravagance is impossible.

A gracious and dignified manner in woman is something which we all admire; it gives to her her finest charm. The man who touches his hat to his little daughter, who steps back and allows her to enter the room first because she is a lady, does much to cultivate this manner; for a girl cannot be in the habit of receiving and acknowledging such attentions without acquiring that grace which we desire for her, and the influence of it does not stop there. The little girl who is treated with such consideration invariably responds with a loving service which must endear her to her father's heart. What another child must be bidden to do, she does spontaneously. Her feet are ready to run, and her hands to work for him, so that courtesy becomes what it should be, not merely a form, but the expression of love itself, and it is the habit of her life.

Perhaps the truest gentleman I ever knew brought up his little daughter by the same standard of manly honor and courage that he did his son. Did he hear her retailing some bit of foolish gossip, "A gentleman never tells tales," would be his grave rebuke. Did she bump her head or pinch her chubby finger, her refuge was his arms, but his word was, "Courage, my soldier!" And sometimes when she had resisted a sharp temptation, or acted with spirit and decision in a sudden crisis, he would say, proudly, "That was done like a gentleman. Allow me to shake hands." Kisses were for every day. She was foolish and naughty, but when he said, "Allow me to shake hands," she felt that she had come up to his own high standard, and had acted as he would have done in similar circumstances, and her small heart swelled with such pride and joy that it was almost like pain. Every one acknowledges that such training is good for sons; why not for daughters also?

When a girl is a child no longer, but has crossed the border-land which leads to young womanhood, then a father's care and influence are, if possible, more valuable still. There would be fewer foolish marriages in this world if fathers possessed their daughters' confidence more completely, and girls had greater faith in their father's good judgment and affection.
—ELEANOR A. HUNTER.

DICTIONARY OF DISCONTENT.

SCIENCE, Dear Lady Betty, has diminished hope, knowledge destroyed our illusions and experience has deprived us of interest. Here, then, is the authorized dictionary of discontent:
What is creation? A failure.
What is life? A bore.
What is man? A fraud.
What is woman? Both a fraud and a bore.
What is beauty? A deception.
What is love? A disease.
What is marriage? A mistake.
What is a wife? A trial.
What is a child? A nuisance.
What is the devil? A fable.
What is good? Hypocrisy.
What is evil? Detection.
What is wisdom? Selfishness.

What is happiness? A delusion.
What is friendship? Humbug.
What is generosity? Imbecility.
What is money? Everything.
And what is everything? Nothing.
Were we, perhaps, not happier when we were monkeys?
—LONDON TRUTH.

A WEAVER.

YES, I'm a weaver and each day,
　The threads of life I spin;
And be the colors what they may,
　I still must weave them in.

With morning light then comes the thought,
　As I my task begin;
The Lord to me new threads has brought,
　And bids me weave them in.

Sometimes He brings me threads of gold,
　To brighten up the day;
Then sombre tints so bleak and cold,
　That turn the gold to gray.

His love, alas, I oft forget,
　As these dark threads I spin,
They give me grief and pain,
　But still He bids me weave them in.

And thus my shuttle swiftly flies,
　With threads both dark and light;
And on I toil till daylight flies,
　And fades away the night.

Oh! when at last my day of toil is o'er,
　And I shall cease to spin;
He'll open wide His father's door,
　And bid me enter in.

Then safe at home in heavenly light,
　How clearly I shall see:
That all the threads, the dark and light,
　Each one had need to be.

THE STAR-SPANGLED BANNER.

THERE is no better time than the present for every person, child or adult, who does not know the words of this grand national hymn to learn them. Here they are:

OH, say, can you see by the dawn's early light,
What so proudly we hailed at the twilight's last gleaming?
Whose broad stripes and bright stars through the perilous fight,
O'er the ramparts we watched, were so gallantly streaming?
And the rockets' red glare, the bombs bursting in air,
Gave proof through the night that our flag was still there;
Oh, say, does that star-spangled banner yet wave
O'er the land of the free and the home of the brave?

On the shore, dimly seen through the mists of the deep,
Where the foe's haughty host in dread silence reposes,
What is that which the breeze, o'er the towering steep,
As it fitfully blows, half conceals, half discloses?
Now it catches the gleam of the morning's first beam;
In full glory reflected, now shines on the stream;
'Tis the star-spangled banner; oh, long may it wave
O'er the land of the free and the home of the brave!

And where is the band who so vauntingly swore,
'Mid the havoc of war and the battle's confusion,
A home and a country they'd leave us no more?
Their blood hath washed out their foul footsteps' pollution;
No refuge could save the hireling and slave
From the terror of flight, or the gloom of the grave;
And the star-spangled banner in triumph doth wave
O'er the land of the free and the home of the brave!

Oh, thus be it ever, when freemen shall stand
Between their loved home and the war's desolation!
Blest with victory and peace, may the heaven-rescued land
Praise the Power that hath made and preserved us a nation!
Then conquer we must, for our cause it is just;
And this be our motto, " In God is our trust;"
And the star-spangled banner in triumph shall wave
O'er the land of the free and the home of the brave!
—FRANCIS SCOTT KEY.

JESUS WEPT.

THERE is no sin in tears; nor is it sinful to mourn and weep. Tears are but the sign of grief and sorrow, and of a sympathetic heart. We weep because of sorrow, and we shed tears when in grief. Jesus wept in sympathy with sorrowing friends, for he was "a man of sorrows and acquainted with grief." Who has not lost a friend, a relative, a brother, a sister, a son, a daughter, a father, a mother? O how real death is! The sharp pang it gives the heart is proof of its sad reality. No wonder Mary and Martha mourned! But would they have shed such bitter tears had they known how soon Lazarus would rise from the dead. Let us, therefore, remember that our dead shall soon rise. Life is but a short while, and if we be "in Christ" we shall soon see those who have gone to be "with Christ." Now they do not need our pity. And, truth to say, we should try and let grief for them die out, but not love. They are better off than we are. Let our aim be to join them in the heavenly home, where we shall "sing such songs in such sweet company" that sorrow will be remembered no more.

WEAVING.

DAILY, hourly, we weave and weave,
And whether we sing, or sit and grieve,
The weaving goes on without delay,
Shaping our robe for the judgment day.

Our smiles and our tears in blended sheen,
All through the woof of the fabric gleam;
And the garment glitters with threads of gold,
Wrought in by a patience manifold.

The kindness that won an erring soul
Strengthens the strands and brightens the whole;
While the deed was deemed not worth a place
In the finished web with joy we trace.

Our very thoughts in the pattern fair,
Now light'ned with love, now dark'ned with care,
The weaver's mystical shuttle throws,
Till into the robe their likeness grows.

The tangled threads, the knots and the ends,
All into the woof the Master blends;
And with a touch of His skilful hand
Brings into its place each straying strand.

* * * * *

A beautiful garment, thou sheen of pure gold,
Reflecting God's glory from seam and from fold!
Environ my soul with thy beauty and light,
That, approved, I may stand in Heaven's clear light.
—Elmira Advertiser.

BROTHERLY KINDNESS.

Oh, kindly judge thy erring friend or foe,
We cannot tell the current's undertow
Which, while he calm and upright seems to stand,
May wash away from him the ebbing sand

Beneath the surface of a quiet life
There may be waging oft a bitter strife
Between the ranks of duty onward led
And those led on by passion's hydra head.

And we look on the while with careless eyes,
As those who watch the calm of starry skies.
Anon the veil is drawn from tragedy unseen
As we behold the drama's closing scene.

We then are quick to shed the friendly tear
Upon the wrecks completed by despair,
With bated breath we speak the words of praise
Which we withheld in dark, despondent days.

We gladly bring the blossoms rare and sweet,
His deadened senses, as we hope to greet,
And fashioned into cross they gently rest,
A mocking tribute on his pulseless breast.

Ah, better far the smile of kindly cheer,
To lift from living heart its care and fear,
And words of sympathy that quickly fly
Like angel messengers from on high.

A little leaf, enhanced by generous trust;
A rosebud, fragrant in its crumbling dust—
By them the funeral gifts are only dross;
By them we ease the spirit's heavy cross.

Extend thy hand with ever ready clasp,
You know not who amid the throng may grasp
Its firm support to help him bear the load
Of hidden woe along life's rugged road.

Let charity with countless graces crown
O'er human weakness, sin and guilt abound.
A vestal virgin, still may she impart
The flame of love to every sinking heart.

So may we charge each glance and word
   and act
With that sweet, wondrous, magic,
   nameless tact,
Which peace and comfort yield to those
   oppressed,
And guide the weary ones to promised
   rest.
      —A. WILLIS LIGHTBOURN.

SOME DAY.

SOME day, some gladder day my hand
   will touch
The chords that now are silent in my
   harp,
And that sweet song that I could never
   sing
Will burst in raptures from my happy
   heart,
    Some day, some happy day.

Some day the voices that have called to
   me
Long from the mystic realms of
   shadowland,
Will woo me nearer, and my ears will
   catch
Some message sweet that I will understand,
    Some day, some happy day.

Some day the blooms of hope that
   would not bear
For me, though 'tended well, the rosy
   fruit
Will bloom again about my 'pathway
   fair,
In summer climes will ripen rich and
   sweet,
    Some day, some happy day.

Some day, I know not where or when
   'twill be,
But all the radiant glow that lit the
   skies
Of my lost childhood will shine forth
   again,
And that to me will be fair paradise,
    Some day, some happy day
      —MEMPHIS COMMERCIAL APPEAL.

WEDDED.

WELL, you are wedded, and around
   your life
Twine two great joys; for some one
   calls you wife,
And child-lips murmur; "Mother!"
   and you smile
After long years of sorrow and heart
   strife.

Smile up into the eyes that meet your
   own—
Feel the strong, sheltering arm around
   you thrown;
And with the loveliest words of love,
   you while
The hours away, no longer dark and
   lone.

You feel the clinging of your child; you
   feel
His arms about your neck; his kisses
   steal
Away the sigh that trembles to your
   lips
When faithful Memory doth some face
   reveal

From out the fading past; but tears or
   sighs
Are not for your sweet lips—for your
   bright eyes.
What earthly joy can now your joy
   eclipse?
For, choosing well, your love could be
   but wise.

And yet, I fancy that upon your brow
There is a faint, sad shadow resting
   now;
The bended knee droops lower, till
   at last
Your weeping face in your pale hands
   you bow.

And give yourself to grief! Is it not
   so?
A voice calls to you from the long
   ago—
A hand is stretched toward you from
   the past,
And joy is lost in bitterness and woe!

You wonder why the tears your eyes
  should fill;
You whisper to your breaking heart:
  " Be still!"
But the heart moans with yearning
  unsufficed—
Vague yearning, which the world can
  never fill!

For women love but once; and if
  denied
That first, sweet love, they live un-
  satisfied,
Clinging to it as to the cross of
  Christ—
A cross whereon their hearts are cruci-
  fied!

And this is life—the life which we
  must lead;
A life of dire distress and sorest need;
A life which longs, but vainly longs,
  for rest—
Rest for the hands that toil—the hearts
  that bleed!

Aye! this is life. Heaven's mercy on
  us, sweet!
Be it that you and I no more shall
  meet
Until the grass is green above the
  breast,
And God's white daisies grow at head
  and feet!
  —FRANK L. STANTON.

AN OLD SONG.

SHALL I, wasting in despair,
Die because a woman's fair?
Or make pale my cheeks with care,
'Cause another's rosy are?
Be she fairer than the day,
Or the flowery meads of May,
  If she be not fair for me,
  What care I how fair she be?

Great, or good, or kind, or fair,
I will ne'er the more despair,
If she love me, this believe,
I will die ere she shall grieve!
If she slight me when I woo,
I can scorn and let her go;
  For if she be not for me,
  What care I for whom she be?
    —GEORGE WITHER.

DEPARTURE.

WELL, Bill, shake han's 'n' say good-
  bye afore ye go away,
We hate t' see ye leavin'; we'd lots
  ruther hev' ye stay.
Mother 'n' me's a gittin' ole; we caint
  be with ye long;
She's bin porely fer some time now,
  'n'll never be ez strong
Ez she wuz afore the ager laid 'er up s'
  long in bed,
'N' more 'n likely when ye git back
  ye'll find yer mother dead.
Her pore ole lips 'uz quiverin' when
  she went t' say good-bye,
'N' tears splashed on the pillers when
  she axed ye ef ye'd try
'N' be a good boy fer her sake, Bill,
  when ye git fur away.
We hate t' see ye go, Bill; we'd lots
  ruther hev' ye stay.

Look et them pore young 'n's 'way up
  yander on the hill
Wavin' ther hats 'n' apurns 'n' throwin'
  kisses et ye, Bill.
Ther little throats 'uz choakin', they
  could har'ly help but cry
When ye went up 'n' shuck ther han's
  'n' kissed 'em all good-by.
They'll be mighty sad o' evenin's circled
  round the ole fireplace,
'N' they'll miss the tales ye tole 'em
  'bout yer early boyhood days;
They'll be listenin' fer yer whis'le ez ye
  done yer evenin' chores,
'N' they'll hev' no one to swing 'em in
  'at ole rope swing o' yours,
'N' ther little eyes'll water nowcher fiddle's quit its play;
Oh, they hate t' see ye go, Bill; they'd
  a heap ruther hev' ye stay.

Now, Bill, yer train's a-comin'; here's
  some scraps the chil'ren sent;
Dress goods, more'n likely; 'n' me 'n'
  mother went
'N' hed our picters taken so ez we
  could give ye one
T' 'member us by in after years when
  we'll be dead 'n' gone.
Now, here's a little Bible mother said
  to give to you;
She cou'dn't spend much money, but I
  reckon it'll do

Ez well ez ef we wuzn't pore 'n' her
  more change t' spare ;
So take it, Bill, 'ith mother's love, 'n'
  try 'n' keep it where
It'll allers be the handiest when ye're
  fur away.
We hate t' see ye go, Bill ; we'd lots
  ruther hev' ye stay.
                    —CHICAGO RECORD.

A NEGRO ON BLIND TOM.

DE beatenest niggah I eber seed yit
For playin' the whi' folks for all he
  can git,
An' dressin' in broad-clauf, an' eatin'
  fine grub,
An' knockin' pianer keys down wid a
  club,
An' makin' fine music an' all sich as dat,
Was brack as de debbil an' bline as a
  bat.

Whoop, niggah, don't talk ! Blind Tom
  is de stuff
To show dat de whi' folks is done
  bragged a-nuff
About dem musicians wid pompydo har,
Dat plays in de concerts an' sings in de
  quar,
An' tinks de bes' music is wrote in de
  books,
An' niggahs ain't fitten fur nuffin but
  cooks.

Shucks ! Dat niggah wouldn't be
  foolin' his time
A-huntin' up music to play wid a hyme,
An' lookin' to see how de music wus
  wrote,
An' practisin' up how to play it by note,
He des doubles up his ole brack rusty
  fis'
An' knocks out de music like grindin'
  out gris'.

Lawd, didn't he knock music out by de
  tons,
A-playin' dat battle, an' shootin' dem
  guns,
An' bustin' dem bombshells, an' marchin' dem troops,
An' makin dem keys gib de reg'lar war-
  whoops,

An' slashin' an' killin' ob folks right an,
  lef—
Gosh, niggah, dat playin' mos' skeered
  me to def !

Now, s'pose he'd a' had all dot music
  wrote out,
An' spent half his life-time a-foolin'
  about,
An' practisin' up how it o'rt to be
  played,
An' seein' which note repisent which
  bergade,
You couldn't 'a' tole when he got troo
  de playin'
Whedder it was a battle or somebody
  prayin'.

Dat's des whut I says 'bout de people
  I sees
A-playin' ob music by modern idees ;
Dey bounces about like a fish on a hook,
An' pulls up dey coat sleeves, an' fixes
  de book,
An' makes mo' to do dan a dozen
  police—
An' gibs you de jim-jams a-playin' de
  piece.

I bet ef King David was libbin' to-day,
An' had dat ole harp whut he t'ought
  he could play,
He'd hab him a law passed in less dan
  a week
To fro all de music books into de
  creek,
An' I bet he would kick dat ole harp
  out ob sight
An' get him a niggah to play music
  right.
                      —BOOTH LOWREY.

A BOY'S WORST FOE.

DON'T send my boy where your girl
  can't go,
And say, " There's no danger for boys,
  you know,
Because they all have their wild oats to
  sow."
There is no more excuse for my boy to
  be low
Than your girl. Then please do not
  tell him so.

Don't send my boy where your girl can't go,
For a boy or a girl sin is sin, you know,
And my baby boy's hands are as clean and white,
And his heart is as pure as your girl's to-night.
—WOMAN'S VOICE.

SUNNY PEOPLE.

THERE is a certain old lady, who lives in a little old house, with very little in it to make her comfortable. She is rather deaf and she cannot see very well, either. Her hands and feet are all out of shape and full of pain because of her rheumatism. But in spite of all this, you would find her full of sunshine, and as cheery as a robin in June, and it would do you good to see her. I found out one day what keeps her so cheerful.

"When I was a child," she said, "my mother taught me every morning, before I got out of bed, to thank God for every good thing that I could think of that He had given me, for a comfortable bed, for each article of clothing, for my breakfast, for a pleasant home, for my friends; and for all my blessings, calling each by name; and so I begin every day with a heart full of praise to God for all He has done and is doing for me."

Here is the secret, then, of a happy life, this having one's heart full of praise, and when we do as this dear little old lady does—that is, count our blessings every day, in a spirit of thanksgiving for them—we shall find many a reason why we should praise God

CREEDS.

LONG years I've spent in study over creeds;
Perplexed by questions deep beyond reply;
Now tempted to affirm, now to deny;
Sad, paralyzing influence on good deeds.

What joy to follow where calm Nature leads!
And roam in woods or fields which round us lie;
To gather flowers, or behold the sky;
And thence invoke that peace the spirit needs.

All Nature speaks to man with tranquil voice;
He, too, her child, is nurtured on her breast;
She shows, full oft, for him a smiling face.

But not alone for him. The fields rejoice,
Birds sing, sun shines, vexed ocean sinks to rest,
Bright stars roll on in the vast sea of space.
—PROF. E. EMERSON, *in The Open Court.*

HAGAR.

Go back! How dare you follow me beyond
The door of my poor tent? Are you afraid
That I have stolen something? See! my hands
Are empty like my heart. I am no thief!
The bracelets and the golden finger rings
And silver anklets that you gave to me
I cast upon the mat before my door,
And trod upon them. I would scorn to take
One trinket with me in my banishment
That would recall a look or tone of yours,
My lord, my generous lord, who sends me forth,
A loving woman, with a loaf of bread
And jug of water on my shoulder laid,
To thirst and hunger in the wilderness!
Go back!
Go back to Sara! See! she stands
Watching us there, behind the flowering date,
With jealous eyes, lest my poor hands should steal
One farewell touch from yours. Go back to her,

Hagar.
My lord, my generous lord, who sends me forth,
A loving monan, with a loaf of bread
And jug of water on my shoulder laid,
To thirst and hunger in the wilderness !

—*Page 230.*

And say that Hagar has a heart as proud,
If not so cold, as hers; and, though it breaks
It breaks without the sound of sobs, without
The balm of tears to ease its pain. It breaks—
It breaks, my lord, like iron; hard but clean;
And, breaking, asks no pity. If my lips
Should let one plea for mercy slip between
These words that lash you with a woman's scorn,
My teeth should bite them off, and I would spit
Them at you, laughing, though all red and warm with blood,
"Cease!" do you say? No, by the gods
Of Egypt, I do swear that if my eyes
Should let one tear melt through their burning lids,
My hands should pluck them out; and if these hands,
Groping outstretched in blindness, should by chance
Touch yours, and cling to them against my will,
My Ishmael should cut them off, and blind
And maimed, my little son should lead me forth
Into the wilderness to die. Go back!

Does Sara love you as I did, my lord?
Does Sara clasp and kiss your feet, and bend
Her haughty head in worship at your knee?
Ah! Abraham, you were a god to me.
If you but touched my hand my foolish heart
Ran down into the palm, and throbbed, and thrilled;
Grew hot and cold, and trembled there; and when
You spoke, though not to me, my heart ran out
To listen through my eager ears and catch
The music of your voice and prison it
In memory's murmuring shell, I saw no fault

Nor blemish in you, and your flesh to me
Was dearer than my own. There is no vein
That branches from your heart, whose azure course
I have not followed with my kissing lips.
I would have bared my bosom like a shield
To any lance of pain that sought your breast.
And once, when you lay ill within your tent,
No taste of water, or of bread or wine
Passed through my lips; and all night long I lay
Upon the mat before your door to catch
The sound of your dear voice, and scarcely dared
To breathe, lest she, my mistress, should come forth
And drive me angrily away; and when
The stars looked down with eyes that only stared
And hurt me with their lack of sympathy,
Weeping, I threw my longing arms around
Benammi's neck. Your good horse understood
And gently rubbed his face against my head,
To comfort me. But if you had one kind,
One loving thought of me in all that time,
That long, heart-breaking time, you kept it shut
Close in your bosom as a tender bud
And did not let it blossom into words.
Your tenderness was all for Sara. Through
The door, kept shut against my love, there came
No message to poor Hagar, almost crazed
With grief lest you should die. Ah! you have been
So cruel and so cold to me, my lord;
And now you send me forth with Ishmael,
Not on a journey through a pleasant land
Upon a camel, as my mistress rides,

With kisses, and sweet words, and dates and wine,
But cast me off, and sternly send me forth
Into the wilderness with these poor gifts—
A jug of water, and—a loaf of bread—
That sound was not a sob; I only lost
My breath and caught it hard again.
    Go back!
Why do you follow me? I am a poor Bondswoman, but a woman still, and these
Sad memories, so bitter and so sweet,
Weigh heavily upon my breaking heart
And make it hard, my lord—for me to go.
"Your God commands it?" Then my gods, the gods
Of Egypt, are more merciful than yours.
Isis and good Osiris never gave
Command like this, that breaks a woman's heart,
To any prince in Egypt. Come with me
And let us go and worship them, dear lord.
Leave all your wealth to Sara. Sara loves
The touch of costly linen and the scent
Of precious Chaldean spices, and to bind
Her brow with golden fillets, and perfume
Her hair with oint. Sara loves the sound
Of many cattle lowing on the hills;
And Sara loves the slow and stealthy tread
Of many camels moving on the plains.
Hagar loves—you. Oh! come with me, dear lord.
Take but your staff and come with me!
Your mouth
Shall drink my share of water from this jug
And eat my share of bread with Ishmael;
And from your lips I will refresh myself
With love's wine from tender kisses pressed.
Ah! come, dear lord. Oh! come, my Abraham.
Nay, do not bend your cold, stern brows on me
So frowningly; it was not Hagar's voice
That spoke those pleading words.
Go back! Go back!
And tell your God I hate Him, I hate Him
The cruel, craven heart that worships Him
And dare not disobey. Ha! I believe
'Tis not your far-off, bloodless God you fear,
But Sara. Coward! Cease to follow me!
Go back to Sara. See! she beckons now,
Hagar loves not a coward; you do well
To send me forth into the wilderness,
Where hatred hath no weapon keen enough
That held within a woman's slender hand
Could stab a coward to the heart!
    I go!
I go, my lord; proud that I take with me
Of all your countless herds by Hebron's brook,
Of all your Canaan riches, naught but this—
A jug of water and a loaf of bread.
And now, by all of Egypt's Gods I swear
If it were not for Ishmael's dear sake
My feet would tread upon this bitter bread,
My hands would pour this water on the sands;
And leave this jug as empty as my heart
Is empty now of all the reverence
And overflowing love it held for you,
    I go!
But I will teach my Ishmael
To hate his father for his mother's sake.
His bow shall be the truest bow that flies
Its arrows through the desert air. His feet,
The fleetest on the desert's burning sands;
Aye! Hagar's son a desert prince shall be,
Whose hands shall be against all other men;
And he shall rule a fierce and mighty tribe,

Whose fiery hearts and supple limbs shall scorn
The chafing curb of bondage, like the fleet wild horses of Arabia.
   I go!
But like this loaf that you have given me,
So shall your bread taste bitter with my hate ;
And like the water in this jug, my lord,
So shall the sweetest water that you draw
From Canaan's wells taste salty with my tears.

Farewell! I go, but Egypt's mighty gods
Will go with me, and my avengers be,
And in whatever distant land your God,
Your cruel God of Israel, is known.
There, too, the wrongs that you have done this day
To Hagar and your first-born, Ishmael,
Shall waken and uncoil themselves, and hiss
Like adders at the name of Abraham.
   —ELIZA POISEVENT NICHOLSON,
       "*Pearl Rivers.*"

DESTINY.

THE workings of Providence are truly mysterious and are clearly not for man to understand. At times they appear to work hardships where they are least deserved, and where they can be most illy borne. So far as their connections with man, they envelop his life in mystery from his cradle to his grave. We are told by the ancients, that every one is the maker of his own fortune. It has been often quoted and by some adopted as a truism. Yet, it is only true in part, and is believed only by those who in their imaginations have fashioned their own. The history of the average man convinces him that, after all, he really takes but little part in shaping his future, but that "there is a destiny that shapes our ends, rough hew them as we may."

The idea of each being the maker of his own fortune disappears as he advances in life and runs counter to the workings of Providence. When the wild dreams of youth have disappeared, and he drifts really into the whirlpool of life he often finds himself in new roads, in strange paths and amid different surroundings than, as a maker of his own fortune, he would have ever selected. How, or why, he cannot tell. What is the end, or object, he cannot guess. He finds it so, and if he is a philosopher, accepts the situation. He observes that the good have died, the bad still live ; the unexpected has happened, the expected never took place. Such are the daily occurrences in spite of the human will. And hence, no one can be truly said to be the maker of his own fortune amid such circumstances, and no sane person should demonstrate such folly as to so imagine. Such are only lessons which teach the frailty of man, and the Divinity of God.

A TRIBUTE TO WOMANHOOD.

As backward we turn life's pages,
   And look through the vista of years,
Accompanying each nation's victories
   A woman's name appears.
The soft white hand of woman
   The greatest deeds have done,
And every tribute paid to her
   Has been most nobly won,

When the pitiless hand of war
   Held France with cruel force,
Blotting out peace and happiness,
   Spreading ruin in its course ;
'Twas a woman then that rose,
   The terrors of battle braved,
And by her dauntless courage
   La Belle France was saved.

And what has Columbia's woman
   Done for the "Land of the Free ?"
That her name should be synonymous
   For courage and dexterity.
She showed to our many heroes
   Where the path of honor lies,
Sending them out to win
   The freedom that we prize.

Hers is the first ear to listen
   To the pleading of distress ;
She is ever first to hasten,
   Tired and weary hands to press.

Philanthropic, true and tender,
  Virtue's champion is she—
Then first in her nation's history
  May she ever be.

Not a labyrinth has there been
  In this turbulent voyage of life,
But a woman's steps have tread,
  Leaving solace in the strife.
O, womanhood ! true womanhood ;
  Adversity ne'er weighs thee down ;
To thee as well as man belongs
  The sceptre and the crown.
    —PEARL MARKEY.

A COLORADO PHILOSOPHER.

HE stood by the fence of a mountain
    ranch,
  A pitiful, sad-eyed burro ;
There wasn't an edible leaf or branch,
    And the alkali ground
  For miles around
Had never a sign of furrow.
" Ah me ! " he sighed, " I'm sad it's so,
  But life is an endless tussle ;
They've let me go in the storm and
    snow,
  For they know I am used to rustle.

" I can go a day on a sardine can
  And two on a scrap of leather ;
I have lived a week on a chinese fan,
    And it's even plain
    That I sometimes gain
On only a change of weather.
The lazy ones feed on hay, indeed !
  But I, who have nerve and muscle—
They say : ' He'll do ; he will worry
    through ;
He's a wonderful brute to rustle ! ' "

O ! sorrowful burro, thin and sad !
  I feel to you like a brother.
With the human race it's just as bad,
    For the tramp and shirk
    Must escape from work,
  By the bountiful sweat of another.
There are some that stand with glove in
    hand
  In the infinite toil and bustle ;
They sing and play, but they've lots of
    hay—
  They never have learned to rustle !
    —CHARLES P. ALLEN.

A RURAL CHRISTMAS.

WE uns is as solid as rocks ;
  Old Christmas, jest come when you
      choose !
Mammy's a-knittin' of socks,
  An' daddy's a-makin' of shoes !

The house got another room built
  Fer comp'ny—what comes by sur-
      prise ;
Molly's a-quiltin' a quilt,
  An' Mary's a-bakin' of pies.

The hogs is done kilt, an' the mules
  Laid off fer the holiday time ;
Play theatre now in the schools,
  An' see all you want fer a dime.

Thar's fun till a feller can't rest !
  The boys is hurrahin' all day ;
An' then, when it's night, why—they
    jest
  Git a fiddle an' shuffle away !
    —ATLANTA CONSTITUTION.

HOLIDAY ATTENTIONS.

" MY dear, you're looking very tired to-
    night."
  (That means a Christmas cloak.)
" I'll get your slippers and your pipe—
    a light."
  (That's business and no joke !)

" You'll kill yourself if you keep work-
    ing so ! "
  (That speech is bound to win !)
" Darling, I could not live if you should
    go ! "
  (That means a diamond pin.)

" I've had the girl make just the nicest
    tea ! "
  (My head has fallen back !)
" The kind you liked best when you
    married me ! "
  (Mercy ! a fur trimmed sacque !)

" Poor, tired dear ! I'll rub your head
    for you ! "
  (In mute despair I look.)
" When I go shopping I'll be tired,
    too ! "
  (That means—my pocketbook !)
    —CONSTITUTION.

"HE'LL SEE IT WHEN HE WAKES."

WE remember at the Wilderness a gallant Mississippian had fallen, and at night, just before burying him, there came a letter from her he loved best. One of the group around his body—a minister, whose tenderness was womanly—broke the silent tearfulness with which he saw the dead letter; he took it and laid it upon the breast of him whose heroic heart was still.

"Bury it with him. He will see it when he wakes."

It was the sublimest sentence of his funeral service.

Amid the clouds of battle smoke,
 The sun had died away;
And where the storm of battle broke,
 A thousand warriors lay.
A band of friends upon the field,
 Stood round a youthful form, [peal'd
Who, when the war cloud's thunder
 Had perish'd in the storm—
Upon his forehead, on his hair,
 The coming moonlight breaks,
And each dear brother standing there
 A tender farewell takes.

But ere they lay him in his home,
 There came a comrade near,
And gave a token that had come
 From her the dead held dear.
A moment's doubt upon them press'd,
 Then one the letter takes,
And lays it low upon his breast—
 "He'll see it when he wakes."
O thou who dost in sorrow wait,
 Whose heart with anguish breaks,
Though thy dear message came too late,
 "He'll see it when he wakes."

Ne'er more amid the fiery storm
 Shall his strong arm be seen;
No more his young and manly form
 Tread Mississippian green.
Then even thy tender words of love—
 The words affection speaks—
Came all too late; but oh! thy love
 "Will see them when he wakes!"
No jars disturb his gentle rest,
 No noise his slumber breaks,
But thy words sleep upon his breast—
 "He'll see them when he wakes."
         —FRANK LEE.

A GOOD OLD CANDY PULL.

YOU talk about your husking bees—
Who've lived in Yankeedom,
And guess of all the season's sport,
There's none that gives such fun
As those good, old-fashioned parties,
Where boys and girls so dear,
With song and shout and laughter
Husk out each golden ear.
But away down south, in Dixie,
The sport of greatest gain
Is where the boys go with the girls
To see the mill grind cane;
And while they're at a grinding
Their cup of joy is full
If they only have a "hand in"
A
    Good
        Old
            Candy
                Pull.

You talk about your spelling schools,
Who've grown up in the west,
And reckon, of all the season's fun,
They surely were the best.
You think no times are equal to
Those good old days of bliss,
When boys and girls stood up in line
And spelled until they missed.
But away down south, in Dixie,
The land of corn and wine,
The season here we hold so dear
Is when the cane we grind.
If you could go to a "stir off"
And see a kettle full
You would say there was nothing like
A
    Good
        Old
            Candy
                Pull.

THE OLD KITCHEN FIRE.

IT doesn't make no difference how fur
 away I go,
I still can see that ruddy blaze and feel
 its cheerful glow,
An' hear the voices hushed long since
 a-talkin' as of yore,
An' me a happy, rompin' child upon the
 poplar floor;

The cat a-sittin' on the hearth, the
  cheers a-standin' round—
Content was there if anywhere on earth
  it can be found !
An' theyn't no other happiness I'd any
  more desire
Than jist to be a boy again aroun' the
  kitchin fire.

No matter what I'm doin' of, I always
  try to feel
A boy agen with mother who, while
  cookin' of the meal,
Would kiss me now an' then an' speak
  some kind word in 'my ear
In such a tone as somehow now I cannot ever hear ;
If, I could only for awhile feel glad as I
  felt then,
I'd give a long, long life to live the old
  days o'er agen ;
For theyn't no other happiness I'd any
  more desire
Than jist to be a boy agen aroun' the
  kitchin fire.
—WILL T. HALE.

HUMAN LILIES.

IN a black slough, floored with mire and filth, roofed with heavy, damp vegetation, and vile with unhealthy odors, a lily put up tender green leaves, and lifted a slender, graceful throat and a white, pure face. Day by day she grew in grace and beauty, and all the vile things about her could not steal her perfect bloom or her rare perfume, or soil her spotlessness. The slimy drops that fell ever from the vines overhead ran from her fair petals, leaving no stain ; nor did she once stoop to the mire and the noisome thing that tried to drag her down. Proud and cool and sweet, she lifted her white face to heaven—or rather to the heaven of her imagination, for the gloomy branches and mosses above her shut God's blue from her yearning eyes. But by and by, they grew to a bitter envy of her— those low, slimy things that could not climb to her height—and they conspired to her ruin. But still she stood daunt- less against their attacks until, vine on vine and cactus on cactus, they twined about her and their weight became too heavy to be borne ; and so, at last, with- out an instant's warning, her frail body broke and her proud head sunk prone, dying, into the mire. But even then her face shone out, white and clear, in that filthy place ; and the things that had hated her, and had brought about her ruin, were still unsatisfied : they had broken her body, but they could not soil her purity or lower her brave, true soul. Woman, born of low and coarse parentage, untaught, uncared for, often—ah, me !—unloved ; accus- tomed to bad manners and low habits and vile language in your very home ; with wrong teaching and wrong example on all sides of you—my story of the lily is for you ! I have seen women grow up, white and pure and beautiful, through the very dregs and slime and filth of life ; I have seen them hold up their heads above those who hated them and tried to drag them down ; I have seen them shun evils that they rec- ognized as such, not from any teaching, but from the innate, unquenchable purity of their souls ; and O, thank God ! I have seen them stand in the face of temptation firm and strong as the rock that feels the warm arms of his sea and loves her, but yields to her never. Each woman that lives, whatever the disadvantages of her early life and edu- cation, may, if she will, stand up, proud and strong and free, under God's blue heaven and let nothing drag her down. Somewhere within reach of my pen, there may be one woman—only one—who was born in the lower ranks of life ; who knew, through a loveless childhood and maidenhood, only poverty and struggle and care ; who was used to a coarse and unhappy home life, to quarreling, wrangling, violent language, oaths—to all the horrible things that dwell in the homes that lack refinement, education, gentleness and love. If any such woman read these lines, I say to her that it is never too late for a woman to stand upright and live a pure, spot- less, honest life. Let them wear out your strength trying to drag you down until your life-thread snaps and all is over, but do not ever yield to them, do not ever stoop to them, do not ever let them soil your spotlessness. You may even have stumbled and fallen, but I tell you, poor heart, it is not yet too late. Do not tell me that man may be forgiven a sin for which woman is eternally cursed—I will not believe it. You may both stand upright once more if only you have the will and the honesty and the unfaltering purpose. If you help yourself, the world will help you; for the world loves nothing—nothing—so much as it loves a pure and honest and virtuous woman. And if the lily is pure when she is set among velvets and laces, I tell you she is ten times purer when she lifts her white head through the mire and filth of the gutter and shines out clear and sweet as one of God's own stars in the black vault of midnight.

—ELLA HIGGINSON.

NAMELESS.

THERE is a name so sweet, so dear,
That I could never write it here,
Where careless eyes, perchance might see—
The name a loved one gave to me;
A little name, one simple word,
Soft as the twitter of a bird,
Brooding above her tiny nest;
But, oh! it is the dearest, best;
And softly I'll that name repeat
Until my heart shall cease to beat!

There is a little, plaintive song,
My heart repeats the whole day long;
I heard it once at day's decline,
Low breath'd by lips close pressed to mine.
I would not that a careless ear
Should catch the song I love to hear;
So my heart's throbbings, come and go
As to myself I breathe it low;
Soul-music holy, glad and deep,
Within my heart of hearts I keep.

There is a heart so warm and true,
And eyes of pure and tender hue;
I know full well I need not fear
What fate may bring, if they are near.

Oh! fond, true faith, on which I rest,
And own myself so richly blest!
Oh! faithful friend, for whom I yearn,
And count the hours till they return;
The name, the song, the heart I own,
I keep for thee, and thee alone!

HOME AFFECTIONS.

THE heart has affections that never die. The rough rubs of the world never obliterate them. They are memories of home. There is the old tree under which the light-hearted boy swung many a day; yonder is the river in which he learned to swim; there is the house in which he knew a parent's protection; nay, there is the room in which brother and sister long since laid in the yard in which we must soon be gathered, ever shadowed by yon old church, whither, with a joyous troop like himself, he has often followed his parents to worship, and hear the good old man who ministered at the altar. Even the very school house associated in youthful days with thoughts of task, now comes to bring pleasant remembrances of many occasions that called forth some generous exhibition of noble traits of human nature. There is where he learned to feel some of his emotions. There, perchance, he first met the being who, by her love and tenderness in life, has made a home for him happier than that which his childhood had known. There are certain feelings of humanity and those, too, among the best, that can find no appropriate place for their exercise only at one's fireside.

HOW SCHOLARS ARE MADE.

COSTLY apparatus and splendid cabinets have no magical power to make scholars. In all circumstances, as a man is, under God, the master of his own fortune, so he is master of his own mind. The Creator has so constituted the human intellect that it can only grow by its own action and free will—it will certainly and necessarily grow. Every man must, therefore, educate him-

self. His book and teacher are but helps; the work is his. A man is not educated until he has the ability to summon, in an emergency, all his mental powers in vigorous exercise to effect his proposed object. It is not the man who has seen most, or read most, who can do this; such a one is in danger of being borne down like a beast of burden, by an over-loaded mass of other men's thoughts. Nor is it the man who can boast of native vigor and capacity. The greatest of all warriors in the siege of Troy had the pre-eminence because self-discipline had taught him how to use his bow.
—Daniel Webster.

HEALTH.

Health is perpetual youth—that is, a state of positive health. Merely negative health, the mere keeping out of the hospital for a number of years, is not health. Health is to feel the body of luxury, as every vigorous child does, as the bird does when it shoots and quivers through the air, not flying for the sake of the goal, but for the sake of flight; as the dog does when he scours madly across the meadows, or plunges into the muddy blissfulness of the stream, but neither the bird nor dog nor child enjoys his cup of physical happiness—let the dull or the worldly say what they will—with a felicity so cordial as the educated palate of conscious manhood. To "feel one's life in every limb," this is the secret bliss of which all forms of athletic exercise are merely varying disguises; and is absurd to say that we cannot possess this when character is mature, but only when it is half developed. As the flower is better than the bud, so should the fruit be better than the flower.

EVERY YEAR.

The Spring has less of brightness,
    Every year;
And the snow a ghastlier whiteness,
    Every year;
Nor do summer-flowers quicken,
Nor autumn-fruitage thicken,
As they once did, for they sicken,
    Every year.

It is growing darker, colder,
    Every year
As the heart and soul grow older,
    Every year;
I care not now for dancing,
Or for eyes with passion glancing,
Love is less and less entrancing,
    Every year.

Of loves and sorrows blended
    Every year;
Of the charms of friendship ended
    Every year;
Of the ties that still might bind me,
Until Time to Death resigns me,
My infirmities remind me,
    Every year.

Ah! how sad to look before us,
    Every year;
While the cloud grows darker o'er us,
    Every year;
When we see the blossoms faded,
That to bloom we might have aided,
And immortal garlands braided,
    Every year.

To the past go more dead faces,
    Every year;
As the loved leave vacant places,
    Every year.
Everywhere the sad eyes meet us,
In the evening's dusk they greet us,
And to come to them entreat us,
    Every year.

"You growing old," they tell us,
    "Every year;
"You are more alone," they tell us
    "Every year
You can win no new affection,
You have only recollection,
Deeper sorrow and dejection,
    Every year."

Yes! the shores of life are shifting,
    Every year;
And we are seaward drifting,
    Every year;

Old places, changing, fret us,
The living more forget us,
There are fewer to regret us,
　　Every year.

But the truer life draws nigher,
　　Every year;
And its morning star climbs higher,
　　Every year;
Earth's hold on us grows slighter,
And the heavy burden lighter,
And the Dawn Immortal brighter,
　　Every year.
　　　　—ALBERT PIKE.

THE WAY OF IT.

DRINK and the gang drinks with you;
　Swear off and you go it alone;
For the bar room bum who drinks your rum
　Has a quenchless thirst of his own.
Feast, and they cut you dead;
　They'll not get mad if you use them bad,
So long as their stomach's fed,
Steal, if you get a million,
For then you can furnish bail;
　It's the great big thief gets out on leave,
While the little ones go to jail.

A MOTHER'S FAREWELL.

Go forth into the world, my boy,
　It beckons now to thee,
And be as pure amid the strife
　As at thy mother's knee;
Let no desire bid thee turn
　Or quit the path of right,
But fix thy gaze on duty's goal
　And keep thy armor bright.

You'll miss the farmhouse and the brook,
　Each charm thy childhood knew;
The vine whose breath around thy feet
　Its wild aroma threw.
And oh, amid life's fevered toil,
　Its sorrow and its pain,
Thy lips will often sigh, my boy,
　To breathe its scent again.

'Twill not be easy to succeed
　And foes thy strength will try,
But think of home, and strive, my boy,
　Resolved to do or die.

Recall the withered face of one
　Who loves you day and night,
And pray that God may give you grace
　To keey your armor bright.

The world may laugh at you and say:
　" Look at the parson, boys,
His wings are sprouting on his back "—
　But lightly heed the noise.
No ridicule can hurt the man
　Whose heart is pure within;
Remember this, my boy, and fear
　No mockery but sin.

Think always twice before you speak,
　No provocation lend.
'Tis better to prevent a wrong
　Than have a wrong to mend.
Life is too short to while away
　Its sweet and solemn light;
Oh, guard its sacred moments well.
　And keep thy armor bright.

I may be sleeping ere thy brow
　By fortune's wreath is bound,
But triumph never scorns a crest
　In duty's armor found.
Then, forth into the world, my boy,
　I send thee from my breast,
This sums it all: do well thy part,
　And time will do the rest.
　　　　—L. L. KNIGHT.

THE SCYTHE OF TIME.

KIND reader! it has been a long time since we had an interview,—so long that, no doubt, you have, ere this, numbered me with those who were; yet, thanks to kind Providence, I still linger on the shore of Time, and have not forgotten past associations. Just now the Future, painted by the delicate finger of Fancy, in the most beautiful and attractive colors, looms up before my eager gaze, while Imagination hies away down the dusky lane of the Past, to bring in review, once again, forms and faces, scenes and occurrences, long since enveloped in the mystic folds of the dark mantle of oblivion. As I look upon the train, and contemplate the picture, with the history of each, I cannot refrain from the repetition of those earnest words of an unassuming Montgomery;—

> "Yonder his shadow flits away;
> Thou shalt not thus depart;
> Stay thou transcendent spirit, stay,
> And tell me who thou art."

Since last we interchanged thoughts and sentiments, gentle reader, I have passed through lands and scenes new and strange to me, and again revisited the lovely spot of my nativity—the place where the halcyon days of my early life were spent in the innocent mirth and thoughtless sports of my childhood—I have stood upon the verge of those beautiful plains of the far South-West, and gazed with delight upon their wide expanse, dotted o'er with sporting flocks and grazing herds; I have penetrated the depths of her magnificent forests, and retired at "twilight's balmy hour," beneath her sweet scented groves of orange and magnolia—listening to the plaintive, evening lay of the sleepless nightingale, while the mellow beams of night's pale queen streamed softly and noiselessly down through the long gray moss that invested the giant arms of the majestic cypress,—all conspiring to harmonize the discordant feelings of the human breast, and elevate the thoughts of the most sordid mind to the true Source of grandeur, beauty, and power. I have floated upon the bright bosom of earth's expansive waters, and mingled with the busy throngs and gay circles of her thriving towns and populous cities, where all seemed flush with life and animation, and buoyant with hopes of a protracted and bright future; yet, in the "desert waste and city full"—in the unbroken forest—upon each beautiful field and plain, I have observed, with feelings of melancholy sadness, traces of some stealthy, sure and certain devastation. Here a decaying bough or mouldering trunk—there a ruined wall or tottering column—yonder a silent group of white and sculptured stones—all bearing testimony to the crushing tread of some resistless conqueror. Borne onward by the panting engine and rattling car, I once more stood at the threshold of the old homestead. It was the same spot—I knew it was the same—and I was the same personage, of a larger growth, who went out thence of yore; but it requires no inconsiderable effort of the feelings to realize it. Long years had gone to join the cycles of Eternity, leaving a mighty chasm behind, which imagination alone can overleap. A favorite old oak had gone down in the storm's rude blast: the broad arms of a friendly elm, that stood by the rippling water's side, lay scattered upon the ground; the stone wall of the huge old mill, and the "cot that stood by it," had tottered and fallen; in short, everything, once so pleasant and dear to my heart, bore marks of the same destructive agent observed elsewhere, and seemed invested with a strangeness to me incomprehensible. Such were the externals of the old paternal grounds; but, oh! change stopped not there. Had a few old oaks and elms—sacred enough to me indeed—been the only objects devastated, their loss could have been repaired. But, reader, a more sad and solemn change have I yet to record to you. The once large and happy circle that used to gather, at eventide, beneath that old moss-covered roof, was broken and scattered for *all time*. Fond brothers and sister, though not in the grave, were in other lands; an aged sire, with trembling limbs and whitened locks, grasped me by the hand, and once more welcomed me into the venerable mansion of my childhood. With one hand raised to his wrinkled brow, he, with the other, pointed to the vacant "old arm chair," which still kept its place in the corner, and then softly retired, leaving me to divine the rest.

Kind reader! need I tell you that my heart *did* divine it! For a few moments I stood fixed and motionless as the marble statue that marked the spot where she lies. She had gone from the walks of life, to join the happy throngs of blissful eternity. Soon my eager steps were bending toward that sacred spot—the family graveyard. There a little mound of earth, and a plain, but neatly engraved stone, told a short, sad tale, which bowed my head, in sorrow down, till it was pillowed upon the cold clay which shut out the mortal remains of my sainted mother from my fond embrace. After an outgush of prayers and tears, I slowly arose, involuntarily exclaiming, What cruel power is it which thus rudely severs the tenderest ties, and blights the fairest prospects of earth? A still small voice whisperingly replied—" 'Tis the Scythe of Time. Then bled my heart afresh, while I felt

" That soon beneath the inevitable blow,
I, too, should lie in dust and darkness low.

" When Time, the conqueror, will suspend
His scythe, a trophy o'er my tomb,
Whose waving shadow shall portend
Each frail beholder's doom."

THOUGH LOST TO SIGHT, TO MEMORY DEAR.

[The oft-quoted line, "Though lost to sight, to memory dear," originated with Ruthven Jenkyns, and was first published in the *Greenwich Magazine for Mariners*, 1701 or 1702. We give the whole poem.]

SWEET heart, good-bye! that flut'ring sail
Is spread to waft me far from thee,
And soon before the farth'ring gale
My ship shall bound upon the sea.
Perchance all des'late and forlorn,
These eyes shall miss thee many a year;
But unforgotten every charm—
Though lost to sight, to memory dear.

Sweet heart, good-bye! one last embrace!
Ah, cruel fate, two souls to sever!
Yet in this heart's most sacred place
Thou, thou alone, shalt dwell forever;
And still shall recollection trace
In fancy's mirror, ever near,
Each smile, each tear, that form, that face—
Though lost to sight, to memory dear.

SWEETHEART, GOOD-BYE.

SWEETHEART, good-bye! Our varied day
Is closing into twilight gray,
And up from bare, bleak wastes of sea,
The storm-wind rises mournfully;
A mystic prescience strange and drear,
Doth haunt the shuddering twilight air;
It fills the earth, it chills the sky—
Sweetheart, good-bye!

Sweetheart, good-bye! Our joys are past,
And night with silence comes at last—
Old things must end—yea, even love—
Nor know we if re-born above
The earth-blooms of our earthly prime,
Shall bloom beyond these bounds of time,
" Ah! death alone is sure," we cry—
Sweetheart, good-bye!

Sweet-heart, good-bye! Though midst tears,
Pass the pale phantoms of our years,
Once bright with spring, or subtly strong
When summer's noontide thrilled with song;
Now, wan, wild-eyed, forlornly bowed,
Each rayless as an autumn cloud
Fading on dull September's sky—
Sweetheart, good-bye!

Sweetheart, good-bye! The vapors roll
Across yon distant, darkening wold
Are types of what our world doth know
Of tenderest loves of long ago;
And thus when all is done and said,
Our life lived out, our passions dead,
What can their wavering record be
But tinted mists of memory?
Oh! clasp and kiss me ere we die—
Sweetheart, good-bye!

FULLY DECIDED.

"THE curfew shall not ring tonight!"
She said it loud enough
To make them know for blocks away
It was no idle bluff.

The curfew-ringers hastened thence
And labored hard with her,
To get her to recall her words;
She firmly said, "Ump-er!"

They tried her yet again, for they
Could scarce their ears believe;
" Oh, let us ring the curfew!"
She answered, " Not this eve."

Rebuffed, chagrined, in silence they
   Disconsolately sat ;
And sitting thus, they wrung their hands
   And let it go at that.
                —EXCHANGE.

LOOK ON THE BRIGHT SIDE.

LOOK on the bright side of things ; it is the right side. The times may be hard, but it will make them no easier to wear a gloomy face. It is the sunshine and not the cloud that makes the flower. Full one-half our ills exist only in imagination. There is always that before or around us that should cheer and fill the heart with warmth. The sky is blue ten times where it is black once. You have troubles it may be ; so have others. None are free from them, and perhaps it is well that none should be. They give sinew and tone to life, fortitude and courage to man. That would be a dull sea, and the sailor would never become skillful, where there was nothing to disturb the ocean. It is the duty of every one to extract all the happiness and enjoyment he can without and within him. Above all, he should look on the bright side of things. What though appearances do look a little dark—the lane will turn and the night end in broad day. In the long run, and very often in the short, the great balance of life will right itself. Men were not made to hang down either head or hands, and those who do, only show that they are departing from the path of true common sense and right. There is more virtue in one sunbeam than in a whole hemisphere of clouds and gloom. Therefore, look on the bright side of things. Cultivate what is warm and genial, and shun what is cold and repulsive, dark and morose.—

THE HABIT OF READING.

"I HAVE no time to read," is the common complaint, and especially of women, whose occupations are such as to prevent continuous book perusal. They seem to think, because they cannot devote as much attention to books as they are compelled to devote to their avocations, that they cannot read anything. But this is a great mistake. It isn't the books we finish at a sitting which always do us the most good. Those we devour in the odd moments, half a dozen pages at a time, often give us more satisfaction, and are more thoroughly digested than those we make a particular effort to read. The men who have made their mark in the world have generally been the men who have in boyhood formed the habit of reading at every available moment, whether for five minutes or five hours.

It is the habit of reading rather than the time at our command that helps us on the road to learning. Many of the most cultivated persons, whose names have been famous as students, have given only two or three hours a day to their books. If we make use of spare minutes in the midst of our work, and read a little, if but a page or paragraph, we shall find our brains quickened and our toil lightened by just so much increased satisfaction as the book gives us. Nothing helps along the monotonous daily round so much as fresh and striking thoughts, to be considered while our hands are busy. A new idea from a new volume is like oil which reduces the friction of the machinery of life. What we remember from brief glimpses into books often serves as a stimulus to action, and becomes one of the most precious deposits in the treasury of our recollection. All knowledge is made up of small parts, which would seem insignificant in themselves, but which taken together, are valuable weapons for the mind and substantial armor for the soul. " Read anything continuously," says Dr. Johnson, " and you will be learned." The odd minutes which we are inclined to waste, if carefully availed of for instruction, will, in the long run, make golden hours and golden days, that we shall be ever thankful for,

A LEAF

FROM THE CALENDAR TORN.

OVER me gently steals the thought
   Of life's sacred and solemn care
As in calm, breathless silence I
   A leaf from the calendar tear.

The thought of fruitless moments fled,
  Sends thro' my heart a dart of pain,
And comes o'er me a long sad thought
  Of days that'll ne'er return again.

Like leaves from the calendar torn,
  Had they also their missioned lot,
And when they had their blessings borne,
  Were half enjoyed and soon forgot.

Go, dear old leaf, thy mission's done,
  And fruits to thy creator borne,—
May ours be such report as thine,
  When we're from life's calendar torn

KEEP A MERRY HEART.

No use to whine and worry
  'Cause the sun don't shine to-day,
No use to fume an' flurry
  'Cause misfortune cloud the way.
The skies will surely brighten,
  The shadows all depart.
'Jes' go on straight and learn to wait
  An' keep a merry heart.

There is no use o' growlin';
  It costs no more to smile.
Tho' winter's storms are howlin'
  Spring'll be here after a while.
There is no use o' kickin'
  Jes' go on with your part;
Be stanch an' true in all you do
  An' keep a merry heart.

There is no use o' wearin'
  A melancholy air.
The world is not a-carin'
  Your grief and woe to share.
Altho' some grievous sorrow
  Should cause a tear to start,
Jes' let good cheer drive back the tear
  An' keep a merry heart.
  —WILLIAM WEST.

A SMALL SWEET WAY.

THERE'S never a rose in the world
  But makes some green spray sweeter;
There's never a wind in all the sky
  But makes some bird wing fleeter;

There's never a star but brings to heaven
  Some silver radiance tender;
And never a rosy cloud but helps
  To crown the sunset splendor;
No robin but may thrill some heart,
  His dawnlike gladness voicing;
God gives us all some small sweet way
  To set the world rejoicing.

THE MODEL WIFE.

SHE rises every morning,
  Just when the roosters crow;
She gently splits the kindling—
  And makes the old stove puff and blow.

She puts the breakfast on to cook,
  And sings as if at play;
And while the batter-cakes are made,
  Her husband snores away.

The children show her gentle care,
  Their nightly slumbers o'er;
She dresses half a dozen,
  And she wipes a dozen more.

Then to the room she doth repair;
  Her husband hears her say:
"I've almost worked myself to death;
  Are you goin' to sleep all day?"

THE MODEL HUSBAND—A WEAK SATIRE.

HE rises every morning,
  Just at the break of dawn;
He lights the kitchen fire,
  And he puts the kettle on.

He washes all the dishes,
  Put biscuits in to bake,
And calmly as a cyclone
  Beats to tenderness the steak.

Then he dresses all the children,
  Hears 'em say their prayers,
And let's 'em go to take the air,
  Or tumble down the stairs.

He sweeps the house all over,
  Knocks the dust from every shelf;
His wife—she runs for office,
  And he just can't help himself.

"WHEN TIMES ARE HARD."

When times are hard and crops are spoiled
And debts are overdue,
And no matter how you've toiled
Things look pretty blue;
Just remember that away up there
Is a Lord that knows it all,
And when it gets too hard to bear
Why just give him a call.

I've heard a lot what folks have said,
And read what some did write;
'Bout a "stiff lip" and "keep your head"
And "coming out all right."
But if you've reached your last rope's end
Just let me say a word,
Now if you want affairs to mend
Why, call upon the Lord.

He can fix it don't you doubt it,
He can give you what you need;
Just you tell Him all about it,
Then you follow, let Him lead,
He can pass a bill and sign it,
While you're blinking of your eye;
Make a law, put power behind it,
That shall never fail or die.

You can pin your faith to Grover,
Or any other of that horde;
But you'll find before its over
That there's no one like the Lord.
—C. Clayton Brown.

"ROCK OF AGES."

"Rock of Ages cleft for me,
Let me hide myself in thee!"
Sang the lady, soft and low,
And the melancholy flow
Of her voice so sweet and clear,
Rose upon the evening air
With that sweet and solemn prayer:
"Rock of Ages, cleft for me,
Let me hide myself in thee!"

Yet she sang, as oft she had,
When her thoughtless heart was glad;
Sang because she felt alone—
Sang because her soul had grown
Weary with the tedious day—
Sang to while the hours away:
"Rock of Ages cleft for me,
Let me hide myself in thee!"

Where the trembling starlight falls
On her mansion's stately walls;
On the chill and echoing street—
Where the lights and shadows meet—
There the lady's voice was heard,
As the breath of Night was stirred
With that music floating free:
"Rock of Ages, cleft for me."

Wandering, homeless, through the night,
Praying for the morning light—
Pale and haggard, wan and weak,
With the death-hue on her cheek,
Went a woman—one whose life,
Had been wrecked in sin and strife;
One of whom, in one far land
Wrote the Master on the sand!
And her soul, by Sorrow wrung,
Heard the lady as she sung:
Rock of Ages, cleft for me,
Let me hide myself in thee!"

On the marble steps she knelt,
And her soul that instant felt
Mercy's healing touch was there;
Quivering, moved her lips in prayer!
And the God she had forgot
Smiled upon her lonely lot—
Heard her as she murmured oft,
With an accent sweet and soft:
"Rock of Ages, cleft for me,
Let me hide myself in thee!"

Little knew the lady fair,
As she sang so sweetly there,
That her voice had reached a soul
Which had lived in sin's control!
Little knew, when she was done,
That a lost and erring one
Heard her as she breathed that strain
And returned to God again!
—Frank L. Stanton, *in Atlanta Constitution.*

OH, HAD I KNOWN!

If I had thought so soon she would have died,
He said, I had been tenderer in my speech,
I had a moment lingered at her side,
And held her, ere she passed beyond my reach
If I had thought so soon she would have died.

That day she looked up with her startled
    eyes,
Like some hurt creature where the
    woods are deep,
With kisses I had stilled those breaking
    sighs,
With kisses closed those eyelids into
    sleep,
That day she looked up with her
    startled eyes.

Oh, had I known she would have died
    so soon,
Love had not wasted on a barren
    land,
Love, like those rivers under torrid
    noon,
Lost on the desert, poured out on the
    sand—
Oh, had I known she would have died
    so soon!

SOME FAMOUS HYMNS.

NEARLY ALL GREAT RELIGIOUS SONGS
THE RESULT OF INSPIRATION.

It is more true, perhaps, of hymns than of any form of poetry that they owe their origin to some sudden inspiration that seldom is repeated, says the *Chicago Tribune*. The great "Te Deum," that pæan of Christianity, is said to have been first sung at the baptism of St. Augustine. Certain it is, that it was the first hymn which Columbus and his sailors sang when they set foot on the New World and planted the flag of Spain.

Thomas di Celano, a scholar of St. Francis, of Assisi, wrote "Dies Iræ." One of the best versions in English is that of Lord Roscommon, who died with two lines of it on his lips.

The "Veni, Sanctu Spiritus" came from King Robert of France.

They still show in Cornwall those features of the landscape which proved an inspiration to Wesley. He wrote many hymns, however, and this article has to do only with those who were obscure and had but one or two great moments of inspiration.

"Rock of Ages," a hymn which has been a great comfort to Christians, was written by Augustus Toplady in 1778.

The author's life was a troubled one; his creed underwent changes; his temper was fiery. The better part of his nature seems to have blossomed forever in this hymn.

Bishop Heber wrote much besides the missionary hymn "From Greenland's Icy Mountains;" but it is by that he will be chiefly remembered.

Although John Howard Payne, the author of "Home, Sweet Home" never had a home, he had the most brilliant realization of the ideal Home, Sweet Home.

Joseph Hart, a native of London, where he was born in 1712, was the author of "Come ye Sinners, Poor and Needy."

Sir Walter Shirley, an English Knight and preacher, who died in 1796, composed the beautiful hymn, known as "Sweet the Moments, Rich in Blessing."

Dr. Timothy Dwight, one of the early presidents of Yale, wrote many ponderous and learned works on theology; but the reason why he will be longer remembered than many another theologian is that he was the author of, "I Love Thy Kingdom, Lord."

"Nearer, My God! to Thee" was composed by Sarah Fuller Flower. She married a civil engineer named Adams in 1834. She died in 1849 at the age of forty-four, and lies buried near Harlow, in Essex.

John Keble, the eminent English divine, wrote many learned volumes. He lives in the affections of his countrymen, however, as the author of "Sun of My Soul, Thou Saviour Dear."

"Just as I Am, Without One Plea" was written by Miss Charlotte Elliott, of Clapham, Eng. How she came to compose it was curious. A clergyman asked her one day if she were a Christian. She replied that she felt unworthy to approach the Lord. "But come just as you are," suggested the clergyman. The words touched her and she put them in the form by which they are known to Christians all over the world. Miss Elliott died in 1871.

"I would Not Live Alway" was written fifty years ago by Rev. Dr. Muhlenberg. It is a hymn which has comforted many mourners and given its author a lasting fame.

"Ninety and Nine," a hymn which was a great favorite with Moody and Sankey congregations, was written by Miss Elizabeth C. Clephane, a Scottish lady. Mr. Sankey supplied the music.

The "Lead, Kindly Light" of Dr. John Henry Newman (afterwards Cardinal Newman) was written during a voyage to England. This hymn is said to be a great favorite with Queen Victoria. It seems to be loved equally by all Christian sects.

The late Matthew Arnold severely criticised those hymns of a Salvation Army order in which, however commendable may have been the intention of the author, the language descends to a vulgar plane. "Bad music and bad poetry in the end are dangerous," said Mr. Arnold. Among hymns that have been degraded to common-place uses is the "Sweet By and By." Its history is a curious one:

Prof. Joseph P. Webster, the author of the music, was at times subject to deep melancholy. Entering his office one day in one of his blue fits his partner, Bennett, asked him:

"What is the matter now?"

"No matter," was the answer; "it will be all right in the sweet by and by."

"Sweet by and by!" echoed Bennett. "That's a good sentiment for a hymn. I'll try it."

He turned to his desk, wrote three stanzas rapidly, and handed them to Webster. The latter was surprised and moved. He immediately made a draft of a musical staff and began to fill it with notes.

"Bennett," he said, "I've set music to your words; come, let us sing it."

And in a few weeks, throughout the length and breadth of the country, old and young were singing "Sweet By and By."

GUESTS OF THE HEART.

Soft falls through the gathering twilight
The rain from the dripping eaves,
And stirs with a tremulous rustle
The dead and dying leaves;

While afar, in the midst of the shadows,
I hear the sweet voices of bells,
Come borne on the wind of Autumn,
That fitfully rises and swells.

They call and they answer each other,
They answer and mingle again,
As the deep and the shrill in an anthem
Make harmony still in their strain,
As the voices of sentinels mingle
In mountainous regions of snow,
Till from hill-top to hill-top a chorus
Floats down to the valleys below.

The shadows, the firelight of even.
The sound of the rain's distant chime
Come bringing, with rain softly dropping,
Sweet thoughts of a shadowy time;
The slumberous sense of seclusion
From storms and intruders aloof,
We feel when we hear in the midnight
The patter of rain on the roof.

When the spirit goes forth in its yearnings
To take all its wanderers home;
Or, afar in the regions of fancy,
Delights on swift pinions to roam,
I quietly sit by the firelight—
The firelight so bright and so warm—
For I know that those only who love me
Will seek me through shadow and storm.

But should they be absent this evening,
Should even the household depart,
Deserted, I should not be lonely,
There still would be guests in my heart
The faces of friends that I cherish,
The smile, and the glance, and the tone,
Will haunt me wherever I wander,
And thus I am never alone.

With those who have left behind them
The joys and sorrows of time—
Who sing the sweet songs of angels
In purer and holier clime!
Then darkly, O evening of Autumn,
Your rain and your shadows may fall;
My loved and my lost ones you bring me,
My heart holds a feast with them all.

A QUESTION.

WHICH will you do, smile and make others happy, or be crabbed and make everybody around you miserable ? You can live among flowers and singing birds, or in the mire surrounded by fogs and frogs. The amount of happiness which you can produce is incalculable, if you will only show a smiling face, a kind heart, and pleasant words. On the other hand, by sour looks, cross words and a fretful disposition, you can make others unhappy almost beyond endurance. Which will you do ? Wear a pleasant countenance ; let joy and love beam in your eye ? There is no joy so great as that which springs from a kind act or a pleasant deed ; and if you do a kind act during the day whereby some fellow mortal has been made happy, you will feel its glorious influence at night when you rest, and throughout the day when about your daily business.

A SERMON IN A PARAGRAPH.

PRESIDENT PORTER of Yale College gave the following advice the other day to the students : " Young men, you are the architects of your own fortunes. Rely on your own strength of body and soul. Take for your guiding star self-reliance. Inscribe on your banner ; " Luck is a fool ; Pluck is a hero." Don't take too much advice—keep at helm and steer your own ship, and remember that the great art of commanding is to take a fair share of the work. Think well of yourself. Strike out. Assume your own position. Put potatoes in a cart, over a rough road, and the small ones go to the bottom. Rise above the envious and jealous. Fire above the mark you intend to hit. Energy, invincible determination, with a right motive, are the levers that move the world. Don't drink. Don't chew. Don't smoke. Don't swear. Don't deceive. Don't read novels. Don't marry until you can support a wife. Be in earnest. Be self-reliant. Be generous. Be civil. Read the papers. Advertise your business. Make money and do good with it. Love your God and fellow-men. Love truth and virtue. Love your country and obey its laws."

GOOD-BYE.

IT is a hard word to speak. Some may laugh that it should be, but let them. Icy hearts are never kind. It is a word that has choked many an utterance, and started many a tear. The hand is clasped, the word is spoken, and we part and are out on the ocean of time—we go, to meet again, when ? God only knows. It may be soon, and it may be never ! Take care that your good-bye be not a cold one—it may be the last you can give, ere you meet again. Death's cold hands may have seized him and he died thinking you loved him not. Again, it may be a long separation. Friends crowd and give you their hands. How do you detect in each good-bye the love that lingers there ; and how may you bear with you the memory of those parting words many days ? We must often separate. Tear not yourself away with a careless boldness that defies all love, but make your words linger—give your heart full utterance—and if tears fall, what of it ? Tears are not unmanly.

LET BYGONES BE BYGONES.

LET bygones be bygones ; if bygones
    were clouded
By aught that occasioned a pang of
    regret,
Oh, let them in darkest oblivion be
    shrouded ;
'Tis wise and 'tis kind to forgive and
    forget.

Let bygones be bygones, and good be
    extracted
From ill over which it is folly to
    fret ;
The wisest of mortals have foolishly
    acted—
The kindest are those who forgive
    and forget.

Let bygones be bygones; oh, cherish no longer
  The thought that the sun of affection has set;
Eclipsed for a moment, its rays will be stronger,
  If you, like a Christian, forgive and forget.

Let bygones be bygones; your heart will be lighter
  When kindness of yours with reception has met;
The flame of your love will be purer and brighter
  If, Godlike, you strive to forgive and forget,

Let bygones be bygones; oh, purge out the leaven
  Of malice, and try an example to set
To others, who, craving the mercy of heaven,
  Are sadly too slow to forgive and forget.

Let bygones be bygones; remember how deeply
  To Heaven's forbearance we all are in debt;
They value God's infinite goodness too cheaply
  Who heed not the precept, "Forgive and forget."
    —CHAMBERS'S JOURNAL.

THE HEN-PECKED MAN.

Now, ain't there one o' human kind
  In all this glorious lan',
That's got a word of kindness for
      The
        Hen-
          Pecked
            Man?

From Adam to the present day,
  Without a break or span,
He's had to tread a thorny way—
      The
        Hen-
          Pecked
            Man.

He gets but little joy from life,
  For, do whate'er he can,
The world is always prone to guy
      The
        Hen-
          Pecked
            Man.

He needs a lot o' sympathy,
  So, take him by the han',
And speak a word of comfort to
      The
        Hen-
          Pecked
            Man.
              —ROBERT L. BLALOCK.

THE OTHER POINT OF VIEW.

THERE are many stories written of wives hungering for their husbands' love, and living and dying unsatisfied. We want a story which will represent the husband hungering for his wife's love, and living unsatisfied for want of it. It is not an uncommon experience.

Perhaps the wife is a professional reformer. She is so busy caring for the world that she has no time to care for her household. She expends all her love on Humanity, and has none left for her husband. She is a woman with a mission, and her own home is left a foreign missionary field for some one else to cultivate. Or she is devoted to society; receptions, visits, balls, at-homes, so absorb her that she is never at home to her husband and her children. She lives on admiration, not on love. Or she does not know the difference between a housekeeper and a homekeeper. The house is admirably kept. She is a good cook, an excellent housemaid,—but not a wife. She ministers to her husband's stomach and to his eye,—but never to his heart. She shrinks from a kiss which will disarrange her hair, or an embrace that threatens to disorder her dress. Or she is of Puritan temper and training. She loves, but she knows not how to say that she loves. She does not know how to say to him, I thank you, and quite unwittingly receives every caress and every courtesy which her husband's love pays to her, as though it were a debt overdue.

HAPPY HUSBAND.

IT is a man's own fault if he is unhappy with his wife, in nine cases out of ten.—The great men of this world have been wretched in their domestic relations, while common men have been exceedingly happy. Absorbed in themselves, those who desired the world's applause were careless of the little world at home ; while those who had none of this egotism strove to keep the hearts that were their own, and were happy in their tenderness. No woman will love a man the better for being renowned and prominent. Though he be first among men, she will be prouder, not fonder ; and if she loses him through his renown, as is often the case, she will not even be prouder. But give her love, appreciation, kindness,—and there is no sacrifice she would not make for his content and comfort. The man who loves her well is her hero and king. No less a hero to her, though he is not to any other ; no less a king, though his kingdom is her heart and home.
—BOSTON CULTIVATOR.

REST.

BY FATHER RYAN.

MY feet are wearied and my hands are tired,
    My soul oppressed ;
And with desire have I long desired
    Rest—only Rest.

'Tis hard to toil, when toil is almost vain,
    In barren ways ;
'Tis hard to sow and never garner grain
    In harvest days ;

The burden of my days is hard to bear,
    But God knows best,
And I have prayed but vain has been my prayer
    For Rest—sweet Rest.

'Tis hard to plant in Spring and never reap
    The Autumn yield ;
'Tis hard to till, and when 'tis tilled to weep
    O'er fruitless field.

And so I cry a weak and human cry,
    So heart-oppressed
And so I sigh a weak and human sigh,
    For Rest—for Rest.

My way has wound across the desert years,
    And cares infest
My path, and through the flowing of hot tears
    I pine for Rest.

'Twas always so ; when still a child I laid
    On mother's breast
My wearied little head, e'en then I prayed,
    As now, for Rest.

And I am restless still ; 'twill soon be o'er,
    For down the West
Life's sun is setting, and I see the shore
    Where I shall Rest.

ONE SAD DAY,

ONE sad day when the sun's gold crown
    Jeweled and splendored the dreamy west,
I came with a burden and laid it down—
    Under the lilies and leaves—to rest ;
And, weeping, I left it and went my way—twilight
With the whispering : " God knows best."

One sad day ! It was long ago,
    And thorny the paths that my feet have pressed,
Since with tears and kisses I laid it low—
    Soul of my soul and life of my breast !
And, kneeling now in the dark to pray,
    There comes with a voice from the sunless west,
The same sweet voice that I heard that day—
    The twilight whispering : " God knows best.' "

THE RUNAWAY BOY.

Wunst I sassed my pa, an' he
Won't stand that, an' he punished me—
Nen when he wuz gone that day,
I slipped out an' runned away.
I took all my copper cents,
An' climbed over our back fence
In the jimson weeds 'at growed
Ever'where all down the road.
Nen I got out there, an' nen
I runned some—an' runned again,
When I met a man 'at led
A big cow 'at shooked her head,
I went down a long, long lane,
Where wuz little pigs a-playin';
And a great big pig went " booh !"
An' jumped up, an' skeered me, too,
Nen I scampered past, an' they
Was somebody hollered " Hey !"
An' just looked ever'where,
An' they wuz nobody there.
I want to, but I'm afraid to try
To go back * * * An' by an' by
Somepin' hurts my th'oat inside—
An' I want my ma—an' cried.
Nen a grea' big girl come through
Where's a gate, an' telled me who
Am I ? an' ef I tell where
My home's at she'll show me there,
But I couldn't ist but tell
What's my name ; an' he says " Well,
An' ist tooked me up an' says
" She know where I live, she guess."
Nen she telled me hug wite close
Round her neck !—an' on she goes
Skippin' up the street ! An' nen
Purty soon I'm home again.
An' ma, when she kissed me,
Kissed the big girl, too, an' she
Kissed me—ef I p'omise shore
I won't run away no more !
—James Whitcomb Riley.

LET IT PASS.

Be not swift to take offence,
  Let it pass, let it pass ;
Anger is a foe to sense,
  Let it pass, let it pass.
Brood not darkly o'er the wrong,
Which will disappear ere long ;
Rather sing this cheery song,
  Let it pass, let it pass.

Swift corrodes the purest mind,
  Let it pass, let it pass,
As the unrecorded wind,
  Let it pass, let it pass.
All the vulgar souls that live
May condemn without reprieve,
'Tis the noble who forgive,
  Let it pass, let it pass.

If for good you've taken ill,
  Let it pass ; let it pass ;
Oh ! be kind and gentle still,
  Let it pass, let it pass.
Time at last makes all things right
Let us not resent, but wait,
And our triumph shall be great,
  Let it pass, let it pass.

COUNTING APPLE-SEEDS.

Beside the hearth one winter night
Made rosy by the great log's light,
That, flaming up the chimney dark,
Hit every cranny, every nook,
Upon the rug a little maid
Sat curled, in pose demure and staid.

In pensive mood, with dreamy eyes
She sits, while up the chimney flies
A thought with every fiery spark
Glinting and flashing through the dark,
Till with a sigh profound and deep
She moves, as one moves in her sleep.

A rosy apple in her hand
A weight of thought seems to demand.
She taps it with a finger light,
Then carefully she takes a bite.
Another bite, now one, now two—
The core is thus exposed to view.

Another sigh ! what can it be,
My little maid, what aileth thee ?
Ah ! what is this ? some incantation ?
Muttered with such reiteration ?
Hark ! as each seed her bright eyes see,
These are the words that come to me :

  " One I love, two I love,
      Three I love I say !
  Four I love with all my heart,
      Five—I cast away—"

Here a tear rolls brightly down,
What's the secret she has won ?

I once knew all the birds that came
And nestled in our orchard trees.

--Page 241.

Who can say! But just behind
Sounds a voice so soft and kind:
"Look again! Thou must indeed
Find for me another seed!"

Rosier her bright cheeks glow
In the firelight's ruddy glow.
Sure enough a culprit seed!
Finds she in the core indeed—
"From thy lips I fain would hear
What the sixth one means, my dear."

"Six he loves," she murmured low,
And the firelight's flickering glow
Two happy faces now disclose
With cheeks aglowing like the rose.
But here we'll let the curtain fall,
For the end is best of all.
   SACRAMENTO UNION.

SOME COMFORT.

WHEN the snow is on the garden,
 And the ice is on the walk,
And the monthly bill for fuel
 Brings about a painful shock,
There's a pleasing consolation,
 And we feel inclined to sing,
For it's cheering to remember
 That we're one day nearer Spring.

When we slip on icy pavement
 And go down with fearful crash,
Then arise in indignation,
 Using language that is rash,
It is soothing to remember
 Spring is coming on the hop,
With its mud to serve as cushion
 When the walker takes a drop.

When the mercury is tumbling
 And the northern breezes roar,
And we're howling at the scoundrel
 Who neglects to shut the door,
It is helpful to remember,
 Ere a chair at him we fling,
That the door he now leaves open
 He'll be closing in the Spring.

When before the fire we shiver,
 With a bad attack of chills,
And at intervals we're gulping
 Down a lot of quinine pills,
It's some comfort to remember,
 As we bolt the bitter stuff,
That the balmy Spring is coming
 And we'll soon be warm enough.

Yes, the gentle Spring is coming,
 With its flowers, birds, and bees,
With sweet odors of the blossoms
 Borne upon each passing breeze.
And though now the blasts of Winter
 Rush and roar and sharply sting,
It is cheering to remember
 That we're one day nearer Spring.
  —PITTSBURG CHRONICLE TELEGRAPH.

A RAILROADER'S PRAYER.

A RAILROAD man is responsible for the following prayer:

"O Lord, now that I have flagged thee, lift my feet from off the road of life and plant them safely on deck of the train of salvation! Let me use the safety lamp known as prudence, make all couplings in the train with the strong links of thy love and let my lamp be the Bible. And, Heavenly Father, keep all switches closed that lead off on the sidings, especially those with a blind end! O Lord, if it be thy pleasure, have every semaphore block along the line to show the white light of hope that I may make the run of life without stopping. And, Lord, give us the Ten Commandments as a schedule, and when I have finished the run, and have on schedule time pulled into the great station of death, may Thou, the Superintendent of the Universe, say with a smile: 'Well done, Thou good and faithful servant. Come and sign the pay roll and receive your check for eternal happiness.'"
  —REHOBOTH SUNDAY HERALD.

DREAMS OF THE ROYAL NOON.

I GAZE upon the river of my dream;
'Tis noon—and I am on the upland
 path,
Far in the temples of the russet dell
With unseen druids for sweet com-
 pany,
Shuddering anon as by a careless step,
I find my feet upon the yawning brink;
And far below the image of the pool,
Glassy, but that the last of autumn
 leaves
Have gathered thick upon its smiling
 brow.

There, in far reaches, see the glimmer-
    ing stream,
O golden mirror of my hopes and
    dreams !
Beyond, the hills, which in ascending
    scale
To mountains, grow in fearful terraces,
Till o'er all else in cold, majestic peaks
The giant monarch of the purple host
Rears his bare brow, while o'er the
    billowy plain
The glory of the last autumnal haze
Lies like a robe of airiest gossamer,
And there a pile of stately, rough-hewn
    stone,
Lost in the semi-darkness of the haze
Transfigured to the gaze, Aladdin's
    hall,
Or Kremlin seems, or Spain's Escurial.

A thousand things of minor relevance,
Like sparks too soon extinguished, fall
    beside
The pathway of my tense and prisoned
    gaze
Without a recognition—royal dream
Of noon in more than royal orient
    court,
Of noon upon the death-bed of the year.
Oh, leaves that soon go whirling in the
    gale,
Torn from the sweet companionship of
    limbs
That bore you long with all of mother's
    care,
Oh, waning days, oh, hills upon whose
    brow
The silver threads of Yule's untrodden
    snow
Shall shortly lie—oh, river of my dream,
Flash kind farewell athwart the noon-
    tide beam !
          —*Waverley Magazine.*

POETRY.—Poetry is the interpreter of the soul, and translates all thought into one language. While we eat the fruit of autumn, it reminds us of the blossoms of spring; and when we inhale the odorous breath of May, it foretells the frosts of December. It makes the marble of the sculptor breathe, the canvas of the painter speak, and the anvil of the artisan ring a chime. It is the handmaid of religion ; the rose in the wreath of the bride, and the chaplet of the dead ; the mirth and music of the marriage, and the awe and silence of the burial. It is the voice of peace, the song of love, and the sigh of sorrow. It sparkles in the smile of hope, and glitters in tears of regret. It is seen in the downcast eyes of modesty, or the ingenuous expression of manhood. It is heard in the shape of a dove, or felt in the down of a swan, it is the truly beautiful, and the beautiful truth.

RISE HIGHER.—When the birds are flying over, and the fowler lies in wait for them, if they fly low, at every discharge of the fowler's gun some fall, some are wounded, and some, swerving sideways plunge into the thicket and hide themselves. But you will find that immediately after the first discharge of the gun the flock rise and fly higher. And at the next discharge they rise and fly still higher. And not many times has the plunging shot thinned their number before they take so high a level that no longer the fowler aims at them because they are out of the reach of his shot. When troubles come upon you, fly higher, and if they strike you, fly still, And by and by you will rise so high in spiritual life, that your afflictions will be set on things so entirely above that these troubles shall not be able to touch you. So long as the shot strikes you, so long hear the word of God saying to you, " Rise higher."

THE AUTUMN OF LIFE.—It is the solemn thought connected with middle life that life's last business is begun in earnest, and it is then, midway between the cradle and the grave, that a man begins to marvel that he let the days of youth go by so half enjoyed. It is the positive autumn feeling, it is the sensation of half sadness that we experience when the longest day of the year is passed and every day that follows is shorter, and the light fainter and feebler ; shadows tell that Nature is hastening with gigantic footsteps to her winter grave. So does man look back upon his youth. When the first gray hairs become visible, when the unwelcome truth fastens itself upon the mind that a man is no longer going up hill, but down, and that the sun is always westering, he looks back on things behind. When we were children we thought as children. But now there lies before us manhood, with its earnest work, and then old age, and then the grave, and then Home. There is a second youth for man, better and holier than his first, if he will look on, and not look back.

MY FAVORITE PAPER.

There's a little country paper that I love to sit and read,—
A paper poorly printed and behind the times, indeed,
With pages small and narrow, and ink inclined to spread—
And here and there a letter gravely standing on its head.

Or caps, a bit erratic boldly popping into view—
In unexpected places, and knocking things askew.
A real old-fashioned paper, from my little native town ;
Each week I hail its coming, and I never put it down—

Till I've read its every column, all the local news, you know,
About the dear old country folks I lived with long ago.
I note whose barn is painted—whose cattle took the prize,
And how Uriah Potts has raised a squash of wondrous size.

How Farmer Martin's daughter takes the school another year—
At this I pause and smile a bit and feel a trifle queer,
Remembering how, in bygone days when life seemed made for mirth,
I thought this schoolma'am's mother was the sweetest girl on earth.

And now and then, perchance, I read that one I knew is dead,
Or find, again, some boyhood chum the second time has wed ;

And so it goes, and none can know what memories sad and sweet,
Come back to me whene'er I read this homely little sheet.

"THE RIDDLE OF THINGS THAT ARE."

We walk in a world where no man reads
The riddle of things that are—
From a tiny fern in the valley's heart
To the light of the largest star—
Yet we know that the pressure of Life is hard
And the silence of Death is deep,
As we fall and rise on the tangled way
That leads to the gate of Sleep.

We know that the problems of Sin and Pain,
And the passions that lead to crime,
Are the mysteries locked from age to age
In the awful vault of Time ;—
Yet we lift our weary feet and strive
Through the mire and mist to grope
And find a ledge on the mount of Faith
In the morning-land of Hope.
—Harper's Weekly.

THE DATE OF CHRISTMAS.

Those who do not lose sight of the religious aspect of Christmas may be interested to have the fact recalled that the 25th of December has not always been the day fixed as that upon which Christ was born. Before the fourth century many people believed that April 20 was the eventful day, others, May 20, and in Egypt the belief prevailed that it was January 6. The Greek Church for a long time had no settled feast, but merely commemorated the great event on the Epiphany. St. John Chrysostom, in a Christmas sermon, preached on December 25, 386, said that this day had not been clearly known to them longer than ten years, " but it has been familiar from the beginning to those who dwelt in the West." From this it appears evident

that December 25 was in the fourth century adopted by the Church in the East, in conformity with the traditional custom in Western Europe.
—LONDON CHRONICLE.

DON'T STAY LATE TO-NIGHT.

The hearth of home is beaming,
  With rays of rosy light;
And lovely eyes are gleaming,
  As falls the shades of night;
And while thy steps are leaving
  The circle pure and bright,
A tender voice half grieving
  Says, "Don't stay late to-night."

The world in which thou movest
  Is busy, brave and wide;
The world of her thou lovest
  Is at the ingle side;
She waits for thy warm greeting;
  Thy smile is her delight;
Her gentle voice entreating,
  Says, "Don't stay late to-night."

The world so cold, inhuman,
  Will spurn thee if thou fail;
The love of one poor woman
  Outlasts and shames them all;
Thy children will cling 'round thee,
  Let fate be dark or bright;
At home no shaft will wound thee,
  Then "Don't stay late to-night."

MY FRIEND.

Your letter, lady, came too late,
  For Heaven had claimed its own;
Ah! sudden change from prison bars
  Unto the great white throne!
And yet I think he might have stayed
  To live for his disdain,
Could he have read the careless words
  Which you have sent in vain.

So full of patience did he wait
  Through many a weary hour,
That o'er his simple soldier faith
  Not even death had power,
And you! did others whisper low
  Their homage in your ear,
As though amongst their shallow throng
  His spirit had a peer?

I would that you were by me now,
  To draw the sheet aside,
And see how pure the look he wore
  The moment when he died.
The sorrow that you gave to him
  Had left its weary trace
As 'twere the shadows of the cross
  Upon his pallid face.

"Her love," he said, could "change
  for me
The winter's cold to spring."
Ah, trust a fickle maiden's love,
  Thou art a bitter thing;
For when these valleys, bright in May,
  Once more with blossoms wave,
The Northern violets shall grow
  Above his lonely grave.

Your dole of scanty words had been
  But one more pang to bear,
For him who kissed unto the last
  Your tress of golden hair,
I did not put it where he said,
  For when the angels come
I would not have them find the sign
  Of falsehood in the tomb.

I've read your letter and I know,
  The wiles that you had wrought,
To win that noble heart of his
  And gained in—cruel thoughts!
What lavish wealth men sometime
  give
For what is worthless all;
What manly bosoms beat for truth
  In folly's falsest thrall.

You shall not pity him, for now
  His sorrow has an end;
Yet would that you could stand with
  me
Beside my fallen friend,
And I forgive you for his sake,
  And he—if it be given—
May e'en be pleading grace for you
  Before the court of heaven.

To-night the cold winds whistle by,
  As I my vigil keep
Within the prison dead-house, where
  Few mourners come to weep.
A rude plank coffin holds his form,
  But death exalts his face,
And I would rather see him thus
  Than clasped in your embrace.

To-night your home may shine with lights,
And ring with merry song,
And you be smiling as your soul
Had done no deadly wrong,
Your hand so fair, that none would think
It penned these words of pain,
Your skin so white—would God your heart
Were half so free from stain.

I'd rather be my comrade dead
Than you in life supreme,
For yours, the sinner's waking dead,
And his, the martyr's dream ;
Whom serve we in this life, we serve
In that which is to come,
He chose his way ; you yours ; let God
Pronounce the fitting doom !

HEAR BOTH SIDES.

YONDER speaker gains your ear !
He seems right, there's no denying ?
Yet my friend, before replying,
Hear both sides to make it clear.

Each one thinks his cause is just,
Be he titled lord or minion !
Prides himself on his opinion !
Takes his story first on trust.

"List ! a weeping wife has " wrongs "
Sad, indeed, seems her condition ;
Ere you favor her petition,
Find out where the blame belongs.

Hear both sides if you would save,
Wedded hearts in their probation,
Jealousy may have foundation
Cold and " cruel as the grave ! "

Judge no man by what you hear
From the tongues that dare assail him,
Power to contradict may fail him,
Or to save the name held dear.

As you meet the human tides,
Pause, my friend, ere you pass sentence
Lest, too late, you feel repentance,
In all cases hear both sides.

"CURFEW MUST NOT RING TO NIGHT,"

SLOWLY England's sun was setting, o'er the hill tops far away.
Filling all the land with beauty at the close of one sad day,
And the last rays kissed the forehead of a man and maiden fair,—
He with footsteps slow and weary, she with sunny floating hair,
He with bowed head, sad and thoughtful, she with lips all cold and white,
Struggled to keep back the murmur,—
" Curfew must not ring to-night."

" Sexton," Bessie's white lips faltered, pointing to the prison old,
With its turrets tall and gloomy, with its wall dark, damp and cold,
" I've a lover in that prison, doomed this night to die,
At the ringing of the curfew, and no earthly help is nigh,
Cromwell will not come till sunset," and her lips grew strangely white
As she breathed the husky whisper,—
" Curfew must not ring to-night."

" Bessie," calmly spoke the sexton, every word pierced her young heart
Like the piercing of an arrow, like a deadly, poisoned dart,
" Long, long years I've rung the curfew from that gloomy, shadowed tower ;
Every evening, just at sunset, it has told the twilight hour ;
I have done my duty ever, tried to do it just and right,
Now I'm old I still must do it,
Curfew it must ring to-night."

Wild her cries and pale her features, stern and white her thoughtful brow,
And within her sacred bosom, Bessie made a solemn vow.
She had listened while the judges read without a tear or sigh,
" At the ring of the curfew, Basil Underwood must die."

And her breath came fast and faster, and
   her eyes grew large and bright—
In an undertone she murmured—
   "Curfew must not ring to-night."

She with quick steps bounded forward,
   sprang within the old church
   door,
Left the old man treading softly paths
   so oft he'd trod before ;
Not one moment paused the maiden,
   but with eyes and cheek aglow,
Mounted up the gloomy tower where the
   bell swang to and fro,
And she climbed the dusty ladder on
   which fell no ray of light,
Up and up—her white lips saying—
   "Curfew shall not ring to-night."

She has reached the topmost ladder, o'er
   her hangs the great dark bell ;
Awful is the gloom beneath her, like a
   pathway down to hell.
Lo, the ponderous tongue is swinging,
   'tis the hour of curfew now,
And the sight has chilled her bosom,
   stopped her breath and paled her
   brow.
Shall she let it ring ? No, never. Flash
   her eyes with sudden light,
And she springs and grasps it firmly—
   "Curfew shall not ring to-night."

Out she swung, the city seemed a speck
   of light below,
'Twixt heaven and earth her form sus-
   pended, as the bell swung to and
   fro,
And the sexton, at the bell-rope, old and
   deaf, heard not the bell,
But he thought it still was ringing fair
   young Basil's funeral knell.
Still the maiden clung most firmly, and
   with trembling lips and white,
Said to stop her heart's wild beating,—
   Curfew shall not ring to-night."

It was o'er, the bell ceased swaying, and
   the maiden stepped once more
Firmly on the dark old ladder, where
   for hundred years before,
Human foot had not been planted. The
   brave deed that she had done

Should illumine the sky with beauty ;
   aged sires with heads of white,
Long should tell the little children,
   Curfew did not ring that night.

O'er the distant hills came Cromwell ;
   Bessie sees him, and her brow,
Full of hope and full of gladness, shows
   her anxious traces now.
At his feet she tells her story, shows her
   hands all bruised and torn ;
And her face so sweet and pleading, yet
   with sorrow pale and worn,
Touched his heart with sudden pity, lit
   his eye with misty light ;
"Go, your lover lives," said Cromwell.
   " Curfew shall not ring to-night."

LOCKE ON HUMAN PLEASURES.

THUS I think :—It is a man's proper business to seek happiness and avoid misery. Happiness consists in what delights and contents the mind ; misery in what disturbs, discomposes, or torments it. I will therefore make it my business to seek satisfaction and delight, and avoid uneasiness and disquiet ; to have as much of the one, and as little of the other, as may be. But here I must have a care I mistake not, for if I prefer a short pleasure to a lasting one, it is plain I cross my own happiness. Let me then see wherein consists the most lasting pleasures of this life, and that, as far as I can observe, is in these things : 1st. Health, without which no sensual pleasure can have any relish. 2d. Reputation—for that I find everybody is pleased with, and the want of it is a constant torment. 3d. Knowledge—for the little knowledge I have I find I would not sell at any rate nor part with for any other pleasure. 4th. Doing good—for I find the well-cooked meat I eat to-day does now no more delight me any. I am diseased after a full meal ; the perfumes I smelt yesterday now no more affect me with any pleasure ; but the good turn I did yesterday, a year, seven years since, continues still to please and delight me as often as I reflect on it. 5th. The expectation of eternal and incomprehensible happiness in another world is that also which carries a constant pleasure

with it. If then I will faithfully pursue that happiness I propose to myself, whatever pleasure offers itself to me, I must carefully look that it cross not any of those five great and constant pleasures above mentioned. For example, the fruit I see tempts me with the taste of it that I love, but if it endanger my health, I part with a constant and lasting for a very short and transient pleasure, and so foolishly make myself unhappy, and am not true to my own interest. Hunting, plays, and other innocent diversions delight me; if I make use of them to refresh myself after study and business, they preserve my health, restore the vigor of my mind, and increase my pleasure; but if I spend all, or the greatest part of my time in them, they hinder my improvement in knowledge and useful arts, they blast my credit, and give me up to the uneasy state of shame, ignorance, and contempt, in which I cannot but be very unhappy. Drinking, gaming, and vicious delights will do me this mischief not only by wasting my time, but by a positive efficacy endanger my health, impair my parts, imprint ill habits, lessen my esteem, and leave a constant lasting torment on my conscience. Therefore all vicious and unlawful pleasures I will always avoid, because such a mastery of my passions will afford me a constant pleasure greater than any such enjoyments; and also deliver me from the certain evil of several kinds, that by indulging myself in a present temptation I shall certainly afterward suffer. All innocent diversions and delights, as far as they will contribute to my health, and consist with my improvement, condition, and my other more solid pleasures of knowledge and reputation, I will enjoy, but no further, and this I will certainly watch and examine, that I may not be deceived by the flattery of a present pleasure to lose a greater.
—Fox Bourne's Life of John Locke.

PADDLE YOUR OWN CANOE.

I have travelled about a bit in my time,
   And of troubles I've seen a few,
But found it better in every clime
   To paddle my own canoe.
My wants are small, I care not at all
   If my debts are paid when due ;
I drive away strife, in the ocean of life,
   While I paddle my own canoe.

Chorus.—Then love your neighbor as yourself,
   As the world you go travelling through,
And never sit down, with a tear or a frown,
   But paddle your own canoe.

I have no wife to bother my life,
   No lover to prove untrue ;
But the whole day long, with a laugh and a song,
   I paddle my own canoe.
I rise with the lark, and from daylight till dark,
   I do what I have to do,
I'm careless of wealth, if I've only the health
   To paddle my own canoe.
        Then love your, etc.

It's all very well to depend on a friend
   That is, if you've proved him true ;
But you'll find it better by far, in the end,
   To paddle your own canoe.
To borrow is dearer by far than to buy,
   A maxim though old, still true ;
You never will sigh, if you only will try
   To paddle your own canoe.
        Then love your, etc.

If a hurricane rise in the midday skies,
   And the sun is lost to view,
Move steadily by, with a steadfast eye,
   And paddle your own canoe.
The daisies that grow in the bright green fields,
Are blooming so sweet for you ;
So never sit down, with a tear or a frown,
   But paddle your own canoe.
        Then love your, etc.

WOMAN'S LOVE.

Oh, woman's love is a holy light,
And when 'tis kindled ne'er can die,
It lives—though treachery and slight
To quench the constant flame may try.

Like ivy, where it grows, 'tis seen
To wear an everlasting green;
Like ivy, too, 'tis found to cling
Too often round a worthless thing.

Oh, woman's love—at times it may
Seem cold or clouded, but it burns
With true, undeviating ray,
Nor ever from its idol turns.

Its sweetest place on which to rest,
A constant and confiding breast,
Its joy to meet—its death to part—
Its sepulchre—a broken heart.

A BEAUTIFUL IDEA.

It cannot be that this earth is man's only abiding place; it cannot be that our life is a bubble, cast upon the ocean of eternity to float for a moment on its waves, then sink into nothingness. Else why is it that the glorious aspirations which leap like angels from the temple of our hearts are forever wandering about unsatisfied? Why is it that the rainbow and the cloud come over us with a beauty that is not of earth, and then pass off and leave us to muse upon their faded loveliness? Why is it that the stars which hold their festivals around the midnight throne, are set so far above the grasp of our limited faculties, forever mocking us with their unapproachable glory? And finally, why is it that the bright forms of human beauty are presented to our view but for a moment and then taken from us, leaving the thousand streams of our affections to flow back in Alpine torrents upon our hearts? We are born for a higher destiny than that of death; there is a realm where the rainbow never fades—where the stars will be spread out before us like the islands that slumber on the ocean, and where the beautiful beings that here pass before us like shadows, will stay in our presence forever.

TWO MOTHERS.

Two mothers wept one, fair and young,
  With tender longing fondly clung
Unto the little form just hid
  Beneath the tiny coffin lid.

The other woman, old and gray,
With stricken heart for feet astray,
Sobbed in her grief: "O God! had he,
When but a baby, gone to Thee!"
—Kathleen Kavanagh.

AUTUMN LEAVES.

Shadowed with russet and gleaming
    with gold,
  Brightened with crimsoned array;
Loos'ed at the west wind's softest touch
  The leaves are floating away,—
    Beautiful leaves!
    Nature grieves
Through days that are cold and gray.

Falling in sunshine, falling in shadow,
  Rustling in twilights dim;
Seeking a grave 'mongst the low, green
    grasses
  To a murmurous requiem,—
    To the cricket's plaint,
    In the grasses faint,
Lone notes of nature's hymn.

Knee deep do they lie in the hollows,
  They whirl through the open glade
Like partridges startled from feeding,
  To settle again in the shade.
    Drifting leaves,
    Dying leaves,
That the wild winds have betrayed.

Already their beauty is fading fast,
  Their colors to russet turn,
No longer with brilliance of raiment
  In crimson and and gold they burn;
    Buried leaves,
    Forgotten leaves,
Sleep 'neath the bramble and fern!
—F. Hamilton.

THE SOMETIME LAND.

We say, when we sigh and our hearts
    grow sad,
  That sometime the sky will show
    after rain;
We hope, when we lose those who make
    life glad,
  To sometime gaze on their faces
    again.

Our cross may cause us to swoon by the way,
But sometime the burden will surely fall;
And sometime, sometime, and sometime, we may
See the infinite love of God in all.

Ah, Sometime Land! lying ever beyond
The now with its tortures and trials sore!
We note thee from Nebo with glances fond
As the old seer cast toward Canaan's shore.
And e'en though our steps may never be heard
With the footfalls of angels along thy strand—
Still waft us the song of the sometime bird!
Aye shine and encourage us, Sometime Land.
—WILL T. HALE.

THE FLOOD OF YEARS.

A MIGHTY Hand, from an exhaustless urn,
Pours forth the never-ending Flood of Years
Among the nations. How the rushing waves
Bear all before them! On their foremost edge,
And there alone, is Life; the Present there
Tosses and foams and fills the air with roar
Of mingled noises. There are they who toil,
And they who strive, and they who feast, and they
Who hurry to and fro. The sturdy hind—
Woodman and delver with the spade—are there,
And busy artisan beside his bench,
And pallid student with his written roll,
A moment on the mounting billow seen—
The flood sweeps over them and they are gone.
There groups of revellers, whose brows are twined
With roses, ride the topmost swell awhile,
And as they raise their flowing cups to touch
The clinking brim to brim, are whirled beneath
The waves and disappear. I hear the jar
Of beaten drums, and thunders that break forth
From cannon, where the advancing billow sends
Up to the sight long files of armèd men,
That hurry to the charge through flame and smoke.
The torrent bears them under, whelmed and hid,
Slayer and slain, in heaps of bloody foam.
Down go the steed and rider; the plumed chief
Sinks with his followers: the head that wears
The imperial diadem goes down beside
The felon's with cropped ear and branded cheek.
A funeral train—the torrent sweeps away
Bearers and bier and mourners. By the bed
Of one who dies men gather sorrowing,
And women weep aloud! the flood rolls on;
The wail is stifled, and the sobbing group
Borne under. Hark to that shrill sudden shout—
The cry of an applauding multitude
Swayed by some loud-tongued orator who wields
The living mass as if he were its soul.
The waters choke the shout and all is still.
Lo, next, a kneeling crowd and one who spreads
The hands in prayer; the engulfing wave o'ertakes
And swallows them and him. A sculptor wields
The chisel, and the stricken marble grows
To beauty; at his easel, eager-eyed,

A painter stands, and sunshine, at his touch,
Gathers upon the canvas, and life glows;
A poet, as he paces to and fro,
Murmurs his sounding lines. Awhile they ride
The advancing billow, till its tossing crest
Strikes them and flings them under while their tasks
Are yet unfinished. See a mother smile
On her young babe that smiles to her again—
The torrent wrests it from her arms; she shrieks,
And weeps, and midst her tears is carried down.
A beam like that of moonlight turns the spray
To glistening pearls; two lovers, hand in hand,
Rise on the billowy swell and fondly look
Into each other's eyes. The rushing flood
Flings them apart; the youth goes down; the maid,
With hands outstretched in vain and streaming eyes,
Waits for the next high wave to follow him.
An aged man succeeds; his bending form
Sinks slowly; mingling with the sullen stream
Gleam the white locks and then are seen no more.
Lo, wider grows the stream; a sea-like flood
Saps earth's walled cities; massive palaces
Crumble before it; fortresses and towers
Dissolve in the swift waters; populous realms
Swept by the torrent, see their ancient tribes
Engulfed and lost, their very languages
Stifled and never to be uttered more.
  I pause and turn my eyes and, looking back,
Where that tumultuous flood has passed, I see
The silent Ocean of the Past, a waste
Of waters weltering over graves, its shores
Strewn with the wreck of fleets, where mast and hull
Drop away piecemeal; battlemented walls
Frown idly, green with moss, and temples stand
Unroofed, forsaken by the worshippers.
There lie memorial stones, whence time has gnawed
The graven legends, thrones of kings o'erturned,
The broken altars of forgotten gods,
Foundations of old cities and long streets
Where never fall of human foot is heard
Upon the desolate pavement. I behold
Dim glimmerings of lost jewels far within
The sleeping waters, diamond, sardonyx,
Ruby and topaz, pearl and chrysolite,
Once glittering at the banquet on fair brows
That long ago were dust; and all around,
Strown on the waters of that silent sea,
Are withering bridal wreaths, and glossy locks
Shorn from fair brows by loving hands, and scrolls
O'erwritten—haply with fond words of love
And vows of friendship—and fair pages flung
Fresh from the printer's engine. There they lie
A moment and then sink away from sight.
  I look, and the quick tears are in my eyes,
For I behold, in every one of these,
A blighted hope, a separate history
Of human sorrow, telling of dear ties
Suddenly broken, dreams of happiness
Dissolved in air, and happy days, too brief,
That sorrowfully ended, and I think
How painfully must the poor hearts have beat
In bosoms without number, as the blow
Was struck that slew their hope or broke their peace.

Sadly I turn, and look before, where yet
The flood must pass, and I behold a mist
Where swarm dissolving forms, the brood of Hope,
Divinely fair, that rest on banks of flowers
Or wander among rainbows, fading soon
And reappearing, haply giving place
To shapes of grisly aspect, such as Fear
Molds from the idle air; where serpents lift
The head to strike, and skeletons stretch forth
The bony arm in menace. Further on
A belt of darkness seems to bar the way,
Long, low and distant, where the Life that is
Touches the Life to Come. The Flood of Years
Rolls toward it, near and nearer. It must pass.
That dismal barrier. What is there beyond?
Hear what the wise and good have said. Beyond
That belt of darkness still the years roll on
More gently, but with not less mighty sweep.
They gather up again and softly bear
All the sweet lives that late were overwhelmed
And lost to sight—all that in them was good,
Noble, and truly great and worthy of love—
The lives of infants and ingenuous youths,
Sages and saintly women who have made
Their households happy—all are raised and borne
By that great current in its onward sweep,
Wandering and rippling with caressing waves
Around green islands, fragrant with the breath
Of flowers that never wither. So they pass,
From stage to stage, along the shining course
Of that fair river broadening like a sea.
As its smooth eddies curl along their way,
They bring old friends together; hands are clasped
In joy unspeakable; the mother's arms
Again are folded round the child she loved
And lost. Old sorrows are forgotten now,
Or but remembered to make sweet the hour
That overpays them; wounded hearts that bled
Or broke are healed forever. In the room
Of this grief-shadowed Present there shall be
A Present in whose reign no grief shall gnaw
The heart, and never shall a tender tie
Be broken—in whose reign the eternal Change
That waits on growth and action shall proceed
With everlasting Concord hand in hand.
—WILLIAM CULLEN BRYANT.

RISING IN THE WORLD.

EXPERIENCE continually contradicts the notion that a poor young man cannot rise. If we look over the list of rich men, we find that nearly all of them began life worth little or nothing. To any person familiar with the millionaires of the United States, a score of examples will occur. On the other hand, the sons of rich men, who began life with the capital which so many poor young men covet, frequently die beggars. It would probably not be going too far to say that a large majority of such moneyed individuals either fail outright or gradually eat up the capital with which they commence their career.

And the reason is plain. Brought up in expensive habits, they spend entirely too much. Educated with high notions of personal importance, they will not, as they phrase it, stoop to hard work. Is it astonishing, therefore, that they are passed in the race of life by others with less capital originally, but more energy thrift and industry? For these virtues, after all, are worth more than money, They make money, in fact. Nay, after it is made, they enable the possessor to keep it, which most rich men pronounce to be more difficult than the making. The young man who begins life with a resolution always to lay by part of his income is sure, even without extraordinary ability, gradually to acquire a sufficiency, especially as habits of economy, which the resolution renders necessary, will make that a competence for him which would be quite insufficient for an extravagant person. It is really what we save, more than what we make, which leads us to fortune. He who enlarges his expenses as fast as his earnings increase must always be poor, no matter what his abilities. And content may be had on comparatively little. It is not in luxurious living that men find real happiness.

FLOWERS THAT NEVER WITHER.

There are flowers that never wither,
   There are skies that never fade,
There are trees that cast forever
   Cooling bowers of leafy shade.
There are silver wavelets flowing
   With a lulling sound of rest,
Where the west wind, softly blowing,
   Fans the far lands of the blest.

Thitherward our steps are tending,
   Oft through dim, oppressive fears,
More of grief than pleasure blending
   In the darkening woof of years.
Often would our footsteps weary,
   Sink upon the winding way,
But that when all looks most dreary,
   O'er us beams a cheering ray.

Thus the Father who hath made us
   Tenants of this world of care
Knoweth how to kindly aid us
   With the burdens we must bear;
Knoweth how to cause the spirit
   Hopefully to raise its eyes
Toward the home it doth inherit
   Far beyond the azure skies.

There is a voice that whispers lowly
   Down within this heart of mine,
Where emotions the most holy
   Ever make their sacred shrine,
And it tells a thrilling story
   Of the great Redeemer's love,
And the all-bewildering glory
   Of the better land above.

Oh, this life, with all its sorrows,
   Hasteth onward to a close!
In a few more brief to-morrows
   Will have ended all our woes.
Then o'er death the part immortal
   Shall sublimely rise and soar,
O'er the star-resplendent portal,
   There to dwell forevermore.

TURNING GRAY.

Life's sands are running fast away,
   The buoyant step of youth has gone,
The falling hair is turning gray,
   And time seems now to hurry on
More fleetly than in days of yore,
   Before the heart became its prey,
Before 'twas saddened to the core,
   Before the hair was turning gray.

Yes, turning gray! age comes like snow,
   As still, and carves each careworn line;
Its wrinkles on the brow will grow,
   The hair with silvery streaks will shine,
The eyes their brightness lose, the hand
   Grow dry and tremulous and thin;
For life, alas! is quickly spanned,
   And death its gates soon closes in!

Ah, turning gray! we fain would hide
   This sign how long with time we've been;
These deepened wrinkles side by side
   Cut by the sorrows we have seen.
For feeble beats the heart as years
   More thickly cluster on our head,
As autumn raindrops hang like tears,
   On some fair flower that's nearly dead!

Like perished petals from the flower
   Our hopes and wildest joys are laid,
Born only for a day or hour,
   Sweet gambols by the fancy played.

As age comes on, we long for rest,
As saints near shrines will long to pray;
But still! we love that time the best,
Before the hair was turning gray!

BOYS, WAKE UP!

Boys, wake up! Don't sit dozing as though the world was just made to sleep in. Don't imagine somebody is going to clothe and feed you while you do nothing but read love stories. Have more ambition than to part your hair in the middle, carry a cane, wear fine boots, and flourish a cigar. Don't belittle yourselves by using tobacco in any form. It will make you filthy, create an appetite for liquor, and make you old and nervous.

Wake up! Try to be somebody. Try to do something. Try to be noble, honest and industrious. By being somebody, we do not mean simply being rich, or just like the rest of the boys. Step out boldly into new paths that other boys are too indolent and timid to try. In doing this you may not be like Ned, who uses oaths; or Fred, who plays cards; or Tom, who calls his father "the old man," and his mother "the old woman"; or like scores of other boys, who do about the same way for fear the rest will laugh at them.

To do something is to shovel coal or run errands; indeed anything that is right, rather than lounge on hotel steps or hang around saloons. If you would rather tell a little falsehood, or smoke or drink, than to be seen in plain clothes, coarse boots, and at work—you are nobody.

Truth, temperance and good deeds make men; clothes have nothing to do with it. If the lads you associate with talk sneeringly of their mothers and sisters, avoid them as you would deadly poison. The influence of low, vulgar language may lead you to infamy. Be pure. O, how pleasant it is to look into the face of a lad who is chaste and virtuous! Take care of your bodies; do not abuse them. Keep them sacredly pure, clean and wholesome.

Don't think that because you are only a lad it will not make any difference if you do just as you please. Don't think that God cares very little about you, when the most trifling act you may do is held in His everlasting remembrance. He says: "Even a child is known by his doings, whether his works be pure or whether they be right.". Just think of that! Oh how good, and right, and pure then, ought every child to be, because for such God is fitting up a beautiful mansion in glory!

Keep doing, always doing—remembering that wishing, dreaming, intending, murmuring, talking, sighing, and repining are all idle and profitless employments.

"LIGHT AT EVENING TIME."

'Tis evening time. The shadows gathering fast
Around my footsteps, as they onward move,
Admonish me life's day is nearly past.
But, lo! I see light shining from above!

They say I'm growing old. 'Tis true, I know—
For I have numbered over threescore years—
How blest!—My heavenward pathway brightens so,
And not a shade of darkening gloom appears!

'Tis evening time, indeed! and soon I'll rest—
And yet it seems but yesterday begun
My life's bright morning—now, far in the west—
So rapidly declines my cloudless sun!

Yes, cloudless! Thanks to God! All bright and clear:
And even in death's valley light doth shine!
With Jesus by my side I cannot fear,
Encircled by the loving arms divine.

I've looked within the vale, and even when
Upon the brink of its dark shadow's gloom,
Stood face to face with death—victorious then—
Exulting o'er the monster and the tomb.

Oh, hallelujah to the blessed Lamb!—
Death's wondrous Conqueror!—My soul adore
In ceaseless praises His all-glorious name,
Through life, in death, in Heaven, forevermore.
— MARY D. JAMES,
in Christian Woman.

HOPE.

HOPE! sweetest messenger of Heaven,
To animate our drooping soul,
Blest boon to rebel nature given
To soothe, sustain and make us whole.

How dark would be the brightest sky
That ever smiled o'er all the world,
How pale the rosebud's richest dye,
If Hope were from our bosoms hurled.

Without its warm benignant beams,
To raise our dark, despairing hearts,
How soon would life's bright purling streams
Congeal before Death's icy dart.
— BIRDIE.

TWENTY YEARS AGO.

I HAVE wandered by the village, Tom
—I've sat beneath the tree,
Upon the school-house playing-ground, which sheltered you and me;
But none are left to greet me, Tom, and few are left to know
That played with us upon the green just Twenty Years Ago.
The grass is just as green, dear Tom; bare-footed boys at play
Are sporting just as we were then, with spirits just as gay;

But master sleeps upon the hill, all coated o'er with snow,
That afforded us a sliding place just Twenty Years Ago.

The old school-house is altered some, the benches are replaced
By new ones, very like the same our pen-knives had defaced;
But the same old bricks are in the wall, the bell swings to and fro,
The music just the same, dear Tom, 'twas Twenty Years Ago.
The river is running just as still—the willows on its side
Are larger than they were, dear Tom, the stream appears less wide;
The grape-vine swing is ruined now, where once we played the beau,
And swung our sweethearts, pretty girls, just Twenty Years Ago.

The spring that bubbled 'neath the hill, close by the spreading beech,
Is very high—'twas once so low that we could almost reach;
But in kneeling down to get a drink, dear Tom, I started so
To see how sadly I am changed since Twenty Years Ago.
Down by the spring, upon an elm, you know I cut your name—
Your sweetheart's just beneath it, Tom, and you did mine the same:
Some heartless wretch has peeled the bark—'twas dying sure but slow,
Just as the one whose name you cut, died Twenty Years Ago.

My lids have long been dry, dear Tom, but tears come in my eyes;
I thought of her I loved so well—those early broken ties;
I visited the old churchyard and took some flowers to strew
Upon the graves of those we loved some Twenty Years Ago.
Some are in the churchyard laid, some sleep beneath the sea;
But few are left of our old class, excepting you and me;
But when our time shall come, dear Tom, and we are called to go,
I hope they'll lay us where we played just Twenty Years Ago.

MY MOTHER, TOO, GROWS OLD.

WHILE sitting by my father's side,
  Whose days are almost told,
Another aged form is there—
  My mother, too, grows old.
She toiled with him life's sunny glades,
  Life's sultry noon away;
She's resting now in life's cool shades,
  The shades of evening day.

Chorus—Upon Eternity's dread shore
    I see death's angel stay,
  And which I scarcely dare to
      think
    He first will call away.

The warm affections of her heart,
  With time nor age grow cold;
Her eye such love-light still imparts,
  I scarce can think her old,
But when beneath her cap of snow
  Some whitened locks unfold,
And as I watch her steps, I know
  My mother, too, grows old.

Chorus—Upon Eternity's, etc.

Engraven on her furrowed brow,
  The peace of God I see;
His peace has kept her heart till now
  From grief and sorrow free;
They've weather'd all the storms of life,
  Together sailed life's sea,
And calmly may their ships now sail
  To the haven where they'd be.

Chorus—Upon Eternity's, etc.

LAST ROSE OF SUMMER.

'TIS the last rose of summer,
  Left blooming alone,
All her lovely companions
  Are faded and gone;
No flower of her kindred,
  No rosebud is nigh
To reflect back her blushes,
  Or give sigh for sigh.

I'll not leave thee, thou lone one,
  To pine on the stem,
Since the lovely are sleeping,
  Go, sleep thou with them;

Thus kindly I scatter
  Thy leaves o'er the bed,
Where thy mates of the garden
  Lie scentless and dead.

So soon may I follow,
  When friendships decay,
And from love's shining circle
  The gems drop away;
When true hearts lie wither'd
  And fond ones are flown,
Oh, who could inhabit
  This bleak world alone?
      —MOORE.

THE SCHOOLHOUSE.

YES, John, our district well may brag
  On this new schoolhouse. I brag
      too.
I'm for improvement. I don't lag
  Behind when things want putting
      through.

But that old, battered, wooden shell
  That stood on this spot fifty year,—
I'd learned to know its face so well
  That somehow—John, it's mighty
      queer.

But when you pulled the old house
      down,—
  The time this new one was begun,—
I had to go to lower town;
  I couldn't stand to see it done.

For there I studied A, B, C,
  Got licked and learned, by hook and
      crook,
To read about the apple-tree
  In Webster's old blue spelling-book.

And, where that church stands, many a
      morn
  ('Twas a field then)—a love-sick fool,
I stood behind a shock of corn
  To see the schoolma'am come to
      school,

Her cheeks, as she the cornfield crossed,
  Were redder than the scrub-oak
      leaves;
Her eyes were brighter than the frost
  That sparkled on the tasseled sheaves.

And in among the noisy throng
  Of barefoot youngsters she would
    go,—
And, as I watched her, I allowed
  It wasn't strange they loved her so.

But when just at the schoolhouse door,
  Each urchin claimed his kiss, ah!
    then
I longed to go barefoot once more,
  And read the spelling book again.

Sweet Lucy! How came it to pass
  I can't explain,—but any way,
I might as well have joined a class,
  For I hung round there half the day.

At noon I'd take her nuts, a pear,
  Or apples,—my best grafted fruit,—
To trade for smiles; she traded fair,
  And gave me many thanks to boot.

And sometimes, after study hours,
  When Lucy led her merry throng
Into the woods for late wildflowers
  And autumn leaves, I'd go along.

She had some dozen boys, half grown,
  That loved her well. They shamed
    me though,
For I loved too, and I alone
  Had not the pluck to tell her so.

"You happy boys!" I thought, "you
    swap
  Wildflowers for kisses from her lips;
I'd harvest the whole flower crop
  To kiss her very finger-tips."

But winter came, and when the ground
  And the big hills with snow were
    white,
I'd hitch my colt up and go round
To take her home from school at night,

One frosty evening, riding slow
  Through Johnson's woods, her rosy
    cheek
Lay close to mine and thrilled me so
That I determined I would speak.

"Lucy!" I said, "dear Lucy!"—
    Here
Her eyes met mine and flustered me,
  As awkward as a yearling steer
I backed and tried again. "You see,

I want to ask you "—a big lump
Came in my throat—"Whoa, Bill, you
    fool!
That's nothing but a hemlock stump!
  If—if you love—the boys in school."

"Twan't what I meant; but, anyway,
  She dropped her eyes, and I could
    see
She guessed what I had tried to say,
  She said, "Of course. They all love
    me."

Boldened by this, her hand I pressed
  And cried, "Dear Lucy, couldn't
    you
Love me a little with the rest?
  For I—I love the schoolma'am too;

See, yonder comes my schoolma'am
    wife;
Her cheeks are fresh and rosy yet;
And, for our happy married life,
  We bless this spot where we first
    met

THE FALL O' THE YEAR.

OH! the elms are yellow,
The apples are mellow,
  The corn is ripe in the ear;
The birds leave off nesting,
The earth begins resting,
  Because 'tis the Fall o' the year.

The crickets are calling,
The red leaves are falling
  In the fields the stubble is sere;
The day of the clover
And wild bee is over,
  Because 'tis the Fall o' the year.

Since Summer is flitting,
Dear friend, it is fitting
  The heart should make double
    cheer;
So let us go smiling,
With love, life beguiling,
  Because 'tis the Fall of the year.
    —Mrs. M. F. Butts.

A BEAUTIFUL EXTRACT.

I SAW a temple reared by the hand of man, standing with its high pinnacles in the distant plain. The streams beat upon it—the God of Nature hurried His thunderbolts against it—and yet it stood as firm as adamant. Revelry was within its halls, the gay, the happy and the beautiful were there. I returned, and the temple was no more; its high walls lay scattered in ruins; moss and wild grass grew there. The young and the gay that revelled there had passed away.

I saw a child rejoicing in his youth—the idol of his mother, the pride of his father. I returned; the child had become old—trembling with the weight of years, he stood the last of his generation—a stranger amidst the desolation around him.

I saw an old oak standing in all its pride on the mountains—the birds were carolling on its boughs. I returned; the oak was leafless and sapless, the winds were playing at their pastime through its branches.

"Who is the destroyer?" said I to my guardian angel.

"It is Time," said he. "When the morning stars sang together in joy over the new made world, he commenced his course. And when he shall have destroyed all that is beautiful of the earth—plucked the sun from his sphere, veiled the moon in blood; yea, when he shall have rolled heaven and earth away as a scroll; then shall an angel from the throne of God come forth, and with one foot on the sea and the other on the land, lift up his hand towards Heaven eternal, and say, Time is, Time was, but Time shall be no more!"

LOOKING FORWARD.

WHY turn, faint spirit, to the vanished past?
Why grieve that some vain longing might have been?
Why brood o'er broken hours no longer thine,
Or sigh for conquests thou may'st never win?
Leave the poor faded hope and trust long dead,
And nurse the heart's unfolding bloom instead.

Fling your misgivings to the idle wind!
Fruition is the patient soul's reward—
Thy path through trouble to the good man's goal
Let not these petty weaknesses retard—
Tread with unfaltering step the rugged way
That leads this trial to the perfect day!

Press not thy bosom, like the imprisoned bird,
In sad repinings 'gainst the bars of fate;
What though the skies are sometimes hung in cloud,
Deem not, therefore, thy whole life desolate;
Make thy own destiny, though dangers throng—
Fearless advance, with every step grow strong!

Turn not thy mind's eye inward, where a waste
Spreads 'neath the spirit's sky of doubtful gloom,
But look thou rather to the scenes without,
Where all God's fairest, holiest treasures bloom;
Forget thyself—cast each dull clog aside—
And look in trust above, whate'er betide!

Fold not thy hands in weary, dull despair,
Whatever shadows thy fair hopes enshroud—
Sleep not thy life away in idle dreams;
Nerve thee for God's own work—nor heed the cloud
That breaks above thee; toil will bring release,
Care fade away and struggle end in peace!

—C. C. Cox.

LIFE'S SPINNERS.

Cotton spinners, watch your bobbins,
  See they all do smoothly run ;
Watch 'gainst snarls and vexing tangles
  Till the work of day is done.
When they all seem spinning smoothest
  Watch them with most careful eyes,
For you know not at what moment
  Snarls and tangles may arise ;
Now they run so smooth and even
  That you almost idle stand,
But next moment lo ! a tangle
  Needs a careful patient hand.

Friends, we all of us are spinners ;
  Look around and you will find
That on many a twirling bobbin
  We the yarn of life do wind.
See the thread of love that's purest
  Spun from out a mother's heart,
Winding round her household idols,
  Of her very life a part ;
Smooth and even it is running—
  Lo ! a little snarl appears,
O ! my friends, with patience meet it,
  Or 'twill tangle on for years.
Threads from heart and brain and spirit,
  Through our lives we all must spin—
Some of joy and some of sorrow,
  Some alas ! of death and sin ;
Some are smooth and some are tangled,
  Let us patient watch them all,
Trusting that our spools of sorrow
  And of sin may both be small.
    —Mrs. Mary Bayard Clark.

GROWING OLD.

It is the solemn thought connected with middle life, that life's last business is begun in earnest ; and it is then, midway between the cradle and the grave, that man begins to marvel that he let the days of youth go by so half enjoyed. It is the pensive autumn feeling ; it is the sensation of half sadness that we experience when the longest day of the year is past, and every day that follows is shorter, and the light fainter, and the feeble shadows tell that nature is hastening with gigantic footsteps to her winter grave. So does man look back upon his youth. When the first gray hairs become visible, when the unwelcome truth fastens itself upon the mind that a man is no longer going up hill but down, and that the sun is always westering, he looks back on things behind. When we were children, we thought as children. But now there lies before us manhood, with its earnest work, and then old age, and then the grave, and then home. There is a second youth for man, better and holier than the first, if he will look on, and not look back.

ACT FROM PRINCIPLE.

How few persons there are whose lives are governed entirely by principle, rather than inclination. Even those of us who may be endeavoring to live for high purposes, come far short of our aspirations ; alas ! how very far short. How often we find our convictions of right and duty, questioning if it might not be as well for us to yield to inclination just for the time, promising our disturbed consciences that we will make up for the present indulgence by more rigorous self-denial and more strict attention to duty. Vain, fallacious reasoning of a weak nature ! we can never make up for a neglected opportunity, one misspent hour, one wrong selfish act. Once past, the opportunity unimproved, the hour wasted, the act committed, it is beyond reach or recall, except in thoughts of regret. We may atone for it, but we can never change the past. Alas ! how painfully are we aware of this fact. Then should we all endeavor the more earnestly to make our lives the ornament of principle ; for we all know that, after all, the path of duty, though sometimes rugged, is not without sweet pleasure ; and let us never follow our inclinations if they would lead us away from right. Then shall we be permitted at the last to look back upon our lives with satisfaction, feeling that we have "done what we could," and that Our Father regards us with smiles of approbation.

NO ONE COMES HOME TO ME.

I SIT in the still autumn evening,
   As the shades of night draw anigh;
And with a dull, heart-faint feeling,
   I gaze on the passers-by
All lonely I look thro' the shadows,
   As lonely as life can be;
For each one has some face to look for,
   But—no one comes home to me.

I know there are heart-happy faces,
   That eagerly watch all aglow,
Awaiting the steps of some loved one—
   Some form that they fondly know;
I list to the hurrying footsteps,
   But none bring a thrill to me;
For, from all the plenty of passers,
   No one comes home to me.

My heart fills up with emotions
   Full many and strange to tell,
Till, like all woe-stricken women,
   The tears to my eyelids well;
And I wonder if others are ever
   As lonely and heartsick as I,
And if, thro' the shadows and the silence,
   Their hearts ever hungrily cry.

With no one to share in my sorrows,
   No one my efforts to share;
Always alone thro' the shadows,
   The burden of living to bear;
Yet, see I hearts all around me,
   E'er gladsome and full of glee—
Aye, each one has some face to look for,
   But—no one comes home to me.

I question if life's worth the living
   Without a companion—a heart
That responds to our every emotion
   And forms of our fibre a part.
The soul's constant call is for kinship,
   Of close and divinest degree—
The many may pluck and possess it;
   But—no one comes home to me.

All helpless and hopeless I ponder,
   Till dreary and dazed is my brain,
'Till the shadows grow thicker and thicker,
   And close all within me my pain;
So turn I, in sorrow, around me,
   As far as the eye can see,
And each one has some face to look for,
   Still—no one comes home to me.
      —JOSIE FRAZEE CAPPLEMAN.

ADVICE TO LADIES.

IN marrying make your own match; do not marry any man to get rid of him, or to oblige him, or to save him. The man who would go to destruction without you will quite as likely go with you, and perhaps drag you along. Do not marry in haste, lest you repent at leisure. Do not marry for a home and a living, when by taking care of your health you can be strong enough to earn your own living. Do not let aunts, fathers or mothers sell you for money or a position into bondage, tears and lifelong misery, which you alone must endure. Do not place yourself habitually in the society of any suitor until you have decided the question of marriage; human wills are weak, and people often become bewildered and do not know their error until it is too late. Get away from their influence, settle your head, and make up your mind alone. A promise may be made in a moment of sympathy, or even half delirious ecstasy which must be redeemed through years of sorrow, toil and pain. Do not trust your happiness in the keeping of one who has no heart, no head, no health. Beware of insane blood. Do not rush thoughtlessly, hastily, into wedded life, contrary to the counsel of your best friends. Love can wait; that which cannot wait is something of a very different character.

RETROSPECTION.

LISTEN, listen, gentle river,
   Stay one moment in thy flow!
Cease, oh! cease thy happy murmurings
   While my heart pours forth its woe!
Down beside a western prairie,
   Where the vine and roses blend,
Where the proud magnolias waving,
   And the stately poplars bend—

There, in early joyous childhood,
   Wandered I for many a day,
Culling flowers of richest odor,
   Blooming round my happy way.
There, within that fairy dwelling,
   Sweet affection kept her throne;

There in prayer loved voices mingled ;
  Ah ! where are those treasures gone ?

In that graveyard 'neath the willow
  Side by side, in dreamless sleep,
Where the mock-birds sing their requiem,
Where the low green clover creeps,
Are those loved ones sweetly resting,
  Lost to sorrow and to tears,
Heedless of the tempest gathering
  Round the gloom of coming years.

On my young brow care is leaving
  Traces of her cruel tread,
Pleasure's roses all have withered,
  Hope's sweet dreams forever fled.
And I'd fain, when life is ended,
  Lay me where I'm kneeling now ;
Sweet I'd rest, clear, placid river,
  On thy green bank's mossy brow.

SONG OF EGLA.

Day in melting purple dying,
Blossoms all around me sighing,
Fragrance from the lilies straying,
Zephyr with my ringlets playing,
  Ye but waken my distress :
  I am sick of loneliness.

Thou to whom I love to hearken,
Come ere night around me darken,
Though thy softness but deceive me,
Say thou'rt true, and I'll believe thee ;
  Veil, if ill, thy soul's intent,
  Let me think it innocent.

Save thy toiling, spare thy treasure ;
All I ask is friendship's pleasure,
Let the shining ore lie darkling,
Bring no gem in lustre sparkling ;
  Gifts and gold are naught to me,
  I would only look on thee ;

Tell to thee the high wrought feeling,
Ecstasy but in revealing ;
Paint to thee the deep sensation,
Rapture in participation,
  Yet but torture if compressed
  In a lone unfriended breast.

Absent still ? Ah, come and bless me !
Let these eyes again caress thee,
Once in caution I could fly thee,

Now I nothing could deny thee ;
  In a look if death there be,
  Come ! and I will gaze on thee !
    —Maria Brooks.

YOUR FIRST SWEETHEART.

You can never forget her. She is so young and innocent and pretty. She had such a way of looking at you over her book at church. She alone, of all the world, did not think you a boy of eighteen, but wondered at your size and learning, and your faint foreshadowing of a sandy moustache, and believed you every inch a man. When at those stupid evening parties, where boys and girls who should have been eating suppers of bread and milk, and gone to sleep hours before, waltzed and flirted, and made themselves sick over oysters and champagne, you were favored with a glance of her eye, or a whisper of her lip, you ascended to the seventh heaven immediately. When once upon a memorable eve, she polked with young Smith, and never even looked at you, how miserable you were. It is funny to think of now ; but it was not funny then, for you were awfully in earnest. Once, at a picnic, she wore a white dress, and had roses twined in her hair, and she looked so much like a bride you fairly trembled. Sometimes you thought, in just such snowy costume, with just such blosssoms in her hair, she might stand before the altar, and you, most blessed of all mortals, might place a gold ring upon her finger ; and when you were left alone with her for a moment, some of your thoughts would form themselves into words, and though she blushed and ran away, and would not let you kiss her, she did not seem to be angry. And then, when you were somewhat parted a little while, and when you met again she was walking with a gentleman, a large, full grown, whiskered man, of twenty-eight or thirty, and had neither word nor smile for you, and some well-meaning gossip informed you soon afterward that she was " engaged " to the tall gentleman with black whiskers, and that " it was a splendid match "—it was terrible news to you, then, and sent you off to some busy town far from your native place, where, after a good deal of youthful grief, and many resolutions to die and haunt her, you recovered your equanimity, and began to call love stuff and nonsense.

BARRIERS.

BETWEEN thy life and mine
Rugged and strong, resistless barriers rise ;
Day after day they shown a sterner front
   Uplifted to the skies,
   Shutting me out from thee,
Ofttimes there comes a blinding mist and rain,
But through the darkest, thickest cloud I know
   The sun will shine again !

   Between thy life and mine
Sullen and cold the turbid waters roll ;
Beneath their angry waves hope's bark was wrecked
   Long e'er it reached its goal.
   Yet in the quiet deep
"Faith's anchor holds," fast with its golden chain
Binding two hearts, that else would drift away
   Upon a sea of pain !

   Between thy life and mine
Stretches afar a wide and dreary plain,
Across the waste we gaze with longing eyes ;
   Heart cries to heart—in vain ;
   The echoes answer back
"In vain, in vain ; " and so we turn away,
With one long, shivering sigh of agony,
   In loneliness to stray !

   Between thy life and mine
The hand of faith has woven some bright threads,
Whose glittering radiance thro' these shadowed days
   A steadfast lustre sheds.
   Parted though we must be,
These golden fibres shall our hearts entwine,
The sweetness of unspoken sympathy
   Blending thy life and mine.
            —M. L. M.

A SONG OF PEACE.

THE grass is green on Bunker Hill,
  The waters sweet on Brandywine ;
The sword sleeps in the scabbard still,
  The farmer keeps his flocks and vine ;
Then who could mar the scene to-day
  With vaunt of battlefield or fray ?

The brave corn lifts its regiments,
  Ten thousand sabres in the sun ;
The ricks replace the battle tents,
  The bannered tassels toss and run,
The neighing steed, the bugle's blast—
  These be our stories of the past.

The earth has healed her wounded breast,
  The cannon plough the fields no more,
The heroes rest. O, let them rest
  In peace along the peaceful shore !
They fought for peace, for peace they fell ;
  They sleep in peace, and all is well.

The fields forget the battles fought,
  The trenches wave in golden grain ;
Still we neglect the lessons taught,
  And tear the wounds agape again !
Sweet Mother Nature, nurse the land,
  And heal her wounds with gentle hand.

Lo! peace on earth ; lo ! flock and fold ;
  Lo ! rich abundance, fat increase,
And valleys clad in sheens of gold.
  Oh ! rise and sing a song of peace,
For Theseus roams the land no more,
  And Janus rests with rusted door.
            —JOAQUIN MILLER.

CULTIVATE A TASTE FOR READING.

YOUNG men with excellent purposes sometimes make a great mistake in thinking they ought to give up every moment of their time to business, and to neglect everything else. This is a sad error. Every young man entering life ought to give some portion of his time regularly—I don't care if it is only half an hour a day—to the development of his mind, to the gaining of useful information, to the cultivation of some innocent and ennobling taste. Why, a man who has no soul except for his business is a "poor stick," a mere machine. A taste for reading is worth more than a hundred thousand dollars to him who has it—nay, worth more than any sum I could name. A rich man, without that or some similar taste, does not know how to enjoy his money. His only resource is to keep on making money, unless he prefers to spend it; and a mind that is not well developed does not know how to spend it wisely. A man worth his two millions used to tell me he would gladly give it all if he could only have the education which his lazy and stupid boy refused to acquire. If you will pardon the advice, I would say: Make it a rule—never to be broken —to devote at least half an hour a day to the reading of some useful book— not stories chiefly, either. Stories are good in their places; but every man needs a knowledge of history, the elements of science and other useful subjects; and, if he has only half an hour to give to reading, he will be very foolish to give it all to novels. Be hungry and thirsty after knowledge of all kinds; and be sure you will be none the worse, but all the better as business men.

—F. E. ABBOT.

KEEP STRAIGHT AHEAD.

PAY no attention to slanderers and gossipmongers. Keep straight on in your course, and let their backbiting die the death of neglect. What is the use of lying awake nights brooding over the remark of some false friend, that runs through your brain like forked lightning? What the use of getting into a worry and fret over gossip that has been set afloat to your disadvantage, by some meddlesome busybody, who has more time than character. These things can't possibly injure you, unless, indeed, you take notice of them, and in combating them give them standing and character. If what is said about you is true, set yourself right at once; if it is false, let it go for what it will fetch. If a bee sting you, would you go to the hive and destroy it? Would not a thousand come upon you? It is wisdom to say little respecting the injuries you have received. We are generally losers in the end, if we stop to refute all the backbitings and gossipings we may hear by the way. They are annoying, it's true, but not dangerous so long as we do not stop to expostulate and scold. Our characters are formed and sustained by ourselves, and by our own actions and purposes, and not by others. Let us always bear in mind that calumniators may usually be trusted to time, and the slow but steady justice of public opinion.

WITHOUT AN ENEMY.

HEAVEN help the man who imagines he can dodge enemies by trying to please everybody! If such an individual ever succeeded, we should be glad of it —nor that one should be going through the world trying to find the beams to knock and thump against, disputing every man's opinion, fighting and elbowing and crowding all who differ from him. That again is another extreme. Other people have their opinion, so have you; don't fall into the error of supposing that they will respect you more for turning your coat every day to match theirs. Wear your own colors in spite of wind and weather, storm and sunshine. It costs the irresolute and vacillating ten times the trouble to wind and twist and shuffle than honest, manly independence to stand its ground.

IT MATTERS NOT.

IF we could know,
Which of us, darling, would be first to go,
Who would be first to breast the swelling tide,
And step upon the other side—
If we could know!

We cannot know,
My darling, which of us must bear the woe,
Of struggling through life's closing years alone,

From which sad heart will burst the
    anguished groan ;
        We cannot know.
        Until that hour
Of parting, may sweet Love, with chas-
    tening power,
Dwell in our hearts, and guide our steps
    aright,
Baptizing us in His celestial light,
        Until that hour.

        Hand clasped in hand,
And heart-throb answering heart-throb,
    then we'll stand,
Unfaltering amid the storms of life,
With hearts forever pure from stain of
    strife—
        Hand clasped in hand.

        The God of Love
At last will send from far-off courts
    above,
Bright spirits to this dark and storm-
    swept shore,
Who'll bear us where we'll praise for-
    evermore,
        The God of Love.

        'Twill not be long,
My darling, ere we both shall swell the
    throng
Of God's immortals on the golden shore,
Until we meet where partings are no
    more,
        'Twill not be long.

        It matters not,
Then, darling, on which one shall fall
    the lot,   [Death ;
Since Love will triumph even over
Which brow shall first be chilled by
    His cold breath ;
        It matters not.

BROKEN TIES.

People often see small things that make an impression on them for life. We never will forget one of them. It was on a beautiful evening in early spring, and a hunter was the actor in the tragedy. He had been out gunning, and was just returning from an almost fruitless hunt. Just as he had nearly reached the limits of the town in which he lived, a lone pair of wild ducks came flying over, perhaps innocently seeking their place of rest for the night. They were flying high in the air, and they had doubtless calculated they were safely out of the reach of gunshot. But they were not, at least one of them was not ; for the aim and gun of the hunter were good, and at the discharge, it was painfully evident that from then on must widen the course of the pair.

The wounded bird began to sink in its flight, and fell dead a few rods from the hunter. In his eagerness to get the fallen bird, the hunter left his gun, and ran for it, unnoticing its mate, which seemed to prefer death to the fate which had befallen it, though it was otherwise unharmed. As the hunter picked up the dead bird, the other seemed to give up its last hope of companionship, and arose from near the side of its fallen comrade, and thence started out upon a new life, alone !

There was more of sadness in this picture than the huntsman saw. He only wished for his gun to bring down the other. Was it not a pity he didn't have it ? Would it not have been preferable to both the living, as well as to the dead bird ? Did the hunter ever have a pang of regret for the heart he had broken, though it were only that of a bird ?

AND THERE SHALL BE LIGHT.

O dark, so dark may hang the night ;
  O dark, so dark without a star ;
No gleam upon thy longing sight
  To tell thee morning comes afar,
Look up then, heart, and crush thy
    fear,
At darkest time the dawn is near.

The way of life for thee may seem
  An endless race from dawn till dusk ;
For thee to wake while others dream,
  And yet the harvest—barren husk,
Toil on, brave heart, though others
    jeer,
At darkest time the dawn is near.

At darkest time, when courages dies,
  And tears unto the eyelids well,
When frowning sorrow silent flies
  To ring for hope the parting knell,

Then shall the wondrous light appear—
At darkest time the dawn is near.

We do not look for golden grain
 When we commit the seed to earth.
Ah, no! we wait till sun and rain
 To mystic life has given birth.
Learn then to smile through toil and
  tear,
At darkest time the dawn is near.

For in my heart's philosophy
 I hold that conscientious strife
Must bring reward to you and me,
 Both now and in a higher life,
Though years may pass ere fruit appear,
At darkest time the dawn is near.
 —NATTIE BONNER.

LONELY.

SITTING lonely, ever lonely,
 Waiting, waiting for one only,
Thus I count the weary moments pass-
  ing by ;
 And the heavy evening gloom
 Gathers slowly in the room,
And the chill November darkness dims
  the sky.
 Now the countless busy feet
 Cross each other in the street,
And I watch the faces fluttering past
  my door ;
 But the step that lingered nightly,
 And the hand that rapp'd so lightly,
And the face that beamed so brightly
  Come no more.

By the firelight's fitful gleaming,
I am dreaming, ever dreaming,
And the rain is slowly falling all
  around ;
 And the voices that are nearest,
 Of the friends the best and dearest,
Appear to have a strange and distant
  sound.
 Now the weary wind is sighing,
 And the murky day is dying,
And the wither'd leaves lie scatter'd
  round my door ;
 But that voice, whose gentle greeting
 Set this heart so wildly beating
At each fond and frequent meeting,
  Comes no more.

TAKE IT IN.

IF you'd make life worth living
 In this valley here below,
Take the fun in with the labor—
 Take enjoyment as you go.
If you'd live the noblest, truest,
 Keeping cheerful, brave and strong,
Be no slave for future pleasures ;
 Take them as you go along,

Do not lay up all your treasure,
 After years of life to bless ;
Do not wait until your efforts
 Meet the fulness of success ;
Do not drudge till your position
 Is the richest men among ;
Ere you taste of life's sweet nectars,
 Sip them as you go along,

Pleasure makes your work more easy,
 Work shows pleasure at its best,
Rest will nerve the arm to labor,
 Labor, too, brings sweetest rest.
Work with steady, earnest effort
 In the pushing, crowding throng ;
But do not forget the pleasures,
 Take them as you go along.
 —SMILEY'S ENTERPRISE.

THE MOCKING BIRD.

WITH the advent of spring comes again the mocking bird, the royal songster of the Southland. Or, rather, he starts afresh his new songs, for he is really with us at all seasons. In winter, they usually remain in pairs in some sequestered spot, about which they linger until the dawn of spring. They seem to wish to divide up their beauty and usefulness to humanity by pairing off, and each pair taking a location, or neighborhood, or farm-yard to themselves. The cedar or holly tree is their favorite resort for winter quarters, around which they may be seen any month in the year. Less frequently in the summer, when all nature is his home, but at no time does he forget the home which sheltered him from the winter's storms. At the dawn of spring he is the first to discover it, and at once begins to harbinger its coming. Near by his winter home, which he protects from the trespasses of other birds with all the vigor of a Southern soldier, he will perch upon some twig the first warm day, and smooth his plumage and begin to run over the scales of his new spring songs. He is small, not larger than a robin, of a blue-lead and white color, but is a strong, game and active little fellow. He is fond of the yard and garden, and while destructive to nothing useful or ornamental, he is valuable and is regarded as the gardeners' and farmers' friend, He seems to recognize this, for while he prefers his native American liberty, he courts the protection and admiration of his human friends, which he amply repays by choice music, often day and night, from March to August, and often even during the beautiful Indian summer. But during the months of April, May and June is he at his best. It is then he begins with his own native notes, and to which he adds in mimicry surpassing the original notes of all of his tribe. And strange to say, he never forgets the borrowed notes of his feathered neighbors. He not only sings his own music, but equally as well does he read and repeat the strains of all his neighbor, or visiting birds. His loyalty to his mate is remarkable and especially commendable After helping to build the nest in some favored fruit tree or bush, he guards it well from the approach of other birds, and while his better half is occupying the nest, his favorite place is on some limb, or tree-top near by, from which he sings his choicest selections in the most ecstatic manner. The young birds are greeted by food first from the male, and then from the female bird, and between meals are they made glad by the choicest music of the mimic choir.

These birds are found in nearly all the Southern States, and especially do they delight to live in the Gulf and Atlantic States, as far North as Maryland. They are often caught and caged, though to see the pride of the Southern songster in all his glory, you should see him in his native air, and hear him repeat the notes of his native Southland.

"ABIDE WITH ME."

A MOTHER rocked her little ones to sleep,
  Rocked them, and sang softly and tenderly,
Sang o'er and o'er again the same sweet strain,
  "Fast falls the eventide. Abide with me."
Sang, as the twilight fell upon the hills,
  Sang, as the sunlight faded in the west,
"The darkness deepens, Lord, with me abide,"
  Then stole out softly, leaving them to rest.

And each succeeding day as twilight fell,
  We saw her hush her little ones to rest,
Stroking the curls that on the pillow lay,
  Kissing the face that lay upon her breast.
But still she always sang those same sweet words,
  That seemed to her loving heart so dear to be,
"I need Thy presence every passing hour,
  Through cloud and sunshine, Lord, abide with me."

And some one asked her why she always sang
  Those words, to hush her little ones to rest,
And she had smiled half sadly as she said:
  "Why? I think only that I love them best;
And then too, I have sometimes prayed," she said,
  "That when my darlings have to manhood grown,
They'll not forget the song that mother loved:
  I trust that they will take it for their own."

Then sorrows came. Her dearest friend was dead,
  And years rolled on, and turned her hair to gray;

But still she sang the song she loved so well,
As trustingly as on her wedding day;
Sang it as she had sung it years gone by;
Sang it, but not above the little bed;
Nay, for her darlings left that long ago;
And two of them were men, but one was dead.

Jack, noble, manly Jack, had gone to war,
But Ned—none knew but God where he had gone;
And none but God and mother knew the prayers
That she had breathed for this wild, wayward son,
One night, as twilight fell upon the hills,
Some one came up the path with quiet tread;
A wounded soldier came to bring sad news,
To tell her that her soldier boy was dead.

Only a moment was her gray head bent,
I saw the tears fall on her wrinkled hand;
And then she spoke—her voice was firm and clear,
As one in battle giving a command:
"Tell me, was he a coward ere he died?
Or was he brave and true unto the last?
Tell me, was he afraid to meet his death?
Speak, stranger, tell me truly all thou hast."

"A coward? Nay. He fought beneath the flag,
Followed it till he died beneath its stars,
Covered with wounds, with glory, and with scars."

Never shall I forget her eager look—
As she rose, tottering quickly to his side,
And whispered: "Say, were these the words he sang:
'Abide with me, fast falls the eventide'?"

And when he answered, "Yes, yes, them's the words,"
Her silver head was bent upon the sill,
I thought that she was weeping, and bent down;
But nay, her song, her faith upheld her still.

Morning. The sunlight breaks upon the hill,
And wakes the lark and robin from their nest.
It steals softly through the window bars
To kiss the face of one who is at rest.
Resting. And so we found her, by and by,
Her face as peaceful as in childhood's hour;
Kissed her for those that she had loved best,
And laid her out to sleep among the flowers.
Only a few steps from the cottage door,
Where the winds sobbed above her tenderly,
We buried her, and wrote beneath her name
Only three little words, "Abide with me."

Some one came up the garden path one day,
Some one who oft had trod that path before;
Some one whose face lit up with eager hope,
Now, as he stood again beside the door.
But why was all so lonely and so still,
And where was mother, that the door was fast,
For surely she had waited for her boy,
Had prayed for him and loved him to the last.

A child played just beyond the church-yard gate,
Ah! she should tell him what he wished to know
And so he hurried quickly down the path,
That he had known so many years ago.
She listened to his question in surprise,
And looked at him in wonder as she said:

"Where are they? Why the soldier boy was killed,
The other one was rough and wild, they said."
And every day his mother watched for him,
I've seen her often with her silver hair,
There by the window, but he never came,
And then she died, her grave is over there."
Ah! such a cry as fell upon the air ;
A wail of pain and deepest agony,
It made the startled birds fly off their nests ;
It made the child shrink back and steal away.

"Dead! mother dead? Then I have broke her heart,
Dead, and I have come home to be forgiven,
Dead, then her boy's repentance comes too late."
He sobbed aloud, and raised his eyes to heaven,
Then turning, strode along the narrow path
To where the child had said his mother slept,
And falling down beside the simple stone
Sobbed until pitying angels might have wept.

"O mother, I've come back to thee," he said,
"Come back to love thee and be loved by thee,
Come back to find," he paused, his eyes had caught
The words beneath her name, "Abide with me."
A moment and the fierce wild sobbing ceased
Although the warm tears still fell thick and fast,
But when he spoke again his voice was calm,
Just as the sea's when a storm is past.

"O mother, I will take thy song," he cried,
"I'll take thy faith, thy Bible, and thy God,
I'll live as thou didst teach me how to live,
I'll follow in the path thy feet have trod."
And some one passing by the churchyard gate
Heard a man's voice, paused in the twilight dim
To listen, but the only words he heard,
Were the dear words of the old cradle hymn :

" Hold thou thy Cross before my closing eyes,
Shine through the gloom and point me to the skies,
Heaven's morning breaks, and earth's vain shadows flee,
In life, in death, O Lord, abide with me."
—PHILA FARVEY BUTLER.

FISHING.

A YOUTH beside the water sits,
The noonday sun is warmly beaming ;
His nose and neck are turkey red,
His eye with radiant hope is gleaming,
He watches close the bobbing cork
Advance upon the tiny billows ;
A jerk, a swish, and high above
He lands a sucker in the willows.
    That's fishing.

A fair maid trips the tennis court,
A dozen eyes admire her going ;
Her black and yellow blazer burns
A hole right through the sunset's glowing.
She drives the ball across the net,
And into hearts consumed with wishing
She drives a dart from Cupid's bow ;
She'll land a sucker, too. She's fishing.
    That's fishing.

My little wife beside me stands
And steals a dimpled arm around me ;
A kiss upon my lips—that's bait—
Some information to astound me.

Her bonnet is quite out of style,
  Her summer wrap quite past the using;
That lovely one—so cheap at Brown's—
  Is just the one she would be choosing,
        That's fishing.

So, whether the game be fish or men,
  The bait be kisses, worms or blushes;
The place at home, by sunny pool,
  Or tennis ground at evening's hushes;
'Tis the old game the serpent played
  With Mother Eve in Eden's bowers,
And Adam's sons and daughters all
  Will love the sport to time's last hours.
        That's fishing.
            AMERICAN ANGLER.

"THE DAYS ARE GROWING LONG AGAIN."

THE days are growing long again;
  Still later fall the shades of night;
Still earlier breaks the golden dawn:
  And, darting, through the sunshine bright,
The sparrows strain their little throats,
  To tell, in joyous chirruping,
How songs in earth and air portend
  The glad returning of the spring.

And as I note how winter's spell
  Is broken, note the budding trees
And soft moist earth and balmy air,
  My heart draws sweet analogies.
Far in my life seems broken, too,
  The winter spell of grief and pain,
And with the coming of the spring
  My days grow long and bright again.
—HELEN E. STARRET, *in Interior*.

EASTER BELLS.

OUT upon the rosy dawning
  Break the gladdening Easter bells,
In the gray of Easter morning
  Clear and sweet, their notes they swell.

Telling of that sweet old story,
  In their quaint and curious chimes,
Of our Saviour's death and glory
  In the olden, olden times.

How the angel at the entrance
  Opened wide the gate of stone,
Throwing bars of heavenly glory
  In the sepulchre alone.

How he burst all bars asunder,
  Tore the veil of death away,
Shedding beams of golden splendor,
  In the morn of Easter day.

Rose o'er all the world victorious,
  Borne on wondrous clouds of light,
To the heights of love and mercy,
  To the home so fair and bright.

Ring out, ring on, ye silvery bells,
  Your story dear to tell,
Till earth and sky shall echo back
  The chime of Easter bells.

MA AND ME.

I MAY be partial, perhaps I be;
But there ain't no wife in this town I see
That is anything near to my Hepsy Ann,—
She never changes, and never can.
She's heatin' the old brick oven now,
While I'm goin' on at the tail of the plow,
There's gingernuts, apples, and pies to bake,
And a loaf of brown bread, and a pan o' cake,
And beans, that for thirty long years and nine
We've had every Saturday, rain or shine.
I may be partial, perhaps I be,
But never a daughter like mine, I see,
With rose in her cheek and laugh in her eye,
Both jolly and modest, both merry and shy,
With lips full of kisses—But stop right thar!
Them kisses are only for me and ma!
She'll wash an' iron an' laugh an' sing,
An' milk our Daisy, and—everything!
I tell you, our Kitty is good to see,
And a real treasure to ma and me!
I may be partial, perhaps I am;
But there ain't no boy that is just like Sam.
Sam's goin' to Congress some futur day
A risin' man, so the papers say;

A lawyer, an' lucky as he can be—
Sends money often to ma and me.
He ain't ashamed of his origin,
Like some o' those monkeyish city men ;
He stands right up for the crowds that toil ;
An' he calls himself a son o' the soil.

I may be partial as most things go,
But there ain't no fruit like the fruit I grow,
The branches groan with them yeller pears
And the red-cheeked apples they put on airs,
'Cause they are a kind that is scarce an' high,
And my trees never gin out an' die.
Perhaps I'm old-fashioned ; there be a few
Who think that trees and cattle, too,
Needs jest as much tendin' as humans do.
I guess I'm partial, I know I be,
But a happier household you wouldn't see
Than Sam an' Kitty and ma and me.
—MARY A. DENNISON, *in New York Ledger.*

HIS CONSCIENCE.

I SAT alone with my conscience
In a place where time was o'er,
And we talked of my former living
In the land of the evermore ;
And I felt I should have to answer
The question if put to me,
And to face the answer and question
Throughout eternity.

The ghosts of forgotten action
Came floating before my sight,
And things that I thought had perished
Were alive with a terrible might ;
And the vision of life's dark record
Was an awful thing to face—
Alone with my conscience sitting
In that solemnly silent place.

And I thought of a far-away warning,
Of a sorrow that was to be mine,
In a land that then was the future,
But now is the present time ;

And I thought of my former thinking
Of the judgment day to be ;
But sitting alone with my conscience
Seemed judgment enough for me.

And I wondered if there was a future
To this land beyond the grave ;
But no one gave me an answer,
And no one came to save ;
Then I felt that the future was present,
And the present would never go by—
For it was but the thought of a future
Become an eternity.

Then I woke from my timely dreaming,
And the vision passed away,
And I knew the far-way warning
Was a warning of yesterday ;
And I prayed that I may not forget it,
In this land before the grave—
That I may not cry in the future,
And no one come to save ;
I have learned a solemn lesson
Which I ought to have learned before,
And which, tho' I learned it in dreaming,
I hope to forget no more.

So I sit alone with my conscience,
In the place where the years increase,
And I try to fathom the future,
In the land where time will cease ;
And I know of a future judgment,
How dreadful soe'er it be,
That to sit alone with my conscience,
Will be judgment enough for me.

GRAMMAR IN RHYME.

NOUNS are names of things or men,
As John and William, ink and pen.
Pronouns take the place of names,
As she for Mary, he for James.
An adjective describes a thing,
The quiet country, bubbling spring.
Verbs can tell us what is done,
We read and write, and walk and run.
Adverbs tell us how, when or where,
Now, answer truly, what goes there ?
Interjections hop right out
Before you think, as "Oh ! No doubt ! "
Conjunctions fasten words together,
As "Clear and cold but pleasant weather."

Prepositions fasten words
And show their bearings, "Wings on birds."

THE MONEYLESS MAN.

Is there no secret place on the face of the earth
Where charity dwelleth, where virtue hath birth,
Where bosoms in mercy and kindness will heave,
Where the poor and the wretched may ask and receive?
Is there no place at all where a knock from the poor
Will bring some kind angel to open the door?
Ah! search the wide world wherever you can,
There is no open door for a moneyless man.

Then go to the halls where the chandelier's light
Drives back with its splendor the darkness of night,
Where the rich hanging curtains in shadowy folds
Sweep gracefully down with their trimmings of gold,
Where mirrors in silver take up and renew
In long, lighted vistas the 'wildering view—
Go there to the banquet and find if you can
A welcoming smile for a moneyless man.

And go to the church with its cloud-reaching spire,
Which gives back to the sun his great look of red fire,
Where the columns and arches are gorgeous within,
And the walls seem as pure as a saint within sin,
Walk down the long aisles, see the rich and the great
In the pomp and the pride of their worldly estate—
Walk down down in your patches and find if you can
Who'll open a pew for a moneyless man.

You may go to the banks where Mammon has told
His hundreds of thousands of silver and gold,
Where, safe from the hands of the starving and poor,
Lie piles upon piles of the glittering ore.
Walk up to the counter; ah! there you may stay
Till your limbs grow old and your hair turn gray,
And you'll find at the bank not one of the clan
With money to lend to the moneyless man.

Then go to your judge with his dark flowing gown,
With his scales whereon law weigheth equity down,
Where he frowns on the weak and smiles on the strong,
And punishes right while he justifies wrong.
Where juries their lips to the Bible have laid
To render a verdict they have already made—
Go there in the court-room and find if you can
Any law for the cause of the moneyless man.

Then go to your hovel, where no raven has fed
The wife who has suffered so long for her bread,
Kneel down by her pallet and kiss the death-frost
From the lips of the angel your poverty lost;
Then turn in your agony upward to God
And bless while it smites you the chastening rod,
And you'll find at the end of life's little span
A welcome above for a moneyless man.

GRANDFATHER.

GRANDFATHER sits in his large easy chair,
Where the sun kisses his thin whitened hair;

In the warm sunlight he rocks to and
    fro,
Thinking of days in the long, long ago,
The days of his youth when he was a
    boy,
Full of youth's pleasures, a fond
    mother's joy;
Now as he sits rocking there to and
    fro—
He's living again in that long, long ago.

In all of those years, now nearly four-
    score,
With all of the scenes his mind hath in
    store,
There is none so vivid in memory's
    glow
As those of his youth in that long, long
    ago;
The face of each playmate as fair and
    as bright
As the red sunset glow on a yesterday
    night;
The form and the voice, each face and
    each name,
In his memory's eye are ever the same.

As he rocks to and fro he's living once
    more
The pleasures his memory holdeth in
    store,
He feels not the weight of his fourscore
    years,
His eye is not dimmed by the mist of
    tears;
There's rather a smile in his fading
    eyes,
As thoughts of his youth in his mind
    arise;
The deep-wrinkled face grows brighter
    and fair,
As thoughts leave their sweetest expres-
    sion there.

Rock, grandfather, rock and live over
    again,
Those days of your youth that bring
    you no pain;
The years of your toil, their troubles
    and care,
In memory find no resting-place there,
How dear to the aged those scenes of
    their youth,
They live, ever live, immortal as truth;
Fresh in the mind as the sunlight's
    bright ray,
Give blessings to age by night and by
    day
—J. L. ANDERSON, *in Inter-Ocean.*

LONGING FOR HOME.

O, how I am longing for the home of my
    childhood,
The days when my happiness knew
    no bound;
Tho' sorrow and sadness had entered
    the doorway,
A happier home could scarce have
    been found.

Now, when the voyage of life is almost
    o'er,
I sit dreaming of the days that are
    gone;
Dreaming of the loved ones who've
    passed on before me,
Whose days of sorrow and sadness
    are done.

I long for the days when in innocent
    childhood
I walked through the paths, with sweet
    flowers strewn;
I had not a care or a thought for the
    morrow,
Each hour and moment I counted as
    my own.

And now, when old age with its cares
    are upon me,
And, I, dreaming, look up through the
    soft moonlight,
At the millions of stars which are stud-
    ding the heavens,
And pin to the sky the black curtains
    of night.

Ah, yes, I am longing for the days of
    my childhood,
With life's varied dreams to live over
    again;
Then at last to enter the portals of
    heaven,
Where we shall be free from all sorrow
    and pain.
—CARRIE E. GLENN.

"SLEEPING, I DREAMED."

Dreaming, I float on a billowy sea,
　Past willowy isles and shadowy shore,
Wrapped in the folds of life's mystery,
　Spreading white sails without rudder or oar;
Beautiful forms—though long in the grave—
Silently beckon me over the wave,
Smiling with eyes that nevermore weep—
Beautiful phantasies woven of sleep:

Upward I wing to a heavenly crest,
　By mountains that lift to the azurine skies,
Away to the circles of infinite rest,
　Where fountains of youth perpetually rise;
Friends of old days are trooping about me,
Scenes of fair childhood are dawning upon me,
Faintly and sweet, angels' voices are blent,
Fragments of bliss to night's day that are lent.

Mother and father from over the plain
Are chanting their joy with welcoming strain,
Bending, their white hands are held out to greet me:
Oh, vision so rare! the gray morn will break thee—
Back to earth's worry I'm wafted once more,
Back to its toilings I thought had been o'er;
Jostlings of strife and throes of life's pain
Wake me from sleep and from dreams that are vain!
　　　　—Inda Barton Hays.

VICTOR HUGO ON THE IMMORTAL SOUL.

At a dinner given to Victor Hugo in Paris, some years ago, says *L'Universe*, he delivered an impromptu address, in which he gave expression to his faith in the Infinite and in the soul's immortality. His friend, Houssaye, who was present, says:

"Hugo at that time was a man of steel, with no sign of old age about him, but with all the agility, the suppleness, the ease and grace of his best years." He was contradicting the atheists, and his friend says "his face was bright with the heavenly halo, and his eyes shone like burning coals."

"'There are no occult forces,' he said; 'there are only luminous forces. Occult force is chaos; the luminous force is God. Man is an infinite little copy of God; this is glory enough for man. I am a man, an invisible atom, a drop in the ocean, a grain of sand on the shore. Little as I am, I feel the God in me, because I can also bring forth out of my chaos. I make books, which are creations. I feel in myself that future life; I am like a forest which has been more than once cut down; the new shoots are stronger and livelier than ever,

"'I am rising, I know, towards the sky. The sunshine is on my head. The earth gives me its generous sap, but heaven lights me with the reflection of unknown words. You say the soul is nothing but the result of bodily powers. Why, then, is my soul more luminous when my bodily powers begin to fail? Winter is on my head, and eternal spring is in my heart. There I breathe at this hour the fragrance of the lilacs, the violets and the roses as at twenty years ago. The nearer I approach the end, the plainer I hear around me the immortal symphonies of the worlds which invite me.

"'It is marvellous, yet simple. It is a fairy tale, and it is historic. For half a century I have been writing my thoughts in prose and verse—history, philosophy, drama, romance, tradition, satire, ode and song, I have tried all, but I feel I have not said a thousandth part of what is in me. When I go down to the grave, I can say, like many others, I have finished my day's work, but I cannot say, I have finished my life. My days will begin again the next morning The tomb is not a blind alley. It is a thoroughfare. It closes on the twilight to open on the dawn.'"

A SWARM OF BEES.

B hopeful, B happy, B cheerful, B kind,
B busy of body, B modest of mind,
B earnest, B truthful, B firm and B fair,
Of all Miss B Havior B sure and B ware.
B think ere you stumble for what may B fall.
B true to yourself, and B faithful to all ;
B brave and B ware of the sins that B set.
B sure that one sin will another B get.
B watchful, B ready, B open, B frank,
B manly to all men, whatever B their rank ;
B just and B generous, B honest, B wise,
B mindful of time, and B certain it flies.
B prudent, B liberal, of order B fond,
B uy less than you need B fore B uying B yond ;
B careful, but yet B the first to B stow,
B temperate, B steadfast, to anger B slow.
B thoughtful, B thankful, whate'er may B tide.
B justful, B joyful, B cleanly B side ;
B pleasant, B patient, B fervent to all,
B best if you can, but B humble withal.
B prompt and B dutiful, still B polite ;
B reverent, B quiet, and B sure and B right ;
B calm, B retiring, B ne'er led astray,
B grateful, B cautious of those who B tray.
B tender, B loving, B good and B nign,
B loved thou shalt B, and all else B thine.

BETTY AND THE BABY.

MY home seems deserted, I'm lonely and sad,
I miss all the pleasures of home I once had,
I try to be cheerful, I fail to be glad,
Since Betty left home with the baby.

I sit in the rooms, and I read and I write,
I whistle and sing, but the only delight
That is mine is to joyfully dream every night
Of Betty, who's gone with the baby.

It seems that a mother's sweet face I can see
As I dandle the baby in joy on my knee ;
But no man was ever more lonesome than me,
Since Betty's been gone with the baby.

The house is a picture of silence and gloom,
As I walk though its halls that are still as a tomb,
Like a crazy man, silently searching each room
For Betty, who's gone with the baby.

She has "gone to see ma," and it's many a mile ;
Every day that she stays seems a terrible while,
And I'll never be happy or able to smile
Until Betty comes home with the baby.

'Twill be joy to my heart when the message shall come
That the hen and our chicken no longer will roam.
Gee ! won't this old rooster crow loudly at home
When Betty gets back with the baby ?
—WILL S. HAYS, *in Louisville Times.*

WEAKNESS.

"IF I should try to take a kiss," says he,
"Tell me what would you do ? "
"You ought not to attempt it, John," said she ;
"I'm not as strong as you."
—CAPE COD ITEM.

THE COMING MAN.

A PAIR of very chubby legs,
Encased in scarlet hose ;
A pair of little stubby boots,
With rather doubtful toes ;
A little kilt, a little coat,
Cut as mother can—

And lo! before us stands in state
   The future "coming man."

His eyes, perchance, will read the stars,
   And search their unknown ways;
Perchance the human heart and soul
   Will open to their gaze;
Perchance their keen and flashing glance
   Will be a nation's light—
Those eyes that are now wistful bent
   On some "big fellow's" kite.

Those hands—those little busy hands—
   So sticky, small and brown;
Those hands whose only mission seems
   To pull all order down —
Who knows what hidden strength may be
   Hidden within their clasp,
Though now 'tis but a taffy stick
   In sturdy hold they grasp.

Ah, blessings on those little hands,
   Whose work is yet undone!
And blessings on those little feet,
   Whose race is yet unrun!
And blessings on that little brain,
   That has not learned to plan!
Whate'er the future holds in store,
   God bless the "coming man!"
      —SOMERVILLE JOURNAL.

TALK'S CHEAP.

THERE'S lots o' quaint ol' sayin's
   I've noticed in my day—
Big truths and solid principles
   Told in the shortest way.
My father ust to have one,
   An' this is how it ran:
"Talk's cheap, my boy," he ust to say;
   "But money buys the lan'."

I own the sayin's homely,
   Undignified and rough;
But then, it tells just what you mean,
   An' tells it brief enough.
An' when you git to thinkin'
   How short is life's thin span,
It's well to min' "that talk is cheap,
   But money buys the lan'."

'Twon't do to boast an' bluster
   An' brag an' try to bluff;

An' don't you git to thinkin'
   This world "ain't up to snuff."
It is; an' while you're blowin'
   Your own bazoo, my man,
There's some one sneerin', "Talk is cheap,
   "But money buys the lan'."
      —CHICAGO NEWS RECORD.

ONE WORD.

"WRITE me an epic," the warrior said—
"Victory, valor and glory wed."

"Prithee, a ballad," exclaimed the knight—
"Prowess, adventure and faith unite."

"An ode to Freedom," the patriot, cried—
"Liberty won and wrong defied."

"Give me a drama," the scholar asked—
"The inner world in the outer masked."

"Frame me a sonnet," the artist prayed—
"Power and passion in harmony played."

"Sing me a lyric," the maiden sighed—
"A lark not waking the morning wide."

"Nay, all too long," said the busy age—
"Write me a line, instead of a page."

The swift years spoke, the poet heard,
"Your poem write in a single word."

He looked in the maiden's glowing eyes,
A moment glanced at the starlit skies;

From the lights below to the lights above,
And wrote the one-word poem—Love.
      —BLACKWOOD.

THE TRUE GENTLEMAN.

THE true gentleman carefully avoids whatever may cause a jar or a jolt in the minds of those with whom he is cast—all clashing of opinion, or collision of feeling, all restraint or suspicion, or gloom, or resentment; his great concern being to make every one at their ease and at home. He has eyes on all his company, he is tender toward the bashful, gentle toward the distant, and merciful toward the absurd. He can recollect to whom he is speaking, he guards against unreasonable allusions or topics which may irritate, he is seldom prominent in conversation and never wearisome. He makes light of favors when he does them and seems to be receiving when he is conferring. He never speaks of himself, except when compelled, never defends himself by a mere retort; he has no ears for slander or gossip, is scrupulous in imputing motives to those who interfere with him, and interprets everything for the best. He is never mean or little in disputes, never takes unfair advantage, never mistakes personalities or sharp sayings for argument or insinuates evil which he dare not say out. From a long-sighted prudence he observes the maxim of the ancient sage, that we should ever conduct ourselves toward our enemy as if he were one day to be our friend. He has too much sense to be affronted at insults; he is too indolent to bear malice. He is patient, forbearing and resigned on philosophical principles; he submits to pain because it is inevitable, to bereavement because it is irreparable, and to death because it is his destiny. If he engages in controversy of any kind his disciplined intellect preserves him from the blundering discourtesy of better, perhaps, but less educated minds, who, like blunt weapons, tear and hack instead of cutting clean, who mistake the point in argument, waste their strength on trifles, misconceive their adversary and leave the question more involved than they hear by the way. They are annoying, it is true, but not dangerous so long as we do not stop to expostulate and scold. Our characters are formed and sustained by ourselves, by our own actions and purposes, and not by others. Let us always bear in mind that calumniators may usually be trusted to time and the slow but steady justice of public opinion.

EMBER FACES.

As I gaze into the embers of the fire
   burning low,
Faces fair, and yet fantastic, come and
   fade with every glow;
Faces dead and those still living, starting, shaping on the coals—
Faces dear and half forgotten, waking
   thoughts in mem'ry's folds.

Smiling ones I see among them, welcoming my gaze intent,
And sadder ones look out upon me with
   soulful eyes of sorrow pent;
And here and there I see a face that
   brings to me some boyhood dream,
Some sweet, pure face of love or friend
   that cheers me with a kindly beam.

And now and then a glowing spectre
   touches on some tender chord,
Hidden in the great Forgotten, op'ning
   floods of memory broad;
Fond ones dead and oft regretted in
   the hallowed long ago,
But by time interred as many of those
   thoughts which deeply flow.

Ah, but lurking brightest 'mongst them,
   glowing warmly, do I see
Sweet, sweet face, which tender mem'ry
   brings with sadness unto me;
And as I look with heart o'erflowing,
   surging, longing, deep I sigh—
All the faces fade from memory, all save
   hers grow gray and die.

Burning in that single ember, crowned
   by halo rich and bright,
Is the memory of a dead past, bringing
   with it sorrow's night;
Calmly looking, calmly watching, gazing in my dimming eye
Is that face of sweet remembrance,
   answ'ring to my heart's death cry.

Oh, with utter, boundless yearning, look
   I in that sweet face there,
All that held I on earth dearest—now
   my bitter deep despair.
The ember glows, and with its pulsing
   throbs my heart in aching tense—
I drink the sweets of recollection, gray
   ashes but my recompense.

And just as far from out my life is she as
  is that ember face.
Athwart we live, and ever will, until we
  shall all time outpace.
I look again, the face is there, my heart
  is bursting—anguish, doubt ;
It glows, and as in life, so there it fades,
  it flickers, falters, and—goes out.

* * * * * *

A long-suppressed moan—a sigh, but
  half aloud ;
O'er that sweet face dead ashes form the
  shroud.
—M. B. F., Jr.

THE BIVOUAC OF THE DEAD.

THE muffled drum's sad roll has beat
  The soldier's last tattoo !
No more on life's parade shall meet
  The brave and fallen few ;
On fame's eternal camping-ground
  Their silent tents are spread,
And Glory guards, with solemn round,
  The bivouac of the dead.

No rumor of the foe's advance
  Now swells upon the wind,
No troubled thought at midnight haunts
  Of loved ones left behind.
No vision of to-morrow's strife
  The warrior's dread alarms.
No braying horn or screaming fife
  At dawn shall call to arms.

Their shivered swords are red with rust,
  Their plumed heads are bowed,
Their haughty banner trailed in dust
  Is now their martial shroud ;
And plenteous funeral tears have washed
  The red stains from each brow,
And the proud forms by battle gashed
  Are free from anguish now.

The neighing troop, the flashing blade,
  The bugle's stirring blast ;
The charge, the dreadful cannonade,
  The din and shout are past
Nor War's wild note, nor Glory's peal,
  Shall thrill with fierce delight
Those breasts that never more may feel
  The rapture of the fight.

Rest on, embalmed and sainted dead !
  Dear as the blood ye gave :
No impious footsteps here shall tread
  The herbage of your grave ;
Nor shall your glory be forgot
  While fame her record keeps,
Or Honor points the hallowed spot
  Where Valor proudly sleeps,

Yon marble minstrel's voiceless tone
  In deathless song shall tell,
When many a vanished year hath flown,
  The story how ye fell :
Nor wreck, nor change, nor winter's
  blight,
Nor time's remorseless doom,
Can dim one ray of holy light
  That gilds your glorious tomb.
—THEODORE O'HARA.

THE TERRIBLE FIRE.

I WILL tell you a tale of the terrible fire ;
It springs from the earth ; it is dreadful and dire.

  In the dark
  Wintry sky,
  See the spark
  Upward fly ;
  See it grow
  In its frame ;
  See it glow
  Into flame !

See it burning and blazing ;
  See it springing into life
With a vigor amazing—
  How it longs for the strife !
Hear the noise and the rattle—
  How it swells, how it grows,
Like the crash of a battle,
  Like the clash of the foes !

See it rushing, and rising, and roaring !
  See it trying to touch a tall star ;
It seems in the sky to be soaring
  Like a flag of fierce flame from far.
See it turning, and burning, and braving—
  See it streaming and gleaming and red !
Ah ! the smoke in the air now is waving
  Like a winding-sheet of dull lead.

Hear it laugh with wild glee at each
  futile endeavor
To quench or to quell its exuberant
  force ;

It is flaming, and free, and fantastic
  forever.
It delights and exults with no pang of
  remorse ;
With no pain, with but passion—mad
  passion—it quivers,
With its pennon of scarlet, the blood-
  iest hue ;
With its gleaming streams and roaring
  rivers.
It dares to do all things that flames
  dare to do.
How it darts, how it dances, and dashes,
  As though it had taken for aim,
To reduce all the world into ashes
  And to fling all the stars into flame !
It is glittering and glowing, and glar-
  ing—
  And raging it rings its own knell ;
It is showing its wonderful daring—
  It is turning the sky into hell !

  How it lazily lingers,
    With its swell and its fall ;
  With its fiery fingers
    Weirdly weaving a pall ;
  With its horrible hisses,
    Like the wind in a storm ;
  With its blistering kisses
    On face and on form !

        Of its flashes
          Bereft,
        Only ashes
          Are left :
        Till its cries
          Tell its doom—
        And it dies
          In the gloom.

I have told you the tale of the terrible
  fire ;
It has sung its last song to its luminous
  lyre—
It has sung its last song, it has breathed
  its last breath ;
It has lived without life, it has died
  without death.
        APPLETON'S JOURNAL.

WHO SHALL GO FIRST TO THE SHADOWY LAND?

WHO shall go first to the shadowy land,
        My love or I ?
Whose will it be in grief to stand,
And press the cold, unanswering hand,
Wipe from the brow the dew of death,
And catch the softly fluttering breath,
Breathe the loved name, nor hear reply,
In anguish watch the glazing eye ;
        His or mine ?

Which shall bend over the wounded sod,
        My love or I ?
Commending the precious soul to God,
Till the doleful fall of the muffled clod
Startles the mind to a consciousness
Of its bitter anguish, and life distress,
Dropping the pall o'er the love-lit past
With a mournful murmur " The last—
  the last ; "
        My love or I ?

Which shall return to the desolate home,
        My love or I ?
And list for a step that shall never come,
And hark for a voice that must still be
  dumb,
While the half-stunned senses wander
  back
To the cheerless life and the thorny
  track.
Where the silent room and the vacant
  chair
Have memories sweet, but hard to bear ;
        My love or I ?

Ah ! then, perchance to that mourner
  there !
        My love or I !
Wrestling with anguished and deep
  despair
An Angel shall come through the gates
  of prayer,
And the burning eyes shall cease to
  weep,
And the sobs melt down in a sea of
  sleep,
While fancy freed from the chains of day
Through the shadowy dreamland floats
  away ;
        My love or I ?

And then, methinks, on that boundary
  land,
        My love and I,
The *mourn'd* and the *mourner* together
  shall stand
Or walk by those rivers of shining sand,
Till the dreamer awakened at dawn of
  day

Finds the stone of the sepulchre rolled away,
And over the cold, dull waste of Death,
The warm, bright sunlight of holy Faith,
  My love and I!

THE LIGHT OF OTHER DAYS.

How sweet to sit at eventide
  And ponder o'er the past;
Fond memory's dream recalls again,
  Those hours too bright to last,
She draws her curtain round the mind,
  Excluding every care,
And spreads before our fancied gaze,
  Home visions bright and fair.

The kitchen hearthstone's cheery light,
  E'en now I plainly see,
And little ones with joyous smiles,
  Come tripping up to me;
Their prattling, tongues and ringing laugh,
  Make all the inmates gay,
As o'er the room they freely bound,
  Exultant in their play.

The old clock ticks upon the shelf,
  As one in days before,
And purring puss with quiet look,
  Lies stretched upon the floor;
The watch-dog from his kennel barks,
  At every passing sound,
And home-like scenes grow merrier,
  As fast as the hours speed round.

But every evening has its close,
  And loving friends must part,
Farewell, sweet vision of an hour,
  That's lightened my sad heart.
Farewell, but not forever—no,
  Come oft with thy bright rays,
And bring back to my wearied mind,
  The light of other days.
    —MRS. WILLIAM WEBSTER.

WISHT I COULD.

WISHT I could go back a little, 'n be a boy agin,
A-jerkin' o' the minners with a little crooked pin;
'N hear the frogs a-gruntin' as I git 'em on the jump,
'N me skeered wusser'n they was, when they hit the water plump.

Wisht I could go loafin' 'cross the medder smellin' sweet,
'N feel the sassy daisies a 'tickling o' my feet,
All the while a-noddin' 'n a-smiling up at me—
Wisht I could go back 'n be like I uster be.

Wisht I could go t'morrer, 'n find 'em all the same,
As they was the day I lef' t' make a bigger name;
'N see dear old mother—always skeery —at the gate,
Like she uster wait fer me, whenever I was late.

Wisht I could look in heaven 'n see her there t'day,
'N git a tender smile o' love, like when I went away;
I feel like it ud help me to battle here with sin—
Wisht I could go back awhile, 'n be a boy agin.
    —ATLANTA CONSTITUTION.

DREAMING BY THE RIVER.

SITTING by the silent river, gliding softly, gently by,
List'ning to the mournful cadence of the trees that sough and sigh;
Dreaming of the days departed, musing on the long ago,
Thinking how the long years vanished swiftly as the river's flow.

Longing for the old home-spot that I have not seen for years,
Where the loving mother's waiting with her patient hope and prayers;
Waiting for the boy who left her, through the wide, wide world to roam,
Praying God to guide his footsteps, and to bring him safely home.

Dreaming of the gladsome childhood
   spent among the fields and flowers,
Where the merry brooklet babbled
   through the shady nooks and
   bowers ;
Where the daisies and the blue-bells
   dotted fields and hill-side o'er,
And the roses and the lilies bloomed
   beside the cottage door.

But, alas ! those days have vanished,
   vanished in the silent past,
As all happy hours must vanish, nothing
   in this world can last !
Brightest days of joys and pleasure
   must give place to care and pain,
As the sunny skies of morning oft at
   eve bring clouds and rain.
        —ANONYMOUS.

THE OLD FIREPLACE.

'TWAS built in days so long ago,
   This fireplace, tall and wide ;
And no one now can ever know
   Who, in the winter-tide,
Sat by the warm ingle
And heard the wind mingle
   With snow and sleet outside.

Upon the stones now black with time
   Stretches the golden glow,
The shining flames that redly climb
   Their jagged shadows throw,
The log's drowsy humming
In monotone coming
   Sounds weirdly soft and low.

Along the vistas of the past,
   Faint visions seem to stray,
The print of many feet is cast
   Upon the hearthstone gray,
In dark crannies keeping,
Dim secrets lie sleeping
   There watch the stones alway.

The dreams that come within its light,
   The fire-lit silence fill,
While shadows flit from out the night
   And steal o'er time's doorsill,
Through memory's paths, weary
Come thought phantoms eerie
   Around us wan and still.

Amid the night there falls a spell
   Weaved where the firelight plays,
For fancies past and future dwell
   Where shines the ruddy blaze ;
Aloft, in our dreaming,
Air castles are gleaming,
   Alight with lambent rays.

And when the long cold nights begin,
   Near to the fireplace wide,
We sit, when evening-light creeps in,
   Its cozy hearth beside,
Close by the bright ingle
And hear the wind mingle
   With snow and sleet outside.
        —ELLEN BRAINERD PECK.

POETRY AND RELIGION.

POETRY is virtue expressed in figures of speech. Poetry, I would say, is the religion of words, while religion is the poetry of deeds. So that a truly religious man is a living poem. There is rhythm in his voice, meter and measure in his conduct, ideality in his thoughts and sublimity in his emotions. His life becomes a poem set to the music of harmonious action. To ascend still higher in the affinity between religion and poetry, I would say that both are based on revelation, religion on the direct revelations of God to man—poetry on the revelations of that beauty and loveliness that lie hidden in nature and man. In fact, had we no religion to teach us of a God, poetry would unfold to us his everlasting manifestations. As there is a beautiful image in every piece of marble which the sculptor's art may bring forth, so there are God's secrets and lessons in the rocks and rills, in the flowers and trees, which a poet only can truly depict. The ancients were right in making their prophets and poets identical, as is shown by the word *vates*, which expresses both ; for the poet, as the prophet, is a priest of God.

The soul requires its proper nourishment as well as the body. It is poetry which feeds the hunger of the human heart for immortality. All things physical teach decay and death. Poetry idealizes and symbolizes all our surroundings and transfigures even the sad

habiliments of death with life immortal. None can read Wordsworth's "Ode to Immortality" without being transported from this vale of tears and sadness into a happier world of thought and feeling. We should, however, cherish and foster poetry; not only for its own sake and its own beauty, not only as the handmaid of religion, a teacher of idealism and morality, as a revealer of the secrets of nature and hence as a priest of God; not only as a comforter and messenger of good tidings of another world and better life, but for the sake of religion itself as its strongest bulwark. Poetry is one of the most conservative of influences. It preserves the scenes of the past and the evanescent feelings and emotions, and is perpetuating those lessons and hidden meanings of things already old and which would otherwise be lost. This fact is especially serviceable with regard to the forms and ceremonies of religion. They are an essential part of faith, but seem often useless from a prosaic handling. Poetry envelops them with renewed meaning and life, and by carrying the form in ever roseate habiliments perpetuates at the same time the lesson and the doctrine. Poetry invigorates the Sabbath and holidays, every prayer and fast, with the new idea of modern life. Especially in times of doubt and skepticism is this a great service to religion. And in another direction poetry can demolish the very stronghold of doubt by poetizing science as Tennyson has done in his "In Memoriam." Here the poet has sought to discover a unity beneath all the discordant part of nature which the scientist with his crucible and microscope could never find. And it seems strange, yet wonderfully true, that while poetry thus naturally seeks to elevate faith and draw it nearer to God, it elevates itself also. No great poet ever lived but stood on the vantage ground of faith and aspired to reach the throne of God. If Whittier and Tennyson have gained the ear of mankind it was by this intense religious fervor which breathes through their verses. Of ancient Hebrew poetry, notably, the Psalms of David have been truly called "gorgeous palaces, the materials of which have been supplied by faith."
—REV. DR. JOSEPH SILVERMAN.

GET ACQUAINTED WITH YOURSELF.

YOUNG man the books will bid you read
The seers from Kant to Plato,
But get acquainted with yourself,
You are no small potato;
And though you sling a blacksmith's sledge
Or dig within the trenches,
Hold up your head with those that sit
Upon the highest benches.
Oh! read the sages of the world
And let their wisdom win you,
But get acquainted with yourself
And find what you've got in you.

In modest arrogance of soul
Make your own valuation,
Then slowly make the sluggish world
Accept your estimation.
Go, get acquainted with yourself
Before your leaf is yellow,
You'll find the man beneath your hat
Is something of a fellow.
Then stir him out and prod him up
Before his force has fainted,
Go, get acquainted with yourself,
Then make the world acquainted.

Then trust the man beneath your hat,
And when you come to know him
You'll find a fellow fit to grace
A novel or a poem.
Go, get acquainted with yourself,
You'll find that very few are,
For tasks for which you were designed,
A better man than you are.
Young man the books will bid you read,
The seers from Kant to Plato,
But get acquainted with yourself,
You are no small potato.
—SAM WALTER FOSS, *in Boston Globe.*

LET US FORGET.

Let us forget
The memories that bind us fast
To our mistakes, outgrown and past;
The trust betrayed, the tarnished name,
The look of scorn, the blush of shame,
Let us forget.

Let us forget
That once we strove for selfish gain,
Regardless of another's pain ;
The vain remorse, the sense of loss,
The burden of our self-made cross,
  Let us forget.

Let us forget
The slights, the stings, the anguished tears
That marked the paths of by-gone years ;
The bitter cup, the dark despair,
The one sad hour which none might share
  Let us forget.

Let us forget
All but the love, the grace, the light
That bore us to our present height,
And haunting ghosts of grief and care
The guise of angel hosts shall wear,
  Let us forget.
  —IDA W. WHEELER.

THE REASON WHY.

" 'TIS strange that it always is easy
  For a man when he is flirting, you know,
To swear to a woman he loves her,
  By all that's above and below.

" But when he is truly in earnest,
  Tell me the reason, I pray,
'Tis awfully hard to utter
  The words that he fain would say ? "

She replied, as her dimples deepened,
  " The reason is simple, forsooth ;
'Tis because it is awfully hard, sir,"
  For a man to utter the truth."
    —LIFE.

THE SECRET CHAMBER.

IN my soul there's a secret chamber
  Fast locked with a golden key,
A chamber filled with treasures
  That are hidden even from me.

I know, in that mystical chamber,
  There are dreams that are true and sweet ;
There are songs like the songs the angels
  Sing at the Father's feet.

There are longings and hopes and passions,
  There are thoughts that are white and fair ;
There are poems as great and tender,
  And holy and pure as prayer.

Songs that would speak in music
  To many an aching heart ;
Dreams that would bring fruition
  Of the passionate hopes of Art.

There are treasures of all high feeling ;
  There are jewels of mercy and grace ;
There are ingots of brave ambitions
  Laid away in that mystical place.

And never a song do I fashion,
  But I long for the music that's there,
And never a line do I measure
  But I sigh in a futile despair.

For the treasures are locked in that chamber,
  And never will open to me,
Lest thou, in thy mercy, shouldst listen
  And bring me the mystical key.

Thy love is the key of that chamber,
  And all of its treasures were free,
If thou wouldst design only to hearken
  And give thy dear love unto me.

Then, the dreams and the thoughts and the fancies,
  The hopes and the longings were mine ;
To set in my songs till their music
  Should swell in a beauty divine !

Then, the gems and the jewels of passion,
  That are locked in that chamber away,
I should bind in a circlet of glory
  And all at thy feet I should lay.

For thou art my only ambition,
  And thou art my life and my art—
Who holdest the key to my treasures
  And keepest the door of my heart.
    —HOWARD HAWTHORNE M'GEE.
An das blondlockiges Liebchen geschrieben.

OLD "BOB WHITE."

WHEN peas are ripe you hear the call ;
    "Bob White ! "
In music sweet the clear notes fall :
    "Bob White ! "
(He wants to let his sweetheart know—
That's why he keeps a callin' so.)

Acrost the medder an' the swamp :
    "Bob White ! "
From woodlan's where the rabbits romp ;
    "Bob White ! "
Still, still he calls that name o' his
(I wonder where his sweetheart is ?)

From dewy mornin' up to night :
    "Bob White ! "
An' ringin' down the sweet twilight :
    "Bob White ! "
From break o' day to evenin' dim,
He calls his sweetheart home to him !

AN OLD SCENE.

THERE'S a spot that ever brings
    Dreams of days I used to know,
Where the rose of memory springs
    From the grave of long ago.

Where youth's visions fair arise,
    With its love and hope and trust,
Where I meet the long-closed eyes,
    Clasp the hands that now are dust.

Where the phantoms of the past
    Loving message to me wave ;
Gleams from skies long over-cast,
    Tender greeting from the grave,

While beneath the olden spell
    Beats my heart grown free from care ;
Life is young and all is well,
    And the silver leaves my hair.

Though the feet that trod the path
    Echo lightly there no more ;
Though the sea that rose in wrath,
    Ebbing, left a storm-swept shore.

Still mine eyes gazed thro' the mist
    And the cloudless dawn behold,
When life's sea was amethyst—
    By the sunbeams flecked with gold.

Still this spot forever brings
    Dreams of days I used to know,
And the rose of memory springs
    From the days of long ago.
        CHICAGO INTER-OCEAN.

IN AFTER DAYS.

IN after days, when you and I are parted,—
    When death's mysterious veil is drawn between
Our fateful lives,—will you, still loving-hearted,
    Think tenderly sometimes of what has been ?

Not in your busy hours ;—life is too real
    Always to wear the tinge of fond regret;
And men must work ; and so to your heart, tho' leal,
    Will come some moments when you will forget.

But when you watch the golden daylight dying,—
    When o'er the earth the lengthening shadows creep,—
When down the hill the evening breeze comes sighing
    To kiss the silent waters as they sleep ;

When through the darkening skies the stars break slowly,
    Remote and still, like quivering points of light,—
And Nature's throbbing heart, in slumber holy,
    Rests tremulously in the arms of Night ;—

Ah, will you then look back, with tender yearning,
    To dream of one whose web of life is spun?—
One who grew weary of forever learning
    The hopeless tasks that Fate commanded done.

Or is love, with all its beauty, only
    "A dream and a forgetting," fond and fleet ?
Nay, dear ; methinks your heart—still, true, tho' lonely—
    Will keep remembrance of a past so sweet.

So from that past some words by dead lips spoken
Shall come to say it has not been in vain,
While one by one the slender threads are broken
That Fate has knotted in Life's tangled skein.
—STELLA G. FLORENCE.

LAY OF THE CROAKER.

GOIN' to build an elevator, I hear the folks say.
I warn you now, stranger, 'twon't never pay,
And if you try it on, I'll bet my skin,
You'll sink every dollar that you put in.
Billville's superior, according to my tell,
And Waycross town will beat it all to— well,
'Thout any talkin', you can chalk it down.
An elevator 'll never pay in this here town.

There's people livin' about here who really say
A north and south railroad's comin' this way,
And boast about the size the town's goin' to git.
Some even claim 'twill make a city yit.
City nothin'! I'll jest bet a speckled cow
'Twon't be this big twenty years from now,
Talk that to them, and they look mad and frown,
Bet there'll be no railroad in this here town.

The people that live here? All a sorry lot;
The preacher's a hypocrite, deacon's a sot,
The doctors all quacks, the lawyer a fool,
The teacher's the biggest dolt that ever taught a school:
Boys are all vicious and full of deviltry;
Gals ain't just what they railly ought to be.
Oh, for meanness we've got great renown,
And it's a bad one—this here town.

They say that factories are comin' 'thout fail;
Darned sight better build a good jail,
A poorhouse, reform school and penitentiary,
And let our thieving merchants get in free.
So, stranger, you had better take my advice—
I give it to you 'thout money or 'thout price—
If you want to get done and get done brown,
Just invest your money in this here town.
—JACK CRAYTON.

THE UNFETTERED MUSE.

ARKAN saw and Tennes see,
Past and present you'll agree,
What things do Tennes see?
What was it Arkan saw?
Now let your answers be
Guided by truth and law.

What do we saw in Tennessee?
Logs, saw logs; that's the idee.
What do we see in Arkansas?
Southern kindness without a flaw,
And genuine hospitality
Is scattered around in Tennessee.

Grand as the river that rolls between
Are the kindness shown and the goodness seen.
Grace and beauty everywhere
Are vying with this sunny air.
The flower of Southern chivalry lies
Within this zone of genial skies.
—A. NONYMOUS.

THE LAND OF LONG AGO.

THE Land of the Long Ago, they say,
Lies over the hills of the Far Away,
In the Country of the Past.
'Tis filled with ghosts of the vanished years,
Bent with their load of sorrow and tears,
That people a graveyard vast.

Yet memory paints it fair and sweet
And we wander back with our weary feet
From the gateways of To-day.

To watch the birds in the shady nooks,
To fish again in the rippling brooks,
When the twilight hours grow gray.

"Tis a land of long-forgotten dreams,
The ghosts that lurk by the rippled streams,
Are the shapes we used to know
When the hills of the Far Away seemed near
And hope smiled right in the face of Fear,
In the lands of the Long Ago.
—CHICAGO DISPATCH.

NAMES OF STATES AND THEIR MEANING.

MAINE takes its name from the Province of Maine, in France, and was so called as a compliment to the queen of Charles I., Henrietta, who was its owner.

New Hampshire took its name from Hampshire, England. New Hampshire was originally called Laconia.

Vermont is French (Verd Mont), signifying Green Mountain.

Massachusetts is an Indian word signifying "Country about the Great Hills."

Rhode Island gets its name because of its fancied resemblance to the Island of Rhodes, in the Mediterranean.

The real name of Connecticut is "Quon-eh-ta-cut." It is a Mohican word, and means "Long River."

New York was so named as a compliment to the Duke of York, whose brother, Charles II., granted him that territory.

New Jersey was named for Sir George Carteret, who was at that time governor of the Island of Jersey, in the British Channel.

Pennsylvania, as is generally known, takes its name from William Penn, the "sylvania" part of it meaning woods. Literally, it is "Penn's Woods."

Delaware derives its name from Thomas West, Lord de la Ware.

Maryland was named in honor of Henrietta Maria, queen of Charles I.

Virginia got its name from Queen Elizabeth, the "Virgin Queen."

The Carolinas were named for Charles (Carolus) II.

Florida gets its name from Kanunas de Flores, or "Feast of the Flowers."

Alabama comes from a Greek word, and signifies "Here we rest."

Louisiana was so named in honor of Louis XIV.

Mississippi is a Natchez word and means "Father of Waters."

Three or four Indian interpretations have been given to the word Arkansas, the best being that it signifies "Smoke Waters," the French prefix "Ark" meaning bow.

Tennessee, according to some writers, is from Tenasea, an Indian chief; others have it that it means "River of the Big Bend."

Kentucky does not mean "Dark and Bloody Ground," but is derived from the Indian word "Kain-tuk-ae," signifying "Land at the head of the River."

Ohio has had several meanings fitted to it. Some say that it is a Suwanee word, meaning "The Beautiful River." Others refer to the Wyandotte word Oheza, which signified "Something Great."

Indiana means land of Indians.

Illinois is supposed to be derived from an Indian word which was intended to refer to a superior class of men.

Wisconsin is an Indian word meaning "Wild, Rushing Waters."

Missouri means "Muddy Water."

Michigan is from an Indian word meaning "Great Lake."

The name of Kansas is based on the same as that of Arkansas.

Iowa is named from an Indian tribe, the Kiowas; the Kiowas were so called by the Illinois Indians because they were "across the River."

The name of California is a matter of much dispute. Some writers say that it first appeared in a Spanish romance of 1530, the heroine being an Amazonian named "California."

Colorado is a Spanish word, applied to that portion of the Rocky Mountains on account of its many-colored peaks.

Nebraska means shallow waters.

Nevada is a Spanish word signifying "snow-covered mountains."

Georgia had its name bestowed when it was a colony, in honor of George II.

The Spanish missionaries of 1524 called the country now known as Texas "Mixtecapah," and the people Mixtecas. From this last word the name of Texas is supposed to have been derived.

Oregon is a Spanish word signifying "vales of wild thyme."

Dakota means "leagued" or "allied tribes."

Wyoming is the Indian word for "Big Plains."

Washington gets its name from our first President.

Montana means mountainous,

Idaho, gem of the mountains (Indian).

COURTSHIP.

COURTSHIP is the last brilliant scene in the maiden life of a woman. It is, to her, a garden where no weeds mingle with the flowers, but all is lovely and beautiful to the senses. It is a dish of nightingales served up by moonlight to the mingled music of many tendernesses and gentle whisperings—and eagerness that does not outstep the bounds of delicacy, and a series of flutterings, throbbings, high pulses, burning cheeks, and drooping lashes. But, however delightful it may be, courtship is, nevertheless, a serious business; it is the first turning point in the life of a woman, crowded with perils and temptations. There is as much danger in the strength of love as its weakness. The kindled hope requires watching. The rose tints of affection dazzle and bewilder the imagination, and while always bearing in mind that life without love is a wilderness; it should not be overlooked that true affection requires solid supports. Discretion tempers passion, and it is precisely that quality which, oftener than any other, is found to be absent in courtship. Young ladies in love, therefore, require wise counsellors. They should not trust too much to the impulses of the heart, nor be too easily captivated by a winning exterior. In the selection of a husband, character should be considered more than appearance. Young men inclined to intemperate habits, even but slightly so—rarely make good husbands to the end; they have not sufficient moral stamina to enable them to resist temptation even in its incipient stages and, being thus deficient in self-respect, they cannot possess that pure, uncontaminated feeling which alone capacitates a man for rightly appreciating the tender and loving nature of a true woman. The irreligious man is like a ship without a rudder, and he never can make a good husband, for a house darkened by cold scepticism or an indifference to religion and its duties is never a home—it is merely a shelter; but there is little warmth in the atmosphere of the rooms, and every object in them looks chill and chilling. The indolent man, likewise, cannot be expected to make a good husband, for he neglects his time and wastes his estate, allowing it to be overrun with thistles and brambles, and subsists on the industry of others. Every precaution, then, is necessary in the selection of a husband.

"THY WILL BE DONE."

SHE begged so hard to go with me,
  Dear little one, that busy day—
I told her long I should not be,
  Yet still her tears she would not stay.

To-day I'm begging, begging so,
  Of her, my baby white and still,
To let me only with her go,—
  O Father, were it but Thy will!
    —NEW ORLEANS PICAYUNE.

THE LAND OF DREAMS.

THE twilight deepens, the shadows creep,
  The moonlight quivers in silver beams,
And silent we step in the boat of sleep
  And drift to the shadowy land of dreams.

Oh, mystic land, where the dead return,
  And warm lips cling to the deathless kiss;
And the years are not and the weary learn,
  That anguish dies in the arm of bliss.

Afar, in that holy, unknown land
  Ambition gathers the flowers of fame,
And fortune reaches her golden wand,
  And pure and white is the soul of shame.

The shackles fall from the prisoners there,
  The peasant sits on the throne, a king;
The blind eyes open to all that's fair,
  And deaf ears hear, and dumb lips sing.

Dreams! Who can tell what messengers stray
  Around us all in the hush of night,
When the form lies still as the soulless clay
  And we follow ourselves through love and light?

And who shall say but the land of dreams
  Is the land of the living, after all,
And daily life, with the scars and seams,
  Is only a dream when the shadows fall?
                    —MARTHA BONNER.

EVER NEAR.

O LOVE, thy face, though far, is ever present,
  And thy kind smile, like the soft moon at night,
Shines on my life, and maketh safe and pleasant
  Every rough way, with its soul-kindling light;
And all my dearest thoughts fly out to thee—
Light of my life, thou'rt never far from me.

When on the hills the day is slowly dying,
  And the pale stars peep shyly from the skies,
When 'mid white clouds the winged moon is flying,
  And gray woods to the wind sing symphonies.
Still as I gaze on nature's face so fair,
Heart's dearest love! thy smile is ever there.

And through the long and lonesome midnight hours,
  Dreaming, my soul still hears thy tender voice,
And as the flow'rets smile in sun and showers,
  So doth my heart grow stronger and rejoice.
Thus day and night, wherever thou may'st be,
Light of my life, thou'rt never far from me.
                    —SPRINGFIELD REPUBLICAN.

SOUL TO BODY.

So we must part, my body, you and I,
  Who've spent so many pleasant years together;
'Tis sorry work to lose your company,
  Who clove to me so close, what'er the weather,
From Winter unto Winter, wet or dry;
  But you have reached the limit of your tether,
And I must journey on my way alone,
And leave you quietly beneath a stone.

They say that you are altogether bad,
  Forgive me, 'tis not my experience,
And think me very wicked to be sad
  At leaving you, a clod, a prison, whence
To get quite free I should be very glad.
  Perhaps I may be so a few days hence;
But now, methinks, 'twere graceless not to spend
A tear or two on my departing friend.

Now our long partnership is near completed,
  And I look back upon its history;
I greatly fear I have not always treated
  You with the honesty you showed to me.
And I must own that you have oft defeated
  Unworthy schemes by your sincerity,
And by a blush, or stammering tongue have tried
To make me think again before I lied.

'Tis true you're not so handsome as you were,
But that's not your fault, and is partly mine.
You might have lasted longer, with more care,
And still looked something like your first design.
And even now, with all your wear and tear,
'Tis pitiful to think I must resign
You to the friendless grave, the patient prey
Of all the hungry legions of decay.

But you must stay, dear body, and I go,
And I was once so very proud of you ;
You made my mother's eyes to overflow
When first she saw you, wonderful and new,
And now, with all your faults, 'twere hard to find
A slave more willing, or a friend more true,
Ay—even they who say the worst about you
Can scarcely tell what I shall do without you.

A BEAUTIFUL THOUGHT.

WE know not the author of the following, but it is one of the most beautiful productions we ever read : "Nature will be reported. All things are engaged in writing their own history. The plant and pebble go attended by their own shadow. The rock leaves its scratches on the mountain side, the river its bed in the soil ; the animal leaves bone in the stratum, the fern and the leaf their modest epitaph in the coal. The falling drop makes its epitaph in the sand or stone ; not a footstep in the snow or along the ground but prints in characters more or less lasting a map of its march ; every act of man inscribes itself on the memories of its followers and in his own face. The air is full of sound ; the ground is all memoranda signatures ; and every object is covered over with hints which speak to the intelligent."

YOU WILL MISS ME.

"SOMETIME you will miss me, darling,
When the long night shadows fall,
I shall be beyond the starlight,
And I shall not hear you call,
You will oftimes wake at midnight,
And will think of one dear head
That your bosom softly pillowed—
Resting among the dead !

"All the precious love you gave me
In the olden, happy time,
You will think of, and weave it
Deftly into heartfelt rhyme.
You will miss me—it must be so,
But perhaps our God will give
Unto me the power to cheer you
And watch o'er you while you live.

"I shall come if he is willing,
At the lonely midnight hour,
And my presence soft around you
Shall enfold when storm-clouds lower,
Shielding you from every evil,
Though you may not see my face,
I will never leave you lonely—
There shall be no vacant place.

"All the hopes and aspirations,
All the precious love we've known,
This shall draw our souls together
Round the great Eternal Throne.
Do not mourn for me, my darling,
Meekly bear the chastening rod—
Think that I am with you always
I, who love you next to God."

MISS GUSHER ABROAD.

A DELAYED LETTER.

ST. PETTYSBUG, Feb. 9.

HOME ov mi burth ! dearest on earth !
Land of the brave and free ! !
Yoar own Soo Gusher, over in Rusher,
Pens these lines to thee !

She travels abroad with earl and lord—
Of coarse i mean with their wives—
To spy and look and 'rite her book,
On Youropean manners and lives.

This country, u kno', is rapt up in sno',
And the people are rapt up in furs ;
The soljers u meet are han'som' and neat,
With enormous big boots on and spurs.

You kno' the ole 'Zar ? 'twas whispered afar—
" He's almost de'd with afrite ;
His polish naybor has given him the aguer,
And turned his da' into nite ! "

So i went to his villar with mi Hill's Chill Killer,
And filled him f'om he'd to toe ;
And now, they tell, he's up and well,
And merry as Old Black Joe !

With feelings ov sorrer i leave on the morrer,
This land of serfdom and sno' ;
But I'll 'rite u againe f'om mi vesterbul train,
And pitch u the dots as i go.
     Yours in Rusher,
       Bound for Prusher,
         SOOSAN GUSHER.

AN INITIATED DRUMMER.

ONE thing I like about these " Knights of the Road " is that they are great fellows for secret societies. Most all of the drummers belong to everything going, from the " Grand Knights of the Diamond Garter " down to the " Sons of Temperance." I am quite a hand for all such mysterious things myself, so I get solid with all the boys. My old friend Crookston called on me t'other day to see if I needed any drugs and to have a visit. We had a jolly old time. While we were settin' in the office a chap came in and wanted to borrow $2 on account of a remittance not coming to him as he expected. I told him my $2 I kept to lend was in now, being sent in the day before by Johnnie McIntire, but I never lent it except to drummers. He said " That's me." I gave him the grand hailing sign of an Odd Fellow, which he tumbled to. Then I came the great " hair in the soot " grip of a Pythonic. He tumbled. Then, Crook gave him the G. B. of the Sons of Malta. He was on to it. Then I gave him the hair-poking signal of a Good Tippler, He smiled and said " H. 2O." This is a chemical term meaning " water." Then Crook struck out his hand and gave him the noted P. D. Q. sign of a Royal Arch Brick Mason. He " got thar " on that. Then Crookston examined him as follows to make sure he was a drummer :

" From whence cometh thou, pard ? "
" From the Lodge of the Holy St. Johns, Michigan."
" What seek ye here to do ? "
" To obtain a few orders for cigars."
" Then you are a drummer ? "
" I am so taken and accepted by all the boys."
" How may I know you to be a drummer ? "
" By my cheek and my fifty-pound sample case. Try me."
" How shall you be tried ? "
" By the 'squire."
" Why by the 'squire ? "
" Because the 'squire is a magistrate and an emblem of stupidity."
" Where were you first prepared to be a drummer ? "
" In my mind."
" Where next ? "
" In a printing-office, adjoining a regular post of drummers.
" How were you prepared ? "
" By being divested of my last cent, my cheek rubbed down with a brick, a bunion plastered over each eye, and a heavy sample case in each hand. In this fix I was conducted to the door of the post."
" How did you know it was a door, being blind ? "
" By first stepping in a coal scuttle and afterwards bumping my head against the door knob."
" How gained you admission ? "
" By benefit of my cheek."
" Had you the required cheek? "
" I had not, but Steve Oars had it for me."
" How were you received ? "
" On the sharp toe of a boot, applied to my natural trousers."

"What did this teach you?"
"Not to fool around too much."
"What happened next?"
"I was set down on a cake of ice, and asked if I put my trust in mercantile reports."
"Your answer?"
"Not if I know myself, I don't."
"What happened next?"
"I was put a-straddle of a goat made out of a 2 x 4, and trotted nine times around the room by four worthy brothers, and then brought in front of the Left Bower for further instructions."
"How did he instruct you?"
"To approach a customer in three upright, regular steps, with my business card extended at right angles, my arms forming a regular square."
"How were you then disposed of?"
"I was again seated on the cake of ice in front of a dry-goods box, and made to take the following horrible and binding oath:
"'I, Charles S. Robinson, do hereby and herein most everlastingly and diabolically swear by the Great Bob-Tail Flush, that I will never reveal and always steal all the trade secrets I can for the use and benefit of this Most August Order. And I further swear by the Bald-Headed Jack of Clubs, that I will never give, carve, make, hold, take or cut prices below the regular rates. And I further swear by the Pipers that played before Moses, to never have any commercial dealings with any man, or his wife, sister, grandmother, old maid aunt or uncle, unless they, he, she or it, is sound as a goose. Binding myself under no less a penalty than to have my grip-sack slit from top to bottom, my dirty shirts and socks taken out, and my reputation removed and buried beneath the Pearl Street bridge, where the Salvation Army ebbs and flows every two and one-half hours. So help me Bob Ingersoll, and keep me in backbone.'
"I was then asked what I most needed."
"What was your reply?"
"Money!"
"What did you then behold?"
"A copy of Dunn & Co.'s reports,

open at chapter 'Muskegon.' Upon the one book rested a pair of drug scales, in one pan of which reposed ten pounds of concentrated lye, and in the other sat a small silver jackass."
"What did this emblem signify?"
"The scales indicated the balance between debtor and creditor. The other emblems represented the lie-abilities and ass-sets of bankrupts."
"Did this teach you any lesson?"
"You bet! It taught me the fact that the former are generally so almighty much better than the latter."
"Shake! Brother! * * * Will you be off or from?"
"Both, if I can borrow enough money to get out of town on."
"Have you any cigars?"
"I have."
"Give 'em to me."
"I did not so receive 'em, neither will I so impart 'em."
"How will you dispose of 'em?"
"On sixty days' time or 2 per cent. off for cash, F. O. B."
"All right, begin."
"No, begin you."
"No, you begin."
"Up." "Em." "Set."
"'Set 'em up.' The words and sign are right. Brother Snooks, he is a yard wide and all wool, and you can bet on him."

Brother Crookstone and I both lent the chap $5, and he left with many thanks and kind wishes.

Now you see by this, what a help it is to a fellow when he gets dead broke among strangers, to have these little things to fall back on.
—GRAND RAPIDS TIMES.

OFF YONDER.

ALWAYS just beyond; "off yonder!"
  Where the curtains of life's skies
Part at rosy dawn; with wonder
  Watch we all, with eager eyes.

Watch we with the heart uplifting;
  For the promise as a star
Fixed is, and we're onward drifting
  To the hope beyond the bar.

"Off yonder!" never lying nearer
　Is the gift with longing heart
We reach out for; strangely dearer
　All because so far apart!

Always just beyond! fulfilment
　Of our hopes and happiest dreams.
Could we know a full perfectment,
　Would we watch for Heaven's gleam?

SWEETHEARTS STILL.

Do you think of the long ago, sweetheart,
　As we stand by the old brook's side,
And russet and brown, the leaves float down
　To drift away with the tide?
Do you think of the days gone by,
　When we sat by this dimpled stream
Dreaming for hours 'mid its gay, wild flowers,
　As only youth can dream?

The haws are ripe on the fading boughs
　Where the thrushes used to sing,
When the sky was blue and the blossom new
　In the fresh and joyful spring;
And I dared to plead my love
　Till your lips sweet answer gave,
While, rich and bright, the quivering light,
　Lay on the silvery wave.

You say you are older now—and wise;
　And the time of dreams is o'er,
For our children play on the sunny way
　Where we kept our tryst before.
So you pluck the crimson haws,
　Which are stirred by no brown wing,
And give a sigh to the days gone by,
　And the vanished bloom of spring.

But look up into my face, sweetheart!
　You have been my wife for years;
We have had our share of toil and care,
　And wept together some tears.
Yet our hearts have aye been bound
　In a bond so truly blest,
That I cannot tell (I love so well)
　If autumn or spring is best.
　　　—E. MATHESON, *in Chambers's Journal.*

THE HAND THAT ROCKS THE CRADLE, RULES THE WORLD.

BLESSINGS on the hand of woman!
　Angels guard its strength and grace,
In the palace, cottage, hovel—
　Oh! no matter where the place!
Would that never storms assailed it,
　Rainbows ever gently curled;
For the hand that rocks the cradle
　Is the hand that rules the world!

Woman! how divine your mission
　Here upon our natal sod!
Keep, oh! keep the young heart open
　Always to the breath of God!
All true trophies of the ages
　Are from mother-love impearled;
For the hand that rocks the cradle
　Is the hand that rules the world!

Blessings on the hand of woman!
　Fathers, sons and brothers cry,
And the sacred song is mingled
　With the worship of the sky;
Mingled where no tempest darkens,
　Rainbows ever are unfurled;
For the hand that rocks the cradle
　Is the hand that rules the world!

THE FAREWELL OF HOPE.

I HAVE been to the funeral of all my hopes,
　And entombed them one by one;
　　Not a word was said,
　　Not a tear was shed,
　When the mournful task was done.

Slowly and sadly I turned me round,
　And sought my silent room;
　　And there alone
　　By the cold hearthstone
　I wooed the midnight gloom.

And as the night wind's deepening shade
　Lowered above my brow;
　　I wept o'er days
　　When manhood rays
　Were brighter far than now.

The dying embers on the hearth
　Gave out their flickering light,
　　As if to say
　　This is the way
　The life shall close in night.

I wept aloud in anguish sore
O'er the blight of prospects fair;
　While demons laughed
　And eager quaffed
My tears like nectar rare.

Through hell's red halls an echo ran—
An echo loud and long—
　As in the bowl,
　I plunged my soul,
In the might of madness strong.

And there within that sparkling glass
I knew the cause to lie;
　This all men own
　From zone to zone,
Yet millions drink and die.

　　　　　　　　　R. L.

THE DAYS THAT ARE NO MORE.

Tears, idle tears, I know not what they mean,
Tears from the depth of some divine despair
Rise in the heart and gather in the eyes,
In looking on the happy autumn fields
And thinking of the days that are no more.

Fresh as the first beam glittering on a sail,
That brings our friends up from the under world.
Sad as the last, which reddens over one
That sinks with all we love below the verge.
So sad, so fresh, the days that are no more.

Ah, sad and strange, as in dark summer dawns
The earliest pipes of half-awakened birds
To dying ears, when unto dying eyes
The casement slowly grows a glimmering square;
So sad, so strange, the days that are no more.

Dear as remember'd kisses after death,
And sweet as those in hopeless fancy feign'd
On lips that are for others; deep as love—
Deep as first love, and wild with all regret;
Oh, death in life! the days that are no more.

　　　　　　　Alfred Tennyson.

BY AND BYE.

What will it matter by and bye,
　Whether my path below was bright,
　Whether it wound through dark or light,
Under a gray or golden sky,
When I look on it by and bye?

What will it matter by and bye,
　Whether uphelped I toiled alone,
　Dashing my foot against a stone,
Missing the charge of the angel high,
Bidding me think of the by and bye?

What will it matter by and bye,
　Whether with dancing joy I went,
　Down through the years with a gay content,
Never believing—nay, not I,
Tears would be sweeter by and bye!

What will it matter by and bye,
　Whether with cheek to cheek I've lain,
　Close to the pallid angel, pain,
Soothing myself with sob and sigh—
"All will be elsewise by and bye!"

What will it matter—nought if I
　Only am sure the way I've trod,
　Gloomy or gladdened, leads to God,
Questioning not of the how, the why,
If I but reach him by and bye.

What will I care for the unshared sigh,
　If, in my fear of lapse or fall,
　Close I have clung to Christ through all,
Mindless how rough the road might lie,
Sure he will smoothen it by and bye.

What will it matter by and bye?
  Nothing but this—That joy or pain
  Lifted me skyward—helped to gain,
  Whether through rack, or smile or sigh,
Heaven—home—all in all—by and bye!
  —Mrs. Preston.

ONE FRIEND.

How pleasant it is to have one friend to whom we can go and unbosom our feelings when the world is harsh with us, and darkness has settled on the fair face of nature. At such a time a heart to advise and counsel with us—that will manifest feeling and sympathy—is above a price. The outgushings of love and tenderness revive and cheer us—drive away sadness from the bosom, and brighten the heavens again. He who has one to whom he can go in the hour of adversity, can never be wholly cast down; dark as it may sometimes be, it will always be a bright spot, beautiful, it will grow brighter, and brighter, till the stricken desolate heart partakes of the fulness of joy and is cast down no more forever.

THE CLOSING YEAR.

'Tis midnight's holy hour—and silence now
Is brooding, like a gentle spirit, o'er
The still and pulseless world. Hark! on the winds
The bell's deep tones are swelling; 'tis the knell
Of the departed year. No funeral train
Is sweeping past; yet on the stream and wood,
With melancholy light, the moonbeams rest,
Like a pale, spotless shroud; the air is stir'd
As by a mourner's sigh; and on yon cloud,
That floats so still and placidly through heaven,
The spirits of the seasons seem to stand,
Young Spring, bright Summer, Autumn's solemn form,
And Winter with his aged locks, and breath
In mournful cadences, that come abroad
Like the far wind-harp's wild and touching wail,
A melancholy dirge o'er the dead year,
Gone from the earth forever. 'Tis a time
For memory and for tears. Within the deep,
Still chambers of the heart, a spectre dim
Whose tones are like the wizard voice of Time,
Heard from the tomb of ages, points its cold
And solemn finger to the beautiful
And holy visions that have pass'd away,
And left no shadow of their loveliness
On the dead waste of life. That spectre lifts
The coffin-lid of hope, and joy, and love,
And, bending mournfully above the pale
Sweet forms that slumber there, scatters dead flowers
O'er what has pass'd to nothingness. The year
Has gone, and, with it, many a glorious throng
Of happy dreams. Its mark is on each brow,
Its shadow in each heart. In its swift course,
It waved its sceptre o'er the beautiful,
And they are not. It laid its pallid hand
Upon the strong man, and the haughty form
Is fallen, and the flashing eye is dim.
It trod the hall of revelry, where throng'd
The bright and joyous, and the tearful wail
Of stricken ones is heard, where erst the song
And reckless shout resounded. It pass'd o'er
The battle plain, where sword and spear and shield
Flash'd in the light of midday—and the strength
Of serried hosts is shiver'd, and the grass,
Green from the soil of carnage, waves above
The crush'd and mouldering skeleton. It came
And faded like a wreath of mist at eve;

Yet, ere it melted in the viewless air ;
It heralded its millions to their home
In the dim land of dreams. Remorseless Time—
Fierce spirit of the glass and scythe—what power
Can stay him in his silent course, or melt
His iron heart to pity ? On, still on
He presses, and forever. The proud bird,
The condor of the Andes, that can soar
Through heaven's unfathomable depths, or brave
The fury of the northern hurricane,
And bathe his plumage in the thunder's home,
Furls his broad wings at nightfall, and sinks down
To rest upon his mountain-crag,—but Time
Knows not the weight of sleep or weariness,
And night's deep darkness has no chain to bind
His rushing pinion. Revolutions sweep
O'er earth, like troubled visions o'er the breast
Of dreaming sorrow ; cities rise and sink,
Like bubbles on the water ; fiery isles
Spring, blazing, from the ocean, and go back
To their mysterious caverns ; mountains rear
To heaven their bald and blacken'd cliffs, and bow
Their tall heads to the plain ; new empires rise,
Gathering the strength of hoary centuries,
And rush down like the Alpine avalanche,
Startling the nations ; and the very stars,
Yon bright and burning blazonry of God,
Glitter a while in their eternal depths,
And, like the Pleiad, loveliest of their train,
Shoot from their glorious spheres, and pass away,
To darkle in the trackless void :—yet Time—
Time, the tomb-builder, holds his fierce career,
Dark, stern, all-pitiless, and pauses not
Amid the mighty wrecks that strew his path,
To sit and muse, like other conquerors,
Upon the fearful ruin he has wrought.
—GEORGE D. PRENTICE.

NOTHING BUT LEAVES.

NOTHING but leaves ! The spirit grieves
Over a wasted life ;
Sins committed while conscience slept,
Promises made but never kept ;
Hatred, battle, and strife,
Nothing but leaves !

Nothing but leaves ! No garnered sheaves
Of life's fair ripened grain,
Words, idle words, for earnest deeds.
We sow our seeds, lo ! tares and weeds,
To reap, with toil and pain,
Nothing but leaves !

Nothing but leaves ! Memory weaves
No veil to cover the past,
As we return our weary way,
Counting each lost and misspent day,
We find sadly at last
Nothing but leaves !

And shall we meet the Master so ?
Bearing our withered leaves ?
The Saviour looks for perfect fruit ;
We stand before Him, humbled, mute,
Waiting the word He breathes,
Nothing but leaves !

LOST THINGS.

THERE are a great many things lost that are found again, and a great many others that are lost and never found. There are reputations lost, which cannot be regained ; there are hopes lost, which come not back again ; there are joys and friendships lost ; there are thoughts and talents lost, which are never found. Every man has at some time lost something, which he would give the world, if it was his, to recover. It may have been but a single pearl from the thread of friendship, or a mere hope of his soul, but it was preciously dear to him, and smallest things are ofttimes the dearest to the heart of man, as for instance, a little wife, a little heir, a fortune, a little home. What wonder, then, that, when they are lost, he would give everything he had for their recovery?

SOCIABILITY.

THINK how much happiness you convey to each other by kindly notice and a cheerful conversation. Think how much sunshine such sociability lets back into your own soul. Who does not feel more cheerful and contented for receiving a polite bow, and a genial "good morning with a hearty shake of the hand?" Who does not make himself happier by these little expressions of feeling and good will? Silence, and a stiff, unbending reserve are essentially selfish and vulgar. The generous and polite man has pleasant recognition and cheerful words for all he meets. He paves the paths of others with smiles. He makes society seem genial, and the world delightful to those who would else find them cold, selfish, and forlorn. And what he gives is but a tithe of what he receives. Be social wherever you go, and wrap your lightest words in tones that are sweet and a spirit that is genial.

IN MEMORIAM.

("OUR MOTHER").

WE walk life's pathway, each with purer feeling,
Knowing her presence lingers round us still,
Feeling her spirit is a light revealing
  A truer knowledge of the Eternal will.
We miss her ever, yet a sweet communion
Bringeth a compensation unto each,
Binding our spirits in a tender union,
  Too deep for utterance—too pure for speech.

In all the years which yet may lie before us
  We know no higher love than her's will be,
Oh, that some hearts as fondly may deplore us,
  When we have crossed, like her, the Eternal Sea!
Faithful and true, through all her sad hereavements,
She walked with uncomplaining step life's way,
Building a monument of pure achievements,
  Far more enduring than the things of clay.

To live each day, for each day's humble duty;
To bear the cross, yet never show the pain—
To wear upon one's brow the spirit's beauty—
  To die, and leave a record without stain!
These are the tests which stamp upon our being
  A more enduring impress than earth's fame,
A spotless passport to the Great All-Seeing,
  A crown imperishable as His great name.

Thus was her life, from whom we late have parted,
  Full of all loving ministries and grace—
So patient, kind, gentle and tenderhearted
That dying we saw the angel in her face.
Rest thee, oh mother, in thy sweet seclusion!
We murmur not, Oh! God, at Thy decree,
We only hope when freed from life's illusion,
We may, like her, dear Father, come to Thee.
    —APPLETON OAKSMITH.

WAYWORN.

I AM alone, sweet friends—be not unkind!
Of all my earthly benefits bereft.
A weary traveller, I have left behind
  All that I loved, and now have nothing left!

Way down the darkening dingle,
The cows come slowly home.

Sorrow and Sin have made me what I am,
And from their cruel thralldom I would flee!
Suffer my soul to feel a little calm—
For the sweet Christ be merciful to me!
I fain would rest along the rugged way;
May I not tarry with you for a day?

I am but human; by temptation led,
I may have known what ye have never known!
But, wist ye not of what the Master said:
"Let him that hath not sinned first cast a stone"?
The way is rough; behold my bleeding feet—
Thorn-pierced, yet struggling still the goal to win!
Open your hearts and hear my sad heart beat!
Be pitiful, and take the wanderer in!
I need your care—my sufferings you mark;
A wayworn brother, dying in the dark!
—F. L. STANTON.

WHEN THE COWS COME HOME.

"When klingle klangle, klingle,
Way down the dusty dingle,
The cows are coming home;
Now sweet and clear, and faint and low,
The airy tinklings come and go,
Like chimings from the far-off tower,
Or patterings of an April shower.
That makes the daisies grow;
Ko-ling, ko-lang, kolingle lingle.
Way down the darkening dingle,
The cows come slowly home;
(And old-time friends, and twilight plays,
And starry nights and sunny days,
Come trooping up the misty ways,
When the cows come home,)
With jingle, jangle, jingle,
Soft notes that sweetly mingle,
The cows are coming home;
Malvine, and Pearl and Florimel,
De Kamp, Redrose and Gretchen Schell,
Queen Bess and Sylph, and Spangled Sue

Across the fields I hear her "loo-oo"
And clang her silver bell:
Go-ling, go-lang, golingle dingle,
With faint far sounds that mingle,
The cows come slowly home;
(And mother-songs of long-gone years,
And baby joys and childish fears,
And youthful hopes and youthful tears,
When the cows come home)
With ringle, rangle, ringle,
With twos and threes and single
The cows are coming home;
Through violet air we see the town,
And the summer air a-slipping down,
And the maple in the hazel glade,
Throws down the path a longer shade,
And the hills are growing brown:
To-ring, to-ring, toringeringle
By threes and fours and single,
The cows come slowly home;
(The same sweet sound of wordless psalm.
The same sweet June-day rest and calm,
The same sweet rest of buds and balm,
When the cows come home,)
With tinkle, tankle tinkle
Through fern and periwinkle,
The cows are coming home;
A-loitering in the checkered stream,
Where the sun rays glance and gleam,
Clarvin, Peach-bloom and Phebe Phillis
Stand knee-deep in the creamy lilies,
In a drowsy dream:
To-link, to-lank, tolinkle linkle
O'er banks with butter-cups a-twinkle,
The cows come slowly home;
(And up through memory's dim ravine
Come the brook's old song, and its old-time sheen,
And the crescent of the Silver Queen,
When the cows come home.)
With klingle, klangle, klingle,
With loo-oo, and moo-oo, and jingle,
The cows are coming home;
And over there on Merlin Hill,
Hear the plaintive cry of the whip-poor-will
And the dew-drops lie on the tangled vines,
And over the poplars Venus shines,
And over the silent mill;
Ko-ling, ko-lang, kolingle lingle,
With ting-a-ling and jingle
The cows come slowly home;

Let down the bars; let in the train
Of long gone songs, and flowers and rain,
For dear old times come back again,
When the cows come home.)"

M-PHATIC.

"My Madeline! my Madeline!
Mark my melodious midnight moans;
Much may my melting music mean,
My modulated monotones.

"My mandolin's mild minstrelsy,
My mental muse's magazine,
My mouth, my mind, my memory,
Must, mingling, murmur 'Madeline!'

"Muster 'mid midnight's masquerade,
Mark, Moorish maiden, matron's mein;
'Mongst Murcia's most majestic maids,
Match me my matchless Madeline.

"Mankind's malevolence may make
Much melancholy music mine;
Many my motives may mistake,
My modest merits much malign.

"My Madeline's most mirthful mood
Much mortifies my mind's machine;
My mournfulness's magnitude
Melts—makes me merry, Madeline!

"Match-making ma's may machinate,
Manœuvring misses me misween;
More money may make many mate,
My magic motto's—Madeline!

"Meet, most mellifluous melody,
'Midst Murcia's misty mounts marine,
Meet me by moonlight, marry me,
Madonna mia!—Madeline!"

HEART WOUNDS.

THE wounds, that are made into the hidden depths of the bosom, are hard to heal. We may try the emollient poultice of time, and hope that its gentle soothing will bring relief in blessed oblivion. We may, even, try the balm to be found in the higher remedy of religious comfort. But human nature is so weak and in spite of all our efforts, it is impossible to so wean our thoughts from things that are passion-crowned as to find all the consolation we may need in mere spiritual relief. The wounds are still there —deep down in the heart—and though they may have been covered over, they are yet tender and sore, and will quicken again at the first touch of remembrance.

Let the smitten heart seek what source of forgetfulness it will—whether it seeks distraction amid scenes of excitement and dissipation, or perhaps, turns to another and purer shrine for its worship, there will, at times, gleam forth little stars in the twilight of memory, which will lighten up the slumbering depths of feeling, and bring back to view, in overwhelming sorrow, that "olden time" with its wealth of smiles and joys which once brightened life with Heaven-borrowed hues, only to fade away and leave our future pathway more bleak and desolate than ever.

A LITERARY CURIOSITY.

THE following remarkable little poem is a contribution to the San Francisco Times from the pen of Mrs. H. A. Deming. The reader will notice that each line is a quotation from some one of the standard authors of England and America. This is the result of a year's laborious search among the voluminous writings of thirty-eight leading poets of the past and present. The number of each line refers to its author below:

LIFE.

1. WHY all this toil for triumphs of an hour?
2. Life's a short Summer, man a flower.
3. By turns we catch the vital breath and die—
4. The cradle and the tomb, alas! so nigh.
5. To be, is better far than not to be,
6. Though all man's life may seem a tragedy;
7. But light cares speak when mighty griefs are dumb,
8. The bottom is but shallow whence they come.

9. Your fate is but the common fate of all ;
10. Unmingled joys here to no man befall.

11. Nature to each allots its proper sphere ;
12. Fortune makes folly her peculiar care.

13. Custom does often reason overrule,
14. And throw a cruel sunshine on a fool.

15. Live well ; how long or short, permit to Heaven ;
16. They who forgive most shall be most forgiven.

17. Sin may be clasped so close we cannot see its face—
18. Vile intercourse, where virtue has no place.

19. Then keep each passion down, however dear,
20. Thou pendulum betwixt a smile and tear.

21. Her sensual snares let faithless pleasure lay,
22. With craft and skill, to ruin and betray.

23. Soar not too high to fall, but stoop to rise ;
24. We masters grow of all that we despise.

25. Oh, then, I renounce that impious self-esteem ;
26. Riches have wings, and grandeur is a dream.

27. Think not ambition wise because 'tis brave :
28. The paths of glory lead but to the grave,

29. What is ambition ? 'Tis a glorious cheat—
30. Only destructive to the brave and great.

31. What's all the gaudy glitter of a crown ?
32. The way to bliss lies not on beds of down.

33. How long we live, not years, but actions tell ;
34. That man lives twice who lives the first life well.

35. Make then, while yet ye may, your God your friend,
36. Whom Christians worship, yet not comprehend.

37. The trust that's given guard, and to yourself be just :
38. For, live we how we can, die we must.

1, Young ; 2, Dr. Johnson ; 3, Pope ; 4, Prior ; 5, Sewell ; 6, Spenser ; 7, Daniell ; 8, Sir Walter Raleigh ; 9, Longfellow ; 10, Southwell ; 11, Congreve ; 12, Churchill ; 13, Rochester ; 14, Armstrong ; 15, Milton ; 16, Bailey ; 17, Trench ; 18, Somerville ; 19, Thomson ; 20, Byron ; 21, Smollett ; 22, Crabbe ; 23, Massinger ; 24, Cowley ; 25, Beattie ; 26, Cowper ; 27, Sir Walter Davenant ; 28, Gray ; 29, Willis ; 30, Addison ; 31, Dryden ; 32, Francis Quarles ; 33, Watkins ; 34, Herrick ; 35, William Mason ; 36, Hill ; 37, Dana ; 38, Shakespeare.

DOES ANY ONE CARE FOR FATHER ?

Does any one care aught for father ?
Does any one think of the one
Upon whose tired, bent shoulders
The cares of the family come ?

The father who strives for your comfort,
And toils on from day unto day,
Although his steps ever grow slower,
And his dark locks are turning to gray.

Does any one think of the due bills
He's called upon daily to pay,
Milliner bills, college bills, doctor's bills ?
There are some kind of bills every day,

Like a patient old horse in a treadmill,
  He works on from morning till night—
Does any one think he is tired?
Does any one makes his home bright?

Is it right, just because he looks troubled,
  To say he's as cross as a bear?
Kind words, little actions of kindness,
  Might banish his burden of care.

'Tis for you he is ever so anxious—
  He will toil for you while he may live;
In return he will only ask kindness,
  And such pay it is easy to give.
—Mrs. H. Spencer.

THE GILDED AGE

Man is much of chronic grumbler, and truly "never is, but always to be blessed." He is very much like the pig in an orchard,—no matter on which side of the orchard he is turned in, he imagines the best pickings are on the other side! With him the present never counts for much, but it is either the past that was, or the future that is to be, glorious. In his youth it is usually the future. In his older age it is the past that becomes the gilded age. The real truth is, both are gilded ages, and the future will be but an improved continuation of the past and present. Even though death intervenes, the harvest can but be of the seed sown, and nature and plans will go on repeating themselves. But little attention is paid to the youth's fabulous and fantastic dreams. Everybody knows he is guessing, and in the absence of prophesy, feel that they have as much right to guess as he. So he has his say and nobody is hurt by it. But can as much be said of the old man's say? He will have an audience. In consequence of his age, and the assumption that old men know much that no one else does, their individual experience, and uncontradicted wisdom, often passes for truth and history when it is really very far from it. The old man forgets he lives in the past and sees no reason why his boy should rise on tiptoes and try to peer into the future, if only in his imagination. To him the past is familiar, and no times were so good, no man so smart, and no deed so great, as those of the past. Everything of the past had a better taste and richer flavor to him than at present. As a matter of fact, he has forgotten the many bad tastes and flavors and only remembers the good ones. Still his mind goes back on all occasions to the good things and good old times of the past, until his boy almost doubts his father's strength of mind, and concludes that he, himself had inherited a great propensity for tale-telling!

Yet, is it a fact that the past had so many enchantments that the present does not have? To the savage, whose only aim was hunting, it had. To the hermit, who wished much of the world to himself, it is perhaps also true. Indeed, in the race of the survival of the fittest, the crushed out have always held on tenaciously, and felt that it was a hardship to make way for the fittest. Yet, make way they must, for such is the inevitable law of God and nature. The crushed out had their "Good old days," and, the fittest, which survive them, will also have their good old days; and in turn, become the crushed out for the still more fit. It is but the plan and wisdom of the Creator of all that progress asserts itself and that the world grows better and happier, as the flower unfolds itself, leaf by leaf. We need not go very far back to see this, for the ruins of the extinct are everywhere, although our limitations only extend to a few hundred years at best. To the past century, they almost stop, and yet during that time, what do we find? All countries proportionally limited, and this one no where crossing the Mississippi, and nowhere touching the Gulf of Mexico. At that time its fifteen states did not average as many million of people, and it could boast of no city of fifty thousand inhabitants. It had no water-works, no fire-departments, no police forces, and only a very few newspapers, and almost no books to read. It all has been but quite a short while ago, and yet there were then no envelopes, no postage stamps, no railroads, no steamboats, no telegraph, no matches, no bicycles, and thousand and one things that are to-day very commonplace and go largely to make up the happiness and comfort of man. It is not claimed that there have been any special visitations of Providence for this century; yet, it was only in 1828 that the first locomotive was made, and later since the first steamship crossed the ocean; and later since the cotton-gin, reaper, steam loom, modern printing-press, ice machine, telephone, photographic camera, and thousands of other things, too numerous to mention, were given to the world, and which it now appears that no age could get on without. All of them not only brought the benefits of their use, but created a demand for engineers, firemen, coal-diggers, mechanics and laborers, in a thousand fields that did not exist, and without which many must have been crowded out of employment. With them came also new wants and employments, and a thousand of comforts and luxuries that our predecessors, in their gilded ages, could not have had anywhere, or at any price. The man of to-day enjoys those of the past and many more: and still we are told of those "good old times." They were "good old times," but in the living present are better times; and in the coming future, will, in all probability, be still better times. It may have been well for the lover then to "take his pen in hand," although it was only a goose-quill: yet, think of the later days of "taking his typewriter in his arms!" And don't forget that he also paid twenty-five cents postage on his letters, and felt in luck if she ever got them. Think also of the branding-iron, the pillory, the stocks and the lash, to say nothing of the burning of "witches," and other things which were common in many countries that the bad and terrible present would not tolerate for a moment.

Yes, if the common, everyday man, who is known as the "tin bucket brigade," and upon whom good or bad times so largely depend, is disposed to be dissatisfied with his present condition, let him ask the old man, who lives in the past, how was it then? If he tells you the truth, he will say they were either slaves, or but little better. If your wages are low now, they were still lower then. In fact, only from six to twelve dollars a month, in many cases, and that payable monthly, instead weekly, and a day's work from "sun to sun," instead of ten hours. If the old man talks of stage-coaches, and says inventions and machinery have taken away labor, ask him if the railroads, which took the place of the stage-coach, do not give employment to more people now than were in the country then? If the making of machinery does not give employment to more people than there were to employ at that time? If he insists that hunting had been ruined, ask him if the manufactory of timber from the hunting grounds did not feed more people than the game thereon? If he says the fishing is spoiled by the mills, factories and steamboats on the steams, ask him if the mill, factories and steamboats do not employ more laborers than there were fishermen, and if the fishing does not still go on, though the fish be artificially hatched before being caught.

Yes, ask him if it is not a fact that the dwellings of men are not far better now than then; and are there not in them thousands of things for comfort that did not then exist, or were attainable only by the rich? As a matter of fact, he now gets his clothes, sugar, coffee, ice, and hundreds of other things, at far cheaper prices than then, while the asylum, hospital, library, newspaper and public schools are everywhere open to him. His wife now aids him by her sewing machine, "kitchen piano," or patent range, instead of in the field; while the boys help make a living by the sale of books and papers before riding to school on a bicycle,—the poor man's horse, that does not have to be fed!

Indeed, the evidences are too numerous to believe that all the good times, or even the best times existed in the past; or that people live longer or were happier, except on the principle that where "ignorance is bliss, 'tis folly to be wise," and that the early years of any life are the happiest of it. This was always true, and the visionary view of it will continue to depend upon which side of the hill of life the individual looks at it. To one the mirage is in front of him; to the other it is behind him. The real object of the reflection, however, is the gilded, living, present.

That is the age of all the ages with which we have to do, It has its blessings, and which were never before equalled. It is ours. The future is God's,—who will doubtless unfold newer, perhaps better, blessings, for those still fitter than we.

THE OLD HOMESTEAD.

THE darling, dear old Homestead, the
    sunniest and best,
Where wanderers from every clime
    found welcome and sweet rest,

Where footprints in the yielding sand
    Were long since swept away;
And hearts and hands which toiled for us
    Seemed but as yesterday.

Where mourning ones were sooth'd and warmed
    By many a soft caress,
And children's soulful laugh rang out
    In song and happiness.

Long, long ago, when young, I watched,
    From my dear sunlit room,
The day's bright glory hasten
    To dissipate night's gloom.

And often from the dear old home
    Beneath gray Kaatskill's mount,
I watched him through his gorgeous tints,
    Drop in his golden fount.

In waking dreams, it comes to me
    Like sunbeams, on my track,
And misty wreaths from mountain tops
    Seem rolling gently back.

And the Hudson, with it silvery waves,
    All placid, proud and free—
And so the dear old homestead,
    In my youth comes back to me.

No house so large in all the place,
    Two dizzy stories high!
Looking with hospitable ease
    Upon each passer-by.

Five windows ranging from above,
    And four upon the ground,
The massive door, once painted white,
    The frontal entrance crowned.

The lilac bush which proudly
    Beside the bee-house stood,
An open fountain for the toilers,
    Gathering winter food;

The morning glories in their robes
    Of rose and purple hue,
Twin'd sweetly 'bout the window panes
    And drank the early dew.

The old brown school-house on the hill
    Beside the poplar trees,
Where teachers, armed with birchen toys,
    The scholars ne'er could please.

Where Daboll's sums were ciphered out
    Through many sighs and tears;
And Murray's rules, though learned by heart,
    Were mysteries for years.

Still, fabled wayside shrine ne'er gain'd
    More loyal devotees
Than this, where men of high renown
    First learned their A B C's.

The treasured, dear old homestead,
    What fountain depths are stirred,
What hallowed memories thrill the soul
    At that one sacred word!

What tearful eyes watched o'er us then,
    Hearts changeless, true and warm,
And loving arms that clasped us round
    To shield us from life's storm.

There too, within the hallowed walls
    Whence flow sweet rills of grace,
By faith, the covenant seal, upon
    My infant brow was plac'd.

In the deep hush of quenchless love
    The mother bore her part,
While from the aged pastor's hand,
    The sacred symbols dropt.

The walk of smooth gray flagstone,
  The Balm of Gilead tree,
Where birds sang 'mongst quivering
    leaves,
  The sweetest minstrelsy.

The elm, beneath whose graceful
    boughs
  Our play-house used to be,
Beside the huge old grindstone
  Where we played—" Come to see."

The ancient damask rose, which
    bloom'd
  Beneath my mother's eye,
Like her, diffusing choicest sweets
  On all so royally.

The plat of ground for summer flowers
  Where golden sunshine lay,
The dill and fennel aroma,
  And old-time caraway.

The orchards, with their weight of
    fruit—
  Of golden, green and red—
The grove of pines, in summer time,
  Where sheep were watched and fed.

The well-worn path across the green,
  Where we so often rov'd ;
The little brook that murmured by
  Life's daily mission prov'd.

The meadow grass, which fell beneath
  The mower's cruel hand,
I almost feel the aroma
  Which thrilled my senses then.

The sheaves from out the autumn fields
  Were gathered in the barn ;
And neighbor men and boys came in
  To husk the yellow corn.

But ah ! the peach and apple blooms
  Were sweeter far than now,
And oft we plucked the tiny buds
  From some deep hidden bough,

And tied them with gay ribbon grass
  Within our streaming hair.
Oh ! happier far than royalty
  Decked in their jewels rare.

We cannot tell the father's toil
  In honest manly pride,
Or the mother's patient lullaby
  Sung sweetly by his side,

While wielding nobly plough and hoe
  She plied the busy wheel,
And together sought the Mercy-seat,
  To ask the pardon sealed.

The well ! O what were homesteads
  Without the dear old well !
Where we learned to draw the bucket
  From its stony cell.

And laid our hands upon the curb
  So mossy, old and brown,
And wondered how it could be built,
  So many fathoms down.

And oft as twilight shadows fell,
  Upon the dark brown hill,
We stole out silently to hear—
  To hear the whistling whippoorwill,

The robin's morning carolee,
  The meadow lark's refrain,
The many home-born melodies
  We shall not hear again.

Nor as the twilight shadows fall
  Upon the dark brown hill,
Shall we step softly out to hear,
  The whistling whippoorwill !

O pleasant sounds ! O cherished sights !
  As seen through memory's sheen,
Was the darling, dear Old Homestead,'
  Our Homestead on the green.
                        MRS. C. B. V.

A DAY DREAM.

I CAN see her now, how plainly to my
    memory comes the sight
  Of that sweet old wrinkled face, to
    me so dear ;
Framed in curls that formed a halo of
    the softest, purest white ;
  Lighted up by eyes so tender, blue
    and clear.
Oh, the wondrous tales she told,
  Of the robber knights of old,
That used to fill my boyish scul with
    dread.
  But she brushed away all fear
  With each tangled lock of hair,
As she kissed and tucked me in my
    trundle bed.

What a tender, loving smile was always
    on that dear old face ;
And what music did that thin, sweet
    voice employ ;
What a world of consolation found I in
    that boundless grace,
That would let her see no evil in her
    boy.
    Oh, how bountifully blessed,
    Was the curly head that pressed
That bosom, as she crooned some
    quaint old song :
    Gently rocking to and fro
    In the evening's firelight glow,
Safely shielded from all chance of
    harm or wrong.

Many years have come and gone since
    I saw that dear old face ;
Many years of toil and blessing, pain
    and joy ;
But there always will remain within my
    heart a tender place,
For that guardian angel to a way-
    ward boy.
    Little prayers learned at her knee,
    Little stories told to me,
In those early days, come crowding
    back the while ;
    And, oh, what would I not give
    O'er those days again to live,
Basking in my dear old granny's
    tender smile.
    —ARTHUR C. TURNER, *in Detroit Free Press.*

ONE BY ONE.

THEY are gathering homeward from
    every land,
        One by one,
As their weary feet touch the shining
    strand,
        One by one,
Their brows are bound with a golden
    crown ;
Their travel stained garments are all
    laid down,
And clothed in white raiment they rest
    on the mead,
Where the Lamb loveth his children to
    lead,
        One by one.

Before they rest they pass through the
    strife,
        One by one
Through the waters of death they enter
    life,
        One by one,
To some are the floods of the river still
As they ford their way to the Heavenly
    hill ;
To others the waves run fiercely wild,
Yet all reach the home of the undefiled,
        One by one.

We, too, shall come to that river side,
        One by one,
We are nearer its waters each even-
    tide.
        One by one,
We can hear the noise and the dash of
    the stream,
Now and again, through our life's deep
    dream ;
Sometimes the flood all its banks o'er-
    flow,
Sometimes in ripples the small waves
    go,
        One by one.

Jesus, Redeemer, we look to Thee,
        One by one ;
We lift up our voices tremblingly
        One by one.
The waves of the rivers are dark and
    cold,
We know not the spot where our feet
    may hold ;
Thou who did'st pass through in dark
    midnight,
Strengthen us, send us Thy staff and
    Thy light
        One by one.

Plant Thou Thy feet beside as we tread,
        One by one ;
On Thee let us lean each drooping
    head,
        One by one.
Let but Thy strong arms around us be
    twined.
We shall cast our cares and fears to
    the wind ;
Saviour, Redeemer, be Thou in full
    view,
Smilingly, gladsomely shall we **pass**
    through,
        One by one.

HOPE AGAIN.

O, MY soul, why are thou sad ?
  Life hath earnest work to do ;
"Hope again !" hope maketh glad,
  Gird thine armor on anew,—
Life hath much for thee to do.

Bravely stand the battle's jar ;
  Like a valiant soldier fight
In life's tangled maze of war,
  Knowing well thy course is right,
Soon will dawn the morning light.

Though creation should unite
  To wrench thy banner from the sky,
Never turn to take thy flight,
  For to turn is but to die ;
Let thy course then onward lie.

Fight for truth, and strive for right—
  Let error, base deceit and pride
Quickly vanish from thy sight
  As thy car doth onward ride—
With truth and justice as thy guide.

Then, when life's combat 's o'er,
  Thou a pensioner shalt be,
On a bright and radiant shore,
  Far beyond life's boisterous sea,—
From gloomy sorrow ever free.

"ENDLESS STRIFE."

So weary of life—careworn by sin,
So tired of strife—and worn out by din—
Ceaselessly striving to act some part—
Veiling the soul and shrouding the heart,
Loving the world, yet longing to be
At last at peace, untrammell'd and free :
Still ever struggling in Endless Strife—
FATHER IN HEAVEN—I'm weary of life !

Weary of life that was once so bright
With its dazzling dreams of heav'nly light—
Its promising buds in childhood's days—
The rose's blush of its noonday blaze :
Thoughtlessly smiling—when I would weep,
While life's petals were dropping to sleep—
Defying the clouds to dark'n my life—
FATHER IN HEAVEN—I'm tired of strife !

Weary of life that hath grown so dark,
Battling, storm-toss'd on a battered barque :
Weary, my GOD, as was once yon dove
Longing to find the dry land above—
Seeking some spot where the feet may rest
Above the deluge that whelms my breast ;
Struggling 'midst waves—forever at strife
FATHER IN HEAVEN—I'm weary of life !

THE PICTURE IN MY HEART.

IN each man's soul there lives a dream
  Lit by a woman's eyes.
Whose glance thrills the tender gleam
  That thrills the evening skies.
It is a dream that never faints
  Though weal or woe befalls,
But haunts the heart, and softly paints
  A picture on its walls.

    It is my dream at midnight,
    And in the crowded mart,
      That darling face
      With gentle grace—
    The picture in my heart !

In each man's heart there floats a voice,
  That speaks to him alone,
The voice of her, his spirit's choice,
  He longs to call his own.
The days may hasten like the wind,
  Or lag with sullen feet,
Some day his wondering heart shall find
  The face he longs to meet.

    It is my dream at midnight,
    Its dear eyes ne'er depart,
      Oh, where is she,
      My bride to be—
    The picture in my heart !

Oh, some hearts range the wide world through
  And through to find their mate,
And some amid the darkness rue
  That they have met too late ;
A wistful glance betrays to each
  What neither dares to sigh ;
A wedded bond forbids the speech
  That's uttered by the eye.

It is my dream at midnight,
It makes my pulses start,
Oh, Fate, be kind
And let me find
The picture in my heart!
—SAMUEL MINTURN PECK.

MY MOTHER'S GRAVE.

SHE has left me, priceless treasure,
　More than all the world beside ;
Oh ! my heart is sad and lonely
　Since my gentle mother died.
How I miss her tender accents—
　How her love I fondly crave ;
When my life work here is ended,
　Let me rest beside her grave.

Sweet the message that she gave me,
　As she clasped me to her breast ;
"God will comfort, guide and keep
　　you—
　In His arms there's perfect rest ;
Do not grieve that I must leave you,
　We shall meet to part no more,"—
Then a band of white-robed angels
　Bore her to the golden shore.

She is free from all earth's sorrow,
　Free from all earth's pain and woe ;
Safe in heaven, her ransomed spirit
　Only joy and peace shall know.
Soon I'll hear the angels calling,
　Soon death's waters I must brave ;
When life's journey shall be over,
　Let me sleep beside her grave.

THE BABY OVER THE WAY.

ACROSS in my neighbor's window,
　With its folds of satin and lace,
I see with crown of ringlets,
　A baby's innocent face.
The throng in the street look upward,
　And every one, grave and gay,
Has a nod and a smile for the baby
　In the mansion over the way.

Just here in my cottage window,
　His chin in his dimpled hands,
And a patch on his faded apron,
　The child that I lived for stands
He has kept my heart from breaking
　For many a weary day ;
And his face is as pure and handsome
　As the baby's over the way.

Sometimes when we sit together,
　My grave little man of three
Sore vexes me with the question :
　" Does God up in Heaven like me ? "
And I say. " Yes, yes, my darling,"
　Though I almost answer " Nay,"
As I see the nursery candles
　In the mansion over the way.

And oft when I draw the stockings
　From his little tired feet,
And loosen the clumsy garments
　From his limbs so round and sweet,
I grow too bitter for singing,
　My heart too heavy to pray,
As I think of the dainty raiment
　Of the baby over the way.
　　　　* * *
Oh, God in Heaven, forgive me
　For all I have thought and said !
My envious heart is humbled ;
　My neighbor's baby is dead !
I saw the little white coffin
　As they carried it out to-day,
And the heart of the mother is breaking
　In the mansion over the way.

The light is fair in my window,
　The flowers bloom at my door ;
My boy is chasing the sunbeams
　That dance on the cottage floor.
The roses of health are crowning
　My darling's forehead to-day ;
But the baby is gone from the window
　Of the mansion over the way.
　　　　—MARY RILEY SMITH.

THANKSGIVING DAY.

FAULT has been found with the Constitution of the United States because the Deity was not alluded to in that great document. Yet before the adoption of that great platform of liberty, was the example of the Pilgrim Fathers greater than their precepts, and everywhere was special homage paid to that Deity. And ever since that time, the impress has been upon the hearts of the people, as well as upon the coins of the country, " In God we trust."

Without any particular church, or peculiar creed, has the American people required no documentary vows, or constitutional obligations to be a God-loving and God-fearing people. This fact has doubtless had much to do with its great success as a nation, and surely has done much towards gaining for it the profound respect of all nations. It was and is apparent that a great nation, like the United States, was truly invincible to any foe, so long as God was retained as a silent partner. So far, has that partnership been retained. It is to be hoped it ever will be. It is one of the strongest firms the world has ever known. It is invincible, so long as it is retained.—" In union there is strength."

So many are the blessings of the United States that the average citizen chews his own tobacco, smokes his own pipe, eats, drinks, and is merry and never stops to consider the blessings his great country endows him with; and never does he fully appreciate his blessings until he realizes the hardships and illiberalities of less favored countries. While we enjoy our heritage as a matter of course the subjects of other countries are continually surrendering their loyalty to their own native colors to get beneath the protecting folds of the Stars and Stripes. Their subjects love ours, better than their own native lands, while all nations envy its blessings and respect its greatness.

Cognizant of its own greatness, and proud of its heritage, the United States, recognizing the brotherhood of man and the fatherhood of God, enjoy the blessings of nature and invite those of the Deity.

THE PASSING YEAR.

MY door stands open wide to-night,
   In token of a parting guest,
Whom twelve months since, with keen delight,
   I welcomed to my homely rest.

He stands there now, wan, wasted, old,
   His race quite run, his mission o'er,
And when the midnight hour is tolled
   We part to meet no more.

He came to me in merry guise,
   With hopes and promises not a few;
Ah! who could look within those eyes
   And deem that they were all untrue?

But expectations all have fled,
   The promises are broken, too,
The hopes lie withered, crushed and dead—
   Not one of all but proved untrue.

And there he stands, decrepit, wan,
   Who came to me a merry elf;
A few sands more he will be gone,
   And with him gone part of myself.

So come and go the passing years
   That bear us to the silent sea,
But bright with smiles, or dim with tears,
   They come in love, Dear Lord, from Thee.

ENGAGED.

ENGAGED to marry—to help one another over the rough places of life's journey; to guard one another over its pitfalls; to help one another in striving for the fair heights of Beatitude. Is it not for this the world marries? To illuminate with sunshiny hope the dark places? To gild with the sunshine of faith the threatening clouds of difficulty? To bridge the chasms of gloomy failures with the strong spans of mutual charity? Is it not for this the world marries? the wedded hands and hearts may build up lofty cathedrals of soul, that the Divine love may come down and dwell therein.

THE DYING WIFE.

LAY the gem upon my bosom,
   Let me feel her warm breath,
For a strong chill o'er me passes,
   And I know that it is death.
I would gaze upon the treasure—
   Scarcely given ere I go—
Feel her rosy, dimpled fingers
   Wander o'er my cheek of snow.

I am passing through the waters,
　But a blessed shore appears ;
Kneel beside me, husband dearest,
　Let me kiss away thy tears ;
Wrestle with thy grief ; my husband,
　Strive from midnight unto day ;
It may leave an angel's blessing
　When it vanishes away.

Lay the gem upon my bosom,
　'Tis not long she can be there ;
See ! how to my heart she nestles,
　'Tis the pearl I love to wear.
If in after years beside thee
　Sits another in my chair,
Though her voice be sweeter music.
　And her face than mine more fair.

If a cherub call thee "Father,"
　Far more beautiful than this,
Love thy first-born, oh ! my husband !
　Turn not from the motherless ;
Tell her something of her mother—
　You may call her by my name !
Shield her from the winds of sorrow !
　If she errs, oh ! gently blame.

Lead her sometimes, where I'm sleeping
　I will answer if she calls,
And my breath will stir her ringlets,
　When my voice in blessing falls ;
Then her soft, black eyes will brighten,
　And shall wonder whence it came ;
In her heart when years pass o'er her
　She will find her mother's name.

It is said that every mortal
　Walks between two angels here,
One records the ill, but blots it,
　If before the midnight drear
Man repenteth—if uncancelled,
　Then the right hand angel weepeth,
Bowing low with veiled eyes.

I will be her right hand angel,
　Sealing up the good for Heaven ;
Striving that the midnight watches
　Find no misdeeds unforgiven.
You will not forget me, husband,
　When I'm sleeping 'neath the sod ;
Oh, love the jewel to us given,
　As I love thee—next to God !

THE NEW YEAR.

Silent and white
Thro' the dim night
Fell the soft snow,
Now fast, now slow,
Making the posts
Like sheeted ghosts,
Robing the woods
In finer goods
Than ever were spun by mortal skill,
And bleach'd on the sunny side of the hill
Where fringes were woven by weavers,
Where warp is mist and the woof is air ;
The world is dressed like a bird in white,
Altho' the poor old year died last night.
　Drop not a tear
　On the cold bier
　Of the brave year
　Whose course is here
　His work is done,
　And battles won,
　And he will be
　Named with the free
　Thro' future time
　For deeds sublime.
　We welcome here
　The new-born year,
　The snow that falls
　From the gray walls
　Of the thick clouds
　Is not for shrouds
　For the days fled,
　Or the years dead,
　'Tis the white fleece,
　Emblem of peace,
　Sent down to cheer
　The soft young year
　May no red vein
　Make a red stain
　On the robe white
　Wove last night.
　So ring the soft
　Sweet bells aloft.
　Ring the true chime
　Of the good time.
　Ring loud and clear
　For this New Year.

IF YOU WANT A KISS, TAKE IT.

THERE is a jolly Saxon proverb
　That is pretty much like this :
That a man is half in heaven
　When he has a woman's kiss,

If you want a kiss, take it

—Page 36.

But there is danger in delaying,
  And the sweetness may forsake it;
So I tell you, bashful lover,
  If you want a kiss, why, take it

Never let another fellow
  Steal a march on you in this;
Never let a laughing maiden
  See you spoiling for a kiss.
There's a royal way of kissing,
  And the jolly ones who make it
Have a motto that is winning;
  If you want a kiss, why, take it.

Any fool may face a cannon,
  Anybody wear a crown,
But a man must win a woman
  If he'd have her for his own.
Would you have a golden apple,
  You must find the tree and shake it;
If a thing is worth the having,
  And you want a kiss, why, take it.

Who would burn upon a desert,
  With a forest running by?
Who would give his sunny summer
  For a bleak and wintry sky?
O! I tell you there is magic,
  And you cannot, cannot break it;
For the sweetest part of loving
  Is to want a kiss, and take it.

THINKING.

THINKING is not dreaming. The world is full of dreamers. A few men do most of its thinking. Thinking is manufacturing. It is taking mental tools, and hammering, and filing, and molding, and shaping, until ideas have grown into fully developed realities of the brain, with dimensions and clearly marked outlines. The reason there are not more thinkers is because thinking is work; it wears away tissue and muscle. It is tiresome. It requires time and purpose. Men can dream while they sleep; to work they must be awake. Dreaming is tearing away the flood-gate and allowing the flood to pour through; if anything remains it is only driftwood that may chance to hang on the way. Minds fill with driftwood because they are not thinking. Thinking is measuring chances, weighing principles, watching the operation of law; it is a process of creeping upon things and taking them by surprise before they have time to get away. A thinker is a hunter. He must live alone. He must be satisfied with small daily fare and often see his game fly before he has time to shoot. He must have courage to face chasms, and dark places, and climb steep mountains. He must love solitude on an outpost hidden in the rocks.

And here is the reason this age is not prolific of good thinkers. It is an age of company, of travel, of theatre-going, of corporations and speculations, Men live in crowds. It is a day of double houses. Too much man and not enough of God. Communion with nature is shut out. There are no sparks because the flint and steel are not in contact. We are following the college drones, "ponying" through life. Everybody wants to ride. Going to the spring for water is out of fashion. The spring must come up the hill. We want to turn the faucet and have things run out to our hand and the faucet must be on castors, that it may be convenient.

For these reasons most people are only sponges; they live wholly by absorption and are like the thing they touched last. They wait for things to "turn up;" but the only thing they ever find turning up especially for them, is a little sod in a lone corner of the graveyard, and they are at last laid away, while the great multitude, having never missed them, asked in wonder, "When did he die?"

FALLING LEAVES.

THEY are falling, slowly falling,
  Thick upon the forest side—
Severed from the noble branches
  Where they waved in beauteous pride,
They are falling in the valleys
  Where the early violets spring,
And the birds in sunny springtime
  First their dulcet music ring.

They are falling, sadly falling,
  Close beside our cottage door—
Pale and faded, like the loved ones
  That have gone forevermore.
They are falling, and the sunbeams
  Shine in beauty soft around;
Yet the faded leaves are falling—
  Falling on the grassy mound.

They are falling on the streamlet
  Where the silvery waters flow,
And upon its placid bosom
  Onward with the waters go.
They are falling in the churchyard
  Where our kindred sweetly sleep—
Where the idle winds of summer
  Softly o'er the loved ones sweep.

They are falling, ever falling,
  When the autumn breezes sigh—
When the stars in beauty glisten
  Bright upon the midnight sky.
They are falling when the tempest
  Moans like Ocean's hollow roar—
When the tuneless winds and billows
  Sadly sigh for evermore.

They are falling, they are falling,
  While our saddened thoughts still go
To the sunny days of childhood,
  In the dreamy long ago,
And their faded hues remind us
  Of the blighted hopes and dreams—
Faded like the falling leaflets
  Cast upon the icy streams.

THE RIGHTS OF WOMAN.

The rights of woman, what are they?
The right to labor, love and pray,
The right to weep when others weep,
The right to wake when others sleep.

The right to dry the falling tear,
The right to quell the rising fear;
The right to smooth the brow of care,
And whisper comfort to despair.

The right to watch the parting breath,
To soothe and cheer the bed of death.
The right, when earthly hopes all fail,
To point to that within the vail.

The right the wanderer to reclaim,
And win the lost from paths of shame;
The right to comfort and to bless
The widow and the fatherless.

The right the little ones to guide,
In simple faith to Him who died;
With earnest love and gentle praise
To bless and cheer their youthful days.

The right to live for those we love,
The right to die that love to prove;
The right to brighten earthly homes
With pleasant smiles and gentle tones.

Are these thy rights? then use them well;
Thy silent influence none can tell
If these are thine, why ask for more—
Thou hast enough to answer for.
        —ALICE OLIVER.

UNDER THE SNOW.

THE brown old earth lies quiet and still
  Under the snow;
The furrows are hid on the broken hill
  Under the snow;
Every twig is fringed with mossy pearl.
  The drooping cedars bend to the ground,
  The rosebush is drifted to the mound,
  And still from the silent sky to the ground
The white flakes noiselessly whirl.

The roads and fields are buried deep
  Under the snow;
The hedges lie in a tangled heap
  Under the snow;
And the little gray rabbits under them creep,
While the twittering sparrows cunningly peep,
From the sheltering briers and cozily sleep
  Under the snow,

The rough old barn and the sheds near by,
The mounded straws of the wheat and rye,
  Are covered with snow;
The straggling fences are softened with down,
Every part is white, with a beautiful crown
  Of drifted snow.

And I think, as I sit in the gloaming here,
Watching the objects disappear,
How many things are folded low
Under the drift of the falling snow!

There are hearts that once were full of love
  Under the snow;

There are eyes that glowed with the
   soul of love
     Under the snow ;
There are faded tresses of golden hair
And locks that were bleached with the
   frost of care—
There are lips that once were like the
   rose,
There are bosoms that were stung with
   woes.
There are breasts that once were true
   and strong.
There are forms that once were praised
   in song,
O, there's a strange and a mighty throng
     Under the snow !

Another mound will once lie deep
     Under the snow !
And I will with the pale ones sleep
     Under the snow.
O, God, transform my soul with grace
That in the love-light of thy face
I may stand pure when Death shall
   place,
My pulseless heart and body low
     Under the snow.
        —JOHN H. BONNER.

LIGHT.

FROM the quickened womb of the
   primal gloom
   The sun rolled bleak and bare,
Till I wove him a vest for his Ethiop
   breast
Of the threads of my golden hair ;
And when the broad tent of the firma-
   ment
   Arose on its airy bars
I pencilled the hue of the matchless blue
And spangled it round the stars.

I painted the flowers of Eden bowers,
   And their leaves of living green,
And mine were the dyes in the sinless
   eyes
   Of Eden's virgin queen ;
And when the fiend's art on the trustful
   heart
   Had fastened its mortal spell,
In the silvery sphere of the first-born
   tear
   To the trembling earth I fell.

When the waves that burst o'er a world
   accursed
   Their work of wrath had sped,
And the ark's lone few, the tried and
   true,
   Came forth among the dead.
With the wondrous gleams of my bridal
   beams
   I bade their terrors cease,
As I wrote on the roll of the storm's
   dark scroll
   God's covenant of Peace.

Like a pall at rest on a senseless breast,
   Night's funeral shadows slept—
When Shepherd swains on Bethlehem's
   plains
   Their lowly vigils kept—
Then I flashed on their sight the heralds
   bright
   Of Heaven's redeeming plan,
As they chanted the morn of a Saviour
   born—
   Joy, joy to the outcast man !

Equal favor I show to the lofty and low,
   On the just and unjust I descend ;
E'en the blind, whose vain spheres roll
   in darkness and tears ;
Feel my smile, the best smile of a
   friend ;
Nay, the flower of the waste by my love
   is embraced
As the rose in the garden of kings,
At the chrysalis bier of the worm I ap-
   pear,
And lo ! the gay butterfly wings.

The desolate morn, like a mourner for-
   lorn,
   Conceals all the pride of her charms,
Till I bid the bright hours chase the
   night from her bowers
   And lead her young day to her arms !
And when the gay rover seeks Eve for
   his lover
   And sinks to her balmy repose,
I wrap the soft rest by the zephyr-fanned
   West,
   In curtains of amber and rose !

From my sentinel sleep by the night-
   dreaded deep
   I gaze with unslumbering eyes,
When the cynosure star of the mariner
   Is blotted from out the sky !

And guided by me through the merciless sea,
Though sped by the hurricane's wings,
His compassless, dark, lone, weltering bark
To the haven home safely he brings.

I waken the flowers in their dew-spangled bowers
The birds in their chambers of green,
And mountain and plain glow with beauty again,
As they bask in the matinal sheen.
O, if such the glad worth of my presence on earth,
Though fretful and fleeting the while,
What glories must rest on the home of the blest,
Ever bright with the Deity's smile!

THE PATTER OF BABY'S FEET.

I REMEMBER once readin' a tender, sweet refrain
Woven from the fancy of some dreamin' poet's brain,
Tellin' of the joy that comes when, lyin' in your bed,
You hear the raindrops fallin' on the shingles overhead.
Some folks may not think so, but with him I quite agree,
That the simple sounds of nature hold the sweetest melody;
And that is why I'm thinkin' that there's no tune quite as sweet
As the soft, melodious patter of baby's little feet.

From early mornin's brightness till evenin's gatherin' gloom
We hear the tuneful patter of his footsteps in each room;
Now along the hallway, now upon the stair,
Up and down, come and go, wanderin' here and there,
Fillin' all the hours with the music of his tread,
Till sleep o'ercomes and bears him a captive to his bed.
'Tis with joy I leave the hustle and the bustle of the street
For the gentle, restful patter of baby's little feet.

They have worn a pathway that winds all through my breast,
And their soothin', patterin' music lulls me to my nightly rest;
And even when sleep has claimed me I hear it in my dreams,
Like symphonies of angels, so mellow-like it seems.
There is somethin' very pleasin' in the whisperin' of the trees;
In the murmurin' of a mountain brook, in the sighin' of the breeze;
But in all of art or nature there is no tune that can beat
The smooth, harmonious patter of baby's little feet.
—WILLIAM WEST.

I WISH HE'D MAKE UP HIS MIND.

I WISH he would make up his mind, ma,
For I don't care longer to wait;
I'm sure I have hinted quite strongly,
That I thought of changing my state;
For a sweetheart he's really so backward
I can't bring him out, though I try;
I own that he's very good-tempered,
But then he's dreadfully shy!

When I speak about love in a cottage,
He gives me a look of surprise;
And if I but hint at a marriage,
He blushes quite up to his eyes.
I can't make him jealous—I've tried it—
And 'tis no use my being unkind,
For that's not the way, I am certain,
To get him to make up his mind.

I've sung him love sonnets by dozens,
I've worked him both slippers and hose,
And we've walked by moonlight together,
Yet he never attempts to propose!
You must really ask his intention,
Or some other beau I must find,
For indeed I won't tarry much longer
For one who can't make up his mind.

DISAPPOINTMENTS.

DISAPPOINTMENTS are so common in this life that it is the part of prudence to school one's self to bear them patiently. Those who are of sanguine temperament and especially the young and inexperienced find it difficult to accept disappointments with a cheerful mind, but that is one reason why they should endeavor to train themselves to do so, for they cannot be sure of happiness until they have reached some degree of stoicism. Time is the great healer for all kinds of grief, but only the observant have faith in it. Sorrows that seem unbearable are overcome by time, and there is scarcely any grief or disappointment that will not yield to its soothing influences.

It is the first force of the grief or disappointment that must be overcome by will-power and that can be strengthened by faith in the influence of time and hope for the future. Unfortunately one cannot become a philosopher by thinking; one needs hard experience to chasten the spirit and reveal the vanities of life. Emerging from that experience with a cheerful, hopeful disposition, as some do, it is an easy matter to bear griefs and disappointments. One who has done so knows that there is compensating good in nearly every evil, and instead of allowing his mind to dwell upon the evil he seeks the good.

There is no greater grief than that which follows the death of a loved one; no greater disappointment than that which pierces a parent's heart when death or other cause ends or wrecks the career of a child for whom bright plans had been cherished for years. But when the grief has been mastered, soothing reflections come to the philosophic mind, picturing the happy past or the still more happy future or recounting the sorrows the loved one has escaped in the present.

It is too much to expect that young children shall accept disappointments, even in trivial matters, with the philosophic calm of their elders. Their age and inexperience combine to make them much too sanguine, and hence they suffer more when disappointed, but no child is too young to be admonished against giving way to grief. It should, indeed, be a part of the training of the young, this teaching them to bear disappointments with philosophic calm and to seek relief in some new enterprise which shall absorb the attention while time is healing the wound.

When this kind of training is neglected a petulant disposition is developed and the victim becomes a hypochondriac magnifying the disappointments and sorrows of life and making himself and others unhappy by his continual moanings. Instead of being strengthened while young to bear the greater griefs and disappointments which will surely come to him in his mature years, his peevishness is increased to such a degree that he is unfitted to bear the trials of life.

But a child taught to turn with some degree of cheerfulness away from disappointments, to dismiss them from memory and seek new enterprises or amusements, is made cheerful and develops a disposition and habit of mind that will be of the greatest service to him when the real trials and sorrows of life come upon him. It is impossible to avoid disappointments if one preserves as he should, a hopeful disposition, but it is possible to control one's manner of dealing with disappointments so as to set them aside and allow time to efface even the recollection of them.

BORROWING TROUBLE.

WHAT a vast proportion of our lives is spent in anxious and useless forebodings concerning the future, either our own or that of our dear ones. Present joys, present blessings, slip by, and we lose half their sweet flavor, and all for want of faith in Him who provides for the tiniest insect in the sunbeams. Oh, when shall we learn the sweet trust in God that our little children teach us every day, by their confiding faith in us! We, who are so mutable, so faulty, so terrible, so unjust; and he who is so watchful, so pitiful, so loving, so forgiving! Why cannot we, slipping our hand in His, each day walk trustingly over that day's appointed path, thorny or flowery, crooked or straight, knowing that evening will bring us sleep, and peace and home. Why told distrustfully to gather up manna for days yet to come, when every dewy morning shall find it freshly sprinkled at our feet! When we do get near "Our Father" how wonderful seems this, our distrust, how our eyes overflow, that we could make so mean a return for that all-embracing, all-bountiful, generous kindness, which is measureless as the ocean, though our shortcomings are numerous as its tossing waves.

A WOMAN'S SMILE.

A BEAUTIFUL smile is to the female countenance what the sunbeam is to the landscape; it embellishes an inferior face, and redeems an ugly one. A smile, however, should not become habitual, or insipidity is the result; nor should the mouth break into a smile on one side, the other remaining passive and unmoved, for this imparts an air of deceitful grotesqueness to the face. A disagreeable smile distorts the line of beauty, and is more repulsive than a frown. There are many kinds of smiles, each having a distinctive character; some announce goodness and sweetness; others betray sarcasm, bitterness and pride; some soften the countenance by their languishing tenderness; others brighten it by their brilliant and spiritual vivacity. Gazing and poring over a mirror cannot aid in acquiring beautiful smiles half so well as to turn the gaze inward to watch that the heart keeps unsullied from the reflection of evil, and is illumined and beautified by all sweet thoughts.

RECOLLECTIONS.

Do you remember all the sunny places,
  Where in bright days, long past, we played together?
Do you remember all the old home faces
That gathered round the hearth in wintry weather?

Do you remember all the happy meetings,
  In summer evenings round the open door
Kind looks, kind hearts, kind words and tender greetings,
And clasped hands whose pulses beat no more?
  Do you remember them?

Do you remember all the merry laughter;
  The voices round the swing in our old garden;
The dog that, when we ran, still followed after;
The teasing frolic sure of speedy pardon?
We were but children *then*, young, happy creatures,
  And hardly knew how much we had to lose—
But *now* the dreamlike memory of those features
Comes back, and bids my darkened spirit muse.
  Do you remember them?

Do you remember when we first departed
  From the old companions who were round us,
How very soon again we grew light-hearted,
And talked with smiles of all the links which bound us?
And after when our footsteps were returning,
  With unfelt weariness o'er hills and plain;
How our young hearts kept boiling up, and burning,
To think how soon we'd be at home again?
  Do you remember this?

Do you remember how the dreams of glory
  Kept fading from us, like a fairy treasure;
How we thought less of being famed in story;
And more of those to whom our fame give pleasure?

Do you remember in far countries, weeping,
When a light breeze, a flower, hath brought to mind
Old, happy thoughts, which till that hour were sleeping,
And made us yearn for those we left behind?
Do you remember this?

Do you remember when no sound woke gladly
But desolate echoes through our homes were ringing,
How for awhile we talked—then paused full sadly,
Because our voices bitter thoughts were bringing?
Ah me! those days—those days! my friend, my brother,
Sit down and let us talk of all our woe,
For we have nothing left but one another;
Yet where *they* went, old playmate, *we* shall go—
Let us remember this.

A GEM FOR EVERY MONTH.

JANUARY.

By her who in this month is born
No gem save garnets should be worn;
They will insure her constancy,
True friendship and fidelity.

FEBRUARY.

The February born will find
Sincerity and peace of mind;
Freedom from passion and from care,
If they the amethyst will wear.

MARCH.

Who on this world of ours their eyes
In March first open shall be wise;
In days of peril firm and brave,
And wear a bloodstone to their grave.

APRIL.

She who from April dates her years,
Diamonds should wear, lest bitter tears
For vain repentance flow; this stone
Emblem of innocence is known,

MAY.

Who first beholds the light of day
In spring's sweet flowery month of May,
And wears an emerald all her life,
Shall be a loved and happy wife.

JUNE.

Who comes with summer to this earth,
And owes to June her day of birth,
With ring of agate on her hand,
Can health, wealth, and long life command.

JULY.

The glowing ruby should adorn
Those who in warm July are born;
Then will they be exempt and free
From love's doubt and anxiety.

AUGUST.

Wear a sardonyx, or for thee
No conjugal felicity,
The August-born without this stone,
'Tis said must live unloved and lone.

SEPTEMBER.

A maiden born when autumn leaves
Are rustling in September's breeze,
A sapphire on her brow should bind—
'Twill cure diseases of the mind.

OCTOBER.

October's child is born for woe,
And life's vicissitudes must know;
But lay an opal on her breast,
And hope will lull those woes to rest.

NOVEMBER.

Who first comes to this world below
With drear November's fog and snow,
Should prize the topaz amber hue—
Emblem of friends and lovers true.

DECEMBER.

If cold December gave you birth,
The month of snow and ice and mirth,
Place on your hand a turquoise blue,
Success will bless whate'er you do.

THAT DREADFUL GET-UP BELL.

Hear the ringing of the bell—
    Rising bell !
What a world of misery its harsh sound
    doth foretell !
How it clatters—clatters—clatters on
    the icy air of morn,
Till all pleasant dreams it scatters—
    wakes us up to thoughts forlorn !
Though 'tis far from our desire,
We must rise to light the fire,
While we shiver—shiver—shiver—
And the stars all seem to quiver.
And the stars and moon all bright
Seem to grin at us and quiver in a comi-
    cal delight.
As we grumble, as we stumble, and we
    tumble out of bed—
As we pour forth ice-cold water and
    bathe therewith our head,
While we listen to the ringing
    Of the bell—bell—bell—
As we listen to the dinging
    Of that dreadful get-up bell.

Hear the merry breakfast-bell !
    Cheerful bell !
It brings us thoughts of good things,
    and with it comes the smell
Of coffee and of beefsteaks, and potatoes
    smoking hot
For the punctual early risers who are
    ready on the spot ;
For those who heard the rising-bell, and
    got up in a hurry,
And did not take another nap and then
    commence to skurry.
But the slothful—ah ! the slothful—
Be they old, or be they youthful ;
They who, half-an-hour too late,
Fear they 'll find an empty plate ;--
How they shudder at the bell !
And it seems to them a knell
As they listen to its swell
    With a groan !
Ah ! what anguish do they feel as they
    listen to the peal
Of the bell—bell—bell—bell—bell !
As they hear the folks go down—
Tramp of boots and rustling gown—
    Left alone !
Then they view their sloth with
    sorrow,
Vow they'll rise betimes to-morrow,
As they listen to the ringing of the
    bell—
To the ringing and the dinging of the
    bell !

A NEW YEAR GREETING.

" A HAPPY New Year " So we lightly
    cry
To those around, in careless, idle
    phrase,
But, ah ! what years are happy 'neath
    the sky ?
Whose paths are altogether pleasant
    ways ?

And so to you, my friend, I fain would
    give
Another greeting for the coming
    year—
A greeting that through all its days
    may live,
As tender music lingers on the ear.

We know the year that holds the
    summer's prime—
Holds, too, the winter's icy storm and
    frost,
The changing blasts of spring's capri-
    cious time,
The mellow autumn, when the world
    is lost,

In beauty like a dream, when golden
    days
Fall softly on us with the falling
    leaves
And purple hills are wrapped in radiant
    haze.
Like the enchanted mist that Fancy
    weaves.

So, too, the years of changing human
    life
Hold many a season clasped in their
    embrace,

Days bright with hope, days dark with
    weary strife,
And days serene with fair, pathetic
    grace,

Shall I, who fain would call upon your
    way
Life's highest blessing, wish for smiles
    alone
From sunny skies on flowery meadows?
    Nay,
Not so, God blesses those he makes
    his own.

Souls lapped in glowing sunshine sel-
    dom rise
To face unblenched the driving storm
    and rain;
And hearts most truly and most gently
    wise
Have learned their wisdom in the
    school of pain.

Therefore, O steadfast soul! I ask for
    you
Courage and strength to meet the
    fiercest blast;
And God's best sunshine, faithful heart
    and true,
To gild your pathway when the storm
    is past.
        —BY CHRISTIAN REID.

YOUNG LADIES' "PSALM OF LIFE."

Tell us not in idle jingle,
  " Marriage is an empty dream,"
For the girl is dead that's single,
  And things are not what they seem.

Life is real, life is earnest;
  Single blessedness a fib;
" Man thou art, to man returnest,"
  Has been spoken of the rib.

Not enjoyment, and not sorrow,
  Is our destined end or way,
But to act that each to-morrow
  Finds us nearer marriage day.

Life is long and youth is fleeting,
  And our hearts, though light and gay,
Still like pleasant drums are beating
  Wedding marches all the way.

In the world's broad field of battle,
  In the bivouac of life,
Be not like dumb driven cattle,
  Be a heroine—a wife.

Trust no future, howe'er pleasant;
  Let the dead past bury its dead!
Act, act in the living present
  Heart within and hope ahead.

Lives of married folks remind us
  We can live our lives as well;
And, departing, leave behind us
  Such examples as will "tell."

Such examples as another,
  Wasting time in idle sport,
A forlorn, unmarried brother,
  Seeing, shall take heart and court.

Let us, then, be up and doing,
  With a heart on triumph set;
Still contriving, still pursuing,
  And each one a husband get.

OUR MOTHER'S GRAVE.

We are standing now at the foot of mother's grave, and oh, what a precious spot it is! It is a heart-link in that hallowed chain which binds the past and the present together in such a sad and sweet and holy communion. And standing now above her precious dust we feel her spirit's presence near, and hear, as in long days gone by, the music of her dear, sweet cheer. Yes, indeed, the memories of her goodness, her kindness, her gentleness, her sweetness and her loving indulgence and forbearance and tender sympathies floats to us now like the delicious perfume of some woodland blossoms. The music of other voices may be lost, but the entrancing memory of hers will echo in our souls forever. Other faces will fade away and be forgotten, but hers will shine on until the light from Heaven's portals shall glorify our own. Years have filled great drifts between her and us, but they have not hidden from our sight the glory of her pure, unselfish love, for that love emptied into our life all the blessings that earth could possibly hold. It gave glory light to existence. It gave beauty to earth. It transformed the dull prose of life into the poetry of a rhythmic flow of rapturous emotions It was as inexhaustible as the waters of the ocean. It was as drainless as the glittering showers of falling sunbeams. It was as true and as sweet as the odors are to the flowers in Spring, and as cheering and as constant as the stars are to the shadows of the night. Like a fountain, it never ran dry. It was ever flowing in the silveriest ripples of cheer and delight. Its sparkling tides carried those lulling strains which always soothed and comforted. Under its blessed ministry all the hurts and bruises and pains were eased and cured and healed. Its spray was a balm. The memory of this love flings a halo of comfort around this blessed grave, and standing within the circle of its radiance a light of ineffable softness and beauty and glory comes stealing down from Heavens above, and drowns all earthly shadows in her remembered lover.

BLOUNT.

CASUAL IMPRESSIONS.

SONGS OF THE PAST.

You'D smile, my friend, if you could see
   how I my glasses don,
To read the journal sent which tells how
   you are getting on !
Now does it seem so many years have
   come and gone their way
Since we were only boys that thought
   of little else but play,
And never stopped to think for once
   'twould not be long until
Impartial Time would leave his scars
   on even Jim and Bill ?

I've done but little yet—but may, in
   some of these good times :
A fellow somehow always hopes, however
   slow he climbs !
It sounds so queer—does't make you
   feel a man among the men
To have them call you "Colonel," now,
   and "leading citizen ?"

For I can think of you alone, strive
   strongly as I will,
But as the boyish friend I knew when
   we were Jim and Bill.

When summer comes and blesses earth,
   and all the world is green,
Do bud and bloom remind you then of
   summers that have been ?
Do bird-songs warbled near you bring
   the haw hills back again—
The homes, though humble, which appeared
   the holiest places, then ?
And do you long to look once more
   upon each vale and rill
Near which our happy boyhood romped
   when we were Jim and Bill ?

And while you sit by winter's hearth,
   does memory e'er recall
The boyish loves we used to know—
   the maids who held us thrall ?
Ah, some of them are dead long since,
   forgotten and entombed—
Soon-perished flowers that since made
   bright the spheres in which they bloomed ;
The glory of their guileless lives the
   past will ever fill,
And gild the dreams we dreamed, old
   friend, when we were Jim and Bill.

But, seriously, I'd like to meet and talk
   an hour or two
About the time that had few clouds—
   when roses thornless grew;
When thought scarce winged beyond
   where sky met earth in fondest kiss,
And fields and woods and streams held
   all the world could hold of bliss;
For though the future have in store some
   things to please us—still
No days can rival those old days when
   we were Jim and Bill !

—WILL T. HALE.

ISLE OF THE PAST.

THERE'S a green, emerald isle up the
   river of Time,
Where life's roses blossom and die,
Where bright waters flow o'er the shell-decked
   shore,
With a low, sweet, musical sigh.

There are locks of hair, some silvery
    gray,
And some of pale golden hue,
There are snowy bosoms and clasping
    hands,
And eyes of melting blue.

There 're a few tiny teeth in a wee rosy
    mouth
A baby face bright with a smile ;
A small waxen form laid away with the
    flowers
That bloom on that magical isle.

There's an old wrinkled form, Oh ! we
    loved it so !
And a voice grown faint and low,
Ah ! tremulous tones of age and grief,
Mingle sad on that star-lit shore.

There's a song unsung and a lute un-
    swept.
And words of love half spoken ;
There are light tripping feet and wild
    music sweet,
And blood-pulsing hearts half-broken.

A circle bright, a bridal dress,
    Two hearts made one forever,
See ! a broken ring, a silken tress,
    Where the cypress' dark boughs
        quiver.

The sparkling cup, and green laurels
    are there,
And bright eyes are looking upward.
And withered leaves and chaplets torn,
    And proud heads bowing earthward.

There are witching dreams, and rain-
    bow hopes,
And gleams of noon-day breaking,
There are meaningless words and faith-
    less vows,
And hearts in silence breaking.

Life's sky-lights are there, its night-
    shadows dim,
    Joy's greeting, and sorrow's farewell ;
The snowy shroud's there, the slow-
    moving hearse,
    And toll of Life's vesper bell.

Oh ! Magical Isle—Oh ! wondrous
    Isle—
Ripe with life and death's desola-
    tion—
May the soul draw strength from thy
    long day night,
And Memory's holy creation !
—Mrs. S. W. Fletcher.

A SIMILAR CASE.

Jack, I hear you've gone and done it,
Yes, I know ; most fellows will :
Went and tried it once myself, sir,
Though you see, I'm single still.
    And you met her—did you tell me ?
    Down at Newport last July,
    And resolved to ask the question,
    At a *soiree ?* So did I.

I suppose you left the ball-room
With its music and its light ;
For they say love's flame is brightest
In the darkness of the night.
    Well, you walked along together.
    Overhead the starlit sky,
    And I'll bet—old man confess it—
    You were frightened. So was I.

So you strolled along the terrace.
And the summer moon did pour,
All its radiance on the waters
As they rippled on the shore :
    Till at length you gathered courage,
    When you saw that none were nigh—
    Did you draw her close and tell her
    That you loved her ? So did I.

Well, I needn't ask you further,
And I'm sure I wish you joy,
Think I'll wander down and see you
When you're married—eh, my boy ?
    When the honeymoon is over
    And you're settled down, we'll try—
    What ? The deuce you say ! Rejected,
    You rejected ? So was I !

ONLY A PICTURE.

Under the snow-white sheet she lies,
    Helen, my beautiful Helen, my true !
Softly the morning breaks over the
    skies ;

Softly regretful stars kiss her adieu!
  Lies she there seeming
  So blissfully dreaming,
Fragrant her rose-lips as breath of the morn,
  No one shall lisp her
  Name even in whisper—
She's roaming where fairyland fancies are born.

Clustering clouds of dark, passionate hair,
  Frown back the venturous beams of the sun,
  Hidden, but meagrely—shapely and rare—
  Round, white, soft mysteries, wait to be won,
    Seemingly bolder
    One Parian shoulder,
Purity's self dims the pillow below—
    While thrown above her
    Head—who could but love her?—
A round arm lies white as the shimmering snow

Parting, as clouds part when summer winds blow—
  Heavenly wonders unveiling above—
So part the gauze clouds, revealing below
  Opaline mountains in gardens of love—
    Soft undulations,
    Like music's vibrations—
Coursing light-footed the silvery strings—
    Seen like the ocean
    In jubilant motion—
Breaking its burden of beautiful things.

Waking, as wakes the young bird in its nest,
Baby "Nell" opens her wondering eyes—
Climbs where the lush mountains bear on their crest
  Strawberries ripe as the ruddiest skies,
    There among treasures
    In beautiful measures,
Roguish-eyed, cherry-lipped, pink-footed Nell,
  Drinks from a chalice,
  The King in his palace
Might barter his crown for; and barter it well.

THE UNIVERSAL PRAYER.

FATHER of all! in every age,
  In every clime adored,
By saint, by savage, and by sage,
  Jehovah, Jove, or Lord!

Thou Great First Cause, least understood,
  Who all my sense confined
To know by this that Thou art good,
  And that myself am blind.

Yet gave me, in this dark estate,
  To see the good from ill;
And, binding Nature fast in Fate
  Left free the human will.

What conscience dictates to be done,
  Or warns me not to do,
This, teach me more than hell to shun,
  That, more than heaven pursue.

What blessings thy free bounty gives,
  Let me not cast away;
For God is paid when man receives:
  To enjoy is to obey.

Yet not to earth's contracted span
  Thy goodness let me bound,
Or think thee Lord alone of man,
  When thousand worlds are round,

Let not this weak, unknowing hand
  Presume thy bolts to throw,
And deal damnation round the land,
  On each I judge thy foe.

If I am right, thy grace impart,
  Still in the right to stay;
If I am wrong, Oh, teach my heart
  To find that better way.

Save me alike from foolish pride,
  Or impious discontent,
At aught thy wisdom has denied,
  Or aught thy goodness lent.

Teach me to feel another's woe,
  To hide the fault I see ;
That mercy I to others show,
  That mercy show to me.

Mean though I am, not wholly so,
  Since quicken'd by thy breath ;
Oh, lead me, wheresoe'er I go,
  Through this day's life or death.

This day, be bread and peace my lot ;
  All else beneath the sun,
Thou know'st best bestow'd or not,
  And let thy will be done.

To thee, whose temple is all space,
  Whose altar, earth, sea, skies !
One chorus let all Being raise !
  All Nature's incense rise !
    —ALEXANDER POPE.

REMEMBER THY MOTHER.

LEAD thy mother tenderly
  Down life's steep decline ;
Once her arm was thy support,
  Now she leans on thine.
See upon her loving face
  These deep lines of care,
Think, it was her toil for thee
  Left that record there.

Ne'er forget her tireless watch,
  Kept by day and night ;
Taking from her step the grace,
  From her eye the light.
Cherish well her faithful heart,
  Which through weary years
Echoed with its sympathies
  All thy smiles and tears,

Thank God for thy mother's love,
  Guard the priceless boon,
For the parting hour
  Cometh all too soon.
When thy grateful tenderness
  Loses power to save,
Earth will hold no dearer spot
  Than thy mother's grave.

THE DYING WIFE.

RAISE my pillow, husband, dearest—
  Fainter and fainter comes my breath ;
And those shadows stealing slowly,
  Must I know, be those of death,

Sit down close beside me, darling,
  Let me clasp your warm, strong hand,
Yours that ever has sustained me,
  To the borders of this land.

For your God and mine—our Father
  Thence shall ever lead me on :
Where upon a throne eternal,
  Sits His loved and only Son ;
I've had visions and been dreaming
  O'er the past of joy and pain ;
Year by year I've wandered backward,
  Till I was a child again.

Dreaming of girlhood, and the moment
  When I stood your wife and bride,
How my heart thrilled Love's triumph,
  In that hour of woman's pride.
Dreaming of thee and all the earth chords
Firmly twined about my heart—
  Oh ! the bitter burning anguish.
When I first knew we must part.

It has passed—and God has promised,
  All thy footsteps to attend ;
He that's more than friend or brother,
  He'll be with you to the end.
There's no shadow o'er the portals,
  Leading to my heavenly home—
Christ has promised life immortal,
  And 'tis He that bids me come.

When life's trials wait around thee,
  And its chilling billows swell ;
Thou'lt thank Heaven that I am spared them
Thou'lt then feel that "all is well."
Bring our boys unto my bedside :
  My last blessing let them keep—
But they're sleeping—do not wake them ;
  They'll learn soon enough to weep.

Tell them often of their mother,
  Kiss them for me when they wake,
Lead them gently in life's pathway,
  Love them doubly for my sake,
Clasp my hand still closer, darling,
  This, the last night of my life ;
For to-morrow I shall never
  Answer, when you call me " wife,"
Fare thee well, my noble husband,
  Faint not 'neath the chast'ning rod :
Throw your strong arm round our children
Keep them close to thee and God.

I LOVE THE PAST.

I LOVE the past, the dear old past,
  The days of chivalry and song,
My eyes thereon are sweetly cast,
  As time in circles speeds along.
It is so fair so glorious there,
  That all my heart is beating fast,
And these for me are friendships free
  I love, I love the dear old past.

I love the past, those quiet times,
  So hallowed by the poets' lay,
The charm of song, the sweetest rhymes
  Wherewith to bless a summer day.
The men so bold we there behold
  Their fortunes free with beauty cast
Ah, there to me pure friendships be,
I love, I love the dear old past.

I love the past, those warlike days,
  When men possessed a purpose strong,
And filled with faith a thousand ways
  Pursued the life of noble song,
Then hearts were true and bright as dew,
  Then hope through loss and death could last,
Ah, there to me brave friendships be,
I love, I love the dear old past.

I love the past, and would that I
  Could turn and live within its pale,
That I might see its golden sky,
  And all its fair surroundings hail!
My heart is there, I breathe its air,
  And cling to all its skill amassed,
Ah, there to me fond friendships be,
I love, I love the dear old past.

RECONCILED.

TO-NIGHT my darling said to me,
  Her bright eyes glancing shyly down,
" Forgive me, dear, that I o'erreach,
  Or even seem to pass, the bound
Of perfect trust—but tell me true,
  " If," placing both her hands in mine,
" Some dire mishap should chance to mar
  This face you ofttimes call divine—
" Some stroke of harm sharp smite and spoil
  This girlish form, these lightsome ways;
Or sickness rob my cheeks of bloom,
  Or blindness blot the passing days.
If all were gone—e'en youth and strength!"
Deep grew the shadow on her brow—
" Answer from out your heart of hearts,
  Say, would you love me then as now?"

With gentle force I gravely laid
  The sunny head upon my breast,
Noting, meanwhile, the sigh that gave
  Sure token of her sad unrest.
" Strange questioning this, O sweet," I cried;
  " Wrong, wrong to thus perplex and dim
The finer feelings of the mind—
  To jar by such an idle whim

" Love's confidence." This my reply.—
  The pale face lit with eager glow—
" A soul that in another finds
  Each hope, each purpose blend and flow
Responsive, ne'er, though ill betide,
  Proves false. Affliction's bitter blast
But firmer binds, a charm creates
  Unfading to the very last."

I ceased—then sudden felt the clasp
  Of two white arms my neck about,
While two lips murmured, faint and low,
  " Pardon—forget my foolish doubt."
Dear child! Dear, loving little pet!
  How could I choose but kiss, and say,
" My own! God grant thus easy we
  May end all griefs through life's brief day!"

"SOMETIME."

SOMETIME
These lonely heartaches will be o'er,
And I shall find a peaceful, quiet rest
Beyond the sea that stretches out before
And I shall lean upon the Master's breast
    Sometime.

Sometime,
When all life's tearful toils are done,
I know this brow a starry crown shall wear;
And this poor heart, its last long battle won
Shall dwell forever with its leader there,
    Sometime.

Sometime,
Earth's night shall break in Heaven's day—
And bright, O Christ! shall be Thy glorious dawn!
And, when these changing scenes have passed away,
Tohis own home He'll lead His children on,
    Sometime.

Sometime
He'll turn life's bitter into sweet,
And give us laughter for our burning tears;
Prayer shall be lost in praising at His feet,
And faith be changed to sight when He appears,
    Sometime!

Sometime
These garments, spotted and impure,
And torn and tattered with the thorns of sin,
Shall be exchanged for vesture white and pure
That his own hand will clothe His children in,
    Sometime.

Sometime
The loved and cherished dreams of earth
That His dear hand hath broke in gentle love—
Because I thought them of too great a worth—
He'll give me back in beauty new above,
    Sometime.

Sometime
Dead hopes shall spring to life again,
And all that's lost on earth, in heaven be found;
Our faded flowers, beneath God's vernal rain
Shall bloom afresh in Eden's holy ground,
    Sometime!

Sometime,
Within the quiet house of death—
But, no! I look not for that cheerless home;
My Saviour promised with his latest breath,
To come *Himself* and take me with Him home
    Sometime!

Sometime
Will come, to this long-waiting heart,
The sweet "sometime" I look and long for so;
And I shall be dear, Saviour, where Thou art,
And as Thou art shall see Thee and shall know
    Sometime.

"Sometime!"
O God! when *will* Thy "sometime be?
When will Thy blessed promised "morrow" come?
Lord, keep me patient to wait for Thee—
All ready, when Thou comest, to go home,
    Sometime.
      —Bertie Bliss.

THE CHILDREN'S LAND.

I know a land, a beautiful land,
  Fairer than isles of the east;
Where the farthest hills are rainbow-spanned,
  And mirth holds an endless feast;
Where tears are dried like the morning dew,
  And joys are many, and griefs are few;
Where the old each day grows glad and new,
  And life rings clear as a bell;
Oh! the land where the chimes speak sweet and true
  Is the land where the children dwell!

There are beautiful lands where the rivers flow
Through valleys of ripened grain;
There are lands where armies of worshippers know
No God but the God of Gain
The chink of gold is the song they sing,
And all their life-time harvesting
Are the glittering joys that gold may bring,
In measures they buy and sell;
But the land where love is the coin and king
Is the land where the children dwell!

They romp in troops through this beautiful land
From morning till set of sun,
And the Drowsy Fairies have sweet dreams planned
When the little tasks are done.
Here are no strivings for power and place,
The last are first in the mimic race,
All hearts are trusted, all life is grace,
And Peace sings; "All goes well"—
For God walks daily with unveiled face
In the land where the children dwell!
—JOHN JEROME ROONEY,
in Catholic World.

ARE THE ORATORS ALL DEAD?

A WRITER discusses this question and virtually decides it in the affirmative. Alas, that it is too true! Like the poets, the orators have made way for a more practical, new order of things.

The poets have starved out, and the orators have been read out. Indeed the day and mission of the orator have past. In the days of the ancients, the forum was their instructor; their orator, their newspaper. The day of printing had not come, and they were accustomed to hear, rather than to read. Their oratory had more responsibilities resting upon it, than that of the present day. And hence, it is still said that the eloquence of the Roman and Athenian people has been rarely equalled, and never surpassed. Indeed it is apparent that the eloquence of the Athenian orators has surpassed that of all other ages in true and irresistible spirit, which, at a period of two thousand years, stirs our blood and excites us to action.

For years, and even centuries, after the Greeks and Romans, was oratory the principal mode of conveying and disseminating thought to the public, and not until the fifteenth century, when Gutenberg gave to the world the use of printers' types, did it lose its mission. When that art became known, and in general use, oratory lost its mission and the world gradually became accustomed to read, rather than to hear. From that time, the circular begat the pamphlet, the pamphlet, the quarterly, the quarterly, the weekly, the weekly, the daily, until now the record of the day is laid at almost every man's door within a few hours after the occurrence of the news it contains. And hence, besides the mighty aid of the millions of books that are being issued from the presses of the world, do the legislator, the politician, and even the orator himself, address themselves rather to the press of the country, than to their hearers; regarding their many readers more than their comparatively few hearers. And thus has the sword gradually surrendered its sceptre to the pen, and gradually relegated to the past that once debated question: "Resolved, That the pen is mightier than the sword."

Yes, the day of the orator has passed. He can now better fulfil his mission by the pen, than at the forum or on the hustings. In the South, perhaps, better than elsewhere, has this comparatively lost art held its tenacity, and continued its usefulness. Having a large class of non-readers, and the greatest per cent. of native orators, the art has been cherished for its beauty and utility. Yet, even here, it is acknowledged to be on the wane, and fast surrendering its sacred responsibilities to the press and pen.

It may be sad, yet it is nevertheless a fact, that the orators are either dead, or have concluded that the pen is, at the present day, a more effective weapon.

REFLECTIONS ON A SKULL

[The following poem is the production of Captain Howe, of Alabama, a Confederate officer in the late war, and published directly after the surrender :]

AND this was man ! imperious man !
  Who laughed, defied and scorned—
And this the chamber where the mind
  Bright visions once adorned.
And this the socket, where the eye
Bespoke his immortality.

And here the mouth, the fleshless mouth,
  Whence music issued forth,
And there the shapeless nose that once
  Inhaled the scents of earth,
And here the ear where joyous sound
Once made the happy heart rebound.

And this the cranium, where reigned
  The passions of the soul ;
Yea ! burning eloquence and thought,
  Too great for earth's control ;
'Twas here where Reason poised her wings
O'er Passion's sleepless lightnings.

Yea ! from the summit Conscience sent
  The thunders of its law,
And radiant thoughts like lightning gleamed
  O'er all they felt or saw ;
Here glowing hopes once kindled bright,
Like frosty crystals in moonlight.

Here realms of fancy rose and fell
  Like rainbows in a cloud,
And cunning schemes and grand designs
  With God-like power endowed ;
Here love and hate, and hopes and ire,
Impaled the soul with wall of fire.

'Twas here where Science lit the mind
  To track the solar light,
To measure worlds and systems vast,
  And comets in their flight,
Yea ! darkly brooding evermore
On Law's phenomenon and lore.

'Twas here where subtle Falsehood chained
  The spirit to the earth,
In cankers, rags and filthy dross,
  A thing of little worth,
Till Truth, uprising, burst the bond
And pointed to the far beyond.

Where now, thou lone, deserted cell,
  Which once was Reason's throne,
Tell me, if echo's voice can tell,
  Where is thy monarch flown ?
What ! Silent ! E'en thy ghastly grin
Derides and mocks me from within.

No tongue hast thou thy tale of love
  In anguish to relate,
To utter threatenings on the bard,
  Who wantons with thy fate ;
Thou need'st no voice—thy orbless eye
Speaks more than tongue or poetry.

The power of thought, the flash of wit,
  The language of the eye,
The influence of the spirit power,
  Can they, too, fail and die ?
In savage mood thou seem'st to laugh
To scorn each human epitaph.

I do not like thy lipless grin,
  Thou mockery of death !
It indicates what I shall be
  When I have lost my breath,
O death ! thou monitor, I see
Pride's hollow pomp and pageantry.

Still would I live, endure the pain
  Which racks the human frame,
When sheer old age has lost the sweets
  To which my youth lays claim ;
I'd live, and yet I know not why
I dread thy touch, Mortality.

Grim spectacle, good night ! my lamp
  Burns dimly in this midnight hour,
And thy cold, hollow grin, doth mock
  Ambition, fame and human power,
Since Death permits the worm to crawl
And revel in proud Reason's hall !

KISS ME GOOD NIGHT, MAMMA.

DEAR mamma, I've put all my playthings away,
I've been such a good little darling to-day :

I know that you love me, for often you've said
That I was your angel. now put me to bed.
The stars have come out, and, mamma, you told me
They were windows thro' which all angels could see ;
And now while their smiling on us with delight,
Oh! kiss me, dear mamma, come kiss me good night.

Chorus.

    Angels watch over me, thy vigils keep
    Guard and protect me while I am asleep.
    O! bring me a message in dreams from papa
    Waiting in heaven for me and mamma.

Dear mamma, you kissed me and told me today
That if I'd kneel down you would teach me to pray.
I heard you last night, won't you teach me the same?
"Our Father in heaven, hallowed be thy name."
I'll kneel when you kneel, I'll look as you look,
So that God can write down both our prayers in one book,
And papa can read them while God holds the light,
Oh! kiss me, dear mamma, come kiss me good night,

Chorus,

Dear mamma, look up, O! don't look so sad,
To know he is in heaven should make your heart glad ;
O! kiss me but once, and then smooth down my hair,
And tell me that some day we'll meet papa there,
You know that he's waiting, and happy he'll be,
When he comes with the angels to meet you and me.

Ah! then we'll be happy in God's pleasing sight,
O! kiss me, dear mamma, come kiss me good night.

Chorus.

BY THE SUMMER SEA.

I THOUGHT I had surely conquered and lived down this sharp old pain,
Till the mighty voice of the ocean wakes it to life again—
Wakes it to throb and torture, to burn with its fire anew,
As I sit on the sands, O Philip, and long and yearn for you.

There are fancies strangely bitter in the surge of this restless sea,
And hopes, and dreams, and memories, all rising mournfully ;
The waves that are softly breaking, with starry lustre kissed,
Summon a host of phantoms out of the ocean mist.

In the years that have fled forever since you and I first met,
The long years of hopeless passion, the long years of vain regret,
I have fondly dreamed, O Philip, that I had mastered quite
The heart that rises up once more in bitterness to-night.

I have thrust away in silence each loving thought of you ;
I have laid to rest each memory so tender and so true ;
I have prayed upon my bended knees for power to forget,
And the answer to that prayer is this—
I love you, love you, yet.

You put me from you sternly, in those bitter words which said,
That love for me was hopeless, since trust in me was dead :
I am nowise better, Philip, than I was so long ago—
But I love you more, my darling, than you will ever know.

Is love so very plenty in this weary world of pain,
That you cannot let all else go by and trust me once again?
I would never wrong you, Philip, nor ever pain you more—
You see I cast all pride away, here on this ocean shore.

My heart seems breaking, Philip, as I linger all alone,
And there comes no sound of comfort, save the ocean's restless moan!
I stretch my hands to Heaven, and pray for your return,
But the hope that dies, and the love that lives, can only pant and yearn.

The cruel sea's between us, with its ceaseless ebb and flow,
And I sigh, and wonder, and question, will it be ever so?
Will the distance loom, my darling, ever as great as now,
When time has left his silver threads athwart my pallid brow?

Will there come no end, O Philip, to the weariness and strife?
Will there dawn no day of gladness upon my saddened life?
Will the sun go down in darkness, and peace be only given,
When the aching heart is laid to rest, and the sinful soul is shriven?

You cannot blame me, Philip, that I remember still—
For they err who tell us all things are possible to will!
I would gladly crush forever the heart which madly clings,
Dog-like, unto the cruel hand, that only strikes and stings!

But love, which is sorely bitter, is very mighty, too,
And faith is like a needle—to its magnet ever true;
I would fain be fickle, Philip, and false as false can be,
As I sit alone and desolate, beside the summer sea.

But the Past is here beside me, in this purple, starry night,
And her great eyes shine upon me, with tender, mournful light—
Sweet eyes, so full of gentleness, so lovely in their pain,
That I clasp her back, O Philip, to my faithful heart again!
—Christian Reid.

CHASING BUTTERFLIES.

As I pass'd a child one day,
  It was busy in care,
Gliding youth's moments away
  Chasing butterflies fair.

Said I to him, while passing—
  "Say, what's the use, my youth,
Of all such foolish chasing?
  Pray your answer, in truth?"

Then, thought I, how many who
  Live life through in disguise,
And all they act, all they do,
  "Is chasing butterflies!"

YOU OR I.

If we could know!
Which of us, darling, would be first to go,
Who would be first to breast the swelling tide,
And step alone upon the other side—
  If we could know.

If it were you,
Should I walk softly, keeping death in view?
Should I my love to you more oft express?
Or should I give you, darling, only less—
  If it were you?

If it were I,
Should I improve the moments slipping by?
Should I more closely follow God's great plan?
Be filled with a sweeter charity to man—
  If it were I?

If we could know !
We cannot, darling, and 'tis better so.
I should forget, just as I do to-day,
And walk along the same old stumbling way—
If I could know.

I would not know
Which of us, darling, will be first to go,
I only wish the space may not be long
Between the parting and the greeting song ;
But when, or where, or how, we're called to go—
I would not know.
—Detroit Free Press.

WOMAN.

No subject was ever more abused than Woman. The gosling youth begins on it early, and never lets up. The penny-a-liner finds her a fruitful theme from birth, through the divorce court, and even after her death inflicts the world with something he calls obituary. Even the most prosaic and arctic hearted, at times, thaws out and has his pen as well as his heart directed at her. And the dudes and the poets,—why they simply couldn't exist without her ! With them, she is made the subject of a lot of gush upon the slightest provocation. A two-season-Widower, or second-hand politician couldn't waste more adjectives on her than they. She is a "peach," she is a "daisy," she is "a jewel." she is an "angel," and all that class of stuff. No matter how pale or how freckled her face, "Her cheeks are like the cherry." No matter if her eyes are crossed, and of different colors, they are "Diamonds sparkling fair." If her feet resemble canal boats, they are "Little mice, stealing in and out." Her hair is always in ringlets, golden waves, etc, etc,—and the "sweet, girl graduates," why, they are all angels,—just perfect, the last one of them."
And still, Woman has survived it all, perhaps the cholera infantum included ! Yes, thank God, she is with us, and has brought her knitting and come to stay ! It is not surprising that some of them survived, however, as children and imbeciles are said to do well on gruel and taffy. But how the others got along on it, as the downeasterner says, is a caution ! It can only be explained by their taking it, like the bad children used to take medicine,—by throwing it behind the bed !—Fortunately, like the "bad children," those turned out the best.

But isn't it wonderful what inflictions of this character have been heaped on that sex ? Many of them, actually intended as compliments !—The spring poets, dudes, and young lovers, might be excused, on account of previous condition ; but the others, never ! In the absence of an early introduction to their corkscrew-curled Aunt's slipper, they should have been introduced to the opposite sex at an early age, and assured that she was neither an idiot, a toy, nor a dupe. They should have been taught better long ago, and if their training had been begun two or three generations before they were born, it would have been all the more effectual. And, insomuch as similar training has not been taught, isn't it time to begin ? Why continue to insult woman's intelligence ? Why assume that she is a fool, or admit yourself to be one ? Why not introduce the sexes to each other, and assure the one that he is only a male-woman, and she really a female-man ? This is simply the truth of it, and why not out with it, and have both understand it ? It may be policy for some to persuade woman that she was only made out of scrap material, and intended as man's pudding-headed plaything ; but there are others who have a different notion of it, and have always had the idea that when God made man and was pleased with his work, that it was the female portion of it, with which he was especially pleased, and in which He worked His picked clay ! And, with due respect to the story of creation, we have always been ashamed of our great grandfather's moral cowardice in trying to hide behind grandma's petticoat of fig leaves. In keeping with the ancients' idea of woman, it did no credit to her, and reflected on the man for whom she is said to have been created.

This idea was started then, and has been kept up ever since. All history, myth, story and fiction have really been for the Big Ike, man, while the Mrs. Adams, Mrs. Alexanders, Mrs. Columbuses, Mrs. Washingtons, and Mrs. So-and-sos have been but zeros in the column. Where did these Big Ikes come from, and why so great? It is a wonder that Woman was permitted to bear them —and in case of the founder of Rome, even that honor was transferred to a She-Wolf;—and still another wonder is, that it hadn't been a he-wolf! Such was the ancients' idea of woman, and like in many other things, the thought of the past still clings to the present. Yet, is it not time to relegate such rot to where it belongs? Woman can't use her usual good taste and write or speak very much of herself; so let us insist that if it is to be done by man, that he use some sense in doing it. And if he will not do so of his own accord, we hope she will demand it,— whether she belongs to a Woman's rights convention, or not. If he insults your intelligence, tell him so. If he come buzzing around, like a June-bug in the spring, telling you your cheeks are like the cherry, tell him that his mind runs on cherries and other green things, and to hunt some other pasture, or cherry tree. If he quotes poetry, and talks about all kinds of flowers, ask him if he has read of the hum of industry, and will please substitute the bouquets for a barrel of Pittsburg's best,—warranted 196 pounds? If he says you are an angel, ask him what he would look like yoked up with an angel? Remind him that angels would be very lonesome on earth, especially as all seem to be female angels; and that your mother and father, who know you best, had never discovered that you were one: and that you really doubted it yourself, in so much as you had no recollection of the great white throne, and wings; that you really felt quite at home down here, and that even an angel might be addressed intelligently, and perhaps entitled to a good and sensible husband.

If he goes to talking about your teeth being pearls, and your eyes diamonds, tell him to rent a hall and see how many he'll get to hear him at popular prices, as the bent of his mind seems in that direction; or tell him to go to a jewelry store, and take along the price; that you and your father are not in the business, and have none to exchange for a dollar marriage license, nor dude clothes, and unpaid bills.

If he vows that he would do anything for you, even lose his last drop of blood, don't believe it. Tell him that the sacrifice of his last drop of blood would not be much, after the others were gone, and might be attended with his funeral expenses, which you did not care to incur. Back this up by questions about living for you, instead of dying for you, and test his doing anything for you, by a request that he take the ox-cart and bring a load of cordwood to keep you warm, and to make a fire for himself to sit by.

These tests are worth a good deal, and one dose will usually cure the worst cases of "love-sickness," and are convincing that a Woman may be a good doctor.

Again, he may desire to ape the English, or be original by breaking out in a new place by telling you that you are worth millions,—yes, all the world to him:—Keep cool, and don't think he has placed a very high value on you. The balance of the world is probably not worth over fifty dollars to him, after his debts are paid, so sixty dollars is your estimate, which is less than the value of a good horse. But ask him how he learned you were worth so much. Has he consulted Dun and Bradstreet on your father? Assure him that his information may be at fault, as the foreign title clubs have made no propositions, or investigations, as yet. Then ask him, as an evidence of good faith, to show you the corners of a dozen or two hundred-dollar bills while you get your breath, and more maturely consider his proposition of marriage.—He may never comply with your last very simple request, but you will have time for reflection, and probably to select a better husband.

There are thousands of ways they will come at you, and shock your intelligence; but then, even sensible women must have amusement; and fool-men must have excuses for wives, though the excuses often repent of their folly. And, sometimes, they make powerful well of a bad bargain! Yet, the truth of it is, after all, that a man or woman only meets one or two in a lifetime that they really love, and with whom they can be thoroughly congenial and perfectly happy. There are people, however, who are very much like an old shoe.—Most anybody can wear and get along with them.

The real mate, however, only the individual can name. Strange as it may seem, that one "cometh like a thief in the night," and like "the wind, bloweth where it listeth." Yet, this kindred spirit can always tell when he comes, and where he blows! Such a one not only appears, but is, different from all the rest. When he meets his counterpart, he needs but little courtship, and is the least prepared to give it. He simply finds the wind is out of his sails, the propeller lifeless, and that he has only the anchor to cling to. Both seem to have had the same bug crawl down their backs, and each has an "Inward inexpressibleness of an outward all-overishness!" They recognize, without reasoning, that Cupid has them captive, and yield, and give up the ghost!

This one may not be so smart, or handsome as the others. He may talk glibly to others but to you, he is silent eloquence. He gets red in the face, twists and turns in his chair, discovers for the first time that his hands are all in his way, while his tongue swells up in his mouth as a roll of biscuit dough, and to swallow is as difficult as to work a force pump. He swells up, and looks as if he had lost a collar button, or had forgotten something, but cannot even think of angels, cherries, diamonds, or pearls. You feel half sorry for him and realize that the Vesuvius within him,—like the measles,—must break out. He finally drawls out something about the weather, and for relief you get up and hand him a fan, yourself forgetting that it is really cold, and that the fire has died out.—Poor fellow, he "has it bad!" You both should stroll out in the fresh air and have your story "continued in our next!"

But permit us to draw the curtain and say, there are probable elements of a man and husband in this fellow. He isn't a coward because he behaves so; for a real man can lead in battle, and face all kinds of dangers better, and more gracefully, than he can the woman he really loves: or her father, in asking for her. Such a one will probably be actually brave enough not only to protect her, but to bring the wood and water, kindle the fires, and appreciate a mother-in-law. He will probably not send any spring poetry, but will provide lots of spring-salad, and say but little about living or dying, cherries, diamonds, angels, or pearls, but he will doubtless accord to woman all the honors God intended, and convince her, that after all, there are men worth having.

THE SURPRISE.

SOFTLY and slowly I crept in the door
   Of the parlor; and there was seen,
All wrapp'd in the arms of the God of
    Sleep,
   The object of my love—my queen!

Gently, right up to the sofa I stole
   On which she, like a bride did lie.
There I, quietly kneeling by her side,
   Cast a word of the heart—a sigh.

Her tresses in beautiful graces fell,
   Her hands were folded on her breast,
And like the tidal waves of the ocean,
   Their heav'nly motion gave them rest.

Beneath the kerchief, which o'erspread
   her face,
   Her ringlets fell in silent grace;
Her form, none fairer that God ever
   made—
   A perfect type of Grecian race.

Thought I, as she lay in silent beauty,
  Was angel to angel e'er fairer?
Then rushed upon me the coquettish
    thought
  I'd kiss her, would it not scare her!

So, drawing nearer, where she lay
    dreaming
  I proceeded with that intent—
And behold! I found her eyes were
    beaming—
  And up she jump'd, and out she
    went!

FAITH, HOPE AND CHARITY.

To a mother was born one day
  Fair daughters numbering three,
Which for the want of better names,
  Were called Faith, Hope and Charity,
Fairer than they were never seen,—
  The mother's heart swelled with joy,
Although she half-way sighed because
  At least one was not a boy.

Hope, round, jolly, little cherub,
  Grew stronger both night and day,
And, like her fair sister, Faith,
  Was just full of mirth and play.
Charity pined, lingered long and then,
  She without a single sigh,
Left father, mother, Faith and Hope
  For her kind and home on high,

Faith, more beautiful than Charity,—
  And seemingly the stronger,—
Sad as it may seem, also died,
  Tho' she lingered much the longer,
Mother, tender and true, weep not,
  For Hope is still left with thee,—
That constant lives, and will live on,
  Heaven's home for Faith and Charity.

THE WEDDING BELLS.

O, THE bells! The wedding bells!
What a happiness their ringing tells!
How the music from them swells!
What melody in them dwells!
  O, what smoothness in their swing-
    ing!
  O, what sweetness in their ringing,
  As love's message to us bringing,
  They keep on ringing, ringing!

They fill our hearts with pure delight
As they ring out clear and bright
And shed abroad their golden light
And dispel the gloom of night.
  O, the bells! the wedding bells!
  How they weave their magic spells
  Around our heart, and fill its cells
  With the love that in them dwells.
    Let them swing the altar o'er,
    Let them ring for evermore,
    Let them sing the song in store
    For all lovers the wide word o'er.
  There is joy within those bells,
  There is peace within those bells,
  There is love within those bells,
  There is heaven in those bells,
        —WILLIAM HENRY TUCKER.

THE GOOD WE ALL MAY DO.

OH, the good we all may do,
  While the days are going by!

There are lonely hearts to cherish,
  While the days are going by;
There are weary souls who perish,
  While the days are going by!

If a smile we can renew,
  As our journey we pursue;
Oh, the good we all may do,
  While the days are going by!

There's no time for idle scorning,
  While the days are going by;
Let your face be like the morning,
  While the days are going by!

Oh, the world is full of sighs,
  Full of sad and weeping eyes;
Help your fallen brother rise,
  While the days are going by!

All the loving links that bind us,
  While the days are going by;
One by one we leave behind us,
  While the days are going by!

But the seeds of good we sow,
  Both in shade and sun will grow,
And will keep our heart's aglow,
  While the days are going by!
Oh, the good we all may do,
  While the days are going by!
        —ROSA BELL HOLT.

A GOOD BOOK.

We recently saw a good book, and it is of such rare occurrence, we can but stop to make a note of it. Now to make a good book it must have good paper and be well bound. This one was. There were many in the collection, but none better bound, and of better paper. It was doubtless a popular book, or at least one in universal demand; and this cannot be said of many books. It contained about six hundred pages, and was elegantly bound in sheep. We do not know who was its author, for he seems to have been too modest to have attached his name to it.

But we have seen many really similar books, by various authors; yet, none quite so good. The special charm to this book was, that instead of having its pages marred by rot, abortive thoughts and ink, they were left blank. Instead of being a nest of rotten eggs, it was a nice, clean nest for some hen or rooster to lay thoughts in!

But if the Sunday papers would only imitate the example of this great and unknown author, and send out their papers unprinted, all will be forgiven, and no questions asked!

FORGOTTEN.

Please let me hold your dolly, dear,
   She's got a beautiful head;
Santa Claus didn't bring me one,
   'Cause my papa is dead.

I lay awake the livelong night
   To hear him on our shed;
I guess he went the other way,
   'Cause my papa is dead.

He brought Sue Jones a picture-book,
   The cover was gold and red;
I 'spec he thought I couldn't read,
   'Cause my papa is dead.

And Mary Smith got fruit and nuts,
   French candy, too, she said;
I didn't even get a sugar mouse,
   'Cause my papa is dead.
     —Mrs. LaSalle *in Age Herald.*

SILENT GRIEFS.

There are sighs unheaved, there are tears unwept,
There are lutes unstrung, there are harps unswept,
There are griefs unknown, there are thoughts untold,
There are hearts that beat warm when they seem but cold;
There are loves unlost when they seem so dead,
There are wounds unseen that have often bled,
For the soul feels most when in silence deep
It lives unheard as the winds in their sleep.

There are sorrows very dark that o'ercloud our way,
And that shade the heart in our life's glad day,
There are joys unfelt, there are hopes unfed,
There are pledges hushed, there are vows unsaid,
There are flowers dead among the spring leaves,
There are treasures lost among the golden sheaves,
There are memories sweet, and we love them well,
But the eye grows dim as their currents swell,

There are friendships gone like the dews of morn,
There are smiles now turned to the coldest scorn,
There are dreams we loved in the days gone by,
When the sun was warm, and so bright our sky,
That are past like spray on the ocean's breast,
When the storm has ceased and her waters rest,
And the heart grows sad that its loves have fled,
That its hopes are gone and its garlands dead.

There are scenes we knew that are faded now,
There are gathered wreaths and a shaded brow,
There are songs unsung that we loved to hear,
When the heart was fresh and its pleasures near,
There are footsteps hid in the sands of Time,
There are voices stilled in this earthly clime,
But the echoes come from the boundless shore
That lies beyond, in the vast evermore.

There are prayers we breathe for the ones we love,
While we linger here from our home above,
Yet we smile to think that our griefs will cease,
And our hearts rejoice in an endless peace.
Far away above the ethereal blue.
Where each soul is glad and each heart is true,
We will live in Love, and her radiant beam
Will inspire the soul with a heavenly dream.
—*Richmond Dispatch.*

A GOOD WOMAN.

A GOOD woman never grows old. Years may go over her head, but if benevolence and virtue dwell in her heart, she is as cheerful as when the Spring of life first opened to her view. When we look upon a good woman we never think of her age—she looks as charming as when the rose of youth first bloomed upon her cheek. That rose has not faded yet; it will never fade. In her neighborhood she is the friend and benefactor, in the church the devout worshipper and exemplary Christian. Who does not love and respect the woman who has passed her days in acts of kindness and mercy—who has been the friend of man and God—whose whole life has been a scene of kindness and love, a devotion of love and religion? We repeat, such a woman cannot grow old. She will always be fresh and buoyant in spirit and active in humble deeds of mercy and benevolence. If the young lady desires to retain the bloom and beauty of youth let her not yield to the sway of fashion and folly; let her love truth and virtue; and to the close of life she will retain those feelings which now make life appear a garden of sweets, ever fresh and ever new.

VALUE OF BOOKS.

BOOKS are the windows through which the soul looks out. A house without books is like a house without windows. The love of knowledge comes with reading and grows upon it; and the love of knowledge in a young mind is almost a warrant against low vices and vulgar tastes. Among the earliest ambitions to be excited among all who are struggling up in life from nothing to something, is that of owning and constantly attending to a library of good books. A little library growing larger every year is an honorable part of a young man's history. If such works as "Our Father's House," "Night Scenes," or "Science and the Bible" be seen upon the shelves of the gradually forming library the tastes and habits of the owner are happily molded.

REMARKABLE FACTS.

EVERYTHING in nature indulges in an amusement of some kind. The lightnings play, the winds whistle, the thunders roll, the snow flies, the rills and cascades sing and dance, the waves leap, the fields smile, the vines creep and run, and the buds shoot. But some of them have their seasons of melancholy. The tempests moan, the zephyrs sigh, the brooks murmur, and the mountains look blue.

LAND OF THE SOUTH

LAND of the South—imperial land—
How proud thy mountains rise—
How sweet thy scenes on every hand;
How fair thy covering skies!

But for this—ah, not for these—
  I love thy fields to roam,
Thou hast a dearer spell to me,
  Thou art my native home!

The rivers roll their liquid wealth,
  Unequalled to the sea—
Thy hills and valleys bloom with health,
  And green with verdure be;
But not for thy proud ocean streams;
  Not for thine azure dome,
Sweet, Sunny South—I cling to thee—
  Thou art my native home!

I've stood beneath Italia's clime
  Beloved of tale and song,
On Helvyn's hills, proud and sublime,
  Where nature's wonders throng;
By Tempe's classic sunlit streams,
  Where gods of old did roam,
But ne'er have found so fair a land
  As thou—my native home!

And thou hast prouder glories too,
  Than nature ever gave;
Peace sheds o'er thee her genial dew,
  And freedom's pinions wave,—
Fair science flings her pearls around;
  Religion lifts her dome,—
These, these endear thee to my heart,
  My own, loved, native home!

And "heaven's best gift to man" is
    thine;
  God bless the rosy girls!—
Like sylvan flowers, they sweetly shine;
  Their hearts as pure as pearls!
And grace and goodness circle them,
  Where'er their footsteps roam—
How can I then, whilst loving them,
  Not love my native home!

HOW CAN A WOMAN TELL?

He told me his love this morning,
  With his dear hand clasped in mine,
And he said, "God speed the dawning
  When, darling, I call thee mine."
But my fond heart is questioned softly,
  Though loving him true and well,
Will his love outlast any changes?
  Ah! how can a woman tell?

When the years shall bridge their trials,
  And the cares and pains outweigh
The joys in the little household,
  As clouds might obscure the day—
Will the hand that has led me fondly
  When maidenly ills befell,
As earnestly shield from sorrow?
  Ah! how can a woman tell?

When the silver threads are creeping
  Through my tresses one by one;
When I lose my youth and beauty,
  As many a wife has done;
Will his heart be mine as truly,
  As when in the flowery dell
He gave me his trusted promise!
  Ah! how can a woman tell?

I glance at my sweetheart waiting,
  His eyes they are clear and true;
"I will love him," my heart says gladly
  "I will trust him the wide world
    through,
I will be to him joy and comfort,
  I will other wives excel;
I will keep him with love's magic—"
  This much may a woman tell.

THE STORY OF THE GATE.

Across the pathway, myrtle-fringed,
Under the maple, it was hinged—
  The little wooden gate;
'Twas there, within the quiet gloom,
When I had strolled with Nelly home,
  I used to pause and wait.

Before I said to her good night.
Yet loath to leave the winsome sprite
  Within the garden's pale,
And there, the gate between us two,
We'd linger, as all lovers do,
  And lean upon the rail,

And face to face, eyes close to eyes,
Hands meeting hands in feigned sur-
    prise
  After a stealthy quest—
So close I'd bend ere she'd retreat—
That I'd grow drunken from the sweet
  Tuberose upon her breast.

We'd talk—in fitful style, I ween—
With many a meeting glance between
The tender words and low:
We'd whisper some dear, sweet conceit,
Some idle gossip we'd repeat;
And then I'd move to go.

"Good-night," I'd say; "Good-night—good-bye!"
"Good-night"—from her, with half a sigh—
"Good-night!" Good-night!"
And then—
And then I do not go, but stand,
Again lean on the railing, and—
Begin it all again!

Ah! that was many a day ago—
That pleasant summer time—although
The gate is standing yet;
A little cranky it may be,
A little weatherworn—like me—
Who never ean forget!

The happy—"End?" My cynic friend,
Pray save your sneers—there was no "end"
Watch yonder chubby thing!
That is our youngest, hers and mine;
See how he climbs, his legs to twine
About the gate and swing.

SCRIBNER'S MAGAZINE.

THE ERRING.

THINK gently of the erring!
Ye know not of the power
With which the dark temptation came,
In some unguarded hour.
Ye may not know how earnestly
The struggle, or how well,
Until the hour of weakness came,
And sadly thus they fell.

Deal gently with the erring!
Oh, do not thou forget,
However darkly stained by sin,
He is thy brother yet;
Heir of the self-same heritage;
Child of the self-same God,
He hath but stumbled in the path,
Thou hast in weakness trod.

Speak gently to the erring!
For it is not enough
That innocence and peace have gone
Without thy censure rough?
It sure must be a weary lot
That sin-crushed heart to bear,
And they who share a happier fate
Their chidings well may spare.

Speak kindly to the erring!
Thou yet may'st win them back,
With holy words and tones of love,
From misery's thorny track,
Forget not thou hast often sinned,
And sinful yet must be—
Deal gently with the erring one,
As God has dealt with thee!

NIGHT.

'TWAS on one eve in September as I took my accustomed walk, I was awakened to the grandeur of a Southern sunset. The herd had begun to wind along their woodland paths homeward; and as they went on the tinkle, tinkle of the bell served as enchanting music to speed their progress. The sun's journey was now completed. The partridge had whistled its mate to its side and retired for the night. The mountain and hills with their autumn-tinged foliage were now bathed in "amber light." The golden stripes were extending up from the west—mingled with the stars of Heaven—representing our nationality. The stars that were now appearing, were reflected back again to Heaven by the crystal waters of the neighboring brook. Some showed their brilliancy, others, like the pale watchers by a dead man's corpse, looked down as if upon a world of corruption, and flickered, and flickered away. Soon the moon arose and asserted its dominion over the scene. The weather was warm and the sight enchanting. A gentle breeze stirred the air from the southeast. The moon and stars showed palely through the trees, and made the whole one poetical scene. I thought if the grandeurs would only remain until morning, I would rise and see them then. Next morning I arose, and a dense fog shrouded the whole. The birds sat with folded wings. The moss hung in gloomy festoons from the stirless trees. No breath of air stole over forest or wave; but everywhere there brooded a still and awful calm. In the valley the murky vapors shaped themselves into the dim outlines of some huge monster, and as rapidly as they shaped themselves into form, they passed as the scenes of some panorama, and another took its place. The beauty of the landscape has been hidden by mysterious vapor. The brook no longer chants its poetical tune. Night has its terrors—and how fitly may it be compared with human life! At times the skies are clear and the star of hope beams brightly to direct our course; again they are darkened by clouds. At times there is a light to illuminate our footsteps, again a vapor to wrap them in darkness. But the scene is becoming bright. There beams the light of day, and the sun puts the vapors and darkness to shame. Thus if our lives are properly spent will the eternal sun banish the shadows and vapors of our lives, and we shall enjoy eternal day!

THE LOVER'S PARAGON.

Just fair enough to be pretty,
  Just gentle enough to be sweet,
Just saucy enough to be witty,
  Just dainty enough to be neat,
Just tall enough to be graceful,
  Just slight enough for a fay,
Just dressy enough to be tasteful,
  Just merry enough to be gay.

Just tears enough to be tender,
  Just sighs enough to be sad,
Tones sad enough to remember,
  Your heart through their cadence made glad,
Just meek enough for submission,
  Just bold enough to be brave,
Just pride enough for ambition,
  Just thoughtful enough to be grave.

A tongue that can talk without harming
  Just mischief enough to tease,
Manners pleasant enough to be charming,
  That put you at once at your ease,
Disdain to put down presumption.
  Sarcasm to answer a fool,
Cool contempt enough shown to assumption,
  Proper dignity always the rule.

Flights of the fair fancy ethereal,
  Devotion to science full paid,
Stuff of the sort of material
  That really good wives are made.
Generous enough and kind-hearted,
  Pure as the angels above—
Oh! from her may I never be parted,
  For such is the maiden I love.

THE CALM THAT COMES AT EVENING.

There's a calm that comes at evening,
  When the weary day is o'er,
That's as soothing as the lullaby
  Our mothers sang of yore;
And though the day be dreary,
  I can just forget it all,
In the calm that comes at evening,
  When the twilight shadows fall.

I can see my sweetheart's signal
  From her waving window blinds;
I can feel her perfumed presence
  Wafted to me on the winds;
When I hush my heart to hear her,
  I can almost understand
Her sweet welcome in the wimple
  Of the wind-wave from her hand.

When she laughs it's like the music
  Of the ripples on the rills,
And her breath is like the fragrance
  Of the flowers that deck the hills.
And though the day be dreary,
  I can just forget it all,
In the calm that comes at evening,
  When the twilight shadows fall.
    —Cy Warman.

"DOES DEATH END ALL?"

"Does death end all?" Oh, mighty sage!
The years to you have wisdom given.
When from Life's Book is torn our page,
  Is that the end? Is there no Heaven?

Just fair enough to be pretty,
  Just gentle enough to be sweet,
Just saucy enough to be witty,
  Just dainty enough to be neat.

—*Page 334.*

Stroking his thin, white hair he said,
  With voice both sad and low,
"On graves of their dead, wise men
    have laid
  This answer: 'We do not know!'"
"Does death end all?" dear doubting
    Tom,
  Is that what science teaches?
When this life ends, is none to come?
  A lie the Bible preaches?
"The brain's the soul, and when man
    dies,
  Like autumn leaves do fall,
All life is gone, they cannot rise,
  'Tis sad, but 'death ends all.'"

"Does death end all?" thou man of
    God,
  Who points us to His Throne;
When we are laid beneath the sod,
  Is there no resurrection morn?
"I only know in Book of Light
  God promises to save;
That death is not an endless night,
  There's life beyond the grave."

"Does death end all?" Oh, mystery!
  The greatest in this world!
Beyond man's ken or history,
  The secret lies unfurled.
"Life's fitful fever" o'er at last,
  The grave, the bier, the pall;
Ah, then we'll know, when all is past,
  Does death indeed end all.
    —JAMES E. FISHER.

WHEN YOU ARE OLD.

WHEN you are old, and I am passed
    away—
  Passed, and your face, your golden
    face is gray—
I think, whate'er the end, this dream
    of mine,
  Comforting you, a friendly star will
    shine
Down the dim slope where still you
    stumble and stray.

So may it be; that so dead Yesterday,
  No sad-eyed ghost, but generous and
    gay
May serve your memories, like almighty
    wine
      When you are old.

Dear Heart, it shall be so. Under the
    sway
Of death the past's enormous disarray
Lies hushed and dark. Yet though
    there come no sign,
  Live on well pleased! Immortal and
    divine,
Love shall still tend you, as God's
    angels may,
      When you are old.
        —W. E. HENLEY.

FOR COMING MERCIES.

DEAR Lord, are we ever so thankful,
  As thankful we should be to Thee,
For Thine angels sent down to defend
    us
  From dangers our eyes never see;
From perils that lurk unsuspected,
  The powers of earth and of air,
The while we are heaven protected
  And guided from evil and snare?

Are we grateful as grateful we should
    be
For commonplace days of delight,
  When safe we fare forth to our labor
And safe we fare homeward at night;
For the weeks in which nothing has
    happened
  Save commonplace toiling and play,
When we've worked at the tasks of the
    household
  And peace hushed the house day by
    day?

Dear Lord, that the terror at midnight,
  The weird of the wind and the flame,
Hath passed by our dwelling, we praise
    Thee
  And lift up our hearts in Thy name;
That the circle of darlings unbroken
  Yet gathers in bliss round the board,
That commonplace love is our portion,
  We give Thee our praises, dear Lord.

Forgive us who live by Thy bounty
  That often our lives are so bare
Of the garlands of praise that should
    render
  All votive and fragrant each prayer.

Dear Lord in the sharpness of trouble
  We cry from the depths to the throne !
In the long days of gladness and beauty
  Take Thou the glad hearts as Thine own.

Oh, common are sunshine and flowers,
  And common are raindrop and dew,
And the gay little footsteps of children,
  And common the love that holds true,
So, Lord, for our commonplace mercies,
  That straight from Thy hand are bestowed,
We are fain to uplift our thanksgivings—
  Take, Lord, the long debt we have owed.
—MARGARET E. SANGSTER

A WIFE'S PRAYER.

THE following is the prayer of Mrs. Martin Luther for her husband, which contains the sentiment, less beautifully expressed, doubtless, of that of many a wife:

"Lord bless and preserve my husband; let his life be long, comfortable and holy; and let me also become a great blessing and comfort unto him, a sharer in all his sorrows, a meet helper for him in all the accidents and changes of the world; make me amiable forever in his eyes, and very dear to him. Unite his heart to me in the dearest union of love and holiness, and mine to him in all the sweetness of charity and compliance. Keep me from all ungentleness, and discontentedness and unreasonableness of passion and humor; and make me humble and obedient, charitable and loving, patient and contented, useful and observant, that we may delight in each other according to Thy blessed word and ordinance, and both of us may rejoice in Thee, having our portion in the love and service of God forever."

THE OLD FARM.

THE dear old farm ! Its every rod
  Is fraught with memories sweet to me;
Each spot recalls some by-gone hour
  Of joyous childhood, gay and free.

Here nature seemed to speak herself,
  In hill and stream and sunny field ;
In them I find companionship
  The crowded city cannot yield.

What are its shallow joys to me,
  Its pomp and show, its sordid wealth.
Given in exchange, for heaven's pure air,
  For boundless freedom and rugged health.

Let him who loves the sickly shade
  Behind the counter scrape and bow;
To me it seems a better thing
  To feel the sunlight on my brow.

And to the one who falsely scorns
  The manly farmer's honest toil,
Degrading deems the work that gains
  A living from the generous soil,

I'll point him to some famous names,
  Our country's pride and glory now,
Of men whose youth did not disdain
  To wield the axe or drive the plow,

But let the farmer know his worth,
  Lofty and bold his mien should be,
His will full strong, and clear his mind,
  His duty and opinions free.

Thus careful thought and industry
  Work wonders with the fertile sod ;
His labors high and approval win
  From man, from conscience and from God.
—ANNE TAYLOR.

THE SINS OF OMISSION.

IT isn't the things you do, dear.
  It's the thing you've left undone,
Which gives you a bit of heartache
  At the setting of the sun.
The tender word forgotten,
  The letter you did not write,
The flower you might have sent, dear,
  Are your haunting ghosts to-night.

The stone you might have lifted
  Out of a brother's way,
The bit of hearts we counsel
  You were hurried too much to say,

The loving touch of the hand, dear,
  The gentle and winsome tone
That you had no time or thought for
  With troubles enough of your own.

The little act of kindness
  So easily out of mind ;
Those chances to be angels
  Which every mortal finds.
They come in night and silence,
  Each chill, reproachful wraith,
When hope is faint and flagging,
  And a blight has dropped on faith.

For life is all too short, dear,
  And sorrow is all too great,
To suffer our slow compassion
  That tarries until too late,
And it's not the thing you do, dear,
  It's the thing you leave undone,
Which gives you the bit of heartache
  At the setting of the sun.
  —MARGARET E. SANGSTER.

WHAT THE LORD EXPECTS OF US.

CHRIST never asks of us such busy labor [feet ;
As leaves no time for resting at his
The waiting attitude of expectation
  He ofttimes counts a service most complete.

He sometimes wants our ear—our rapt attention— [impart ;
  That he some sweetest secret may
'Tis always in the time of deepest silence, [with heart.
  That heart finds deepest fellowship

We sometimes wonder why our Lord has placed us [obscure,
  Within a sphere so narrow, so
That nothing we call work can find an entrance ; [dure.
  There's only room to suffer—to en-

Well, God loves patience ; souls that dwell in stillness,
  Doing the little things, or resting quite,
May just as perfectly fulfil their mission, [sight,
  Be just as useful in the Father's
As they who grapple with some giant evil, [see.
  Clearing a path that every eye may

Our Saviour cares for cheerful acquiescence,
  Rather than for a busy ministry.
And yet—he does love service, when 'tis given [deed ;
  By grateful love that clothes itself in
But work that's done beneath the scourge of duty, [heed.
  Be sure to such he gives but little

Then seek to please him, whatsoe'er he bids thee ;
  Whether to do, to suffer, to lie still !
'Twill matter little by what path he led us,
  If in it all we sought to do his will.
  —CHICAGO INTER-OCEAN.

SHADOWS.

EV'NING shadows in their flitting,
  In their flitting to and fro,
Seem to whisper and to beckon,
  Beckon us to come and go.
For they tell in noiseless cadence,
  In a noiseless, mystic rhyme,
To the heart of joy and sorrow
  Soon or late there comes a time
When the daylight fades to twilight
  And the twilight into night
And the shadows gently bury
  Earthly memories from sight,
When the day of life is ended,
  When the gulf of life is spanned,
And the soul returns forever
  To the silent shadow land.
  —CLIFFORD HOWARD.

YOU'D BETTER CHERISH HIM.

THERE are husbands who are pretty,
There are husbands who are witty,
There are husbands who in public are
  as smiling as the morn ;
There are husbands who are healthy,
There are husbands who are wealthy,
But the real angelic husband, well, he's
  never yet been born.

Some for strength of love are noted,
Who are really so devoted
That whene'er their wives are absent,
  they are lonesome and forlorn ;
And while now and then you'll find one
Who's a fairly good and kind one,
Yet the real angelic husband, oh, he's
  never yet been born !

So the woman who is mated
To the man who may be rated
As pretty fair, should cherish him forever and a day.
For the real angelic creature,
Perfect, quite, in every feature.
He has never been discovered, and he won't be, so they say.
—INCOGNITO.

CHRISTMAS.

ORIGINALLY Christmas was strictly a day of religious praise, feasting and thanksgiving. It is, perhaps, a little unfortunate that it has lost something of its strictly religious cast as it has become a day of more general observance. Yet it is a day for all, and even the atheist answers the question, "If a man die shall he live again?" once a year, as he enters into the joys of the Christmas season; for without the Christmas story, all hope of a more blissful eternity closes with the day. It matters not whether one be Christian or pagan, Jew or Gentile, it is the recognition of that great vital principle that "though he be dead, yet shall he live again."

In all ages and among all nationalities there has been a wonderfully concurring idea, similar, at least, to the story of the cross, that it was not all of life to live, nor of death to die. Even the untutored Indian had some thought that there was a future beyond the grasp of his mind, the joys of which were beyond his experience, and that the truly "Happy Hunting Ground" was beyond life's confines.

The ancients had their idols and and worshipped their typical and representative gods, because of their instinct, or intuitive conception, of a true and living God. Their idols were not worshipped or represented as their real god, but as representatives of the ideal, which was conclusive of their having at least some idea, however vague, of the Godhead.

Everywhere, and in all ages, has mankind, had some idea of the existence of the Deity, and some conception of an eventually better future state. In all ages has the inward monitor of man suggested that there was a corresponding reward for the good and for the evil deeds of the body. That the body was a physical and earthly being, and that the mind, or soul of man, was a spark of the Divinity itself. That the one was satisfied by the things of earth, that the other went out in the search of its kindred, and built its hopes in an immortality beyond.

In this beautiful hope has all mankind, even the atheist, shared. Yet, until nearly two thousand years ago, the word had gone forth, but the day had not dawned for the coming "Light of the World." Ages after ages have rolled by in their countless flight, until the faithful grew weary of watching, and had stationed sentinels in the watchtowers to note the coming of the promised morn, of which this is the anniversary. Their impatient voices were heard to cry, "Watchman, what of the night?" This question was asked again and again, and the solemn sound died away with its echo. But growing more impatient as the hour approached, the voice was once more heard at Bethlehem: "Watchman, what of the night?"—The time the watchman gave not, but replied, "The morning cometh!"—Just then the star of Bethlehem sought its new-born God as the orient lighted its pathway with heavenly blushes.—The angels rejoiced, the earth was glad, and the heavens were lighted with a new brilliancy at dawn of the story of the cross—of the coming of the age of " Peace on earth, good will towards men."

Since that time has this day been one of great rejoicing to all Christians of all lands and nations. Since that time not only do Christians. but the people of all climes unite in celebrating this day as the anniversary of the hope of a blissful immortality, until it matters not about any special creed or faith, wherever there rests in the breasts of men the hope that somehow, or where, at some future time, a happier future state awaits them, do men unite in celebrating this day, as the anniversary of the hope of a better and brighter day beyond.

FAITHFUL.

It is something, sweet, when the world goes ill,
To know you are faithful and love me still ;
To feel, when the sunshine has left the skies,
That the light is shining in your dear eyes—
Beautiful eyes ! more dear to me
Than all the wealth of the world could be !

It is something, dearest, to see you near
When life with its sorrows seems hard to bear ;
To feel when I falter, the clasp divine
Or your tender and trusting clasp in mine—
Beautiful hand ! more dear to me
Than the tenderest thing of earth could be !

Sometimes, dearest, the world goes wrong,
For God gives grief with His gift of song,
And poverty, too ! But your love is more
To me than riches and golden store.
Beautiful love ! until death shall part,
It is mine—as you are—my own sweetheart !

—Frank L. Stanton.

THOU SHALT KNOW HEREAFTER.

(John xiii, 7.)

'Tis easy, when the skies are bright
To trust our loving Father's care,
To say that all He does is right,
And pledge to follow anywhere.

But faith alone can dry our tears
When baby fingers cease to move,
And all our hopes of future years
Are buried with the ones we love.

How good can come from grief like this
We cannot understand, nor know ;
How tears and sighs are turned to bliss,
And made to help us, He will show.

When in our Father's presence, blest
With clearer vision, we shall see
That love has given what is best
To fit us for eternity.
—G. A. Warburton.

WHEN A FELLER'S GOIN' UNDER.

Seen the chap 'at hangs aroun'
 Gapin' like a fish, and blinkin',
Makin' nary move nur soun',
 When a feller-man is sinkin' ?
Nawthin' seems to bring him to,
 There he'll set, an' loll an' wonder,
Nuvver knowin' what to do
 When a feller's goin' under.

Folks may sink, er folks may swim,
 Braver men might giv' up tryin' ;
Nuvver seems to trouble him,
 Who's a livin' er who's dyin',
Can't no more nur drool an' shake,
 Starin' paralyzed out yunder,
Studyin' ef he's still awake,
 When a feller's goin' under.

But he ain't the on'y chap
 Sets and watches men a-drownin',
There is him 'at takes his nap
 When the sky is black an' frownin'
Can't see lightnin' strikin' near,
 Ain't a bit afeard of thunder,
Looks ez ef he didn't keer
 When a feller's goin' under.

He's the chap 'at wouldn't toss
 Ary plank ter help a neighbor,
'Fore he figgers up his loss
 An' the extra 'mount o' labor.
An' he stan's there safe on shore,
 An' he nuvver sees his blunder
Tell his help ain't ast no more,
 An' the drownin' man's gone under.
—Frank Walcott Hutt.

BANKS OF RHINE.

The castled crag of Drachenfels
Frowns o'er the wide and winding Rhine,
Whose breast of waters broadly swells
Between the banks which bear the vine,
And hills all rich with blossom'd trees,
And fields which promise corn and wine,

And scatter'd cities crowning these,
Whose far white walls along them shine,
Have strew'd a scene, which I should see
With double joy wert *thou* with me!

And peasant girls, with deep-blue eyes,
And hands which offer early flowers,
Walk smiling o'er this paradise;
Above, the frequent feudal towers
Through green leaves lift their walls of gray,
And many a rock which steeply lours,
And noble arch in proud decay,
Look o'er this vale of vintage bowers;
But one thing want these banks of Rhine,—
Thy gentle hand to clasp in mine!

I send the lilies given to me;
Though long before thy hand they touch,
I know that they must wither'd be,
But yet reject them not as such;
For I have cherished them as dear,
Because they yet may meet thine eye,
And guide thy soul to mine even here,
When thou behold'st them drooping nigh,
And know'st them gathered by the [Rhine,
And offer'd from my heart to thine!

. . . .

Through life to dwell delighted here;
Nor could on earth a spot be found
To nature and to me so dear,
Could thy dear eyes in following mine
Still sweeten more these banks of Rhine!
—LORD BYRON.

NEARER TO GOD AND TO THEE.

Go make thee a mark far above me,
  Near the top of the temple of fame;
Say that thou'lt endeavor to love me,
  When there I have written my name.
Think not of the hearts that have fainted
  While striving for what I would be,
For I shall be better for striving,
  And nearer to God and to thee.

No burden could e'er be too heavy,
  No task ever seem too great,
No journey too long or too lonely,
  No hour too early or late.
For matchless love would be thriving
  On the hopes of the bliss to be,
And I should be better for striving,
  And nearer to God and to thee.

All the long way from noontime till midnight,
  And back from the midnight till noon;
By the bright light of love I'd be toiling,
  And hoping the end would be soon.
And when time of hope had bereft me,
  Tossed wildly on life's troubled sea,
I should know the struggle had left me
  Still nearer to God and to thee.
—CY WARMAN.

THE TRIBUNAL.

LIFE, stand thou at my soul's tribunal to-night
In account of thy actions of wrong or right.

Hast thou walked in the path which thy conscience prescribed?
Or hast thou, poor weak one, turned blindly aside?

That vow which thou pledged but this morning to keep;
That troth to more patience—hast kept it?—Speak!

Alas and alas! Thou cowerest, poor life;
Thou hast sunk as the grass in the wind's maddened strife.

Vows, pledges and hopes thou'st forgot at the feast,
And to-day's western sun marks no more than the east.

Yet, penitent, up! Look with gladness above;
The morrow is pleading thy help and thy love.
—GRACE HEWETT SHARP.

FACES THAT ARE GONE.

How we long to see the faces
  That have crossed the silent tide—
Faces marked with care and sorrow,
  Faces full of joy and pride.
Some with furrowed brow and hoary,
  Some in youth's lamented bloom—
One by one from us departed,
  For the cold and silent tomb.

Birds employ their notes of gladness
  As they flutter to and fro,
Flow'rs display their wealth of beauty,
  As they used to long ago;
But the birds might sing forever,
  And the flow'rs forever bloom—
They can ne'er bring back the faces,
  That are hidden in the tomb.

Silently death steals upon us,
  Silently time speedeth on—
Soon we, too, shall all be numbered
  With the faces that are gone;
Each and all must shortly follow
  Thro' the shadows and the gloom,
To the loved ones who are waiting,
  In the light beyond the tomb.
        —HENRY R. CONANT.

WHY IRVING NEVER MARRIED.

IT was while engaged in writing his history of New York that Irving, then a a young man of twenty-six, was called to mourn the somewhat sudden death of Matilda Hoffman, whom he had hoped to call his wife. This young lady was the second daughter of Josiah Ogden Hoffman, the eloquent jurist. In her father's office Washington Irving had essayed to study law, and with every prospect, if industrious and studious, of partnership with Mr. Hoffman, as well as a matrimonial alliance with Matilda. Those high hopes were disappointed by the decease of the young lady on the 27th of April, 1809, in the eighteenth year of her age. There is a pathos about Irving's recital of the circumstances of her death, and of his own feelings, that is truly painful and tear-impelling. He says: "She was taken ill with a cold. Nothing was thought of it at first, but she grew rapidly worse, and fell into a consumption. I cannot tell you what I suffered. * * * I saw her fade rapidly away—beautiful and more beautiful, and more angelic to the very last. I was often by her bedside, and in her wandering state of mind she would talk to me with a sweet, natural and affecting eloquence that was overpowering. I saw more of the beauty of her mind in that delirious state than I had ever known before. Her malady was rapid in its career, and hurried her off in two months. Her dying struggles were painful and protracted. For three days and nights I did not leave the house and scarcely slept. I was by her when she died; all the family were assembled around her, some praying, others weeping, for she was adored by them all. I was the last one she looked upon. I cannot tell you what a horrid state of mind I was in for a long time. I seemed to care for nothing; the world was a blank to me. I abandoned all thoughts of the law. I went into the country, yet could not enjoy society. There was a dismal horror continually in my mind that made me fear to be alone. I had to get up in the night and seek the room of my brother, as if the having a human being by me would relieve me from the frightful gloom of my own thoughts. Months elapsed before my mind would resume any tone; but the despondency I had suffered for a long time in the course of this attachment, and the anguish that attended its catastrophe, seemed to give a turn to my whole character, and then throw some clouds into my disposition, which have ever since hung about it. I seemed to drift about without aim or object, at the mercy of every breeze; my heart wanted anchorage. I was naturally susceptible, and tried to form other attachments, but my heart would not hold on; it would continually recur to what it had lost; and whenever there was pause in the hurry of novelty and excitement, I would sink into dismal dejection. For years I could not talk on the subject of this hopeless regret; I could not even mention her name, but her image was constantly before me, and I dreamt of her incessantly." Such was the language in which Irving poured forth his sorrows and sad memories in a letter written many years ago to a lady who wondered at his celibacy and expressed a wish to know why he never married. Can words more graphically describe the shipwreck of hope, or more tenderly depict the chivalric devotion of a faithful lover? How sweetly, too, does Irving portray with his artist pen the lineaments of his loved one! He says, in the same letter:—"The more I saw of her, the more I had reason to admire her. Her mind seemed to unfold itself, leaf by leaf, and every time to discover new sweetness. Nobody knew her so well as I, for she was so timid and silent; but I, in a manner, studied her excellence. Never did I meet with a more intuitive rectitude of mind, more native delicacy, more exquisite propriety of thought and action, than in this young creature. I am not exaggerating; what I say was acknowledged by all who knew her. Her brilliant little sister used to say that people began by admiring her, but ended by loving Matilda. For my part, I idolized her. I felt at times rebuked by her superior delicacy and purity, and felt as if I were a coarse, unworthy being in comparison."

MY SISTER.

WHO was it climbed the tallest trees,
And tore her frocks and grazed her knees,
Which did her teacher much displease?
My sister.

Who was it stole the lemon pie,
Hid on the pantry shelf so high,
And gave me half upon the sly?
My sister.

Who was it in the mill-pond fell
And lost her thimble in the well,
And cried for fear that I would tell?
My sister.

And who, at last, long dresses wore
And had of beaux a half a score,
And voted boys a perfect bore?
My sister.

Who coaxed me once to go to bed,
Because she had an aching head,
And then sat up with cousin Fred?
My sister.

Who sews the buttons on my clothes,
And with me to the opera goes,
And then neglects me for the beaux?
My sister.

Who always scolds me when I swear,
And does a nobby pullback wear,
All plaited, looped and puffed with care?
My sister.

Who brushes, dusts and darns my clothes,
And all my little failings knows,
And kisses me before her beaux?
My sister.

And who, with all her crimps and curls,
And silks and velvet, rings and pearls,
Is just the jolliest of girls?
My sister.
—REHOBOTH SUNDAY HERALD.

INCAPABLE.

I'VE frazzled out—thar ain't no doubtin' that—
Plum failed in all I've uvver undertaken; [trouble's at
An' blame my time! jes' whar ther
It ain't my natu'al luck to l'arn, I reckin! [my skull
Tho' it's kind uv got ter thumpin' 'bout
Thet it's my fault—I'm jes' incaperbul.

. . . . . .

I've worked—hard—nuvver drunk, or bet, or swore;
I never smoked, nur even chawed, terbacker; [pore
I've spent no money foolish; still I'm
As anny rat 'ith but one ha'f-e't cracker— [hull—
I'm wo'th no more'n er em'ty hick'-nut
I've hed my chance—I'm jes' incaperbul.

Thar warn't no fire nur freeze, no flood nur drout' [failin';
On which ter lay the causes uv my
Whut I hev' sowed wus allus free ter sprout [ailin'
An' flourish—not er cussed thing wus
'Cept me—I nuvver 'peared ter hev' the pull [caperbul.
Ter fetch things straight—I'm jes' in-

I'd ruther now that I hed drunk an' bet,
An' be'n as triflin' es er Georgy nigger; [set
I'd ruther cyclones, fires an' drout' hed
Ag'in me—then I'd hev' some show ter figger [ful
I warn't ter blame—by gum! it's piter-
Ter think merse'f jes' durn incaperbul.
—W. D. FOX.

EPITAPH.

Here lies a rose, a budding rose,
  Blasted before its bloom ;
Whose Innocence did sweets disclose
  Beyond that flower's perfume.
To those who for her loss are grieved,
  This consolation's given—
She's from a world of woe relieved,
  And blooms a rose in Heaven.
—Burns

THE ANGELUS.

After all it is a beautiful sight to behold the wonderful hold religious customs have fixed upon the people of some of the nations. In Belgium and other Catholic countries the old custom of ringing the bell at six and twelve o'clock is still observed with great beauty and regularity, and even the unbeliever is caught with its beneficent influence, and naturally joins in private worship. Whether in the field, at the workshop, at play or at work, when the Angelus ring out—morning, noon, or night—all play is ceased, all work stopped, and, there and then, the prayers of saints and sinners unite in thanks and praise to Almighty God for His blessings and mercies. And while it is a form of worship to Virgin Mary, it is nevertheless an old and beautiful custom, in which the Deity is always recognized, and perhaps more often than by the more modern, if less truly Christian, religions. Indeed, we Protestants may get many standards of charity and good works, as well as beautiful customs, from our Catholic friends.

This particular one is perpetuated by a painting by one of the noted artists; which was regarded as one of the great paintings of the world, and when sold brought a fabulous sum. It represented a couple of peasants working in a field at a beautiful purple sunset, when the Angelus hour arrived, and just as the bell gave notice of the time for devotion, their hoes were dropped, a supplicating attitude was struck, all cares forgot, save the higher duties of the hour. In this position, and amid these beautiful surroundings, the artist catches the picture, and imprints it on canvas, to live, doubtless, long after its artist is forgot. It is a beautiful picture ; and the custom might be well imitated in some form by the more modern orthodox churches.

A BEAUTIFUL PRAYER.

Our Father, while our hearts unlearn
  The creeds that wrong thy name,
Still let our hallowed altars burn
  With faith's undying flame.

Not by the lightning-gleams of wrath
  Our souls Thy face shall see ;
The star of love must light the path
  That leads to heaven and Thee.

Help us to read our Master's will
  Through every darkening stain
That clouds his sacred image still,
  And see Him once again.

The brother man, the pitying friend,
  Who weeps for human woes ;
Whose pleading words of pardon blend
  With cries of raging foes.

If 'mid the gathering storms of doubt
  Our hearts grow faint and cold,
The strength we cannot live without,
  Thy love will not withhold.

Our prayers accept, our sins forgive.
  Our youthful zeal renew ;
Shape for us holier lives to live,
  And nobler work to do.
    [Dr Oliver Wendell Holmes,
      before the Y. M. C. U.]

UNREST.

The farther you journey and wander
  From the sweet, simple faith of your
    youth,
The more you peer into the yonder,
  And search for the root of all truth,
No matter what secrets uncover
  Their veiled mystic brows in your
    quest,
Or close on your astral sight hover,
  Still, still shall you walk with unrest.

If you seek for strange things you shall
find them,
  But the finding shall bring you to
grief;
The dead lock the portals behind them,
  And he who breaks through is a
thief.
The soul with such ill-gotten plunder
  With its premature knowledge oppressed,
Shall grope in unsatisfied wonder
  Alway by the shore of unrest.

Though bold hands lift up the thin
curtain
  That hides the unknown from our
sight;
Though a shadowy faith become certain
  Of the new light that follows death's
night;
Though miracles past comprehending
  Shall startle the heart in your breast,
Still, still will your thirst be unending
  And your soul will be sad with unrest.

There are truths too sublime and too holy
  To grasp with a mortal mind's touch.
We are happier far to be lowly;
  Content means not knowing too
much.
Peace dwells not with hearts that are
yearning
  To fathom all labyrinths unguessed,
And the soul that is bent on vast learning
  Shall find with its knowledge—unrest.

RUTH AND NAOMI.

A rabbi's child and Puritan's once met
And like those fabled mates with each
a wing
That only soar when they together
cling,
These comrades happy joyed in mutual
debt
For rich ancestral stores most alien.
Yet—
As greatest pleasures know no lasting
spring,
Death came, but sunny mem'ry comforting,
In tears with brightest rays her rainbow
set.

Might Naomi not often glean with Ruth.
And thus give time a double joy and
worth?
It takes the each and all from every
clime
To cull auspiciously the seeds of truth;
To win anew a paradise for earth,
And reap in joy the harvest—truth
sublime.
                LOWELL COURIER.

THE END.

INDEX.

A.

A Beautiful Idea, 248
A Beautiful Thought, 287
A Beautiful Prayer, 336
A Beautiful Extract, 149
A Beautiful Picture, 257
A Benediction, 204
Abide With Me, 265
Angelus, The, 343
A Boy's Worst Foe, 219
A Book of Dreams, 59
Accomplished Girls, 85
A Colorado Philosopher, 224
A Chansonnette, 202
A Business Letter, 28
A Blamed Sight Worse, 206
Act From Principle, 258
Advice to Ladies, 259
A Day Dream, 301
After Hiawatha, 115
Ages, the Seven, 80
A Good Woman, 331
A Gem for Every Month, 312
A Game of Euchre, 157
A Gentleman Defined, 185
A Good Old Candy Pull, 225
A Good Prayer, 70
A Good-Bye, 109
A Kiss—Definitions of, 40
A Kiss, If you Want, Take it, 307
A Kiss—Love's First, 18
A Leaf From the Calendar Torn, 231
Alone in the Gloaming, 67
A Life Story, 75
A Lost Type, 91
Alphabetical Wooing, An, 102
A Literary Curiosity, 296
Alone, 122
A Maiden's Love, 126
A Metamorphosis, 111
And There Shall be Light, 263
A Mother's Picture, 7
A Mother's Farewell, 229
A Mistake Often Made, 81
A Negro on Blind Tom, 219
A Name in the Sand, 150
A New Year Greeting, 314
An Initiated Drummer, 288
And You'll Remember Me, 52
And There Shall be Light, 263
Anniversary, Our Wedding 38
An Old Scene, 282
An Old Song, 218
An Old Fashioned Calendar, 43
A Note of Hope, 62
Antony and Cleopatra, 64
An Out-of-date Couple, 90
Apart with God, 77
A Psalm of Life, 92
A Prayer of the Heart, 74
A Poor Rich Man, 98
Apple Seeds, Counting, 240
A Question, 194
A Question, 237

A Queer Marriage Ceremony, 199
A Railroader's Prayer, 241
Are the Orators All Dead? 322
A Rural Christmas, 224
Arbitrary English Language, 76
As Age Comes On, 33
Arm-chair, The Little, 202
A Similar Case, 317
A Sermon in a Paragraph, 237
A Small, Sweet Way, 233
A Song of Peace,
A Song for the Future, 171
A Swarm of B's, 273
A Touching Poem, 141
A Student's Love Letter, 87
A True Gentleman, 274
A Tribute to Womanhood, 223
At the Garden Gate, 332
At the Baby's Bed-time, 191
Autumn, 144
Autumn's Arrival, 93
Autumn Leaves, 248
A Voice of the Night, 57
A Weaver, 214
A Wife's Prayer, 336
A Wish for My Friend, 130
A Woman's Smile, 312
A Woman's Question, 100
A Woman's Nay, 158
A Printer's Love-Letter, 152

B.

Banks of Rhine, 339
Baby, Measuring the, 177
Baby, The News, 18
Baby—What is It? 16
Broken Ties, 263
Baby's Bed-time, At the, 191
Baby's Feet,—The Patter of, 310
Baby Over the Way, 304
Baby, When, was Dead, 78
Barriers, 261
B's, A Swarm of, 273
Be Good to Yourself, 209
Benediction, A, 204
Being in Debt, 204
Beautiful Hands, 161
Big Words—Don't Use, 9
Bible, Cards as a, 19
Bivouac of the Dead, 276
Beautiful Gate, 54
Beautiful Idea, 248
Beautiful Extract, 149
Beautiful Snow, The, 24
Beautiful Things, 63
Better than Gold, 60
Betty and the Baby, 273
Betrothed—The Prayer of a, 121
Blind Tom—A Negro on, 219
Bliss Interrupted, 158
Boarders, Mr. Tompkins on his, 89
Blue Back Speller, 36
Blue and Gray, 128
Blue and Gray, 132
Blue and Gray, Knot of, 175

345

//INDEX.//

Bob White, Old, 282
Books, Choice of, 96
Boston Girl, The, 154
Borrowing Trouble, 311
Boy, The Battle Scarred, 191
Boys, Wake up, 253
Boy's Worst Foe, A, 229
Boy Runaway, The, 240
Brotherly Kindness, 216
Bell, The Dreadful Get Up, 314
By and By, 291
By the Summer Sea, 324
Butterflies, Chasing, 325
Bells, Wedding, 329
Book, The Evolution of the, 167

C.

Chamber, The Secret, 281
Church Bells, The Old, 179
Candy Pull, A Good Old, 225
Cradle, The Empty, 8
Calendar, A Leaf from the Torn, 232
Calendar, An Old-fashioned, 43
Cards as a Bible, 19
Care for Father, 13
Casual Impressions, 316
Changes, 79
Chasing Butterflies, 325
Checkers, Playing, 62
Cheap Pleasures, 70
Cherish Him, 337
Childhood, 182
Childhood's Land, 211
Childhood's Song, 198
Chansonnette, A, 202
Christmas, 338
Christmas, A Rural, 224
Choose Your Friend Wisely, 118
Colonel Bluegrass, Kentucky, 142
Closing Year, 292
Come Unto Me, 75
Coming Man, 273
Common Mercies, 335
Conscience, His, 269
Country Editors, 85
Country Editors, 92
Counting Apple Seeds, 240
Courtship, 285
Courage, Moral, 22
Creeds, 22
Cultivate a Taste for Reading, 261
Curfew Must Not Ring To-night, 245
Cemetery, The Old, 151
Cradle, The Hand that Rocks, 290
Cows Come Home, When the, 295

D.

Dad's Old Grindstone, 202
Darling, 131
Daughters and Fathers, 213
Day Dream, A, 301
Dead Leaves Whisper, 170
Days that are No More, 291
Dead—The Beautiful Land of the, 105
Death, 63
Death, Does it End All? 334
Death, What People Call, 110
Death, Unto, 184
Debt, Being in, 204
Definition of Home, 85
Definition of a Kiss, 40
Does Death End All? 334
Departure, 218
Destiny, 223
Dictionary of Discontent, 214
Distant, 101
Disappointments, 311
Dixie—Original Words of, 68
Does Anyone Care for Father? 297
Dog, the Little, under the Wagon, 56

Don't Forget the Rainy Day, 14
Don't Scold, 165
Don't Stay Late To-night, 243
Dove, The, 181
Don't Throw Cudgels at Your Town, 91
Don't Use Big Words, 9
Dot Long-Handled Dipper, 212
Dreaming, 53
Dreaming, 144
Dreams, A Book of, 59
Dreams, The Land of, 285
Dreaming of Home, 35
Dreaming by the River, 278
Dreams of the Royal Noon, 241
Drummer, An Initiated, 288
Drifting, 87
Drifting in the Dark, 61
Driftweed, 32
Dying Words of Noted Men, 188
Dying Wife, 319
Dying Wife, 305
Duck, How Father Carves, The, 161

E.

Eve, Why She had no Help, 45
Easter, 196
Ecstasy of Kisses, The, 141
Easter Bells, 268
Editors, Country, 85
Editors, Country, 92
Ember Faces, 275
Empty Cradle, The, 8
Endless Strife, 303
Engineer's Signal, 186
Eternity of God, 30
Erring, The, 333
Evening, 14
Endurance, 187
Ever Near, 286
Exile's Song, The, 175
Every Year, 228
Eyes that Cannot Weep, 169
Engaged, 305
English, Arbitrary Language, 78

F

Fare Thee Well, 10
Faces, Ember, 275
Faces at the Fire, 145
Faces that are Gone, 340
Fading, 51
Failure, 123
Faithful, 339
Faith, Hope and Charity, 329
Falling Leaves, 104
Falling Leaves, 307
Falling Star, 198
Fancy, My Temple of, 45
Farm, The Old, 336
Fallen, 14
Farm, Living on the, 53
Famous Hymns, Some, 235
Fate, 65
Fate, 117
Fatherhood of God, 54
Father's Grave, My, 145
Fathers and Daughters, 213
Father, Does Anyone Care Aught for, 13
Farewell, 151
Farewell of Hope, The, 290
First Sweetheart, My, 120
First Gray Hair, The, 101
Fire, The Terrible, 276
Fishing, 267
Flood of Years, 249
Flowers that Never Wither, 252
Frank L. Stanton, 83
Friendship, 118
Foreshadowings, 35
For Common Mercies, 335
Forget, Trying to, 4

INDEX. 347

Forgotten, 330
For Love's Sake Only, 183
From the Workshop "Home," 94
From Sofa to Hammock, 149
Four Leaf Clover, 170
Fully Decided, 231
Friend, Choose Your, Wisely, 118
First Telegraphic Despatch, The, 124

G.

Goblets and Glasses and Mugs, 187
Gambling, 55
Gate, the Story of the, 332
Gem for Every Month, A, 313
Gentleman Defined, 185
Gentleman, the True, 274
Get Acquainted with Yourself, 280
Get-up Bell, That Dreadful, 314
God's-Acre, 71
Give a Kind Word When You Can, 113
Gloaming, Alone in the, 67
God, 46
God, Apart with, 77
God, Eternity of, 30
God Knows Best, 107
God, Keep, on Your Side, 86
Good-Bye, 237
Good-Bye, Sweetheart, 231
Good Husband, Recipe for, 175
Good Motto, 45
Good-Night, 147
Good-Night, 150
Gilded Age, The, 298
Grindstone, Dad's Old, 202
Grammar, in Rhyme, 269
Grammar School, Extraordinary, 153
Grandfather, 270
Grandmothers—Master Ralph's Opinion, 201
Grandma's Birthday, 156
Grandma, How Danced, 98
Growing Old, 258
Growing Old Gracefully, 163
Growing Old, 19
Growing Old, I'm, 209
Guests of the Heart, 236
Gray Hair, The First, 101
Greeting, A New Year, 314
Griefs, Silent, 330
Good Book, A, 330

H.

Help the Homeless, 11
Hagar, 220
Habit of Reading, The, 232
Had I Known, 234
Hang up the Baby's Stocking, 206
Helping on the Track, 115
Helping Husband, 239
Helping Every Day, 52
Hasty Word, The, 87
Heart-wounds, 296
Health, 228
Heart, The Picture in My, 303
Hear Both Sides, 245
He Has Not Lived in Vain, 206
Her Secret, 13
Her Wish, 98
Her Name, 74
Her Picture, 102
Her Proposal, 162
Her Heart is True, 94
His Conscience, 269
Hereafter Thou Shalt Know, 339
Holiday Attentions, 224
Home, 146
Home, The Old, Old, 178
Home, My, 42
Home Affections, 227
Home, Definition of, 85
Home Together, 21

Home, Memories of, 105
Home, We Can Make Happy, 109
Home, From the Work-Shop, 94
Home, Longing for, 171
Home, Sweet Home, 106
Home-Ranch across the Big Divide, 164
Hope, 59
Hope, 88
Hope, 254
Hope, A Note of, 62
Hope, 107
Hope, Farewell of, 290
Hope Again, 303
Horse Trade, Uncle Eph's, 84
Horse, What he would Say, 68
How Grandma Danced, 98
How Beautiful, 82
How Scholars are Made, 227
How Sweet 'Tis True, 190
How Can a Woman Tell, 332
Hours Wasted,
Homestead, The Old, 300
Hymns, Some Famous, 235
Human Lilies, 226
Human Pleasures, Locke on, 246
How Father Carves the Duck, 161
Husband, Recipe for a Good, 175
Husband, The Model, 233
He'll See It When He Wakes, 225

I.

If She Had Lived, 20
Idaho, 183
If I But Knew, 88
If You Want a Kiss, Take it, 306
I'm Growing Old, 209
I Love the Past, 320
In Memoriam, 65
Interrupted Bliss, 158
In the Twilight, 177
In the Gloaming, Alone, 67
In After Days, 284
In Memoriam (Mother), 294
Indian Summer, 106
Isle of the Past, 316
It Matters Not, 262
I Wish He'd Make Up His Mind, 310
Impressions, Casual, 316
Irving, Why he Never Married, 341
Incapable, 342

J.

John's Wife, 134
Jesus Wept, 215

K.

Kentucky, Col. Bluegrass, of, 142
Keep a Merry Heart, 233
Keep God on Your Side, 86
Keep Straight Ahead, 262
King's Kiss, The, 183
Keep Me Awake, Mother, 112
Kindness, Brotherly, 216
Kiss, Definitions of a, 40
Kiss Her and Tell Her So, 71
Kiss, If You Want One, Take it, 306
Kiss Me, Darling, 135
Kiss Me Good-Night, Mamma, 323
Kisses, The Ecstasies of, 141
Kitchen Fire, The Old, 225
Kind Word, Give When You Can, 113

L.

Land, The Children's, 321
Land of the South, 331
Land of Long Ago, The, 287
Latter Day Preaching, 81
Last Rose of Summer, 254

Laugh, 91
Laugh, 147
Laughing Children, 187
Lay of the Croaker, 283
Lead Thou Me On, 81
Learn a Trade, 47
Leaves, Falling, 104
Leaves, Autumn, 248
Let Us Forget, 280
Let it Pass, 240
Let Bygones be Bygones, 237
Level and the Square, The, 60
Life, A Lost, 91
Life's Spinners, 258
Life, The Game of, 95
Life, The Sweetest Part of, 165
Lite's Onward Current, 13
Lives, Our, 116
Life, a Tangled Skein, 138
Light, 140
Light, 309
Light, of Other Days, The, 278
Light at Evening Time, 253
Lightning Age, The, 152
Lilies of the Field, The, 131
Lines to a Skeleton, 95
Literary Curiosity, A, 297
Living the Past, 137
Living on the Farm, 53
Little Arm Chair, The, 202
Locke on Human Pleasures, 246
Long Ago, The Sweet, 139
Long Afore he Knowed, 58
Longing for Home, 271
Lonely, 264
Long Handled Dipper, Dot, 212
Look on the Bright Side, 232
Looking off Unto Jesus, 67
Looking Forward, 257
Lord's Prayer, The, 10
Lost Type, 91
Lodge Room, The Old, 71
Lost Things, 293
Lover's Limit, 174
Love Letter, A Student's, 87
Love Letter, A Printer's, 152
Love has its Way, 203
Love My Angel, 132
Love, Woman's, 247
Love's First Kiss, 18
Love's Paragon, 334

M.

Mason, She would be a, 208
Marriage Ceremony, a Queer, 159
Ma and Me, 268
Maiden's Love, A, 126
Mammy Gets the Boy to Sleep, 39
Man, the Kicker, 113
Man, The Coming, 278
Man in the Moon, 169
Marry, Three Ways to, 34
Mammy, The Southern, 83
Mamma, Old, 97
Master Ralph's Opinion of Grandmothers, 201
Me an' Mary, 7
Man and his Shoes, 163
Memory, 111
Men who Lose, The, 77
Memories of Home, 105
Measure for Measure, 24
Measuring the Baby, 177
Mixed Metaphor, 130
Mill, The Old, 12
Miss Gusher Abroad, 287
Mocking Bird, 264
Model Wife, 233
Model Husband, 233
Memories of Home, 105
Mortgage, The, 102
Motto, A Good, 45

Memory, Thy Holy, 130
Moneyless Man, 270
Mother, Somebody's, 174
Mrs. Lofty and I, 166
Mother's Song, My, 80
Mother's Grave, My, 304
Mother's Grave, My, 136
Mother's Grave, Our, 315
Mother's Farewell, A, 229
Mother's Old Steel Thimble, 51
Mother at Prayer, 11
Mother at Home, The, 193
Mother, Keep me Awake, 112
Mother, Rock me to Sleep, 111
Mother, Where Used to Sit, 119
My Angel, Love, 132
My Father's Grave, 145
My Favorite Paper, 243
My Husband, 137
My First Sweetheart, 120
My Daughter's Learned to Cook, 73
My Home, 42
My Little Girl, 90
My Musical Maid, 192
My Mother, 136
My Mother's Song, 80
My Mother's Song, 304
My Mother, too, Grows Old, 255
My Sister, 342
My Sweetheart, 58
My Sweetheart, 77
My Sweetheart, 123
My Temple of Fancy, 45
M—phatic, 296
Motto in a Wedding Ring, The, 107
Mr. Tompkins on his Boarders, 89
Musings in the Twilight, 119
My Vanished Past, 166
Musical Maid, My, 192
Music, Old Time, 193
Moral Courage, 22

N.

Nameless, 227
Name in the Sand, 150
Names of States, and Their Meaning, 284
Nearer to God and to Thee, 340
Never Trouble Trouble, 32
Never, The House of, 19
Never Mind What "They" Say, 139
New-Year, 200
New-Year Greeting, A, 306
New Church Organ, 172
Night, 335
Night, Scenes in, 140
No One Comes Home to Me, 259
Not Fought for, 207
Nothing Lost but a Heart, 99
No Telephone in Heaven, 57
No Time for Hating, 178
Nothing but Leaves, 293
Noted Men, Dying Words of, 188

O.

Off Yonder, 289
Of the Old Back Stair, 114
Old Jingle, 28
Old Mamma, 97
Old Oaken Bucket, 177
Old-Time Music, 193
Oh, Had I Known, 234
O Promise Me, 86
O Loving Hearts, 132
Old Bob White, 282
Old Back Stair, of the, 114
Old Church Bells, 179
Old Time Religion, 48
Old Fireplace, 279
Old Folks at Home, 170
Old Lodge Room, 71

INDEX.

Old Homestead, 300
Old Mill, The, 12
Old Time Circus Clown, The, 122
Old Scene, An, 282
One Friend, 292
One Sad Day, 239
Original Words of Dixie, 68
One by One, 203
One by One, 302
One Word, 274
Only, 99
Only a Picture, 317
Orators Are All Dead, 322
Our Lives, 116
Our Mother's Grave, 315
Our Mother, In Memoriam, 65
Our Little Boy 'at's Gone, 207
Our Wedding Anniversary, 38
Out-of-Date Couple, 90
Over and Over Again, 133

P.

Paragon, The Lover's, 334
Paddle Your Own Canoe, 247
Past and Present, 197
Past, Isle of the, 316
Playing Checkers, 62
Poetry, 242
Poetry and Religion, 279
Poor Rich Man, The, 98
Prayer of the Heart, 74
Procrastination, 191
Printer's Love-Letter, 152
Psalm of Life, 92
Psalm of Life, Young Ladies' 315
Paper, my Favorite, 243
Paragraph, A Sermon in a, 237
Past, 320
Past, My Vanished, 166
Past, Living, the, 137
Past, I Love the, 320
Patter of Baby's Feet, 310
Peace, Song of, 261
People, Sunny, 220
Picture, Her, 102
Picture, A Beautiful, 62
Picture, Only a, 317
Picture in My Heart, 303
Pleasures, Cheap, 41
Pleasures, Locke on, 246
Playground, the Old, 135
Prayer, Universal, 318
Prayer, Mother at, 11
Prayer, The Lord's, 10
Prayer, A Railroader's, 241
Prayer, The, of a Betrothed, 121
Prayer, A Beautiful, 343
Preaching, Latter Day, 81
Promise Me, 50

Q.

Quits, 128

R.

Rice Throwing at Weddings, 162
Rainy Day, The, 19
Railroader's Prayer, 241
Recollections, 312
Rich Man, a Poor, 98
Recipe for a Good Husband, 175
Reconciled, 320
Regret, 124
Regret, 148
Rest, 239
Reflections on a Skull, 323
Remarkable Facts, 331
Remember Thy Mother, 319
Render Home Pleasant,

Retrospection, 176
Retrospection, 259
Right Will Right Itself, The, 48
Rights of Woman, 308
Rise Higher, 242
Rising in the World, 251
Religion, The Old Time, 48
Rock Me to Sleep, Mother, 111
Rock of Ages, 234
Romantic Marriage, 82
Ruth, 103
Ruth, 194
Ruth and Naomi, 344
Rural Christmas, A, 224
Runaway Boy, The, 240
Reading, The Habit of, 232
Reading, Cultivate a Taste for, 261
Recessional, 39

S.

Sea, By the Summer, 324
Shadows, 337
Schoolhouse, 255
Saxby to Ingersoll, 37
Secret Chamber, The, 281
Sermon in a Paragraph, 237
September, 33
Seven Ages, The, 88
Sleeping, I Dreamed, 272
Shadows and Sunshine, 128
She Waited by the River, 158
Shoes, Man and His, 163
She was Willing, 166
She Kissed Me Good-Night, 179
She Would be a Mason, 208
Skull, Reflections on a, 323
Silent Griefs, 330
Similar Case, A, 317
Sitting in Silence, 117
Sister, My, 342
Signal, The Engineer's, 186
Skeleton, Lines to a, 95
Surprise, The, 328
Sociability, 294
Some Day, 66
Some Day, 115
Some Day, 158
Some Day, 217
Sometime, 22
Sometime, Land, The, 248
Sometime, 39
Sometime, 320
Small Things, 184
Sometime, Somewhere, 76
Some Other Day, 9
Some Comfort, 241
Some of these Days, 45
Some Famous Hymns, 235
Somebody's Sunbeam, 159
Somebody's Mother, 174
So Much of Life Behind me Lies, 145
Somebody Else, 124
So We Grow Old, 32
Song for the Future, 171
Square and The Level, 60
Spinning Wheel, The Old, 180
Song of Egla, 260
Soul to Body, 286
Soul, Hugo on, 272
Snap Shots, 193
South, Land of the, 331
Stanton, Frank L., 83
States, The Names of, 284
Star Spangled Banner, 215
Student's, A Love-Letter, 87
St. Patrick's Day, 199
Stone the Woman, Let the Man go Free, 133
Stub Ends of Thought, 123
Steel Thimble, Mother's Old, 51
Sweethearts, Still, 290

INDEX.

Sweet Long Ago, The, 139
Sweetheart, My, 123
Sweetheart, Good-Bye, 231
Sweetheart, My First, 120
Sunny People, 220
Sunday, Thank God for, 134
Sundays Long Ago, 199
Scythe of Time, 229
Steer, The Beautiful, 118
Stair, The Old Back, 114

T.

Take It In, 264
Talk's Cheap, 274
Terrible Fire, The, 276
Time, The Scythe of, 229
Temple of Fancy, My, 45
Telephone, No, in Heaven, 57
Telegraphic Dispatch, The First, 124
Thank God for Sunday, 134
Thanksgiving Day, 304
Thanksgiving on the Farm, 92
Thanksgiving, 160
That Dreadful Get-up Bell, 314
Till Death Us Part, 136
The Angelus, 343
The Autumn of Life, 242
The Baby Over the Way, 304
The Baby, What is it? 16
The Battle-Scarred Boy, 191
The Beautiful Gate, 54
The Beautiful Snow, 24
The Beautiful Land of the Dead, 105
The Beautiful Steer, 118
The After Glow, 43
The Bible, Cards as, 19
The Bivouac of the Dead, 276
The Blue Back-Speller, 36
The Blue and the Gray, 128
The Blue and the Gray, 182
The Bravest of Battles, 170
The Burro, A Colorado Philosopher, 224
The Boston Girl, 154
The Busy Man, 29
The Calm that Comes at Evening, 334
The Children's Land, 321
The Choice of Books, 96
The Coming Man, 273
The Cows, When the, Come Home, 295
The Croaker, Lay of, 283
The Closing Year, 292
The Country Editor, 92
The Days Gone By, 65
The Days that are No More, 291
The Days are Growing Long Again, 268
The Dove, 181
The Dead, The Beautiful Land of, 105
The Difference, 165
The Drummer's Grip, 44
The Drummer Initiated, 288
The Dying Wife, 305
The Dying Wife, 319
The Ecstasy of Kisses, 141
The Empty Cradle, 8
The Engineer's Signal, 186
The Eyes that Cannot Weep, 169
The Eternity of God, 30
The Erring, 335
The Evolution of the Book, 167
The Exile's Song, 175
The Face o' the Year, 256
The First Telegraphic Dispatch, 124
The Falling Star, 198
The Farewell of Hope, 290
The Flood of Years, 249
The Farm, Living on, 53
The Family Clock, 76
The Game of Life, 95
The Garden of Dreams, 200
The Gilded Age, 298
The First Gray Hair, 101

The Good We all May Do, 329
The Good Old Things, 75
The Habit of Reading, 232
The Hand that Rocks the Cradle, 290
The Hasty Word, 87
The Hen-Pecked Man, 238
The Knot of Blue and Gray, 175
The House of Never, 19
The Humming Top, 243
The King's Kiss, 183
The Lord's Prayer, 10
The Land of Dreams, 10
The Little Arm Chair, 202
The Language of Precious Stones, 155
The Land of Dreams, 285
The Land of Dreams, 339
The Land of Long Ago, 283
The Little Woman, 161
The Level and the Square, 60
The Light of Other Days, 278
The Little Dog Under the Wagon, 56
The Lightning Age, 152
The Long Ago, 241
The Lover's Paragon, 334
The Prayer of a Betrothed, 121
The Men Who Lose, 77
The Moneyless Man, 270
The Motto in a Wedding Ring, 107
The Model Wife, 233
The Model Husband, 233
The Mortgage, 102
The Mocking Bird, 264
The Mother at Home, 193
The Mystical Sea, 17
The Mystical River, 62
The New Year, 200
The New Year, 306
The New Baby, 18
The New Woman, 28
The New Church Organ, 172
The Ol' Barlow Knife, 82
The Old Kitchen Fire, 225
The Names of States, 284
The Old Back Stair, of, 114
The Old Mill, 12
The Old Lodge Room, 71
The Old Lady Speaks, 93
The Old Time Circus Clown, 122
The Old Cemetery, 151
The Old Playground, 135
The Old Folks at Home, 170
The Old Oaken Bucket, 177
The Old Farm, 336
The Old Trundle Bed, 23
The Old Hand Press, 79
The Old Homestead, 300
The Old Rail Fence, 20
The Old Time Brinnel Cur, 34
The Old Time Religion, 48
The Old Fireplace, 279
The Old Home, 178
The Old Spinning Wheel, 180
The Other Point of View, 238
The Past, I Love the, 320
The Past, Isle of, 316
The Picture in My Heart, 303
The Patter of Baby's Feet, 310
The Passing Year, 305
The Printer's Prayer, 29
The Prayer of a Betrothed, 121
The Rainy Day, 19
The Reason, 171
The Reason Why, 281
The Rights of Woman, 308
The Right will Right Itself, 48
The Runaway Boy, 240
The River Time, 26
The Soul's Flight, 149
The Sweet Long Ago, 139
The Sweet Sad Years, 109
The Seven Ages, 80
The Southern Mammy, 88

The Riddle of Things That Are, 243
The Song I Never Sing, 69
The Star Spangled Banner, 214
The Sweetest Part of Life, 105
The Sometime Land, 248
The Sins of Omission, 336
The Scenes of Childhood, 25
The Schoolhouse, 255
The Soul, Victor Hugo on, 272
The Surprise, 328
The Spinning Wheel, 157
The Story of the Gate, 332
The Scythe of Time, 229
The Secret Chamber, 281
The Tramp, 125
The Tribunal, 340
The True Wife, 100
The True Gentleman, 274
The Terrible Fire, 276
The Unfettered Muse, 283
The Universal Prayer, 318
The Virgin's Refrain, 203
The Way of it, 228
The Wedding, 159
The World is Full of Beauty, 73
The Westward Window, 108
The Wedding Bells, 329
The Young Widow, 36
There Are, 152
They Met and Kissed and Parted, 132
Theology and Religion, 195
They Are Dead, 52
Three Ways to Marry, 34
There Shall be Light, And, 263
Thinking, 307
Thimble, Mother's Old Steel, 51
Thou Shalt Know Hereafter, 339
To-Day, 93
To an Inquirer, 166
This Little Wife of Mine, 198
Thoughts of Other Days, 43
Tho' Lost to Sight, to Memory Dear, 231
"Thy Will be Done," 284
Thy Holy Memory, 132
Thy Name is Still the Magic Spell, 101
To a Kiss, 26
To a Mocking Bird, 173
To Those Who Fail, 148
To Know and Hear, 55
To Grown-up Land, 155
Touching Poem, A, 141
Trade, Learn a, 47
Tribute to Womanhood, 223
Trust Me, Darling, 129
Thou Shalt Know Hereafter, 330
Trying to Forget, 42
Turning Gray, 252
Twenty Years Ago, 254
Trouble, Borrowing, 311
Twilight, 108
Two Mothers, 248
Two Mysteries, 38
Trust in God, and Do the Right, 159
Tramp, The, 125

U.

Unanswered, 11
Uncle Eph's Horse Trade, 84
Under the Snow, 308
Under a Crazy Quilt, 156
Unfettered Muse, 283
Universal Prayer, 318
Unrest, 343
Until Death, 27
Unto Death, 184

V.

Value of Books, 331
Victor Hugo on the Soul, 272
Violin and Song, 194

Voice of the Night, A, 57
Virgin's Refrain, The, 203

W.

Wanted, 63
Wait Till Trouble Comes, 121
Wasted Hours,
Way-Worn, 294
Weariness, 185
Weaver, A, 214
Weaving, 215
We Can Make Home Happy, 109
Wedded, 217
Wedding Bells, The, 329
Westward Window, The, 109
Woman's Rights, 158
Wedding, The, 159
Weakness, 273
We've All Been There Before, 205
We's Twinnies, 64
We May be Happy Yet, 69
Weep Not for the Past, 123
What the Lord Expects of Us, 337
Wife, The Dying, 305
Wife, The Dying, 319
Wife, The True, 100
Wife, The Model, 233
Wife and I, 13
Wife's Prayer, 336
What Can You Do? 120
What Matters It? 165
What I Live for, 174
What People Call Death, 110
What a Horse Would Say, 68
What Wives are for, 66
What is a Year? 184
What Dreams May Come? 44
Whatever Comes, 33
When the Cows Come Home, 295
When Baby was Dead, 78
"When the Devil was Sick, 127
When Times are Hard, 234
When Sam'wel Led the Singing, 171
When She Came Home, 92
W'en Ma's Away, 8
When the Circus was In Town, 3
When the Dawsons Moved Away, 212
When a Fellow's Going Under, 339
When the Skies Clear Off, 17
When You are Old, 335
When Day is Done, 105
When the River Flows, 74
Wives, What are, for, 66
Where Mother Used to Sit, 119
Who Knows? 29
With the Baby in Her Arms, 198
Without an E, 107
Wish't I Could, 278
Wish for My Friend, A, 130
Without an Enemy, 262
Who Shall Go First, 277
Why, 109
Why Eve had No Help, 45
Why Irving Never Married, 341
Woman, 326
Woman, 190
Woman, 203
Woman, The Little, 161
Woman's Love, 247
Woman's Smile, A, 312
Womanhood, A Tribute to, 223
Woman's Question, 100
Woman Tell, How Can a, 332
Worse, A Blamed Sight, 206

Y.

Yesterday, 65
Yesterday, 210
You Know You Do, 26

INDEX.

You or I, 325
You Will Miss Me, 287
You'd Better Cherish Him, 337
Young Ladies' Psalm of Life, 315
Your First Sweetheart, 260
Years, The Sweet, Sad, 109
Years, The Flood of, 249

Year, The Closing, 292
Year, The Passing, 305
Year, The New, 200
Year, The New, 306
Year, The New Year Greeting, 314
Year, What is a, 184

INDEX OF AUTHORS.

A

	PAGE
Abbot, F. E.	
Cultivate a Taste for Reading	261
Aker, Elizabeth.	
Rock Me to Sleep, Mother	111
Allen, Charles P.	
Colorado Philosopher, A	224
Allen, E. A.	
Endurance	187
Anderson, J. L.	
Grandfather	270
Arnold, Sir Edwin.	
Young Widow, The	36

B

Bacon, Carolyn L.	
My Sweetheart	123
Bangs, Egbert L.	
Her Wish	99
Banks, F. Linnaeus.	
What I Live for	174
Barnes, Mary C.	
Little Woman, The	161
Barton, Elizabeth.	
Garden of Dreams, The	200
Bayne, Mrs.	
Lost Life, A	91
Bean, Sam.	
Sweetest Part of Life, The	205
Thoughts of Other Days	43
When the Circus was in Town	8
Bell, Rev. Chas. D.	
Sweet, Sad Years, The	109
Bennett, Georgia E.	
After Glow, The	43
Birdie.	
Hope	254
Blackwood	
One Word	274
Blalock, Robert L.	
Hen-Pecked Man, The	238
Bliss, Bertie.	
"Sometime"	320
Blount.	
Our Mother's Grave	315
Bly, Nellie.	
Death	63
Bolton, Sarah K.	
Whatever Comes	33
Bonner, John H.	
Under the Snow	308
Bonner, Martha.	
Land of Dreams, The	285
Bonner, Mattie.	
And There Shall be Light	263
Bourne, Fox.	
Locke on Human Pleasures	246
Bowles, Fred. G.	
Dead Leaves Whisper	170
Brag, Bachelor.	
My First Sweetheart	120
Broadhurst, George H.	
Men Who Lose, The	77

	PAGE
Brooks, Maria.	
Song of Egla	260
Brown, A. L.	
With the Baby in Her Arms	198
Brown, C. Clayton.	
"When Times are Hard"	234
Brown, Emma Alice.	
Measuring the Baby	177
Browne, Julius H.	
Romantic Marriages	80
Browning, Elizabeth Barrett.	
For Love's Sake Only	183
Bryant, William Cullen.	
Flood of Years, The	249
Buckham, James.	
Apart with God	77
Burdette, Robert J.	
Alone	122
Burdette, R. T.	
Not Fought For	207
Butler, Phila Farvey.	
"Abide with Me"	265
Butts, Mrs. M. F.	
Fall o' the Year, The	256
Byron, Lord.	
Banks of Rhine	339
Fare Thee Well	10
Soul's Flight, The	149

C

Campbell, James Edwin.	
Uncle Eph's Horse Trade	84
Cappleman, Josie Frazel.	
No One Comes Home to Me	259
Carleton, W. C.	
New Church Organ, The	172
Carpenter, Theo.	
Falling Leaves	104
Challiss, Court.	
My Daughter's Learned to Cook	73
Chapman, Arthur.	
W'en Ma's Away	81
Clark, L. G.	
River Time, The	26
Clark, Mrs. Mary Bayard.	
Life's Spinners	258
Cohen, Jacob.	
Three Ways to Marry	34
Conant, Henry R.	
Faces that are Gone	340
Cox, C. C.	
Looking Forward	257
Crayton, Jack.	
Lay of the Croaker	283
Curtiss, F. H.	
Her Picture	102

D

Deming, Mrs. H. A.	
Life—A Literary Curiosity	296
Dennis, Amanda Elizabeth.	
Shadows and Sunshine	128

INDEX OF AUTHORS.

Dennison, Mary A.
  Ma and Me................................ 268
Denton, Joel.
  Spinning Wheel, The.................. 157
Dorr, Julia C. R.
  Benediction, A............................ 204
Driver, S. P.
  Blue and the Gray, The............... 128
Duganne, A. J. H.
  No Time for Hating..................... 136

E

Ellison, Alfred.
  Some Other Day........................ 9
Emerson, Prof. E.
  Creeds..................................... 220

F

Fields, Rufus M'Clain.
  Old-Time Brinnel Cur, The.......... 34
Finch, M. E. P.
  Blue and the Gray, The............... 182
Fisher, James E.
  "Does Death End All?".............. 334
Fletcher, Mrs. S. W.
  Isle of the Past........................ 316
Florence, Stella G.
  In After Days........................... 282
Folsom, Montgomery M.
  O, Promise Me!........................ 86
Foss, Sam. Walter.
  Get Acquainted with Yourself...... 280
  Life Story, A........................... 75
Fox, W. D.
  Incapable................................ 342
Frost, Mrs. L. J. H.
  To Know and Hear..................... 55
Fuller, Minnie Martin.
  Empty Cradle, The..................... 8
Fuller, Mrs. W. A.
  September............................... 33

G

Gildersleeve, Mrs. C.
  Mrs. Lofty and I....................... 160
Glenn, Carrie E.
  Longing for Home..................... 271
Goldberry, Louise Dunham.
  Beautiful Gate, The................... 54

H

Haire, Elizabeth Cherry.
  We's Twinnies......................... 64
Hale, Will T.
  Casual Impressions................... 316
  Country Editors....................... 85
  Old Kitchen Fire, The................ 225
  Sometime Land, The.................. 248
  Where Mother Used to Sit........... 119
Hall, Margaret Scott.
  Help the Homeless.................... 11
Hamilton, F.
  Autumn Leaves........................ 248
Harbaugh, T. C.
  When the Dawsons Moved Away.... 212
Hardie, Harry.
  This Little Wife of Mine.............. 198
Harrington, Fred.
  Until Death............................ 27
Harwell, Aubrey.
  Her Heart is True..................... 94
  Lights are Growing Dimmer, The... 66
Hatcher, G. Edmund.
  How Sweet 'tis True.................. 190
Hayne, William H.
  Falling Star, The..................... 198

Hays, Inda Barton.
  "Sleeping, I Dreamed".............. 272
  Southern Mammy, The.............. 88
Hays, Will S.
  Betty and the Baby................... 273
  Penitent's Prayer, The............... 29
Hazletine, Walter M.
  Where the River Flows.............. 74
Henley, W. E.
  When You are Old..................... 335
Higginson, Ella
  "Eyes that Cannot Weep, The"... 169
  Four-Leaf Clover...................... 170
  From the Workshop "Home"....... 94
  Human Lilies..........................226
  Living the Past....................... 137
  Prayer of the Heart, A............... 74
Hill, Barton.
  To A. E. E............................ 141
Hills, William H.
  Busy Man, The........................ 29
Holt, Rosa Bell.
  Good We All May Do................. 329
Holmes, Oliver Wendell.
  Beautiful Prayer, A.................. 343
  True Wife, The....................... 100
Howard, Clifford.
  Chansonnette, A..................... 202
  Shadows................................ 337
Hubner, Charles W.
  My Mother............................. 136
Hugo, Victor.
  Immortal Soul, The................... 272
Humphries, Joseph W.
  Sitting in Silence..................... 117
Hunter, Eleanor A.
  Fathers and Daughters.............. 213
Hutt, Frank Walcott.
  When a Feller's Goin' Under....... 339

J

Jacob, Mary Agnes.
  My Temple of Fancy................. 45
James, Mary D.
  "Light at Evening Time"........... 253
Jay, Emel.
  Hang up the Baby's Stocking...... 206
Jay, Hamilton.
  "Come unto Me".................... 75
Jenkyns, Ruthven.
  Though Lost to Sight, to Memory Dear........ 231
Johnson, Philander.
  Past and Present..................... 197
Jonas, S. A.
  He has not Lived in Vain............ 206
  Retrospection......................... 176
Jones, I. Edgar.
  What Matters It....................... 165
Judson, Mrs. Emily C.
  "My Angel Love".................... 132

K

Kavanagh, Kathleen.
  Two Mothers.......................... 248
Kellogg, Nellie K.
  Grandma's Birthday................. 156
Key, Francis Scott.
  Star-Spangled Banner, The......... 214
Kidder, Mrs. M. A.
  Keep God on your Side.............. 86
Kipling, Rudyard.
  Recessional........................... 39
Kiser, S. E.
  "When the Devil was Sick"........ 127
Knight, L. L.
  Mother's Farewell, A................ 229
  Woman................................. 190
  Yesterday............................. 65

L

La Flamboy, Jeannette.
  They are Dead 52
Lee, Gen. E. G.
  To a Mocking-Bird 173
Lee, Frank.
  "He'll See it when he Wakes" 225
Lightbourn, A Willis.
  Brotherly Kindness 216
Long, Dr. Howard W.
  Memory 111
Longfellow, Henry W.
  God's-Acre 71
  Psalm of Life 92
  Rainy Day, The 19
Lowe, E. B.
  When Day is Done 105
Lowrey, Booth.
  Negro on Blind Tom, A 219
Lytle Gen. Wm. Haines, U. S. A.
  Antony and Cleopatra 64

M

Mackay, Charles.
  Inquiry, The 53
Markey, Pearl.
  Tribute to Womanhood, A 223
Marston, Philip Bourke.
  Procrastination 191
Martin, Elizabeth Stewart.
  Unanswered 11
Martin, Rev. J. H., D. D.
  Dove, The 181
Mashile.
  "Some Day" 158
Mason, J. S.
  Wish for My Friend, A 130
Matheson, E.
  "Out of date" Couple, An 90
  Sweethearts Still 290
May, Joseph Lee.
  My Musical Maid 192
May, Julia H.
  Two Mysteries 38
McLeod, Norman.
  Trust in God, and Do the Right 159
Meredith, Owen.
  Changes 79
M'Gee, Howard Hawthorne.
  Book of Dreams, A 59
  Secret Chamber, The 281
  St. Patrick's Day 199
  Sundays Long Ago 199
Miller, Elma Sydem.
  Colonel Blue Grass, Kentucky 142
Miller, Joaquin.
  Bravest of Battles, The 170
  Song of Peace, A 261
Miller, Mollie.
  You Know You Do 26
Mills, Henry Talcott.
  Game of Euchre, A 157
Mitchell, Louise.
  Alone in the Gloaming 67
Morehead, D. H.
  Song for the Future, A 171
Moore, Thomas.
  Last Rose of Summer 255

N

Naden, Constance C. W.
  Twilight 108
Nicholson, Eliza Poisevent.
  Hagar 220

O

Oaksmith, Appleton.
  nMIemoriam 294

O'Hara, Theodore.
  Bivouac of the Dead, The 276
Oliver, Alice.
  Rights of Woman, The 308
O'Neil, Charles S.
  Sometime, Somewhere 76

P

Paine, Albert B.
  Mystical Sea, The 17
Palmer, Arthur Cleveland.
  If She Had Lived 20
Parke, J. R.
  There Are 152
Peck, Ellen Brainerd.
  Old Fireplace, The 279
Peck, Samuel Minturn.
  My Sweetheart 58
  Picture In My heart, The 303
Peeler, Chas. G.
  New Baby, The 18
Perry, Dora.
  King's Kiss, The 183
Pike Albert.
  Every Year 228
  Level and Square, The 60
Pope, Alexander.
  Universal Prayer, The 318
Prentice, George D.
  Closing Year, The 292
  Name in the Sand, A 150
Preston, Mrs.
  By and Bye 291

R

Rawlins, Frances.
  Memories of Home 105
Read, Chas. A.
  Our Wedding Anniversary 38
Reid, Christian.
  By the Summer Sea 324
  New Year Greeting, A 314
  Regret 148
Rexford, Eben E.
  At the Baby's Bedtime 191
  Home Together 21
Riggs, Luther G.
  We May be Happy Yet 69
Riley, James Whitcomb.
  Days Gone By 65
  Long Afore He Knowed 58
  Man in the Moon 169
  Old Trundle Bed, The 23
  Runaway Boy, The 240
  Song I Never Sing, The 69
Rittenberry, Alma.
  Old Rail Fence, The 20
Roberts, Rev. P.
  Old, Old Home, The 178
Rock, M.
  My Mother's Song 80
Rooney, John Jerome.
  Children's Land, The 321
Rossetti, Christina.
  Who Knows? 29
Ryan, Father.
  Better than Gold 61
  Rest 239

S

Sangster, Margaret E.
  For Coming Mercies 335
  Little Arm-chair, The 202
  Reason, The 171
  Sins of Omission, The 336
Saxby, Howard.
  Saxby to Ingersoll 37

INDEX OF AUTHORS.

Saxe, John G.
  I'm Growing Old 209
Seabrook, Whitemarsh.
  Old Mauma 97
Sexton, Ella M.
  What Dreams May Come 44
Sharp, Grace Hewett.
  Tribunal, The 340
Silvernian, Rev. Dr. Joseph.
  Poetry and Religion 279
Smith, Eva MacDonagh.
  Foreshadowings 35
Smith, Florence E.
  Drifting 87
Smith, Rev. J. B., D. D.
  Westward Window, The 108
Smith, Mary Riley.
  Baby over the Way, The 304
Smith, Mrs. May Riley.
  Some Time 22
Spencer, Mrs. H.
  Does Any One Care for Father? 297
Spencer, John D.
  Frank L. Stanton 83
Spinney, Elenor.
  Fate 117
Stanton, Frank L.
  Dreamin' of Home 35
  Faithful 339
  Love's First Kiss 18
  Old-Time Circus Clown, The 122
  Playin' Checkers 62
  "Rock of Ages" 234
  Some of these Days 45
  Wayworn 294
  Wedded 217
Starret, Helen E.
  "Days are Growing Long Again, The" 268
Stevens, Rear-Admiral.
  Hope 107
Stratton, Mrs. M. W.
  Keep Me Awake, Mother 112

T

Taylor, Anne.
  Old Farm, The 336

Tennyson, Alfred.
  Days that are No More, The 291
Thayer, Louis E.
  "Mother's Picture, A" 7
Thurson, Grant C.
  Home Ranch Across the Big Divide .. 164
Tucker, William Henry.
  Wedding Bells, The 329
Turner, Arthur C.
  Day Dream, A 301

W

Warburton, G. A.
  Thou Shalt Know Hereafter 339
Ward, Katie.
  Yesterday 210
Warman, Cy.
  "And You'll Remember Me" 52
  Calm that Comes at Evening, The ... 334
  Nearer to God and to Thee 340
Watson, J. W.
  Beautiful Snow, The 24
Webster, Daniel.
  How Scholars are Made 227
Webster, Mrs. William.
  Light of Other Days, The 278
Welsh, Robert Charles.
  Exile's Song, The 175
West, William.
  Keep a Merry Heart 233
  Patter of Baby's Feet, The 310
Wheeler, Ida W.
  Let us Forget 280
Whitney, Emma Clark.
  God Knows Best 107
Wither, George.
  Old Song, An 218
Womack, Nellie.
  Mystical River, The 62
Wood, Edward N.
  Lead Thou Me On 81
  No Telephone in Heaven 57
  One by One 203
  When Baby was Dead 78
Wordsworth, Samuel.
  Old Oaken Bucket, The 177

ANONYMOUS.

A

	PAGE
Accomplished Girls	85
Act from Principle	258
Advice to Ladies	259
After Hiawatha	115
Alphabetical Wooing, An	102
Angelus, The	343
Arbitrary English Language	78
Are the Orators All Dead?	322
As Age Comes On	33
Autumn	144
Autumn of Life, The	242
Autumn's Arrival	93

B

Baby, The—What is it?	16
Barriers	261
Battle-Scarred Boy, The	191
Beautiful Extract, A	149
Beautiful Extract, A	257
Beautiful Hands	161
Beautiful Idea, A	248
Beautiful Land of the Dead, The	105
Beautiful Picture, A	201
Beautiful Steer, The	118
Beautiful Things	63
Beautiful Thought, A	287
Be Good to Yourself	209
Being in Debt	204
Blamed Sight Worse, A	206
Bliss Interrupted	158
Blue-Back Speller, The	36
Borrowing Trouble	311
Boston Girl, The	154
Boys, Wake Up!	253
Boy's Worst Foe, A	219
Broken Ties	263
Business Letter, A	28

C

Cards as a Bible	19
Care for Father	13
Chasing Butterflies	325
Cheap Pleasures	70
Childhood	182
Childhood's Song	198
Choice of Books, The	96
Choose your Friend Wisely	118
Christmas	338
Coming Man, The	273
Counting Apple-Seeds	240
Country Editor, The	92
Courtship	285
"Curfew Must not Ring To-night"	245

D

Dad's Old Grindstone	202
Darling	131
Date of Christmas, The	243
Definition of Home	85
Definitions of a Kiss	40
Departure	218
Destiny	223
Dictionary of Discontent	214
Difference, The	165
Disappointments	311
Distant	101
Do not Throw Cudgels at your Town	91
Don't Forget the Rainy Day	14
Don't Scold	165
Don't Stay Late To-Night	243
Don't Use Big Words	9
Dot Long-handled Dipper	212
Dreaming	53
Dreaming	144
Dreaming by the River	278
Dreams of the Royal Noon	241
Drifting in the Dark	61
Driftweed	32
Drummer's Grip, The	44
Dying Wife, The	305
Dying Wife, The	319
Dying Words of Noted Men	188

E

Easter	196
Easter Bells	268
Ecstasy of Kisses, The	141
Ember Faces	275
"Endless Strife"	303
Engaged	305
Engineer's Signal, The	186
Erring, The	335
Eternity of God, The	30
Evening	14
Ever Near	286
Evolution of the Book, The	167

F

Faces at the Fire	145
Fading	51
Failure	123
Faith, Hope and Charity	329
Fallen	14
Falling Leaves	307
"Family Clock, The"	76
Farewell	151
Farewell of Hope, The	290
Fate	65
Fatherhood of God, and Brotherhood of Man	54
First Gray Hair, The	101
First Telegraphic Despatch, The	124
Fishing	267
Flowers that Never Wither	252
Forgotten	330
Friendship	118
From Sofa to Hammock	149
Fully Decided	231

357

G

	PAGE
Gambling	55
Game of Life, The	95
Gem for Every Month, A	313
Gentleman Defined, A	185
Gilded Age, The	298
Give a Kind Word When You Can	113
Goblets and Glasses and Mugs	187
God	46
Good Book, A	330
Good-Bye	237
Good-Bye, A	109
Good Motto	45
Good-Night	147
Good-Night	150
Good Old Candy Pull, A	225
Good Old Things, The	75
Good Prayer, A	70
Good Woman, A	331
Grammar in Rhyme	269
Grammar School Extraordinary	153
Growing Old	18
Growing Old	258
Growing Old Gracefully	163
Guests of the Heart	236

H

Habit of Reading, The	232
Hand that Rocks the Cradle, Rules the World, The	290
Happy Every Day	52
Happy Husband	239
Hasty Word, The	87
Health	228
Hear both Sides	245
Heart Wounds	296
Helping on the Track	115
Her Name	74
Her Proposal	162
Her Secret	13
His Conscience	269
Holiday Attentions	224
Home	146
Home Affections	227
Home, Sweet Home	106
Hope	59
Hope	88
Hope Again	303
House of Never, The	19
How Beautiful	82
How Can a Woman Tell	332
How Father Carves the Duck	161
How Grandma Danced	98

I

Idaho	183
If I But Knew	88
If you Want a Kiss, Take it	306
I Love the Past	320
Indian Summer	106
Initiated Drummer, An	288
In Memoriam	65
In the Twilight	177
It Matters Not	262
I Wish He'd Make up his Mind	310

J

Jesus Wept	215
John's Wife	134

K

Keep Straight Ahead	262
Kiss Her and Tell Her so	71
Kiss Me, Darling	135
Kiss Me, Good-Night, Mamma	323
Knot of Blue and Gray, The	175

L

	PAGE
Land of Long Ago, The	283
Land of the South	331
Language of Precious Stones, The	155
Latter Day Preaching	61
Laugh	91
Laugh	147
Laughing Children	187
Leaf, A	232
Learn a Trade	47
Let Bygones be Bygones	237
Let it Pass	240
Life, a Tangled Skein	138
Life's Onward Current	13
Light	140
Light	309
Lightning Age, The	152
Lilies of the Field, The	131
Lines to a Skeleton	95
Little Dog under the Wagon, The	56
Living on the Farm	53
Lonely	264
Looking Off Unto Jesus	67
Look on the Bright Side	232
Lord's Prayer, The	10
Lost Things	293
Love Has its Way	203
Lover's Limit	114
Lover's Paragon, The	334

M

Maiden's Love, A	126
Mammy Gets the Boy to Sleep	39
Man and His Shoes	163
Man, the Kicker	113
Master Ralph's Opinion of Grandmothers	201
Me and Mary	7
Measure for Measure	24
Metamorphosis, A	110
Miss Gusher Abroad	287
Mistake Often Made, A	81
Mixed Metaphor	130
Mocking Bird, The	264
Model Husband—A weak Satire, The	233
Model Wife, The	233
Moneyless Man, The	270
Moral Courage	22
Mortgage, The	102
Mother at Home, The	193
Mother at Prayer	11
Mother's Old Steel Thimble	51
Motto in a Wedding Ring, The	107
M-Phatic	296
Mr. Tompkins on his Boarders	89
Musings in the Twilight	119
My Father's Grave	145
My Favorite Paper	243
My Home	42
My Husband	137
My Little Girl	90
My Mother's Grave	304
My Mother, too, Grows Old	255
My Sister	342
My Sweetheart	77
My Vanished Past	166

N

Nameless	227
Names of States and their Meaning	284
Never Mind What "They" Say	139
Never Trouble Trouble	32
New Woman, The	28
New Year, The	200
New Year, The	306
Night	333
Night Scenes in ——	140
Note of Hope, A	62
Nothing but Leaves	293
Nothing Lost but a Heart	99

O

	PAGE
Off Yonder	289
Of the Old Back Stair	114
Oh! Had I Known!	234
Ol' Barlow Knife, The	82
Old "Bob White"	282
Old Cemetery, The	151
Old Church Bells	179
Old-Fashioned Calendar, An	43
Old Folks at Home, The	170
Old Hand-Press, The	79
Old Homestead, The	300
Old Jingles	28
Old Lady Speaks, The	93
Old Lodge Room, The	71
Old Mill, The	12
Old Play-Ground, The	135
Old Scene, An	282
Old Spinning-Wheel, The	180
Old-Time Music	193
Old-Time Religion, The	48
O Loving Hearts	132
One by One	302
One Friend	292
One Sad Day	239
Only	99
Only a Picture	317
Original Words of "Dixie"	68
Other Point of View, The	238
Our Little Boy 'at's Gone	207
Our Lives	116
Over and Over Again	133

P

Paddle Your Own Canoe	247
Passing Year, The	305
Poetry	242
"Poor" Rich Man, A	98
Prayer of a Betrothed, The	121
Printer's Love Letter, A	152

Q

Queer Marriage Ceremony, A	159
Question, A	194
Question, A	237
Quits	128

R

Railroader's Prayer, A	
Reason Why, The	281
Recipe for a Good Husband	175
Recollections	312
Reconciled	320
Reflections on a Skull	323
Regret	124
Remarkable Facts	331
Remember Thy Mother	319
Retrospection	259
Rice-Throwers at Weddings	162
"Riddle of Things That Are, The"	243
Right Will Right Itself, The	48
Rise Higher	242
Rising in the World	251
Rural Christmas, A	224
Ruth	103
Ruth	194
Ruth and Naomi	344

S

Scenes of Childhood, The	25
Schoolhouse, The	255
Scythe of Time, The	229
Selection	95
Selection	123
Selection	147

	PAGE
Selection	164
Sermon in a Paragraph, A	237
Seven Ages, The	89
She Kissed Me Good-Night	179
She Waited by the River	156
She Was Willing	166
She Would be a Mason	208
Silent Griefs	330
Similar Case, A	317
Small Sweet Way, A	233
Small Things	184
Snap Shots	193
Sociability	294
Somebody Else	124
Somebody's Mother	174
Somebody's Sunbeam	159
Some Comfort	241
Some Day	66
Some Day	115
Some Day	217
Some Famous Hymns	235
Sometime	39
So Much of Life Behind Me Lies	145
Soul to Body	286
So We Grow Old	32
"Stone the Woman—Let the Man Go Free"	133
Story of the Gate, The	332
Stub Ends of Thought	123
Student's Love Letter, A	87
Sunny People	220
Surprise, The	328
Swarm of Bees, A	273
Sweetheart, Good-Bye	231
Sweet Long Ago, The	139

T

Take It In	264
Talk's Cheap	274
Terrible Fire, The	276
Thank God for Sunday	134
Thanksgiving	160
Thanksgiving Day	304
Thanksgiving on the Farm	92
That Dreadful Get-up Bell	314
Theology and Religion	195
They Met and Kissed and Parted	132
Thinking	307
Thy Holy Memory	130
Thy Name is Still the Magic Spell	101
"Thy Will be Done"	285
Till Death Us Part	136
To a Kiss	26
To an Inquirer	166
To-day	93
To Grown Up Lands	155
To Those Who Fail	148
Tramp, The	125
True Gentleman, The	274
Trust Me, Darling, I'll be True	129
Trying to Forget	42
Turning Gray	252
Twenty Years Ago	254

U

Under a Crazy Quilt	156
Unfettered Muse, The	283
Unrest	343
Unto Death	184
Unto the Editor's Room he Went	68

V

Value of Books	331
Violin and Song	194
Virgin's Refrain, The	203
Voice of the Night, A	57

W

	PAGE
Wait till Trouble Comes	121
Wanted	63
Way of it, The	229
Weakness	273
Weariness	185
Weaver, A	214
Weaving	215
We Can Make Home Happy	109
Wedding, The	159
Weep not for the Past	143
We've All Been There Before	205
What a Horse Would Say if He Could	68
What Can You Do?	120
What is a Year?	184
What the Lord Expects of Us	337
What People Call Death	110
What Wives are for	66
When the Cows Come Home	295
When Sam'wel Led the Singin'	17
When She Came Home	92
When the Skies Clear Off	17
Who Shall go First to the Shadowy Land?	277
Why?	109
Why Eve had no Help	45
Why Irving never Married	341
Wife and I	13
Wife's Prayer, A	336
Wisht I Could	278
Without an E	107
Without an Enemy	262
Woman	203
Woman	326
Woman's Love	247
Woman's Nay, A	158
Woman's Question, A	100
Woman's Rights	158
Woman's Smile, A	312
World is Full of Beauty, The	73

Y

	PAGE
Years and Years he Spent at College	86
You'd Better Cherish him	337
Young Ladies' "Psalm of Life"	315
You or I	325
Your First Sweetheart	260
You Will Miss Me	287

www.ingramcontent.com/pod-product-compliance
Lightning Source LLC
Chambersburg PA
CBHW030423300426
44112CB00009B/818